Bonds of Secrecy

THE MIDDLE AGES SERIES

Ruth Mazo Karras, Series Editor

Edward Peters, Founding Editor

A complete list of books in the series
is available from the publisher.

BONDS OF SECRECY

Law, Spirituality,
and the Literature of Concealment
in Early Medieval England

Benjamin A. Saltzman

PENN

UNIVERSITY OF PENNSYLVANIA PRESS

PHILADELPHIA

Copyright © 2019 University of Pennsylvania Press

All rights reserved. Except for brief quotations used for purposes of review or scholarly citation, none of this book may be reproduced in any form by any means without written permission from the publisher.

Published by
University of Pennsylvania Press
Philadelphia, Pennsylvania 19104-4112
www.upenn.edu/pennpress

Printed in the United States of America on acid-free paper

1 3 5 7 9 10 8 6 4 2

Library of Congress Cataloging-in-Publication Data

Names: Saltzman, Benjamin A., author.
Title: Bonds of secrecy : law, spirituality, and the literature of concealment in early medieval England / Benjamin A. Saltzman.
Other titles: Middle Ages series.
Description: 1st edition. | Philadelphia : University of Pennsylvania Press, [2019] | Series: The Middle Ages series. | Includes bibliographical references and index.
Identifiers: LCCN 2019017142| ISBN 9780812251616 (hardcover : alk. paper) | ISBN 081225161X (hardcover : alk. paper)
Subjects: LCSH: Secrecy—England—History—To 1500. | Secrecy—Law and legislation—England—History—To 1500. | Concealment (Criminal law)—England—History—To 1500. | Secrecy—Religious aspects—Christianity—History—To 1500. | God (Christianity)—Omniscience—History of doctrines—Middle Ages, 600–1500. | Monastic and religious life—England—History—To 1500. | Spirituality—Christianity—History—Middle Ages, 600–1500. | Christian hagiography—History—To 1500. | Riddles, English (Old)—History and criticism. | Latin poetry, Medieval and modern—England—History and criticism.
Classification: LCC BJ1429.5 .S25 2019 | DDC 303.3/7—dc23
LC record available at https://lccn.loc.gov/2019017142

For Sidney

Contents

A Note on References and Translations	ix
List of Abbreviations	xi
Introduction	1

PART I. LAW

Chapter 1. Political Epistemology and Crimes of Concealment in Anglo-Saxon Law	19
Chapter 2. The Secret Seized: Theft, Death, and Testimony	45

PART II. SPIRITUALITY

Chapter 3. Monastic Life and the Regulation of Secrecy	65
Chapter 4. Making Space for Spiritual Secrecy	95
Chapter 5. Seeing in Secret: Saints, Hagiography, and the Ethics of Concealment and Discovery	124

PART III. LITERATURE

Chapter 6. Binding Secrets, Solving Riddles	161
Chapter 7. Worldly Concealment, Divine Knowledge, and the Hermeneutics of Faith	184
Chapter 8. Reading Hidden Meaning: Between Interpretive Pride and Eschatological Humility	207
Afterword	244
Notes	255
Bibliography	303
Index	325
Acknowledgments	337

A Note on References and Translations

Unless otherwise noted, punctuation, spelling, and capitalization of Old English and Latin texts follow the cited editions, abbreviations have been silently expanded, and editorial emendations have been silently adopted. All biblical references are to Weber and Gryson, eds., *Biblia Sacra iuxta vulgatam versionem*. All translations of the Bible are from *The Holy Bible: Douay-Rheims Version*. When reliable translations have been available for other foreign language texts, I have typically consulted and adopted them here with silent modifications. All remaining translations are my own.

Abbreviations

Abbreviations for books of the Bible follow those in Weber and Gryson, eds., *Biblia Sacra iuxta vulgatam versionem*.

Æthelberht	The Laws of King Æthelberht, in Liebermann, ed., *Die Gesetze der Angelsachsen*, 1:3–8; Attenborough, trans., *Laws of the Earliest English Kings*, 4–17; cited by law number
I–X Æthelred	The Laws (I–X) of King Æthelred, in Liebermann, ed., *Die Gesetze der Angelsachsen*, 1:216–70; Robertson, trans., *Laws of the Kings of England*, 52–133; cited by law number
I–VI Æthelstan	The Laws (I–VI) of King Æthelstan, in Liebermann, ed., *Die Gesetze der Angelsachsen*, 1:146–83; Attenborough, trans., *Laws of the Earliest English Kings*, 122–69; cited by law number
Aldhelm, *Aenigm.*	Aldhelm, *Aenigmata*, ed. Glorie; *Poetic Works*, trans., Lapidge and Rosier, 70–94
Alfred	The Laws of King Alfred, in Liebermann, ed., *Die Gesetze der Angelsachsen*, 1:16–88; Attenborough, trans., *Laws of the Earliest English Kings*, 62–93; cited by law number. Unless otherwise noted, quotations are from MS E (CCCC 173; Ker, no. 39; Gneuss-Lapidge, no. 52).
ALL 1	Lapidge, *Anglo-Latin Literature, 600–899*
ALL 2	Lapidge, *Anglo-Latin Literature, 900–1066*
ASE	*Anglo-Saxon England*
ASPR 1	Krapp, ed., *Junius Manuscript*. Anglo-Saxon Poetic Records 1; individual poems cited by ASPR volume, page, and line
ASPR 2	Krapp, ed., *Vercelli Book*. Anglo-Saxon Poetic Records 2; individual poems cited by ASPR volume, page, and line

ASPR 3	Krapp and Dobbie, eds., *Exeter Book*. Anglo-Saxon Poetic Records 3; individual poems cited by ASPR volume, page, and line
ASPR 4	Dobbie, ed., *Beowulf and Judith*. Anglo-Saxon Poetic Records 4; individual poems cited by ASPR volume, page, and line
ASPR 5	Krapp, ed., *Paris Psalter and the Meters of Boethius*. Anglo Saxon Poetic Records 5; individual poems cited by ASPR volume, page, and line
ASPR 6	Dobbie, ed., *Anglo-Saxon Minor Poems*. Anglo-Saxon Poetic Records 6; individual poems cited by ASPR volume, page, and line
Beo	Klaeber, *Klaeber's "Beowulf*," ed. Fulk, Bjork, and Niles; cited by line
Boniface, *Aenigm.*	Boniface, *Aenigmata*, ed. Glorie
BL	London, British Library
BT, BTS	Bosworth and Toller, *Anglo-Saxon Dictionary*; *Supplement* by Toller; *Enlarged Addenda and Corrigenda to the Supplement* by Campbell
cap.	*capitulum, capitula*
CCCC	Cambridge, Corpus Christi College
CCM	Corpus Consuetudinum Monasticarum
CCSL	Corpus Christianorum, Series Latina
CH I	Ælfric, First Series of *Catholic Homilies*, ed. Clemoes
CH II	Ælfric, Second Series of *Catholic Homilies*, ed. Godden
CH III	Godden, *Ælfric's Catholic Homilies: Introduction, Commentary and Glossary*
CLA	E. A. Lowe, *Codices Latini Antiquiores*, 11 vols. and supplement, cited by volume and item number
I, II Cnut	The Laws (I and II) of King Cnut, in Liebermann, ed., *Die Gesetze der Angelsachsen*, 1:273–371; Robertson, trans., *Laws of the Kings of England*, 154–219; cited by law number
Conlationes	Cassian, *Conlationes*, ed. Petschenig; *Conferences*, trans. Ramsey
CPG	Geerard, ed., *Clavis Patrum Graecorum*, 5 vols.
CSASE	Cambridge Studies in Anglo-Saxon England

CSEL	Corpus Scriptorum Ecclesiasticorum Latinorum
CSML	Cambridge Studies in Medieval Literature
CUL	Cambridge, Cambridge University Library
De institutis	Cassian, *De institutis coenobiorum*, ed. Petschenig; *Institutes,* trans. Ramsey
DOE	*Dictionary of Old English: A to I*, ed. Cameron et al.
DOE Corpus	*Dictionary of Old English Web Corpus*, compiled by Healey et al.
DMLBS	Latham and Howlett, *Dictionary of Medieval Latin from British Sources*
DOML	Dumbarton Oaks Medieval Library
I, II Edward	The Laws (I and II) of King Edward, in Liebermann, ed., *Die Gesetze der Angelsachsen*, 1:138–45; Attenborough, trans., *Laws of the Earliest English Kings*, 114–21; cited by law number
Edward & Guthrum	The Laws of Kings Edward and Guthrum, in Liebermann, ed., *Die Gesetze der Angelsachsen*, 1:128–35; Attenborough, trans., *Laws of the Earliest English Kings*, 102–9; cited by law number
EETS	Early English Text Society
o.s.	old series
s.s.	supplementary series
El	*Elene*, ASPR 2; cited by page and line
ep., epp.	*epistola(e)*
Epi.	*Epigramma*
Eusebius, *Aenigm.*	Eusebius, *Aenigmata*, ed. Glorie
fol., fols.	folio(s)
frag., frags.	fragment(s)
Gneuss-Lapidge	Gneuss and Lapidge, *Anglo-Saxon Manuscripts*; cited by item number
HE	Bede, *Historia Ecclesiastica*, ed. and trans. Colgrave and Mynors
Hlothhere & Eadric	The Laws of Kings Hlothhere and Eadric, in Liebermann, ed., *Die Gesetze der Angelsachsen*, 1:9–11; Attenborough, trans., *Laws of the Earliest English Kings*, 18–23; cited by law number

Ine	The Laws of King Ine, in Liebermann, ed., *Die Gesetze der Angelsachsen*, 1:88–123; Attenborough, trans., *Laws of the Earliest English Kings*, 36–61; cited by law number. Unless otherwise noted, quotations are from MS *E* (CCCC 173; Ker, no. 39; Gneuss-Lapidge, no. 52).
Isidore, *Etymologiae*	Isidore of Seville, *Etymologiarum sive Originum libri XX*, ed. Lindsay; *Etymologies*, trans. Barney et al.
JEGP	*Journal of English and Germanic Philology*
JMEMS	*Journal of Medieval and Early Modern Studies*
Ker	Ker, *Catalogue of Manuscripts Containing Anglo-Saxon*; cited by item number
MGH	Monumenta Germaniae Historica
Auct. ant.	Auctores antiquissimi
Briefe d. dt. Kaiserzeit	Die Briefe der deutschen Kaiserzeit
Capit.	Capitularia regum Francorum
Capit. episc.	Capitula episcoporum
Conc.	Concilia
Epp.	Epistolae
Epp. sel.	Epistolae selectae
Fontes iuris N.S.	Fontes iuris Germanici antiqui, Nova series
LL nat. Germ.	Leges nationum Germanicarum
Poetae	Poetae Latini aevi Carolini
SS	Scriptores
SS rer. Merov.	Scriptores rerum Merovingicarum
SS rer. Germ.	Scriptores rerum Germanicarum
MS, MSS	manuscript(s)
n.s.	new series, nuova serie
OE	Old English
OED	*Oxford English Dictionary Online*, www.oed.com
OMT	Oxford Medieval Texts
PG	J.-P. Migne, ed. *Patrologia Graeca*
PL	J.-P. Migne, ed. *Patrologia Latina*; cited by vol. and col.
RegC	*Regularis concordia*, ed. and trans. Symons; cited by *capitulum*

Rid.	Exeter Book *Riddle(s)*, ASPR 3; cited by number, page, and line
RM	*Regula magistri*, ed. de Vogüé; cited by *capitulum*; trans. Eberle, *Rule of the Master*
RSB	Benedict of Nursia, *Regula Sancti Benedicti*, ed. Hanslik; cited by *capitulum*; trans. Fry, *Rule of St. Benedict*
SC	Sources chrétiennes
Symphosius, *Aenigm.*	Symphosius, *Aenigmata*, ed. Glorie
Swerian	*Swerian* (anonymous legal tract), in Liebermann, ed., *Die Gesetze der Angelsachsen*, 1:396–99; cited by law number
Tatwine, *Aenigm.*	Tatwine, *Aenigmata*, ed. Glorie
VCA	Anonymous of Lindisfarne, *Vita Sancti Cuthberti*, ed. Colgrave
VCM	Bede, *Vita Sancti Cuthberti*, metrical version, ed. Jaager
VCP	Bede, *Vita Sancti Cuthberti*, prose version, ed. Colgrave
Wihtred	The Laws of King Wihtred, in Liebermann, ed., *Die Gesetze der Angelsachsen*, 1:12–14; Attenborough, trans., *Laws of the Earliest English Kings*, 24–31; cited by law number

Introduction

> Abscondit se Adam et uxor ejus a facie Domini Dei in medio ligni paradisi.
>
> —Genesis 3:8

On discovering their nakedness, they covered themselves; on hearing the voice of God, they hid amid the trees of paradise. This primordial moment of concealment—the moment in which Adam and Eve attempt to hide themselves from the face of God—was clearly an impracticable endeavor from the start. The intangibility of God's face and the disembodiment of his voice would render his omniscience at once distant and ubiquitous, at once secret and manifest. Those physical trees of paradise, placed there by the Creator himself, could hardly conceal the shameful couple from his scrutiny. Yet still they tried.

The lavishly illustrated vernacular translation of the first six books of the Old Testament known as the Old English Hexateuch (a manuscript produced in the eleventh century at Canterbury, probably at Saint Augustine's Abbey) makes that futile attempt to hide from God uncannily palpable.[1] In the top frame on fol. 7v (fig. 1), God stands at the left looking from a distance through the tree that divides the frame and separates him from Adam and Eve, as they entangle themselves with one another in a nest of serpentine branches. With his hands clasped at his heart, Adam looks in God's direction with an expression of profound confusion and regret—a tear even seems to flow from his eye. It is as though Adam recognizes not only his act of betrayal but also the failure of his own attempt at concealment, as he tries to glance back at his Creator only to set his eyes on this solid tree, an object that occludes Adam's vision but not God's. In contrast to Adam's longing gesture, Eve grasps a loose branch in one hand and holds her face in the other, looking downward and away. As Adam clutches his heart and Eve grasps her face, they are together held and fettered by the foliage that inadequately conceals them.

Figure 1. London, British Library, Cotton Claudius B. iv, fol. 7v,
illustrating Gen. 3:8. © British Library Board.

Sin and Omniscience

Capturing the dynamic relationship between God's omniscience and the couple's act of hiding, this illustration encapsulates several larger early medieval attitudes about the human inclination toward secrecy and concealment. One such perspective, to borrow from Pope Gregory the Great (d. 604), is that the act of hiding is itself both a basis for and a magnifier of sin, an *augmentum nequitiae*.[2] Another is that this original "occultationis culpa" (sin of concealment) is proper to humankind ("hominis . . . proprium"); it is the customary vice of human kind ("usitatum humani generis uitium") inherited from our ancient parents ("parentis ueteris imitatione descendit").[3] According to this model, secrecy is intrinsic to our postlapsarian identity, and it must therefore be resisted just as one ought to resist sin. Commenting on the above passage from Genesis, for example, Bede (d. 735) explains how all sin ultimately equates to an act of hiding from God: "Abscondunt se namque a facie Dei qui peccant, quia indignos se diuinae pietatis reddunt aspectu. Abscondunt se a facie Dei, non ut ipsorum conscientiam internus arbiter non uideat, sed ut ipsi gloriam uultus eius numquam nisi resipiscendo conspiciant" (In fact, those who sin hide themselves from the face of God because they render themselves unworthy of the sight of divine goodness. They hide themselves from the face of God not in such a way that the inward Judge does not see their conscience, but that they may never see the glory of his face except by repentance).[4] By Bede's analysis, to presume to hide from God is to commit a sin, *and* to commit a sin is to hide from God. Because the inward Judge ("internus arbiter") witnesses everything, one can certainly *attempt* to hide, but the attempt will necessarily fail and will thereby only impair the sinner from being able, as it were, to look back.[5] In the Old English Illustrated Hexateuch, Adam tries to do just that, as he returns his gaze in the direction of God. But if we follow Bede's logic, Adam's sin is precisely what prevents him from seeing his Creator through the arboreal veil that stands between them. To borrow from Gregory once again, the trees of paradise "uidelicet occultatione non se Domino, sed Dominum abscondit sibi" (clearly did not conceal him from God, but concealed God from him).[6] The sin of concealment and the concealment of sin are thus two concomitant descendants of the same ancient failure to perceive and recognize God as the Judge who is *always* within.

The theological picture offered by Gregory and Bede does much to explain the significance of the scene that we encounter visually in the Old English Illustrated Hexateuch. They present us with a sweeping sense of God's omniscience and convey the futility and moral danger in attempting to hide from him, as that first couple so infamously experienced. They construct an image of our ancestral subjectivity—tied as it is to that original moment of sin and the perverted attempt at hiding—and they encourage a humble resistance against the inborn human tendency to carry out similar acts of concealment. This encouragement and the corresponding image of subjectivity rest on a complex system of belief, one that demands an individual's acknowledgment both that God always has access *within the self* and that his scrutiny persists *regardless of the self*. At its core, the theological problem posed by the human appetite for secrecy therefore reflects a matter of faith: attempting to hide from God signals a treacherous form of unbelief. Put another way, no one—at least theoretically—would attempt to hide from God if he or she fully *believed* it to be impossible. But in actuality, as we will see over the course of this book, some believers still tried to conceal themselves and their sins even while claiming to believe in the omnipotence of God. Regulating this kind of paradoxical psychology of belief (believing that one's actions are always seen, while simultaneously trying to conceal them) would become a complex and pivotal social concern, engaged in different ways by secular law (the efficacy of which often relied on a cultural belief in God's omniscience) and by monastic rules (where theological admonitions and regulatory reinforcement went hand in hand). Ultimately, these regulations hinge on a moral paradigm that quickly becomes inescapable: to step outside of it is to attempt to hide from God, and to attempt to hide from God is to sin, and to sin is to hide from God, and to hide from God is to step outside of it, *ad infinitum*. That there can be no outside to this infinite loop is only reaffirmed by Gregory's and

Bede's insistence that, no matter where one falls inside it, God still always perceives from *within* as the *internus arbiter*.

Psychologies of Concealment

The effect of this *internus arbiter* on the experience of secrecy emerges within two intertwined domains: the institutional and the psychological. In the latter, secrecy is often understood as the possession of control over oneself, over one's own thoughts, one's words, one's mind and body. This notion of "keeping" a secret would in fact become far more prevalent after the Enlightenment. Georg Simmel's famous sociological study of secrecy thus takes secrecy principally as a form of possession: "the strongly accentuated exclusion of all not within the circle of secrecy results in a correspondingly accentuated feeling of personal possession. For many natures possession acquires its proper significance, not from the mere fact of having, but besides that there must be the consciousness that others must forego the possession."[7] To some degree, this possessive form of secrecy can already be seen in Anglo-Saxon references to the mind. When the Exeter Book poem *Maxims I*, for instance, insists that "hyge sceal gehealden" (the mind must be held) or *The Wanderer* praises the noble custom of the man who "his ferðlocan fæste binde, / healde his hordcofan" (binds fast his mind, holds his hoard-coffer), they are drawing on a familiar poetic trope in order to express the social *desideratum* of keeping thoughts to oneself and retaining them in one's mind.[8] In one sense, this trope may reflect an Anglo-Saxon virtue of possessing a tempered *mod* (mind), which is necessary for resisting sinful temptations and recalcitrant emotions such as ire.[9] In another sense, it may reflect a principle like that Sedulius Scottus borrowed from Pseudo-Seneca's *De moribus*: "Quod tacitum uelis esse, nemini dixeris. A quo enim exigis silentium, quod tibi ipsi non imperasti?" (If you wish for secrecy, tell no one. Can you demand from someone else a silence which you have not imposed on yourself?).[10] Students would have learned something similar from the *Disticha Catonis* early in their educational careers: "Virtutem primam esse puta conpescere linguam; / proximus ille deo est, qui scit ratione tacere" (Consider that the first virtue is to restrain your tongue; nearest to God is he who knows how to be prudently silent).[11] These gnomic lessons clearly promote the virtue of reticence and restraint, as a tactical kind of secrecy that entails concealment from other human beings.

These metaphors of ownership and control, moreover, align such tactical or strategic forms of secrecy with the materialist psychology that prevailed in early medieval England. Scholars such as Leslie Lockett and Britt Mize have shown us how Anglo-Saxon notions of psychology relied on a cardiocentric model of the mind as a kind of container and enclosure, physically and corporally located in the chest and capable of being locked and fastened.[12] These findings have positively changed the way the field now approaches the conceptions of mind and mentality during this period. However, what these studies and others have tended to take for granted is the very present—perhaps almost too present and therefore easily overlooked—influence of God in the psychological landscape of early medieval England. There can be no doubt that the mind was regarded as a container and enclosure located in the heart or chest, but the nature of that enclosure changes dramatically when it houses not just the self, but also the *internus arbiter*, that divine, internal Judge.[13] What place do these metaphors of binding, holding, and fettering—bodily metaphors that convey a sense of physical control and possession—have, then, in light of God's abstracted and internalized presence? In a world where God always has access to the interior of one's mind, such possession and control mean something radically different.

There is a distinction, clearly, between keeping a secret from God and keeping one from a fellow human being. Likewise, a distinction also needs to be drawn between the human experience of secrecy under divine omniscience and the forms of secrecy that entail the guarding of divine mysteries or esoteric knowledge.[14] While these distinctions are critical to my argument in the chapters that follow, the forms of secrecy they represent are also often impossible to separate: the interiority forged by the poetic and gnomic admiration of fastening one's mind is an interiority that can never escape God's omniscience—at least in the logic of early medieval Christianity. But when we account for the belief in divine omniscience, human modes of concealment begin to look weak in light of its logic. Not only do the poems ironically fail to meet the very standard of silence they have set, as the speaker of *The Wanderer* goes on to confess his sorrow, and the sage of *Maxims I* professes the very secrets ("degol" and "dyrne") that ought only to be shared between wise men,[15] but as we will see, this notion of interiority—the yearning for control over the mind as an object fettered and bound—also comes into tension with the very real belief that those secrets *belonged* ultimately to God. And since they belonged to God, no matter how tightly held or forcefully they were bound, those secrets could at any point be extracted and publicly announced, whether by a mad demoniac (such as the one we will encounter in Chapter 3) or through the judicial ordeal (as we will see in Chapter 1) or eventually at the Last Judgment, when all secrets would be revealed before everyone (an inevitability considered in Chapter 8). Metaphors of binding and servitude, as Megan Cavell has comprehensively shown, pervade early medieval English literature, but these metaphors also figure extensively in legal, monastic, and literary descriptions of secrecy, sometimes rendering secrets as that which one might attempt to restrain or bind (as in *The Wanderer*), but more often reflecting a tension between weak human attempts to restrain thoughts and God's ultimate possession over those thoughts.[16] This tension becomes strikingly apparent if we return to the Old English Illustrated Hexateuch (fig. 1). In the depiction of that first couple, there emerges a crucial paradox that will become a recurring theme of the present study: rather than an *act of binding*, secrecy is more frequently understood as a state of *being bound*, a state of being held captive, of being fettered, enslaved, trapped. To attempt to hide or conceal a secret was thus to be enslaved or bound by the power of the secret, a power superbly exemplified by the illustrations of Adam and Eve attempting to hide from God, entangled with one another amid those serpentine branches.

Cultures of Scrutiny

This tension between divine omniscience and the psychological mechanics of secrecy played out most perspicaciously in two of early medieval England's major institutional settings: secular law and monastic life. These are two very different institutions, each with much internal variety. But their role in shaping behavior at the intersection of psychology and belief is mutually illuminating. Today, in our secularized, post-Enlightenment world, the belief in a divine witness has been replaced with other more tangible systems and mechanisms of surveillance. Jeremy Bentham's panopticon, to select a well-known and generalizable example, is the ultimate man-made expression of this godlike omniscience: the guard in the darkened tower can see the prisoners in their illuminated cells, but the prisoners cannot see the guard. The design is, in Bentham's own words, "a new mode of obtaining power of mind over mind, in a quantity hitherto without example."[17] This "new mode" achieved through a "simple idea in Architecture" allows an institution—such as a prison, hospital, or school—to enact constant observation over its subjects:

> The more constantly the persons to be inspected are under the eyes of the persons who should inspect them, the more perfectly will the purpose of the establishment have been attained. Ideal perfection, if that were the object, would require that each person should actually be in that predicament, during every instant of time. This being impossible, the next thing to be wished for is, that, at every instant, seeing reasons to believe as such, and not being able to satisfy himself to the contrary, he should conceive himself so.[18]

Bentham's system, of course, dreams of a benevolent establishment whose indispensable agency might keep the disorderly public in check. That agency reaches its height of power by relying on the faith of each of its subjects: his ability to "believe as such" and not "to satisfy himself to the contrary." The subject's faith in the "fiction of God" (to borrow a phrase from Miram Božovič's reading of Bentham) sustains the effectiveness of the panopticon; without that fiction in the mind of the prisoner, the system of surveillance would immediately collapse.[19] As Bentham theorized and Foucault famously argued, such panoptic arrangements carry tremendous power to shape and alter the behavior of the subjects under their gaze, as the concealment of the observer ensures that any awareness of being under observation occurs entirely in the imagination of the one observed and that such awareness is independent of the actual whereabouts, actions, and personality of the observer.[20] The panopticon produces the effect, in other words, of Bede's *internus arbiter*.

Suddenly, Bentham's claim to have produced something "hitherto without example" and Foucault's argument that the seventeenth and eighteenth centuries saw the invention of this new form of discipline (as a departure from the principle of "judicial investigation" invented by the late Middle Ages) both appear to miss the crucial theological precedent of divine omniscience.[21] This is not to say that from the late Middle Ages onward Christians stopped believing in God's omniscience (which of course is not true), but rather that God's judgment was slowly removed from the mobilizing position in institutional power that it held during the early Middle Ages—only to be replaced in the Enlightenment with a similar form of institutional power itself.[22] In early medieval England, the judicial ordeal and the judicial reliance on the oath as sources of proof are two examples of this institutional mobilization of God's omniscience (to be discussed in Chapter 1): these practices relied on and cultivated a culture that operated under God's constant observation, recourse to which was fundamental to legal authority during the period. These practices, in other words, yielded a culture in which an individual's secrets were not only known by God but could also be revealed at any moment before a larger worldly audience with worldly consequences.

There are, of course, significant differences between Bentham's panopticon and the early medieval belief in God's omniscience (the role of sovereignty is but one such difference), and there are crucial similarities as well (such as the conviction held in both systems that the observer is necessarily benevolent). But my point is not to project a kind of Foucauldian system of power onto a period where it does not quite belong; as I mentioned above, Foucault's interest in the Middle Ages tends toward the later rather than the earlier parts of the period. Nevertheless, this Benthamian example—now generalized into newer and more modern forms of surveillance—illustrates just how radically such systems of surveillance can affect social behavior. In early medieval England, it was the double-edged belief in God's omniscience—that God knows all human secrets, yet his secrets remain fundamentally unknowable to human beings—that had such a profound, diverse, and widespread effect on the social and institutional dynamics of the period. Within those institutions emerged a culture of scrutiny in which every oath and ordeal, every monk caught stealing or confession extracted, every rhetorical reference to God as a witness or as the future judge would exploit and further instill the deeply entrenched belief in the power and immediacy of God's omniscience, and it would condition the way believers acted and thought as subjects under the law, as religious within monasteries, and as readers before books.

Bonds of Secrecy

In the chapters that follow, we will encounter various acts of concealment as they transpired in Anglo-Saxon legal, monastic, and literary sources; we will explore how some of these acts were forbidden and regulated, how others were encouraged, and how the very idea of secrecy was negotiated and formed in the process. My central argument is that this legal and monastic culture of scrutiny—which developed in relation to and sometimes in tension with the belief in God's omniscience—profoundly shaped the practices of literary interpretation during the period. It was a culture in which the capacity for human beings to conceal anything, whether physically or mentally, was severely limited by the institutional and social reliance on the belief that God had ultimate control over the concealment and revelation of secrets. Law codes, for example, harnessed this belief in order to facilitate the management of proof, adjudicate wrongs, and preclude criminal acts of concealment; monastic rules used it to forbid monks from even attempting to conceal their thoughts, while the actions of saints and abbots frequently reminded them that some such secrets were already quite known or could be made known at any moment. But despite these prohibitions and regulations, despite the reiteration of God as a constant witness, people still attempted to conceal things, authors still wrote about the lures of secrecy, and texts still laid claim to hidden meanings, begging to be uncovered by their readers. It is in these moments of defiance and imagination that the story becomes most intriguing.

Bonds of Secrecy begins by investigating how acts of concealment were regulated in Anglo-Saxon law and monastic life, respectively. Chapter 1 examines the secular law codes of the period—legislation produced under kings such as Ine (688–726), Alfred (849–899), Æthelstan (895–939), Cnut (990–1035), and others—and finds throughout these codes various preoccupations with crimes that entailed secrecy, such as murder (distinguished from manslaughter by the concealment of the deed) and theft (etymologically and pragmatically defined by its secrecy). Numerous laws require that transactions be conducted openly, while others establish highly particular rules for the delivery of testimony and the swearing of oaths. In these codes, acts of concealment converge into a criminal category that not only demands intense legal proscription but also threatens the limits of sovereign power and political epistemology. The solution: Anglo-Saxon legal procedures repeatedly utilized, concretized, and reinforced preexisting but abstract beliefs in divine omniscience through rituals such as the judicial ordeal; this process established a distinctive legal hermeneutic, which always had recourse to God as the ultimate witness and judge. Chapter 2 continues this examination of Anglo-Saxon law and illustrates one mode of legal hermeneutics with a case study of a law from the code of King Ine concerning a stolen slave whose previous owner is not alive to testify. This is a case that raises important questions about not only the relationship between secrecy and sovereignty but also the intertwined relationships between secrecy and death, theft, and servitude that will become central to the discussions that follow.

Chapter 3 then turns to the monastic traditions and practices of Anglo-Saxon England. From the *Rule of Saint Benedict* to the *Regularis concordia*, from Cassian's *Conferences* to the *uitae* of several Anglo-Saxon saints, together these texts and others reveal one side of an underlying tension in monastic life, where the scrutiny we find in the secular law codes is intensified and where secrecy is even more strictly regulated through the requirements of immediate confession to the abbot, the interdictions against keeping thoughts to oneself, and even the occasional employment of a *circa* whose job it is to weasel out secrets and infractions among the brethren. And yet, as I go on to argue in Chapter 4, these normative regulations and their theological underpinnings operated alongside the virtuous encouragement of a very different kind of secrecy—what I call "spiritual secrecy"—in which a monk separates himself from other human beings in order to communicate openly with God. I demonstrate the prevalence of this form of secrecy through a study of private prayer and Anglo-Saxon church architecture that reveals the sorts of places within a monastery that would have allowed a monk to pray *in secreto*. Several Old English and Latin narratives (such as Felix's *Vita Sancti Guthlaci* and the Old English poems *Guthlac A* and *B*) reveal the kinds of social reactions incited by and justifications raised in defense of the often problematic solitary behavior of monks, abbots, and saints who would leave the communal space of the monastery to inhabit and pray in *loci secretiores*. The tension between the monastic regulation of secrets (discussed in Chapter 3) and the encouragement of spiritual secrecy (discussed in Chapter 4) often centers around a concern over ownership and possession: monks, as servants of God (*serui Dei*), forfeit their proper servitude and become slaves to sin when they try to conceal a secret from the abbot or, by extension, from God. The spiritual secrecy of private prayer and of eremitism was, on the other hand, specifically characterized as the epitome of that proper, noble servitude to God.

At this point, we reach the crux of the book, and I should therefore pause to explain the argument that links the first half to the second. Like much of this project, understanding the relationship between the concept of secrecy and these forms of solitude—"spiritual secrecy," as I have termed it—in early medieval England requires a critical readjustment, on our part, about the meaning of secrecy itself. The historian's perennial challenge is to describe the past using and while constrained by the language of the present; the latter rarely fits the former and inevitably risks contorting it. Secrecy—a multifaceted concept rich in contemporary meaning and pervasive in contemporary life and discourse—is particularly vulnerable to this kind of contortion. Worse, it is the kind of thing that almost asks to be treated as a universal human phenomenon, and thus often is. It is all the more vital, therefore, that when we set out to think about past experiences of secrecy, we put aside any current preconceptions without forgetting how they might nevertheless persist in shaping our ideas about the past; let us put them aside, for the time being, so as to leave space for the concept to develop on its own as we explore its various early medieval manifestations. One of the broader lessons from this book will therefore be about the importance of attending to the historical specificity of the concept and experience of secrecy: I do not believe we can speak of a generic and universal Secrecy, but can instead only really speak about how the forms and experiences of secrecy function at any given time, in any given place or institution or culture or religion.

To begin this process, we might recall that the word *secretus* takes its etymology from the Latin *secernere*, meaning "to separate." It is to this general sense of separation that the concept of secrecy in early medieval England is most closely connected, and it is therefore with this sense that my use of the word will most often align. The act of praying *in secreto*, as one such example, both implies an act of separation (from fellow brethren, from distractions, from the world) and shapes the meaning and conceptual limits of secrecy itself, as the secret rooms of a church become metaphors for the interior space of one's heart where prayer can always take place *in secreto*.

More importantly, understanding the concept of secrecy in early medieval England also requires a reconsideration of ethics. Secrecy and concealment are morally ambiguous concepts.[23] In itself, secrecy is neither inherently right nor inherently wrong; the ethical status of a secret is typically contingent on its content, its effect, and the circumstances in which it is performed. As Simmel puts it, "Secrecy is a universal sociological form, which, as such, has nothing to do with the moral valuations of its contents."[24] Yet, as I will show, the form of secrecy itself and the moral valuation of its form—not merely its content— is in fact historically contingent. The monastic tension uncovered in Chapters 3 and 4, for example, produced a distinctive ethical relationship between the self and the world in early medieval England—an ethics of secrecy radically different from its modern reflex, which Simmel and others assume as sociologically universal. In contemporary Anglo-American culture, people or institutions are judged based on the content of the secrets they keep or disclose, judged (in a utilitarian model, for instance) for the effect that the content of a given secret might have on others. State secrets, to take an example of current interest, are thus either justified or condemned based on how many lives they might save or how many lives they put at risk, indeed sometimes even based on *whose* lives are at stake. From a different, if equally cogent perspective, the preservation of an individual's right to privacy—essentially the right to keep secrets—is understood to be ethically imperative, unless, for instance, it puts other rights at risk.[25] The nuances of these contemporary debates over the ethics of state secrets and surveillance are too complex and too expansive to allow for a more detailed discussion here, as are the other varieties of ethical situations involving secrecy (which have already been extensively studied by Sissela Bok and others). However, the critical point remains that a contemporary ethics of secrecy is almost always evaluated by weighing consequences or rights. This admittedly simplistic characterization (and its distinction from the early medieval model that I will posit below) corresponds more generally with the emergence in the Enlightenment of deontological and utilitarian models of ethics and the attendant displacement of an ethics of virtue that had dominated since antiquity.[26] This shift in normative ethics is one way to understand how and why a contemporary ethics of secrecy might have come to differ from its early medieval predecessor.

The morality of concealment in the early Middle Ages, on the other hand, was shaped not by the same concern for consequences and rights (both of which were somewhat foreign concepts at the time)[27] but by a concern for the intention or mindset of the individual engaged in acting secretly. I argue that the monastic tension discussed in Chapters 3 and 4 reflects an underlying distinction between moral and sinful modes of concealment. On the one hand, spiritual secrecy—the secrecy that characterized private prayer and eremitic monasticism—was encouraged and often upheld as a hallmark of spiritual virtue precisely because it entailed a deliberate openness to God's constant observation. But on the other hand, as Bede and Gregory make eminently clear in their discussions of Adam and Eve, any attempt to hide from God was (besides an attempt at the impossible) ultimately an act of evil, since it signaled a dangerous and sinful disbelief in God's omniscience.

For example, in his commentary on Genesis, Bede emphasizes the significance of Cain's decision to kill his brother "in agro" (in the field), since his attempt to commit the crime in what Bede refers to as a *locus secretior* represents the assumption that he could evade the notice of God.[28] For Bede, this assumption demonstrates Cain's particular treachery and faithlessness ("perfidia"), for he "occisurus fratrem foras ducit, quasi in loco secretiori diuinam possit declinare praesentiam, non recogitans neque intellegens quia qui occulta cordis sui quae redarguit nouerat, etiam quo ipse secederet quidue in abdito gereret posset intueri" (leads his brother, whom he is about to kill, out of doors, as if he could avoid the divine presence in a more remote/secret place, neither reflecting on the fact, nor understanding, that he who knew the secrets of his heart, which he rebuked, could also observe whither he withdrew himself and what he was doing in secret).[29] Cain's primary crime is obviously the act of murder. But like the sinner in Psalm 9, for instance, who acts secretly ("digollice" in the Old English; "in abscondito" in the Vulgate) and thinks that "Ne geþencð God þyllices, ac ahwyrfð his eagan þæt he hit næfre ne gesyhð" (God will not mind it and will turn his eyes away so that he never has to see it), Cain enables and exacerbates the treachery of his crime by thinking that he can conceal it from God.[30] However, within this exegetical paradigm, what is most striking is Bede's decision to describe the field as a *locus secretior*, rendering that place of sin with language identical to that typically used by hagiographers (including Bede himself) to describe the sorts of holy places where monks go off to pray alone, those more remote and secret spaces, which can separate and remove them from the scrutiny of other human beings, but never from God.

This brief exegetical passage illustrates the way early medieval ideas about secrecy were keyed to specific spatial and bodily metaphors and configured around God's ability to transcend those physical boundaries: the secret interiority of the heart is always open to God, no matter where the physical body happens to be located. This spatio-bodily arrangement is also brilliantly reflected in the illustration of Adam and Eve in the Old English Hexateuch (fig. 1), where the tree is placed as a barrier between God and the couple, where the branches ensnare their bodies, where Adam grasps at his chest (indicating either remorse or containment), where Eve holds her face in her hand. And yet, the architectural and bodily representations of Adam and Eve's concealment are implicitly transcended by God, for whom such barriers are no obstacle. The key to this ethics of secrecy therefore lies in an acknowledgment of that spatial transcendence, enabling and indeed promoting a type of secrecy that is distinctly *not secret* to God.

Goscelin of Saint-Bertin gives us, for example, a particularly sharp, if pithy, picture of what this acknowledgment would have entailed. When he composed his *Liber confortatorius* in the eleventh century, he addressed the lengthy letter to the anchoress Eva of Wilton, explicitly forbidding it to be read by anyone other than its intended recipient (his request evidently went unheeded). Nevertheless, he describes the letter as an "archanum duorum . . . Christo medio signatum" (secret of two, sealed with Christ as mediator).[31] Eva's newfound anchoritic life, as Goscelin frequently reminds her, would require the same kind of spiritual secrecy that he applies to their mutual epistolary secret; his deliberate openness to Christ's watchful presence in the midst of their secret correspondence is precisely what sustains that correspondence as a morally exemplary form of secrecy. Goscelin's letter to Eva is but one example of a kind of textual secrecy that is deliberately opened up to God's mediation, yet this ethics of secrecy crops up in numerous other literary contexts as well.

As I go on to argue in the second half of this book, the hagiography, poetry, and riddles of early medieval England exhibit a keen interest in the mechanics of secrecy and disclosure. In the process, they establish their own systems of hermeneutics that confront the limits of human perception and the potency of God's knowledge. Chapter 5 thus initiates a transition from a study of the cultural practices in Anglo-Saxon law and monasticism to a study of literary interpretation by examining several hagiographic sources—including the *uitae* of Saints Cuthbert (d. 687), Columba (d. 597), and Oswald (d. 992)—and arguing that saints and their hagiographers offer a model for understanding how secrets that are governed by God can be negotiated and disseminated by humans. Here, we find that the moral distinction between sinful and spiritual forms of secrecy governed not only acts of concealment but also acts of discovery and acts interpretation—both in the lives of saints and in the recording of their lives by hagiographers.

The final three chapters go on to demonstrate how these ethical conditions of secrecy further insinuate themselves into the production and consumption of literature. In Anglo-Saxon England, monastic culture was of central importance in forming not only religious ideals but also literary taste. Much of the literature extant from the period was produced in monasteries or at least copied and preserved in their scriptoria and libraries. Amid the literary material that does survive, riddles constituted a vast genre that was extremely popular and especially so in monasteries. Chapter 6 begins an investigation into the large and unwieldy corpus of Anglo-Saxon riddles, a corpus that reveals in all its variety a particular and tenacious interest in the literary mechanics of concealment and hermeneutic discovery. I argue that these mechanics—as we will see in the Old English *Apollonius of Tyre* (a narrative that centers around a particularly vicious riddle) and the *Riddles* of the Exeter Book—take their shape through images of servitude and metaphors of binding and fettering, which relate the solving of a riddle to the loosing (*soluere*) of the fetters that bind a servant to a master. Like the knots of the riddles, the bonds of servitude—which are often, as we have already seen above, used as a metaphor for "binding fast" (*fæste bindan*) the mind in secrecy—become subject to hermeneutic pressure; the bonds of riddles, as with the bonds of servitude, and as with the bonds of the mind, are never quite as strong as the master tends to presume, unless that master is God. These riddles thus further challenge the notion that a human being can fully possess and control a secret, which—so long as it is bound to language—remains open to interpretation and unlocking.

Chapter 7 continues this investigation of Anglo-Saxon riddles to show how literary concealment taught the reader to approach the unknowable mysteries of God. It begins, however, not with riddles but with an excursus into the poetry of Cynewulf, in particular his poem *Elene*. The poem, which tells the story of Constantine's mother's search for the True Cross, is fundamentally concerned with ideas of secrecy, a concern that manifests itself in the concealment of the Cross and culminates in Cynewulf's enigmatic concealment of his own signature in the final lines. It is also a poem about the strategies available for uncovering those secrets, presenting a distinction between two forms of hermeneutics—interrogative and faithful—that become central to the role of riddles and their readership in the intellectual landscape.

Chapter 8 returns to the corpus of Anglo-Latin riddles and asks how their readers experienced the synthesis and, more often, the tensions between these two hermeneutic methods. In representing the objects of the world, both mundane and extraordinary, the collection of *Aenigmata* by Aldhelm of Malmesbury (d. 709 or 710) comes to exemplify a decipherable form of concealment that enables the reader to approach those divine *aenigmata* that would otherwise rest beyond the immediate hermeneutic reach of human observers. By examining the manuscripts in which these riddles survive, I show how the glosses and neighboring texts inform the ways they were read, sometimes with a blind and proud desire to decrypt a scientific kind of knowledge (a practice Aldhelm subtly condemns) and sometimes with a keen awareness of the place that these texts and the lowly reader occupy within the larger scope of the universe. Such an awareness becomes evident in what might otherwise appear to be a perplexing coincidence: these riddles often accompany reflections on the Day of Judgment and the revelation of all secrets that the end of time will bring. This codicological fact has gone unnoticed by modern scholars, yet to the early readers of these manuscripts it must have brought the interpretation of texts and of human acts of concealment into cosmic perspective.

In a larger literary context, the force of the belief in God's omniscience demands an acknowledgment that any meaning concealed or hidden in a text must already be known by God, which in turn invites an alternative method of interpretation. Textually hidden meaning becomes subject not merely to hermeneutic pressure—brute intellectual suspicion or force—but also and more effectively to humble expressions of faith: the same kind of faith used to distinguish a moral mode of concealment from a sinful one. In some literary contexts, such a hermeneutic of faith is unmistakably fostered and encouraged;

but in others, as in the multifaceted corpus of Anglo-Saxon riddles and the evidence left behind by readers in their manuscripts, we see these two modes of interpretation chafe against one another, abrading away their surfaces to reveal a crucial distinction between the ways in which Anglo-Saxons understood the process of reading and our own contemporary approaches to literary criticism.

PART I

Law

Chapter 1

Political Epistemology and Crimes of Concealment in Anglo-Saxon Law

No matter how thoroughly a legal code manages to anticipate its potential limitations and inconsistencies, insofar as it relies on some pursuit of truth—whether in determining the rightful owner of a piece of land or in prosecuting a thief or even in adjudicating grievances—the greatest barrier to its enforcement will always be the human capacity for concealment. To the juridical powers that be, an act of concealment and the potential for secrecy constitute serious threats to practical and theoretical management in the rule of law: what is unknown to the sovereign cannot be governed; what is unknown to the judge cannot be adjudicated. The proof such acts of governing and judgment require can easily be perverted, destroyed, or obscured, and these are inevitabilities that early medieval legislation aggressively sought to undermine. Particularly in Anglo-Saxon England, the act of concealing a crime (whether deliberate or accidental) significantly magnified the impact of the crime by removing it from the epistemological reach of the legal apparatus. Such concealment posed a serious problem, and it could take place on any number of different levels, including the level of the crime itself (as when a thief secretly steals a piece of property) and the level of the witness (as when an individual hides a thief after the fact or later testifies falsely). And when proof becomes dependent on the testimony or oath of a witness, as it often does, it also becomes dependent on the will of that witness to remember and report it accurately. With that, the distinction between concealment and perjury becomes especially fraught, as the law codes of early medieval England attempt to regulate, negotiate, and manage the inevitable secrecy of their subjects.[1]

Modern law tends to establish certain rights—such as the right to privacy or the right to remain silent—that grant individuals a degree of tolerable secrecy and regulate the circumstances under which such secrecy must be forfeited (for example, when innocent life is immediately or, in the case of terrorism, potentially at stake).[2] Balancing the right to privacy with the need for justice and security has become a complex and weighty ethical issue.[3] However, as we will see in the course of this chapter, Anglo-Saxon law was far less forgiving in its regulation of secrecy. It gives no such right to privacy or to silence, it consistently treats concealed crimes more severely than open ones, and it often regards the act of concealing a crime as tantamount to the crime itself, or worse. The site of testimony—an epistemological space established and guaranteed by the swearing of an oath—is particularly hospitable to deliberate acts of concealment. Even when events are not deliberately concealed, they are always at risk of falling out of knowledge: witnesses can be lost (their whereabouts forgotten or untraced), they can fall ill (thereby becoming unable to testify in person), or they can die (to be buried along with their knowledge). Even if witnesses are at hand and able to swear an oath, their testimony always teeters on the edges of good-faith error, on the one hand, and of deceitful perjury, on the other. In order to preempt, as best as possible, the irreversible occlusion of knowledge inherent to the very process of bearing witness, Anglo-Saxon law codes set up a variety of methods for compelling, managing, and valuating different forms of testimony, as a procedural act in which the swearing of an oath could confirm or deny the claims of the plaintiff or of the defendant. For while ostensibly an act of disclosure, testimony always carries the potential for concealment.

The fact that error and perjury "must always be *possible* at the moment of bearing witness" is why, in one reading of the phenomenon, the act of testimony "must not essentially consist in proving, in confirming a knowledge, in ensuring a theoretical certitude, a determinant judgment."[4] Far from a consideration of medieval jurisprudence, this is Jacques Derrida's way of recognizing the singularity of the testimonial experience, which consists of a fundamental and counterintuitive paradox: "*as soon as* it is guaranteed, certain as a *theoretical proof*, a testimony *can no longer* be guaranteed *as* testimony. For it to be guaranteed as testimony, it cannot, it must not, be absolutely certain."[5] For Derrida, testimony can rather "only appeal to an act of faith."[6] Its role in proving, confirming, ensuring, and determining the truth of an event is first and foremost predicated on the willingness of the addressee to *believe* that the testimony is neither erroneous nor perjured, even though both error and perjury are entirely within the realm of possibility—to remove that possibility is to remove the possibility of testimony itself.[7]

Although Derrida would disassociate this "act of faith" from the "grand appearance of so-called religious faith,"[8] in the earliest stages of English law we discover precisely such an appeal to the latter, where a substrate of religious faith served to establish and assure, among other things, the absolute authenticity of doubtful testimony and where it shaped the underlying mechanics of political epistemology. This epistemology works on two levels: the law codes carefully and creatively negotiate these situations of testimonial uncertainty first by establishing parameters for reducing the possibility of criminal concealment and then, if testimonial concealment is deemed likely, by deferring to a divine form of mediation and judgment. The religious faith required by such judgment in turn provides the necessary grounds for doubtful testimony to be considered not merely believable but *certain* (even if that certainty must still sometimes be refereed by a priest's interpretation of divine judgment or by trusting that the testimony will eventually come before the judgment of God).[9] The judicial ordeal is a superb example, since, in the words of one of its leading historians, it was a "device for dealing with situations in which certain knowledge was impossible but uncertainty was intolerable."[10] Under these circumstances, the source of proof was found not in testimony that demands faith in the witness (as Derrida construes it) but rather in testimony that demands faith in God (as entailed by Anglo-Saxon law).

As we will see, early medieval law established a complex and rigorous hierarchy for evaluating the circumstances and quality of testimony, proof, oaths, and pledges. Indeed, the function of witnesses then was significantly different from their function today. Because the oath of witnesses functioned as a form of proof in itself (as opposed to the more open-ended first-person testimony sought from witnesses in today's Anglo-American legal system), the Anglo-Saxon law codes had to set out rules for determining whose testimony would be considered valid and what to do when an essential witness was likely to produce invalid testimony, or when two witnesses represented contradictory positions, or even when a witness was simply unavailable to be present at a legal proceeding. For cases in which the oath of a witness was the only obtainable form of proof—and in Anglo-Saxon law, oaths were formulated *as* proof—but in which the oath or the witness was in doubt or deficient, the law resorted to forms of testimonial proof that employed divine judgment instead. For example, witnesses who were known to be perjurers or who had been repeatedly accused of theft were required to undergo the ordeal essentially as a way for God to render judgment on their behalf.[11] When the law hits the limits of testimony and the limits of political epistemology, those limits are brought to the eternal Judge, whose judgment is always certain (because omniscient) and always reliable (because God *is* truth, as in John 14:6), thereby producing a testimonial experience that completely inverts the one described by Derrida. Yet even that early medieval testimonial experience still relied on a similar albeit much grander form of faith.

I have chosen to begin this book in an admittedly counterintuitive manner, starting not with Anglo-Saxon ideas about individual consciousness or interiority (as one might expect to find in a study of secrecy) but rather with institutional forms of power as they interpret, act on, and shape the behavior of their subjects. This choice is predominantly governed by the type of evidence that survives: most encounters with secrecy and concealment during the period are told from the perspective of those institutions (whether secular or religious, legal or monastic) that had the most at stake in governing and regulating individual acts of secrecy. Moreover, this choice enables us to see secrecy as a cultural phenomenon that extends beyond the individual; it enables us to see, for instance, the way secrecy was shaped by and in relation to structures of sovereignty, the way those structures of sovereignty approached acts of secrecy through a particular form of hermeneutics, and the way such hermeneutic approaches often claimed authority from God's omniscience. In this phenomenon, the centrality of institutional power is twofold. On the one hand, acts of secrecy (such as the concealment of a crime) become especially problematic and therefore elaborately regulated because they strike at the epistemic heart of the institution (in this case, the legal institution). On the other hand, the institution benefits immensely whenever its subjects internalize God's omniscience as the underlying beat of its epistemic heart (much like Bentham's panopticon, the potency of which depends merely on the subject's internalized *belief* in the unseen yet all-seeing observer).[12] But of course, these institutional mechanisms were far from uniform and far from absolute. As one of the goals of this book is to demonstrate how the early medieval forms of this belief in God's omniscience had a profound and complex effect on the behavior of those who subscribed to its logic, this effect is most immediately and intensely apparent in secular law and monastic practices. However, unlike the monastic culture of Anglo-Saxon England, where this internalization tends to be more extreme and absolute (see below, Chapters 3 and 4), the emerging secular legal infrastructure could not always take this internalization for granted, even if the infrastructure frequently relied on God's omniscience for its epistemological authority. This rudimentary and imperfect feature of the law makes it an especially worthwhile place to begin because it reveals a practical and procedural concern over secrecy that at times functions independently of God's knowledge (for instance, when determining a trustworthy witness), yet often ultimately turns to depend on it (for instance, when an untrustworthy witness is the only available witness). Anglo-Saxon ideas about secrecy took shape amid these hermeneutic exchanges between individuals, institutions, and God. And as we will see, the concepts that emerge from these exchanges spill over from strictly legal settings into the literary culture of the period, informing the literature with Anglo-Saxon legalistic conceptions of sovereignty. Whether in the recurring themes of mastery and servitude or in the legal implications of theft, these juridical ideas turn up in monastic and literary contexts as nuanced metaphors that further manipulate Anglo-Saxon ideas about secrecy.

The Emergence of Political Epistemology

In examining these juridical approaches to secrecy, we discover that crimes of concealment (such as theft, murder, and perjury) were a serious concern in the law codes produced by Anglo-Saxon kings. These codes, taken together, comprise an enormous, diverse, and challenging body of material, and yet they constitute only a fraction of the legal sources that survive from the period (not to mention those of canon law and other ecclesiastical statutes). Despite the diversity of this genre of historical evidence, however, these codes often occlude the realities of legal practice: it is their nature to prescribe a highly normative and regulated social model that is both responsive to practical concerns but also abstracted from those concerns as well as from the details of its own implementation and enforcement.[13] If we turn, however, to those charters, wills, lawsuits, and other documents that scholars would typically use to discern more localized legal procedures and practices,[14] we encounter by comparison very few explicit references to acts of concealment. While this paucity of references to concealment in Anglo-Saxon charters is certainly limiting, it is also revealing. It suggests either that local practices lacked the ability and perhaps the inclination to regulate such acts of concealment (although some evidence to the contrary will be considered below), or that such concealment was a concern that fell predominantly into royal jurisdiction, reflecting the particular position from which the law codes were promulgated along with the authority they tended to reinforce. Together, these two possibilities reveal a crucial aspect of Anglo-Saxon political epistemology: secrecy and concealment emerge as a legal problem primarily in relation to sovereign attempts at maintaining epistemological authority. This changes the debate about the relative strength of royal authority during the period, allowing us—whether we take a minimalist approach or a maximalist one—to see more precisely that the emerging Anglo-Saxon "state" was at its strongest when attempting to regulate and enforce against crimes of concealment.[15]

By the eleventh century, the concealment of crimes will come to approach treason, as it does, for example, in one of Cnut's laws: if someone neglects an audible call for help in apprehending a thief, he must pay a fine to the king for insubordination ("oferhyrnesse").[16] This obligation to come to the aid of someone raising a hue and cry has its origins, as Paul Hyams argues, as a public response to private wrongs, but it eventually was taken under royal power.[17] Patrick Wormald has summarized the numerous instances of legislation that treats and punishes theft as a form of treason, but it remains difficult to see why.[18] By the time Cnut institutes the above law, a theft need not directly involve the king's person or property; instead, the king's subjects become an extension of his juridical authority in attempting to apprehend the thief. Impeding or ignoring the apprehension of a thief is thus tantamount to insubordination to the king. This extension of authority was greatest when the king's epistemological capacity was somehow limited or threatened, especially in cases of theft and other crimes that utilize concealment in one form or another. To impede the apprehension of a thief, even to do so passively by ignoring a call for help, is thus to participate in the further concealment of the thief from the king's legal apparatus.

But these concerns really begin to develop at a much earlier point in the period (as early as the reign of King Æthelberht in the seventh century), and they can be seen in laws that demand forfeiture of property or the payment of fines to the king as punishment for certain crimes as well as in those laws that authorize imprisonment or execution. Offenses committed directly against the king or destructive acts committed in the king's presence are an obvious impetus for such royal involvement; the former tended to be treated as personal wrongs (albeit of an especially grave variety), and the latter called for elevated penalties.[19] But numerous laws also assigned such penalties for crimes not directly involving the king's person, allowing the king to decide, for instance, whether a thief be executed or allowed to live: a seemingly harsh punishment that has posed a problem for how we understand early medieval law.[20] Many of these crimes—a term I use deliberately, because they are met with royal involvement despite their apparent distance from the person of the king—involve some form of concealment. In approaching these crimes, the legal culture early in the Anglo-Saxon period moved beyond what Paul Hyams importantly recognized as a culture of undifferentiated wrongs and shifted toward a rudimentary system in which certain wrongs fell under royal jurisdiction and were treated as crimes by virtue of the attempt at secrecy.[21]

This logic—linking political epistemology to the exercise of royal juridical authority—peaks in the tenth century. As Wormald charted, the oath of allegiance underwent development from Alfred through Cnut, but it is the oath, for example, that King Edmund (r. 939–946) required of his subjects that was most likely responsible for formally criminalizing certain acts of concealment in order to establish the king's role in the preservation of peace.[22] The oath begins by requiring fidelity to the king "sine omni controversia et seductione, in manifesto, in occulto" (without any dispute or dissention, whether openly or in secret), and then preempts the primary motive for concealing such a breach of fidelity: "nemo concelet hoc in fratre vel proximo suo plus quam in extraneo" (let no one conceal the breach of it [*scil.* the oath] in a brother or a relation of his, any more than in a stranger).[23] The oath goes on to obligate its subjects, for instance, to aid in apprehending wrongdoers (a principle also embraced in Cnut's law above) and to disclose any knowledge of crimes, particularly those that entailed concealment (such as theft and the harboring of criminals, which we will consider again more closely below).[24] Conducting transactions without the witness ("testimonium") of an official such as a priest or town reeve is forbidden, as is interfering with the tracking of stolen cattle.[25] And refusing to comply with the law ("rectum facere nolit") carries a fine of 120 shillings payable to the king.[26]

If Edmund's oath of allegiance gives us a top-down perspective on the king's power and his attempt at securing epistemological authority, then we might garner a view from the ground by turning to one of the few Anglo-Saxon charters that directly confronts the legal problem of concealment. In the late tenth century, Rochester found itself embroiled in a particularly elaborate land dispute, in which one Æscwyn (widow of Ælfhere) gave to Rochester title deeds for land at Snodland. Shortly thereafter, a few unscrupulous Rochester priests "forstælon þam biscope on Hrofesceastre . 7 gesealdan heo Ælfrice Æescwynne sunu wið feo dearnunga" (stole them [the title deeds] from the bishop of Rochester and sold them to Ælfric, son of Æscwyn, secretly for money).[27] By the time the bishop had discovered the theft, Ælfric had already died, leaving a testimonial vacuum that had to be resolved at a council in London with King Edgar present (along with other important figures, including some we will encounter in Chapter 3, such as Dunstan, Æthelwold, and Ælfstan). At the council, the stolen deeds (along with compensation for the theft) were assigned to the bishop of Rochester, and the estates of Bromley and Fawkham held by Byrhtwaru (Ælfric's widow) were forfeited to the king. The diploma gives no explanation for this forfeiture to the king, but it may have arisen from Ælfric's complicity in the theft suggested by the secret exchange of money. The procedural logic of both Edmund's oath of allegiance and the case of the stolen Snodland deeds suggests that royal involvement in the adjudication of such crimes and wrongs, at least in the tenth century, tends to focus on the potential for subjects to conceal those crimes and obstruct access to pertinent information, thereby interfering with the epistemological reach of the king's legal apparatus and warranting a payment of a fine to the king in addition to redressing the original wrong with the aggrieved party.

A king's legal authority thus resided not only in his production of written law but also in his ability to adjudicate disputes. This authority is evident, for example, in the way King Edgar helped resolve the Rochester dispute by intervening at precisely the moment when knowledge of the case was, owing to the death of Ælfric, most hazy. And a century earlier, King Alfred had a reputation for even greater investigative prowess. Asser, his contemporary biographer, thus extols the virtues of Alfred's judicial enterprise in the way he reformed the disorderly and conflicting varieties of local judgments and adjudicated seemingly impassable conflicts. Parties engaged in a disagreement that could not be resolved by local judges would thus hasten to seek the king's judgment, and parties who resisted his judgment could not do so for long:

> quamuis per uim leg[is] et stipulatione[m] uenire coactus esset, uoluntarie nolebat accedere. Sciebat enim ibidem nihil ex sua malitia confestim posse delitescere; nimirum erat namque rex ille in exequendis iudiciis, sicut in ceteris aliis omnibus rebus, discretissimus indagator.[28]

> [although by force and stipulation of the law he would have been compelled to appear (before the king), he did not wish to approach him, for he knew that none of his malice could remain there unexposed for long—not surprisingly, since the king was a most perceptive investigator in cases needing adjudication as in everything else.]

This romanticized and well-known picture of Alfred's juridical accomplishments is partly owed to the hagiographic conventions of praise. (Even if he wanted to, Asser could hardly have depicted Alfred as an *indagator mediocris*.) But allowing for exaggeration, Alfred's role as *indagator* still suggests that he was not merely instituting written law from a distance but adjudicating cases on the ground, managing the behavior of judges, and imposing himself and his hermeneutic authority on the legal landscape. That authority (even posthumously, as we see in the Fonthill Letter) would have only been reinforced by the reputation that Asser promotes: that nothing could remain hidden (*delitescere*) from the king and his exceptional, almost divine perceptiveness. This perceptiveness is an extreme degree of what I am calling "political epistemology," and for Alfred, as for Edgar, that political epistemology was at the center of their legal authority. Anglo-Saxon legislation leaves us with merely the rough contours of that authority, shaped in response to certain points of epistemological weakness. But in those contours, we begin to see how political systems based on precarious power—as many early medieval ones were—would find the juridical supervision of God an extraordinarily useful mechanism in enabling their authority.

Crimes of Concealment: Theft

But first, let us consider the unlikely legal subject of a cat. This cat vigilantly guards his owner's house from "furibus inuisis" (unseen thieves) and—once given a voice in Aldhelm of Malmesbury's *Aenigmata*—describes his own duty as follows: "Noctibus in furuis caecas lustrabo latebras / Atris haud perdens oculorum lumen in antris" (I survey the blind hideouts in the black nights; the light of my eyes is not lost in the dark caves).²⁹ These lines from Aldhelm's *Aenigma 65* brilliantly capture the drama of a thief in action, as Aldhelm paronomastically synthesizes the darkness and the secrecy of the thieving mice, juxtaposed against the luminous gaze of the cat: the dark caves ("Atris . . . antris") conceal the unseen thieves ("furibus inuisis") in the black nights ("Noctibus in furuis"). Yet those blind hideouts ("caecas . . . latebras") are exposed by the light of the verb *lustrare*, which syntactically falls between the adjective ("caecas") and noun ("latebras"): "caecas lustrabo latebras." The verb exposes and brightens the darkness that surrounds it; moreover, it anticipates the nocturnally illuminated eyesight of the cat ("oculorum lumen") in the subsequent line, eyesight that the cat uses to survey (*lustrare*) his dark surroundings and catch those thieving mice who try to conceal themselves in the shadows.

What makes these rhetorical moves in Aldhelm's poem so compelling is the fact that they reflect the extremely commonplace belief that thieves work at night, in the dark, and in secret: such is the nature of theft. Isidore of Seville thus defines the act of theft (*furtum*) as "rei alienae clandestina contrectatio, a furvo, id est fusco vocatum, quia in obscuro fit" (the secret handling of another's property, derived from "black" [*furvus*], that is, "dark" [*fuscus*], because it takes place in secret).³⁰ This etymological and pragmatic bond between theft and darkness is gnomically captured in the Old English poem *Maxims II*, which states that "Þeof sceal gangan þystrum wederum" (A thief must go about in dark weather).³¹ In another one of Aldhelm's *aenigmata*, Night (*Nox*) claims of herself that "Diri latrones me semper amare solebant" (dreadful robbers are always in the habit of loving me).³² And in *Beowulf*, the thief who steals from the dragon's hoard "to forð gestop / dyrnan cræfte dracan heafde neah" (stepped too close to the dragon's head, in his [*scil*. the thief's] secret craft).³³

This association between theft and secrecy is further implied in the medieval descriptions of death as a thief who comes secretly at night. In the Exeter Book poem *Christ III*, for example, death is a "þeof þristlice, þe on þystre fareð, / on sweartre niht" (terrible thief, who travels about in the dark, in the black night).³⁴ And in Ælfric's *Sermo in natale unius confessoris*, "se dyrna þeof, þe digollice cymð, is se gemænelica deaþ, ðe þæs mannes lichaman mid his digelan tocyme to deaðe gebringð" (common to all, death is the secretive thief, who comes secretly, and who with his clandestine arrival carries the man's body to death).³⁵ These images of death as a secretive thief are ubiquitous in early medieval reflections on the end of life. Not only do they capture the unpredictable and therefore secret arrival of physical death (concealed, as it were, from the person whom it affects the most), but they also reflect a common biblical trope for conveying the unknowability of the second death and the Day of Judgment. As Paul puts it in 1 Thessalonians 5:2, "dies Domini, sicut fur in nocte, ita veniet" (the day of the Lord shall so come, as a thief in the night). The sentiment is put even more tersely in Apocalypse 16:15: "Ecce venio sicut fur" (Behold, I come as a thief). This biblical notion of the second death *qua* thief was clearly also imagined as a metaphor for the unknowable secrecy of the end of time. As one Blickling Homily explains, "We leorniaþ þæt seo tid sie toþæs degol þæt nære næfre nænig toþæs halig mon on þissum middangearde, ne furþum nænig on heofenum þe þæt æfre wiste, hwonne he ure Drihten þisse worlde ende gesettan wolde on domes dæg, buton him Drihtne anum" (We learn that the time is so secret that no man in this world, no matter how holy he may be, nor anyone in heaven either, has ever known when our Lord will decree this world's end on Doomsday, except our Lord alone).[36] The metaphor equating death with theft only works, however, if theft is culturally and pervasively linked with secrecy.

This affinity between theft and secrecy is not merely restricted to the literary and biblical imagination: it also constitutes a fundamental presumption in early medieval English law.[37] For example, from the earliest sources onward, property transactions were required to be conducted before witnesses who could later attest to the fact that the transaction was conducted openly and "un-secretly" ("undeornunga"); if they could not, then the property would be considered stolen (because it was purchased in secret) and on that account returned to its previous owner.[38] Other laws take the perspective of the injured party: according to a law in Ine's code, someone who discovers stolen meat ("forstolen flæsc") that has been hidden ("gedyrned") is permitted to claim the meat as his own by virtue of its concealment.[39] This form of proof is so basic that it even appears in several Old English charms for the theft of cattle, quasi-legal sources that operate on the assumption that thieves act in secret and conceal what they have stolen: "Gif feoh sy undernumen . . . sing on þæt hofrec and ontend .iii. candella drip ðriwa þæt weax . ne mæg hit nan man forhelan" (If cattle is secretly stolen, . . . sing over the hoof track, and light three candles and drip the wax three times. No man will be able to conceal it).[40] And another charm equates stolen goods with the Jewish concealment of the cross on which Christ was crucified: "hi forhelan ne mihton . swa næfre ðeos dæd forholen ne wyrþe" (they concealed what they could not conceal. So may this deed never become concealed).[41] Theft was understood as an act that entails the concealment of both the deed and the stolen object. This logic runs deep in Anglo-Saxon thought, but it is also found in other early medieval legal contexts. For example, the early Continental law codes known as the *Pactus legis Salicae* and the *Lex Salica* stipulate even more directly that "Si quis in domo alterius, ubi clauis est, furtum inuenerit, dominus domus de uita conponat" (If anyone finds stolen goods in another man's house that is under lock and key, the owner of the house shall make composition with his life).[42] While death might seem an excessive penalty for an unproven crime, this law and others like it operate on the assumption that the act of concealing the property is precisely what validates the charge of theft.[43] What makes theft therefore so legally problematic is not only its disruption of the proper order of exchange and transaction but also its removal from legal oversight, threatening the integrity of the legal process as a whole. Given that no legal action can proceed until concealed goods have been uncovered, discovering stolen goods thus often becomes, as the Old English charms suggest, just as much a matter to be resolved by prayer as one to be resolved by legal force.

To be sure, not all crimes of seizure are committed in secret, hence the early medieval distinction between theft (a crime committed secretly) and robbery (the taking of goods in an open and often violent manner).[44] However, the threat posed by furtive theft was of particular concern and finds a striking manifestation in two nearly identical pieces of early Anglo-Saxon legislation (Ine §20 and Wihtred §28), both of which mandate that if a foreigner (i.e., someone from a different kingdom) is traveling through the woods and off the main highway, he must announce himself by shouting or blowing a horn. If he does not do so, then he will be deemed a thief ("ðeof he bið to profianne") to be slain or put to ransom.[45] The choice of the word *profian* (to regard; to prove) in both versions of the law implies that the mere act of behaving secretly is enough to convict and punish the traveler as a thief, and the option of sentencing the thief to death sustains the absolute and irreversible authority of that proof.[46] As we have seen, death is not an especially unusual punishment for acts of theft (especially in early Anglo-Saxon legislation).[47] However, the punishment does imply that the proof is considered incontrovertible, as though the thief were caught in the act. We see the same logic in Wihtred §26, which leaves it up to the king to decide whether someone caught in the act of stealing ("æt hæbbendre handa") should be put to death, sold over the sea, or ransomed for his wergild (the monetary value of a human life based on social status, typically used in Germanic law to determine compensation for the family of the slain victim). Half of the proceeds of the second and third options would be paid to the person who caught the thief, making the first option (death) potentially unprofitable for both the king (if the king were to receive a cut) and the apprehender, as well as starkly unfair to the aggrieved party.[48] In fact, killing the thief could actually turn costly if the thief's family sought retribution for his death. But Ine's code anticipates this potential situation in a revealing way: if the relatives of the dead foreigner attempt to claim the foreigner's wergild, the person who slew him is permitted to declare that he presumed him a thief (because he was traveling secretly) with the effect that no claims could be advanced against him for killing the foreign thief.[49]

However, if he concealed ("dierneð") the killing of the thief, and long afterward it comes to light, then "rymeð he ðam deadan to ðam aðe, þæt hine moton his mægas unsyngian" (he affords an opportunity to the dead man to obtain an oath, by which his relatives may exculpate him).[50] These pieces of legislation illustrate several different ways that concealment can radically change the nature of an action and its relation to the law. If a crime is concealed, it is reasoned and, in fact, proven to have been committed on unjustifiable grounds.

Crimes of Concealment: Murder

If theft by definition is a concealed crime, then the concealment of homicide rests on slightly more ambiguous juridical ground. It has long been recognized that early medieval law—across Continental, Icelandic, Irish, and Anglo-Saxon sources—often distinguished between killing openly and killing in secret, with the former (treated as a defensible form of manslaughter) consistently earning a milder punishment than the latter (treated as a form of murder).[51] The practice of categorizing the crime in this way has a variety of analogues outside of England. In *Egils Saga*, to take a late literary example, King Eirik will not have Egil killed at night, "því at náttvíg eru morðvíg" (because night-slaying is murder-slaying).[52] This simple equation reflects what was perhaps a traditional and longstanding distinction in Icelandic law between *morð* (murder) and the more general term *víg* (manslaughter): "En þa er morð ef maðr leynir eða hylr hræ eða gengr eigi í gegn" (And it is *morð* if a man conceals or hides the corpse or does not admit [to the crime]).[53] If there are no witnesses to the killing (*víg*) and if it is to be found in any way defensible, then the killer must announce it following specific protocols within twelve hours of the event (with exceptions made, for instance, if the killing happens on a mountain or fjord, in which case the announcement must be made within twelve hours of the killer's return).[54] The immediacy and openness of the announcement here is essential for demonstrating innocence.

On the Continent, the *Pactus legis Salicae* makes a similar provision and increases the penalty when the killer tries to conceal the corpse: "Si quis hominem ingenuum siue in silua aut in quolibet loco occiderit et eum ad celandum conburserit et ei fuerit adprobatum, DC solidos conponat" (He who kills a freeman either in a forest or in some other place and burns the body in order to conceal the crime, if it is proved against him, shall pay 600 solidi composition).[55] That amount equates to three times the composition for killing in the open (200 solidi).[56] Another law addresses the problematic secrecy of assassins, referred to as *elocationes in furtum* (secret/furtive hirings), a crime that if discovered—even if the murder never takes place—carries a fine in addition to the penalty for the killing itself of sixty-two and one-half solidi (more than one-third of the composition for an open killing).[57] The recipient of this additional payment is unspecified by the standard phrase *culpabilis iudicetur*, which is used throughout the *Pactus legis Salicae* merely to indicate liability. But as with secret acts of theft, the increased penalty likely corresponds to the increased difficulty of litigating and resolving crimes that have been actively concealed.

Anglo-Saxon law is slightly more ambiguous in its distinction between secret murder and open killing, since implications of secrecy often depend on the terminology of the word *morð*, which is rarely straightforward: sometimes the word designates the secrecy of the act (as in its Old Norse cognate), but more often it refers to acts of killing without any explicit sense of secrecy. Privileging the generality of the latter sense, Bosworth-Toller defines the word *morð* primarily as "death, destruction, perdition" and secondarily as "that which causes death."[58] For the third sense, however, it is defined as a technical term: "slaying with an attempt at concealment of the deed."[59] Editors of the Anglo-Saxon laws, from Schmid to Thorpe to Liebermann, have similarly defined the word so as to capture this sense of secrecy as its primary meaning.[60] However, as Bruce R. O'Brien has reminded us, the Old English words *morð* and *morðor* were not always restricted to the technical sense of "secret murder"; in fact, they carried a much broader and more varied range of meanings. O'Brien goes on to argue that in legal contexts the words have more precision, tending to refer to killings either that could not be compensated (e.g., by payment of wergild or *bot* to the family of the victim) or that constituted treason against a lord.[61] But both of these definitions still rest on an underlying distinction between secret and open homicide.

In examining O'Brien's first category (killings that could not be compensated), we must first consider the shifting principles of compensation in Anglo-Saxon law by turning to the law codes of Æthelred (r. 978–1016) and of Cnut (r. 1016–1035), both of which were composed by Wulfstan, and both of which formalize the category of *botleas* crimes: serious crimes, often involving a breach of peace, that could not be compensated through personal redress and instead involved forfeiture to the king or capital punishment. Before this formalization, the term *bot* applied to compensation owed to the victim or the victim's family; afterward, it was reoriented toward God and the king.[62] An important law in Cnut's code illustrates this tension, wherein *morð* is clearly a concealed act of killing but is also treated as a *botleas* crime that cannot be compensated by payment: "Gif open morð weorðe, þæt man sy amyrred, agyfe man þam magum" (If anyone dies by violence and it becomes open [i.e., manifest] that it is a case of murder, the murderer shall be given up to the kinsmen [of the slain man]).[63] This law reverts back to an older sense of justice and compensation, suggesting that *morð* not only constitutes a crime without remedy (hence *botleas*) but is also specifically an act committed in secret and one that can only be resolved once discovered ("open . . . weorðe"). O'Brien's second interpretation (*morð* as treason) may reflect a correspondence between *morð* and the practice of resolving legal conflicts in secret or outside an official court, a criminal practice sometimes referred to in the laws as "diernum geðingum" (secret compositions).[64] Such extrajudicial or concealed measures were sometimes treated as a crime against the king because they deprived the royal apparatus of its fees and, moreover, because they may have constituted a breach of loyalty.[65] By, for example, slaying a criminal secretly and outside of the confines of the law, the killer will have betrayed his obligation to resolve conflicts through the mediation of the king or through some other open, official avenue, which would protect the killer from retribution. In isolation from these technical legal situations, the literary nature of many of the sources that O'Brien brings to bear on the definition of *morð* almost certainly reflects, as he rightly argues, an expansion and smudging of the terminology; in strictly legal contexts, however, *morð* very often points back to a more limited sense of secret murder, and the law consistently regards such acts of secret murder with particular severity.

But that consistency is slightly complicated by the relationship between secular laws and the penitential texts of the period, in which murder is sometimes defined according to the agent's maliciousness rather than in terms of the crime's concealment. As Stefan Jurasinski has demonstrated, a clause from the *Penitential of Theodore* that defines an act of murder according to the malicious intention of the murderer, who "occiderit odii meditatione"[66] (slays another from a motive of hatred), is translated into the Old English *Scriftboc* where the crime acquires the added quality of concealment, as the killer "slyhð oðerne on morð on eorran mode and mid behydnysse" (slays another by murder with hateful mind and with concealment).[67] The translator, Jurasinski argues, likely supplemented the sanction with his own knowledge of the secular legal tradition in which *morð* requires concealment.[68] Despite O'Brien's findings about the semantic development and breadth of the word *morð*, and despite the fact that maliciousness is occasionally a determining factor (particularly in penitential texts), it is clear that a killing committed in secret or concealed after the fact is generally treated as a greater crime than a killing openly committed. The underlying reason for the severe legal and cultural approach to secret killing is aimed primarily at the danger it poses to the successful implementation of the law itself: a murder without witnesses is much harder to resolve by ordinary means (whether through personal or royal processes) and therefore less likely to yield any compensation or penalty. That difficulty can be countered and the concealment of crimes can be deterred principally by the threat of harsher punishment.

Crimes of Concealment: Arson

Sometimes, despite the fact that theft and murder are substantially different crimes, the two are paired and addressed together under a single law. When this happens, as it does in the anonymous code *Be blaserum*, it reveals a fundamental concern with the means of criminal concealment and the consequences such concealment poses for satisfactory adjudication:[69]

> We cwædon be þam blaserum 7 be þam morþslyhtum, þæt man dypte þone aþ be þryfealdum 7 myclade þæt ordalysen, þæt hit gewege þry pund, 7 eode se man sylf to, þe man tuge. 7 hæbbe se teond cyre swa wæterordal swa ysenordal, swa hwæþer him leofra sy. Gif ðone að forþ-bringan ne mæg 7 he þonne fúl sy, stande on þære yldesta manna dome, hwæþer he lif áge þe nage, þe to ðære byrig hyran.
>
> [We declared about arsonists and murders that the oath be deepened threefold and the ordeal-iron enlarged to a weight of three pounds. And the person charged is to go himself to the ordeal, and the accuser to have a choice between water-ordeal and iron-ordeal, whichever he prefer. If he cannot produce the oath and so be guilty, let it be in the judgment of the most senior men that belong to the borough whether he have life or not.][70]

Why, we might wonder, would arsonists and murderers fall under the umbrella of the same law? The link, I think, rests in the unstated similarity between arson and theft, a link on which Ine §43 sheds some light when it plainly equates the crime of setting fire to a forest with the crime of theft. Fire is a thief ("fyr bið þeof"), the law purports, because it is silent and secret, unlike the felling of trees with an axe, which is more likely to announce the culprit: "sio æsc bið melda, nalles ðeof" (the axe is an informer and not a thief).[71] The two crimes—theft and arson—share similar tactics of secrecy, even if the goals are not exactly the same.[72] One could argue that even the act of stealing lumber with an axe can likewise be concealed; one could also argue that Ine §43.1 concedes the fact that any deforestation—whether by fire or axe—can only be punished after "wyrð eft undierne" (it later becomes manifest). However, Ine §43 still treats arson more severely, likely following the same logic discussed above, that it is far harder to catch an arsonist in the act than it is to catch even the most furtive of lumberjacks. Given the connection between arson and theft as crimes of secrecy, we begin to see why *Be blaserum* would group arson with *morþslyht* (lit., murder-slaying) as categorically similar crimes to be handled with identical protocols. Like *morð*, the word *morþslyht* insinuates the concealment of the act,[73] but the context of this law insinuates why its authors could pair it with arson and thereby unite two very different crimes in accordance with their mutually secretive nature.[74]

Be blaserum is certainly a pragmatic law produced by those who, as Patrick Wormald has suggested, were "locally entrusted with law enforcement and its rewards."[75] As such, it displays a grounded concern for the management of evidence in cases where the practicalities of enforcing the law were impeded by the criminal's efforts at concealment; it is a concern that complicates the picture I have painted above in which concealment primarily falls under the domain of sovereign power. But at the most basic level, grouping together these two furtive crimes—arson and *morðslyht*—effectively allows the law to treat both crimes as forms of perjury, which thereby limits the criminal's ability to produce an oath in his own defense since any such oath must be backed by the authority of a threefold ordeal. *Be blaserum* is not the only law to employ this kind of categorical approach to crimes that interfere with the smooth epistemological operation of the law, particularly crimes that involve concealment from the purview of witnesses.[76] Secrecy was an ingrained aspect of certain criminal activities, and Anglo-Saxon law codes strategically criminalized those actions that had the potential to operate outside of its reach or disrupt the web of sociolegal processes that depended on openness, reflecting a very practical concern for reining in criminal attempts at evasion and concealment. As we will see, such a concern becomes even greater and more acute in the handling of testimony, especially the testimony of those individuals prone to acts of concealment.

Testimony and Concealment

In Anglo-Saxon legal procedure, proof was reached by one of three means: an oath, a document, or the ordeal. Oaths were the primary and, by far, the most common method for accessing and presenting the underlying truth in legal disputes.[77] The swearing of oaths took place at nearly every turn of a proceeding, from the act of accusation to the act of denial to the presentation of witnesses and compurgators. Documents carried equal (if not, in some cases, greater) evidentiary value, particularly where land was concerned, but they were used less frequently than oaths.[78] The ordeal was reserved for situations in which a party was not considered to be oath-worthy, and it involved a physical test that would reveal, by divine intervention, the truth of the party's claim.[79] One method of the ordeal, for example, required a proband to carry a red-hot piece of iron in his bare hands. The hands would be bandaged, and if, following a set period of days, the bandages were removed to find the hands healed, the proband's claim would be judged true and his or her innocence, confirmed.[80] The ordeal and its reliance on God as an omniscient witness and judge will be discussed in more detail below, but for now we should recognize that Anglo-Saxon legal procedure primarily revolved around the swearing of oaths, words spoken by an individual and formulated as proof. Oaths were not just (as in contemporary legal practice) a precondition for the delivery of testimony or the presentation of further evidence to be evaluated and used in demonstrating and building a compelling case, but they were rather the culminating event of a legal proceeding: an oath alone could verify an accusation, just as it could a defense.[81] A case would thus be settled, primarily, according to whosever oath was more worthy (based on the social status and criminal history of the engaged parties) and, secondarily, according to the support that the parties could mount in the form of oath helpers (compurgators or witnesses who could attest to a party's oath-worthiness or who could verify a party's claims).[82]

When proof is dependent on testimony—as spoken language based on subjective experience—it necessarily becomes vulnerable to occlusion and concealment. Given the powerful influence that oaths had over the outcomes of legal cases, how were legal procedures able to credit the truth in the words of one individual or another? How did those procedures mitigate and discourage the inevitable and tempting forms of perjury that must have pervaded the legal scene? How were they able to reach satisfaction over any particular judgment? In other words, what were the limits to testimonial forms of proof, and how did Anglo-Saxon laws develop solutions in order to access and determine the truth as part of a larger process of resolving disputes? On the one hand, the law codes implemented a variety of pragmatic regulations in order to assess and account for the trustworthiness of a given witness. More significant, however, was the reliance on God as a constant witness, which provided reassurance that false testimony would go neither unnoticed nor unpunished, if not in this life, then in the next. Surely, defendants, plaintiffs, and witnesses must have lied; the temptation would have been too great to take advantage of this faith that the legal system placed in the oath bearer's compulsory submission to the divine Judge. The laws against perjury (which we will consider below) further demonstrate that the bearing of false witness must have been a serious and evidently common problem. But at the same time, the combination of pragmatic regulations and the reliance on divine surveillance and judgment (whether the anticipated Last Judgment or the immediate judgment via the ordeal) would, at least in theory, have produced a remarkably efficient system of justice.

The first juridical goal in this system, even before the exercising of oaths and ordeals, was to ensure that crimes were brought within the purview of the law. From early in the period, codes such as King Ine's forbade so-called secret compositions ("diernum geðingum"), arrangements whereby the implicated parties would attempt to resolve a crime outside of the legal system, thereby concealing both the crime and its resolution from the royal legal apparatus.[83] Approaching the crime from a different angle later in the period, Æthelstan (r. 924–939) addressed those bishops and ealdormen who might be inclined out of sheer laziness to permit "dyrnan geþingo" (secret compositions), and as punishment they would forfeit their office along with the king's friendship; they, too, would be required to pay a fine of 120 shillings.[84] Of course, even though these secret compositions were forbidden, the practice must have persisted. Yet what these laws clearly demonstrate is an insistent legal desire to draw such proceedings and their various components (from the initial transactions to the swearing of oaths) into the official domain of royal law.

Not only do secret compositions amount to the theft of profits from the king and other judicial authorities, but they also entail the concealment of a thief and an obstruction of the legal process itself.[85] The crime of harboring a thief or aiding his escape is also addressed frequently throughout Anglo-Saxon law, and several laws in Ine's code expressly forbid the concealment of a criminal. If, for example, a thief is captured and subsequently escapes, his captor becomes responsible for the value of the stolen goods (unless he is able to swear an oath denying his culpability).[86] According to another law, if the thief's captor allows him to escape or in some other way conceals the thief ("ðiefðe gedierne"), he takes on responsibility for the thief's wergild.[87] In other words, these laws treat the act of concealing the theft as tantamount to the crime of theft itself. Later Anglo-Saxon laws also forbid the shielding ("werian") or secret harboring ("dearnunga feormige") of a criminal or thief, and some laws similarly sentence the culprit to the same punishment as the criminal who received his aid.[88] As Wormald argues, these acts of shielding a crime or harboring a criminal were punished as a form of treason against the king, since the establishment of loyalty oaths from Alfred through Cnut enjoined the king's subjects from "concealing the disloyalty of others."[89] Still other laws seek not merely to discourage concealment but instead to encourage testimony by protecting anyone who "dyrne orf ameldað" (informs about concealed cattle) or who "soðre gewitnesse bið" (is a true witness).[90] None of these laws is especially surprising, but they all ultimately establish a crucial differentiation between those good witnesses who are essential to open transactions and those problematic witnesses who are privy to a crime and yet choose to conceal it. That decision to conceal the crime is what distinguishes a witness from an accomplice: the former is indispensable; the latter, immensely disruptive.

The type and quality of the witness makes all the difference between illicit collusion and legitimate oath helping. Ine §7, for example, is concerned with what must have been an extremely common problem: "Gif hwa stalie, swa his wíf nyte 7 his bearn, geselle LX scill. to wite" (If someone steals without the cognizance of his wife and child, he shall pay a fine of sixty shillings).

However, according to the same law, if he "stalie on gewitnesse ealles his hiredes, gongen hie ealle on ðeowot" (steals with the cognizance of all his family, then they all shall go into slavery).[91] The fee of sixty shillings may seem low when compared to other laws in Ine's code (e.g., Ine §12) and elsewhere, which demand the thief's life. Liebermann and others resolve the apparent discrepancy by suggesting that sixty shillings and slavery are punishments for a thief who is not caught in the act ("Die Tat ist nicht handhaft").[92] However, these two punishments (sixty shillings and slavery) actually appear to be aimed at the crime of familial accessory; hence, rather than assigning a punishment to the thief himself, Ine §7 lays out an additional punishment imposed on the family of the thief to account for the possibility that they might have been privy to the crime. If they are not accessories, the thief's family pays sixty shillings from his assets after he has been executed; if the family members are accessories, then they all ("ealle") go into slavery. The word "ealle" likely refers back to the specific phrase "ealles his hiredes," implying that the thief's entire family (save the thief himself, since he would be punished separately) would be sold into slavery. What makes wives and children uniquely different from other witnesses to a crime is that they are expected to keep the secrets of their husbands and fathers. The poem *Maxims I* captures this obligation with gnomic clarity, explaining that a good queen (or woman, or wife) is one who must, among other things, "rune healdan" (keep secrets [or counsel]).[93] A similar assumption is confronted by VI Æthelstan §1.1, which sentences a thief to death, divides his property, and gives a third of it to his wife only "gif heo clæne sy 7 þæs fácnes gewita nære" (if she is innocent and is not privy to the crime). This analogue again helps explain the apparently lenient inconsistency in Ine §7, suggesting that the fee would be imposed *in addition to* the punishment of the thief. Furthermore, Ine §7.2 goes on to specify that "x wintre cniht mæg bion ðiefðe gewita" (a ten-year-old child can be an accessory/witness to a theft). Delineating whose knowledge counts as valid testimony also involves delineating whose knowledge is a threat to the delicate functioning of the law with respect to its reliance on oaths and testimony. The fine line between accessory and witness (*gewita* and *gewitnes*) is particularly evident in the language of these laws, which use the two terms (*gewita* and *gewitnes*) almost interchangeably. But because the witnesses in question are family, they are automatically reasoned to be accessories if they are privy to the crime; they are bound by an obligation (whether satisfied or not) to keep the father's secrets.

Accomplices aside, Anglo-Saxon laws frequently relied on human witnesses, of which there were several different categories. A warrantor (*bond* or *getyma*), for instance, was the person from whom a piece of property was purchased or, sometimes, a third-party witness to a transaction.[94] If the property was found to have been stolen, the current owner would vouch (*getyman*) the warrantor (*getyma*) in order to prove that he rightfully purchased the property and did not steal it (this practice will be discussed in more detail in Chapter 2). Alternatively, many laws consider witnesses (often a *gewitnes*) to be an essential part of any legitimate property transaction. The best protection against accusations of theft would have therefore been to conduct all transactions openly and only before such trustworthy witnesses: a law from King Edward, for example, specifically requires "ungeligene gewitnesse" (trustworthy [i.e., not-lying] witnesses), and another law in Hlothhere & Eadric's code stipulates that a buyer must have two or three trustworthy men ("unfacne ceorlas") or the reeve of the king's estate ("cyninges wicgerefan") as witnesses to a transaction in order to defend against accusations of theft in case the seller cannot later be produced as a warrantor.[95]

The witness in these cases would probably be required to make a statement such as this: "On ælmihtiges Godes naman, swa ic her N. on soðre gewitnesse stande, unabeden 7 ungeboht to, swa ic hit minum egum oferseah 7 minum earum oferhyrde, ðæt ðæt ic him mid sæcge" (In the name of Almighty God, as I here stand for N. in true witness, unsolicited and unbought, so I saw with my own eyes and heard with my own ears that which I declare on his behalf).[96] This formula establishes that the witness remains independent (thus his integrity uncompromised), and yet the statement is also made on behalf of the principal party ("N."). Unlike modern legal practice, which relies on autonomous witnesses to testify to their own experiences of a relevant event (either being summoned by a court or coming forth independently), Anglo-Saxon procedures tended to leave little room for witnesses to act as such. However, a subcategory of witnesses known as "informers" (*meldan*) served to bring information forward. Their role was typically independent and voluntary, but also, in a sense, compulsory: the word *melda* often referred to objects or pieces of property that could somehow attest to their rightful owner or announce their own involvement in a crime, such as a stolen slave who returns as an informer, or a cowbell, dog collar, and a horn used for blowing, or other such announcers of a theft.[97] We have already considered, for instance, the curious axiom "sio æsc bið melda, nalles ðeof" (the axe is an informer and not a thief), which also confirms the notion that a *melda* can announce a crime even if it is otherwise considered to be a mere object.[98] The evidence for the practical use of informers is sparse, but they nevertheless seemed to have been valued across several law codes for their capacity to bring a crime to light, although not necessarily to participate in its juridical resolution.

Oath helpers or compurgators constituted another category of witnesses, who serve to support the oath of the principal party. Since the weight of one oath in relation to an opposing oath was determined primarily by the oath bearer's social status, an oath helper assisted an oath bearer by lending credibility to his status. An oath made with this support was considered, according to one of Æthelred's laws, incontrovertible: "þæt þæt man cyðe mid gewitnesse, þæt nan man þæt ne awende æt cwicon þe ma þe æt deadon" (that which a man declares with witnesses no man shall be able to alter, whether the persons concerned are alive or dead).[99] And with such influence comes responsibility. That particular law thus goes on to insist upon the gravity of acting as such a witness: "7 gang ælc man þæs to gewitnesse, þe he durre on þam haligdome swerian, þe him man on hand sylð" (And a man shall appear as witness to such things only as he is prepared to swear on the relics which are given into his hand).[100] This admonition also divulges the underlying logic of the practice: the efficacy of an oath as a means for accessing the truth was predicated on the assumption that a broken or false oath would be recognized and judged by God, hence the requirement here that the witness be prepared to hold in his hand and swear on relics, and hence the compulsory and formulaic invocation of the deity at the moment of swearing any oath.[101]

Perjury and the bearing of false witness obviously posed a serious problem, because of both their potential to obstruct a legal proceeding and the immediate ease with which that obstruction might have been carried out. Numerous secular laws therefore attempt to discourage perjury by setting relatively high penalties for the crime, if discovered; these penalties, however, only supplemented (and, indeed, often stipulated) a primary reliance on ecclesiastical and penitential forms of discipline.[102] II Æthelstan §26, as one particularly dramatic example, thus forbids a perjurer to be buried in consecrated ground; that is, "buton he hæbbe ðæs biscopes gewitnesse, ðe he on his scriftscire sy, þæt he hit swa gebet hæbbe, swa him his scrift scrife" (unless he has the testimony of the bishop, in whose diocese he is, that he has made such amends as his confessor has prescribed to him). In addition to assigning penitential consequences for acts of perjury, the law codes also show little tolerance for those who might be likely (based on prior actions) to swear a false oath. Since the oath bearer and the oath helpers must all be of good repute in order for their oaths to have any value, the ill reputation of someone who perpetrates certain crimes would automatically disqualify him from later acting as a witness or swearing an oath. For example, proven perjurers are typically exiled from the region in which they were convicted (unless they have properly atoned for the crime), but they also lose the privilege of clearing themselves by oath in the future.[103] Likewise, in Ine's code, those who are repeatedly accused of theft forfeit their oathworthiness.[104] If perjurers or thieves happened to be put to the proof, they would be required to undergo the ordeal in lieu of swearing an oath. Æthelstan's Grately code similarly stipulates that a moneyer accused of counterfeiting would lose the hand used in committing the crime, unless he wished to clear himself by means of the ordeal; for him, swearing an oath was not an option.[105] While any criminal's trustworthiness is automatically called into question by his prior willingness to resort to crime, it is the nature of these particular crimes (perjury, theft, and counterfeiting) that consistently provokes juridical anxiety over the oath-worthiness of their perpetrators. These are crimes that, as we have seen, entail a deliberate attempt to conceal something from the law, and on that basis they raise a red flag about the perpetrator's willingness to conceal information from the law in the future. Oaths were, of course, particularly vulnerable to such concealment.

In the face of this dilemma—a dilemma arising either from the need to extract information out of notoriously untrustworthy individuals (that is, individuals likely to conceal information) or from the need to do so in situations where such information is simply inaccessible and unavailable—the solution is to use the ordeal. By appealing to the indisputability of divine knowledge, the ritual of the ordeal would call on God as both witness and judge to produce a verdict through some form of physical test. For example, one version of the ordeal would require an individual to grab a stone from the bottom of a pot of boiling water. If the wounds were uninfected after three days, he was deemed innocent; if not, then guilty. The healing (or lack thereof) was thus a sign of God's judgment and a demonstration of his omniscience. The varieties of judicial ordeal have been well studied, and scholars have explored the many social ramifications and psychological intricacies of the practice in early medieval England.[106] Within these studies, the ordeal is consistently recognized for its reliance on a system of belief that acknowledges and trusts in God as an omniscient, fair, and omnipotent judge. In his study of the origins of the notion of reasonable doubt, for example, James Q. Whitman has argued that "ordeals were not used as 'magical' means of discovering unknown facts. . . . Instead, what mattered most about the ordeals was their capacity to spare human beings the responsibility for judgment. An ordeal induced God to take the fearsome step of incriminating the accused person, thus allowing human beings to avoid the intimidating obligation of judging their fellows."[107] But the purpose of the ritual was not merely aimed at relieving judges of their duty to impart judgment. After all, the ordeal did still require someone—a human being—to interpret a divine sign: how deeply must the proband's body sink into the holy water? how healed must his scalded hands be?

More importantly, however, the ritual served to reveal the criminal's faithlessness. Indeed, it would distinguish those who believe and submit to God's omniscience from those who do not. Even more forcefully, it would compel those who might waver in their belief to surrender to the totalizing power of God's omniscience, at least eventually. Someone with a guilty conscience may try to hide his crime from the law and from God in order to avoid punishment, but as soon as the possibility of discovery becomes a reality through the divine announcement in the ordeal, the risk of discovery becomes too great. The proband's feeling of guilt (if he is in fact guilty) becomes self-fulfilling. As Patrick Wormald explains, "in so far as the ordeal 'worked', it was through exploiting a guilty conscience."[108] Divine miracles aside, the ordeal worked, in other words, because the proband who feared that the ritual would reveal his crime would be less able to concentrate on swiftly removing the stone from the boiling water or would be more likely to take a deep breath before plunging into the water (thus more likely to float in demonstration of his guilt).[109] This theory cannot account for the fact that some wrongdoers surely had steady enough nerves to evade the test. But it might explain how the truly innocent proband achieved a desirable outcome. By turning to God through prayer, calmly trusting in God's will and benevolence, he would likely take on the challenge of the ordeal with calm, reassured concentration. The ordeal rituals were designed to instill fear in the guilty criminal, whose guilt would prevent him from faithfully turning to God. If, however, the criminal turned to God prior to the ordeal (perhaps even confessing his crime, a desirable outcome induced by the mere threat of the ordeal), that newfound faith—again in practical terms—would probably increase his chances of passing the test (if the test were still deemed necessary). These scenarios demonstrate the importance of belief, but they also demonstrate its complexity. Paradoxically, while the ordeal might reveal the guilt of a criminal who has faithlessly tried to hide his crime from God, the ordeal can only work if that guilty criminal has some inkling of an underlying belief in God's omniscience. In other words, he must have some sense—even if it is deeply suppressed—of the impossibility of concealing his crime from God, and yet he has chosen to do so regardless.

The ordeal rituals, such as *Iudicia Dei II* (one of nine such rituals that survive in various manuscripts), demonstrate the force with which the practice would emphasize God's omnipotent role:

> Deus, qui per ignem signa magna ostendens, Abraham, puerum tuum, de incendio Chaldeorum, quibusdam pereuntibus, eruisti; Deus, qui rubum ardere ante conspectum Moysi et minime conburi permisisti; Deus, qui ab incendio fornacis Chaldaicis, plerisque succensis, tres pueros tuos inlaesos eduxisti; Deus, qui incendio ignis populum sodomae et Gomorrae inuoluens, Loth famulum tuum cum suis saluti donasti; Deus, qui in aduentu sancti Spiritus tui inlustratione ignis fideles tuos ab infidelibus decreuisti, ostende nobis in hoc paruitatis nostrae examine uirtutem eiusdem sancti Spiritus et per huius ignis feruorem discerne fideles et

infideles, *ut a tactu eius furti—uel homicidii uel adulterii—, cuius inquisitio agitur conscii exhorrescant, et manus eorum (uel pedes) comburantur aliquatenus, inmunes uero ab eiusmodi crimine liberentur penitus et inlesi permaneant.*[110]

[God, you who showing great wonders through fire dragged Abraham, your son, from the Chaldean conflagration when others perished; God, you who allowed the bush to burn before the gaze of Moses without being consumed; God, you who led your three boys unscathed from the blaze of the Chaldean furnace, while a great many were burned up; God, you who engulfed the people of Sodom and Gomorrah in an inferno of fire, but gave safety to your servant Lot and his own; God, you who in the advent of your Holy Spirit distinguished the faithful from the unfaithful with the sign of fire: show us in this test of our puniness the strength of that same Holy Spirit, and through the heat of this fire distinguish the faithful from the unfaithful, *so that by its touch those knowing of that theft—or homicide or adultery—whose investigation is proceeding may be terrified*, and their hands (or feet) burned somewhat, but those immune from that charge may be freed completely and remain unharmed.][111]

The rhetorically accentuated list of God's pyrotechnic accomplishments culminates in the anticipation of his next miracle, the immediacy of which is designed to terrify those privy (*conscii*) to the crime at hand and to produce in those *conscii* a kind of fear that betrays their faithlessness. At the same time, it can also produce a kind of fear that has the power to generate a renewed and more compelling form of faith in which the *conscii* recognize and submit to the awe-inspiring power of God. Another prayer in the same ritual thus speaks to precisely this effect on the audience, who "hoc uidentes ab incredulitate sua . . . liberentur" (seeing this [ritual], may be freed of their unbelief).[112] As Wormald notes, "the more the atmosphere was infused with awareness of the Divine Presence and the certainty of His action, through biblical reminiscences of the shattering precedents, the more profound the effect on an uneasy conscience would be."[113]

The ordeal was used especially in those cases where crucial pieces of knowledge were unavailable or when such information could only be provided by someone considered untrustworthy. As Bartlett notes, the ordeal was both convenient and indispensable, especially in cases dealing with crimes that entailed concealment:

The apparent diversity of the situations in which the ordeal was employed should not hide the fact that, beyond this variety, there was common ground. Sexual issues, such as adultery or disputed paternity, are, by their very nature, the cases least usually resolved by witnesses, there being no visible evidence on which to base a judgment. This also explains the frequent use of the ordeal in crimes of stealth—murder as distinct from homicide, theft by night, and so on. Heresy and other cases in which trials of faith were used have a similar "invisible quality"—what was at issue was belief, and belief is intangible.... In all these situations a clear resolution of the issue by normal means was impossible; these cases all share a common tenacious opacity. Yet they were cases which had to be decided—there could be no suspension of judgment.... This was the role of the ordeal.[114]

Judgment is, in part, an act of mediating between what is known and what is unknown. When such mediation cannot otherwise take place—when what is unknowable exceeds what is knowable—the ordeal becomes an absolutely essential tool. It forces the body of the proband to testify and at the same time authenticates that testimony with divine confirmation; it makes God's judgment manifest in the here and now so that earthly judgment might carry on without further delay. If the oath is primarily an oral procedure, then the ordeal is one in which visual signs replace verbal ones, as the body displays its guilt or innocence, sidestepping the always-present risk of spoken deceit and error, the always-present risk of testimonial concealment. But even the oath, as Bartlett recognized, "was, in some sense, an ordeal, but one which relied upon God's eventual rather than his immediate judgment."[115] Both the oath and the ordeal—the two primary forms of proof in Anglo-Saxon law—thus served to make manifest that which God already knows; the ordeal, on the other hand, had the power to make manifest that which was concealed from all but God.

The body becomes a site of that manifestation, as it bears the sign of its own testimony. Katherine O'Brien O'Keeffe has argued that the nature and purpose of this bodily testimony changes over the course of the Anglo-Saxon period, as corporeal mutilation becomes by the eleventh century an important mode of punishment aimed at giving the criminal an opportunity to save his soul by forcing his mutilated body to announce its guilt outwardly for the remainder of his life on earth.[116] The ordeal, when it involves such mutilation, thereby turns into a productive means of inducing repentance and salvation, not merely for torturing the truth out of its target: the body is thus produced "as a site at which secular law and divine power meet."[117] But even when the salvation of the criminal was not explicitly at stake, the body under the ordeal, just like the speaker swearing an oath, still constituted a site where secular law met the divine. The ordeal is, of course, among the most extreme moments in which such a meeting would have taken place. But even though the ordeal was not always used, its efficacy and reality would have reminded any subject of the law that attempting to conceal information from the law—or worse, from God—whether, for instance, by perjury, theft, or counterfeiting, would always and inevitably risk exposure. By resorting to the ordeal as a means to remove doubt and uncertainty from judicial testimony,[118] the legal system harnessed God's omniscience to its own hermeneutic and epistemological advantage, while simultaneously making it all the more perilous to attempt to conceal secrets on earth.

Chapter 2

The Secret Seized: Theft, Death, and Testimony

In the following piece of legislation from the code of King Ine, we catch a glimpse of the testimonial and epistemological complexities often negotiated by Anglo-Saxon law:

> Gif mon forstolenne man befo æt oþrum, 7 sie sio hand oðcwolen, sio hine sealde þam men þe hine mon æt befeng, tieme þonne þone mon to þæs deadan byrgelse, swa oðer fioh swa hit sie, 7 cyðe on þam aðe be LX hida, þæt sio deade hond hine him sealde; þonne hæfð he þæt wite afylled mid þy aðe, agife þam agendfrio þone monnan.
>
> [If a man lays claim to a stolen man (i.e., a slave) who is the property of another, and if the hand (i.e., the previous owner) is dead who has sold him to the man in whose possession he is attached, he shall vouch the dead man's grave to warranty for the slave—just as for any other property, whatever it may be—and declare in his oath of sixty hides that the dead hand sold the man to him; then he shall have freed himself from the fine by the oath, and he shall give back the man to his owner.][1]

This is a strange law, often cited but little discussed. Despite the bizarre legal dilemma that it anticipates, the abstruse language it uses to resolve it, and the surprising solution it prescribes, its forthrightness seems to follow remarkably ordinary procedural logic. At its core, Ine §53 deals with a case of property dispute; the stolen object and the means for recuperating it follow the same fundamental reasoning found in other such Anglo-Saxon legislation. Two aspects of the law, however, make it particularly unusual and problematic. First, the stolen property is a human being ("forstolenne man"), an implied slave—at once human and property—and, as such, always bearing the potential to speak, to testify on its own behalf, and to announce its own history even if the law demands its silence. And second, the law stipulates that if the slave's former owner has died, then the current owner must prove that he rightfully purchased the slave from the former owner (the "deade hond") by vouching his grave or estate to warranty.

In early medieval cases of property dispute, the process of vouching to warranty (*getyman*) was an essential part of proving the rightful ownership of movable goods. The process begins with the understanding, as we have seen in the previous chapter, that all transactions were to be conducted "beforan godum weotum" (before good witnesses) and "undeornunga" (openly, unsecretly), so that the parties involved could easily and thoroughly dispute any charges of theft.[2] Vouching to warranty was one means of doing so: the current owner accused of theft (party A) would call on the former owner of the stolen property (party B, known in Old English as the *hond* and in Latin as the *auctor*); party B would then swear an oath that he legally sold the property to the current owner (party A). This process, known in legal studies as "vouching to warranty," would prove either that the property was not stolen or at least that the current owner (party A) had no knowledge that the property had been stolen at some point prior to his acquisition of it. If the plaintiff continues to claim ownership of the stolen object, the burden then falls on the former owner (party B) to prove that he, too, was unaware that the property was stolen by vouching another warrantor (party C) to verify that he (party B) had lawfully purchased the property before selling it to the current owner (party A).[3] This process ideally produces a transparent chain of testimony that continues until it reaches someone who cannot produce a warrantor and who is thereby determined to have been the thief. Vouching to warranty thus serves as a prerequisite to the prosecution of and defense against any charge of theft.

Despite its somewhat abstruse language, Ine §53 simply negotiates a situation in which a stolen slave is found in someone's possession, and it does so by requiring the current owner (party A) to prove that he legally purchased (hence, did not steal) the slave by vouching the previous owner (party B), and so on and so forth. The party who cannot supply a witness to verify his lawful purchase of the slave is assumed to be the thief (or at least to have been privy to the theft and knowledgeable of the fact that he was purchasing stolen goods, a situation already discussed above). In either case, the property is then returned to its rightful owner. There are various iterations of the procedure of vouching to warranty found throughout early medieval law codes, and much of the variation reflects the complex situations that would inevitably arise when a link is broken in the chain of testimony (a chain in which A ideally vouches B, B ideally vouches C, etc.). Some laws, for example, account for witnesses who claim never to have sold the particular item in question.[4] Others account for cases in which the wrong party is vouched or in which someone is vouched, but he claims himself to be the original owner (thereby stopping the process altogether).[5] Still other laws stipulate the location where the vouching should take place so as not to burden the claimant in the event the property was moved and traded far from his home.[6] Most of the laws emphasize the necessity of physical presence and oral testimony.[7] The death of a former owner, as we find anticipated in Ine §53, must have therefore been a common yet serious break in this theoretically ideal chain of testimony. This serious break arises from the obvious fact that death silences its victims and graves conceal them. The fact that death was considered the most absolute form of secrecy on multiple levels has deep cultural roots that are worth pursuing in order to understand why Ine §53's reliance on the burial place of the dead witness would have been a solution both strikingly implausible and yet legitimately acceptable.

Death and the Secrecy of Encryption

The Greek verb κρύπτω (*kryptō*), meaning "to hide, cover, conceal," is etymologically bound to the word κρύπτη (*kryptē*): "a covered place, vault, crypt."[8] Stone slabs and earthen mounds, tombs and crypts—buried, locked, closed, covered, sealed—embody and announce the secrecy and silence they maintain. In one sense, they topographically conceal and simultaneously publicize the bodily silence of the corpse, now dead, unable to speak, and unable to testify except through the outward display of the grave. Yet this absolute secrecy of death and the associated secrecy of the crypt was also often subverted, as graves are made to testify, relics of saints give signs of divine approval or disapproval, and the dead miraculously speak. This tension between the implied secrecy of death and the occasions of postmortem disclosure at once renders the secrecy of death hardly absolute and those occasions of disclosure all the more spectacular and meaningful.

While the Greek etymology—κρύπτω, κρύπτη—may have been somewhat obscure in early medieval England, it reflects a conceptual and cultural commonplace. The dark and secret topography of crypts, graves, and caverns appears, for instance, in the famous lines of *The Wanderer*, in which the speaker laments the death of his lord: "siþþan geara iu goldwine minne / hrusan heolstre biwrah" (since long ago I covered over my liberal patron with the darkness of the earth).[9] A common Old English word for this kind of concealing darkness, *heolstor* also often conveys the dark concealment of earthen graves.[10] And immediately before this mournful description of his lord's burial, the speaker uses similar language to praise the act of sealing and concealing the thoughts of one's mind, making a clear connection between the locking of thoughts and the locking of a tomb.[11] The latter produces, necessitates, and mirrors the former:

> Forðon domgeorne   dreorigne oft
> in hyra breostcofan   bindað fæste;
> swa ic modsefan   minne sceolde,
> oft earmcearig,   eðle bidæled,   20
> freomægum feor   feterum sælan,
> siþþan geara iu   goldwine minne
> hrusan heolstre biwrah.[12]

[Therefore, those who are eager for glory must often bind fast in their breast-chambers that which is miserable; so must I, so often sorrowful, cut off from my homeland, far from kinsmen, seal my mind with fetters, since long ago I covered my liberal patron with the darkness of the earth.]

The fetters with which the speaker must seal his own mind, binding it fast and keeping his thoughts contained, mirror the isolation of his exile ("eðle bidæled") and the darkness of the sepulchral earth ("hrusan heolstre"): the lord's grave is both cause and model for the wanderer's own intellectual containment and secrecy.[13]

Other poems reflect an even more intimate connection between secrecy and burial. *The Panther*, for example, describes Christ's resurrection with a curious choice of language:

> ond þy þriddan dæge
> of *digle* aras,   þæs þe he deað fore us
> þreo niht þolade.[14]

[On the third day he arose from the *digle* (i.e., tomb), because he suffered death for us three nights before.]

Christ's state of death and his tomb are plainly and simply characterized as a secret ("digle") from which he has broken free.[15] This seemingly unusual and rare metaphor for Christ's death and entombment works in this poem precisely because the scene of resurrection is itself so familiar, allowing the reader to fill in the obvious connection between the word "digle" and the tomb to which it refers. The provocative word thus accentuates those details in the Gospels, where Christ's body is concealed by the great stone secured at the mouth of the sepulcher, even while it remained under the constant surveillance of Pontius Pilate's guards: they "munierunt sepulchrum, signantes lapidem, cum custodibus" (made the sepulcher sure, sealing the stone, and setting guards).[16] The concealment represented by the sealed stone is inverted once the stone has been moved back and the contents of the sepulcher revealed. For Bede, the opening of the tomb even comes to signify a kind of hermeneutic uncovering of the Old Law, since "Mystice autem reuolutio lapidis sacramentorum est reuolutio diuinorum quae quondam littera legis claudebantur occulta" (spiritually, the rolling away of the stone is the uncovering of the divine sacraments, which were formerly sealed up, covered by the letter of the Law).[17] In *The Panther*, Christ's three days in the sepulcher parallel the panther's habit of feasting and then slumbering for three days in "dygle stowe under dunscrafum" (the secret place under the mountain gorge).[18] The panther's secret lair thus becomes an allegory for the secrecy of Christ's tomb. And just as the panther's slumber is followed by a bellowing roar, the silence of Christ's entombment is followed by the promulgation of the news of his resurrection, its "swete stenc" (sweet fragrance) spreading about the entire world ("geond woruld ealle").[19]

Numerous other poetic references further capture this secrecy of death. Using a similarly dark and secret image of interment, for instance, Psalm 142 in the *Paris Psalter* offers a prayer begging for God's ear, even though the enemy has already destroyed and metaphorically buried the supplicant:

> Hi me on digle   deorce stowe
> settan sarlice   samed anlice,
> swa þu worulddeade   wrige mid foldan.[20]

[He has set me sorely in a secret dark place, just like those who are dead in this world, covered with earth.]

In Cynewulf's *Elene*, the True Cross undergoes a similar fate, where it (in one of the poem's several such statements) "þurh feondes searu foldan getyned, / lange legere fæst leodum dyrne / wunode wælreste" (through the fiend's cunning was buried in the earth, resting fast for a long time, secret from the people, it lay buried).[21] In a starkly different context, Beowulf famously announces, prior to his fight with Grendel, that

> Na þu minne þearft   445
> hafalan hydan,   ac he me habban wile
> dreore fahne,   gif mec deað nimeð.[22]

[There will be no need for you to hide my head, but he will have done so to me, gory and bloodstained, if death takes me.]

And *Maxims I* obscurely describes the ocean as the secret place of the dead: "deop deada wæg dyrne bið lengest" (the deep path of the dead is secret the longest).[23] These passages all rely on a shared set of assumptions and imagery:

that regardless of their causes, death and burial entail an inevitable kind of concealment and secrecy.

Indeed, the secrecy in these passages, far from representing the "disintegration of society" associated with the crime of secret murder, as E. J. Christie has proposed in his discussion of *Maxims I*, is in fact an unavoidable kind of secrecy fundamental to all forms of death and burial, whether natural or iniquitous.[24] When the dead were buried on land or at sea (as many surely were), their graves concealed their bodies and symbolized their silence. As Beowulf's statement suggests, even if the chance to bury the corpse was lost, it would still be hidden one way or another. In his discussion, Christie conflates the secrecy of death's unpredictable arrival (as when death is personified as a stealthy thief in the night) with the secrecy of murder (as distinguished from open homicide) and finally with the inevitable secrecy of the corpse's silence.[25] These are three discrete forms of secrecy, as we have seen over the course of this chapter, and the final form of secrecy (the silence of the corpse) was only socially disruptive (and sometimes, we might imagine, advantageous) insofar as the dead may have formerly possessed knowledge that could be beneficial or detrimental to the living, to one's reputation, for instance, or to the outcome of a legal dispute.

In addition to the secrecy associated with burial, we repeatedly encounter images of the silence that death necessarily produces. One of the Blickling Homilies, for instance, gives a rather unpleasant description of the physical reality of death: "Se lichoma þonne on þone heardestan stenc & on þone fulostan bið gecyrred, & his eagan þonne beoþ betynde, & his muþ & his næsþyrlo beoþ belocene, & he þonne se deada byð uneaþe ælcon men on neawsste to hæbbenne" (The body will be turned into the strongest and vilest odor, his eyes will be shut, his mouth and nostrils will be sealed, and then it will be difficult for the corpse to be kept near any [living] men).[26] Poles apart from the "swete stenc" of Christ's resurrection, the very real and gruesome decay of a dead body entails, among other unpleasant things, the sealing or locking ("belocene") of its perceptual and presentational organs. The corpse can neither speak nor hear (and even if it could, people would be inclined to keep their distance). The silenced tongue and sealed ears, moreover, become a motif in the *Soul and Body* poems, where the Soul berates the dead Body for being "dumb ond deaf"[27] and where the savage worms of the grave tear the Body's tongue into ten pieces ("Bið seo tunge totogen on tyn healfe / hungrum to hroþor") so that it can no longer exchange words ("ne mæg . . . wordum wrixlan").[28] And a similar theme is repeated throughout the late Old English poem known as *The Soul's Address to the Body*, in which at one particularly trenchant point the Soul disparages the dead Body, saying "þeo men beoþ þe bliþre, þe arisen ær wiþ þe, / þæt þin muþ is betuned" (people who formerly quarreled with you will be the happier now that your mouth is shut).²⁹ Death renders the body silent even before the grave subjects it to its profound state of concealment.

Vouching the Grave

Clearly, death had a deep association with silence and secrecy, while tombs and crypts externally represented and mirrored the body's absolute state of concealment. But despite the frequency with which the problem of a dead witness must have arisen, very few Anglo-Saxon laws address the issue directly. On the one hand, the scarcity of such laws is especially surprising, given that the death of a witness was, in effect, the accidental concealment of information equivalent to the concealment of a thief or a murderer, since it removed pertinent knowledge from judicial oversight. On the other hand, however, because such concealment-by-loss was in most cases simply unavoidable and for the most part unresolvable, legislators must have had little confidence in measures designed to overcome such a hindrance. The only other Anglo-Saxon example of a similar attempt is found in a piece of legislation that dates to around the year 1000, several centuries after King Ine's reign. II Æthelred §9 explains the process of vouching to warranty in detail and includes a clause specifically addressing the need to vouch a dead warrantor:

> Gyf hwa to deadan tyme—buton he yruenoman hæbbe, ðe hit clænsie—geswutelie mid gewitnysse, gif he mæge, þæt he riht cenne, se ðe hit tyme; 7 clænsnige hine sylfne mid ðam. Ðonne bið se deada besmiten, buton he frind hæbbe, ðe hine mid rihte clænsnian, swa he sylf scolde, gif he mehte oðð liues wære.
>
> [If anyone vouches a dead person—unless he have an heir who can answer the charge—he who vouches him shall show by means of witnesses, if he can, that he is acting justly, and by means of them shall clear himself. Then the dead man will be held guilty, unless he have friends who will clear him according to the law, as he himself would have been obliged to do, had he been able or had he been alive.]³⁰

The scenario in II Æthelred §9.2 is similar to that of Ine §53, since both anticipate the problem of a dead warrantor. Both laws also include a clause that allows the heir of the estate to act in place of the dead man,³¹ and both follow the usual practice of requiring the warrantor (party B) subsequently to clear his own name; if he is dead, his heir must do so on his behalf. However, II Æthelred §9.2 resolves the complication of a dead witness not by using his grave as a symbolic surrogate, but rather by summoning other witnesses or compurgators to attest to the validity of the current owner's claim, presumably either by acting as character witnesses for the current owner or by stating that the former owner had indeed owned and sold the property in question.

Vouching the actual grave of the dead man ("þæs deadan byrgelse"), as required by Ine §53, therefore seems to have been a more unusual practice. The only other Anglo-Saxon evidence of such a practice in action may be found in the so-called Fonthill Letter, which settles a property dispute by sending the defendant to King Alfred's grave ("gesahte he ðines fæder lic" [then he sought your father's body]) to retrieve some sort of seal ("insigle").[32] But although some scholars have suggested a parallel between Ine §53 and the vague procedures of the Fonthill Letter, the precise role of Alfred's body ("lic") and the seal ("insigle") remains unclear.[33] What makes Ine §53 unique and distinct from both the scene in the Fonthill Letter and the directive of II Æthelstan §9.2 is its interpretive ingenuity; Ine §53 relies exclusively and authoritatively on the grave with no recourse to additional witnesses—enacting, as we will see, a remarkable management of various forms of testimonial concealment.

In his edition of the Anglo-Saxon laws, Benjamin Thorpe notes that "this practice of citing the dead to warranty is common to the laws of Germany and Scandinavia."[34] Putting aside for the moment the swearing on saintly relics, which was commonly recounted in hagiographic literature and will be discussed below, the earliest example that I could recover of a law prescribing an act of swearing on a deceased party (that is, someone involved in a case without any special holy status) comes from the Dimetian Code (*Llyfr Blegywryd*) of the Welsh king Hywel Dda (ca. 880–950), which concerns someone who buys property and dies before paying the debt. In order to claim the payment to which he is entitled, the claimant "ef adyly hagen tygu ary seithuet or dynyon nessaf ywerth ar ved y talawdyr ar dichawn ygaffel ac onys dichawn tyget ar yr allawr gyssegredic werthu ohonaw yda hwnnw idaw" (must swear along with six persons nearest to himself in worth, on the grave of the debtor, if he can find it, and, if he cannot, let him swear on the sacred altar, to having sold that property to him).[35] Here the grave clearly has a truth-producing quality, akin to or perhaps better than a sacred altar.[36] All other evidence of the practice comes from several centuries later. The German *Schwabenspiegel*, a vernacular law book compiled in Augsburg, ca. 1275, records a similar practice of swearing on a dead man in the presence of seven witnesses in order to claim any debts owed.[37] And in the fourteenth-century Swedish law code from the province of Uppland, we find a law dealing with cases of accidental death: if a man attempts to shoot an animal but someone gets in the way, the shooter must pay composition for the accidental deed and then swear an oath at three distinct þings, two of which are to be regional þings and the third is to be at the edge of the grave of his victim.³⁸

The practice also apparently persisted in England into the thirteenth century. For example, a document of legal instructions from the reign of King John (1199–1216) states, "E si il auient dedenz cele quinzeine ke li uns de ses testemonies murge, celui qui uiff est, pruuera son testimonie par serrement, e de iluec si iert menez sur la tumbe al mort: e la iurra que se il fust uif cel testemonie portereit" (And if it chance that within the fortnight one of his witnesses dies, he who survives shall prove his testimony on oath, and thence he shall be led to the tomb of the dead man, and there shall swear that if he was alive he would bear his testimony).³⁹ Eventually, the practice was banned by the end of the thirteenth century. The 1268 London charter of Henry III thus allows claimants to settle a dispute, but it expressly prohibits the swearing on the tomb of a dead witness:

> eo tamen excepto quod super tumulos mortuorum de eo quod dicturi essent mortui, si viverent, non liceat precise jurare, sed loco mortuorum qui ante obitum suum electi fuerint ad eos disrationandos qui de rebus ad coronam spectantibus appellati fuerint vel rectati, alii liberi et legales eligantur qui idem sine dilacione facient quod per defunctos memoratos, si viverent, fieri oporteret.⁴⁰

> [With this exception, however, that it shall not be lawful to swear precisely over the tombs of the dead concerning what the dead men would have said, if they were alive, but in the place of the dead men, who before their death were elected to clear those appealed or arraigned of matters relating to the crown, other free and lawful men shall be chosen to do without delay the same that ought to have been done by the said dead men, if they were living.]

This exception was further extended by Henry's son, King Edward.⁴¹ Not coincidentally, the prohibition of swearing on graves coincides with the sharp decline of the use of the judicial ordeal in the decades following the Fourth Lateran Council (1215), suggesting perhaps a perceived association between the use of a grave and the logic of the ordeal.⁴² With the subsequent rise of the jury trial in English common law (and inquisitorial procedures in Continental law) came a decline in the use of practices such as the ordeal and, evidently, the swearing on the graves of dead witnesses. In the five centuries after the establishment of Ine's code, the practice of vouching the graves of dead witnesses had thus become both prevalent and problematic enough to warrant its eventual and deliberate suspension.

However, this technique for recuperating the otherwise lost testimony of a dead witness has received only minimal and dated attention from scholars who have taken to criticizing it as an obviously tenuous form of proof (not unlike the proof supplied by oath or ordeal). The most theoretical assessment to date was made by Henry Charles Lea in his 1866 *Superstition and Force*, where, after briefly discussing the details of the practice, he comments:

> In such cases as these, there could be no doubt as to the absence of testimony, but legal complications are too various and perplexing to render all questions so easy of solution, nor can we expect to find, in the simplicity of primitive laws, elaborate general directions that may guide us in any attempt to investigate thoroughly the principles which the untutored barbarian may have applied to determine the admissibility of this kind of evidence. That they were not always such as would appear rational to us of the nineteenth century may safely be assumed.[43]

Perhaps realizing his own logic to be no more precise that the barbarian legal practices under analysis, Lea ultimately removed this particular passage from later editions of his study. But what it leaves behind is an unwillingness to see a different kind of evidence altogether. All of these laws—Anglo-Saxon, Welsh, Germanic, Scandinavian—are decidedly Christian, and this practice of vouching a grave is no exception. It is based not so much in pagan superstition or in the archaic handling of evidence but rather in an early attempt to reconcile the secular legal requirements of testimony with a Christian system of belief. Clearly, that reconciliation is not yet fully developed in the time of Ine or even by the time the practice lost favor under Henry III.[44]

Perhaps it is not yet fully developed because an oath sworn at the grave does not in itself appeal to God's judgment any more than an ordinary oath sworn in God's name. Swearing an oath on a grave, as in Ine §53, may seem akin to swearing an oath on holy relics, a practice used regularly especially toward the end of the Anglo-Saxon period.[45] But the two are not exactly the same. Relics and the grave of a deceased slave owner may both be composed of human remains, but relics surely held more spiritual and symbolic power than the average merchant's grave. Just as holy water was used as one method of the ordeal (if the proband sank, his claim was deemed true; if he floated, his claim was deemed false, since he was repelled like oil from ordinary water), holy relics would have offered a similar opportunity to test the veracity of the oath bearer's claim. Their power was derived from the saint, and they therefore always had the potential to reveal the truth miraculously (although, as some laws suggest, they did not always effectively do so).[46] Even if the practice of swearing an oath on a grave derived its logic from other related sources and models in early medieval law, such as the ordeal and the swearing on relics, it was still quite unusual: its effectiveness was imagined to derive both from God as a constant witness *and* from the dead as a particular source of memorial authority.

Ine §53, so far as I can tell, is the earliest example of a law that prescribes the act of swearing on the tomb of a dead witness as a substitute for the testimony of that witness.[47] All of the other examples are much later: the earliest written code is Hywel Dda's, but that belongs to the tenth century; the settings of II Æthelstan 9 and the Fonthill Letter likewise belong to the end of the tenth century; and the German *Schwabenspiegel* belongs to the thirteenth century, although it records laws long since in use. No such practices are found in the earlier Carolingian legal codes, such as the *Lex Salica*, or the Roman codes, such as the *Codex Theodosianus*. Two possible conclusions can be drawn from this evidence. On the one hand, as the nineteenth-century legal historians supposed, Ine §53 may have made use of an already widespread, Germanic social practice that assumed graves as truth-authorizing sites. On the other hand, this practice of vouching the grave may have actually originated from a situation precisely like the one that Ine §53 attempts to resolve, a unique instance in which a slave was alleged to have been stolen *and* the key witness had died—a situation, in other words, in which the concealment and loss of information was inevitable; its retrieval, impossible.

The Slave's Silence

Yet such retrieval was not always thought to be impossible. Theft was a serious concern in early medieval jurisprudence, as evidenced by the numerous laws in all of the major codes stipulating various means for preventing, managing, and prosecuting the crime. And the theft of slaves—although more difficult to accomplish and therefore probably less frequently executed than the theft of other forms of property (such as inanimate objects and livestock)—was not especially unusual.[48] Yet among the many other laws in Ine's code pertaining to crimes of theft, it is curious that none should prescribe the vouching of the grave of a dead witness, except for this particular law (§53) concerned with a stolen slave. I propose, therefore, that Ine §53 might go so far as to require the vouching of a grave precisely because the slave—the stolen object—has the potential to speak and therefore to testify. The law thus anticipates or responds to a scenario in which a party might be tempted to call on the slave to testify on account of the death of the key witness and the absence of a more viable alternative. Unlike stolen cattle or other pieces of property, the slave is actually a perfect witness to all of the transactions in which he was bought and sold, a perfect witness up to and including the moment in which he was stolen. That is, except for the fact that he is a slave.

The value of his testimony is undermined by his unfree status. Slaves held a nebulous yet minor legal status that fluctuated from law code to law code and also seems to have expanded with later developments in Anglo-Saxon law.[49] But although undermined by his status, the value of the slave's testimony would not have been completely illusory, as some codes grant slaves the ability to testify. For example, a late tenth-century law states that a slave ("ðeow") could in fact be vouched to warranty,[50] an allowance that seems to have followed the ninth-century development in Anglo-Saxon law that increased a slave's right to retain earnings and by extension to buy and sell property (as we find in Alfred §43).[51] But even in codes as early as the *Lex Salica* on the Continent, a slave who has been enticed away from his master must speak before three witnesses at three separate courts, and those nine total witnesses must then attest to the fact that the slave spoke in those three courts; only then could the slave be returned to his original master.[52] Closer in proximity to Ine §53, the code of Hlothhere & Eadric (which dates to between 685 and 686, only a rough decade earlier than Ine's code) specifically allows a stolen slave to speak as an informer ("stermelda") against his thief:

> Gif frigman mannan forstele, gif he eft cuma stermelda, secge an andweardne; gecænne hine, gif he mæge: hæbbe þare freora rim æwdamanna 7 ænne mid in aþe, æghwilc man æt þam tune þe he tohyre.
>
> [If a freeman steals a person, if he (*scil.* the stolen person) afterward comes as an informer, let him announce it in the presence (of the thief or of witnesses). Let him (the man accused) clear himself if he is able; let each man (so charged) have a number of free oath-men and one with (him) in the oath from the dwelling to which he belongs.][53]

The language that defines the stolen slave in this law ("Gif frigman mannan forstele") is extremely similar to the language of Ine §53 ("Gif mon forstolenne man befo"). And yet, this simple solution of allowing the slave to testify on his own behalf as an informer ("stermelda") in the case of his own theft and to testify to his own history is dismissed in favor of the symbolic warranty of a grave. Perhaps the status of an informant is assigned less legal power than a warrantor, given that the term *melda* (informer) tends to refer to objects that announce a crime as opposed to human warrantors or oath-bearers. Considering, as we have seen above, that an axe is referred to as a "melda" in Ine §43.1 (since the noise it makes announces its own use), and considering that in I Edgar §8 a cowbell, dog's collar, and horn are all also considered to be *meldan* (either metaphorically, or because they can stifle acts of theft by allowing property and potential thieves to announce themselves), it is not surprising that the slave who returns to his original owner would be grouped into this category of property that can somehow inform and testify.[54] However, what is peculiar and revealing about Ine §53 is that the law should altogether sidestep the slave's testimony (or even the slave's ability to serve as an informer) in favor of the authority of the grave.

By turning to a grave, Ine §53 enforces the slave's complete silence by providing an alternative source of testimony. Such silencing is consistent with the rest of Ine's code, which, unlike the other law codes discussed above, very clearly prohibits the vouching of a slave as a witness: "Gif mon forstolenne ceap befehð, ne mot hine mon tieman to ðeowum men" (If a stolen chattel is attached, a slave may not be vouched for it).[55] In the case of a stolen slave, however, the temptation to vouch the slave would have been considerable, and even greater if a key warrantor was dead. In other words, if the previous owner were still alive and could be vouched to warranty, then there would be no need even to consider vouching the slave as a witness. But since the warrantor has died, the law faces a choice between two problematic sources of testimony: one is silenced by death, and the other is civilly dead and barred from testifying.

The problem with a slave's testimony centers on a paradox of agency: the slave has his own will, and yet his will is also understood as subject to the will of his master. On the one hand, slaves could be stolen just like any other form of property, but they could also steal themselves away by escaping from their owner's control.[56] On the other hand, a slave's defense against accusations of theft would often be dependent on an oath sworn by his or her lord.[57] This tension produced by the slave's subjection to the will of his master comes to life in an episode of Lantfred of Winchester's *Miracula Sancti Swithuni*. According to the story, an enslaved woman was stolen and then sold in Winchester, only to be chained up by her new master. When eventually she discovered that her former master happened to be visiting the town of Winchester, "audacter ad priscum loqui uenit dominum—sine illius eri licentia, cuius imperio tum erat subdita" (she boldly came forward to speak to her former master—without the permission of that lord whose control she was then subject to).[58] This episode reveals the problem posed by the slave's obligation to her current master, which necessarily implicates the truthfulness of her testimony. Her ability to speak is contingent on the approval of her current master, even if the slave rightfully belongs to someone else. Here, the slave disobeys her current master's wishes in order to appeal to her former master, but that disobedience is clearly depicted as a scandalous (if noble) breach of her primary (although unjust) obligation. When it comes to speaking more formally as a witness to a crime, is a slave expected to speak on behalf of her own knowledge of the truth, or is she supposed to conceal the truth at the command of her current master, or is she obligated, instead, to the will of her former, rightful master? These possibilities, and the impossibility of determining which path a given slave has chosen to take, automatically render any slave's testimony deficient. Like the family that is privy to the crimes of the father (in Ine §7), the testimony of the slave is assumed to have been corrupted by her obligation to a master.

Although the process of swearing an oath in relation to a grave, altar, or relic is not without its parallels, and although arguments from the absence of evidence are notoriously tenuous, no earlier property dispute law makes an exception for a warrantor or witness who has died. Here, that exception becomes essential because of the slave's potential to speak. By insisting that the grave or the estate of the dead owner be vouched as a witness, the law silences the voice of the slave and voids the slave's potential testimony. It opts instead for the grounded authority of the grave. But that, too, as we have seen, reflects another problematic of concealment, since Ine §53 relies on a symbolic inversion of death's silence.

Testimony in Death

Within an explicitly juridical forum, as we have seen in Ine §53, for example, that outward display of the grave (*byrgels*) can sometimes even be vouched to warranty in lieu of the witness it covers and conceals. The grave—despite its symbolic secrecy—somehow becomes an acceptable compurgator and a legally viable alternative to the living witness. Indeed, despite the frequent cultural connection between death and secrecy, the silence that death imposes is rarely so complete, and countless stories attest to miraculous communications between the dead and the living. Goscelin of Saint-Bertin, for instance, recounts two such stories in his *Liber confortatorius* (a lengthy letter to the recluse Eva of Wilton, written in the years 1082–83).[59] In one derived from the *Vitae patrum*, John the Almoner agrees to allow a woman to confess her sins by means of a sealed, secret letter, which he promises never to open. When the bishop later dies, the woman tries to retrieve her document, fearing that her sins will be discovered and revealed to everyone. She eventually visits the bishop's tomb, where she prays in tears for three days; on the third day, the dead bishop and his dead two neighbors (annoyed with the woman's wailing) rise from their tombs and return the tablets to her with her sins erased.[60] The story staunchly reinforces the notion that death is a state of secrecy, since not only were the tablets and the woman's sin symbolically retained in the bishop's entombed possession, but as a result of her penitential tears, the words of her confession had vanished as well. At the same time, however, the miraculous transmission of the tablets from the dead bishop to the living woman discloses a more fluid boundary between the living and the dead than the woman had originally assumed. Moreover, the story is rich with Christological imagery (such as the three days that parallel the duration of Christ's entombment before his resurrection, a duration also noticeable in the Old English poem *The Panther*), and that imagery further insinuates the centrality of the tomb as the site of fluidity between the living and the dead: the tomb can thus both conceal and, in some circumstances, disclose.

The second story likewise involves a grave that betrays its secrets, although under very different circumstances—circumstances that also reveal an underlying layer of concern over the concealment of particularly heinous crimes. In Goscelin's account of the story, a hermit named Alexander is deceived by the devil into seducing and impregnating the daughter of King Gundoforus. Anxious (at the devil's encouragement) that the scandal would damage the reputation of the entire monastic enterprise, Alexander decides it best to silence his victim and conceal his crime by slitting her throat ("iugularet") and then burying her: "et a conspectu celi omnique humana notitia cum scelere terra obrueret, eum facilius penitere et satisfacere posse apud diuinam clementiam, quam apud humanam uesaniam" (and from the entire view of heaven and human notice, the soil would bury her along with his crime; it would be easier for him to repent and make amends at the house of divine mercy, than before human frenzy).[61] He begins his penance immediately, prostrating himself in tears for three days. Then, something inside an opening in an oak tree catches his attention, and when he reaches both hands in to explore it, "arbor se occlusit et Dei preuaricatorem alligatum tenuit" (the tree closed up and grabbed God's captive transgressor).[62] He remains bound there for fifteen years, until one day King Gundoforus happens across him in the forest. Alexander confesses his crime to the king and nods in the direction of the girl's grave. The king exhumes his daughter's body, finding it undecayed, which in turn prompts Alexander to request her forgiveness. Praying, the king places in his daughter's incorrupt fingers a "festucam remissoriam"[63] (stalk [or straw] used in manumission), with which she makes a gesture of forgiveness, and the oak tree miraculously releases its captive.[64] Like John the Almoner, the dead girl maintains her silence while communicating (or being made to communicate) a message to the living. In this case, it is a message that releases her murderer from his penitential servitude.

We will discover in the next chapter how secrecy is often figured as a kind of captivity and how confession can serve as a form of liberation, but for now these two stories suggest how a tomb or grave or dead body might be *made* to represent the silenced will of the deceased. From its tomb, the dead body of the king's daughter is made to perform a juridical function, much like the function of the grave in Ine §53. The circumstances, objectives, and logistics are clearly different (the process of vouching the grave to warranty in Ine §53 is not intended, for instance, to release the slave from his captivity, but to return him to his proper owner). However, in both cases the symbolic power of the grave—despite the silence it maintains—can supply a legally valid and effective form of testimony. Ine §53 and Goscelin's two miraculous exempla each reify the major cultural assumption that graves are sites of concealment and that death is the profoundest form of silence, and yet at the same time they transcend that assumption.[65]

Anglo-Saxon law was one site where this negotiation frequently took place. We have seen in the previous chapter how aggressively the legislation of the period sought to discourage and regulate away various forms of criminal concealment; murder, theft, the harboring of criminals, and perjury are all crimes distinguished by and punished according to the secrecy with which they are committed. And yet this profound and widely recognized secrecy of death, whether in the form of the grave's concealment or the corpse's silence, was an unavoidable legal obstacle. Witnesses on occasion died, and when they did, the law had to find ways to acquire, manage, and evaluate or somehow compensate for their permanently lost testimony. As we have seen with Ine §53, this inevitability posed a serious problem for effective adjudication, as it should have, given the silence associated with death and the concealment associated with burial. Nevertheless, the problem of a dead witness was, it seems, not as severe as the problem of a slave's potential testimony (and the tangled conflicts of interest that it would raise); nor was it as severe as the secrecy under which the slave was necessarily stolen. The silence of death could be transcended (as we have seen in Ine §53) because the logic of the law was already well suited to a kind of confidence in the symbolic influence and outward authority of a grave and because there was similar cultural confidence in the relics of a saint, such as we have seen exemplified, for instance, by the two short miraculous anecdotes later recounted by Goscelin of Saint-Bertin.

The fact that the secrecy of death could be transcended in these ways changes the concept of secrecy itself away from one of absoluteness in relation to death and toward a form of secrecy in which the silence of the dead body and its grave can be reversed in a process governed and overseen by God. The use of the ordeal in Anglo-Saxon law and the law's underlying trust in the veracity of oaths—both of which fall back on God's omniscience and his immediate or final judgment—primed the law for dealing with situations in which testimony was not just obscured but inaccessible. At the same time, these practices cultivated a culture of scrutiny powered by juridical hermeneutics; indeed, they cultivated a culture in which attempts at concealment were always fleeting and always susceptible to incursion. At any moment, even the most secure of moments (in death), those secrets could be opened if not by the hands of the law and its royal *indagator*, then by the hand of God. Even the silence of death could thus be transcended by the divinely underwritten testimonial authority of the grave.[66]

PART II

Spirituality

Chapter 3

Monastic Life and the Regulation of Secrecy

Early in his *Conlationes*, a text widely influential in the development of Western monasticism, John Cassian (ca. 360–435) relates a story that Abba Serapion frequently told when admonishing younger monks. In his youth, Serapion succumbed to a terrible habit of secretly stealing one biscuit every evening after finishing his meal with the abbot, Abba Theonas. Serapion would hide it in his bosom ("in sinu meo latenter absconderem") and secretly eat it late at night without his abbot's knowledge ("ignorante illo occulte edebam"). He would later compare this habit to work prescribed by the pharaoh's foremen, for he was unable to extract himself from their cruel tyranny ("saeuissima tyrannide") and was ashamed to disclose to his elder this clandestine theft ("clandestinum furtum"). That is, until he could hide it no longer:

> contigit dei nutu de hoc me captiuitatis iugo uolentis eripere, ut quidam fratres cellam senis obtentu aedificationis expeterent. Cumque refectione transacta conlatio spiritalis coepisset agitari respondens que senex propositis interrogationibus eorum de gastrimargiae uitio et occultarum cogitationum dominatione dissereret earum que naturam et atrocissimam uim, quam haberent donec celarentur, exponeret, ego conlationis huius uirtute conpunctus et conscientia redarguente perterritus, uelut qui crederem ob hoc ea fuisse prolata, quod seni dominus secreta mei pectoris reuelasset, in occultos primum gemitus excitatus, dein cordis mei conpunctione crescente in apertos singultus lacrimas que prorumpens paxamatium, quod consuetudine uitiosa subtraxeram clancule comedendum, de sina furti mei conscio ac susceptore produxi, eum que in medium proferens, quemadmodum cotidie latenter ederem, prostratus in terram cum ueniae postulatione confessus sum, et ubertim profusis lacrimis ut absolutionem dirissimae captiuitatis a domino poscerent inploraui.
>
> [by God's will it happened that, in order to snatch me from this yoke of willing captivity, some brothers sought out the old man's cell for the sake

of edification. When the meal was finished, the spiritual conference began to be stirred, as the old man, responding to their proposed questions about the vice of gluttony and the power of hidden thoughts, unlocked their nature and explained the terrible force that they exercise as long as they are concealed. Meanwhile, struck with compunction by the virtue of this conference and terrified by my guilty conscience (for I believed, on account of this occurrence, that these things had happened because the Lord had revealed the secrets of my heart to the old man), I was first shaken by hidden sighs. Then, as my heart's compunction grew, I broke into open sobbing and tears, and from my bosom, the knowing accomplice in my theft, I produced the biscuit that by wicked habit I used to take out to eat secretly, placing it in the center. I threw myself on the ground and with a plea for pardon, confessing how every day I would eat in secret, and with an outpouring of tears I begged them to ask the Lord to free me from my horrible captivity.]*[1]*

The rich and varied vocabulary of secrecy in this cautionary passage ("clandestinum furtum," "occultarum cogitationum," "secreta mei pectoris," "occultos gemitus," "clancule comedendum," "latenter ederem") converges on a single event of concealment: Serapion's youthful act of theft and the various tensions produced by his persistent secrecy. We have observed in the preceding chapters and will encounter repeatedly in the course of this book how secrecy is an intrinsic feature of many acts of theft, but in Serapion's anecdote secrecy also works solidly in opposition to one of the primary goals of monastic life: *discretio*, the idea that through humility a monk learns how to judge himself, but only by first submitting all of his thoughts and deeds to the judgment of his superiors. Here we find, in other words, the foundational basis and justification for regulating acts of secrecy in monastic life.

To this end, Serapion's anecdote has a barbed point. Primarily, it suggests that humility and *discretio* can only be achieved by a monk who conceals nothing from his superior: "cuius humilitatis haec erit prima probatio, si uniuersa non solum quae agenda sunt, sed etiam quae cogitantur, seniorum reseruentur examini, ut nihil suo quis iudicio credens illorum per omnia definitionibus adquiescat" (the first proof of this humility will be if not only everything that is to be done, but also everything that is pondered is offered to the examination of the elders, so that, not trusting in one's own judgment, one may submit in every respect to their pronouncements).[2] Sins can transpire in both deeds and thoughts, and so both must be disclosed. If this lesson is followed, then consequently "ilico namque ut patefacta fuerit cogitatio maligna marcescit, et antequam discretionis iudicium proferatur, serpens taeterrimus uelut e tenebroso ac subterraneo specu uirtute confessionis protractus ad lucem et traductus quodammodo ac dehonestatus abscedit" (as soon as a wicked thought is revealed, it withers away, and even before the judgment of discretion is exercised, the loathsome serpent departs—drawn out as it were into the light from its dark and subterranean cave by the power of confession and paraded around in a certain manner and dishonored).[3] Indeed, secrets are powerful only so long as they are concealed; so much is evident from Cassian's language ("occultarum cogitationum dominatione" and "atrocissimam uim"). But in Cassian's view, this power also equates to a state of captivity ("captiuitatis iugo uolentis" and "dirissimae captiuitatis") in which secrets hold their subjects, not the other way around. The reference to the captivity of the Israelites forced to serve under the pharaoh—as a metaphor for the grip of secrecy—thus subverts the organizing structure of the monastery in which monks, as servants of God, willfully submit to and labor under the supervision of their elders. The monk who tries to conceal a secret thus forfeits his monastic servitude to God as he instead becomes a slave to his secret and to sin. The only way to be released from this captivity is to reveal those secrets to God or, better, to the superior who stands in place of Christ within the monastery, thereby acknowledging willingly and humbly that such acts of concealment are never really under the control of the human will in the first place.

In Serapion's anecdotal lesson, the concealment and the eventual confession of his secretive habit not only illustrate the monastic tradition of regulating secret thoughts; they also reveal a certain tension between the old man and the young Serapion that transforms as Serapion begins to realize, confront, and yield to his belief in God's omniscience. At first, the young Serapion is concerned mainly with his personal act of hiding the theft from the old man and, in retrospect, is unsurprised by his own inability to counsel himself away from the bad habit, both to resist the temptation even though he repeatedly consented to the deed and also to overcome the shame of having concealed the secret from the old man for so long. Eventually, the coincidental conference with the other brethren prompts Serapion to consider God's omniscience in a way that had not factored into his thinking before; the conference itself, Serapion believes, is impelled by God's will, and the discussion of gluttony and hidden thoughts had come about because "seni dominus secreta mei pectoris reuelasset" (the Lord had revealed the secrets of my heart to the old man). But Serapion realizes only later, as he retells the story to his younger subordinates, that God orchestrated the whole conference so that even the old man had no way of knowing that Serapion's secrets were being revealed. In other words, even as the individual wills and intellects danced around Serapion's secret—at one moment still concealed, at the next seemingly open to the whole group—that secret is later reckoned to have never been under the control of anyone but God. It is ultimately Serapion's own realization of God's knowledge that jolts him into confessing that which earlier he thought he could conceal. And even before he confesses, he stirs with hidden sighs ("occultos gemitus"), signaling that up until the moment in which he actually breaks down into tearful compunction, he struggles to conceal his ultimately unconcealable secret.

Monastic Practices

The previous chapter considered the potentiality of secrecy in the legal figure of a slave, who by virtue of his or her conspicuous submission to a higher authority (the owner or lord) lost control over the concealment of his own thoughts and testimony, thereby coming to occupy a compulsory position of silence and secrecy. The present chapter will examine what it means to conceal a secret as a different type of servant, as a servant laboring within a monastery as a servant of the Lord (*seruus Dei*). Secular legislation, as we have seen, attempts to hammer out an ideal model of social behavior and aims to apply and enforce that model collectively across society, a society composed involuntarily of a wide array of classes and individuals. Within that society, monasteries functioned as self-contained spiritual and social organizations with their own sets of rules, practices, and ideals.[4] They, too, were internally organized by hierarchy: on taking vows, a monk's anterior social class was (in an ideal monastic model) wiped away, and ranks within the monastery were instead determined by date of entrance into the community, the virtue of one's life, and the discretion of the abbot.[5] Except in cases of child oblation, the lives of some nuns, and the occasional forcible tonsure of a king, entering the monastic life was also for the most part done on a voluntary basis—even if that basis was thought to be directed by the will of God.[6] Taking monastic vows entailed a chosen commitment to turn away from the world in service of the Lord through total obedience. While secular law and monastic operations occasionally overlapped, they were generally kept discrete. King Ine's law code, for instance, opens by clearing a separate space for those under monastic rules: "Ærest we bebeodað, þætte Godes ðeowas hiora ryhtregol on ryht healdan. Æfter þam we bebeodað þætte ealles folces æw 7 domas ðus sien gehealdene" (In the first place, we command that the servants of God duly observe their proper rule. After this, we command that the law and decrees affecting the whole nation be observed as follows).[7] The rules that govern the separate and important domain of monastic life must therefore be approached in a slightly different, if complementary manner.

As with a study of secular law, a study of Anglo-Saxon monasticism cannot focus exclusively on the prescriptive sets of rules, such as the *Regula Sancti Benedicti*, the *Regula magistri,* or the *Regularis concordia*, that govern an idealized form of monastic practice. As the goal of monastic life is the perfection of one's soul through a commitment to loving God and loving one's neighbors, many of the monastic rules prescribe a specific practice through which to attain that perfection while living within a religious community. Important as they were, these prescriptive texts present only a part of the picture. The other part, as Sarah Foot has argued, is painted in narrative sources where, for instance, hagiographic attention to a saint's extreme piety is contrasted with the mundane behavior of those monks who surround him.[8] At the same time, we can also speak about monastic traditions where the various rules echo one another and where narratives sometimes sharpen, at other times dampen those echoes. The particular tradition that commands my attention at the beginning of this chapter—the tradition of unity, of sharing everything in common, of living as "cor unum et anima una" (one heart and one soul, Acts 4:32), of disclosing every thought of one's heart and soul to the abbot: in short, the tradition of communal scrutiny and transparency—will sound very different by the end of the next chapter, as certain forms of concealment and certain forms of secrecy find their places both within the monastery and at the boundaries between the monastery and the world.

In pursuing a study of secrecy and concealment in Anglo-Saxon monastic practices, several important qualifications must first be made. Unlike the broader, secular context circumscribed by Anglo-Saxon laws and legislation, monasteries provided a more enclosed setting within which modes of secrecy and concealment were discursively constructed, socially enacted, and institutionally regulated in more precise, effective, extreme, and absolute ways. The monk's vow of obedience, his commitment to humility, and his surrender of personal property would make any act of concealment (for instance, casual possession of something unknown by others) by default into an act of secrecy (if we understand secrecy strictly as the deliberate and tactical concealment of something from someone). And such acts of secrecy were carefully regulated through the requirements of confession to the abbot, the injunctions against concealing one's thoughts, and the employment of a *circa* who perused the monastery, weaseling out secrets and infractions.[9] Secrets were also restricted under the general paradigm of monastic unity, against which any secret would inevitably be at odds.[10] Religious who vowed not to keep any personal property and whose community, following the familiar phrase from Acts 4:32, was organized as "one heart and one soul," forfeited private ownership over not only their books and pens but also their thoughts. In the recycled language of the *Regula Sancti Benedicti*, "ne quis praesumat aliquid dare aut accipere sine iussione abbatis, neque aliquid habere proprium, nullam omnino rem, neque codicem, neque tabulas, neque graphium, sed nihil omnino, quippe quibus nec corpora sua nec voluntates licet habere in propria voluntate" (without an order from the abbot, no one may presume to give, receive, or retain anything as his own, nothing at all—not a book, writing tablets, or stylus—in short, not a single item, especially since monks may not have the free disposal even of their own bodies and wills).[11] By entering into a state of spiritual servitude, the monk passes from one legal life to the next, out of the realm of secular law and into the bonds of faith. This passage constitutes a form of dying to the world, like that encapsulated by Paul's statement in Galatians 2:19, "legi mortuus sum, ut Deo vivam" (I am dead to the law, that I may live to God). The monk thus undergoes a sort of civil death when he leaves behind his personal possessions, bonds of kinship, and previous identity to become a servant of God, having freely forfeited his own will to the labor of complete obedience.[12] We might assume that within a monastery the secrets of one's heart—a heart collectively belonging to the whole community ("cor unum et anima una")— would therefore never be permitted to conceal itself either from the abbot or even from fellow brethren.

While partly justifiable, this simplistic assumption poses a serious methodological problem. In the first place, it would be inaccurate to speak of *a* monastic practice or rule that encompassed and characterized the whole of Anglo-Saxon monasticism, nor by extension is it possible to speak of a single paradigm or discourse regarding acts of secrecy and concealment within a monastery. The traditional history of Anglo-Saxon monasticism has it that there were two periods of heightened monastic prominence. The first period runs from the late seventh century to the mid-eighth century, marked roughly on the one end by the Canterbury-based school and monastic reforms under Theodore (602–690) and Hadrian (d. 709 or 710), in the middle by Bede (ca. 673–735) and the flourishing Northumbrian community at Wearmouth-Jarrow, and on the other end by the first Viking age (ca. 780–900). The second period runs from the inception of the Benedictine Reform (mid-tenth century) until shortly after the Norman Conquest (1066). Sarah Foot, John Blair, and others have shown how monastic practices between the years 600 and 900 were quite distinct from those of the later reform period, where the *Regula Sancti Benedicti* served as the primary rule and was strictly followed by all reformed monasteries while more lax houses were actively scrutinized and reformed.[13] The pre-reform period, on the contrary, was especially distinguished by an astonishing diversity of monasteries—or minsters, to use Foot's preferred term, the vernacularity of which encompasses its broadest sense—each following its own particular blend of monastic rules and traditions, as determined by the individual abbot.[14] At the same time, it has also been shown that the *Regula Sancti Benedicti* was very much in circulation and use during this pre-reform period.[15] While the *Regula Sancti Benedicti* will inform many of the arguments in this chapter, it is nevertheless impossible to capture with any certainty the full range of practices in use, especially during this earlier period.[16]

Although it is not possible to make claims about *the* Anglo-Saxon monastery or *an* Anglo-Saxon monastic practice, and although it would be inaccurate on any number of local levels to make comprehensive claims about the practices employed in the monasteries of Anglo-Saxon England, it is important not to underestimate the normative force of the ideal monastery even when it was not realized in practice, for any deviations from the ideal would have necessarily been exercised in relation to it. Additionally, there are certain advantages to taking a broad view that draws on the diversity of monastic practices and the documentary representations of those practices. I will pay particular attention, for example, to the ways in which monastic rules were formed and informed by their predecessors, to the ways in which they were interpreted and refashioned by their commentators and translators, and to the ways in which they were exemplified or contradicted by a number of narrative sources from both early and late Anglo-Saxon England. The argument of these two chapters is thus organized thematically, rather than chronologically. In other words, my purpose is not to show how the concept of secrecy changed in the time between Bede and the Benedictine Reform—the nature of the sources and the traces of the customs are too diverse for profitable comparison—but rather to show how certain experiences and discourses of secrecy developed out of specific monastic traditions and were played out in specific monastic activities.

Alongside this deep tradition of monastic rules are the particular narratives that punctuate these next two chapters. These narratives come primarily from hagiographic sources, which are dynamic in their depictions of acts of concealment. Since many of these sources are the *uitae* of saints who were once monks themselves, they provide insight into the constitution of an ideal religious identity. For according to the *Regularis concordia*, "regulari itaque sancti patris Benedicti norma honestissime suscepta, tam abbates perplurimi quam abbatissae, cum sibi subiectis fratrum sororumque collegiis, sanctorum sequi uestigia . . . studuerunt" (when the rule of the holy Father Benedict had been accepted with the greatest goodwill, very many of the abbots and abbesses with their communities of monks and nuns strived to follow the footsteps of the saints).[17] At the same time as these *uitae* depict the conditions as they were imagined and reputed to have existed in the monasteries of each venerated saint, they also illuminate the discursive range of secrecy available to those monks who themselves produced the *uitae*. Indeed, they often cross the divide of periodicity, as when Ælfric of Eynsham (ca. 950–ca. 1010) writes of Saint Cuthbert (d. 687). In these texts, we discover a more nuanced picture, especially as some saints employ secrecy as a tool for divine work and as a mode of humility, a picture that will become clearer over the course of this book.[18] While some prescriptive and regulatory traditions reveal the intense control over secrets within monastic spaces (as we will see in the present chapter), the possibility for certain necessary, humble, positive, and even compulsory acts of concealment and modes of secrecy emerges in unexpected ways and often alongside encounters with the most absolute experience of secrecy: the secrecy of God.

Regulating Secret Thoughts

The requirement of confessing one's every thought to the abbot runs deep in the history of monastic practice and ideology. For example, the fourth-century and highly influential architect of coenobitic monasticism, Basil of Caesarea (ca. 329–379), maintained that every monk ought "μηδὲν μὲν ψυχῆς κίνημα ἀπόκρυφον φυλάσσειν παρ' ἑαυτῷ" (not to conceal within himself any hidden movement of his soul) but must lay before his superior all matters, even "τὰ κρυπτὰ τῆς καρδίας" (the secrets of the heart).[19] In many ways, Cassian was the conduit between the eastern coenobitic monasticism of Basil and its western iterations. The *Regula Sancti Benedicti*, for instance, similarly discourages such secret thoughts of the heart in its definition of the fifth step of humility, which is accomplished if a monk "omnes cogitationes malas cordi suo advenientes vel mala a se absconse commissa per humilem confessionem abbatem non celaverit suum" (through humble confession, does not conceal from his abbot any sinful thoughts entering his heart or any wrongs committed secretly).[20] Given that the *Regula Sancti Benedicti* encourages monks to read Cassian's *Conlationes*, it should be unsurprising that Benedict links humility to confession in a way that stems almost directly from Cassian's logic of *discretio* discussed above in the context of Serapion's anecdote.[21] Again following Cassian's lead, Benedict also instructs monks to "actus vitae suae omni hora custodire, in omni loco Deum se respicere pro certo scire. Cogitationes malas cordi suo advenientes mox ad Christum allidere et seniori spiritali patefacere" (keep careful watch hour by hour over all of your acts in life, and bear in mind that in every place God himself knows for certain [what is happening]. As soon as wrongful thoughts come into your heart, dash them against Christ and disclose them to your spiritual father).[22] For Benedict, the monk's goal should eventually be to watch over himself as God does—unceasingly and from within.[23] But until the monk has gained the experience necessary for such self-examination, he must entrust that examination to his superior, thereby preempting even the possibility of an interiority within which to conceal a secret: as the *Regula magistri* puts it, "non enim secura possunt esse fossata, ubi intus est hostis" (for entrenchments cannot be secure when the enemy is within).[24]

Assigned responsibility over the care of souls, the abbot is expected to answer on the Day of Judgment for all the misdeeds of his monks, whether disclosed or undisclosed.²⁵ Any secret concealed from the abbot would therefore pose a serious problem both for the structure of the community and for the abbot as he attempts to carry out his duty in this life while anticipating his transition to the next. Benedict's source, Cassian's *De institutis*, even discourages the eventual move to self-examination for monks who are still under the authority of an elder:

> Instituuntur nullas penitus cogitationes prurientes in corde perniciosa confusione celare, sed confestim ut exortae fuerint eas suo patefacere seniori, nec super earum iudicio quicquam suae discretioni committere, sed illud credere malum esse uel bonum, quod discusserit ac pronuntiauerit senioris examen.²⁶

> [They are instructed never to hide any thought deep within that itches in the heart with dangerous shame, but to reveal them to their elder as soon as they surface, nor to judge them in accordance with their own discretion but to credit them as bad or good according to how the elder's examination discloses and makes clear.]

For Cassian, even more so than for Benedict, the thoughts that enter a monk's mind—especially if the monk desires to conceal them—should be submitted to an elder for examination and judgment.

Both Cassian and Benedict employ the verb *patefacere* in describing the act of disclosing one's secrets to the abbot, but that act becomes especially vivid and physical in Benedict's command to "ad Christum allidere" (dash [those evil thoughts] against Christ).²⁷ Here, Benedict is drawing on a typological interpretation of Psalm 136:9: "beatus qui tenebit et adlidet parvulos tuos ad petram" (blessed be he that shall take and dash thy little ones [*scil.* Babylonian babies] against the rock). Accordingly, Christ stands in for the rock against which evil thoughts (in lieu of babies) are smashed, as this rich and startling image reinforces and grounds the role of the abbot, who "Christi enim agere vices in monasterio creditur" (in fact, is believed to hold the place of Christ within the monastery).²⁸ With the abbot holding the place of Christ *qua* rock, God's all-seeing presence is made ever more concrete and immediate. And with their potential to be smashed, evil thoughts become shaped by a certain metaphorical physicality. Combined, these two gestures render the concealment of one's sins theoretically impossible (because God already knows the secrets to be confessed), and yet at the same time they make the immediate confession of one's sins absolutely necessary (because the abbot, despite holding the place of Christ, is still human and bears responsibility for the souls of his monks).

These gestures, moreover, brand secrecy with a metaphor of possession (as one holds a rock) and brand the act of confession with a metaphor of touch, as the secret is handled by the penitent and smashed on the confessor. This conceptualization of confession as the handling of sin (a common later medieval turn of phrase)[29] is perhaps most strongly evidenced in our period by King Alfred's (d. 899) Old English translation of Gregory the Great's (d. 604) *Regula pastoralis*, where confession is described as the washing of the mind's hands (*modes honda*) in the basin of the priest's mind (*sacerdes mod*), which collects the grime of all the sinners that pass through it.[30] Alternately, one Blickling Homily offers a similar though slightly different metaphor of material exchange when admonishing priests not to let a man's wealth influence the process of confession, for "'Eala' cwæþ Sanctus Paulus, 'þæt biþ deofles goldhord, þæt mon his synna dyrne his scrifte.' Forþon þæm wiþerweardan beoþ þæs mannes synna gecwemran þonne eal eorþlic goldhord" ("Oh," said St. Paul, "that a man should conceal his sins from his confessor is the devil's gold hoard." That is because the adversary considers a man's sins more desirable than any earthly gold hoard).[31] The secret treasure of sin, insofar as it remains concealed ("dyrne"), belongs to the devil ("biþ deofles goldhord") and retains its value— a value that far exceeds any material wealth a penitent might offer to share with a priest in order to avoid confessing. The homilist's reading of Paul suggests that the secret gold hoard is held not by the sinner but by the devil. Between the *Regula pastoralis* and the Blickling Homily, then, we see the ways in which secrets are handed back and forth: when concealed they are held by the devil, when confessed they are handed into the basin of the priest's mind. Ultimately, these ways of imagining confession—in which sins can be healed, bashed against a rock, cleansed in a basin, and hoarded as treasure—express the mental experiences of secrecy and confession through metaphors that reflect in physical reality.

Compulsory Confession, or Discovering a Secret

According to Bede, Saint Cuthbert (d. 687) would frequently follow the custom of the time and visit small villages to preach and hear confession from those gathered around. The response of those around him was more than enthusiastic:

> Porro Cuthberto tanta erat docendi peritia, tantus amor persuadendi quae coeperat, tale uultus angelici lumen, ut nullus praesentium latebras ei sui cordis celare praesumeret, omnes palam quae gesserant confitendo proferrent, quia nimirum haec eadem illum latere nullomodo putabant.

[So great was Cuthbert's skill in teaching, so great his love for driving home what he had begun to teach, so bright the light of his angelic countenance, that none of those present would presume to hide from him the secrets of his heart, but all openly brought forth what they had done by confessing, because they thought that these things could certainly never be hidden from him.][32]

Cuthbert's ability to perceive human secrets is imbued with a divine sense of knowledge, which motivates the community's wholesale confession: no one thought that sins could be concealed from him. Regardless of whether the villagers, as imagined and described by Bede, would have actually confessed because they believed Cuthbert already knew their sins, Bede's interpretation itself is infused with a monastic principle of transparency and openness. To Bede, to his contemporary audience, and even more so to his later reform-era audiences, the feeling that concealing one's sins was an impossibility would have been an intimately familiar one. In fact, when Ælfric draws on Bede's narrative in his *Depositio Sancti Cuthberti*, he depicts the impossibility of hiding sins from Cuthbert not as a matter of the villagers' belief but instead as a simple fact: "him men ne mihton heora mod behydan, ac hi eadmodlice him geandetton heora digelnyssa and elles ne dorston, and be his dihte digellice gebetton" (men could not hide their minds from him, but they humbly confessed their secrets to him and dared not do otherwise, and they secretly atoned according to his counsel).[33]

Some took advantage of this mode of belief. In one of his letters, for example, Saint Boniface condemns the mendacious Adelbert of Egmond for making himself into something of a fraudulent saint on the Continent, traveling around the countryside distributing his own fingernail clippings and strands of hair. Worse, to the people who threw themselves at his feet begging to confess, he would declare, "scio omnia peccata vestra, quia mihi cognita sunt occulta vestra. Non est opus confiteri" (I know all your sins, for your secret thoughts are known to me. It is not necessary to confess).[34] The ease with which Adelbert takes advantage of the deep-rooted belief that saints, as agents of God, had access to the recesses of everyone's thoughts together with the trenchant urgency of Boniface's official rebuke of Adelbert attest to what must have been a widely popular conviction that was both necessary (for confession to function properly) and highly problematic.

The monastic practicalities of regulating secret and concealed thoughts, as articulated and experienced in the practice of confession, rarely functioned so smoothly as we see recalled by Bede and Boniface in their respective accounts of Cuthbert and Adelbert. From a normative perspective, we see these practicalities taking shape in early Irish penitential sources. In the ninth chapter of his *Regula monachorum*, Columbanus (543–615) guides his monks toward *mortificatio* (mortification), which—alongside Cassian's model of *discretio*—broadly encompasses the principle that a monk should "sine consilio nihil facias" (do nothing without counsel).[35] Columbanus asserts that, because a monk's primary duty is obedience, he should never presume to judge himself, but rather "semper de ore pendeat alterius" (always hang on the lips of another).[36] Columbanus's perspective is more positive than that found in Cassian, Basil, and Benedict: rather than forbidding the monk from concealing thoughts from the abbot, Columbanus emphasizes instead the act of seeking advice from others. Implied, of course, is that receiving counsel depends on an open flow of thoughts; it depends, in short, on confession.

The situation differs when a monk is engaged in concealing someone else's sins. As Columbanus explains, a monk privy to the sin of a companion has a moral responsibility to correct him:

> Qui scit fratrem suum peccare peccatum ad mortem et non arguit eum, legis evangelii transgressor notetur, donec arguat eum cuius malum reticuit et fateatur sacerdoti, ut quamdiu conscientia mala reticuit tamdiu in afflictione paeniteat.
>
> [He who knows that his brother is committing a mortal sin and does not correct him, must be reckoned a transgressor of the Gospel law until he corrects the man about whose evil he kept silent, and confess to the priest so that for as long as he kept silent in evil conspiracy, so long he may do penance in affliction.][37]

Columbanus obligates the witness to correct the sinner and, moreover, to do so without reprimanding him publicly, thus drawing on the *lex euangelium* of Matthew 18:15–16: "si autem peccaverit in te frater tuus vade et corripe eum inter te et ipsum solum si te audierit lucratus es fratrem tuum si autem non te audierit adhibe tecum adhuc unum vel duos ut in ore duorum testium vel trium stet omne verbum" (if thy brother shall offend against thee, go, and rebuke him between thee and him alone. If he shall hear thee, thou shalt gain thy brother. And if he will not hear thee, take with thee one or two more: that in the mouth of two or three witnesses every word may stand). Failing to correct the sinner would, first and foremost, make the witness complicit in the original crime and require penance keyed to the duration of the witness's silence. But Columbanus's ambiguous phrase—"quamdiu conscientia mala reticuit" (as long as he kept silent in evil conspiracy)—further suggests that the witness's conscience would also be burdened by the knowledge of the sinner's secret and the shame of having concealed it. There is another warning here as well, lest the witness assume that the only way to curtail his own shame would be to take advantage of his position of knowledge and publicly shame the sinner by revealing his secret before the entire community. Matthew 18:15–16 anticipates this contemptible practice of public shaming. However, in a monastic setting, the stakes are slightly different, and the relationship between each individual brother and the community as a whole requires a more delicate handling of such situations in principle, if not also in practice.

In *De poenitentia*, a text attributed to Gildas (d. 570), the author proposes a similar rule but factors in the role of the abbot from whom nothing should be concealed: "Qui uiderit aliquem ex fratribus abatis transgredi praecepta, debet abatem non caelare; sed ante admoneat peccantem ut solus quod male agit confiteatur abati" (One who sees any of his brethren violate the commands of the abbot ought not to conceal the fact from the abbot, but he ought first to admonish the offender to confess alone to the abbot the wrong he is doing).[38] And the *Regula Sancti Benedicti* advances yet another variation on this theme:

> Si quis frater contumax aut inoboediens aut superbus aut murmurans vel in aliquo contrarius exsistens sanctae regulae et praeceptis seniorum suorum contemptor repertus fuerit, hic secundum Domnini nostri praeceptum admoneatur semel et secundo secrete a senioribus suis. Si non emendaverit, obiurgetur publice coram omnibus.
>
> [If a brother is found to be stubborn or disobedient or proud, if he grumbles or in any way despises the holy rule and defies the orders of his seniors, he should be warned twice privately ("secrete") by the seniors in accord with our Lord's injunction (Matt. 18:15–16). If he does not amend, he must be rebuked publicly in the presence of everyone.][39]

While prohibiting the monk from concealing the sin of a brother, all three of these rules draw on Matthew 18:15–16 in order to emphasize the importance of handling some matters privately. In Columbanus's version, to reprimand the sinner publicly before allowing him the chance for privately reconciling his wrong is almost as deplorable as not correcting him at all. In Benedict's version, the brother is only to be rebuked publicly if he does not first amend privately, and the initial private rebuke must specifically be carried out by senior monks. And in Gildas's version, we find the most direct injunction to bring the sin before the abbot.

The dynamic between individual monks and their abbot is complicated by these rules. The requirements of obedience and mortification, for instance, would seem to prohibit two monks of equal standing from counseling one another before bringing a sin to the attention of the community or the abbot. For despite its biblical precedent, such an arrangement of private correction between two brothers may have posed a unique problem within a given monastery. As the *Regula Sancti Benedicti* puts it, "praecavendum est ne quavis occasione praesumat alter alium defendere monachum in monasterio aut quasi tueri, etiam si qualivis consanguinitatis propinquitate iungantur" (it should be avoided that one monk dares to defend another in the monastery at any time or, as it were, to protect another even if they are joined together by some close kinship).[40] The forbidden act of defending another monk—for Benedict and his sources Basil and Pachomius (d. 346)—would probably include turning a blind eye to the sin of a fellow monk; it may also include the quasi-conspiratorial act of private correction if that act of private correction did not ultimately result in the sinner's confession to the abbot. That two monks might resolve a sin between themselves, moreover, would contravene the very core of Columbanus's own commitment to a practice of *mortificatio* in which nothing is to be done without the advice or judgment of the abbot. The dilemma posed by Columbanus's injunction to *mortificatio* and his apparently contradictory statement that monks should first correct one another in private might suggest that Columbanus is *de facto* directing his command for private correction toward an abbot, whose seniority would put him in a position to follow it.[41] Under such an assumption, the abbot would counsel the sinful monk privately rather than upbraid him publicly.

Confronting precisely this dilemma of whether an individual monk should reprove a fellow monk in private or report the monk to the abbot, the *Regularis concordia*—the normative document of the Benedictine Reform in late Anglo-Saxon England—invokes a *circa*: a brother assigned to the task of searching the cloister for slothful, sleepy, or sinful monks. This *circa*, according to the *Regularis concordia*, must not keep silent about any such discoveries but reveal them at chapter before the entire community the following day, unless the fault is slight and the offending monk humbly asks forgiveness.[42] The post-Conquest *Decreta Lanfranci* likewise stipulates that "Circumitores monasterii, quos in alio nomine circas uocant, iuxta sancti Benedicti praeceptum certis horis circumire debent monasterii officinas, obseruantes incurias et negligentias fratrum, et statuti ordinis praeuaricationes" (The roundsmen of the monastery, who are also called *circas*, shall according to the command of Saint Benedict go about at certain times the rounds of the monastery's offices, noting the careless and negligent acts of the brethren and the breaches of regular discipline).[43] The *Decreta* goes on to set out in detail the type of monk who would be suitable for the office, the quantity of *circas* needed in relation to the size of the monastery, and the procedures they must follow when conducting their rounds.

As the passage above hints, the office of the *circa*, sometimes referred to as a *circator*, is thought to originate from *RSB* 48, which outlines the need for one or two senior monks to make rounds ("circumeant") as minor disciplinarians but does not specifically establish the role as an official monastic post.[44] Commenting on this chapter of the *Regula Sancti Benedicti*, Hildemar explains that when a junior monk finds another monk sinning, he is to correct the monk in private ("secrete") so that the monk can then report his own sin directly to the deacon or the abbot.[45] Hildemar's logic accords with the logic of Matthew 18:15. But the practice of bringing the sins before the entire community at chapter, as stipulated in the *Regularis concordia*, highlights a fundamental problem in the task assigned to the *circa* and the enforcement of monastic rules in general.[46] On the one hand, the practical need for a *circa* is obvious: the abbot cannot observe every one of his monks at all times and would therefore benefit from the assistance of one or two senior monks. Hugh Feiss has also suggested that the *circa* served to defuse "some of the annoyances of communal life" while freeing "others from obligations to scrutinize their fellow monastics' behavior" and freeing the "abbot from much petty disciplinary work."[47] On the other hand, we find so few narrative references to the figure of the *circa* that we might even surmise that in practice the task would have been so massively unpopular and unsavory (how could one not despise the *circa*?) that the position was rarely filled except in the idealized schemes laid out in monastic rules.[48] Moreover, the possibility that a *circa* might free the other monks from scrutinizing their fellow brethren ignores the fact that every monk and, indeed, every Christian has a duty to correct a brother or sister out of *caritas* (rather than in slander or out of pride). The point of Matthew 18:15 and Hildemar's interpretation of *RSB* 48 is thus precisely that this responsibility falls on each monk regardless of his seniority and regardless of the presence of an official *circa*. But above all, if the ideal monastery operated as perfectly as the monastic rules would have us believe, then there would be little need for a *circa*, since in principle all of the monks should live under the assumption that their every move and thought is observed if not by the abbot or a senior monk, then certainly by God.

Gregory the Great, for instance, venerated Saint Benedict for the way he "in sua semper custodia *circumspectus*, ante oculos conditoris se semper aspiciens" (always [had] a *watchful* guard over himself, always regarding himself in the Creator's eyes).[49] Benedict, of course, embodies the monastic ideal, having earned the ability to act as a *circa* to himself through persistent piety and *discretio*. Although the closest place to perfection on earth, the average monastery, on the other hand, was still a city of man where temptations might loom among the brethren, theoretically justifying the need for a *circa*. Indeed, the fact that rules such as the ones we find in the *Regularis concordia* were established suggests that in practice the ideals of self-imposed supervision were not always realized; monks did not always succeed in watching themselves "through the eye of the Creator" ("ante oculos conditoris"). In the *Regularis concordia* the role of the *circa*, who both discovers the sins and announces them publicly, remains problematic because it mitigates not only the assumed potency of God's omniscience (the *circa* acts as an extension of the abbot's and thus Christ's *oculi*) but also the *lex euangelium* of Matthew 18:15–16, which Columbanus, Gildas, and Benedict each employ in requiring monks to report their own sins to the abbot voluntarily and not to blather about the sins of others before the whole community. These normative perspectives reveal a delicate balancing act between, on the one hand, the ideal represented by Benedict constantly engaged in self-observation or the villagers who eagerly confess to Cuthbert, and on the other, the practicalities worked out over centuries of monastic rules aimed at managing monks and their inevitable attempts at concealing their sins.

Confessio in secreto

Monks, as we have learned, were instructed to conceal nothing from the abbot, but the organization of the community and the abbot's role as Christ in the monastery required and justified the fact that some secrets, in turn, must be concealed from the community. This tension is especially apparent in the division between public and private forms of penance, a division that is primarily evident in early Irish penitentials but also found its way into Anglo-Saxon practices.[50] The conceptual basis for the division seems straightforward: private confession was reserved for secret sins; public confession, for sins of public consequence. In the words of Ælfric, "ða digelan gyltas man sceal digelice betan & þa openan openlice þæt ða beon getimbrode þurh his behreowsunge þe ær wæron þurh his mandædum geæswicode" (a man must secretly make amends for secret sins and openly for open ones, so that those may be edified through his repentance who before had been seduced by his sins).[51] First of all, we will note the rhetorical correspondence between the type of sin ("digelan") and the mode of penance ("digelice"). The difference between secret and open sins and the corresponding penitential requirements in part reflects the threat that the knowledge of the sin would pose to the community.[52] If the sin itself were committed in secret (without anyone's knowing), then its correction should not be allowed to contaminate the community.[53] But if the community has already been contaminated by knowledge of the sin itself, then an example must be set through public penance.[54] This distinction can be seen, for example, in the passage from Ælfric's *Depositio Sancti Cuthberti* discussed above, in which Saint Cuthbert hears confession from villagers who "be his dihte digellice gebetton" (secretly atoned according to his counsel).⁵⁵ Ælfric alters the nature of the confession and penance from one of openness (Bede's "palam") to one of secrecy ("digellice") presumably to emphasize that the sins themselves were kept secret until Cuthbert's arrival, and according to Ælfric's formulation these sins therefore deserved a private form of atonement.

The difference between open and secret sins is often negotiated on the basis of the example they set for others, as Isidore of Seville advises:

> Maioris est culpae manifeste quam occulte peccare. Dupliciter enim reus est qui aperte delinquit, quia et agit et docet. . . . Multi enim publice delinquentes, sine ullo pudore sua flagitia praedicant. . . . Quaedam enim iam iustitiae portio est iniquitatem suam homini abscondere, et in semetipso de peccatis propriis erubescere.⁵⁶

> [It is a greater transgression to sin openly than to sin in secret. He is doubly at fault who performs the sin openly and sets an example. . . . Indeed, many sinners announce their offenses publicly without any regard for their own shame. For it is a certain portion of justice for a man to hide his sins and feel shame in himself concerning his sins.]

This *sententia* was evidently well known (as it is copied, for instance, into the Pseudo-Bedan *Collectanea*), but it also raises a potential source of conflict.⁵⁷ If, as Gregory argues in the *Moralia in Iob*, the concealment of a sin exacerbates the crime, then on what basis can Isidore claim that a concealed sin is preferable to an open one?⁵⁸ The difference between their two arguments, which ultimately are not incompatible, hinges on the nature of the concealment and the nature of the audience. For Isidore, one should refrain from announcing a sin publicly; but for Gregory, one should never attempt to conceal it from God. The former injunction is socially beneficial; the latter is essential for personal contrition. Relatedly, Marilyn Dunn has argued that many early penitential sources, such as the *Penitential of Finnian*, drew on Cassian and Basil in order to focus the idea of contrition on precisely this interior disposition of the penitent in light of God's omniscience.⁵⁹ Ideally by negotiating the logical overlap between Isidore and Gregory, the sinner becomes engaged in the very tension that this chapter and the next seek to illustrate: the tension between a deliberate and conscientious openness to God combined with separation from other human beings.

Within a monastic context, this theoretical dynamic plays out in far more complicated ways. As just one example, the *Regula magistri* works through these practical considerations to stipulate that "Fratres qui se inmundi per somnum agnouerint, secrete ante fores oratorii . . . abbati ad genua incuruati confiteantur hoc ipsud" (Brothers who are aware that they have defiled themselves in their sleep are to confess this very thing privately to the abbot at the door of the oratory, bent at the knees).⁶⁰ Such a practice was not just prescriptive. Odo of Cluny recounts, for instance, how Saint Gerald of Aurillac (855–909) would naturally on occasion experience a nocturnal emission, and he praises Gerald for handling it so respectfully: a "consecretalis cubicularius" (confidential servant) would bring him a change of clothes, water, and a washcloth, doing so "seorsum" (privately or separately). How Odo came to discover Gerald's secretive though respectable practice remains a mystery, as does his justification for including it in the hagiographic record and thereby contradicting the decency he claims to value in Gerald's discreet conduct.⁶¹ Gerald's behavior is an unusual detail to include in the *uita* of a saint, but its rationalization by Odo speaks to some of the monastic anxieties around human behavior that is sometimes best concealed from the monastic community at large. However, determining the appropriateness of private confession was, it turns out, not always so straightforward, and the arguments related to the practice are sometimes even contradictory. For example, even an early twelfth-century addendum to the Old English translation of the *Regula Sancti Benedicti* instructs that confession of a secret sin specifically must *not* be carried out in a secret location but rather before the eyes of all of the brothers: "gif þara gebroþra hwylc his diglan synna þæm mæssepreoste andettan wille, sy þæt gedon be þæs abbodes leafe innan cirican, *na on digelre stowe*, ac swa, þæt þa gebroþra him onlocian mægen" (if any of the brothers wishes to confess his sins before the mass-priest, let him do so with the abbot's permission in church, *not in a secret place*, so that the brothers might observe him).⁶² There is something to be gained, in other words, by forcing a monk to confess his secret sins before his whole community, both for the sinning monk and the community that surrounds him. Clearly private confession was not a simple or straightforward solution and may have often been quite unsettling for the communal soundness of monastic life.

Forced Confessions: The Case of Ægelward

Sometimes, however, secrets had a way of working themselves out. At the end of the Benedictine Reform, the story of a young monk named Ægelward illustrates the deep concerns around the public revelation of secret sins and, by extension, the necessity of immediate and private confession to the abbot. The story is found in two versions of the *Miracula Sancti Dunstani*—the first by Osbern of Canterbury (d. ca. 1095) and the second by Eadmer of Canterbury (ca. 1060–ca. 1128). The central event takes place in either 1076 or 1077, and it begins in the middle of a mass led by Lanfranc (ca. 1005–1089), the archbishop of Canterbury.⁶³ After the Gospel and the Lord's Prayer, this young monk Ægelward offered the paten to the archbishop and, on doing so, began to see terrible and devilish spirits.⁶⁴ Struck with fear and evidently possessed by a demon, Ægelward suddenly seizes ("apprehendit") Lanfranc with outstretched arms just as the archbishop is attempting to perform the Divine Service. Guards quickly grab the young monk and carry him off to a more secret, private part of the house ("secretiorem domus partem"); in Eadmer's version, Ægelward is carried off ("rapiunt") to the archbishop's chamber ("pontificis cameram").⁶⁵ At this point, the two versions begin to differ. In Osbern's version, Lanfranc visits Ægelward privately and urges him to confess, initiating an important theme in the story. At first the demon prevents Ægelward from confessing his sin: "mox ut ad verbum veniebatur lingua illius a dæmone detinebatur" (as soon as he was on the verge of speaking, the demon restrained his tongue). With the aid of divine power Lanfranc eventually succeeds, and Ægelward confesses. We never learn what the sin actually was—the important point is that he had not confessed it—and we are left wondering how Osbern could have known about this private exchange, carried out as it was in a separate chamber away from the rest of the members of the monastery.

In any case, Ægelward soon relapses as he enters the chapter house with escalating madness and "torvis ac minacibus oculis" (wild and menacing eyes). There, he threatens to declare aloud the sinful deeds that each of his fellow brethren had carried out in secret ("quod unusquisque in secreto operatus fuisset"). This threat has an immediate effect on a certain young monk for whom Archbishop Lanfranc reserved a special degree of affection:

> Hunc ergo inconsolabiliter propter rem quæ acciderat gementem, atque amaras ad Dominum lacrymas profundentem, malignus spiritus compescuit, dicens, "Quid tu," inquit "lacrymaris? Vanæ sunt lacrymæ tuæ, vanus ploratus tuus. Idem nos locus habebit, ambos infernus tenebit." Nolens autem Lanfrancus adolescentem a dæmonio verecundiam pati, confestim de loco surgit, apprehensum illum seorsum ducit prius, ut solitus erat, precibus agens, ut si quid in illo peccati lateret in vera Deo confessione ediceret, ne diabolus illum ligatum teneat, et coram omnibus quæ commisisset valeat improperare. Qui statim quaecunque a pueritia de se scire poterat magna cordis alacritate confitens, tantis archiepiscopum gaudiis replevit ut et manibus confitentis crebra oscula figeret.

[Then, on account of the event—which had weakened this one monk, (who was) grieving inconsolably and pouring out bitter tears to the Lord—the evil spirit silenced him, saying: "Why do you cry? Your tears are in vain; empty is your wailing. The same place will hold us; hell will keep us both." But refusing to allow the young man to suffer such shame from the demon, Lanfranc immediately arose from his place, seizing the young man, and he in front led him separately, as he had been accustomed to do while conducting prayer, in order that he might proclaim to God in true confession if some sins should lie hidden within, so that no devil could keep him bound and be able to taunt him in the presence of all who joined together. At once, with great eagerness of heart he confessed all that which from childhood on he was able to recollect; it filled the archbishop with such great joy that he repeatedly fixed kisses on the hands of him who just confessed.]⁶⁶

Afterwards, Ægelward is brought before Dunstan's tomb, which calms him for a day, but he soon relapses again and attacks Prior Henry. He is brought back to Dunstan's tomb, but again to no avail. They unsuccessfully attempt to restrain him to a bed in the infirmary, where he is visited by many fellow brethren. To all their surprise, he knew "omnes ad se venientes torvis oculis intueri, singulorum occulta detegere, prorsus multam multis verecundiam facere, quos in peccatis suis noverat jacere. Cæterum de iis qui peccata sua confessi fuerant omnino nihil improperando potuit efferre" (how to reveal the secrets of every one of them who was coming to look at him and his savage eyes, to cause entirely such great shame in many, whom he knew wallowed in their sins. To the others who had confessed all of their sins, he was able to do nothing by his taunting).⁶⁷ Confession of secret sins, in other words, prevents the demoniac from revealing them publicly. So when Lanfranc and the young monk visit the infirmary, Ægelward could not even recognize the monk because of the power of confession ("virtutem confessionis"). Eventually, Ægelward becomes madder, and when he is brought to the presence of Dunstan's relics as they are being transported into the refectory, he begins screaming blasphemous things and lifts the heavy bed to which he is restrained, while the evil spirit—not out from hiding and still invisible ("neque ex occulto atque invisibile")—runs around within him like a puppy ("modo catelli discurrentis"). A prayer to Saint Dunstan is offered (again), Ægelward is brought to the saint's venerable body (again), a bystander lays the saint's staff against him, and with one final prayer the demon at last departs. Ægelward recovers and lives a long life.

So exciting was this event that news of it spread quickly, as we learn from a possible reference to it in a letter from Lanfranc to John of Rouen.⁶⁸ But one wonders how much of Osbern's narrative actually demonstrates the miraculous efficacy of Dunstan and his relics.⁶⁹ The chapter certainly pays reverence to Dunstan, and the repeated failures of his assistance could be read (in light of his eventual aid) as a reason to persist in pious devotion. But the emphasis of the chapter really falls on a different miracle: the power of confession. More surprising and compelling than the evidence of Dunstan's saintly potency (and by extension the implication that he should receive one's prayers in times of need) is the notion that if one confesses privately to the archbishop or abbot, one's secret sins will not be revealed before the entire community. That is a fairly good reason to practice confession, even if Osbern's version offers an even better reason: if you do not confess your sins, you may wind up possessed—just like Ægelward. And confession at that point, as the story suggests, is not always effective.[70] Clearly, the event was a disturbing one to the Canterbury community, and the excitement very likely centered on the demoniac and on the personal implications for the members of that community as their individual secrets were nearly divulged. Aside from the fact that he physically assaults the archbishop of Canterbury, what makes Ægelward's actions so criminal—worse than the very sins he threatens to reveal—is the fact that publicly upbraiding his companions would directly violate Matthew 18:15 and the traditions of monastic rules that legislate that *lex euangelium* into practice.

But the demon's ability to peer into and reveal the secrets of others is not all that remarkable. As Cassian explains, for example, only God can perceive all of human secrets, whereas evil spirits can perceive our thoughts only when those thoughts are exposed either by our external and perceptible tells or when the thoughts were instigated by the evil spirit in the first place. In other words, it is fairly easy for demons to perceive human secrets:

> Quemadmodum enim nonnulli latronum in his domibus quas furtim adgredi cupiunt occultas hominum solent explorare substantias, qui per taetras noctis tenebras cauta spargentes manu minutias harenarum reconditas opes, quas uisu peruidere non possunt, tinnitu quodam ad earum lapsum respondente deprehendunt, et sic ad certissimam rei uel metalli cuiusque notitiam quadam elicitae uocis proditione perueniunt, ita hi quoque, ut thesaurum nostri cordis explorent, uelut harenas quasdam suggestiones nobis noxias inspargentes, cum secundum illarum qualitatem adfectum corporeum uiderint emersisse, uelut quodam de intimis conclauibus prodeunte tinnitu quid sit reconditum in adytis interioris hominis recognoscunt.

> [This is reminiscent of those thieves who are accustomed to examine the hidden stores of the people in the homes that they secretly want to break into. In the darkness of the night they carefully sprinkle tiny grains of sand and so discover, thanks to a slight ringing that occurs when they fall, the secret treasures that they are unable to catch a glimpse of. Thus they get an exact knowledge of the thing and of its metal, since it has

been betrayed as it were by the sound that was produced. Likewise, so that these others might explore the treasury of our hearts, they sprinkle certain harmful suggestions in us like grains of sand, and when they see a fleshly disposition emerge in accordance with the character of their suggestions, they recognize what is concealed in the inmost recesses of the inner man, as if by a kind of ringing that comes forth from hidden chambers.][71]

Cassian's fanciful description of the tactics used by demons to gain access to human secrets equates that demonic acquisition of human secrets to an act of theft and a mutual game of secrecy: the individual tries to hide from the hidden thief. It also paints a picture of the false interiority that humans might imagine to be a solid and concealing barrier, but which all along is only engendered by the evil spirit. Just as in Serapion's anecdote or in the Blickling Homily's reference to the devil's gold hoard, here, too, sins always belong to the devil insofar as they remain concealed.

The dynamic changes slightly in Eadmer's version of the *Miracula Sancti Dunstani*, which omits the story of the certain young monk confessing to Lanfranc in private. In its place, Eadmer adds more detail to the scene in the infirmary, which is itself presented as a kind of miracle:

> Inter quae contingebat quodam mirabili modo, ut cum quidam ad eum accederent, ilico si quid grauis peccati de quo necdum ad eum accederent, ilico si quid grauis peccati de quo necdum confessi erant in cordis secreto habebant, detegeret, et illos sibi in poenis perpetuis socios fore futuros, gaudens et hilaris pronunciaret. Ex hoc dum nonnulli grauem contumeliam incurrissent, ipsi semet ipsos grauiter erubescentes, remedium sibi purae confessionis adhibuere. Confessi ergo, et poenitentia cum absolutione peccatorum a praesidente suscepta, iterum se praesentauerunt demonioso.

> [While these things were happening, it came about in some wondrous fashion that when certain men approached him there—ones who kept concealed in their hearts some great sin which they had not yet confessed—he would immediately reveal it, and laughing gleefully he would name them as his future companions in perpetual punishment. When some had received serious rebuke in this way, they became deeply ashamed of themselves and applied the remedy of sincere confession. And when they had confessed and received penance and absolution for their sins from the prior, they presented themselves once again before the possessed man.][72]

Like Osbern, Eadmer goes on to explain that Ægelward was powerless against those who had already confessed, failing to recognize even their identities. Eadmer is clearly drawing on Osbern as his source; however, noticeably absent is the certain young monk, the "adolescens quidam" singled out by Ægelward and pulled aside by Lanfranc. Perhaps Eadmer had trouble substantiating the account, grouping it instead into the collective experience of the larger group of brethren. Or perhaps, as Jay Rubenstein has suggested, Osbern's intimate account of the young monk's confession to Lanfranc is so intimate precisely because that young monk was Osbern himself.[73] This suggestion is particularly compelling because it explains how Osbern would have had access in the first place to the private exchange with the archbishop. As Osbern retains his anonymity, his secrets remain concealed from the community and the readers of the *Miracula*, but not from Lanfranc or from God.

Keeping Secrets, Possessing Souls

This grip of the devil, however, is precisely what drives Ægelward's behavior and keeps individuals from confessing. Eadmer, for example, describes the revelation of sins in the infirmary with language that implies a bond between the demon and any individual who believes that he can actually hold or keep ("habebant") his own secrets. Much like the experience described by Serapion in Cassian's *Conlationes*, the tension centers around the issue of possession: the secret is not actually held by the individual, but instead the individual who tries to conceal the secret is consequently possessed and held captive by the devil. That individual, according to Eadmer, becomes unable to avoid companionship with the devil in perpetual punishment.[74] And Osbern animates this threat with Ægelward's even more forceful rhetoric of possession: "Idem nos locus habebit, ambos infernus tenebit" (The same place will hold us; hell will keep us both).[75] Both hagiographers are making the same point: no matter how well one hides or conceals a sin, the secret of the sin and the person concealing it are in turn held captive by the enemy. Eadmer's phrase referring to the sinners whose sins are "in cordis secreto habebant" (kept concealed in their hearts) takes the *locus* Ægelward will share with the devil and links it back to the act of concealment, changing the place of possession from hell to the heart of the sinner. Eadmer's phrase is one of very few Anglo-Latin examples in which a secret is even described as something held or possessed, and the context implies that such secrets in fact *cannot* be held since all along they belong to the enemy.

In both versions of the *Miracula Sancti Dunstani*, this episode is rife with acts of holding, seizing, and grasping. At the initial mass, Ægelward passes the paten into the hands ("in manus") of the archbishop; Ægelward attacks and wraps his arms ("brachiis") around Lanfranc; the evil spirit takes hold of

Ægelward ("apprehendit"); the guards pry Ægelward from Lanfranc and drag him into a separate chamber; they keep him there until after the mass when they hand him over to Lanfranc; Lanfranc holds down his wild arms ("sæva brachia") while ordering him to confess, but his tongue is held by the demon ("lingua illius a dæmone detinebatur"); when Ægelward is brought before the community, held by very strong men, and makes his threat to the young monk, saying that hell will hold them both, Lanfranc seizes the certain young monk and brings him into a private room to confess so that the devil cannot keep him bound fast ("ligatum teneat"). Once the monk confesses, Lanfranc takes his hands and fastens kisses on them ("et manibus . . . crebra oscula figeret").[76] Rhetoric of this sort continues throughout the episode, especially as Ægelward is dragged about and tied down. The rhetoric is not especially imagistic or creative. Indeed, it is hard to imagine what other words could have been used to describe the sort of action that takes place in this scene. However, amid all of these acts of touching, holding, keeping, and restraining, the only instance in which secrets are even remotely "kept" occurs when the demon holds Ægelward's tongue and prevents him from confessing. Still, Lanfranc persists and with divine assistance manages to compel Ægelward to divulge his sin. In that exchange, the bonds of the devil are traded for the bonds of the abbot, bonds that are physically manifested in Lanfranc's grip ("constringensque sæva brachia"). Beneath this proliferated discourse of possession lies another discourse of captivity and theft. We have already seen in the story of Serapion's secret theft how the act of concealment can be equated to a state of captivity. With Ægelward, we find a similar equation: Ægelward, bound by the fetters of the enemy because he had failed to confess his sin to Lanfranc, in turn binds the young monk (possibly Osbern himself) to an eternity of shared punishment in hell. That young monk is only released from this captivity on confessing everything to Lanfranc, thereby entering into a new or renewed bond of obedience with his archbishop instead. Monastic servitude and obedience (in which monks work as *serui dei*) thus depend on an inversion of the captivity that was once in the hands of the devil when the sin was concealed and then in the hands of the abbot once the sin is confessed.

This exchange of bonds between devil and abbot is made even more explicit in Wulfstan of Winchester's *Vita Sancti Æthelwoldi* and a case of stolen money.[77] After an initial warning, the bishop offers a mild reproof ("modesta"), merely requesting that the money be dropped out in the open where it could be found. But after three days, the guilty monk still had not returned the money, and the bishop addressed the brethren this time with fierce anger: "Noluit sacrilegus ille pecuniam quam furatus est reddere cum benedictione sicut iussimus; reddat eam modo cum Dei omnipotentis maledictione, et sit ipse ligatus, non solum in anima sed etiam in corpore, nostra auctoritate"

(Despite my order, this sacrilegious thief has refused to restore with my blessing the money he took. Now let him return it with the curse of Almighty God upon him, and be bound in body as well as soul by our authority).[78] Immediately, the malediction takes effect and "monachus ille sedens inuisibiliter ligabatur, brachiis sibi inuicem adhaerentibus sub cuculla sua. . . . Omnia tamen reliqua membra sua mobilia et ad usum apta habebat, exceptis brachiis, quae uir sanctus autoritate sibi a Deo collata ligauit et inutilia reddidit" (this monk, while sitting, was invisibly bound up, his arms attached to each other beneath his cowl. . . . All the rest of his limbs had mobility and were able to be used, but the holy man had bound his arms and rendered them useless by the authority conferred on him by God).[79] With his arms bound, the monk approaches Æthelwold to confess his crime in private ("confessus est ei secreto"), and immediately his arms are released.

Once again, theft becomes central to a narrativized admonition against acts of secrecy: the lesson, like the ones discussed above, puts the agent of concealment in a position of captivity. Indeed, the same language is used to describe the binding of the thief in Wulfstan's narrative as is used to describe the binding of Ægelward the demoniac in Osbern's and Eadmer's narratives. The *brachia* of both men are bound (*ligare*), but they are bound from different angles. In the case of Ægelward (like the young Serapion), he is bound by the devil who holds his tongue and keeps him from confessing, and he is physically bound by Lanfranc and by the guards. A similar construction of opposing authorities (the devil and God) holds the thief captive in Wulfstan's *Vita Sancti Æthelwoldi*. The devil, who inspires the monk to commit the theft in the first place, binds him in a state of secrecy, while Bishop Æthelwold— operating under God's authority and the underlying power to bind and loose—reminds the monk, as it were, of his rightful master and his proper servitude to God by miraculously binding his arms, and then unbinding them once he confesses to the crime.

Secrecy as a Form of Theft

At the beginning of this chapter, we looked at a particular act of theft ("furtum") in which Serapion stole biscuits from Abba Theonas. But Serapion's act of hiding the biscuit and eating it secretly actually constituted a theft in another and more serious aspect: acting without the abbot's knowledge ("ignorante illo").[80] This form of secrecy as theft is illustrated even more clearly by another episode in Wulfstan's *Vita Sancti Æthelwoldi*, where Æthelwold assigns a monk named Ælfstan the task of overseeing the preparation of food for the monastery.[81] Ælfstan accomplishes this task with so much enthusiasm that when Æthelwold enters the pristine kitchen, he assumes that Ælfstan must have secretly had the help of a second servant. So Æthelwold declares, "O mi frater Ælfstane, hanc oboedientiam mihi furatus es, quam me ignorante exerces" (O my brother Ælfstan, you have stolen from me this obedience which you practice without my knowledge).[82] He immediately orders the monk to plunge his hand into a nearby cauldron of boiling water and remove a morsel of food from the bottom. Ælfstan obeys without hesitation, and in response Æthelwold instructs him to drop the morsel and tell no living soul ("nemini hoc indicare uiuenti") about what had just taken place. We shall return in Chapter 5 to Æthelwold's command to tell no living soul, but for now let us reflect on the meaning of theft ("furatus") in this scene. According to Katherine O'Brien O'Keeffe's analysis of this episode in her study of monastic agency and obedience, every act of disobedience constitutes an act of theft.[83] It hinges on Ælfstan's interpretation of his abbot's ambiguous command to "praeuidere cibaria artificum monasterii" (oversee/see to/provide the food for the workmen of the monastery):[84]

> By doing more than the abbot's literal order to oversee the food, Ælfstan appears to keep for himself his own will in exceeding what was commanded of him. That excess, appearing to be the product of self-will (however praiseworthy the object of the exercise), would remove him from the structured relation of superior and subject, in that by willing other than he was ordered, he would, in fact, be acting as abbot to himself. In that refiguring of the relation between abbot and subject (where the abbot wills and the subject obeys), through the improper use of his will, Ælfstan would not only steal obedience but would steal his abbot's function.[85]

But in addition to stealing the abbot's function, there is another dimension to Æthelwold's charge of theft. The act of disobedience, in general and in this particular scene, amounts to theft when a subject does something without the knowledge of a superior. Like Serapion who eats the biscuit without his abbot's knowledge ("ignorante illo"), Ælfstan employs his own will in an act of secrecy that leaves his abbot in the dark ("me ignorante"). Whether Ælfstan might have either secretly received the help of additional servants or performed the work himself under his own will, Æthelwold's frustration hinges on the fact that Ælfstan acted without the abbot's knowledge.

The ordeal-like methods used by Æthelwold are therefore not cruel but necessary. As O'Brien O'Keeffe puts it, "Æthelwold's problem as abbot is a problem of knowledge whose resolution can only be achieved by appealing for divine intervention."[86] Ordering Ælfstan to plunge his hand into the boiling water turns Æthelwold's ability to adjudicate the situation over to God, whose knowledge is always more complete. In this way, Æthelwold's actions also resemble those of Abba Theonas when he brought to light Serapion's theft of the biscuit. And they resemble the way Æthelwold himself handles the thief who stole money within the monastery. In all three of these situations, the abbot depends entirely on God's capacity to see and expose the thieves. Of course, the ordeal itself reveals that Ælfstan is not guilty of "stealing the obedience," but in interpreting Ælfstan's actions as a theft, Æthelwold accuses the monk of concealment. Such an act of concealment would have directly violated *Regula Sancti Benedicti*, which stipulates that if someone commits a fault while working in the kitchen, for instance, then he must admit the fault ("prodiderit delictum") to the abbot or the community.[87] As a central figure in the Benedictine Reform, Æthelwold would have likely been aware of this rule and brought it to bear on his initial interpretation of the situation: Ælfstan had failed to make known the fault that Æthelwold presumed him to have committed. That presumption sticks until the moment in which Ælfstan acknowledges that God had been watching all along and submits himself to God's judgment by immediately dropping his hand into the boiling water. Ælfstan is absolved the moment he acknowledges God's omniscience and with it the impossibility of secrecy. But if evaluating acts of concealment is so easy, why does Æthelwold react the way he does? Simply put, any such act of concealment—even if it were ostensibly a positive, good-willed, or beneficial act—would make it impossible for the abbot to satisfy his pastoral duty and lead his flock to salvation. As we have already seen in Cassian and Columbanus, every thought and deed done without counsel equates to a rejection of the monk's vow of obedience. It is the concealment of those thoughts and deeds—regardless of whether they are inherently good or evil—that renders them stolen, and such an act of theft by extension entails disobedience. Secrecy is not only a necessary condition for theft but also a distinct form of theft in itself. As theft, secrecy thus constitutes a crime that demands monastic regulation.

Such regulation has a long tradition. In his *Sermo asceticus et exhortatio de renuntiantione saeculi*, for example, Basil reiterates the importance of seeking judgment from a teacher and figures any deed done apart from that teacher's wisdom as an act of theft:

Εἰ τοίνυν εὕρῃς Θεοῦ χάριτι (πάντως γὰρ ζητήσας εὑρήσεις) ἀγαθῶν ἔργων διδάσκαλον, τήρησον παρ' ἑαυτῷ, μηδὲν παρὰ γνώμην αὐτοῦ διαπράττεσθαι. Ἅπαν γὰρ τὸ ἔξωθεν αὐτοῦ γινόμενον κλοπή τίς ἐστι καὶ ἱεροσυλία πρὸς θάνατον ἄγουσα, οὐ πρὸς ὠφέλειαν, κἂν δοκῇ σοι ἀγαθὸν εἶναι. Εἰ γὰρ ἀγαθὸν, τίνος ἕνεκεν λάθρα, καὶ μὴ ἐν τῷ φανερῷ γίνεται;

[If, then, by the grace of God you have found—and if you look, you shall surely find—a teacher of good works, then guard yourself and do everything according to his judgment. For all that you do apart from him, even if to you it seems good, is a kind of theft and sacrilege leading to death without any benefit. For if it is good, why is it done secretly and not in the open?][88]

Even though Basil's writings would not have been directly known to Wulfstan or to his contemporaries, they were foundational in the construction of Western monastic practices, especially those practices embraced by reformers such as Æthelwold. Conceptually speaking and without suggesting a direct source relationship, the *sacrilegus furatus* (sacrilegious thief) in Æthelwold's monastery thus seems to echo Basil's "κλοπή . . . καὶ ἱεροσυλία" (theft and sacrilege).[89] As a servant of the Lord, the monk becomes the property of both the community and God. Removing himself from that service in an act of disobedience done without the knowledge of his superior or trading that service for a position under the devil in an act of concealing a secret would have been equivalent to stealing himself away from the monastic community and thus from God.[90] Stealing was, of course, forbidden by the Ten Commandments, and its prohibition formed one of the basic principles of monastic life and Christianity more generally.[91] Within a monastery especially, an act of theft was not only a violation of one of the commandments but also an egregious violation of the monk's vow to keep no personal property. But the most effective means for stopping acts of theft in a monastic context was to remind the monks that no matter how secretly a theft is carried out, it will never go unnoticed. In the *Regula magistri*, for instance, the abbot is instructed to warn the kitchen servers in the following way:

Videte, fratres, ne ante orationem communem mensae praebendam aliquid de cibo aut de potu suasione diaboli praesumatis, etsi nos hic positi intus foris uos non uidemus, Deus tamen, qui omni loco praesens est et omnia uidet et nihil est ei occultum, ipse uos conspicit, ne cum uiderit praesumptionem uestram, sensum uestrum tradat in reprobum et ad poenam uobis furta uestra in iudicio consignentur.[92]

[See to it, brothers, that you do not, at the devil's instigation, take any food or drink ahead of time, before the prayer in common at the table. Although we who are inside here do not see you outside, God, who is present everywhere and sees everything, to whom nothing is hidden, does see you. See to it, then, lest when he sees you eating ahead of time he subjects your whim to reprobation, and at Judgment your theft be charged against you for punishment.]

The constant surveillance instilled through the deep-seated belief that nothing is hidden makes any act of secrecy both impossible to conceal and punishable if not by the abbot, then by God.

In many of the examples seen up to this point, the monastic rules that seek in various ways to curtail secrets often target just as much the act of concealing a sin as the sin itself. As Gregory and others make clear, concealing a sin certainly elevates its severity and impedes the sinner's repentance: the longer the sin is concealed, the more powerfully enslaved the sinner becomes. But it is for this reason that numerous monastic thinkers of the period emphasize the importance of confessing immediately no matter how minor the sin. As Columbanus incisively puts it, "Non enim posse aliquem peccare, cum relaturus esset ad alium quæcunque peccasset, et subire pudorem in publicum turpia proferendi" (Indeed, no one can sin when he must report all his sins to someone else and endure the shame of bringing out his repulsive deeds in public).[93] What is more, when secrets are regulated as extended acts of theft—as acts in which a servant of God steals himself away from his monastic responsibility and falls into the captivity of the enemy—any thought or deed concealed from the abbot constitutes a crime even if it seems essentially good to the one who conceals it.[94]

At the same time, the process of regulating secrets within monasteries depended heavily on a practice of confession and penance that often employed a different and necessary kind of secrecy in the form of private confession to the abbot. The injunction in Matthew 18:15–16 that one should correct a brother in secret, Ælfric's distinction between open and secret penance, and the way Lanfranc privately receives the confessions of Ægelward and the terrified young monk: each of these bears witness to the complex negotiations that took place between acceptable and iniquitous forms of secrecy, negotiations that were foundational to the monastic experience and yet so often a source of conflict. In these negotiations, acceptable forms of secrecy were envisioned as the rightful property of the abbot and God, while the iniquitous forms were envisioned as the stolen property—whether treasure or slave—of the devil. At no point does a monk have the ability to hold or keep, to control or possess his own secrets, which while unconfessed belong to the devil and once confessed belong to God. One fundamental difference between these acceptable and iniquitous forms of secrecy, as I will draw out more fully in the next chapter, lies in the deliberate openness to God that the former requires and the latter spurns. And because this difference is largely dependent on the interior disposition of an individual and his or her belief in God's omniscience—in Cassian's terms, the capacity for *discretio*—the constant opportunity for concealment posed a serious challenge to communal scrutiny and thus commanded intense and overarching regulatory energy in

Anglo-Saxon monastic life. Even more powerful than these regulations, however, were the stories of monks such as Ægelward and Serapion, which insist that secrets can always and unexpectedly be made known if not before the monastic community in this life, then inevitably before God and everyone present at the end of time.

Chapter 4

Making Space for Spiritual Secrecy

This book requires us to move beyond any preconceptions we might have about the concept of secrecy. At the opening of the present chapter it is more important than ever that we return to this *tabula rasa* in order to see what was in fact a fundamental tension in monastic life between two different types of secrecy. Serapion's anecdote in the previous chapter illustrates the first type, forbidden and regulated by numerous monastic rules and deliberately hindered by the practice of immediate confession to the abbot. This regulation of secrecy, however, comes up against a different kind of secrecy, which I will call "spiritual secrecy" and which monasticism required of its monks and admired in its saints. This spiritual secrecy, quite distinct from anything we might now associate with the word, takes place when a person removes him- or herself from the perception of fellow human beings to inhabit a *locus secretior* in a process of opening up to God through prayer, reclusion, or contemplation.

The basis for this type of secrecy is to be found in the injunction of Matthew 6:6: "tu autem cum orabis intra in cubiculum tuum et cluso ostio tuo ora Patrem tuum in abscondito et Pater tuus qui videt in abscondito reddet tibi" (But when thou shalt pray, enter into thy chamber, and having shut the door, pray to thy Father in secret: and thy Father who seeth in secret will repay thee). Ultimately, these two types of secrecy not only share the same vocabulary but also employ a similar technique of concealment on the human level. However, while the former was absolutely prohibited, the latter was widely encouraged and upheld as the model of religious life. And the ethical distinction between the two is drawn, I shall argue, not in human or worldly terms (that is, on the basis of the effect that a given secret has on one's earthly companions or one's temporal community) but in terms of the degree of the individual's submission to openness before God.

The requirement of immediate and genuine confession to the abbot was one of the primary means of regulating secrecy within a monastery. The acts of confession surrounding the young Serapion's theft, Saint Cuthbert's pastoral work, Ægelward and the Canterbury community, and the thief in Saint Æthelwold's monastery, to take examples from the previous chapter, all emphasize the importance of confessing to the abbot or to some man of God. However, they generally pass over the question of whether confessing to God alone in private prayer was a sufficient means of resisting the temptation to conceal one's thoughts and one's sins. The effectiveness of private confession was a contested issue for Anglo-Saxon thinkers such as Alcuin of York (ca. 735–804) and Ælfric of Eynsham (ca. 950–ca. 1010), who insisted that in most circumstances it was not enough to confess to God alone and emphasized the importance of sacerdotal mediation.[1] At stake was the risk of having one's sins revealed before the multitudes on the Day of Judgment or even sooner—a prospect narrowly avoided by the young monk whose timely confession to Archbishop Lanfranc in Osbern's *Miracula Sancti Dunstani* made it impossible for the demoniac to recognize him, let alone openly reveal his secrets to the members of the community.[2] In direct contrast to that threat of public revelation, the young monk gave his confession to the archbishop in secret, alone and away from the rest of the community. In that episode and many of the others discussed above, it becomes evident that although concealing secrets from the abbot was absolutely prohibited, not all secrets or modes of secrecy were frowned on, and some were in fact essential to the proper functioning of the monastic community. These constituted a more profound type of monastic secrecy, defined by physical solitude and a separation from other human beings. Whether private confession to an abbot or a prayer said alone in a small chapel, whether the silence of the liturgical *Secretum* or the secret flight and reclusion of holy men and women, these sanctioned forms of secrecy were a salient feature of monastic life.[3]

This notion of secrecy is closely linked to the physical space reserved for seclusion. Adjectives such as the Old English *digol* and the Latin *secretus*, for instance, can be used to denote spaces that are physically discrete and set aside or private and enclosed. And there are varying types and degrees of *loci secreti*. The comparative *secretior*, for example, often signifies those spaces even further removed from human perception and thus all the more suitable to this experience of spiritual secrecy. Such spaces include the bishop's chamber encountered in the previous chapter (the "secretiorem domus partem" where Ægelward is restrained in the early stages of his madness) and the field where Cain murders his brother ("in loco secretiori").[4] It is easy to suppose, as Karma Lochrie does in her study of secrecy in later medieval England, that such secret places would have been problematic for their liability to promote "sexual dangers" or enhance the concealment of any kind of sin. Certainly, as we have seen, such concerns were real. However, secret spaces were also essential for conducting private prayer and for fostering the experience of a kind of secrecy rather different from what we would now typically associate with the term.[5] As we shall see, the range of what constitutes a *locus secretus* is remarkably broad, from the monastery itself (often in the positive form of the adjective, *secretus*) to a more remote hermitage (typically described with the comparative *secretior*), from a physically separate room to the interior space of a supplicant's heart, from the demon-filled wildernesses inhabited by a solitary saint to the field where Cain illicitly kills his brother. With the trenchant exception of Cain's field, many of these *loci* serve the important purpose of allowing the occupant to remove him- or herself from the perception (physical, mental, aural, or visual) of others in order to open up fully and deliberately before the omniscience of God.[6] This simultaneous openness to God and separation from human companions—what I will refer to as the state of "spiritual secrecy"—becomes a fundamental feature of Anglo-Saxon monastic life.

Hermits and the Life of Spiritual Secrecy

The most extreme expression of this spiritual secrecy in religious practice is found in the experience and example of eremitic monks. Partly in response to the distractions inherent to coenobitic living, some of the most devout Anglo-Saxon monks—after sufficient preparation under the supervision of an abbot, sometimes as abbots or bishops themselves, and often while on the path to sainthood—pursued lives of solitude or brief retreats in residence of *loci secretiores*.[7] This practice has a long tradition, dating back to what has been called the "secret flight" motif that we find throughout the *uitae* of the early desert saints who would leave society in order to live in solitude; in fact, it was this form of asceticism that Cassian and Benedict incorporated into the communal practices that form the basis for the monasticism that eventually develops in Anglo-Saxon England.[8] With similar purpose and often with these desert saints as their model, some Anglo-Saxon abbots and bishops took leave from their administrative duties for periods of prayer and contemplation in secret, and in order to do so they often inhabited *mansiones* or *loci secretiores*. The degree to which such secret space was used for spiritual reflection spans a wide range: from temporary retreats in secluded oratories, to special residencies in secret cells within or adjacent to monastic houses, to eremitical habitations of remote islands in the fenlands—England's desert—or on islands off the Northumbrian coast.

The age of the recluse, according to Tom Licence, began to emerge at the end of the eleventh century and ultimately blossomed in the twelfth.[9] But various forms of reclusion, although less common, nevertheless seem to have dotted the landscape of early Anglo-Saxon monasticism, particularly around Northumbria and showing some Irish influence. Having received training in Ireland and Lindisfarne, for example, Saint Chad (d. 672) became bishop of Lichfield and there built himself a more remote dwelling place (*mansio remotior*) not far

from his church, "in qua secretius cum paucis, id est septem siue octo, fratribus
... orare ac legere solebat" (in which he was accustomed to read and pray more
secretly with a few of his brothers, that is to say, seven or eight of them).[10] The
location was isolated and the small group of brothers would meet to pray *in
secreto*, but it offered an opportunity for solitude otherwise precluded by Chad's
administrative duties as bishop.[11] Other bishops did likewise. Aidan (d. 651), the
founder and first bishop of Lindisfarne, would often withdraw to Farne Island
for the purpose of "secretae orationis et silentii" (secret prayer and silence),[12] and
when Archbishop Ælberht of York (767–78) retired from his episcopal office, he,
too, "secreta petivit" (sought solitude).[13] But such retreats were not just available
to the most senior of ecclesiastic ranks, for Bede also describes a Northumbrian
man named Dryhthelm, who (after dying and returning to life) decided to pursue a religious lifestyle and entered the monastery at Melrose where he "accepit
autem in eodem monasterio locum mansionis secretiorem, ubi liberius continuis
in orationibus famulatui sui Conditoris uacaret" (accepted a more secret place of
dwelling within that same monastery, where he, less constrained, would be free
to devote himself to his Maker in constant prayer).[14] The secret space allowed
him to contemplate the secrets of God, which Bede claims he first encountered
during his momentary state of death. But despite its approximation of death,
life as a hermit meant that Dryhthelm was not entirely cut off from others and
was able to consult with neighboring monks who helped him understand his
earlier out-of-body experience.[15] Satellite hermitages tied to particular monastic communities, such as the one at Lichfield used by Chad or at Melrose used
by Dryhthelm, were quite common during the early period of Anglo-Saxon
monasticism, especially in the north of England; they enabled eremitic separation and distance, but still within the periphery of a community.[16] Dryhthelm
and bishops such as Chad, of course, represent two very different brands of
reclusion, but together they illustrate the power of space in enabling certain
experiences of spiritual secrecy.

This practice gradually reaches its pinnacle with Saint Cuthbert (d. 687),
who sought solitude in progressively more secret and remote locations. From
the time he left his more visible post as prior at Melrose for life as a monk at
Lindisfarne, Cuthbert tended toward greater degrees of secrecy; in the words
of his anonymous hagiographer, he "secularem gloriam fugiens clam et occulte
abscedens enauigauit" (sailed away, escaping from worldly glory and withdrawing covertly and secretly).[17] His life was marked by a constant balance
between the active life and the contemplative. After many years spent as a
monk at Lindisfarne and before being appointed as bishop, Cuthbert reached
a point at which he felt worthy to pursue divine contemplation, and as Bede
puts it, "diu concupita, quaestia, ac petita solitudinis secreta, comitante praefati abbatis sui simul et fratrum gratia multum laetabundus adiit" (he entered

greatly rejoicing into the secret solitudes he had long desired, sought, and prayed for, with the good will of his aforementioned abbot and also of the brethren).[18] First he "secessit ad locum quendam qui in exterioribus eius cellae partibus secretior apparet" (withdrew to a certain place in the outer parts of the monastery that seemed more secret).[19] But this *locus secretior*—reminiscent of those utilized by his predecessors, Chad and Aidan—was not secret enough. And after some time, Cuthbert moved to Farne Island where no one before him had been able to dwell on account of its demons (so says Bede, although Aidan had spent some solitary time there). In any case, the island offered a physical barrier between Cuthbert and community at Lindisfarne, and he enhanced that barrier further by building a circular cell with walls that, from the outside, were higher than a person standing upright. Then, by digging the inner room out of the ground, he made the walls much higher from within, so that "ad cohibendam oculorum siue cogitationum lasciuiam, ad erigendam in superna desideria totam mentis intentionem, pius incola nil de sua mansione praeter coelum posset intueri" (for the purpose of restraining the lust of the eyes and thoughts, and in order to lift the whole intention of his mind to higher desires, the pious inhabitant could see nothing except the sky from his dwelling).[20] Although he was at first pleased to see (*uidere*) and be seen (*uideri*) by visiting brethren through his one window, he eventually shut it and would only open it for definite necessities.[21] Cuthbert's spiritual growth develops alongside his progressively greater desire for solitude, and with that solitude comes the contemplative privilege of openness toward God.[22] The design of his cell on Farne Island beautifully represents this experience of spiritual secrecy, as it sharply cuts him off from the sight of visitors and opens him up to the view of the heavens above.

Cuthbert's cell at Farne Island was at some remove from the monastery at Lindisfarne, but the two locations were still linked by institutional association. For Cuthbert, the pursuit of solitude was thus gradual and restrained; at each stage, he inhabited a location only slightly more remote than the last and slowly transformed his retreat on Farne Island so as to increase his isolation. One advantage of these satellite-type hermitages and peripheral chapels tied to established monastic institutions (such as those used by Chad, Dryhthelm, and Cuthbert early in his search for solitude) is that their proximity to the main monastery would have slightly assuaged suspicions about the behavior of those monks who made use of them alone, especially when compared to other more remote and unassociated hermits whose habitation of *loci secretiores* farther away from the supervision of others tended to be faintly problematic. This concern was occasionally voiced by Anglo-Saxon writers, but it can also be seen in the way their lack of supervision was almost always justified with a reassuring mention of God's constant observation.[23]

Saint Guthlac was one of England's most celebrated hermits, whose life is richly recorded in a variety of hagiographic records, some of which, in fact, drew directly on the *uitae* of Cuthbert as a model.²⁴ In the Old English poems *Guthlac A* and *B*, we encounter this justification for remote solitude iterated through a central paradox of spiritual secrecy: "se halga þeow . . . ana gesæt dygle stowe" (the saintly servant . . . settled that secret place alone), and yet "stod seo dygle stow dryhtne in gemyndum" (that secret place remained in the Lord's mind).²⁵ As insinuated by the repeated phrase *dygle stow* (secret place), space is fundamental to the experience of spiritual secrecy. But in the *Guthlac* poems, that space is heavily contested. Although located apart from worldly distractions, these more secret and more remote parts of the world were also notoriously thought to be inhabited by demons.²⁶ But even though demons inhabit the landscape prior to Guthlac's arrival, the poet depicts the land as ultimately belonging to God. Stephanie Clark has argued that Guthlac's conflict with the demonic inhabitants is imagined as "a land dispute between spiritually unworthy tenants who have held the land through temporary loan and a warrior of God who is granted permanent tenure as his reward for faithful service."²⁷ The poem thus presents a narrative of exchange in which Guthlac, as the better guardian or shepherd ("betran hyrdes"), takes over the secret land ("dygle stowe") from the possession of the devils. The dynamics of secret space offer a particular challenge to any proven servant of God and with it an opportunity for further demonstrating exceptional piety.

With the exchange of land comes an exchange of the type of secrecy that it represents. Formerly the secrecy of the fenlands is controlled by the devil; eventually, it becomes the kind symbolized by the spiritual secrecy of Matthew 6:6, a secrecy deliberately and actively opened up to God. That God perceives every human secret (especially in those secret places far from the eyes of most human beings) is even recognized and admitted by one of the demons, who approaches Guthlac in feigned friendship, saying,

> Fela ge fore monnum miþað   þæs þe ge in mode gehycgað;   465
> ne beoð eowre dæda dyrne,   þeah þe ge hy in dygle gefremme.²⁸

> [before other men, you (*scil*. humankind) conceal much of what you are contemplating in your mind; although you practice them in secret, your deeds are not secret].

The demon's dissimulation makes the passage particularly ambiguous: either he is pretending to recite the doctrinal view that God sees all secrets (as expressed in Matthew 6:6 and elsewhere) or he is suggesting that demons are more perceptive than Guthlac may have assumed (in the vein of Cassian's description of the way demons gain access to human secrets like thieves at night).²⁹ The difference between the devil's two possible intentions is that the former should be understood to be always true (that is, God always sees everyone's secrets), while the latter is dependent on whether the person concealing those secrets willingly opens them up to God. Either way, it acknowledges that although Guthlac conceals his secret practices, those practices cannot remain entirely secret. Guthlac's solitary life is thus justified by the fact that God is always watching and more importantly by the saint's awareness of that constant observation. For Guthlac, as one of the more exceptional hermits in the Anglo-Saxon tradition, the secrecy of his life is defined not just by the isolated location of his dwelling place, but also by his active contemplation of and openness toward God.

This contemplation becomes especially evident as Guthlac nears his death and anticipates the heavenly kingdom:

> þær is sib ond blis,
> domfæstra dream,   dryhten ondweard,
> þam ic georne   *gæstgerynum*,
> in þas dreorgan tid   dædum cwemde,   1085
> mode ond mægne.³⁰

[there is peace and happiness, the joy of those steadfast in judgment, where present is the Lord whom I have eagerly pleased in *gæstgerynum* and in deeds, in mind and in might, during this dreary time.]

Guthlac looks back on his life as a servant of God, laboring on his Lord's behalf in deed and in "gæstgerynum." The meaning of *gæstgeryne* is not exactly clear; it is a word typically defined as "spiritual mystery," a joining of *gæst* (spirit) and *run* (secret; mystery). Here it could certainly refer to the spiritual mysteries of the Mass or of scripture—the kinds of mysteries subject to exegetical interpretation. But the poet's use of the term implies a certain human experience of spirituality and contemplation that such a definition fails to convey.³¹ It seems to conflate, in other words, divine mystery with contemplative secrecy, where God and human converge in the mind of the supplicant. "Gæstgerynum" and "dædum" (deeds) are placed in apposition to "mode ond mægne" (mind and might), suggesting that *gæstgeryne* signifies thought as opposed to deed, the product of one's mind as opposed to one's might (lines 1084–86a). Bosworth-Toller accordingly defines the word as not only "spiritual mystery" but also "mystery of the mind."³² But in the experience of Guthlac, the word really seems to carry both meanings at once as it hovers between the spiritual mysteries of God on the one hand and Guthlac's own secret thoughts on the other. It thus conveys a private communion with God—in the form of secret prayer and contemplation—that is both incomprehensible to others and yet absolutely open to the Lord.³³

This conflation is especially evident a few lines later, as Guthlac prepares to expound scripture for his faithful follower, Beccel; it is a gift enabled by the fact that the saint is "deophycgende dryhtne to willan / gæstgerynum" (deeply mindful of *gæstgerynum* according to the Lord's will).³⁴ Guthlac's explanation of the mystery of God ("dryhtnes geryne") does not disappoint:

>   ne swa deoplice   dryhtnes *geryne*
>   þurh menniscne   muð areccan
>   on sidum sefan.³⁵

[never through a human mouth (had the) *mystery* of the Lord been so deeply expounded in an expanse of wisdom.]

Here the poet inverts the construction set up in the preceding lines: "deophycgende dryhtne to willan / *gæstgerynum*" becomes "swa deoplice dryhtnes *geryne*." Guthlac's deep contemplation enabled through spiritual secrecy translates into his deep interpretation of divine secrets.³⁶ *Gæstgeryne* comes to signify an experience of secrecy that takes place when contemplating diving mysteries in solitude. Yet it is a form of solitude in which Guthlac is never really alone. Fending off the devils that claim the island as their own, Guthlac thus announces:

>   Ne eam ic swa fealog,   swa ic eow fore stonde,
>   monna weorudes,   ac me mara dæl
>   in godcundum   *gæstgerynum*
>   wunað ond weaxeð,   se me wraþe healdeð.
>   Ic me anum her   eaðe getimbre   250
>   hus ond hleonað.³⁷

[I am not so destitute of a company of men as I appear standing before you, but a greater contingent dwells and grows in my divine *gæstgerynum*, which will fiercely support me. I will easily build a house and shelter here for me alone.]

The poet alternates between images of Guthlac alone and perpetually supported by a host of angels.³⁸ In Guthlac's solitude, his state of spiritual secrecy ("gæstgerynum") brings forth troops of angels that accompany him and carry him closer to the company of God.³⁹ Ultimately, this motif of solitude amid angels becomes so central to Guthlac's hagiographic identity that even his brief entry in the *Old English Martyrology* ends by describing the angel who spoke to the saint every evening and morning, sharing with him "heofonlico geryno" (heavenly mysteries).[40]

The Monastery as a Secret Space and the Secret Spaces Within the Monastery

Loci secretiores are not restricted to fenlands and islands or even chapels on the outskirts of monastic lands: they are also found within Anglo-Saxon monasteries. Indeed, even the monastery itself is traditionally conceptualized as separate, secluded, and in a sense secret from the world outside.[41] According to the *Regula magistri*—in a decidedly idealistic formulation—the monastery as a whole is imagined as a secret space where God's secrets are encountered through the rituals of daily life. The daily reading of the Rule is thus suspended in the presence of non-monks to avoid "detractionem futuram in saeculo, cum secreta Dei saecularis agnouerit" (defamation afterward in the world should a layperson learn the secrets of God) and, moreover, so that "secretum monasterii uel mensuras uitae sanctae constitutas in disciplinam ab inrisoribus non sciatur" (the secret of the monastery and the established norms for leading a holy life in accordance with the teaching may not be learned by scoffers).[42] There are exceptions, of course, but the Rule is regarded and treated as a kind of secret, privileged because it dictates how members of a monastic community might bring themselves closer to the secrets of God. The Rule mirrors the secrecy of the monastic space as a space that is physically separated from the worldly community that surrounds it.

This institutional secrecy of the monastic enterprise has a long tradition that goes back to the desert fathers but was well recognized in Anglo-Saxon England. In the Old English *Vita* of Saint Mary of Egypt, for example, Zosimus's monastery in Palestine "wæs swa westen and swa digle þæt næs na þæt an þæt heo wæs ungewunelic ac eac swilce uncuð þam landleodum him sylfum" (was so deserted and so secret that it was not only unfrequented, but it was entirely unknown to the people of the land themselves).[43] Similarly, in Ælfric's *Vita* of Saint Martin, the saint "gestaðelode him mynster twa mila of þære byrig, and seo stow wæs swa digle þæt he ne gewilnode nanes oþres wæstenes" (established a monastery two miles outside of the city, and the place was so secret that he never desired another desert).[44] And in Werferth's translation of the preface to Gregory's *Dialogi*, he records Gregory's recollection of his time in a monastery: "þa gelyste me þære diglan stowe (*secretum locum*), þe ic ær on wæs on mynstre. Seo is þære gnornunge freond, forþam man simle mæg his sares & his unrihtes mæst geþencean, gif he ana bið on digolnysse" (then I longed for that secret place, where I formerly was in the monastery; that is the friend of sorrow because a man can always think over his sadness and his wrongs best if he is alone in secrecy).[45] Of course, Gregory's nostalgic isolation and the remote monastic sites established by Zosimus and Martin were an ideal admired but not always realized in early medieval England.

Most monasteries in Anglo-Saxon England were enclosed by some kind of physical wall that both concealed the monks and their activities from the world and concealed the world and its distractions from the monks.[46] But even though an ideal monastery (as promoted by the *Regula magistri* or the *Regula Sancti Benedicti*, for instance) would have been a completely self-sufficient one, interaction with the outside world and the laity was often unavoidable.[47] Indeed, we have already seen one instance in which guards ("milites") readily materialized during Lanfranc's mass in order to apprehend the mad Ægelward.[48] Monasteries, especially in the early Anglo-Saxon period, were in general not as conducive as we might expect to contemplative activities and the separation from worldly distractions that such activities would require.[49] Such activity and distractions may very well have been responsible early in the Anglo-Saxon period for the desire of some extraordinarily devout monks—such as Cuthbert and Guthlac—to adopt solitary lives in order to come closer to God through seclusion and contemplation. And as I will discuss in more detail below, something similar may have also been responsible for the architectural changes that coincided with the Benedictine Reform later in the period.[50] The want of complete tranquility in many areas of a monastic house called for spaces designated for private prayer, or at least the adoption of any number of different small spaces for precisely that purpose within monasteries and churches.[51]

In theory, the oratory—*oratorium* in Latin, *gebedhus* in Old English—would have been one such space, a perfect *locus secretior*. A rather nebulous and broad architectural category, any discrete room reserved for the purpose of prayer could have served as an oratory, which *Regula Sancti Benedicti* describes as follows:

> Oratorium hoc sit quod dicitur, nec ibi quicquam aliud geratur aut condatur. Expleto opere Dei, omnes cum summo silentio exeant, et habeatur reverentia Deo, ut frater qui forte sibi peculiariter vult orare non impediatur alterius improbitate. Sed et si aliter vult sibi forte secretius orare, simpliciter intret et oret, non in clamosa voce, sed in lacrimis et intentione cordis.
>
> [The oratory ought to be what it is called, and nothing else is to be done or stored there. After the Work of God, all must leave in complete silence and with reverence for God, so that a brother who may wish to pray alone will not be disturbed by the insensitivity of another. Moreover, if

at other times a brother chooses to pray secretly, he may simply go in and pray, not in a loud voice, but with tears and heartfelt devotion.]⁵²

The oratory, then, is a place of complete silence; it is a place where anyone may pray alone or in the presence of others; it is a place where one can pray more secretly ("secretius orare"). This means that even if there are other brethren in the room, the monk who wishes to pray alone ("peculiariter") will be alone with God.

The experience of secrecy within the oratory is clearly different from the kinds of secrecy that the monastic rules and the abbots enforcing those rules worked hard to prevent; it is also different from the kind of secrecy found in those acts of private penance (*secreta poenitentia*) discussed in the previous chapter. In part, the first of these differences manifests itself in the nature of the thing concealed: on the surface, a concealed sin would seem to pose a problem that a concealed prayer does not. However, as we have seen, the line between the two is often blurred, especially for those monks who are not yet able to judge for themselves what constitutes a good or evil thought, and who must therefore always defer to counsel and never conceal anything from their superiors: the case of Ælfstan's stolen obedience is exemplary in this respect. But the greater difference is located not so much in the nature of the thing concealed but rather in the monk's state of contrition and acceptance of God's omniscience. As Adalbert de Vogüé elegantly comments, "since the heart has become the place of secret prayer, this prayer is set against not only ostentation, but also irreverence and superficiality. To pray loudly would be to insult God by supposing that he needs to hear our voices. To pray in silence is to recognize that his glance penetrates to the depths of the heart."⁵³ For Benedict, the space of the oratory is identified by the silence it requires of those within, and that silence is an implicit acknowledgment of God's omniscience.

Echoing and expanding on Benedict's description of the oratory and brilliantly illustrating de Vogüé's logic, the *Regularis concordia* made this spatial design a fundamental part of reformed monasteries in tenth-century England. All monks were instructed accordingly:

> secretis oratorii locis, in quantum Sancti Spiritus gratia clementer instigauerit, peculiaribus teste Deo cum bonorum operum uigilantia consulte utatur orationibus.

> [Insofar as the grace of the Holy Spirit shall mercifully inspire him, he should practice private prayer prudently in the secret spaces of the oratory, with God as his witness and with a zeal for good works.]⁵⁴

The permissibility, indeed encouragement of solitary prayer ("peculiaribus orationibus") in the secret places of the oratory ("secretis oratorii locis") directly contrasts with the open ("palam") way in which the monastic customs should generally be carried out (as the *Regularis concordia* suggests just before the passage quoted). But this contrast is promptly qualified from two crucial directions: first, by the fact that God is always a witness ("teste") even in those *loci secreti* that are hidden from the eyes of others and, second, by the requirement of vigilance ("vigilantia"), that the monk be watchful of himself.

Prayer in Secret

Private prayer and contemplation held an important place in Anglo-Saxon monastic practice, providing an opportunity for monks to exercise spiritual devotion by the means and to the degree that was personally necessary while complementing the corporate worship of God through the liturgy. Indeed, not only were private forms of prayer often derived from communal ones,[55] but elements of the liturgy also took on private forms. For example, the Secret or *Secretum* (the silent offertory prayer belonging to the Proper of the Mass) gets its name from the silence with which it is performed, as the celebrant's communion with God is sonically concealed from the earthly audience in the church. This important role of silence and spiritual secrecy in the various practices of private prayer is ultimately founded on the words spoken by Christ in the Sermon on the Mount: "Tu autem cum oraveris, intra in cubiculum tuum, et clauso ostio, ora Patrem tuum in abscondito" (when thou shalt pray, enter into thy chamber, and having shut the door, pray to thy Father in secret).[56] Prayer in secret is at once a mode of humility that distinguishes Christians from the hypocrites and heathens who pray on street corners, and at the same time, it is a method of appealing to God alone so that "Pater tuus, qui videt in abscondito, reddet tibi" (thy Father who sees in secret will repay thee).[57] The rhetorical reciprocity in Matthew 6:6 between the prayer in secret ("in abscondito") and the Father who sees in secret ("in abscondito") implies precisely the point made by de Vogüé above: that secret prayer affirms God's inexorable access to the depths of the heart.

We tend to disassociate private prayer from any notion of secrecy; indeed, we might even prefer to translate *secretus* when it appears in descriptions of such prayer with words such as "private," "silent," or "solitary." However, Anglo-Saxon religious seem to have drawn a strong connection, as I will demonstrate, between such prayer and the spatial separation intrinsic to early medieval conceptions of secrecy. On the one hand, the secrecy of private prayer evolves from the separation from other human beings that the spiritual life and the work of contemplation require, as we have seen in the *Regula magistri* and in Gregory's recollection of his monastic background. On the other hand, this particular notion of prayer in secret also evolves out of the proximity to God that is fostered through such solitude and separation. "Omnes culpe meae a te non sunt abscondite" (all of my faults are not hidden from you), the supplicant says in one private prayer, echoing Psalm 68:6.[58] In another, God is invoked as the "occultorum cognitor" and "digla oncnawend" (knower of secrets).[59] Even Alcuin, who was largely skeptical of solitary, nonsacerdotal forms of confession, wrote a private confessional prayer for Charlemagne that similarly acknowledges God's omniscience: "Sed tu, domine, occultorum cognitor, qui dixisti, paenitentiam te malle peccatorum quam mortem, Tibi omnia cordis mei reuelabo archana" (But you, Lord, the knower of secrets, who said that you prefer the repentance of sins over death, to you I will reveal all the secrets of my heart).[60] There are countless other examples like these (some of them even based on Alcuin's prayer), in which the secrecy of private prayer depends on an acknowledgment of God's knowledge.[61] Paradoxically, such prayer thus entails an experience of secrecy in which one's secrets are deliberately opened to God.

References to such acts of secret prayer abound in a variety of Anglo-Saxon texts. Take, for example, the late Anglo-Saxon Handbook for the Confessor, which requires that the penitent with no means to give alms pray "on diglum gecneowige gelome" (kneeling frequently in secret places).[62] On the other hand, take the *Visio Leofrici*, which recounts how, when Earl Leofric of Mercia (d. 1057) "wiste þæt menn fæste slæpen, he wolde on dihlum stowum hine georne gebiddan" (knew that people were fast asleep, he would earnestly pray in secret places).[63] These two examples, both of which share a connection to eleventh-century Worcester, reveal the range of such secret prayer even outside a strictly monastic setting and regardless of whether the supplicant was a poor layperson or a pious earl. At the same time, these examples also show both the influence of monastic practice and language on lay experiences of spiritual devotion and the extent to which private and secret spaces ("diglum stowum") resonated with spiritual meaning.

In the distinctly monastic context of Saint Augustine's Abbey (which we will explore in more detail below), Saint Dunstan (d. 988) sought the same kind of secrecy. According to B.'s *Vita Sancti Dunstani*, while Dunstan was the archbishop of Canterbury, "fuit ut in secretis noctium temporibus sancta loca, propter multimodam populorum ad se uenientium inhesionem uel etiam aliorum multorum occupationem, sancta semper psalmodia decantando lustraret" (he would go around the holy places in the secret times of the night, ever singing sacred psalms; [he did this] because of the constant attendance of visitors and his preoccupation with many other matters).[64] Late one night, he went to the eastern chapel of Saint Mary (see below, fig. 3) whence he heard unfamiliar voices singing with delicate harmony ("subtili modulamine").

Looking in, he saw bands of virgins dancing and singing a hymn by Sedulius.[65] At the right time, especially at night ("in secretis noctium temporibus"), any place could become a *locus secretus*, and in such a *locus* someone as holy as Dunstan might encounter divine company in unexpected ("ex insperato") ways.

The role of private prayer underwent some transformations during the tenth-century Benedictine Reform, in which Dunstan was an instrumental figure. As Thomas H. Bestul has shown, the devotional spirituality sometimes associated with Anselm and the twelfth century was actually part of a longer tradition that developed around Canterbury and Winchester.[66] Although communal and liturgical ritual became more unified, regularized, and intensified during the monastic reforms advanced on the Continent by Benedict of Aniane and in England by Æthelwold and Dunstan, private prayer seems hardly to have vanished from monastic life.[67] Indeed, as we have seen in the language of the *Regularis concordia* (itself the keystone of Æthelwold's reform movement), there was still space for private devotion in the reformed monasteries of later Anglo-Saxon England; in fact, it encouraged such prayer. And moreover, manuscript evidence from the period supports an argument for a continuance, if not a proliferation of the practice.[68] Sets of private prayers abound in the eleventh-century codices such as the Galba Prayerbook,[69] the Portiforium of Saint Wulfstan,[70] and Ælfwine's Prayerbook,[71] where, for example, the so-called Directions for Private Devotion clearly instruct the reader to pray in secret: "do þis dihlice, þær ðu sylf sy" (do this secretly, where you are by yourself).[72] But what would following such an instruction entail?

It hardly needs saying that private prayer and contemplation may have also (perhaps predominantly) been dependent on nonwritten forms of oration, such as in meditations on memorized psalms.[73] Indeed, one wonders whether the writing down of a prayer for others to read automatically renders it less secret and less personal, less *digollic* and less *peculiaris*. If so, then the key to a prayer's secrecy (in the sense akin to the liturgical *Secretum*) must be located in the performance of the prayer and the location of that performance, rather than its textual or idiomatic shape. The Directions for Private Devotion in Ælfwine's Prayerbook thus guide the extemporaneous supplicant to pray secretly ("do þis dihlice"), while also reminding him or her that "ne mæg ænig mann on his agen geþeode . . . Gode swa fulfremedlice areccan, ne his mildheortnesse biddan, swa he mæg mid þillicum sealmum 7 mid oþrum swilcum" (no man can express so fully to God, nor request His mercy in his own words as he can with this or any other psalm).[74] We have to assume that most private prayer would have very likely included some use of the Psalms simply because they were the religious text that young monks tended to memorize first. There is no reason to doubt their significance and usage, but it is important to consider how the internalization of the Psalms from a young age operates as a private internalization of God in which the supplicant is reminded of God's always-observant presence from within.⁷⁵ Praying with the internalized words of the Psalms in secret ("dihlice"), in silence, and alone—perhaps even simultaneously during moments of communal psalmody—would have thus transcended the distinction between public and private, liturgical and solitary.

When monastic writers refer to an act of secret prayer (*oratio in secreto*), the references tend to be concerned with the particular and singular disposition of the supplicant in relation to God. Alcuin accordingly reassures the bishop and community of Hexham that "etiam et singularis uniuscuiusque in secreto oratio ad aures omnipotentis Dei pervenire non dubitandum est" (it is not to be doubted that even the individual prayer of each person in secret reaches the ears of the Almighty God).⁷⁶ And Bede uses the sacrificial offering of turtledoves and pigeons in Luke 2:24 to distinguish allegorically between public and private prayer: because the turtledove wanders by itself and the pigeon huddles in a flock, the former represents the "secretas orationum lacrimas" (secret tears of prayers) while the latter represents the "publicos ecclesiae conuentus" (Church's public gatherings).⁷⁷ Communal and private prayer are different, to be sure, but the difference has everything to do with the reflexive disposition of the supplicant as opposed to the external actions of the community. Prayer in secret does not so much entail the concealment of the prayer from the view of others (a turtledove can still be seen even though it flies alone) as it does disassociation and separation from others, ignoring their presence and thoughts in favor of focusing on the self's relation to God. This singular and particular nature of private prayer is even applied collectively, as when the *Regularis concordia* (echoing its earlier architectural language) requires that for thirty days following the death of a brother "cotidie sacerdotum unusquisque secretis oratorii locis specialiter pro eo Missas celebret" (each priest shall daily celebrate a Mass specifically for the dead brother, in the secret places of the oratory).⁷⁸ And similarly in Ælfwine's Prayerbook, the generic injunction to "do þis dihlice, þær ðu sylf sy" (do this secretly, where you are by yourself) again captures this state of being with one's self, as such prayer takes place wherever one happens to be, but also automatically designates that location as a site of secrecy.⁷⁹

But if we turn our attention to the kinds of physical and architectural spaces that would have been particularly conducive to this mode of prayer, what we find is that despite the emphasis on the collective liturgy, the Benedictine Reform—far from suppressing private prayer—saw a reconfiguration of spiritual space, whereby the secrecy of the monastic life (idealized, for instance, in the *Regula magistri* and eremitic isolation) was built into the fabric of major churches as they were expanded to accommodate a burgeoning culture of private prayer. The language of the rules and the experiences described in narrative sources point to a monastic preoccupation with the nature of the space in which private prayer was conducted and what that space meant for the monastic enterprise as a whole. In the process, these architectural forms of secrecy shaped a monk's connection to God.

The Architecture of Secret Space

According to Isidore of Seville, the most sacred parts of a building are its most secret, its *loci secretiores*.[80] And almost any place designated for private prayer, as we have seen, will often be referred to as a *locus secretus* or a *digle stow*.[81] Oratories and other such spaces can be found in a wide variety of possible locations: a chapel, for instance, within a church or in a field. And they can have various architectural features, shapes, sizes, and layouts, none of which is as important for defining a space as an oratory as the activity of prayer that takes place inside. To complicate the picture, the number of oratories contained within a given monastic foundation varied widely in Anglo-Saxon England. Abbot Ceolfrith (d. 716) supposedly built many oratories ("plura fecit oratoria") around the monasteries of Monkwearmouth and Jarrow.[82] And according to Alcuin, York's *Alma Sophia* contained thirty altars and was "porticibus . . . circumdata multis" (surrounded by many a *porticus*).[83] Especially during this early period of Anglo-Saxon monasticism, these chapels were supplemented by "free-standing oratories" scattered throughout the country, many of which have vanished: since they were unassociated with larger monastic foundations, they were simply more vulnerable both to physical threats and to gaps in memory and records.[84] And even while monastic churches often survive, other Anglo-Saxon monastic buildings have not tended to fare so well. It is difficult, therefore, to begin imagining or charting the full range of what Anglo-Saxon oratories might have looked like, where within the monastic topography they might have been located, and especially how they might have been used.[85] There has been outstanding work, especially by Helen Gittos, that has tackled this challenge on a broad scale, not only showing us how features of Anglo-Saxon church architecture corresponded to certain liturgical practices but also reminding us of the dangers in drawing particular connections between architecture and lived experience, especially where surviving evidence on either side is sparse.[86] The search for the secret spaces where prayer took place is in many ways a perilous one, made worse by the private and secret nature of such prayer: but from the remnants of Anglo-Saxon churches a picture begins to emerge that gives us a sense of how such solitude might have been experienced even within monastic walls.

With the exception of the small single- and double-cell churches that dotted the Anglo-Saxon landscape, many moderate and large institutions had churches with multiple rooms of various sizes. The terminology for and use of such rooms is far from consistent, even though they become a typical feature of Anglo-Saxon church architecture.⁸⁷ Working in the early Northumbrian and Irish tradition, for example, Adomnán refers in his *Vita Sancti Columbae* to such a space as an *exedra*, which seems to have been a small room attached to the outside wall of the main church with an entrance from the nave.⁸⁸ In his *De locis sanctis*, however, we find an *exedra* as a detached building containing relics and a shrine.⁸⁹ If the word *exedra* is somewhat rare and imprecise, the word *porticus* is far more common but often no less ambiguous. In insular usage, *exedra* seems to be synonymous with *porticus* in referring to any side chapel, whereas on the Continent *exedra* tends to refer specifically to a building separated from the main church.⁹⁰ For example, the Carolingian Walahfrid Strabo (ca. 807–849) explains that an *exedra* is "absida quaedam separata modicum quid a templo vel palatio et dicta inde, quod extra haereat" (a kind of apse separated a little way from the temple or palace, and [it] is called this because it is attached outside), whereas a *porticus* functions "ut per eam intretur et transeatur" (to allow one to enter through it and step across it).⁹¹ In England, on the other hand, *porticus* were side chapels typically attached to the main building, and rather than serving as a covered walkway (like that described by Strabo), they tended to be enclosed on all sides and would rarely have more than one doorway. Some *porticus* may have also been used for choral participation in the liturgy: Ælfric thus clarifies the *Regularis concordia* at one point to note that boys should sing responses to the *Kyrie eleison* from the north *porticus*, the south *porticus*, and the western end of the church.⁹² (Arnold W. Klukas has suggested the intriguing possibility that this arrangement would require a second story, as at Deerhurst, so that the voices would sound as if they were coming from above.)⁹³ Aside from their use in producing these liturgical sound effects, varieties of *porticus* are found in many English churches from the earliest to the latest periods of Anglo-Saxon monasticism. Whether the thirty York chapels described by Alcuin or the particular chapels we will encounter in Bede, Ædiluulf, and William of Malmesbury, the term *porticus* frequently delineates a place of prayer in the form of a compact and separate chapel that opens to the nave or chancel through a small doorway.⁹⁴

As a major, continuous seat of Anglo-Saxon monastic life and administration, Canterbury offers a useful collection of buildings for exploring the range of architecture suitable for private prayer. Just after the arrival of the missionaries led by Saint Augustine, the Church of Saint Martin (fig. 2) was converted into a place of prayer for Bertha, the Christian wife of the pagan King Æthelberht of Kent (d. 616). Æthelberht allowed her and the missionaries to meet in the church, where they would pray and say Mass, baptize, and preach.⁹⁵ Once the king was converted and baptized, he allowed them to preach more widely and to build and restore additional churches in Kent. Until then,

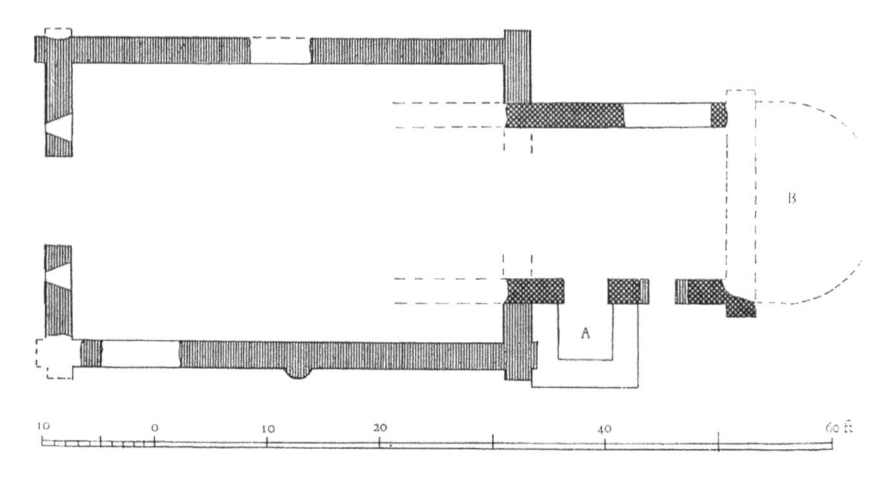

Figure 2. Ground plan of the Church of Saint Martin, Canterbury. Taylor and Taylor, *Anglo-Saxon Architecture*, 1:144, fig. 63.

the Church of Saint Martin remained their base camp and to this day represents the oldest surviving church in England still in use (some parts having been rebuilt). Originally, the church was a Roman building, although there is some debate about which parts of the surviving church were Roman, if any; it is also possible that the church was simply rebuilt from existing Roman materials in the sixth century under the direction of Bertha, whose Frankish ancestry might account for the foreign appearance of the construction methods.[96] Regardless of the precise date and circumstances of construction, scholars agree that the existing chancel is the earliest part of the church. Contemporary with the construction of the south wall of the western part of the chancel is a doorway to a small room (A), making it possibly the earliest Anglo-Saxon example of such a room, dating to the year 600 at the very latest (shortly before or after the arrival of Saint Augustine). It is likely the model for the construction of similar spaces in other Kentish churches built by Augustine after receiving Æthelberht's blessing.[97]

Nearby on the grounds of Saint Augustine's, Canterbury, several later buildings seem to have used features of Saint Martin's as a model. For example, the Church of Saint Pancras (the easternmost building depicted in fig. 3) was perhaps one of the churches first constructed (or reconstructed) by Saint Augustine after the conversion of King Æthelberht. In the mid-eighth century, two small *porticus* were then added to the north and south walls in the middle of the nave; these would become a typical feature of Kentish church architecture and, during the late eighth and ninth centuries, would rapidly

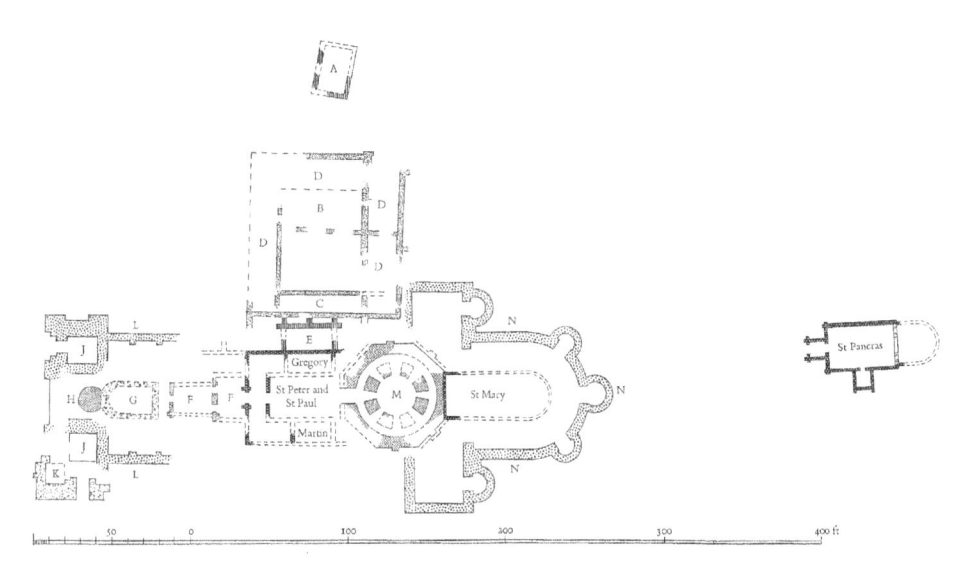

Figure 3. Ground plan of Saint Augustine's Abbey and the Church of Saint Pancras, Canterbury. Taylor and Taylor, *Anglo-Saxon Architecture*, 1:136, fig. 61.

become a common addition to churches throughout England.[98] Nothing survives of the northern *porticus* at Saint Pancras, but of the one on the south side of the nave, we can see the base of each wall, the threshold to the nave, and the remains of a small altar (figs. 4 and 5).[99] The *porticus* is a relatively small space with enough room for one person to pray comfortably if alone.[100] To the west of Saint Pancras (in fig. 3) lies the much larger Church of Saint Peter and Saint Paul, within which the *porticus* of Saint Gregory and Saint Martin run along the north and south sides of the nave, respectively. These side chapels were used as burial places for important figures in the early history of the abbey (including Saint Augustine himself), and they date to the late seventh century (built therefore shortly before the *porticus* at Saint Pancras). As spaces separate from yet enclosed within the main church, these *porticus*—whether the more intimate one at the Church of Saint Pancras or the larger ones at the Church of Saint Peter and Saint Paul, where, according to Bede, a priest would say Mass privately every Saturday at the altar of Saint Gregory in the north *porticus* for the archbishops buried there—must have been highly conducive to private prayer.[101]

These three Canterbury churches were part of a major and important Anglo-Saxon monastic center, and their *porticus* demonstrate an early and architecturally persistent type of chapel that would have been available to monks wishing to pray in the more secret places (*loci secretiores*) within a church. To be

Figure 4. Ruins of the Church of Saint Pancras, Canterbury.
Photograph by Benjamin A. Saltzman.

Figure 5. Southern *porticus* of the Church of Saint Pancras, Canterbury.
Photograph by Benjamin A. Saltzman.

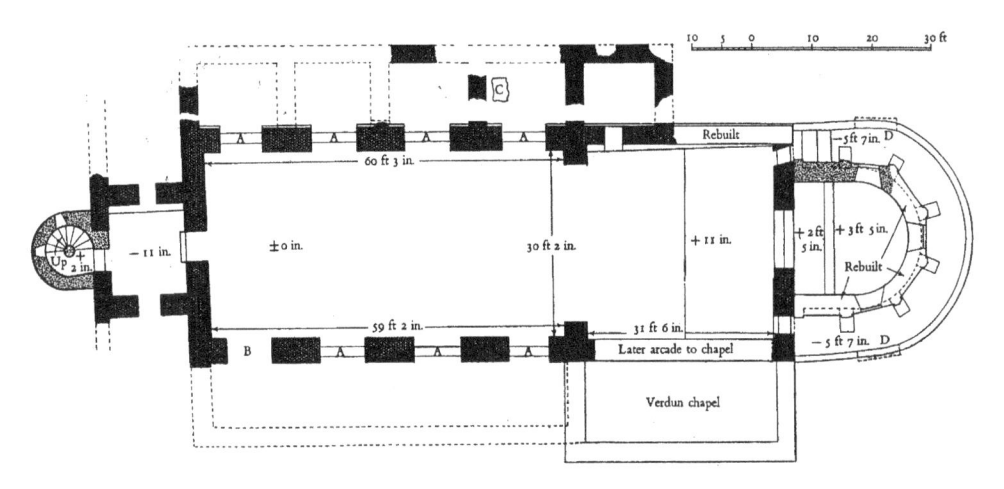

Figure 6. Ground plan of All Saints Church, Brixworth, Northamptonshire, showing doorways to the *porticus* (A) off of the nave. Taylor and Taylor, *Anglo-Saxon Architecture*, 1:110, fig. 49.

sure, these buildings cannot speak for all Anglo-Saxon monastic churches. Many pre-Conquest church buildings, especially those attached to smaller foundations, were constructed in a two-cell fashion with a rectangular nave and a small chancel.[102] However, numerous churches did contain simple twin *porticus* such as the ones at Canterbury, representing a relatively widespread and typical style that especially flourished in southern England during the early to middle period of Anglo-Saxon church construction.[103] Even some notable early Anglo-Saxon churches built around the seventh century and at some remove from Kent—such as Brixworth in Mercia (fig. 6) and Jarrow in Northumbria—seem to have had four or five chapels flanking each side of the nave.[104] Literary sources, too, tell us something about the early construction and use of these chapels. For example, Ædiluulf's poem *De abbatibus* (written between 803 and 821) concerns an abbey connected to Lindisfarne and describes several *porticus*. Sigbald, the fourth abbot of the abbey, built a church containing "prepulchris mensa tabellis, / porticus in medio" (an altar distinguished by very lovely pictures in the midst of a *porticus*).[105] And later in the poem, Ædiluulf describes a vision of a church that was "domus exterius magnis minimisque per omne / porticibus spatium muri subfulta manebat" (supported all the way around the wall outside by large and small *porticus*).[106] In the vision, he is then led by his teacher Eadfrith into these great and small *porticus* ("porticibus magnis minimis induxit"), each of which had bright candles burning at its altar, clearly illuminating all of the *porticus* ("porticibus cunctis ardebant lumina clara"). And the *porticus* to the west was particularly brilliant ("magno splendebat honore") on account of its golden altar.[107] There, in that western *porticus*, the poet encounters Abbot Wulfsig praying alone, shining with the same clear and wondrous light ("lumine clarum") that illuminated the *porticus* itself.[108] This behavior, we are led to believe, was not especially unusual, as earlier in the poem Ædiluulf informs us that Wulfsig would often supplicate privately when all the other brothers had gone to lunch and at other times when he could be alone.[109]

While many early Anglo-Saxon churches contain these simple side chapels off of the nave (such as those at Brixworth or those envisioned by Ædiluulf), we eventually see an expansion and increase in complexity of these secret spaces during the Benedictine Reform in the tenth century. For example, the early church at Glastonbury constructed during the reign of King Ine around the year 700 had a simple nave flanked by two *porticus*; shortly afterward, two additional *porticus* were added to the west end of the church, and under Dunstan in the mid-tenth century, two more *porticus* (dedicated to Saint John the Baptist and Saint Andrew) were added to the eastern end of the church as part of his larger project of expansion (fig. 7).[110] Glastonbury thus underwent gradual growth in the number of small chapels added around the periphery of the church in the period leading up to the Benedictine Reform, in some sense paralleling Dunstan's own early and foundational role in the reform movement itself.

During the late tenth century, Bishop Æthelwold and his successor, Ælfheah, oversaw similar expansion at Winchester. The expeditious timing of these improvements suggests that when Æthelwold was compiling the *Regularis concordia* around the year 973, he must have had some sense of what sort of secret places would have been available to the monks and priests at Winchester for saying private prayers and special masses, as he uses the phrase "secretis oratorii locis" not once but twice.[111] If he had any concrete spaces in mind, he could have been thinking of Glastonbury (where he spent more than a decade studying and working under Dunstan) or he may very well have been thinking of the layout of Old Minster, Winchester, which had recently undergone a number of architectural changes, the most substantial of which were carried out under his leadership.

Old Minster began with a structure much like that of Saint Pancras, in which the nave was flanked on both sides with two small transeptal *porticus* (fig. 8). At some point early in the tenth century (see fig. 9), a series of three small chapels (F) were added onto the north wall at the western end of the nave (three more were probably mirrored on the south wall); these chapels would have been there just prior to Æthelwold's tenure as bishop and may

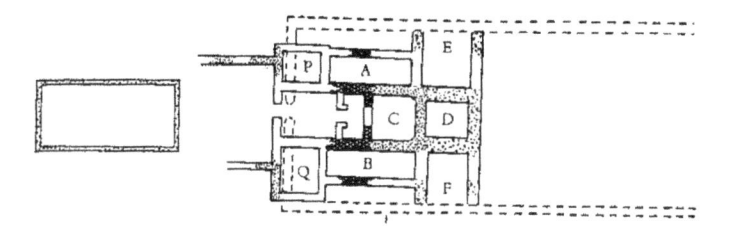

Figure 7. Ground plan of Glastonbury, showing lateral *porticus* (A and B) flanking Ine's nave (c. 700); later chancel (C) and lateral *porticus* (P and Q) from the period 700 and 950; and Dunstan's tower built over a crypt (D) and the lateral *porticus* of Saint John the Baptist (E) and Saint Andrew (F) in Dunstan's extended church (c. 950). Taylor and Taylor, *Anglo-Saxon Architecture*, 1:253, fig. 110.

have influenced his design for monastic life and the architecture that would sustain it. Even more significant is the massive structure that Æthelwold would build onto the west end of the church (fig. 9, B and C) around Saint Swithun's original tomb (fig. 9, 2). This addition was constructed between the years 971 and 974, corresponding quite closely with the date of the *Regularis concordia*, and was then further augmented around the later years of Æthelwold's tenure as bishop (structure D, fig. 9, was built between the years 974 and 980). The genius of Æthelwold's western structure, as Wulfstan of Winchester reports, was the labyrinthine assortment of chapels that greeted those who sought to enter the church:

> Istius antiqui reparauit et atria templi
>   moenibus excelsis culminibusque nouis,
> partibus hoc austri firmans et partibus arcti
>   porticibus solidis, arcubus et uariis.
> Addidit et plures sacris altaribus edes;
>   quae retinent dubium liminis introitum,
> quisquis ut ignotis hec deambulat atria plantis
>   nesciat unde meat quoue pedem referat,
> omni parte fores quia conspiciuntur apertae
>   nec patet ulla sibi semita certa uiae
> Huc illucque uagos stans circumducit ocellos

>   attica Dedalei tecta stupetque soli,
> certior adueniat donec sibi ductor et ipsum
>   ducat ad extremi limina uestibuili.

> [Æthelwold also rebuilt the building of the Old Minster with lofty walls and new roofs, strengthening it on its southern and northern sides with solid *porticus* and arches of various kinds. Similarly, he added numerous chapels to house holy altars; these disguise the entrance of the main doorway so that, if someone were to walk through the interior of the church with unfamiliar steps, he would not know whence he came, nor how to retrace his steps, because in every direction open doorways may be seen and there is no sure route apparent to him. Stopping, he casts his wandering eyes around here and there, and marvels (as it were) at the classical structures of the one and only Daedaelus, until an experienced guide comes to him and leads him to the threshold of the one remaining door (i.e., the main entrance).][112]

If the *Regula magistri* gave early monasticism its idealized secrecy by concealing the reading of the Rule from outsiders,[113] then Æthelwold's entranceway to Old Minster realized that ideal in stone. The uninitiated who walked into the church with "ignotis . . . plantis" faced a daunting maze of doorways, small rooms, and chapels; only with the guidance of an experienced "ductor" could one hope to make it through the actual entrance and into the main church. Wulfstan says nothing of the sorts of activities that went on in these chapels and rooms, but even allowing for exaggeration, the presence of "sacris altaribus" suggests that when these *porticus* were not in the service of confounding outsiders, they must have at times been used for prayer.[114] Surely, they constituted "secretis oratorii locis" in more than one sense.

Æthelwold's architectural vision was taken even further by Ælfheah, who as bishop of Winchester from 984 to 1006 immediately picked up where his predecessor left off, adding onto the eastern end of the church by building the apsidal lateral chapels (fig. 9, E) and a crypt under the altar (fig. 9, 5), which Wulfstan describes in remarkably similar terms:

>   Insuper occultas studuistis et addere criptas
>   quas sic Dedaleum struxerat ingenium,
>   quisquis ut ignotus ueniens intrauerit illas
>   nesciat unde meat quoue pedem referat.
>   Sunt quibus occultae latitant que hinc inde latebrae;
>   quarum tecta patent, intus et antra latent.

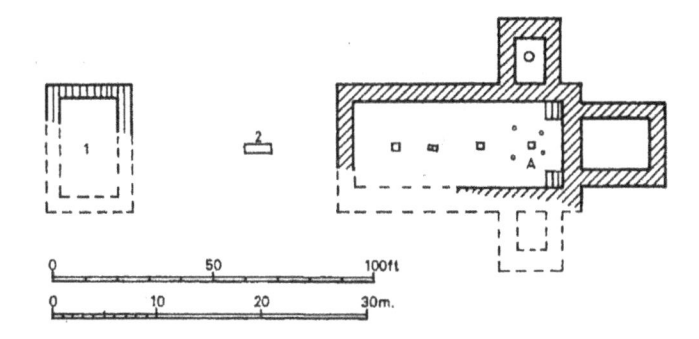

Figure 8. Ground plan of Old Minster, Winchester, showing the earliest buildings from the seventh century. Taylor and Taylor, *Anglo-Saxon Architecture*, 3:744, fig. 644.

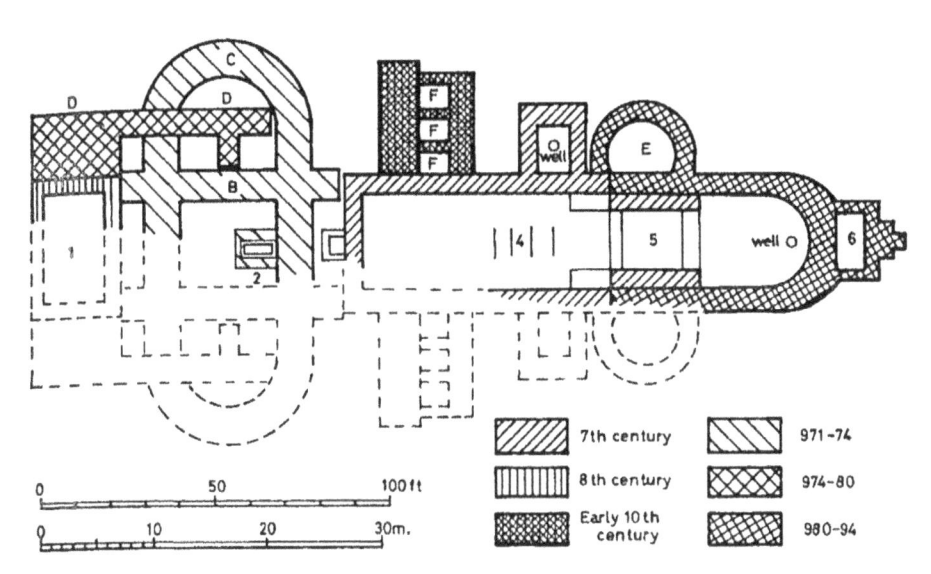

Figure 9. Ground plan of Old Minster, Winchester, showing the three northern *porticus* (F) probably built before Æthelwold's arrival; the western entrance built around Saint Swithun's tomb (2), composed of the large apsidal structure (C and B) and additional west work (D); the eastern apsidal chapels (E) and extension (6) built by Ælfheah, including the crypt below the main altar (5). Taylor and Taylor, *Anglo-Saxon Architecture*, 3:745, fig. 645.

Introitus quarum stat clausus et exitus harum
   quas homo qui ignorat luce carere putat,
nocte sub obscura quae stare uidentur et umbra.
   Sed tamen occulti lumina solis habent:
cuius in exortu, cum spicula prima resultant,
   lucifer ingrediens spargit ubique iubar
et penetrat cunctas lucis splendore cauernas,
   donec in hesperium sol ruat oceanum.
machina stat quarum, sacram subportant et aram
   sanctorumque pias ordine reliquias;
multipliciqua modo manet utile culmen earum:
   exteriora gerens, interiora tegens.

[What is more, you have taken care to add hidden crypts which Daedalian wit had constructed in such a way that, should any unfamiliar visitor enter them he would not know whence he came nor how to retrace his steps. They have unseen recesses which lie hidden on this side and that; their roofs are open, but inside their compartments lie hidden. Their entrance and exit is sealed, but someone who does not know these crypts—which seem to subsist in the depth of night, in darkness and shadow—might think them devoid of light. Nevertheless, they have the light of the unseen sun; at day-break, when the first rays glimmer, the sun enters and scatters its radiance everywhere, and with the brilliance of its light reaches into all the compartments until it sinks into the western ocean. Their structure is such that they each in turn contain a holy altar and the holy relics of saints; and their roof remains useful in many ways: supporting what is without, yet covering what is within.][115]

The combination of Æthelwold's chapel-laden entrance and all the unseen hidden recesses of Ælfheah's crypt clearly produced a building that was not only extremely conducive to private prayer, on account of the numerous *loci secreti*, but was also designed to conceal the interior of the church from the uninitiated: even if an outsider made it through Æthelwold's entranceway and into Ælfheah's crypts, charting an exit from there has every indication of futility. Wulfstan may have overstated the dauntingly Daedalian nature of the entrance and crypts of Old Minster, but his description of the chapels tells us something about the experience of prayer that members of the community could have had within the church—a secret space that was already deliberately separated from the outside. To the uninitiated, these hidden compartments might seem dark and devoid of light ("luce carere"), but in fact they are designed to be lit with the light of the sun from the time it rises until it sets below the horizon; yet the dark cells of the crypt are also always illuminated by God's light, as the "occulti lumina solis" (the light of the unseen sun) implies both the actual sunlight whose source is concealed by the architectural structure and the light of God who is unseen. This dynamic of secret space and private prayer—in which the supplicant is secluded but remains open to God—was manifested in the architectural design and structure: the *tecta* (roofs, coverings) oxymoronically remain open ("tecta patent"), while the interior cavities are concealed ("intus et antra latent") and the entrance and exit is sealed ("Introitus quarum stat clausus et exitus harum"). It is possible that Wulfstan is thinking of a labyrinthine structure where there are only walls and no ceilings, but it is also possible (indeed, more likely) that he is thinking about the ways that even in an enclosed space such as a crypt, a monk could look up toward God and feel constantly looked down upon by him. This horizontal concealment and vertical openness physically represent the very structure of spiritual secrecy.

If hidden rooms in the depths of a crypt offered supplicants one opportunity for solitary prayer, a similar architectural logic may have also governed the construction of chapels in the upper stories of monastic buildings.[116] According to Wulfstan, for example, the five-story tower at Old Minster was remarkable for its striking physical separation and profound openness and visibility:

Insuper excelsum fecistis et addere templum
    quo sine nocte manet continuata dies.
Turris ab axe micat qua sol oriendo coruscat
    et spargit lucis spicula prima suae. . . .
Luna coronato quotiens radiauerit ortu
    alterum ab ede sacra surgit ad astra iubar.
Si nocte inspiciat hanc pretereundo uiator
    et terram stellas credit habere suas.

[Moreover, you have undertaken to add a lofty structure where perpetual day abides without the intervention of night. From the summit of heaven a tower gleams, on which the rising sun shimmers and sprinkles the first rays of its light. . . . Every time the moon shines down from its crowned origin, a reciprocal gleam rises from the holy church to the stars. If a traveler passing by night would gaze upon this, he might think that the earth had stars of its own.][117]

The tower could be seen from a great distance and also afforded those inside the ability to see far and wide. Its heavenly position in proximity to the stars and its quality as a kind of star itself reflect the luminous experience of light that one might have within. It thus shares with the crypt a striking similarity, for a supplicant attuned to God's constant radiance would be immersed in that perpetual day whether in the darkest depths of the church or the highest room in its tower.[118]

A product of the Benedictine Reform, Wulfstan of Worcester (d. 1095) seems to have embodied this very experience of spiritual secrecy through interactions with the architecture of his surroundings. For instance, he would frequently pray in the west *porticus* of Saint Mary's church ("in occidentali porticu aecclesiae"), where he would "obserato aditu Christum uocare, lacrimis pulsare caelum, aethera onerare planctibus" (bar up the entrance, and calling on Christ knock at heaven with his tears and burden the sky with his laments).[119] There were eighteen other altars in that church, and Wulfstan evidently prostrated himself before each one seven times a day. And if that devotion were not sufficient in itself, Wulfstan also frequently traveled by night to nearby churches where he would pray to God, guided there by Christ so that "nullae illum turbarent tenebrae, nulla quateretur solitudine" (no darkness could confound him, nor solitude unsettle him).[120] We might now look again at the photograph of the southern *porticus* at Saint Pancras (fig. 5), as we call to mind the scene of Wulfstan praying. Although Wulfstan's *porticus* at Saint Mary's would have been part of a large and complex array of chapels and altars compared to the small and simple layout of Saint Pancras, we can still imagine what it must have felt like to walk through the nave, step inside the *porticus*, and kneel before the altar, to bolt the door to the church and beat at the door of heaven. It was undoubtedly a feeling of profound solitude (a feeling that remains even though the walls of the Saint Pancras *porticus* no longer stand), and yet it must have also been a feeling of exposure and openness that only such solitude can provide.

The Secret Architecture of the Heart

As much as the early period of Anglo-Saxon monasticism witnessed numerous bishops, abbots, and monks practicing eremitic solitude, and as much as the later Benedictine Reform may have opted to facilitate private prayer through the construction of designated *loci secretiores* within monastic churches, it is important to realize that such prayer was never fully restricted to physically separate spaces and rooms. In describing the ideal oratory, Benedict himself envisioned a room in which, regardless of its actual size and usage, the mandatory silence is what separates one supplicant from another. And yet the architectural structures that fortified the practice of private prayer—whether the imaginary ones of the *Regula Sancti Benedicti* or those constructed during the Benedictine Reform—remained central to the conceptualization and experience of spiritual secrecy. Long before the English Benedictine Reform, Cassian thus proposed a foundational logic of private prayer that would have been particularly compelling and valuable to a coenobitic monk without access to a solitary chapel. By conceiving of the personal space of the heart metaphorically through the secret space of the oratory, Cassian equates any silent prayer to a prayer in secret:

> Intra nostrum cubiculum supplicamus, cum ab omnium cogitationum siue sollicitudinum strepitu cor nostrum penitus amouentes secreto quodammodo ac familiariter preces nostras domino reseramus. clauso oramus ostio, cum strictis labiis omni que silentio supplicamus non uocum, sed cordium scrutatori. in abscondito oramus, quando corde tantum et intenta mente petitiones nostras soli pandimus deo, ita ut ne ipsae quidem aduersae ualeant potestates genus nostrae petitionis agnoscere.[121]

> [We pray in our room when we withdraw our hearts completely from the clatter of every thought and concern and open up our prayers to the Lord in secret and, as it were, intimately. We pray with the door shut when, with closed lips and in total silence, we pray to the Searcher not of voices but of hearts. We pray in secret when, intent in heart and mind alone, we offer our petitions to God alone, so that even the enemy powers themselves cannot discover the nature of our petition.]

Cassian takes up the architectural secrecy implied in Matthew 6:6 ("intra in cubiculum tuum") and applies it to the heart ("intra nostrum cubiculum supplicamus . . . cor nostrum penitus amouentes").[122] This logic allows those living a coenobitic lifestyle to obey the command of Matthew 6:6 even if they never find themselves physically alone. If the purpose of secret prayer is to open up the heart and mind to God, then Cassian further stresses this logic through his phrase "in abscondito oramus" (we pray in secret), echoing the very language of Matthew 6:6 and its command to pray "in abscondito" to the Father who sees "in abscondito." Just as Wulfstan bars the physical door to the *porticus* before praying, Cassian would have his readers bar the metaphorical door to their hearts by shutting their lips or closing off their minds: both entail the crucial act of opening up before God. For Cassian, that act of opening up before God is rendered by the verb *reserare* (to unbar), which is then inverted in Wulfstan's act of shutting the door (*obserare*). These actions ultimately come together in the various spatial experiences of spiritual secrecy, where the will opens the heart and mind to God alone even though he already has access.[123]

Chapter 5

Seeing in Secret: Saints, Hagiography, and the Ethics of Concealment and Discovery

When the faithful follow the command in Matthew 6:6 to pray in secret, the Father observes from a radically different position of secrecy: He sees in secret, "videt in abscondito." This divine position is understood to be secret both because it is located within the supplicant, thereby separated from others, and because God's unknowable secrecy is infinitely removed from the supplicant's own human range of perception. But the supplicant can also pray "in abscondito," in an act of secrecy that is similarly one of separation—although from human beings, never from God. When properly employed in the work of prayer, this spiritual secrecy, as I have termed it in the previous chapter, satisfies the practical and evangelical need for humility and allows the practitioner to avoid the pitfall of hypocrisy. It involves separation—whether mental or physical—from earthly companions, but it engenders proximity to God, who acts as a constant witness, seeing but unseen, knowing but unknown. In Matthew 6:6, the same phrase, "in abscondito," describes both the mode of prayer and the invisibility of God's constant observation, implying a binding relationship between the two, but also an important distinction: that no human being could accomplish a comparable feat of divinely veiled perception (of seeing in secret) because to every human there is always God, the absolute other who sees *all* secrets.

But saints—holy men and women acting as agents of God on earth—present a curious alternative. On the one hand, many saints are remembered for their divinely bestowed ability to see and foresee the secrets of fellow human beings: their *uitae* often communicate the impossibility of hiding from the eyes of these saints, just as one cannot hide from the eyes of God. On the other hand, as we have already seen in the previous chapter, many saints took the injunction of Matthew 6:6 to the extreme in their pursuits of eremitic lifestyles, inhabiting and praying in solitary cells, remote fenlands, and other desertlike places, even in the *loci secreti* of their own minds. And yet some saints hover between these two evangelical pillars, at one moment praying in secret and at another seeing in secret. When combined, these features of Anglo-Saxon saintly life (the tendency toward solitude and the ability to foresee worldly events while concealing that ability from prying eyes) introduce the reality of divine knowledge and divine secrecy—in short, the divine wonder of seeing in secret—into the lives and activities of those individuals and communities still breathing and walking and, indeed, reading in the present life. Whether in those acts narrated by their hagiographers or in the remembrance of and reflection upon those acts by later readers of hagiography, saints brought the immediacy of divine knowledge and divine secrecy down to earth. What emerges, particularly where the active demand and the contemplative ideal meet in the models of sanctity in Anglo-Saxon England, is a productive social and narrative tension between intersecting secrecies—between divine secrecy and divine knowledge, between human secrecy in humble prayer (spiritual secrecy) and insolent attempts to hide from God.

The Secret Witness

Let us take as the primary example of this tension—as it applies to acts of concealment as well as acts of discovery and witnessing—the well-known story of Saint Cuthbert's encounter with the sea animals during his visit to the monastery of Coldingham. The episode, which captures many of the themes to be discussed in this chapter, is itself recounted in all but one of the Anglo-Saxon versions of the *Vita Sancti Cuthberti*, including the Anonymous of Lindisfarne's version (*VCA*), both the metrical (*VCM*) and the prose (*VCP*) versions by Bede (although it is omitted from his *Historia ecclesiastica*),[1] and also the homiletic, vernacular version by Ælfric of Eynsham.[2] According to the Anonymous version (the other versions shall be discussed below), Cuthbert was visiting Coldingham for several days at the invitation of the abbess Æbbe, and every night following his usual custom he would keep vigil and walk along the seashore, singing and praying alone. But a certain cleric of the community became curious about Cuthbert's nocturnal conduct and one night followed him secretly from a distance so as to test him ("occulte de longinquo obsequi eum temptando"). When Cuthbert arrived at the shore and entered the stormy sea up to his armpits, the cleric looked on and was shocked by the sight. What followed was even more alarming: as the saint walked out of the water and kneeled on the sand in prayer, two sea animals approached him and dried his feet with their skins and warmed him with their breath. The next morning at cockcrow, Cuthbert returned to the church to join in communal prayer with the other brethren ("orationem communem cum fratribus"), a form of prayer distinctly in contrast to the private act on the seashore the night before. But among the brethren, the spying cleric was absent:

clericus uero familiae supradictus in scopulosis locis latens, uisu pauidus et tremebundus, tota nocte coangustatus prope mortem accederat. Crastina autem die prosternens se ante pedes hominis Dei, flebili uoce ueniam indulgentiae deprecauit. Cui homo Dei prophetali sermone respondit, Frater mi, quid est tibi? Numquid propius adpropinquasti mihi temptando quam debuisti? Et tamen hoc tibi confitenti uno modo indulgetur, si uotum uoueris, numquam te esse quamdiu uixero narraturum.

[The abovementioned cleric of the community remained hidden in that rocky place, frightened and trembling at the sight (*scil.* of Cuthbert in the sea and of the supplicating sea animals) and, being in anguish all night long, he came close to death. The next day he prostrated himself before the feet of the man of God and, in a tearful voice, prayed for the favor of leniency. The man of God answered him with prophetic words: "My brother, what is the matter with you? Have you approached nearer me, to test me, than you should have done? Nevertheless, since you admit it, you shall receive pardon on one condition; that you vow never to tell the story so long as I am alive."]³

And so the cleric, we are told, kept his vow to tell no one about what he had observed and only recounted the story to others after the saint had passed away. This part of the story—the vow to silence—is the final of four crucial components in the narrative, each of which will be addressed in turn over the course of this chapter and are as follows: Cuthbert's secret and solitary prayer (a theme we have already considered above in Chapter 4), the cleric's furtive pursuit of the saint, Cuthbert's prophetic knowledge of the cleric's behavior, and the common (yet remarkably understudied) trope of the vow to tell no one until after the saint has died.

We begin with the figure of the cleric as a secret witness. In attempting to observe Cuthbert's miraculous and private experience while keeping himself concealed, the cleric ultimately comes to encounter God—through Cuthbert—with fear and trembling ("pauidus et tremebundus"). Theologically, this experience of fear and trembling is a fundamental catalyst of faith: "cum metu et tremore vestram salutem operamini" (with fear and trembling work out your salvation), writes Paul the Apostle.⁴ And in the cleric's rocky hiding place, that fear and trembling signal a spectacular reversal of his original desire. The doubt that motivated the cleric's curiosity and his decision to test (*VCA*: "temptando"; *VCM*: "temptando latenter"; *VCP*: "temptasti") Cuthbert eventually transforms into faith, as the cleric witnesses in a trembling encounter with the divine the faithful actions of the saint and the absurdity—in the Kierkegaardian sense—of the sea creatures.⁵ The cleric's trembling illness that brings him close to death marks a shift in his own relation to the divine; it induces his inevitable confession to the saint and his own realization that he attempted to do what is reserved exclusively for God. By trying to see in secret—to witness the saint's behaviors while hiding from the saint and from God—the cleric betrays his faith in the saint and in God's omniscience; he gives himself over to the mistaken assumption that his own actions and infidelity could go unnoticed by the almighty Judge. This attempted secrecy is identical in principle with the secrecy exemplified by Cain when he takes his brother into the field so as to hide his murder from God (Gen. 4:8–10).[6] And it is also identical with the type of secrecy that monastic rules sought to prohibit, since, as we discovered in Chapter 3, the tendency for some monks to assume that they could conceal their secrets from fellow brethren *and* from God proved a dangerous assumption for both the abbot and the community as a whole.

While God's ability to see in secret ("videt in abscondito") is never impeded by physical boundaries or barriers, nor dependent upon such barriers for concealment, the cleric who spies on Cuthbert must hide behind precisely those things that cannot conceal him before God. To the Anonymous of Lindisfarne, the secrecy of the cleric's pursuit is marked by his distance ("de longinquo") from Cuthbert;[7] in Bede's prose version, the secret pursuit is tied to Cuthbert's footsteps ("clanculo secutus eius uestigia"),[8] and in the metrical version, the cleric is separated by time, having taken the slow path ("lento . . . calle") in following Cuthbert's unknown steps ("incertos . . . gressus");[9] Ælfric combines the stealth of *clanculo* (from Bede's *VCP*) with the slowness of *lentus* (from Bede's *VCM*) in reporting that the cleric "mid sleaccre stalcunge his fotswaðum filigde" (followed his footsteps with slow stalking).[10] Later, the cleric remains hidden amid the rocks (*VCA*: "in scopulosis locis latens"), and in Bede's metrical version, he "Semianimem curvo flatum trahit abditus antro" (draws in a half-alive breath while hidden in his curved cave).[11] In a single verse, Bede's juxtaposition and semantic intertwining of the cleric's breath with the cave that hides him not only highlights the cave's containment of that breath but also suggests that the cleric's loss of breath and potential loss of life have become contingent on his decision to remain concealed. It presents the cleric with an ultimatum: stay hidden and die, or come forward and live. But as brilliantly as this dilemma is articulated here in the metrical version, when Bede later retells the story in prose (followed by Ælfric), he omits the detail of the cleric's proximity to death and also avoids reference to his continued hiding in the rocks through the night.[12] Instead, both Bede (in the *VCP*) and Ælfric shift the emphasis away from the cleric's hiding spot and onto the difficulty of his return home and eventual plea for forgiveness. Ælfric leaves out the return journey altogether, jumping forward and placing the cleric immediately prostrate before Cuthbert the following morning. But for Bede, the difficult walk back to the monastery is marked by the cleric's "nutante gressu" (faltering footsteps), a notable parallel to the metrical description of Cuthbert's "incertos . . . gressus" (unknown footsteps) on the way to the sea earlier in the evening.[13] When read together, Bede's two versions reveal the tension between the cleric's illicit mode of secrecy and Cuthbert's spiritual one. The faltering footsteps of the cleric contrast with the saintly ideal of steadfastness that the cleric earlier witnessed in Cuthbert's unwavering display of faith (*VCA*: "inobstinata mente"). The cleric's footsteps falter as he trembles, realizing his own lack of faith and moving to restore it.[14] The doubt that initially set the cleric's actions in motion is, in the end, overcome when he removes himself from hiding and asks forgiveness, "nil dubitans illum nosse quid ipse noctu egerit, quidue pateretur" (not doubting that Cuthbert knew what he had done that night and why he was suffering), thus acknowledging the impossibility of hiding from the saint and faithfully trembling toward salvation.[15]

But Cuthbert is not alone: several other saints are reported to have had similar experiences with secret spies witnessing their miraculous deeds and visions. The closest parallel is found in the *Vita Sancti Columbae*, which Adomnán, abbot of Iona, composed between 697 and 704, making it nearly contemporaneous with the anonymous version of the *Vita Sancti Cuthberti* (composed between 699 and 705).[16] The precise relationship between the two texts is uncertain,[17] but in Adomnán's *Vita Sancti Columbae*, the saint is observed by a similarly secretive spy. This parallel has attracted some scholarly attention,[18] but what has gone unnoticed is in fact the subtle but important differences between it and the episode with the sea animals in the *Vita Sancti Cuthberti*. Unlike Cuthbert, who regularly prays alone at night while everyone else is asleep, Columba simply decides one day to go off alone ("Hodie . . . solus exire cupio") and orders the brothers not to follow him while specifying exactly where he plans to go: "in occidentalem nostrae campulum insulae" (to the western plain of our island).[19] Columba's desire for solitude is a desire to be free from the observation of his brethren, but his venture is not marked by the same deliberate secrecy as we find in Cuthbert, who acts at night while the others are asleep, and specifically without telling anyone about his destination (as Columba explicitly does). After Columba orders the brothers not to follow him, he goes off alone to pray. All of the monks obey him, with one exception:

> Sed frater quidam callidus explorator alia means uia in cuiusdam monticelli cacumine, qui eidem supereminet campulo, sé occulte conlocat, uidelicet illius causam solitariae beati egresionis uiri explorare cupiens.

Quem cum idem explorator de monticelli uertice in quodam illius campuli colliculo stantem et expansís ad caelum manibus orantem, oculosque ad caelos eleuantem, conspiceret, mirum dictu et ecce subito res miranda apparuit; quam idem supra memoratus homo, ut estimo non sine permisu dei, de propioris monticelli loco oculís etiam corporalibus aspexerat, ut nomen sancti et eius honorificantia quamuis ipso nolente ob hanc manifestatam uisionem postea magis in populís deuulgaretur. Nam sancti angeli caelestis patriae ciues mira aduolantes subitatione sanctum uirum orantem circumstare coeperunt albatís induti uestibus. Et post aliquam cum beato sermocinationem uiro illa caelestis caterua quasi sé exploratam sentiens ad summa citius repedauit caelorum. Beatus et ipse uir post angelicum condictum reuersus ad monasterium, iterum collectís fratribus cum quadam non mediocri obiurgatione inquirit quis de illís esset transgressionis obnoxius. Quibus consequenter se nescisse protestantibus ille conscius sui inexcussabilis transgressus ultra non sustenens delictum celare suum flexís genibus in medio fratrum choro coram sancto ueniam supplex precatur. Quem sanctus seorsum ducens, ingeniculanti cum grandi commendat comminatione ut nulli hominum de illa angelica uisione in diebus eiusdem beati uiri aliquid etiam paruum occultum aperiret. Post egresum uero de corpore sancti uiri illam caelestis coetus apparationem fratribus cum grandi intimauit protestatione.

[But a certain brother, a cunning spy, going by another way, took up a position secretly on the top of a little hill that overlooks that plain, evidently wishing to detect the cause of that solitary expedition of the blessed man. From the top of the little hill the spy saw him standing on a certain knoll of that plain and praying, with his hands outstretched to the sky, and his eyes raised to heaven, and then strange to tell, behold suddenly a marvelous thing appeared, which the same abovementioned man from his position on the nearby hill looked upon, even with bodily eyes; as I think, not without the permission of God, in order that the name of the saint, and his renown, should, although against his will, afterwards be spread more widely among the peoples, because of this vision made manifest. For holy angels, citizens of the heavenly country, flew down with marvelous suddenness, clothed in white raiment, and began to stand about the holy man as he prayed. And after some conversation with the blessed man, that heavenly throng, as if perceiving the spy himself, quickly returned to the highest heaven. The blessed man also, after his conference with the angels returned to the monastery. The brothers were assembled again, and with a not so mild reproach he asked which of them was guilty of a transgression. Thereupon they protested their ignorance; but the one who was conscious of his inexcusable trespass was able to conceal his sin no longer, and with bended knees he prayed humbly for pardon, before the saint, in the midst of the company of the brothers. The saint led him aside and charged him under severe penalties, as he knelt, to disclose to no one, during the days of the blessed man, anything secret, however little, of this angelic vision. But indeed, after the holy man's departure from the body, he revealed to the brothers, with strong affirmation, that apparition of a heavenly assembly.][20]

Columba openly journeys to the plain (a distinctly exposed expanse of space) in broad daylight with the full knowledge of the brethren, and Adomnán carefully constructs the scene so that the secret to be discovered by the spy belongs not to Columba but rather to God; the secret is the "caelestis coetus apparitionem" (apparition of the heavenly assembly). From the beginning, the "callidus explorator" is thus curious not about where Columba is going and what he is doing (for he already well knows that) but about the "causam solitariae . . . egresionis" (cause of the solitary expedition). That cause is, of course, the saint's "angelicum condictum" (conference with the angels) and, specifically, the angels themselves. The spy's ability to witness that conference with bodily eyes, Adomnán comments, must have been specifically granted by God ("ut estimo non sine permisu dei"). Indeed, the whole event seems divinely orchestrated as a way to make the saint's holy status more widely known, while the ostensible solitude of his journey serves to authenticate his humility. Adomnán entirely ignores, for example, the monk's blatant act of disobedience. And when compared to the scene in the anonymous *Vita Sancti Cuthberti*, it is clear that Adomnán is far less concerned with the lack of faith that motivates the disobedient monk and the emotional process by which the disobedient monk comes to a deeper belief in the omnipotence of God; Adomnán merely notes that the brother could not conceal ("celare") his sin any longer. The difficulty of remaining concealed has little bearing on the monk's confession, nor does he experience the fear and trembling that Cuthbert's witness had to suffer while deciding whether to come out of hiding. Adomnán is not concerned with the saint and his relation to one of his disobedient monks, but he is concerned with the divine secret. When Columba pulls the monk aside, therefore, he does not tell him to remain silent about his behavior; he tells him to remain silent about anything secret pertaining to the angelic vision ("angelica uisione . . . aliquid . . . occultum").

Adomnán's emphasis on the divinity of the secret arises in three other episodes in the *Vita Sancti Columbae* that parallel both the scene of Columba on the plain and the scene of Cuthbert on the shore. The episodes occur consecutively in book III of the *Vita*, which is organized around the saint's angelic visions, but together these three differ from the other visions in the way in which they are witnessed by someone who tries to hide himself so as not to be discovered.[21] Unlike Columba's experience on the plain, however, these three episodes depict the saint at night while others are sleeping ("aliis quiescentibus," "aliis dormientibus," and "aliis quiescentibus," respectively). They also depict the utter fear experienced by the witnessing monk. Yet despite their similarities, the three episodes are far from redundant, instead illustrating a concern over the varying degrees of concealment in the act of witnessing the saint's holiness, ranging from accidental observation to intentional (and denied) acts of spying.

In cap. 19, Virgno (then a young monk who would later become the abbot of Iona) is upheld as the ideal witness because he resists the desire to observe the vision by fearfully turning his eyes to the ground:

> Quadam himali nocte supra memoratus Virgnous in dei amore feruens eclesiam orationis studio aliis quiescentibus solus intrat, ibidemque in quadam *exedra*[22] quae oratorii adherebat parieti deuotus orabat. Et post aliquantum quasi horae interuallum unius uir uenerandus Columba eandem sacram ingreditur domum, simulque cum eo aurea lux de summa caeli altitudine discedens totum illud eclesiae spatium replens; sed et illius *exedriolae* separatum conclaue, ubi se Virgnous in quantum potuit latitare conabatur, eiusdem caelestis claritas luminis, per interiorem illius cubiculi ianuam quae ex minore patebat parte erumpens, non sine aliquo formidabili repleuerat terrore.

> [One winter night, the above-named Virgno, enflamed with the love of God, entered the church alone eager for prayer, while others slept. There, in an *exedra* that adjoined the oratory wall, he prayed devoutly. After some space of time, as it were of one hour, the venerable man Columba entered the same sacred building; and along with him there entered a golden light, descending from highest heaven and wholly filling the inside of the church. But also the brightness of that heavenly light filled the enclosed space of the *exedra*, in which Virgno tried to conceal himself as well as he could, streaming through the partly-open inner door of that room, not without some effect of terror.][23]

The terrible light, Adomnán continues, was so bright that Virgno could not endure it. Like the monk who observed Saint Cuthbert, Virgno was overcome by a similar fear:

> Virgnoumque ualde timoratum ad sé crastina aduocat die, hisque breuibus conpellat consulatoriis uerbís: "Bene O filiole," ingeminans, "hac

praeterita nocte in conspectu dei placuisti, oculos ad terram deprimendo claritatis timore perterritus eius. Nam si non ita fecisses, illa inestimabili obcaecarentur tui luce uisa oculi. Sed hoc non neglegenter obseruare debebis, ut talem hanc lucis manifestationem nemini umquam in mea denudes uita."

[And the following day, he (*scil.* Columba) summoned to him the awestricken Virgno, and spoke to him in these few reassuring words: "You have been very pleasing, little son," he repeated, "in the sight of God, this last night, in lowering your eyes to the ground, through dread of his brightness. For if you had not done so, your eyes would have been blinded by seeing that inestimable light. But you must diligently observe this, never in my lifetime to disclose to anyone this so great manifestation of light."][24]

Rather than reprimanding Virgno (as both Columba and Cuthbert do to the other monks who witness their solitary prayers), Columba comforts and commends him for having turned his eyes away from the light, lowering them to the ground out of fear and terror. Of course, Virgno was already innocently praying in the *exedra* prior to Columba's arrival, which indicates that he did not set out with the intention of spying on the saint. Therefore, although Virgno attempts to conceal himself, Columba interprets his actions in a positive way: Virgno tries to conceal himself in an attempt not to hide from God but rather to turn his eyes away from the divine light so as not to witness it without God's permission.

On another night, similarly while others slept, a monk named Colcu happened to come to the door of the church and remained there praying for some time. Then, suddenly:

totam uidet eclesiam caelesti luce repleri, quae silicet fulgoralis lux dicto citius ab eius recessit oculís. Sanctum uero Columbam hora eadem intra eclesiam orantem ignorabat. Postque talem subitam luminis apparationem ualde pertimescens domum reuertitur. Postera die sanctus illum aduocans asperius obiurgauit, inquiens: "De caetero praecauere debes filii ne quasi explorator caeleste lumen quod tibi non est donatum inspicere coneris, quia té effugiet; et ne alicui in meís diebus quod uidisti enarres."

[He saw that the whole church was filled with heavenly light. Quicker than speech, this flash of light vanished from his eyes. He did not know that Saint Columba was at the same hour praying within the church, and after this sudden apparition of light he was much afraid, and returned to his dwelling. On the following day, the saint summoned him and sharply reproved him, saying: "Henceforth take great care, my son, not to attempt like a spy to observe heavenly light that has not been granted to you, for it will flee from you; and not to relate to anyone, in my time, what you have seen."][25]

Colcu's accidental witnessing of the divine light is counteracted by the light's instantaneous retraction and withdrawal from the onlooker's gaze. Like Virgno, Colcu was not granted permission to see it. But although he does not intend to see it, he does not willingly turn away from it, either—hence, Columba's reprimand. Nevertheless, Colcu's unintentional glimpse of the light still sparks that crucial sense of fear that would later function to amplify the force of Columba's admonition.

The final example is quite different. On another day, Columba warns his student, Berchán, not to come near his teacher's lodging that evening, as the student was accustomed to do:

Qui hoc audiens contra interdictum ad domum beati uiri in noctis silentio aliis quiescentibus accessit, *callideque explorans* oculos e regione ad clauium foramina possuit, estimans scilicet, ut res probauit, aliquam intus caelestem uisionem sancto manifestari. Nam eadem hora beati uiri illud hospitiolum caelestis splendore claritudinis erat repletum, quam non sustenens intueri transgressor iuuenis ilico aufugit.

[However, hearing this, he came to the blessed man's house in violation of the interdict, in the silence of the night while others rested. And *craftily spying* he set his eyes in the area near the holes for the keys, supposing that within the house some heavenly vision was being manifested to the saint, as the event showed to be true. For in that hour the blessed man's lodging was filled with the glory of heavenly brightness; the youthful transgressor could not bear to look upon it, and immediately fled away.][26]

Although Berchán could not bear to look at the light, he seems not to have been struck by the same kind of fear experienced by Virgno and Colcu. More importantly, according to Adomnán's interpretation of the event, Berchán believed that he could actually succeed in seeing the heavenly vision by spying, failing to understand that the light is the product of a private exchange between the saint and God, and that only God could authorize participation in the vision. The lesson is the same as that learned by Colcu (and the same as that wisely implemented by Virgno): one cannot observe heavenly light unless it has been granted by God. Applying this logic back to the episode with Columba and the angels on the plain reminds us that the spy's ability to see the angelic conference was entirely the work of God, for the disobedient monk could not have seen the secret vision without divine permission. The consequences for Berchán, on the other hand, are potentially severe:

> Quem die crastina sanctus seorsum dicens cum magna seueritate obiurgans haec ad eum profatur uerba, dicens: "Hac in nocte filii coram deo peccasti; nam tuae infitialis *explorationem calliditatis* a spiritu sancto celari uel abscondi posse inaniter putasti. Nonne ad mei hostium hospitioli té illa in hora appropinquantem et inde redeuntem uidi? Et nisi ego eodem momento pro té orarem, ibidem ante ianuam aut cadens morireris, aut tui de suís foraminibus oculi euerentur."

> [On the following day, the saint took him aside, and reproving him very severely spoke to him these words: "On this night, my son, you have sinned before God; for you have vainly imagined that the *crafty spying* that you have denied could be concealed or hidden from the Holy Spirit. Did I not see you in that hour coming to the door of my lodging and going away from it? And if I had not at that moment prayed for you, there before the door either you would have fallen and died, or your eyes would have been torn from their sockets."][27]

Columba's reaction to Berchán's disobedient act of spying differs markedly from his reaction to the other spies. Unlike with Virgno and Colcu, the saint here intervenes on behalf of the observer, sparing him from blindness and death. But more crucially, Columba does not command Berchán to keep silent about the event. Berchán's actions are similar to the actions of the first spying brother, who disobediently ignores Columba's orders and follows him to the plain. Indeed, both spying brothers are referred to as *exploratores callidi*.[28] The difference, however, is that Berchán imagines that his crafty spying, which he denies doing ("infitialis"), could be hidden from the Holy Spirit. Perhaps the word *infitialis* is meant to imply that the brother had repeatedly denied prior acts of spying.[29] But whether his spying was a repeat offense or a single occurrence, it is clear that Berchán's act of denial sets him apart from the three other spies. Each of the other spies immediately confesses to having observed the saint, thereby recognizing God's omniscience rather than attempting to remain hidden. Columba must therefore handle Berchán by trying to convince him that he actually saw him arrive at his door and saved him from certain blindness. The fact that Berchán could still see is proof that Columba intervened on his behalf. But Berchán's persistent lack of faith requires that Columba condemn the monk—that his face should bear reproach for the rest of *his* life ("exprobrationem facies tua omnibus patietur diebus uitae tuae")—rather than forgive him and invite him to keep silent about the event for the rest of *the saint's* life. One, therefore, who does not believe in God's omniscience cannot be trusted to follow the saint's injunction to silence.[30]

So far, we have encountered secret witnesses only in two early Northumbrian sources, but they also found their way into the circle of Benedictine reformers in southern England several centuries later. We know that the cult of Saint Cuthbert gathered strong momentum in and around Worcester by the tenth century, and so it should be no surprise that Saint Oswald, bishop of Worcester (961–992) and archbishop of York (971–992), might have found himself in a similar position (with a spy observing his communion with an angel) in Eadmer of Canterbury's *Vita Sancti Oswaldi*.[31] As Eadmer reports, Oswald went alone one day to say Mass in the so-called "confessio," a crypt built into the western part of the church where he would frequently pray,[32] and on the way into the *confessio* he asked one of the twelve paupers who typically sat in front of its doors to assist him with the performance of the Mass. After the Gospel, Oswald took the bread and wine into his hands, directed his eyes toward heaven, and with attentive mind he sent forth to God ("intenta mente ad Deum praemitteret") the prayer that begins "Suscipe, sancta trinitas" (Receive, Holy Trinity). This prayer is the part of the *Oblata* (or Offertory) that immediately follows the washing of the priest's hands. As Oswald recited the prayer, the pauper noticed the appearance of a figure to his right, holding a small piece of the purest white bread. The bread began to grow in size while Oswald proceeded with his secret prayers ("in secretis orationibus procedebat"); that is, of course, in reference to the *Secretum*—the proper part of the Mass performed by the celebrant in silence. This scene offers an intriguing perspective on the liturgy and the experience of the priest as he turns away from the congregation (here, the sole pauper) toward God in subvocal prayer.[33] The presence of the angel further suggests that while the *Secretum* is performed in silence and apart from the audience of the congregation, it has its own special audience in God, here represented in angelic form. While Oswald was saying the *Secretum*, the pauper at first remained frozen with fear at the sight of the angel. But once the bread grew to an unaccustomed size ("insolitae magnitudinis"), he fled and slipped out through the door, leaving Oswald alone with the angel for the remainder of the Mass. There, outside the door, the pauper "latitando subsistens" (waited in hiding) and "quid circa altare gereretur trepidus explorabat" (spied with trepidation on what was happening around the altar). When Oswald finished the *Secretum* with the phrase "Per omnia saecula saeculorum"—conventionally sung aloud before the congregation (in this case, the pauper) in anticipation of a responsorial "Amen"—the pauper had already removed himself from the participatory space of the Mass and did not dare reply. Oswald's servant had turned spy; however, motivating his hidden spying ("latitando"; "explorabat") was not doubt but rather fear and trepidation ("pauor"; "trepidus").

On the one hand, the pauper had to turn away from the vision of the angel and flee from the crypt in the same way that Virgno turned his eyes to the ground on seeing Columba's blinding light; yet, on the other hand, the pauper continues to look on, to gaze secretly at the miraculous liturgical scene. Only when the Mass was complete did the pauper "palpitans et tremens" (quivering and trembling) return to Oswald, apologizing for having abandoned him and confessing to having seen the vision. Oswald forgave him and, in conformity to the trope, ordered him not to tell anyone about what had happened as long as Oswald was still alive. One major difference between this scene and the others discussed above is the fact that Oswald invited the pauper to participate in the Mass, which implies that the pauper was given divine (or at least saintly) permission to witness the miraculous vision. Moreover, the pauper's actions (being "obstupuisset" [struck dumb], fleeing, and finally returning to Oswald) are all imbued with the same kind of fear that paralyzed Cuthbert's spy on the shore of Coldingham and later brought him out of hiding. That fear eventually allowed Cuthbert's witness to accept a deeper form of faith, and the fear and trembling of the pauper similarly allowed Oswald to trust that he had submitted to the magnitude of God's power and could in fact be trusted to remain silent about the event. At the same time, the pauper's behavior—of fleeing in fear, but remaining hidden and spying from a safe distance—highlights the tension between the human desire to observe strange things and the apprehension that observing such things might be dangerous or severely punishable.

But punishment does not always transpire. In Ædiluulf's *De abbatibus* (written between 803 and 821), the desire to make sense of the unimaginable plays out—somewhat anticlimactically—in the story of Abbot Sigwine:

> uiderat hunc quidam tetrae sub tempore noctis
> uestibus insolitis indutum tradere dona
> pauperibus miseris, nimium qui frigida membra
> exclusi portis calefacta in rudere ponunt.
> cumque pius tribuit radientis dona metalli,
> precipit obsecrans summi per regna tonantis,
> quatinus haec nulli cuncte per tempora uitae
> dicant; ast miseri testantur dicere numquam,
> ex quo presentis maneat sub tempore uite.
> hoc cernens frater tenebris cumulantibus arua

delituit, fugiensque semel non talia putat
esse, semel poterit quanquam iam cernere uisus.

[Somebody saw him (*scil*. Sigwine) in the hours of the dark night, dressed in clothes not his own, giving gifts to the wretched paupers who, being shut out of the gates, laid their very cold limbs in the rubbish to warm them. And when in piety he gave them gifts of shining metal, he urged and entreated them in the name of the kingdom of the Thunderer on high, that they would tell these things to no man throughout the whole period of their lives, and the poor men vowed never to tell, as long as he remained in the period of his mortal life. The brother, seeing these things, concealed himself in the darkness gathering over the land, and fleeing, thought at one time that such things were not possible, although at another time he could well imagine what he had seen.][34]

There is a categorical difference between the treatment of the secret witness here and the others we have seen: the narrative lacks a miraculous event. In general, Ædiluulf does tend to downplay the supernatural, which might explain why Abbot Sigwine fails to perceive the spying brother or how the brother managed to flee, concealed under the darkness of the night while reflecting on the implications of what he had just witnessed. But while the darkness of night—a common feature of the other episodes—cannot conceal him from God, Sigwine was not a saint (despite his acts of charity) and could not therefore have been expected to receive God's assistance in perceiving the actions of the spying brother. Because that brother never approaches the abbot to ask forgiveness and because the abbot never discovers him, he cannot be bound to the same oath of secrecy that the poor men had already vowed to keep on receiving the gifts; he is presumably free to divulge what he has seen to anyone even during Sigwine's own lifetime.

One lesson from the story of Sigwine is that not all spies get caught, but the more important lesson is that not all spies are necessarily evil. While Berchán (the last of Saint Columba's spies) is clearly disobedient and guilty of enacting a form of doubt that never converts into faith, Sigwine's spy presents a unique case. Violating a privileged exchange between the abbot and the poor men, the brother inverts the conventional relationship between abbot and monk—the brother spies on the abbot *and* conceals his actions from him—thereby inviting an extremely dangerous situation (as we have seen above in Chapter 3). But at the same time, the brother was witnessing not a divine secret (such as those encountered in every episode discussed above) but rather the good deeds of the abbot in spite of the abbot's best attempts to conceal himself humbly with earthly mechanisms ("uestibus insolitis indutum" [dressed in clothes not his own]).

This mode of witnessing is an important hagiographic technique, since it adds scarcity value (derived from the rare privilege of experiencing the saint's deeds firsthand), and at the same time, it authenticates those saintly deeds without calling the humility of the saint into question. Such acts of secret witnessing worked in the other direction as well. Saint Antony, for example, would frequently test Paul the Simple by asking him to wait in prayer outside his cell where Antony would "per fenestram tamen ex occulto . . . videbat" (secretly watch him through the window).[35] In another case, just before receiving the loaf of bread from a raven (a scene famously depicted on the Ruthwell Cross), Antony is like a "callidus explorator" (cunning spy) when he discovers Paul of Thebes in his cave.[36] More often, however, the figure of the cunning spy is a nefarious one. Cuthbert's spy, according to Bede, was an "explorator" but not necessarily a cunning one.[37] And Adomnán uses the phrase "callidus explorator" to describe both the spy who secretly witnesses Columba with the angels on the plain (with God's permission) and Berchán who secretly spies on Columba in his lodging (without God's permission), although in both instances the saint had preemptively forbidden them from doing so.

In the Middle Ages, the figure of a *callidus explorator* would have primarily evoked the serpent in Gen. 3:1, infamously described as "callidior" (more cunning) than all the other creatures, although not specifically an *explorator*. Bede, commenting on Acts 5:3, accordingly explains how Satan enters a person's mind not as God does but rather "quasi callidus quidam et nequam ac fallax fraudulentusque deceptor" (like a cunning, vile, lying, and fraudulent deceiver).[38] And Aldhelm reiterates this theme in his *Aenigma* 88 ("Basiliscus"), where the serpent is more cunning ("callidior") than all creatures who breathe on earth.[39] The church father Peter Chrysologus combines this serpentine image with that of a spy when he calls the devil a "callidus explorator."[40] And Peter Damian in the eleventh century was also particularly fond of the phrase, referring to the tempting devil on one occasion as a "callidus explorator" and on another as a "callidus insidiator" (cunning conspirator) who "explorat" (spies) on us at night.[41] For Damian, monkeys earn the epithet as well, and so do flatterers and adulterers.[42] In the *Vita Quarta Sancti Patricii*, the young Saint Patrick is stalked by a wolf while tending a flock of sheep: "lupus de silua ueniens quasi callidus explorator lento gressu ambulans" (the wolf approached from the forest as a cunning spy, walking at a slow pace).[43] It is tempting to wonder whether Patrick's hagiographer had known of Columba's own "callidus explorator" or had known that the spy in Bede's metrical *Vita Sancti Cuthberti* took the slow path ("lento . . . calle") when following the saint's unknown steps ("incertos . . . gressus").[44] Such linguistic similarities might tempt speculation, but a direct link is dubious and, moreover, beside the point: after all, how else is a wolf supposed to act? And that is precisely the point.

The ambiguous moral valences that surround the figure of the spy, and especially the cunning spy, suggest that when such acts of spying and discovery are done on behalf of God (i.e., by an abbot or a saint such as Saint Antony), they are simply an extension of God's omniscience, but when they are used against or in ignorance of God's omniscience, such acts become particularly animalistic and highly treacherous. This distinction is made strikingly clear in a later chapter of Eadmer's *Vita Sancti Oswaldi*, in which Saint Dunstan "sepe agebat cum eo, non ut firmitudinem animi eius quasi suspectam habens exploraret, sed sicut eam in bono firmam penes se habebat, ita ueraciter esse aliis comprobaret" (continued to spend time with Oswald, not in order to spy on the constancy of his mind, as if suspicious of it, but so that he might truly prove to others that it was as constant in goodness as he himself found it).[45] In other words, it is the suspicious behavior—the doubt and lack of faith—of the secret spy that makes his actions and his identity so reprehensible in the *Vita Sancti Cuthberti* and in the *Vita Sancti Columbae*. But when the observation of others originates in good faith—as Dunstan observes Oswald, as Antony seeks out Paul—the process serves the essential purpose of allowing the otherwise private and humble affairs of a saint to become known more widely. And as we will see, when that process of witnessing is divinely enabled and inspired, it becomes a defining feature of Anglo-Saxon sanctity.

Seeing . . .

In the examples above, the hagiographic trope of the secret witness juxtaposes the privilege that allows saints to behold divine light against the blindness that human onlookers risk when attempting to behold it without the permission of God. As these saints become the mediators between their human companions on earth and the secrets of God above, prophecy is one instrument by which that mediation takes place. Each of these holy men—save for Sigwine (an abbot, but not a saint) in Ædiluulf's *De abbatibus*—is imagined by his hagiographer to have known that he was followed by a spy and on that basis either protect the spy from blindness or confront him about his intrusion and/or disobedience. God thus grants the saints the ability not only to see and experience the miraculous vision of, for instance, angels or divine light but also to see the concealed actions of their brethren. In other words, the saints are granted access both to some of God's secrets and to some of God's knowledge of all human secrets. But that access, as we shall see, remains always partial and always in the hands of God.

Working from an anonymous Latin homily, Ælfric expounds a hierarchy of saints in the first half of his *Sermo in natale omnium sanctorum*. To begin, he distinguishes between saints in the form of men and saints in the form of angels.⁴⁶ Angelic saints resist our knowledge, since "gode anum is to gewitenne hu heora ungesewenlice gecynd buton ælcere besmitennysse oððe wanunge on ecere hluttornysse þurhwunað" (God alone is to know how their invisible nature persists without any pollution or decline in eternal purity).⁴⁷ These saints thus differ from the patriarchs (who have been sent to earth yet are not separated from God) and the prophets (who function like God's satellites in this present world). As Ælfric elsewhere explains, holy men live in such close proximity to the grace of God that God, "on heora heortan swilce on þrymsetle sittende toscæt. 7 demð wunderlice oþra manna dæda" (sitting on their hearts as though on a throne, decides and judges wondrously the deeds of other men).⁴⁸ Their hearts embrace God—fully open to His inward perception—while at the same time, they serve as a seat from which God might observe the actions of those nearby and empower the saint to enact His judgments on them.

By transmitting God's knowledge to their human companions, these saints serve as pivotal reminders that God is always watching. The connection enacted by saints was often immediate and concrete, but their access to God's secrets was understood in a variety of different ways. Representing one view, Ælfric explains how the ancient prophets "wæron godes gesprecan. 7 þam he æteowode his digelnysse. 7 hi onlihte mid gife þæs halgan gastes. swa þæt hi wiston þa toweardan þing 7 mid witigendlicere gyddunge bodedon" (would speak with God, and to them He manifested His secrets, and enlightened them with the grace of the Holy Spirit, so that they knew the things to come and announced them in prophetic song).⁴⁹ A prophet's ability to foresee events on earth is thus enabled by his prior communion with God, and that communion is distinctly bound to speech.⁵⁰ As God ultimately decides what secrets will be revealed to a prophet and manifests them in the form of language, this communion introduces interpretation into the process of accessing divine secrets.

To understand how this process works, Prosper of Aquitaine's *Epigrammata* is a good place to start, given its widely popular use as a classroom text studied by, in the words of Michael Lapidge, "every literate Anglo-Saxon."⁵¹ Prosper's pithy epigrams, all based directly on sayings of Augustine of Hippo, together address a wide range of theological topics while also providing students with exercises in reading verse. The epigrams typically begin with a brief prose introduction to the topic at hand (often taken from Prosper's own *Liber sententiarum*) followed by a more demanding verse incarnation of the same idea. *Sententia* 171 (paired with *Epigramma* 90 [91]) thus presents a simplified and memorable take on the notion that God's workings are unknowable: "In incognitis causis operum diuinorum nonnihil nouimus, cum scimus non sine ratione Omnipotentem facere, unde infirmus humanus animus rationem non potest reddere" (We know something about the unknown causes of divine works, since we know that the Almighty does nothing without reason, concerning which the weak human mind cannot give an explanation).⁵² Although the causes of divine works are unknown and the weak human mind cannot fully comprehend God's actions, rationality provides a link between the human mind and God's secrets. Prosper also takes the view that contemplation of the divine cannot rely on rational effort and sheer intellectual willpower alone but is first and foremost an exercise in faith. Prosper's *Epigramma* 90 (91) reiterates the underlying dilemma of the prose *Sententia* 171:

Divinorum operum secretas noscere causas
    humanis non est possibile ingeniis, . . .
scrutari ne cura procax abstrusa laboret.⁵³

[It is not possible for human minds to know the secret causes of divine works. . . . Let not impudent zeal labor to examine those things which have been concealed (by God).]

The verse *Epigramma*, particularly toward the end, is in some tension with the corresponding prose *Sententia*, undercutting the notion that God's actions can be subject to penetrating reason and concluding that no matter how hard one tries to understand God's secrets, ultimately only God can decide who will be given access and under what circumstances. But even though humans might know something *about* God's works—we might know that nothing is done without reason, for instance—that knowledge *of* God's works is still primarily a matter of faith.

In the *Old English Soliloquies*, which reflects a more uniquely English take on Augustine's thought, the narrator similarly wonders about the means of knowing God. In part, such knowledge is achievable through reason, conceived as a form of mental sense perception in which the eyes of the mind, if healthy and clear, can begin to understand the divine: "Ac se ðe God geseon wille, he scel habban his modes eagan hale: þæt is, ðæt he hebbe festne geleafan and rihtne tohopan and fulle lufe" (But he who wishes to see God, must keep the eyes of his mind healthy: that is, he should have firm faith and true hope and complete love).⁵⁴ In this search for understanding God, the *Old English Soliloquies* is deeply concerned with the complex relationship between belief and knowledge, because as the narrator observes, "we gelyfað eall þæt ðæt we witon, and we nyton fæla þæs þe we gelyfað" (we believe all that we know, and we do not know many things that we believe).⁵⁵ Certain knowledge is the goal, for even after Reason's explanations, the narrator still yearns for knowledge beyond his current state of belief: "Ic hys hæbbe goodne dæl gehyred, and ic hys eac gelife. Ac me lyste hyt nu bet to witanne þonne to gelyfanne" (I have heard a good deal about this, and I believe it as well, but now it would please me better to know it than to believe it).[56] Ultimately, Reason's solution is to encourage the narrator to "gelef þinre agenre gesceadwisnesse, and gelyf Criste, godes sunu, and gelyf eallum hys halgum, forðam hi weron swiðe unlease gewitan, and gelyf þinre agenre sawle" (believe your own faculty of reason, and believe Christ, the son of God, and believe all his saints, because they were very truthful wise men, and believe your own soul).[57] This logic of belief—linked as it is to the firm faith that is essential for clear vision and understanding—ultimately prompts the narrator to let go of his doubts and claim to know that his soul is eternal. The movement between belief and knowledge in the *Old English Soliloquies* is thus negotiated by reason, and faith is clearly treated as the prerequisite for such rational forms of understanding.[58]

When applied to Adomnán's *Vita Sancti Columbae*, these theories help us see the stakes involved in the interactions between the saint and his spies. The first spy, for example, is motivated by a desire to know the *causa* of the saint's solitary journey to the plain, and his overzealous attempt to decipher Columba's interaction with God is motivated by doubt.[59] Like Cuthbert's spy, Columba's first spy seeks knowledge in order to gain faith, when faith is in fact the prerequisite for such knowledge. But Adomnán also infers that God must have granted permission for the spy to have been able to see with his bodily eyes the angels surrounding Saint Columba on the plain: without God's permission, the spy's zealous efforts would have brought him not to faith or understanding but to blindness. Each of the spies investigated in the previous section of this chapter is depicted as having infringed on a private relationship between the saint and God. However, we are led to believe that the saints at the center of these episodes have privileged access to both God's secret grace and God's knowledge, which allows them to know that they have been secretly followed and know that their actions have been secretly observed.

This logic may reflect an unorthodox idea like that found in the Blickling Homilies, where the prophetic capabilities of saints seem to emerge from the fact that "hie wæron gewitan ealra Godes degolra doma" (they were privy to all of God's secret judgments).[60] But Gregory the Great offers a more typical theory (one embraced by Ælfric, for instance), which holds that saints can only access the secrets of God if God has chosen to share them. In the second book of his *Dialogi*, Gregory recounts a time in which Saint Benedict warned a certain cleric never to advance to sacred orders, but when the cleric pretended to forget Benedict's warning after many years, he presented himself for ordination and was immediately seized by the devil and tormented until his death. In amazement at the saint's prophetic capability, Deacon Peter responds, commenting that "iste uir diuinitatis, ut uideo, etiam secreta penetrauit" (as I see it, this man [*scil.* Saint Benedict] penetrated even the secrets [i.e., of God]).⁶¹ Gregory's answer comes in two parts. First he explains why it is possible for someone as holy as Benedict to access the secrets of God:

> Quare diuinitatis secreta non nosset, qui diuinitatis praecepta seruaret, cum scriptum sit: Qui adhaeret Domino, unus spiritus est? . . . Sancti uiri, in quantum cum Domino unum sunt, sensum Domini non ignorant. Nam isdem quoque apostolus dicit: Quis enim scit hominum, quae sunt hominis, nisi spiritus hominis, qui in ipso est? Ita et quae Dei sunt, nemo cognouit, nisi spiritus Dei?⁶²

> [How could he not have known the secrets of God seeing that he kept God's commandments? For it is written, "he who is joined to the Lord is one spirit" (1 Cor. 6:17). . . . In so far as holy men are one with the Lord, they are not ignorant of His thoughts. This is clear from the Apostle's words, "For what man can know the things of a man, but the spirit of a man that is in him? So the things also that are of God no man can know, but the Spirit of God" (1 Cor. 2:11).]

Placing one Pauline expression alongside another, Gregory effectively argues that Benedict's holiness makes him one with God in spirit, which allows him to know God's thoughts as God knows His own. But that logic suggests that achieving access to the abstract mystery of God is reduced to the sole task of keeping His commandments. Potentially, it allows anyone to possess the same range of knowledge as the Creator himself. It renders God's spirit penetrable and thereby affirms Deacon Peter's original theory. Still unsatisfied, however, Peter tests Gregory's response against Paul's statement in the Letter to the Romans that God's judgments are inscrutable ("inconprehensibilia") and his ways are undiscoverable ("investigabiles") (Rom. 11:33). How could God's judgments be at once inscrutable and yet, to Benedict, as accessible as his own thoughts? This realization provokes Peter to take his inquiry a step further, recalling that David the Prophet declares to the Lord in Psalm 118:13: "in labiis meis pronuntiavi omnia iudicia oris tui" (With my lips I have pronounced all the judgments of thy mouth). How, Peter asks, could David know all of God's judgments and even pronounce them with his own lips when Saint Paul regards those same judgments inscrutable?

This dilemma allows Gregory to make the most important distinction yet by introducing a third term into the question of who controls such secrets. It is thus not David who retrieves the judgments from God, but rather God who *speaks* the judgments to David with his own mouth. It follows that, as Gregory goes on to argue, it was not so much Benedict who penetrated the secrets of

God as it was God who placed particular secrets within Benedict's field of vision:

> Occulta itaque Dei iudicia, in quantum coniuncti sunt, sciunt; in quantum disiuncti sunt, nesciunt. Quia enim secreta eius adhuc perfecte non penetrant, inconprehensibilia eius iudicia esse testantur. Quia uero ei mente inhaerent, atque inhaerendo uel sacrae scripturae eloquiis uel occultis reuelationibus, in quantum accipiunt, agnoscunt, haec et norunt et pronuntiant. Iudicia igitur, quae Deus tacet, nesciunt; quae Deus loquitur, sciunt. . . . quoniam sciri ab hominibus et prolata per Deum possunt, et occultata non possunt.[63]

> [They know the hidden judgments of God, therefore, in so far as they are joined to Him, but in so far as they are separated from Him, they do not know them. For since they cannot yet perfectly penetrate his secrets, they bear witness to the fact that his judgments are incomprehensible; however, because their minds are united to Him, by reflecting on the words of Holy Scripture or on such secret revelations insofar as they receive them, they understand them, and know these things and declare them. And so the judgments which God does not utter they do not know, but those which God speaks they do know. . . . For the things that are spoken by God can be known by men, but those which are concealed cannot.]

Here, we encounter the crucial idea that for the judgments of God to be known by a human being, even an exceptionally holy human being, they require communication. God must judge and also decide to reveal the judgments in order for them to be known and proclaimed by the prophet or saint.[64] Elsewhere, Gregory refers to God as the secret or unseen Judge, the *occultus arbiter*—or, in the words of the Alfredian translator of Gregory's *Regula pastoralis*, *se diegla Dema*.[65] God is secret and so are his judgments; that is, until *he* decides to reveal them. He reveals them through scripture and through "occultis reuelationibus" (secret revelations), the secrecy of which can be taken in a number of different ways. The revelations are secret by virtue of having originated in God; they are secret because only the saint (or the intended recipient) has access to them; and they are secret because even the saint, Gregory suggests, cannot see them with total clarity. As long as the saints are living in this present life, they cannot penetrate his secrets perfectly or fully ("perfecte"). This point is often overlooked by modern scholars, who prefer to see the prophetic capabilities of saints as evidence of their spiritual proximity to God. Carole Straw, for example, argues that "the conquest of the flesh enables a participation in God unobstructed by interference from the body. Unencumbered by the confusion of the world and liberated from bodily weakness, holy men obtain direct access to the truth, as Adam once did. Saints can even know God's thoughts 'insofar as they are one with him.'[66] But Gregory's more nuanced point is that even if a saint is united with God in spirit, so long as the saint is still living in the flesh and in this world (no matter how successfully he or she has renounced it), the saint will never have "unobstructed" or perfect access to God's knowledge because that knowledge—from the saint's perspective—is still governed by the laws of worldly concealment. A saint, in other words, does not have the capability to know God as God knows the saint or the world in which he lives. And because God must transmit that knowledge in language or through signs, the knowledge is necessarily susceptible to ambiguity and misinterpretation. Saints are able to understand those inscrutable and secret judgments, to get them right, not because they share the same mind with the omniscient God but because they know how to interpret properly, with *fides*, *spes*, and *caritas* as the beginning, the means, and the end of the hermeneutic process.[67]

For Adomnán, however, prophecy functions predominantly as it does in the first part of Gregory's argument. Book I of the *Vita Sancti Columbae* is organized around Columba's prophetic gift. Describing the nature of that gift, Adomnán draws on Gregory in two ways. First, according to Adomnán, Columba was able to foresee things that took place far away because "quamuis absens corpore praesens tamen spiritu" (although absent in body, he was present in sprit).[68] Like Gregory (and probably emulating him), Adomnán turns to Paul, reminding the reader that "he who is joined to the Lord, is one spirit" (1 Cor. 6:17). But instead of introducing the means by which God communicates with the saint (as Gregory does), Adomnán takes a cue from later in the *Dialogi* to explain that "in aliquantis dialis gratiae speculationibus totum etiam mundum ueluti uno solis radio collectum sinu mentis mirabiliter laxato manifestatum perspiciens speculabatur" (in some speculations of heavenly grace, because the scope of his mind was miraculously enlarged, he saw plainly and contemplated the whole world as if it were caught up in one ray of sun).[69] The godlike expansiveness of Columba's mind, to Adomnán, is what allows him to see what common human beings—corporally restricted as we are in time and space—cannot. Of course, that expansiveness does not come about without the help of "dialis gratiae" (heavenly grace), but it nevertheless removes the interpretive task from the work of prophecy. It assumes that Columba can see as God sees, all at once as though it were a single ray of sun. Gregory uses this same image twice to describe Benedict's experience as he watched Germanus's soul being carried by angels up to heaven. To Benedict, "omnis etiam mundus, uelut sub uno solis radio collectus, ante oculos eius adductus est" (even the whole world, as if collected within a single ray of sun, was drawn together before his eyes).⁷⁰ Although Gregory expounds on this image, explaining that Benedict could see the whole world gathered up because the saint had encountered the magnitude of God, which enlarged his mind and changed his perspective so that everything else was infinitely more minuscule, this vision is marked off as one particular miraculous moment in Benedict's life. Here and when Gregory repeats the story in book IV, it is the specific experience of witnessing the death of Germanus that corresponds with Benedict's ability to see the world in this way for a brief moment.⁷¹ But for Adomnán, this vision is how Columba *always* sees the world, all at once as though it were a single ray of light. It is no wonder Adomnán can supply more than fifty examples of the saint's prophetic gift in the first book alone.

Of saints performing prophetic feats, there are countless examples. Even if we were only to consider those acts of prophecy in which someone tries to hide something from a saint, only to be discovered, the number would still be too large to cover here with any thoroughness. For now, a mere handful must suffice. To take once again from Gregory's *Dialogi*, three consecutive chapters show Saint Benedict, first, warning Exhilaratus not to drink from the bottle of wine he had hidden away for himself while journeying to the saint; second, rebuking a monk for having stashed a handkerchief that was given to him as a gift; and third, reprimanding a young monk (whose father was a high-ranking official) for proudly thinking that he was above holding the lamp while Benedict ate his meal.⁷² These three incidents each highlight a slightly different mode of knowing. In the case of the first, Gregory explains that "facta absentia latere non poterant" (nothing, even what was done in his absence, could be hidden) from Benedict.⁷³ The presence-in-absence motif is very common. On the one hand, we have already seen how Adomnán assigns to Columba a similar (although seemingly more expansive) power of spiritual vision in describing his ability to see all things unencumbered by physical obstacles.⁷⁴ On the other hand, Felix in his *Vita Sancti Guthlaci*, for example, reports that God sent an angel every morning and evening to communicate with the saint, showing him "mysteria, quae non licet homini narrare" (mysteries that it is not lawful for man to utter [cf. 2 Cor. 12:4]) and revealing to him "absentia . . . ut praesentia" (things that were absent as though they were present).⁷⁵ Between Adomnán and Felix we see the range of epistemological power that a hagiographer can assign to a saint with respect to God's role as the controller of knowledge, but Gregory's treatment of Benedict here is slightly more ambiguous since Exhilaratus is subject to not only Benedict's spiritual vision but also the vision of his bodily eyes: Benedict could see in Exhilaratus's expression that he had done something illicit. For Gregory, Benedict's skill is found in the combination of keen insight (what we might today refer to as an ability to "read people") and God-given, spiritual knowledge; how else could he have so precisely known that Exhilaratus would find the wine undrinkable and tainted, as he later discovered, by the presence of a snake? In the second case, Gregory emphasizes the saint's spiritual vision by noting that the monk had entirely forgotten ("egisset oblitus") about receiving the handkerchief, which implies that there was nothing about his external countenance that would have contributed to the saint's suspicion.[76] Carrying the rationale over from the first example, Benedict likewise reminds the monk that he was present ("numquid ego illic praesens non eram?") when he received the handkerchiefs as a gift. But with respect to the final case of the proud, young monk, Gregory explains that Benedict knew what "contra uirum dei uerba per cogitationem tacitus dicebat" (words he spoke silently in thought against the man of God).[77] Here, we see Benedict as a skilled reader of human behavior. No physical distance separates the saint from the monk, and Benedict is able to perceive the monk's pride in what we can only assume was a grunt, a slouch, or a murmur—a subtle external display of his internal sentiment.[78] Yet for Gregory that secret murmur expresses a paradoxical kind of silent speech that only Benedict can understand and interpret. It is this particular ability that incites all the other brethren to realize that "uenerabilem Benedictum latere nihil posset, in cuius aure etiam cogitationis uerba sonuissent" (nothing could be hidden from the venerable Benedict, in whose ear could be heard even the unspoken words of the mind).[79]

These three examples highlight the tension—even within Gregory's own thinking—between the idea that a saint can be present everywhere and know everything just as God does, and the idea that a saint must still receive the information as a message from God, because only God alone can be everywhere and know everything. Benedict's privileged knowledge in each example is garnered either purely from divine inspiration or from having read the body language of the sinner, which in some way disclosed on the surface that which he was concealing beneath. Pastoral work demands that the pastor be able to read the surface of his flock in order to heal the wounds beneath, and in Gregory the Great's *Regula pastoralis* this process of reading is foundational to the metaphor of the pastor as physician that runs throughout the text. In Gregory's *Regula pastoralis* and especially in its Alfredian translation, the pastor is responsible for diagnosing the secret sins of the mind on the basis of the external ailments of the body.[80] And so it is unsurprising, in the final Gregorian example, that Benedict's ability to read the words of the mind (*uerba cogitationis*) should provoke the brethren to believe that nothing could be hidden from the saint. The immediate and physical presence of the holy man who knows their secret thoughts and who can read them as words on a page or hear them as words spoken aloud makes the abstractness of God's omniscience palpable and enforceable.

In Bede's prose *Vita Sancti Cuthberti*, the chapter containing the story of Cuthbert and the sea animals (cap. 10) follows immediately after the chapter in which Bede reports how Cuthbert would visit villages and preach to the people so skillfully that they could not help but confess their sins to him: "Porro Cuthberto tanta erat docendi peritia, tantus amor persuadendi quae coeperat . . . ut nullus praesentium latebras ei sui cordis celare praesumeret, omnes palam quae gesserant confitendo proferrent, quia nimirum haec eadem illum latere nullomodo putabant" (So great was Cuthbert's skill in teaching, so great his love for driving home what he had begun to teach, that none of those present would presume to hide from him the secrets of his heart, but they all made open confession of what they had done, because they thought that these things could certainly never be hidden from him).[81] The language here is unsurprisingly similar to the language in Gregory's description of Benedict. However, the belief held by the villagers that they cannot hide their sins from Cuthbert is derived not specifically from his ability to read the words of their mind (*uerba cogitationis*) but from his ability to read and proclaim the word of God (*uerbum Dei*), which happens to be even more secret than the words of the mind. Everyone confesses to the saint precisely because he is an excellent teacher, pastor, and reader. Of course, the townsfolk would not have necessarily been apprised of this Gregorian line of thought, but Bede certainly was. It makes perfect sense, therefore, that a saint who can expound scripture and the mysteries of Christianity to the *populus* would be imagined as someone who has special access to the secrets of God and, by that virtue, shares with God the knowledge of their sins.

. . . in Secret

The story of Cuthbert's encounter with the sea creatures begins and ends with an expression of secrecy on the part of the saint. He slips off alone at night with unknown footsteps ("incertos . . . gressus") to pray on the shore away from the other members of the community, and the following day he forgives the cleric on the condition that he tell no one about the event until after the saint has died. We have already discussed (in Chapter 4) how secret prayer had an important spiritual and monastic function, but here we encounter a slightly different expression of secrecy in which the saint commands his secret witness—whose act of secrecy itself was a violation not only of monastic rules but also of the faith that should have reminded him that his pursuit of the saint was not secret from God—to keep the event a secret. On the surface, the saint's secret journey and the bond of secrecy between the saint and the cleric might appear to contradict one another—or, put another way, the secrecy of the cleric's pursuit might appear to be aligned with the later bond of secrecy with the saint. Indeed, Ælfric makes it sound like a shady deal: "Ic ðinum gedwylde dearnunge miltsige. gif ðu ða gesihðe mid swigan bediglast. oð þæt min sawul heonon siðige. of andwerdum life gelaðod to heofonan" (I will secretly pardon your misconduct, if you will conceal with silence what you have seen, until my soul will have journeyed hence, called from the present life to heaven).[82] However, if we recall the transformation that the cleric undergoes—from faithless to faithful—as he waits, terrified and trembling in his cave, and if we compare that transformation to the mentality of Berchán and Saint Fintan's spy, then it becomes clear that the silence Cuthbert commands of the cleric is dependent, first and foremost, on the cleric's renewed faith. The saint—or, for that matter, Christ, on whom the saint models his behavior—cannot command a witness to keep a miracle or a vision a secret unless that witness has proven his faith in God; that is, his belief that the secret he is about to receive and conceal until the saint's death is itself sacred precisely because it is known only by him, the saint, and God, and that if he should reveal it before the saint's death, both the saint and God would know what he had done. Only if the recipient of the command to silence has this faith can the saint trust that the secret will actually be maintained.

This hagiographic trope in which a saint commands a witness to keep silent is extraordinarily common, yet it has earned little scholarly consideration. Throughout the *Vitae patrum*, countless holy men and women instruct observers of their miracles and visions to keep silent about them. In Gregory's *Dialogi*, we find Benedict predicting the day of his death to some of his disciples and telling them "per silentium tegerent" (to cloak it through silence) until after he has died.[83] In the Evagrian translation of Athanasius's *Vita Sancti Antonii*, Ammon tells Theodore his secret vision on the condition that he not reveal it to anyone until after Ammon's death.[84] In Bede's prose *Vita Sancti Cuthberti*, the saint predicts the death of King Ecgfrith and his own bishopric, shares the prophecy with Ælfflæd, and bids her not to tell anyone before his death.[85] In Adomnán's *Vita Sancti Columbae*, on five occasions (in addition to the three instances discussed above) the saint makes someone vow to keep secret a vision or miracle until after the saint's death.[86] In Felix's *Vita Guthlaci*, Beccel inquires into Guthlac's conversations with an unknown figure; the dying Guthlac explains that they were conversations with an angel and orders Beccel to "haec dicta mea conserva" (preserve these words of mine).[87] In Bede's *Historia ecclesiastica*, Owine asks Chad a similar question, which Chad answers commanding him to tell no one before his death.[88] Later in the same text, Wilfrid has a vision at Meaux and shares it with Acca, ordering him to "silentio tegere" (cloak it in silence) until he knows what God intends by it.[89] And as we have seen in Chapter 3, after Æthelwold tests the monk Ælfstan by ordering him to plunge his hand into a cauldron of boiling water, he commands the monk "nemini hoc indicare uiuenti" (to tell no living soul).[90] Infinitely more examples could be produced.

However, underlying all of these and the ones left unmentioned is a model rarely cited outright by the hagiographers, although it is often noted by modern editors. That model, of course, is Christ's healing of the sick: when Christ cures the leper, he says: "nemini dixeris" (tell no one) (Mark 1:41–45; Matt. 8:4; Luke 5:14); when he gives hearing and speech to the man who was deaf and mute, he charges the people to tell no one (but the more he charged them, so much the more did they publish it) (Mark 7:36–37); when he brings back the girl from the dead, he tells her parents not to tell anyone what was done (Luke 8:56); when he gives sight to the blind, he says: "vidente ne quis sciat" (see that no man know this) (Matt. 9:27–30); and he most famously orders his disciples to tell no one that he is in fact Christ (Matt. 6:20; Mark 8:30; Luke 9:21), nor likewise to speak of what they had seen in the transfiguration (Matt. 17:1–9; Mark 9:2–8; Luke 9:28–36).[91]

But so far as I have found, Bede, in his usual exegetical style, is the only hagiographer to make explicit the connection between a saint's command to "tell no one" and its precedent in Christ. When the Anonymous of Lindisfarne reports that Cuthbert ordered the spying monk to tell no one about what he had seen on the seashore, he does not mention Christ as his model, nor does Ælfric.[92] Bede, on the other hand, uses Christ to explain the saint's behavior twice. First, in the metrical *Vita Sancti Cuthberti*, Bede proclaims:

> Summique exempla magistri
> Exsequitur, misso renovans qui lumine caecos
> Praecipit auctorem reducis celare salutis.[93]
>
> [Cuthbert followed the example of the great Teacher who, after restoring the blind men with light pouring forth, ordered them to conceal the source of their recovered health.][94]

And in the prose *Vita Sancti Cuthberti*, which Bede wrote after the metrical version, he comments that "In quo nimirum praecepto eius secutus est exemplum, qui discipulis in monte gloriam suae maiestatis ostendens ait, Nemini dixeritis uisionem, donec filius hominis a mortuis resurgat" (In this command, without doubt he [*scil.* Cuthbert] followed the example of Him who, when He showed the glory of His Majesty to the disciples on the mount, said: "tell the vision to no man until the Son of Man be risen again from the dead").[95] The former is a reference to Matthew 9:30; the latter, a reference to Matthew 17:9. Both are equally appropriate examples, to be sure; both enable Bede to capture the figural significance of the saint's actions; both of the commands are expressed by Christ privately (rather than openly to a public audience); and, incidentally, both are concerned with vision and sight: in Matthew 9:30, the blind men whose sight has been restored are told to "*videte* ne quis sciat" (*see* that no man know this), and in Matthew 17:9 Jesus says to his disciples: "Nemini dixeritis *uisionem*" (tell the *vision* to no man). But the examples are also quite different: the former follows a miracle; the latter, a vision. Since the spy is not the recipient of miraculous healing but rather the passive witness to an extraordinary scene, the reference to Matthew 17:9 would seem the more appropriate one for this particular narrative. And yet, while the command in the former is aimed at the two recipients of his miraculous healing, in the latter it is aimed at Christ's own disciples. Does Bede's shift from Matthew 9:30 to Matthew 17:9 indicate an elevation of the spy to the status of a quasi-disciple who, after the saint's death, will actively spread news of his holiness? Clare Stancliffe has argued that Bede departs from his source (the Anonymous of Lindisfarne) by depicting Cuthbert's sanctity with less emphasis on his solitary tendencies and greater emphasis on his pastoral accomplishments.[96] Stancliffe is certainly correct, and Bede's exegetical interpretation of Cuthbert's silencing of the spy shifts the nature of his expedition from a solitary venture to an opportunity for teaching, just like the *summus magister* himself. But Matthew 9:31 holds the key to Bede's metrical reference and its distinction from the prose reference: "illi autem exeuntes diffamauerunt eum in tota terra illa" (But they going out, spread his fame abroad in all that country). Despite Christ's command that no one else know that he had healed the blind man, the people disobeyed him and proclaimed the news widely.

In his homily on Mark 7:31–37, in which Jesus cures a man who is deaf and mute, Bede argues that when Jesus charged the people not to tell anyone ("ne cui dicerent"), God actually wanted the miracle to be proclaimed:

> Numquid aestimandum est quod unigenitus Dei filius signum faciens et abscondi hoc uoluerit et contra uoluntatem illius sit patefactum in turbas nec potuerit *silentio signum tegere* si uellet quod potuit facere cum uoluit? An forte nobis exemplum dare uoluit ut uirtutum opera facientes uitium iactantiae per omnia gloriam que uitemus humanam ne bona nostra actio per inanem uulgi fauorem supernae retributionis munere priuetur?[97]

> [Can we conclude that God's only begotten Son produced this sign and wanted it to remain concealed, that it was revealed to the crowds against his will, and that he could not have *covered this sign in silence* if he wished, since he could do whatever he wanted to do whenever he wanted to do it?

Could it not be that he wanted to give us an example, so that when we perform works of virtue we might avoid the vice of boasting and, above all, we might avoid human vainglory, lest our good deed be deprived of the gift of heavenly reward by the empty approval of the crowd?]

Reporting on the tradition of pious humility that lies behind each of those hagiographic instances in which a saint commands that the knowledge of a miracle or vision not be shared with anyone, here Bede uses the same language (admittedly, a common phrase) to describe both Christ's capability to cloak the sign in silence ("silentio signum tegere") as an example of avoiding vainglory and the monk's success at keeping silent ("silentio tegens") about Cuthbert's miracle for as long as Cuthbert was alive.[98] Relying on this same tradition of humility, the Anonymous of Lindisfarne explains at the outset of his *Vita Sancti Cuthberti* (borrowing a sentence verbatim from Sulpicius Severus's *Vita Sancti Martini*) that "nequaquam ad omnes illius potuerim peruenire uirtutes, adeo ea in quibus ipse tantum sibi conscius fuit nesciuntur, quia laudem ab hominibus non requirens, quantum in ipso fuit, omnes uirtutes suas latere uoluisset" (I have not been able to find out all his miracles by any means; for those, which he alone was aware of are unknown, because, as he did not seek the praise of men, he desired that all his miracles should be hidden so far as this was in his power).[99] And Adomnán, in his *Vita Sancti Columbae*, expands this logic further:

> hoc de uenerabili uiro non est dubitandum, quod ualde numerosiora fuerint quae in notitiam hominum sacramenta interius celata uenire nullo modo poterant quam ea quae quasi quaedam parua aliquando stillicidia ueluti per quasdam rimulas alicuius pleni uassis feruentissimo nouo distillabant uino. Nam sancti et apostolici uiri uanam euitantes gloriam plerumque in quantum possunt interna quaedam arcana sibi intrinsecus a deo manifestata celare festinant. Sed deus nonnulla ex eís, uellint nollint ipsi, deuulgat et in medium quoquo profert modo; uidelicet glorificare uolens glorificantes sé sanctos.

> [It cannot be doubted in the case of the venerable man, that the instances, which inwardly concealed as holy mysteries, could never come to the knowledge of men, were far more numerous than those that from time to time dripped, as it were, like small drops through the cracks of a vessel filled with new strongly-fermenting wine. For holy and apostolic men, shunning vainglory, very often hasten to conceal, as well as they can, such inner secrets as are manifested to them inwardly by God. But whether they will it or not, God makes known, and in one way or another

publicly exposes, some of these things; inasmuch as he wishes to glorify the saints that glorify Him.]¹⁰⁰

When comparing the three authors, we find that Bede departs from the view held by the Anonymous of Lindisfarne (that saints can effectively hide their good deeds if they choose to do so) and seems to align himself with Adomnán, who suggests that if God wishes to make the miracles of a saint known, he can do so regardless of whether the saint tries to conceal them.¹⁰¹ Likewise, for Bede, if a saint performs a miracle or has a vision that is worthy of being known, God will simply *make it known*.

However, when we turn to the metaphors in these passages, Bede's model looks radically different. Whereas the Anonymous (if he had access to a metaphor as brilliant as Adomnán's) would imagine the vessel of wine as perfectly sealed, and Adomnán imagines it as suffering a few inevitable leaks, Bede imagines the work of holy men and women not as wine contained in a vessel (presumably hidden in a cellar) but as a city perched on a mountaintop, as he explains, continuing the thoughts of the homily cited above, that "sciamus opera nostra, si digna imitatione sunt, nullatenus posse celari sed ad utilitatem fraternae correctionis ipso dispensante patefieri qui dicit: non potest ciuitas abscondi supra montem posita" (we should be aware that if our deeds are worthy of imitation they cannot be hidden, but will be revealed for the purpose of fraternal correction, by the divinely arranged plan of the one who said, "a city situated on a mountain top cannot be kept from sight" [Matt. 5:14]).¹⁰² Of course, Bede has in mind a broader notion of good deeds rather than exclusively the kind of private encounters with the divine that we find in Adomnán's *Vita Sancti Columbae*, but the point is the same for both: if God wants the work to be revealed, the saint cannot conceal it. In Bede's versions of Cuthbert's encounter with the sea creatures, the spy's actions become not so much a slip of faith on the part of the cleric as the work of God in proclaiming the saint's pastoral holiness to a wider audience. The Anonymous likewise concludes the episode by commenting that after Cuthbert had died, the cleric was free to share the news and told others how Cuthbert had seen him ("uiderat") with his spiritual eyes ("spiritalibus oculis") while he remained hidden ("latitantem").¹⁰³ The secret witness in the anonymous version shares the story with others by emphasizing his own role as a witness (if not *the* witness), whose secrecy was penetrated by the saint, "sicut uiderat Petrus Annaniam et Saphiram" (just as Peter detected Ananias and Sapphira).¹⁰⁴ The Anonymous places the emphasis on the illicit act of the spying monk, giving that monk almost complete control over the dissemination of the story. Bede simply ends the prose chapter by proclaiming that "post obitum eius plurimis indicare curabat" (after his [*scil*. Cuthbert's] death, he [*scil*. the witness] took care to tell it to many).[105] But the final lines of the episode in Bede's metrical version are clearly the most stunning of all:

> Inque dies meritis crescenti summa tonantis
> Gratia testis adest, pandunt miracula mentem.
> Iam que prophetalis stellanti e culmine virtus
> Candida praerutilo irradiat praecordia flatu.[106]

> [The highest grace of the Thunderer is present as a witness to Cuthbert, growing in merit day by day: his miracles reveal his mind. And now a prophetic power derived from the starry summit of heaven illuminates his shining heart with its golden soul.][107]

As Cuthbert's merits rise, evoking an approach to the city on the mountain from which God displays the good deeds of his saints, the highest grace of God looks down as a witness. And although he is the distant Thunderer, God is also present as a witness, and his presence is located precisely in the ambiguous locus of the saint's mind as that which both witnesses and is witnessed—witnessed by God as he witnesses others, witnessed by others as he witnesses God. Cuthbert's miracles attest to his elevated and spiritual state of mind. At the same time, it signifies that God's miracles spread out from Cuthbert's mind, either by enlarging his mind (as in Gregory's description of Benedict witnessing the death of Germanus) or by his active teaching of others (as when he follows the "summi . . . exempla magistri" [the example of the great Teacher] by counseling and forgiving the spy) or by spreading his intellect throughout the world (through the spy's proclamations after Cuthbert's death). The saint's mind is thus a witness to God and a witness on behalf of God. But God, Bede wants us not to forget, is the ultimate witness, shining and breathing through the illuminated heart of his saint.

Silence and the Role of Hagiography

In the prefatory letter to the monks of the Old Minster, Winchester that accompanies his *Translatio et miracula Sancti Swithuni*, Lantfred (fl. 975) explains that he has chosen to narrate the saint's miracles because, "ut beneficia Dei dignissimum est laudare et iustissimum ea nescientibus predicare, sic impiissimum est illa silendo negare et nequissimum eadem ignorantibus non enarrare" (just as it is most worthwhile to praise God's favors and most appropriate to proclaim them to those who are unaware of them, so it is most wicked to deny them by keeping silence, and most shameful not to expound them to people in ignorance of them).[108] We have seen how this duty to expound what is known about a saint weighs on the shoulders of a hagiographer. As he sets out to compose his *Vita Sancti Cuthberti*, for instance, the Anonymous of Lindisfarne is troubled by the dilemma that, on the one hand, the role of the hagiographer is precisely not a role of silence, and yet, on the other, the hagiographer can neither know nor convey everything that took place in the saint's life.[109] Hence, we commonly find the classical trope "silentio non praetereo" (I cannot pass over in silence) used by hagiographers to introduce a miracle or event of some importance, but we also find "silentio pretereo" (I [must] pass over in silence) used either in paralipsis to condense a large number of miracles into a more manageable sum or to condense a period of the saint's life into a few exemplary moments.[110] In both cases, the rhetoric of the hagiographer echoes the saintly gesture of silencing a witness: "silentio tegens."[111] Indeed, hagiography often works against the saint's own efforts to conceal his deeds. Like the deaf and mute man in Mark 7:36–37 and the two blind men in Matthew 9:30–31 who disobey Christ by proclaiming the news of their miraculous healings, the hagiographer must disobey the saint's desire for silence in order to cultivate praise for the saint's holiness.

Humble secrecy—in which a saint refuses to announce his good deeds, miracles, and visions or protects them from becoming known by pursuing more or less an eremitic lifestyle—is one of the principal characteristics of Anglo-Saxon sainthood: a saint must not proclaim his own good deeds and miracles; rather, he must do everything in his power to ensure that they go unspoken and be concealed in silence. This requirement makes the hagiographer's job all the more challenging, especially if the holy person is still alive as his *uita* is being written. We get a remarkable glimpse into just such a scenario when Eadmer of Canterbury (author of the *Vita Sancti Oswaldi*) describes his process of composing the *Vita Sancti Anselmi*:[112]

> Præterea cum operi manum primo imposuissem, et quæ in cera dictaveram pergamenæ magna ex parte tradidissem; quadam die ipse pater Anselmus secretius me convenit, sciscitans quid dictitarem, quid scriptitarem. Cui cum rem magis silentio tegere quam detegere maluissem; præcepit quatinus aut cœpto desistens aliis intenderem, aut quæ scribebam sibi ostenderem.

> [Moreover, when I had first taken the work (*scil. Vita Sancti Anselmi*) in hand, and had already transcribed onto parchment a great part of what I had drafted in wax, Father Anselm himself one day called me to him privately and asked what it was that I was drafting and copying. And

when I had shown my desire to conceal the subject by silence rather than disclose it, he ordered me either to desist from what I had begun and turn my mind to other things, or to show him what I was writing.]¹¹³

Anselm's private ("secretius") questioning of Eadmer, Eadmer's attempt to conceal the fact that he had been secretly studying Anselm and composing his *uita*, Anselm's intuition that Eadmer had been up to something, and his command that he desist (that is, not share it with anyone except Anselm himself) should all sound like parts of a now-familiar narrative. Even Eadmer's self-silencing earns the same phrase that is often used by saints when silencing their witnesses: "silentio tegere." Is the role of hagiographer, then, akin to the role of spy?

At first, Eadmer attempts to see in secret and conceal his observations from Anselm. But all along, he is seen; Anselm knows what he is writing and knows that he is hiding it. But as much as Eadmer might resemble the spy, the two roles are not exactly the same, either, and the difference between them ultimately comes down to a matter of faith. Whereas the spy seeks knowledge out of doubt and, perhaps, in order to gain faith, Eadmer has faith all along. His writing of the *uita* is an extension of that faith. And like Lantfred, he understands that his duty is to disseminate his particular knowledge of the saint to those who are not so privileged to have lived in such close proximity to the holy archbishop. Recall that the command to silence, *silentio tegere* (*uel sim.*), is only given to those spies and witnesses who have recognized their wrongdoings, realized that they cannot in fact hide from God or from the saint, and accordingly abandoned the doubt that motivated their transgressions in the first place. The command to silence is only used with those who have faith. That Eadmer imposes the same exact command on himself (albeit in an act of hiding a secret from the saint) suggests that he has already grasped the distinction between witnessing with faith and witnessing with doubt.

Of course, one could argue that it is easy for Eadmer to paint himself (and his transgression) in such positively faithful light, which would hardly confirm his fidelity. But what follows is Eadmer's confession of a spectacular act of pious disobedience. Because Anselm had been so generous with his critiques of Eadmer's writings in the past, Eadmer decides to share his work with his mentor; as expected, Anselm makes helpful corrections and improves the work markedly. However:

post paucos correcti operis dies vocato michi ad se pontifex ipse præcepit, quatinus quaterniones in quibus ipsum opus congesseram penitus destruerem, indignum profecto sese judicans, cujus laudem secutura posteritas ex litterarum monimentis pretii cujusvis haberet. Quod nimirum egre tuli. Non audens tamen ipsi precepto funditus inobediens esse, nec opus quod multo labore compegeram volens omnino perditum ire; notatis verbis ejus quaterniones ipsos destruxi, iis quibus scripti erant aliis quaternionibus primo inscriptis. Quod factum meum inobœdientiæ peccato forte non caret. Aliter enim implevi præceptum ejus, ac illum intellexisse sciebam.

[a few days after the work had been corrected, the archbishop himself called me to him and ordered me to destroy entirely the quires in which I had put together the work itself for he considered himself far too unworthy for future ages to consider praise of him in a literary monument to be of any value. This was certainly a severe blow to me. Nevertheless, I dared not entirely disobey his command and yet I was not willing to lose altogether a work which I had put together with much labor. So I observed the letter of his command, and destroyed those quires, having first copied their contents onto other quires. Perhaps my action was not free from the sin of disobedience, for I carried out his order otherwise than I knew that he intended.]¹¹⁴

Eadmer's disobedience hinges on his fine interpretation of Anselm's command: "quaterniones . . . destruerem" (destroy the quires).¹¹⁵ But Eadmer full well knows and admits that his action violates the spirit of Anselm's intention. Even though the disobedience was not total ("non . . . funditus"), Eadmer pleads with his readers that the credit he may have earned by composing the *Vita* will encourage them to intercede on his behalf for, *inter alia*, the specific sin of having disobeyed his superior. He is banking on the likelihood that the benefit of the one will balance out the damage of the other. Although hagiography might be tinged with a degree of disobedience (since by bearing witness to those events in a saint's life, the hagiographer must transgress the saint's principal and essential desire for humility), after death the saint can no longer fall into the sin of vainglory, and the benefit of publication accrues to God and to the church. The writing of a *uita* thus signals the saint's exit from spiritual hiding and entrance into the minds of the *populus*.

As we see in Anselm's veto of Eadmer's *Vita*, no saint—while still alive—can approve or encourage his or her own publicity. And so in spite of Christ's command that no one else learn of the healings he had performed, frequently people disobeyed him: "illi *autem* exeuntes diffamaverunt eum in tota terra illa" (*But* they going out, spread his fame abroad in all that country).¹¹⁶ At the same time, such eventual publicity is essential, for among other things it serves to remind and teach those on earth that holy men and women, perhaps even one's own immediate superior, often serve as conduits for God's secretive scrutiny. While a saint might occasionally receive access to God's secret knowledge, the hagiographer in some ways resembles the secret spy, witnessing and gathering information about the habits of a saint and, after the saint's death, proclaiming them widely, with one crucial distinction: the hagiographer's actions are sparked by faith, rather than doubt.

PART III

Literature

Chapter 6

Binding Secrets, Solving Riddles

The secret deeds of saints and encounters with divine secrets certainly make for compelling hagiographic material. In the narratives we have encountered so far, we see an early medieval ethics of secrecy that governs not merely acts of concealment but also acts of discovery, setting apart, for instance, the doubting spy from the faithful hagiographer as they both seek to uncover and disseminate the secrets of a saint. It follows, then, that this ethical framework may have also applied to the intellectual process of textual interpretation and the discovery of hidden meaning more broadly. To determine precisely how this ethics influenced Anglo-Saxon hermeneutic practices, there is no better place to look than the large and diverse corpus of Old English and Anglo-Latin riddles, which constituted a multifaceted, highly influential, and extremely popular genre committed at the most basic level to experiments in textual forms of concealment and interpretation.[1]

While offering a practical literary experience in encrypting and deciphering textual enigmas, some riddles didactically engage in the religious and spiritual elements of interpretation, which closely correlate to the broader ethical dynamics between secrecy and faith in God's omniscience. But underlying these ethical dynamics are certain metaphors of servitude—of binding and fettering, of ownership and control—that pervade both the logic and rhetoric of a large number of early medieval riddles. For as with the rhetoric of bondage and servitude that emerges in legal and monastic descriptions of secrecy, these metaphors highlight the possibility of and the limits to the holding, guarding, and keeping of a secret both in the literary and textual contexts of the riddles and, by extension, in the social and psychological conditions that circumscribe human experiences of concealment.

Unbinding Servants, Decrypting Death, and Solving Riddles in the Old English *Apollonius of Tyre*

When King Antiochus rapes his daughter in the Old English *Apollonius of Tyre*, he does so on her wedding day by pretending to have a word with her in secret ("sume digle spæce sprecan wolde").² After committing the crime, the king acts both to conceal it ("to bediglianne") and to reveal it: to his subjects he acts as though he were still a devoted father, but among his domestic servants ("hiwcuðum mannum") he openly behaves as a husband to his own daughter. Repugnant as it is, the king's nonchalance before his servants should come as little surprise. Slaves and servants, as we have seen in the previous chapters, were understood to participate in the secrets of their masters. This epistemological relationship is further emphasized here by the component *cuð* (known) in the phrase "hiw*cuðum* mannum," which delineates domestic servants as both known (i.e., familiar to the master) and knowing (i.e., familiar with the master).³ But this polarity between those who know the secret of the king's crime (his servants, his victim, and eventually the reader) and those who do not (his subjects and everyone else) collapses as soon as the king decides to publicize the crime under the concealment of a riddle, which creates a third category of potential "knowers": those given the opportunity to know through a process of interpretation. These themes of knowledge and interpretation weave throughout the romance and introduce a way of thinking about secrecy that will help us understand the very mechanics of riddles.

In the case of Antiochus's riddle, the stakes of knowing here are high: anyone who misinterprets the riddle would suffer beheading; anyone who interprets it correctly through "asmeagunge boclicre snotornesse" (the study of bookish wisdom) would gain the hand of the daughter in marriage, but unofficially would lose his head just the same.⁴ The noble Apollonius soon arrives, agrees to the king's conditions, and listens to the riddle: "Scylde ic þolige, moddrenum flæsce ic bruce" (I suffer wickedness, I enjoy the flesh of the mother).⁵ When Apollonius "smeade ymbe þæt ingehyd, he hit gewan mid wisdome and mid Godes fultume he þæt soð arædde" (thought about the sense, he gained it by wisdom, and with God's help he interpreted the truth).⁶ Three stages mark Apollonius's interpretation: he scrutinizes (*smeagan*) the sense of the riddle, which allows him to conquer (*gewinnan*) it with wisdom and then interpret (*aræddan*) the truth with the help of God. These stages are interdependent.

When Apollonius correctly deciphers the riddle to reveal the incest, the king grows terrified that knowledge of his crime might spread. In order to contain the situation, he judges Apollonius's answer to be wrong and sentences him to beheading unless he can find the "correct" solution within thirty days. But reckoning even that verdict too generous, the king orders his servant, Thaliarcus, to pursue and kill Apollonius. The king's order emphasizes his trust in Thaliarcus: "Thaliarce, ealra mynra digolnessa myn se getrywesta þegn, wite þu þæt apollonius ariht arædde mynne rædels" (Thaliarcus, my servant most trustworthy of all my secrets, you know that Apollonius has correctly interpreted my riddle).[7] Thaliarcus was probably one of the servants privy to the king's secret in the first place, but the king nevertheless reiterates that privilege in his instructions, making sure Thaliarcus is fully aware of his duty. Yet he also offers Thaliarcus his freedom if he should succeed in killing and silencing Apollonius—a conflicted promise for such future freedom presumably would relieve Thaliarcus of his obligation to guard the king's secret. His future freedom is nevertheless contingent and still mitigated by the awkward grammar of Antiochus's phrase, "ealra mynra digolnessa myn se getrywesta þegn," which serves to remind Thaliarcus that his person fundamentally belongs to the king ("myn") as a trustworthy and knowledgeable accomplice in the crime.[8] Moreover, the king's secrets ("mynra digolnessa") are retained and possessed by the servant, who acts as an extension of the king himself; together they are bound to a mutual obligation of concealment even (we might speculate) if Thaliarcus were granted his freedom, or else (we might speculate to the contrary) death would need to accompany Thaliarcus's freedom in order to preserve the king's secret.

But *Apollonius of Tyre* is not particularly concerned with such hypothetical possibilities. Instead, it narrates Apollonius's fugitive travels and shipwrecks, his marriage and the birth of his daughter (Thasia), his separation from his family, and finally their reunion. The narrative then culminates in a scene of judgment: Apollonius and his family return to Tarsus in order to accuse and apprehend Stranguillo and Dionysias—Apollonius's friends and Thasia's guardians—for attempting to steal and murder Thasia. Dionysias responds to the accusation by pointing to Thasia's grave as proof of her natural death: "þu silf aræddest þa stafas ofer hire birgene" (you yourself *read* the lettering over her grave).[9] But Apollonius is an expert reader, as when he "soð arædde" (read the truth) of Antiochus's riddle at the beginning of the romance, and he disproves the deceptive letters on the grave by gesturing for his daughter to come forward. As though "of helle geciged" (called forth from hell), Thasia greets the trembling Dionysias.[10] Seeing Thasia alive terrifies Dionysias not only because she assumed Thasia to be dead but moreover because she believed her secret attempt at murder would be secure with both the death of her victim and the servant whom she ordered to commit the crime. Yet both eventually prove unreliable, as Thasia, still very much alive, in turn calls forth Theophilus (the servant) to testify to Dionysias's murderous plot: "sege hluddre stæfne hwa þe hete me ofslean" (state with a loud voice who commanded you to kill me).[11]

The modes of concealment and assumptions about secrecy at the start of the narrative—as represented by King Antiochus's initial hiding of his crime under the pretense of "secret speech" ("sume digle spæce"), his arbitrary decision to condemn Apollonius's correct interpretation of his riddle, his faith in the secrecy of his servant, Thaliarcus, and his attempt to suppress his criminal secret by having Apollonius murdered—are in the end collectively reversed by someone once thought to be dead and by the loud voice ("hluddre stæfne") of a servant's testimony, blatantly betraying his evil master and announcing the truth to be plainly judged. The bonds of secrecy represented both by death and by servitude are, in other words, not nearly as strong as the characters in the romance want to believe.

The Secrecy of Servants

The assumption is widespread that servants, slaves, and advisors are obligated to keep their master's secrets, either by the weight of duty (in the case of advisors) or by the imposition of law (by which, for instance, servants and slaves were restricted from independently bearing witness).[12] We have already seen in Chapter 2, for instance, how the legal position of the slave would preclude his or her testimony because it is contingent on the will of the master.[13] And in Chapter 3, we have seen how monasticism configured its characteristic piety as a life of servitude in which servants of God (*serui Dei* or *famuli Dei*) labored directly under the authority of and in obedience to the abbot, so that the secrets of their own hearts were no longer their own but instead belonged to the abbot and to God. Even in cases where a monk has a secret, it is generally known by the abbot. We see this dynamic play out, for example, in Ælfric's *Life of Saint Eugenia*, where the saint secretly disguises herself as a man so that she can preserve her virginity by entering the monastic life. Only three people know her secret: the bishop (to whom it was revealed by God) and Eugenia's two servants, who "hyre digol-nysse eallum be-dyrndon" (fully concealed her secret).[14] These assumptions are clearly visible in the narrative of *Apollonius of Tyre*, even if they are ultimately called into question.

Advisors and counselors, too, fill a similar position in relation to the secrets of their principals—a responsibility implied by the medieval Latin titles *secretarius* and *asecretis* (from which derives the modern English word "secretary" as "one who is entrusted with private or secret matters")[15] and by the Old English words *runwita* (a knower of secrets/advice) and *rædels* (which means both "riddle, enigma" in the literary sense and "counsel, advice" in the political sense).[16] The bilingual Antwerp-London glossaries thus link "geruna" with "Asecretis" (privy counselor) and "yldest rædbora" with "Princeps consiliarius" (chief counselor), which the Anglo-Saxon scholia to Priscian's *Excerptiones* links back to *asecretis* by glossing the term as "intimus consiliarius regis" (the most intimate counselor of the king).[17] These terms even arise in *Beowulf*, where Hrothgar laments the dead Æschere with a phrase—"min runwita ond min rædbora" (my secret counselor and my advice giver)—that seems to imply

Æschere's position as both advice giver and knower of Hrothgar's secrets, with the two discrete terms, *runwita* and *rædbora*, conflated in a single character.[18] Positions such as the *runwita* and *rædbora*, or the *asecretis*, by definition come with the responsibility to protect those secrets.

We see this logic with great clarity in the Old English *Apollonius*, as servants are called on to maintain, protect, or participate in the secrecy of their masters. When Antiochus, for example, reminds Thaliarcus that he trusts him with "ealra mynra digolnessa" (all my secrets), his role as a servant is made parallel to the role of the king's riddle (the correct solution to which Thaliarcus already knows).[19] Notably, the king refers to his secrets, his servant, and his riddle with the same possessive pronoun *myn*, reaffirming his assumed possession of each. By confiding in his servants, Antiochus can thus share his secret without letting it become known publicly, since the secret still theoretically remains within the realm of his control. The riddle with which he hopes to conceal his crime ("þæt gefremede man gewilnode to bediglianne") likewise functions as a public and outward display of his secret, at once bound to the rules set by the king (as an extension of his property) and yet subject to external hermeneutic pressure. The problem for Antiochus, as we have seen, is that he assumes his control over the riddle to be more secure than it actually is. His tyrannical attempts to invalidate Apollonius's truly correct answer and have him killed both fail, and the knowledge of the crime that the riddle aims to conceal eventually surfaces: Apollonius goes on to tell others about the king's incestuous deed; even the plebian Hellanicus seems well informed on the matter.[20] At the end of the narrative, that same type of trust in servants and in the unassailable secrecy of death fails Dionysias as well. The secrecy of the crypt is rendered penetrable by Thasia's simulated resurrection, and the secrecy of the servant, Theophilus, is shattered when he is ordered to bear witness in a loud voice and is subsequently freed on account of his testimony. Theophilus's loud speech, moreover, inverts Antiochus's inaugural secret speech ("digle spæce"), as the figure of the servant (albeit a different servant) who ought to protect his master's secrets is released from that obligation. By treating seemingly secure forms of concealment (such as death and servants) as nothing more than encryptions subject to interpretation, *Apollonius of Tyre* thus uses the literary model of the riddle in order to think through the solidity and fragility of secrecy, to put pressure on the assumptions that secrets are entirely controlled by their masters, that servants form an unbreakable extension of those masters, and that murder and death are inviolable forms of concealment. Servants can be unbound, death can be decrypted or misinterpreted or miraculously inverted, and riddles—of course—can be solved.

The duty of the servant, the *seruus*, is in part to *seruare* or *conseruare,* to protect, to preserve, to keep, and to guard.[21] At the same time the servant is also protected, guarded, kept, and taken by the hand of the master, hence the folk etymology offered by Augustine in his *De ciuitate Dei* and reiterated by Isidore in his *Etymologiae*, that slaves are called *serui* because their lives are the ones that the victors in war have not ended but rather preserved (*seruare*).[22] This notion of slaves as conservators of secrets applies not merely to the practical and social relation between actual servants and their masters; it is also metaphorically extended into textual situations as well. When Rufinus translates Origen's *In Numeros homiliae* from the Greek, for example, the sacred meanings of scripture are protected (*seruare*) from inexperienced readers:

> Non enim placuit sancto Spiritui, qui de his scribi voluit, ut palam haec et pedibus, ut ita dicam, imperitorum conculcanda ponerentur, sed ita providit, ut, cum publice haberi videantur, sermonum tamen obscuritate recondita in arcanis et in secretis obtecta *serventur*.[23]

> [For it did not please the Holy Spirit, who did want something to be written about these things, that these things be placed out in the open to be trampled on, so to speak, by the feet of the inexperienced. Instead, He so arranged it that, even though things seem to be treated openly, they nevertheless are *protected*, having been concealed in secrecy and mystery, hidden by the obscurity of the words.]

The final word—*seruentur*—bears the weight of this passage, describing the protective power of verbal obscurity to conceal meaning when presented publicly and openly before experienced and inexperienced readers alike. In other words, the meaning is not removed but is rather preserved by means of concealment. This paradox of open concealment underlies the nature both of servitude and of riddles, which Origen brings together here in the image of obscure words that serve and protect sacred things by concealing their true meanings. Riddles and their formal modes of concealment pervade the Old English *Apollonius* and the *Historia Apollonii*, but they also function alongside other tactical forms of secrecy, particularly the assumption of secrecy applied to servants, as we have seen, producing a symmetrical relationship between the ethical-political figure of the servant and the literary model of the riddle, for both can serve in one way or another as the public and outward preservation of a secret. The servant and the riddle remain outwardly visible, while the knowledge they contain remains concealed or encrypted. If pressed hard enough, however, both riddles and servants can be made to testify, to betray willfully the secrets they are responsible for protecting and conserving.

Apollonius and the Tradition of Anglo-Saxon Riddles

The story of Apollonius is of course not an Anglo-Saxon invention, and the Old English translation remains relatively close to its Latin source (the *Historia Apollonii regis Tyri*).[24] Translation, however, always implies engagement.[25] Indeed, the story of Apollonius was not only read in early medieval England (as attested by the survival of several pre-twelfth-century English manuscripts containing the *Historia Apollonii*), but it must have also been read closely enough to produce at least one surviving version translated into English, which itself is likely a copy from a now-lost exemplar.[26] As for the story's appeal to an Anglo-Saxon audience, several scholars have pointed to the riddles so central to its narrative.[27]

Antiochus's two riddles (only one of which was quoted above) stir the narrative into motion, but the story contains several other riddles as well. Hellanicus, for example, subtly refigures Antiochus's riddle when he warns Apollonius of the threat to his life and offers the following explanation: "Forðam þe þu girndest þæt þu wære þæt se fæder is" (Because you desired to have been what the father is).[28] And Antiochus's own daughter anticipates the king's public riddle when she is approached and comforted by her slow-witted nurse, who has trouble following the daughter's enigmatic account of the event: "forwurdon twegen æðele naman on þisum bure" (two noble names have been destroyed in this chamber).[29] Even after the nurse gets the gist, she dimwittedly asks, "Hwi ne segst þu hit þinum fæder?" (Why not tell this to your father?), to which the daughter responds with another quasi-riddle: "Hwar is se fæder? Soðlice on me earmre is mines fæder nama reowlice forworden" (Where is this father? Truly within me, a wretch, the name of my father has been grievously destroyed).[30] Even more riddles are to be found in the middle of the *Historia Apollonii*, when Thasia is sent to console Apollonius, to draw him out from the darkness of his ship where he is mourning the loss of his family and, both figuratively and literally, bring him into the light. Unaware of their relation, Apollonius sends his daughter away at first, but she returns with an ultimatum: if he resolves the knots of her riddles, she will go away.[31] He despondently agrees, she proceeds with ten riddles, and he answers each of them in turn. The riddles fail to cheer him up, but eventually Thasia tells of her enigmatic tribulations (she was born at sea, her mother was buried at sea, she was given to Stranguillo and Dionysias, who nearly murdered her, etc.), and Apollonius solves that final riddle, coming to realize her true identity.

As the two are reunited, they move from the darkness of the ship's hull into the light of day, from obscurity to revelation.

The riddle exchange between Apollonius and his daughter falls in a section missing from the fragmentary manuscript copy of the Old English *Apollonius*, but it does survive in the one manuscript of the Latin *Historia Apollonii* that is believed to be the closest to the source for the Old English translation.[32] While impossible to determine with any certainty, there is little reason to believe that this riddle exchange was deliberately excised from the Old English translation, especially since all ten of the riddles come from a source that would have been familiar to many educated Anglo-Saxon readers.[33] The riddles are derived verbatim from the Late Latin poet Symphosius,[34] whose collection of one hundred *aenigmata* survives in several Anglo-Saxon manuscripts and is generally regarded as the model for the Anglo-Latin *Aenigmata* by Aldhelm, abbot of Malmesbury and eventually bishop of Sherborne (d. 709 or 710). Indeed, Aldhelm even acknowledges Symphosius by name in his prose prologue,[35] and the immense popularity of Aldhelm's *Aenigmata* as a school text, moreover, influenced the collection of forty *aenigmata* by Tatwine, archbishop of Canterbury (d. 734),[36] which circulate alongside the sixty *aenigmata* by Eusebius, together forming another century collection.[37] Despite Symphosius's pseudonym, which evinces his taste for a good drinking party, despite the playful and inebriated festivities described in his preface as the inspirational context for the creation of these riddles, and despite his own judgment of them as intellectually frivolous *carmina inepta*, we can trace back to Symphosius's *Aenigmata* the healthy interest in riddles that flourished throughout early medieval England, particularly in monastic centers and classrooms.[38] Examples of the genre survive in great variety, some of which are closer in form to Symphosius's collection than others; indeed, some are more somber and others more playful. They are found in Latin and in Old English, in verse and in prose, in collections and in isolation, as lengthy dialogues and as brief trivia. It is a vast genre, the surface of which can only be scratched here and in the subsequent chapters of this book.

Suffice it to say that the riddles in the Old English *Apollonius* would have certainly attracted the attention of Anglo-Saxon readers whose education almost certainly would have put them in touch with the *Aenigmata* of Symphosius or Aldhelm or Tatwine and Eusebius or the many other riddles in circulation, such as those in the Exeter Book,[39] which emerged not just from the traditional sphere of Old English poetics but also from "an intellectual milieu of monastic literature and Latin book-learning."[40] It is impossible to know exactly why the Old English *Apollonius* was copied into Cambridge, Corpus Christi College MS 201, a mid-eleventh-century manuscript, containing chiefly a collection of homilies by Wulfstan (d. 1023) along with a number of other legal and religious items.⁴¹ Many theories about its manuscript context have been proposed, but scholarly consensus is that the *Apollonius* would have been acceptable reading material for clerical or even monastic audiences.⁴² And its riddles would have particularly appealed to that audience, likely the same type of audience that was raised on the *Aenigmata* of Aldhelm and the collection of riddles in the Exeter Book.⁴³

Bonds of Servile Secrecy in the Exeter Book *Riddles*

David Pelteret and David Wyatt have brought our attention to the portrayal of slaves and servitude in the Exeter Book *Riddles* as one source of evidence for demonstrating the prevalence of slavery in Anglo-Saxon society. Edward B. Irving, Jr., has shown how the references to slavery in many riddles reflect an "important and sinister" aspect of the culture.⁴⁴ And Megan Cavell has produced a comprehensive survey of the depictions of servitude and slavery in the Exeter Book *Riddles,* suggesting that they offer a kind of untenable "hope of security and protection" in a "poetic corpus that taps into human concern with its own instability and the instability of nature."⁴⁵ It is, of course, the nature of riddles to depict in extraordinary ways those ordinary, often mundane objects and phenomena are common to the everyday cultural situation of the poet and contemporary reader. Even if some riddles, particularly in the Latin tradition, concern things quite foreign to the daily experience of most English readers—such as Aldhelm's *Minotaurus* (Minotaur) and *Strutio* (Ostrich)—these would have been familiar to anyone with access to Isidore of Seville's *Etymologiae*, as Nicholas Howe has argued.⁴⁶ On the other hand, the frequent references in the *Riddles* to slaves and servants—common to the cultural moment as they would have been—might be unsurprising.⁴⁷ Scholars have frequently noted that these references to servitude and slavery are predominantly isolated to the genre of riddles, with a paucity elsewhere in the Old English poetic corpus. And yet the theme of servitude along with its metaphors of binding and captivity runs far more deeply through the genre—especially as represented by the Exeter Book *Riddles*—than has been noticed to date.⁴⁸

I count at least twenty-seven riddles in the Exeter Book that contain references to servitude, and the number could be higher on the basis of several contested readings.⁴⁹ By contrast, the formula "say what I am called" (variations on "saga hwæt ic hatte") has come to represent a defining feature of the Old English *Riddles*, even though it only occurs eighteen times.⁵⁰ While some of the references to servitude are more extensive than others, the theme of servitude touches almost a third of the riddles in the Exeter Book. Like their Latin counterparts, the vernacular riddles treat such a wide variety of subjects, a variety magnified by the range of metaphors and fluctuations in style, that they tend to resist any all-encompassing theories.[51] Nevertheless, I argue here that this profound interest in servitude and binding in fact shapes the ways that those specific riddles can be read as well as how the techniques of concealment employed in the genre were thought to have functioned.

The first three riddles of the Exeter Book set up a relationship in which the master has complete and absolute control over his servant. In these opening riddles (sometimes treated as a single riddle with three parts), what appears to be a storm together with its constitutive elements is variously depicted as a slave or captive whose master is God.[52] *Riddle* 1, for example, begins by asking "hwa mec on sið wræce, / þonne ic astige strong?" (who drove me on my course when I would rise up with strength?).[53] It ends with the burden of physical labor:

> hæbbe me on hrycge   þæt ær hadas wreah
> foldbuendra,   flæsc ond gæstas,
> somod on sunde.   Saga hwa mec þecce,
> oþþe hu ic hatte,   þe þa hlæst bere.[54]   15

[I carry on my back what once covered the bodies of earth-dwellers, body and soul submerged together in the water. Say who conceals me, or what I, who bear this burden, am called.]

The third *Riddle* once again picks up this language and imagery of the servant's burden and obedience to his master, but it makes more explicit the connection between the work of slaves and the burden of weight on the servant's back ("hæbbe me on hrycge"). It thus ends by rendering the storm as a "þrymful þeow" (mighty slave) who carries a load on his back ("on hrycg hlade") and who is roused and restrained by God alone.[55] While all three riddles play with the analogies of storm as slave and God as lord, it is the beginning of *Riddle* 3 that presents the most awe-inspiring image of captivity at the hands of an almighty master:

> Hwilum mec min frea   fæste genearwað,
> sendeð þonne   under salwonges
> bearm þone bradan,   ond on bid wriceð,
> þrafað on þystrum   þrymma sumne,
> hæste on enge,   þær me heord siteð   5
> hruse on hrycge.[56]

[Sometimes my lord tightly confines me, then sends me under the broad bosom of fertile fields, and holds me in wait, presses certain of my powers in the darkness, forced into prison, there earth sits hard on my back.]

Here, the burden carried on the wind's back (again, "on hrycge") is the earth under which it is confined. Unable to escape, it causes halls to tremble in accordance with the early medieval understanding that earthquakes were caused by winds trapped and running through subterranean caves.[57] It can finally break out of its confinement ("of enge," line 12a), out of its bonds and fetters ("bende ond clomme," line 15a), only when the one who had buried it in the first place decides to uncover it. The poem merges the images of burial and servitude so that both fall under the jurisdiction of God's power to bind and loose, to bury and to resurrect.

The power of God over this instance of servitude and death mirrors the juridical power that Antiochus and Dionysias in the Old English *Apollonius* each assume to hold over their own servants and express with a willingness to kill anyone else who might know and divulge their secrets. While Antiochus and Dionysias both fail in these efforts, *Riddle* 3 paints a picture of the far more profound power behind God's effective and exclusive capacity to capture, release, bury, and uncover. This power is magnified in light of Aldhelm's *Aenigma* 2, which describes the wind (*uentus*) as something that can be neither seen nor touched: "Cernere me nulli possunt nec prendere palmis" (None can see me, nor lay hands on me).[58] The wind is at once invisible and impossible to apprehend, and yet it is nevertheless a captive and servant, apprehended, possessed, and controlled by God alone. The riddles of the Exeter Book thus open with three scenes of absolute control and bondage that maintain a clear and potent hierarchy between the master and his servant.

After these three riddles and beginning immediately with *Riddle* 4, however, the collection begins to entangle the roles of the servant and the master, testing the boundaries of that ostensibly unidirectional power and control. But even the earthquake of *Riddle* 3—with its metaphors of incarceration and binding—begins the process of testing these boundaries by subtly evoking Acts 16:26: "Subito vero terraemotus factus est magnus, ita ut moverentur fundamenta carceris. Et statim aperta sunt omnia ostia: et universorum vincula soluta sunt" (suddenly there was a great earthquake, so that the foundations of the prison were shaken. And immediately all the doors were opened, and the bands of all were loosed). Among the freed prisoners are the apostles Paul and Silas, before whose feet the terrified prison keeper eventually begs, "Domini, quid me oportet facere, ut salvus fiam?" (Masters, what must I do, that I may be saved?).[59] Their roles as prisoner and master are reversed, as the earthquake unbinds (*soluta*) the chains of every inmate. This type of reversal between master and servant is then brought to the surface in *Riddle* 4, which depicts an object—likely a water bucket, although also possibly a bell or millstone—that is "hringum hæfted" (bound with rings) and yet eagerly obeys either its master or, more likely, its servant ("þegne minum"), depending on how one translates the word *þegn*.⁶⁰ Translators of *Riddle* 4 have rendered *þegn* both ways: one critic has even suggested translating the word as "servant/master,"⁶¹ while another explains that "the word *þegne* suggests that (the object) is an article of use employed by a servant while working for his own master."⁶² Although the semantic weight of the word tends to fall more heavily on the side of its sense as "servant," its ambiguity here—made especially apparent following the clear hierarchy of servitude in the previous three riddles—highlights the problematic ease with which these roles of servant and master can be inverted, intertwined, and bound together.

The paradoxes of servants binding masters and masters obeying servants certainly appealed to the poets who produced these riddles, since these sorts of configurations only proliferate as we move deeper into the collection. *Riddle* 12, for example, is frequently cited for its several references to Welsh slaves, but it also depicts a complex relationship between the seemingly opposed acts of binding and serving:

```
Fotum ic fere,      foldan slite,
grene wongas,       þenden ic gæst bere.
Gif me feorh losað,   fæste binde
swearte Wealas,     hwilum sellan men.
Hwilum ic deorum      drincan selle                        5
beorne of bosme,     hwilum mec bryd triedeð
felawlonc fotum,     hwilum feorran broht
wonfeax Wale       wegeð ond þyð,
dol druncmennen      deorcum nihtum,
wæteð in wætre,      wyrmeð hwilum                         10
fægre to fyre;   me on fæðme sticaþ
hygegalan hond,     hwyrfeð geneahhe,
swifeð me geond sweartne.   Saga hwæt ic hatte,
þe ic lifgende     lond reafige
ond æfter deaþe     dryhtum þeowige.⁶³                     15
```

[I travel by foot, trample the ground, the green fields, as long as I carry a spirit. If life departs from me, I bind fast the dark Welshmen, sometimes better men, too. At times I give a bold warrior drink from my breast, other times a proud bride steps on me with her feet; sometimes a dark-haired woman brought far from Wales, a foolish, drunken maidservant, moves and presses me, fills me with water on dark nights, sometimes warms me gently by the fire; a wanton hand puts me in an embrace, turns just enough, sweeps around my dark self. Say what I am called, I who, alive, plunder the land and, dead, enslave multitudes.]

The solution to this riddle is "ox," an animal that is bound in servitude while alive and yet binds the living once it is dead. The rhetoric of servitude is evident throughout the riddle, but especially in the indiscriminate way the leather straps bind not just slaves—the "swearte Wealas" (dark Welshmen) whose very nationality becomes a pejorative term (*wealh*) that signifies their servile status[64]—but better men ("sellan men"), too, presumably prisoners of war. There are a number of other ox riddles in the Exeter Book as well as in the Latin collections, each of which plays with subtle variations on this paradox of living servitude and dead mastery.[65] For example, *Riddle* 72 accentuates the ox's servile status by depicting its submission to the "sweartum hyrde" (dark herdsman) as it plods along the Welsh borderlands and toils "bunden under beama" (bound under a yoke).[66] Like the word *wonfeax* in *Riddle* 12, the pejorative word *swearte* associates slaves with dark-haired Celts, as opposed to the fair-haired Anglo-Saxons.[67] But as Lindy Brady has demonstrated, *Riddle* 72 (as well as *Riddle* 52) plays on the historical paradox of the Welsh as both slaves and slave traders.[68] This paradox is then only reinforced by the paradoxical status of the ox: formerly a servant to a stereotypical slave, the ox eventually becomes the very thing that enslaves others, that "fæste binde" (binds fast) those same Welsh slaves who once worked the plow.

Many other riddles draw on the related paradoxical motif of the dead binding the living. Exeter Book *Riddle* 38 (bull calf) ends thus:

Seo wiht, gif hio gedygeð,   duna briceð;
gif he tobirsteð,   bindeð cwice.[69]

[The creature, if he survives tears up hills, if he is torn apart, he binds the living.]

These antitheses, as Peter Clemoes explains, produce tension "between an endurance (*gedygeð*) which breaks other beings (*briceð*) and a bursting of oneself (*tobirsteð*) which (paradoxically) binds (*bindeð*) others."[70] A similar motif also appears in several Latin *aenigmata* as well, perhaps even serving as one source of inspiration for its vernacular instantiations.[71] For instance, Eusebius's *Aenigma* 37 ends with a similar juxtaposition: "uiuos moriens aut alligo multos" (but dead, I bind many who are living).[72] And Aldhelm's *Aenigma* 83 registers the same idea, just with more words:

At uero linquit dum spiritus algida membra,
Nexibus horrendis homines constringere possum.[73]

[But when the breath leaves my frigid limbs, I can bind men with terrible fetters.]

Again, the relationship between binding and death is expressed in the striking paradox of the dead binding the living; it is both striking and paradoxical precisely because that which is dead should be deprived of agency, bound and held captive by the earth. This point is made especially clear in Eusebius's *Aenigma* 32, which employs the same paradox to describe parchment sheets that announce to the reader, "Viua nihil loquimur, responsum mortua famur" (Alive we do not speak, but dead we give answers).[74] These riddles do their jobs precisely by violating the reader's expectations about the rules of nature and the ways these rules are ordinarily rendered into language. When projected onto the other ox riddles, Eusebius's speaking parchment evokes the fact that the dead—bound as they are—should not be able to respond or speak, but the paradoxical formulation of a riddle is what allows them to do so. Analogously, the dead ox should not be able to bind anything, because it is already bound by death; yet a riddle can open up and unlock this possibility.

Still other riddles play further with the inverted slave imagery introduced in *Riddle* 12. For example, *Riddle* 52 describes a flail as a fettered captive whose master is a Welsh slave:

> Ic seah ræpingas   in ræced fergan
> under hrof sales   hearde twegen,
> þa wæron genamnan,   nearwum bendum
> gefeterade   fæste togædre;
> þara oþrum wæs   an getenge   5
> wonfah Wale,   seo weold hyra
> bega siþe   bendum fæstra.[75]

[I saw a couple of hardy captives carried in the house, under the roof of the hall; they were companions, fettered fast together with tight bonds. One dark-hued Welshwoman was touching the other, a servant who wielded power over the movements of both of them, fast in their bonds.]

The language of bondage and servitude in this riddle echoes several others as well. The tight bonds ("nearwum bendum") that bind the two prisoners fast together ("fæste togædre"), for instance, call to mind the lord who tightly confines ("fæste genearwað") the storm in the first line of *Riddle* 3. The two parts of the flail are "bendum fæstra" (fast in their bonds), a phrase that recalls the way the ox in a common poetic construction "fæste binde" (binds fast) the dark Welshmen in *Riddle* 12; but here, the Welsh servant "weold" (wields power) over the object's restricted movements, whereas in *Riddle* 12 the object dominates the Welshmen. The function of the flail here, moreover, resembles the plow described in *Riddle* 21, which is "bunden cræfte"[76] (bound with skill or power) and yet is served (*þegnian*) by the lord (*hlaford*), not the other way around: the plow is an implement that both binds the ox and is itself bound by power, and it only works properly "gif me teala þenaþ / hindeweardre, þæt biþ hlaford min" (if the one behind me, the one who is my lord, serves me well).[77] The collection of riddles in the Exeter Book displays a profuse interest, therefore, in ideas and symbols of servitude; its entangled and cross-referential treatment also serves to position those servant-master relations (with the significant exception of those in which God is the master) as unavoidably contingent and subject to inversion: the bound can bind and the binder can be bound.

Dissolving the Fetters of a Riddle

How these metaphors of servitude (inverted and knotted as they have become) might relate to the process of interpreting the riddles themselves is subtly introduced by Symphosius's *Aenigma* 5:

> Nexa ligor ferro, multos habitura ligatos;
> Vincior ipsa prius, sed uincio uincta uicissim;
> *Exsolui* multos, nec sum tamen ipsa *soluta*.[78]

> [Fastened with iron, I am bound who shall hold many in bonds; first I myself am bound, but when bound I bind in turn; many I have *loosed*, nor yet myself am *loosed*.]

Not only do these dense lines describe the entanglements of chains (*catena*) as implements of binding that are reflexively and inherently bound themselves, but the *aenigma* is itself tangled up with its own diction and syntax. The polyptoton of each line, for example, is placed squarely on either side of a strong caesura ("ligor . . . ligatos," "uincior . . . uincio uincta," "exsolui . . . soluta") in imitation of the repeated links of a chain. Likewise, the middle line is knotted up with the three forms of the word *uincire*, linked by consonance and sense to the terminal *uicissim*. The third and final line then ties up the *aenigma* by repeating *multos* from the first line and *ipsa* from the second line, thus connecting all three lines of the poem. But it is the epanaleptic rhetoric of solving (*exsolui* and *soluta*) in the third line that calls out the task of the reader. In isolation, this rhetoric of solving (*exsolui* and *soluta*) clearly refers to the unbinding of bound people or other bound implements. However, another sense of the word *soluere* emerges in light of Symphosius's preface, where the poet declares how difficult it is "Ponere diuerse uel *soluere* quaeque *uicissim*" (to set or to *solve* in various ways each [riddle] *in turn*).[79] Symphosius's precise language here anticipates the chains described in *Aenigma* 5 not only with the word *soluere* but also with the *uicissim* that terminates the line. This rhetoric of solving (i.e., loosing) the knots and bonds of riddles is even picked up in the *Historia Apollonii* when Thasia presents several Symphosian riddles to Apollonius: "parabolarum mearum nodos absolveris" (you will have resolved the knots of my riddles), she says.[80] Indeed, as one of the primary models for the Anglo-Saxon riddle tradition—from the *Aenigmata* of Aldhelm to the Exeter Book *Riddles*—Symphosius thus establishes the task of interpreting riddles as essentially an act of unbinding and unraveling: the etymological sense, in other words, of *solving*.

But what exactly does it mean to "solve" (*soluere*) a riddle? Solutions can take various forms, depending on the particular riddle and the context in which it is read. Many early English riddles, for example, travel with their solutions (in the form of rubricated headings, acrostic inscriptions, or marginal annotations), while others simply do not. This is a distinction sometimes posited between the Latin and Old English iterations of the genre, respectively. But as Andy Orchard has cautioned, we must bear in mind that some Latin *aenigmata* circulate without solutions while some of the vernacular riddles actually do.[81] These variations are important because the riddles that are accompanied by their solutions seem to ask a different question of the reader than those, say, of the Exeter Book. Where a riddle commands the reader to "say what I am called" (variations on the formula "saga hwæt ic hatte"), recognizing the name of the object or phenomenon is the ostensible goal.[82] On the other hand, the Anglo-Latin *aenigmata* (by Aldhelm, Tatwine, and Eusebius) are almost always presented with their solutions in the form of rubricated titles, prompting Nicholas Howe to have wondered, like many readers, why these Latin *aenigmata* should violate "from the start the essential quality of any riddle." Howe suggested that Aldhelm in particular seems to be more interested in playing with Isidorian etymologies, which enable many of his *aenigmata* to ask not "what am I called?" (as in the Exeter Book) but "what does my name mean?"[83] Of course, we might also imagine a situation like the one in the *Historia Apollonii* in which someone who has access to the solutions (Thasia) recites the riddles to someone who does not (Apollonius), making the recorded solutions in a given manuscript extraneous to the oral delivery and the process of solving the riddle under such circumstances. But as textual artifacts, those *aenigmata* that circulate with their solutions alter the challenge of resolving them for anyone sitting before such a manuscript. The clear and unconcealed presentation of their solutions determines how the reader must engage with the text. Such *aenigmata* thus ask the reader not merely to provide the name of the object or creature described but rather to untwist and unbind the paradoxes that the riddle presents and the meanings that it conceals, a process that often introduces new and even more knotted enigmas. If the mode of concealment employed by many such riddles is imagined as an act of binding, fettering, or knotting, then solving a riddle involves unbinding it or loosing it from those constraints. But if the riddles that we have examined above tell us anything about the process of binding and loosing, they tell us that the one who unbinds often becomes bound, and the one who is bound often in turn does the binding.

The riddles in the Exeter Book tend to avoid reflecting on their own methods of concealment or their own hermeneutic logic, and they are not contextualized with any sort of preface (as we find with some of the Latin collections). But of all the vernacular riddles, it is *Riddle 42* that offers the most theoretical reflection on the methodology and purpose of riddles as a genre or literary practice. In this capacity, it has attracted much scholarly attention for the way it portrays the riddling process itself. As Patricia Dailey puts it, the riddle "makes its own decoding part of the narrative."[84] And indeed, it is a narrative explicitly concerned with the interplay of secrecy and openness:

Ic seah wyhte	wrætlice twa	
undearnunga	ute plegan	
hæmedlaces;	hwitloc anfeng	
wlanc under wædum,	gif þæs weorces speow,	
fæmne fyllo.	Ic on flette mæg	5
þurh runstafas	rincum secgan,	
þam þe bec witan,	bega ætsomne	
naman þara wihta.	þær sceal Nyd wesan	
twega oþer	ond se torhta Æsc	
an an linan,	Acas twegen,	10
Hægelas swa some.	Hwylc þæs hordgates	
cægan cræfte	þa clamme onleac	
þe þa rædellan	wið rynemenn	
hygefæste heold	heortan bewrigene	
orþoncbendum?	Nu is undyrne	15
werum æt wine	hu þa wihte mid us,	
heanmode twa,	hatne sindon.[85]	

[I saw two wondrous creatures unsecretly play the marriage game; if the deed was successful, the fair-haired maid, proud under her clothes, received her fill. By means of runic letters, I can speak in the hall to men—those who know books—the names of both those creatures together. There must be *nyd* twice over, and a single bright *æsc*, one in the line, two of *ac*, and likewise of *hægel*. Who has unlocked, with the power of the key, the chains of the treasure-gate that held the riddle mind-fast against men skilled in mysteries, concealed in its heart by cunning bonds? Now it is unsecret to men at wine how those two lowly creatures are called among us.]⁸⁶

We discover at the start two creatures who are "plegan hæmedlaces" (playing the marriage game), a game that evokes the (albeit far more repugnant) one played by Antiochus and his unwilling daughter at the beginning of the Old English *Apollonius*.⁸⁷ Here, however, the two creatures are playing their game openly ("undearnunga"), an important distinction that rules out adultery, incest, and other immoral forms of fornication that tend to be characterized by secrecy and are often represented with compound words such as *dyrn-hæmende* (incest; lit. secret marriage), *dyrne-forlegennes* (lit. secret fornication), and *dyrne-liger* (lit. secret fornication).⁸⁸ Their open and unsecret game in *Riddle* 42 is then concealed by a riddle, which (like Antiochus's riddle) is spoken publicly in the hall to be heard or read by those who are book-learned ("þam þe bec witan"). The runes (*Nyd*, *Æsc*, *Ac*, and *Hægel*) that comprise the riddle are entirely visible to everyone, but their meaning can only be deciphered by those "rynemenn" who know how to unlock the metaphorical gates that guard the riddle's solution. The two creatures (which are now made unsecret once again) are a cock and a hen, the words for which in Old English (*hana* and *hæn*) are composed from the aforementioned runic letters (two of the letter *N*, one of the letter *Æ*, two of the letter *A*, and two of the letter *H*).⁸⁹ The process of interpreting the runes, as Dailey has perceived, requires that "the names of the (copulating) cock and hen must be de-assembled (and decoupled) from overlapping letters into two separate semantic units."⁹⁰ What, in the terms I have outlined above, was formerly bound together—both physically and textually—must be unbound by the reader.

Seth Lerer has proposed that the structure of *Riddle* 42 (which moves from unsecret to secret to unsecret) mirrors the material structure of a book.⁹¹ In line 15a, the word "orþoncbendum," another hapax legomenon meaning something like "cunning or original bonds," thus connotes, for Lerer, a book's outer boards, which enclose its inner pages in a way that recalls contemporary techniques of bookbinding such as those described in *Riddle* 26:

                Mec siþþan wrah
hæleð hleobordum,   hyde beþenede,
gierede mec mid golde;   forþon me gliwedon
wrætlic weorc smiþa,   wire bifongen.⁹²

[Then a man covered me with boards, he stretched skin over me and adorned me with gold; the wondrous work of smiths thus ornamented me, held together by wire.]

Lerer's emphasis on book learning leads him to interpret *Riddle* 42 as a poem primarily concerned with the "literate and illiterate ways of interpreting the world," especially in the way it juxtaposes the lewd and the learned; in Lerer's words, "it rephrases the potentially obscene in terms of the patently religious."[93] Such tactics we would expect, given that the riddle, like many in the genre, emerges from a monastic and Latinate tradition of education. It is now, for instance, generally accepted that even the most obscene riddles can be read for their solemn spiritual meanings, as Mercedes Salvador-Bello has shown with this riddle and several of the more vulgar ones that immediately follow it.[94] But literacy and lewdness are unavoidably intertwined in the poem, and it is only the reader who disentangles them in the process of noticing and pronouncing their juxtaposition; in other words, by drawing out the religious connotations, the reader actively calls attention to the more obvious sexual and lewd innuendoes.

Anglo-Saxon riddles no doubt demonstrate an interest in the materiality and tools of book production as well as in the forms of grammar and literacy. But the rhetoric of binding here reflects another layer of poetic interest as well, which has so far gone unnoticed: that of servitude. The metaphors of bookish literacy and of servitude are by no means mutually exclusive, but they instead inform one another through their ambiguity. This ambiguity, the primary device employed in riddles, is displayed most elegantly by those metaphors of binding that are not specifically restricted to the sense of human servitude. For instance, the reference in *Riddle* 42 to the *hordgat* (another hapax legomenon; line 11b) suggests in isolation the protection of locked treasure rather than the binding of servants. However, when returned to the context of the phrase "hordgates . . . clamme" (chains of the treasure gate), the individual meanings of the two words are put in tension with one another. The word *clam* most often refers to fetters or chains applied to the bondage or imprisonment of a person or of some personification (e.g., sin): the word thus tends to imply a mechanism of restriction rather than fortification.[95] For example, in the passage from *Riddle* 3 discussed above, the "bende ond clomme" (line 15a) are the fetters and chains that restrain the storm underground. On the other hand, a *hordgat* would typically serve to limit access to a hoard of treasure and only thereby keep the treasure in its place. The unusual pairing of *hordgat* with the word *clam* in *Riddle* 42 therefore suggests that the "hordgates . . . clamme" is designed just as much to keep the treasure from bursting free as to keep thieves out—just as much, in other words, to keep the hidden meaning of the riddle from announcing itself as to keep readers from deciphering it.

Treasure and slaves may seem ontologically different, yet both are treated as valuable property that can be owned and is worth protecting. The "cægan cræfte" (power of the key) in line 12b of *Riddle* 42 signals one way that such ownership and protection could be both exercised and broken. Keys such as the one in *Riddle* 42 are a common Old English literary motif, representing a tool for metaphorically unlocking the wisdom and meaning of books. Ælfric, for instance, holds that "ðe stæfcræft is seo cæg, ðe ðæra boca andgit unlicð" (grammar is the key that unlocks the meaning of books).[96] Likewise, in the poem *Solomon and Saturn II*, Saturn has the "boca cæga, leornenga locan" (the keys to books in which learning is locked).[97] And in a passage from the poem *Exodus*, spiritual interpretation is only rendered possible if one possesses the "gæstas cægon" (keys of the spirit).[98] But implicit in these all-too-common examples is the notion that keys also represent a form of protection, and the famously obscene *Riddle* 44 makes this connection especially apparent:[99]

> Wrætlic hongað   bi weres þeo,
> *frean* under sceate.   Foran is þyrel.
> Bið stiþ ond heard,   stede hafað godne;
> þonne se *esne*   his agen hrægl
> ofer cneo hefeð,   wile þæt cuþe hol   5
> mid his hangellan   heafde gretan
> þæt he efenlang ær   oft gefylde.[100]

[A wondrous thing hangs by a man's thigh, under the clothes of its *master*. It is pierced in front. It is stiff and hard, has a good place. When the *servant* lifts his own garment over the knee, he wishes to greet with the head of this hanging thing that well known hole, which he—of the same length—often filled before.]

The genteel half of this riddle's double entendre refers to a key that hangs under the clothing of its master ("frean"). Scholars tend to translate *esne* in line 4a as "man" or "young man" (a safe and legitimate rendering of the word), and they do so presumably in order to iron out the inconsistency caused either by the key lifting its own "hrægl" (garment) or by having the *frea* somehow switch from master to servant. But *esne* more specifically refers to a person of a servile class, as in the immediately preceding *Riddle* 43, where the Body is a servant (*esne*) ruled by the Soul, its lord (*frea*).[101] As we have seen before, the riddles of the Exeter Book frequently play with inversions of the master-servant relationship, and the key in *Riddle* 44 is no exception.

The most straightforward interpretation of *Riddle* 44 is that the servant (*esne*) uses his master's key to open his master's property, but the paradox is created by the fact that the *esne* is first and foremost a *frea* (lord, master)—that is, a lord over the key. As the key's master (*frea*) is revealed to be a servant (*esne*), the poem reflects on the way in which keys are both guarded and guardians, servants and masters, just as Symphosius lays out in his *Aenigma* 4:

> Virtutes magnas de uiribus affero paruis.
> Pando domos clausas, iterum sed claudo patentes.
> *Seruo* domum domino, sed rursus *seruor* ab ipso.¹⁰²

> [I carry great powers from little strength. I open closed homes, but again I close those that stand open. I *guard* the house for the master, but in turn am *guarded* by him.]

Like the knotted rhetoric of binding (*uincire*) and loosing (*soluere*) in Symphosius's immediately subsequent chain riddle (*Aenigma* 5), the verb *seruare* here similarly describes the actions of both the key and the master. And the opening description of the surprisingly great power ("uirtutes magnas") held by such a small object captures precisely the surprising logic beneath the phrase "cægan cræfte" (the power of the key) in *Riddle* 42.

Perhaps the best-known keys—and the most powerful—belong to Saint Peter. Any Christian reader encountering Symphosius's *Aenigma* 4 or the "cægan cræfte" in *Riddle* 42 would immediately think of Matthew 16:19: "Et tibi dabo claves regni caelorum. Et quodcumque ligaveris super terram, erit ligatum et in caelis: et quodcumque solveris super terram, erit solutum et in caelis" (And I will give to thee the keys of the kingdom of heaven. And whatsoever thou shalt bind upon earth, it shall be bound also in heaven: and whatsoever thou shalt loose upon earth, it shall be loosed also in heaven).¹⁰³ In Matthew 16:19, the power of the keys not only opens the *hordgat* of heaven but also allows the apostles to bind and loose (to punish and forgive) the bonds of sin. The apostolic key is thus a symbol of the power of judgment both on earth and finally in heaven. And the "cægan cræfte" in *Riddle* 42 by extension gives the reader of the riddle—like both Apollonius and Antiochus, in their own respective ways—the juridical task of loosing and binding.

The legendary complexity of the Old English word *cræft* presents its own problems for the phrase "cægan cræfte." Not only are the word and its related compounds used frequently (sixteen times in the *Riddles* alone), but it is also notoriously difficult to translate, referring both to skill (as in Latin *ars*) and to power.¹⁰⁴ In *Riddle* 42's phrase "cægan cræfte," the word *cræft* seems especially to hover along the full range of its meaning, thus recalling, for instance, the "bunden cræfte" with which the plow in *Riddle* 21 is made into a thing that is powerfully bound and a thing that binds with power. Furthermore, the description of an iceberg in *Riddle* 33 connects the art and power of binding to the textual bonds of riddles themselves. As the iceberg grinds into the side of a ship, it narrates its own origins by speaking a riddle within a riddle:

       Heterune bond,
sægde searocræftig ymb hyre sylfre gesceaft:
"Is min modor mægða cynnes
þæs deorestan, þæt is dohtor min   10
eacen up liden, swa þæt is ældum cuþ,
firum on folce, þæt seo on foldan sceal
on ealra londa gehwam lissum stondan."[105]

[She bound them with a hateful enigma, spoke with cunning skill about her own origins: "My mother is of the most beloved race of women; she is also my daughter, pregnant and lifted up, so that she is known by men, people in multitude, to stand with grace in each and every land."]

The sounds of the iceberg are deceptively powerful and treacherously skillful (*searucræftig*), as they bind (*bindan*) the listeners with their *heterun* (hateful rune, riddle, enigma, mystery, secret). Neither *searocræftig* nor *heterun* exclusively reflects an idea of literacy or textuality, but instead they both refer to sonic and rhetorical bonds spoken ("sægde") by the cryptic sound of the iceberg. These bonds, by extension, correspond with the opacity of the riddle itself as it lures in the minds of its listeners and readers yet resists interpretation.

  The riddles of early medieval England—from those of the Exeter Book to those in the Latin collections to those in the Old English *Apollonius of Tyre*—at once demonstrate the human desire to control, possess, keep, and hold onto our secrets, but they also open that control up to hermeneutic manipulation. The frequently inverted images of binding and loosing and of servitude and mastery map onto the riddles themselves (such as we see in *Riddle* 42 when considered in light of the references to power, servitude, keys, and fetters that surround it): these riddles and their modes of concealment are reimagined as bound possessions, treasure, and servants. In announcing their concealment as a form of bondage, riddles thus lure their readers with an implicit request to be solved, to be loosed, to be unbound, to be released—a request that, if we take the content of the riddles at face value, will only further entangle the reader in their bonds. Hence, the "werum æt wine" (men at wine) to whom the riddle of the cock and hen has been made unsecret in the concluding lines of *Riddle* 42 become woven into the riddle itself, as the two copulating creatures play among us ("mid us"). And in a more violent rendition, the iceberg of *Riddle* 33 binds those who hear her hateful enigma, seafarers who will die at sea and be bound by its depths. These inversions suggest that solving a riddle is in fact not just an act of unbinding but often an act of rebinding as well, for the riddles demand of their readers more than a simple solution, sometimes even requiring the reader to participate in the text's own bonds of secrecy just as a servant or *rædbora* participates in the secrecy of his lord, faithfully protecting (*seruare*) and guarding (*healdan*) it. Indeed, when reading a riddle, one must hold together (*seruare, healdan*) all of the individual pieces and paradoxes in order for it to make sense as a whole.[106] As the plow serves the master who in turn serves the plow, or as the chain binds and unbinds while remaining bound to itself, riddles, too, explore the variety of ways in which human thought and textuality can unbind and bind. But in doing so, the riddles challenge the notion that one can fully possess control over one's secrets, which—so long as they are bound to language—are always open to interpretation and unlocking.

Chapter 7

Worldly Concealment, Divine Knowledge, and the Hermeneutics of Faith

The riddles of early medieval England introduce a way of reading that both reflects and challenges the logic of secrecy discussed in the foregoing pages. As we have seen in the previous chapter, many Anglo-Saxon riddles demonstrate a preoccupation with images of servitude and binding, which become entangled in the very process of unbinding and solving the riddles themselves. Accordingly, the secrecy of some riddles was imagined as a form of servile possession in which textual secrets are at once publicly, even playfully, announced, yet encrypted and guarded in a master-servant relationship that is necessarily weak in the face of hermeneutic pressure; this metaphor of servitude also, as we have seen, corresponds with the mind's limited capacity to possess and retain mastership over its secrets. But then other riddles come to fall within a larger and more profound master-servant relationship, not just between reader and riddle, as it were, but between the reader and God: between the reader of secrets and the knower of all secrets. This relationship between reader, poet, and God—mediated through the text of a riddle—fundamentally challenges the way that such texts can be read.

Some riddles, particularly in the Anglo-Latin tradition surrounding Aldhelm's *Aenigmata*, serve as didactic tools that give the reader an opportunity to encounter and reflect on the mysteriousness of God's Creation in a new and more accessible form, yet in a form that is still linguistically encrypted and obscured. Through their encrypted representations of a variety of creatures, objects, and natural phenomena—together broadly constituting the things (*res*) created by God and falling under his dominion—these riddles thus train the reader to approach the enigmas of scripture and stage the difficulty of interpreting the mysteries of Creation. In the process, some specimens of the genre (a genre as diverse as it is vast) illustrate a deep concern over the role of God's knowledge in the encryption and interpretation of texts. And although, as we will see, some Anglo-Saxon readers failed to appreciate this concern, it is a concern that ultimately draws on the Anglo-Saxon ethics of secrecy that

I have charted in the first half of this book. If an acknowledgment of God's omniscience is what distinguishes a moral mode of secrecy from a sinful one, as I have argued, then monastic texts such as these *aenigmata* (which challenge the reader to discover the secrets that they at once announce and conceal) must begin from a standpoint that no matter how complex the paradox or dense the linguistic veil, God already knows the solution. Reading these and other enigmatic texts—whether the poetry and signatures of Cynewulf or the objects of scriptural exegesis—often thus requires and inspires some combination of both intellectual acumen and faith.

The Hermeneutics of Force and the Hermeneutics of Faith in Cynewulf's *Elene*

It will be helpful to begin first with a poem that is, strictly speaking, not a riddle. In recounting the story of Saint Helena's search for the True Cross, Cynewulf's *Elene* is certainly more hagiographic than enigmatic, but it is nevertheless a poem deeply concerned with the loss and recovery of knowledge in the way it posits the necessary limitations to human acts of concealment and discovery, registering these limitations alongside the epistemological mechanics of divinity and belief. This concern emerges primarily within the narrative of the poem but ultimately culminates in the runic signature of Cynewulf's epilogue: where these literary domains overlap, the poem invites us to think about how an Anglo-Saxon ethics of secrecy (which often manifests itself in hagiography, including *Elene*) might also inform the interpretation of not just riddles but any text that claims title (even unavowedly) to some degree of linguistically or spiritually hidden meaning and thereby elicits attempts at decryption and interpretation.

We tend to think of the Cross as the central figure of Cynewulf's poem, perhaps because it offers thematic continuity between *Elene* and *The Dream of the Rood* in the Vercelli Book, or perhaps because the Cross carries such weighty symbolism and yet evades discovery for so much of the poem. Its concealment draws our attention to it, just as it draws attention from Constantine, Elene, and everyone else on the mission to find it.[1] It must be exhumed from beneath layers of concealment, both geological and psychological, under which it has long been hidden ("lange behyded") and concealed ("lange bedyrned").[2] In part, this concealment is sustained by the soil. Three times the Cross is described as "holy under the earth" ("halig under hrusan").[3] It is also "þurh feondes searu foldan getyned, / lange legere fæst leodum dyrne" (enclosed in the earth through the cunning of the enemy, resting fast for a long time, secret from the people).[4] The earth, in other words, is the physical barrier that conceals the Cross not only from the Christians who seek it but also from the Jews who are responsible for hiding it in the first place. Moreover, the soil profoundly becomes a "foldgræfe" (earthen grave) for the Cross, which had previously been "foldan begræfen" (buried in the earth).[5] This grave further conveys the kind of absolute secrecy associated with death, which we have already seen in a variety of other contexts and which is only penetrable with the assistance of God—an event that will eventually be fulfilled at the climax of the poem.[6]

Along the way, the soil's power of concealment is fortified by the poem's portrayal of a very deliberate secrecy on the part of the Jews. In part, the Jewish secrecy is passive; it is the faded generational memory of the crucifixion, a secret to the Jews for whom knowledge of spiritual mysteries is veiled and long forgotten by the time Elene begins her inquiries. The wise men interrogated by Elene may have access to a deeper knowledge of God's mysteries ("þa ðe deoplicost dryhtnes *geryno*") and may be able to interpret those mysteries through the Old Testament and the Law of Moses ("Moyses æ reccan cuðon").[7] But their proximity to the Law, as Elene comes to realize, necessitates a strictly literal comprehension of it that remains incomplete from the perspective of the New Testament and the Christian faith. And yet, while the Cross is passively concealed from the Jews, it is also actively concealed by the one Jew who happens to know anything about it. Having learned of the crucifixion from his father in a secret dialogue ("leoðorune"),[8] Judas shares this knowledge with his companions and insists on maintaining the secret in response to Elene's questioning:

          Nu is þearf mycel
þæt we fæstlice   ferhð staðelien,
þæt we ðæs morðres   meldan ne weorðen
hwær þæt halige trio   beheled wurde
æfter wigþræce.[9]   430

[Now there is great need that we firmly brace our spirits so that we do not become informants of that murder or as to where that holy tree was concealed after that act of violence.]

Judas pitches his deliberate choice to conceal his knowledge with a combination of rhetoric that—in the contexts we have already seen—would be futile. The notion of "fæstlice ferhð staðelien" (firmly bracing our spirits), for example, may be possible for saints, who frequently embody spiritual fortitude, but such efforts to restrain or possess one's concealed knowledge typically fail. And Cynewulf's choice of the word *melda* reflects the legal role of an informant who, in fact, has little agency over the act of distributing information, as it is typically applied to slaves whose testimony is restricted or to inanimate objects that might announce or reveal a crime in some way (e.g., a bell or an axe).[10] In *Elene*, Judas's outwardly strong rhetoric subtly anticipates the underlying weakness of his secrecy. Indeed, this rhetoric is so strong that it provokes Judas's companions to acknowledge the rarity of the secret:

> Næfre we hyrdon   hæleð ænigne
> on þysse þeode,   butan þec nu ða,
> þegn oðerne   þyslic cyðan   540
> ymb swa dygle wyrd.[11]

[We have never heard any man within this nation, except you just now, nor any other attendant speak out in this way about an event so secret.]

At first, they agree to stand with Judas in guarding the secret, even going so far as to resemble the very earth that conceals the Cross, for they are "stearce" (unyielding) and "stane heardran" (harder than stone) in their desire to conceal that "geryne" (secret).[12] Yet despite their fortitude, Judas's companions ultimately hand him over to Elene as the one who can "onwreon wyrda geryno" (uncover the mystery of those events).[13]

The sepulchral soil, the forgotten Jewish memories, and Judas's deliberate secrecy: these are the layers of concealment that Elene encounters in her search for the Cross. Her approach is aggressive and interrogative, framed from the start as a military expedition led over sea and land by the "guð-cwen" (war-queen).[14] This militancy informs her techniques in both seeking the Cross and interrogating the Jews.[15] In proposing the journey, Constantine thus commands that his mother

> feran foldwege   folca þreate   215
> to Iudeum,   *georne secan*
> wigena þreate   hwær se wuldres beam,
> halig under hrusan,   hyded wære.[16]

[travel the road to the Jews, with a band of people, a retinue of soldiers, *eagerly to seek* where the tree of glory had been hidden, holy under the earth.]

The eagerness of Elene's search crops up frequently with the phrase *georne secan* (eagerly seek), a mode of searching that she exclusively directs toward the discovery of the Cross. As she begins interrogating the Jews, she moves through three progressively smaller groups of progressively wiser men. With each group, her questioning leaves little room for them to speak or respond. Instead, she ends her speech to the first group with threats of condemnation and sends them off to find a more knowledgeable group, "þa me soðlice secgan cunnon, / ondsware cyðan . . . þe ic him to *sece*" (who can truly tell me, reveal the answer . . . the answer I *seek* from them).[17] This group obediently goes off, reenacting Elene's eager mode of searching:

>   *georne sohton*
> þa wisestan   wordgeryno,
> þæt hio þære cwene   oncweðan meahton
> swa tiles swa trages, swa hio him to *sohte*.[18]   325

[they *eagerly sought* those wisest in word-secrets so that they might answer the queen, for better or worse, as she *sought* from them.]

When this second, slightly wiser group arrives, Elene harangues them for their crime, allows a brief response, and then once again orders them to retrieve a wiser group:

>   Ge nu hraðe gangað,
> sundor *asecaþ*   þa ðe snyttro mid eow,
> mægn ond modcræft,   mæste hæbben,
> þæt me þinga gehwylc þriste gecyðan,
> untraglice,   þe ic him to *sece*.[19]   410

[Go now quickly, separately *seek out* those who are wise among you, who have the most strength and wisdom, so that they might boldly reveal to me, with truth, that which I *seek* from them.]

Instead of rushing off to carry out Elene's search (doubly emphasized: "asecaþ" and "sece"), this group "*georne* smeadon" (*eagerly* considered) and "*sohton* searoþancum" (*sought* with cunning thoughts) what sin and crime could possibly be motivating the queen's accusation.[20] In this subtle rhetorical shift, we begin to see a break from Elene's eager search (*georne secan*) directed toward finding the Cross, as the Jews instead eventually turn to reflect and seek wisdom within themselves.

The Jews can then begin to mount resistance once Judas announces that "Ic wat geare / þæt hio wile *secan*" (I well know what she wishes to *seek*).[21] And with this knowledge, Judas leads the Jews in their decision to conceal the secret from Elene even though it is precisely what she seeks. The tension between the collective secret and Elene's search peaks as the Jews try to remain "stane heardran" in the face of her interrogation, refusing to answer her about "þæs hio him to *sohte*" (that which she *sought* from them).[22] The narrative intensity of Elene's quest for the Cross needs little rhetorical reinforcement, yet Cynewulf's repeated use of the word *secan* conveys the persistent direction of her search and the aggressive force of her interrogations.

Elene's method intensifies still further. To the final group of Jews—now privy to the secret of the crucifixion and vowing to support Judas in concealing it—she threatens death by fire and conveys the futility of concealing something so powerful: "ne magon ge þa wyrd bemiðan, / bedyrnan þa deopan mihte" (you cannot cover over that event, conceal that deep power).[23] The threat—a show of force and a claim of command over the secret—is enough for the group to hand over Judas: "he þe mæg soð gecyðan / onwreon wyrda geryno" (he can reveal the truth to you, uncover the mystery of those events).[24] She then takes Judas as her sole prisoner and eagerly ("georne") interrogates him about the Cross, giving him a choice between life and death. Judas confesses the limits of his knowledge: "Ic ne can þæt ic nat, / findan on fyrhðe þæt swa fyrn gewearð" (I cannot find in my heart that which I do not know, what happened so long ago).[25] In other words, he may know *about* the crucifixion from some generational distance, but he has no way of knowing *where* precisely the Cross lies hidden. Elene rebuffs his answer, insisting that he "scealt geagninga / wisdom onwreon" (must uncover the wisdom completely).[26] But this is no longer willful concealment on the part of Judas; it is a lack of knowledge. And it is at this point—as Elene repeatedly demands that Judas make known the truth (e.g., "soð gecyðe") and Judas repeatedly denies knowledge (e.g., "ne can")—that Elene's aggressive search begins to reach its limits, notably, with little gained beyond the knowledge she already had when she first arrived in Jerusalem.[27]

It is also at this point that the nature of Judas's secret begins to change. Whereas formerly he had committed to keeping the secret and compelled his comrades to do the same ("fæstlice ferhð staðelien"), he now as a result finds himself imprisoned in a dry pit and bound with fetters ("clommum beclungen").[28] Not only is he bound by the secret he tried to conceal (much like the similar situations explored in Chapters 3 and 6 of this book), but his physical imprisonment beneath the surface of the ground puts him in much the same situation as the Cross, "foldan getyned, / lange legere fæst leodum dyrne" (enclosed in the earth, long fast in its bed, secret from the people).[29] After Judas endures seven days of captivity and starvation, it is perhaps this grave-like proximity to the secret of the Cross (what Elene previously refers to as the "deopan mihte") along with the solitary separation from the very people who were once his companions that puts Judas in the unique position to confess that he can no longer hide ("helan") the Tree of Life.[30]

We might classify Elene's methods so far as a hermeneutic of force. In some ways, her methods have been effective: she is able to interpret the secret words ("wordgeryno") of the prophets, which in turn gives her the tools to interrogate the Jews, claim ownership over their secret, and threaten them for their knowledge.[31] This is a hermeneutic directed outward, a mode of seeking what is hidden outside of oneself. It partly works: she is able to find Judas, for instance, who otherwise would have had little reason to appear, let alone disclose his knowledge of the crucifixion. But its success is limited.[32] For although she gets Judas to admit his knowledge, he still cannot locate the Cross itself, which, after all, is what she seeks. If the power to conceal in the face of hermeneutic pressure is limited and weak (as the Jews learn through their encounters with Elene), then so, too, is the power to discover by force.

When Elene's forceful hermeneutic hits its limits, it is ultimately Judas's hermeneutic of faith (by contrast) that leads to the discovery of the Cross. To be sure, a hermeneutic of faith can be taken to mean different things. The phrase evokes Paul Ricoeur's argument contrasting the demystifying hermeneutics of Freud and other members of the so-called school of suspicion (e.g., Marx and Nietzsche) with a kind of restorative hermeneutics or hermeneutics of the sacred. This restorative hermeneutics prioritizes faith in an effort to restore meaning and arises from the possibility, in Ricoeur's words, of "an Anselmian type of procedure, i.e., the movement from faith to understanding," the Anselmian aspect of which we will examine more closely below.[33] Here is how Ricoeur puts it:

> The contrary of suspicion, I will say bluntly, is faith. What faith? No longer, to be sure, the first faith of the simple soul, but rather the second faith of one who has engaged in hermeneutics, faith that has undergone criticism, postcritical faith. Let us look for it in the series of philosophic decisions that secretly animate a phenomenology of religion and lie hidden even within its apparent neutrality. It is a rational faith, for it interprets; but it is a faith because it seeks, through interpretation, a second naïveté. . . . "Believe in order to understand, understand in order to believe"—such is its maxim; and its maxim is the hermeneutic circle itself of believing and understanding.[34]

By coupling his hermeneutics to the work of belief, Ricoeur is drawing on not only the precedent set by Hans-Georg Gadamer but also a rich history of medieval thinking on the epistemology of interpretation.[35] The point, then, is that there is a spectrum of faith, from the more religious or sacred forms of faith on the one hand to the more pragmatic or "postcritical" forms of faith on the other, and that therefore one can find a dimension of restoration, faith, and the sacred even in the hermeneutics of, say, Freud; the two modes of reading—the faithful and the forceful—are not finally or fully dissociable. Ultimately, for Ricoeur and Gadamer, respectively, faith and prejudice need not always interfere with rational understanding but instead often complement it.

In the particular context of Cynewulf's *Elene*, this hermeneutic of faith first appears on the more religious end of the spectrum when it arises midway through the poem. Coming to recognize that God is in fact the only one who knows and can reveal the precise location, Judas says a prayer—although in Hebrew, it is directed to a distinctly Christian God—asking that God open ("geopenie") the gold hoard that has long been hidden ("lange behyded").[36] Obviously, this prayer signals Judas's conversion, a pivotal moment in the poem's narrative and, like any conversion, one that entails a shift in faith.[37] He thus ends his prayer with a commitment to belief:

> Ic gelyfe þe sel 795
> ond þy *fæstlicor* *ferhð staðelige*,
> hyht untweondne, on þone ahangnan Crist,
> þæt he sie soðlice sawla nergend,
> ece ælmihtig, Israhela cining,
> walde widan ferhð wuldres on heofenum, 800
> a butan ende ecra gestealda.[38]

[I (will) believe in you better and I *(will) more firmly brace my heart*, my unfaltering hope, on the crucified Christ, that he is truly the savior of souls, the eternal and almighty king of the Israelites, ruling for all time the eternal abodes of glory in the heavens without end.]

Here Judas's earlier attempt to brace his spirit firmly against Elene's interrogations ("fæstlice ferhð staðelien") shifts into a proper and greater Christian mode of spiritual steadfastness ("fæstlicor ferhð staðelige"), in which rather than embracing a secret, he even more firmly embraces God. The nearly identical language is striking, and it suggests a profound tension between the role of faith (such as the faith eventually embraced by Judas) and the desire for knowledge (such as the desire that previously guided Elene's search for the Cross). Translators of this passage often use the future tense ("I *will* believe in you better") to suggest that Judas's belief is conditional on God's revelation of the Cross.[39] And scholars such as Christina M. Heckman have made compelling arguments that, for example, the dialectal exchange between Elene and Judas uses knowledge and proof as a catalyst for converting doubt into belief.[40] The grammar of these lines certainly allows for this possibility, but its ambiguity invites the opposite reading just as easily: remove the futurity and conditionality, and it is Judas's better belief and more steadfast spirit that prompt God to reveal the Cross. The knowledge and proof produced by that revelation then only reaffirm his preexisting faith. Again, both readings are possible, and that is Cynewulf's brilliant way of elucidating an important theological tension between knowledge and belief, which we will consider more thoroughly in the next section of this chapter. Whether Judas needs to see the Cross in order to believe or needs to believe in order to discover the Cross, the two seem to occur almost simultaneously (especially by contrast to Elene's protracted interrogations) and ultimately coalesce into a stronger form of faith.[41]

In response to Judas's prayer, God immediately reveals the location of the Cross with a stream of smoke, and from Judas's perspective the event delivers knowledge, certainty, and proof. He declares about God the savior, "nu ic þurh soð hafu seolf gecnawen" (now through truth I myself have known).[42] What should be a straightforward exclamation of praise turns into a convoluted juxtaposition of truth ("soð") and knowledge ("gecnawen") and past ("hafu") and present ("nu"). The ambiguous temporality suggests that once a belief has been confirmed as knowledge (e.g., by the revelation of the Cross), it begins to look more like proven knowledge all along. But there is still a distinction, as Judas says a few lines later, "nu ic wat þæt ðu eart / gecyðed and acenned allra cyninga þrym" (now I know that you are the known and begotten glory of all kings).[43] The revelation of the Cross has confirmed his knowledge, but it is now distinctly knowledge of the known rather than belief in the unknown.

Elene sees it the other way around, as she marvels at "hu he swa geleafful on swa lytlum fæce / ond swa uncyðig æfre wurde" (how he, in so little time and once so ignorant, could ever become so faithful).[44] If Elene is surprised that ignorance can give way to faith, that is to be expected given her persistent quest for knowledge. But it is at this moment that the poem's attention transitions from the search for knowledge to the search for deeper faith. In other words, faith is what allows Judas to gain the knowledge that subsequently further enriches his faith. At his eventual baptism, for example, "his geleafa wearð / fæst on ferhðe" (his belief became firm in his spirit),[45] a phrase that again recalls his former attempt to keep his knowledge secret by "fæstlice ferhð staðelien" (firmly bracing his spirit): now his *ferhð* embraces no longer a secret but rather belief itself. So when Elene decides that she would like to find the nails that fastened Christ to the Cross, which are still "deope bedolfen dierne sindon, / heolstre behyded" (deeply and secretly buried and hidden in darkness), a "hord under hrusan þæt gehyded gen, / duguðum dyrne, deogol" (a hoard under the earth, that remains hidden, secret, concealed from the multitudes), the hermeneutic tactics undergo a significant shift.[46] The nails are concealed much like the Cross and Elene's request is still quite bold ("bald"), but this time around she asks Judas to petition God with "eallum eaðmedum" (all humility) and Judas immediately does so with "eallum eaðmedum."[47]

This shift toward humility is complemented by a shift in the eagerness with which the search is carried out. Whereas the word *georne* in the first half of the poem often describes Elene's eagerness in seeking the Cross, here Judas eagerly and humbly opens up to God's knowledge: "*geornlice* . . . hleor onhylde, hygerune ne mað" (*eagerly* bowed his head, did not conceal the secret of his heart).[48] And once the nails are found, Elene follows suit, no longer directing her eager search toward knowledge but instead toward her own spiritual piety and faith:

> Ongan þa *geornlice*   gastgerynum
> on sefan *secean*   soðfæstnesse
> weg to wuldre.[49]

[She then, through spiritual mysteries and with faithfulness, *eagerly* began *to seek* the road to glory in her heart.]

And then when she wonders how she might use the nails, she begins eagerly to seek ("georne secan") the will of the Lord ("Dryhtnes willa") and asks the advice of a wise man who might readily know ("*georne* cuðe") what to do.[50] This wise man praises Elene for the way she "holds the word of the Lord, the holy secrets, in her thoughts" ("Dryhtnes word / on hyge healde, halige rune") and, moreover, for the way she "*georne* begange" (eagerly observes) God's requests.[51] The shift is subtle, to be sure, but Cynewulf signals it here by repeatedly invoking the word *georne* (several times alongside *secan*) to describe a radically different approach to the uncovering of hidden meaning and spiritual mysteries.[52]

As Cynewulf orchestrates the tension between these two forms of interpretation—between a hermeneutic of force and a hermeneutic of faith in the narrative of the poem—he invites readers to reflect on their place in other encounters with hidden meaning. As the only Old English poet to hide a runic trace of his identity in his poems, Cynewulf is particularly concerned with the way hidden meaning operates in textual forms of concealment. Indeed, numerous scholars have drawn a variety of similar connections between the narrative of the poem and Cynewulf's textuality: Heckman, for instance, has shown us how the search for knowledge in the poem corresponds to practices of scriptural interpretation in which the Cross and Christianity are fundamentally at odds with Jewish secrecy and tend toward openness; Stacy Klein has demonstrated how Elene's rewriting of history and her interpretive strategies "destabilize any attempt to read the poem's depictions of social and spiritual hierarchy as straightforwardly prescriptive," calling into question "any unequivocal interpretation of a text" and insisting that "characters and events are polysemous"; R. W. V. Elliott drew out thematic connections between Cynewulf's narratives and his signatures; and Martin Irvine has suggested that Elene's search corresponds to the textual hermeneutics and *grammatica* of broader medieval reading practices.[53] Irvine even argues that as the Jews in the narrative lack the codes for properly interpreting the significance of the Cross, the narrative of discovery in the poem is "parallel to interpreting the hidden meaning of an enigma which depends on a code and set of encyclopedic correspondences."[54] These are each compelling and important readings of the poem, for they speak to an epistemological connection between narrative and textuality. To them, however, I would add that the way force and faith entwine in the hermeneutic tensions of the narrative is central to Cynewulf's hermeneutic enterprise.

Cynewulf thus begins his epilogue by describing the process by which he gained the knowledge necessary to compose the poem:

>   Nysse ic gearwe
> be ðære rode riht   ær me rumran geþeaht   1240
> þurh ða mæran miht   on modes þeaht
> wisdom onwreah.[55]

[I did not readily know the truth about the Cross before wisdom, through its powerful virtue, revealed a more expansive understanding to me in the thought of my mind.]

A signature feature of Cynewulf's style, the eccentric and playful rhyming of this passage belies a much more serious reflection on the relationship between wisdom and understanding. Knowledge of the Cross is preceded by the uncovering of wisdom, in which *wisdom* is the subject acting on Cynewulf's mind and opening it up to understanding. This process is inverted earlier in the narrative of the poem, when Elene threatens Judas with death if he does not "wisdom onwreah" (reveal the wisdom). Although identical to the half-line in Cynewulf's epilogue, the context of Elene's command ("wisdom onwreah") reflects her more forceful hermeneutic approach: she expects Judas to reveal his wisdom (*wisdom* is the grammatical object), whereas Cynewulf attributes his understanding to wisdom's capacity to reveal knowledge in the mind of one seeking truth (where *wisdom* is, by contrast, the grammatical subject). Both Cynewulf and Elene have essentially the same goal: to learn the truth about the Cross. But their approaches differ radically.

The revelation of wisdom in both cases is predicated on a shift from sinful physicality to spiritual faith. For Elene's discovery of the Cross, this shift corresponds with Judas's conversion, which replaces a physical search with a prayer to God that opens up the ground where the Cross is buried. For Cynewulf, this shift entails breaking the physical bonds of sin, receiving a gift of knowledge from God, and thereby opening up his mind to poetic expression:

> Ic wæs weorcum fah,
> synnum asæled,   sorgum gewæled,
> bitrum gebunden,   bisgum beþrungen,
> ær me lare onlag   þurh leohtne had   1245
> gamelum to geoce,   gife unscynde
> mægencyning amæt   ond on gemynd begeat,
> torht ontynde,   tidum gerymde,
> bancofan onband,   breostlocan onwand,
> leoðucræft onleac.[56]   1250

[I was stained by deeds, shackled by sins, overwhelmed by sorrows, bound and oppressed by bitter afflictions, before the mighty king gave me learning in a light manner as a comfort for my old age; he meted out the undefiled gift and placed it in my mind, revealed its brightness and sometimes enlarged it, unbound my bone-coffer, unwound my breast-locker, unlocked my poetic skill.]

What stands between Cynewulf's fettered state of bodily sin and his unlocked spiritual expression of knowledge is, of course, God's gift of learning and wisdom.[57] That gift parallels the moment of Judas's conversion as it occasions his release from the physical confines of his prison and the eventual uncovering of the Cross. But if Cynewulf presents his own acquisition of knowledge as a faithful process of unbinding, then what are we to make of his runic signature, which seems to conclude the poem with a far more trivial and ludic form of concealment?

The runes at the end of *Elene*, like those at the end of Cynewulf's other poems, not only conceal the poet's name (a discovery we now take for granted) but also create a more challenging puzzle by representing individual words that must fit into the poem's syntax.[58] Taking the runes for the words they typically represent has frustrated scholars and sparked creative interpretations. Wrestling with phrases such as "·ᚳ· drusende" and "·ᚣ· gnornode" has typically resulted in variations of a torch (*cen*) that falters and bow (*yr*) that mourns, solutions that require gymnastic justifications.[59] Indeed, the latter escaped sense until John D. Niles proposed an altogether different way of reading the runes in Cynewulf's epilogues, arguing that the techniques of encryption vary and rarely correspond to the typical meaning of the runes.⁶⁰ Niles shows, for instance, how in *Christ II* the runic letters merely serve as initialisms pointing the reader to particular Old English words (other than the typical rune names) that elegantly fit into the sense, grammar, and meter of the passage. The runes in *Elene* are more opaque, but Niles offers compelling solutions to these, too. In the case of the two given above, Niles argues that ᚳ (*cen*) could be taken as *cenþu* (courage, boldness, bold spirits), thus "his courage (*cenþu*) had been faltering;" ᚣ (*yr*) could be taken as the adverb *yfele* (grievously), thus "he had been grievously lamenting."⁶¹ What the work by Niles and his predecessors has demonstrated is that solving Cynewulf's runic puzzles requires a tremendous amount of ingenuity, creativity, and persistence: these are the intellectual skills required to move knowledge forward and uncover the meaning Cynewulf has hidden in his signature.

It could even be said that Elene's persistent and forceful hermeneutics offer a model for the reader who wishes to uncover precisely the kind of hidden knowledge found in Cynewulf's signature, which is concealed on a spectrum across textual, linguistic, and physical meaning. Such force can be seen in almost every scholarly attempt at solving the enigma of Cynewulf's runes, whether Thomas Hill's argument that life is often compared to a flickering torch in medieval sapiential literature or R. W. V. Elliott's suggestion that ᚣ is a sensible representation of *yr* (bow) on account of the poem's martial theme.⁶² The runes of Cynewulf's signature are a secret necessarily bound to language and therefore always interpretable through human reason. Indeed, as Victoria Symons has argued, the runes serve "to explore the material nature of the written word . . . and to remind readers of the necessity of correctly interpreting what is read."⁶³ But the forceful hermeneutics they seem to recommend are nevertheless ensconced within Cynewulf's prayers for salvation and a spiritual reflection that more closely aligns with Judas's conversion to a hermeneutic of faith in the way it looks inward to seek God than it does with Elene's hermeneutic of force. The spirituality of Cynewulf's epilogue, in other words, appears to invite a meditative reading practice at odds with those ludic puzzles that have captured the attention of so many readers.⁶⁴ But their relation to faith is more complex. On the one hand, solving these puzzles either distracts from the content of Cynewulf's spiritual reflection or gives the reader fuller access to it, allowing the reader to move beyond textual frustration and toward prayer.

If the narrative of the poem says anything about these two approaches, however, it is to point out their respective limits. Elene may ultimately succeed—she tortures the Jews to the point of breaking their secret and then tortures Judas to the point of breaking his, culminating in his prayer to God and God's exposing of the secret location. But her force alone cannot bring about the discovery of the Cross, nor could Judas's faith alone have done so if it were not for Elene's initial exertion of force. Cynewulf's characteristic signature, then, is thus a final gesture toward the importance of concealment as a tool for producing belief and the importance of belief in producing an epistemology that in turn magnifies faith.

Enigmatic Didacticism and the Enigmas of Scripture

Much like Cynewulf's runic signature, riddles tend to engage the reader in an exchange that is both didactic and playful.[65] For example, as a primary source of inspiration for Anglo-Saxon poets, Symphosius's *Aenigmata* is a collection of Latin riddles framed by lighthearted playfulness, and his preface describes the entertainment and amusement offered by the riddles—so-called *nugae* (trifles)—amid the festively intoxicated circumstances of their creation.[66] It is well known that Aldhelm used Symphosius as a model for his own *Aenigmata*. In fact, Aldhelm even praises his predecessor's metrical skill: "Simfosius poeta, uersificus metricae artis peritia praeditus, occultas enigmatum propositiones exili materia sumpta ludibundis apicibus legitur cecinisse et singulas quasque propositionum formulas tribus uersiculis terminasse" (Symphosius, the poet, the versifier endowed with knowledge of metrical art, is said to have sung the secret propositions of riddles on humble subjects in a playful style and to have restricted the form of each proposition to three verse lines).[67] But despite his acknowledgment of Symphosius, Aldhelm uses the opportunity of Symphosius's playful style—literally, his playful letters ("ludibundis apicibus")—in order to distinguish his own *Aenigmata* as a more serious tool for instruction.

Riddling, as Michael Lapidge puts it, is "an encapsulation of the learning process," and Aldhelm's endeavor to push the genre even further in that direction is well recognized.[68] For Andy Orchard, it is thus "the heavily didactic element which Aldhelm first introduced to the Latin *Enigmata,* and which was to prove his lasting legacy, since an element of the classroom influences all subsequent Anglo-Latin poets in the genre."[69] The fact that the collections of *aenigmata* tended to circulate in manuscripts containing other pedagogical texts such as the *Disticha Catonis* and Prosper of Aquitaine's *Epigrammata* further evidences their role in programs of monastic education.[70] Early library catalogs from Anglo-Saxon centers in Germany suggest *aenigmata* also circulated alongside metrical and grammatical treatises. And as Leslie Lockett has shown, these treatises had a profound and bidirectional effect on the content of the *aenigmata*, and by extension, the ideas contained within the *aenigmata* had a corresponding effect on the impressionable minds of young Anglo-Saxon students.[71]

Aldhelm's *Aenigmata* not only trains the reader in disciplines like the metrical arts;[72] it also offers important preparation for the interpretation and understanding of scripture, as scholars have thoroughly demonstrated.[73] Just as learning grammar, for example, gave students a foundation for reading the Bible, learning the mechanics of a riddle would teach more advanced students skills for interpreting the enigmas of scripture. *Aenigma* is a term that appears throughout biblical commentaries and shows up nine times in the Bible itself: from the "enigmata" of wise men (Prov. 1:6) to the "enigmata" that Job speaks before his companions (Job 13:17) to Ezekiel's presentation of an "enigma" to the Israelites (Ez. 17:2).[74] The frequent use of the term in biblical commentaries arises from the fact that in scripture words and things often symbolize or refer to concepts and objects other than themselves. Augustine refers to these as "aenigmata scripturarum," a category that includes linguistic details (of Hebrew words, for instance) as well as the qualities of things (such as stones and animals), knowledge of which is essential for understanding the figurative significance of any given scriptural passage.[75] A word or thing can always refer to something other than itself. A dove, for instance, is thus not merely a dove but the Holy Spirit (Luke 3:22). Or to take an example from Cassiodorus (d. ca. 585), the fire (*ignem*), lightning (*fulgura*), mountains (*montes*), and heavens (*caelos*) in Psalm 96 signify the Lord in a "schema dicitur aenigma, id est obscura sententia, quando aliud dicit et aliud uult intellegi" (scheme called *aenigma*, that is an obscure sentence, when someone says one thing and wishes another thing to be understood).[76] Cassiodorus's logic not only describes a common biblical trope; it also underlies the mechanics of early medieval riddles.

In his widely circulated definition of *aenigma*, Donatus (fl. 350) describes the trope as an "obscura sententia per occultam similitudinem rerum" (a sentence that is made obscure by the hidden likeness between things).[77] Indeed, Cassiodorus probably derived his explanation from Donatus, who exemplifies the definition with a concise riddle: "mater me genuit, eadem mox gignitur ex me; aquam in glaciem concrescere et ex eadem rursus effluere" (my mother bore me, and soon was born from me; water solidifies into ice, and then flows back out of it).[78] This brief riddle finds its way verbatim into Aldhelm's prose prologue to his *Aenigmata*, and the definition as a whole shows up in a marginal gloss to the title at the head of Aldhelm's verse preface in London, British Library, Royal 12 C. xxiii.[79] Aldhelm and those reading his *Aenigmata*, particularly those reading it in a monastic setting, would have certainly been familiar with Donatus's definition, especially as it extended into the reading of scripture. Bede uses it even more directly than Cassiodorus, but in his *De schematibus et tropiis*, he changes the example from the pithy ice riddle to an extended and complex interpretation of Psalm 67:14.[80]

Such conceptual reciprocity between the enigmas of scripture and those of more humble sources (such as Donatus's popular ice riddle) is a principal justification for the composition and interpretation of riddles such as those that make up Aldhelm's *Aenigmata*. Aldhelm realized this virtue and, for instance, justified his use of prosopopoeia—in which the secret enigma and hidden meaning ("enigma clanculum et latens propositio") inverts the silent nature of insensible objects by making them speak and talk ("loqui et sermocinari fingitur")—by showing first and foremost that the device used throughout his *Aenigmata* has biblical precedent, as when trees anoint a king in the book of Judges (9:8).[81] Numerous other riddles, such as the biblical trivia found throughout versions of the *Ioca monachorum*, directly engage and rely on biblical obscurities and paradoxes: "Dic mihi quis primus obtulit holocaustum Deo? Abel; agnum" (Tell me, who first made an offering to God? Abel; a lamb).[82] And Tatwine's *Aenigma* 3 takes as its solution the four senses of scripture (historical, spiritual, moral, and allegorical), which together guard ("conseruare") the riches of their sister's treasury from ungrateful intruders.[83] Aldhelm's *aenigmata* are less overtly concerned with their relation to scripture; in fact, none of the *aenigmata* refers to exegetical methods or takes the form of straightforward biblical trivia. Instead, what we find is a series of reflections on the mysteries of things and the words that describe them.[84] And these mysteries or enigmas provide the reader with an opportunity to hone his or her interpretive skills, skills particularly useful for the interpretation of more sacred materials.

In Prosper of Aquitaine's *Epigrammata* (a popular text in Anglo-Saxon England, circulating in at least one manuscript alongside Aldhelm's *Aenigmata*),[85] young readers are encouraged to persevere in the face of difficult and obscure passages from scripture:

> Quamvis in sacris libris, quos nosse laboras,
>   plurima sint, lector, clausa et opaca tibi,
> invigilare tamen studio ne desine sancto:
>   exercent animum dona morata tuum.
> Gratior est fructus quem spes productior edit;
>   ultro objectorum vilius est pretium.
> Oblectent adoperta etiam mysteria mentem:
>   Qui dedit ut quaeras, addet ut invenias.[86]

[Reader, although in the sacred books that you labor to know there are many things that are hidden and opaque to you, nonetheless do not cease to be vigilant about your holy study. Moral gifts exercise your mind. The fruit that hope brings forth at length is more welcome: the price of things at hand is far cheaper. Likewise, may concealed mysteries delight the mind: may he, who has granted that you seek, also grant that you find.]⁸⁷

Obscurity is good, for it both requires and encourages diligent study, and such study in turn challenges and nourishes the student. And the importance of struggling with difficult texts to exercise the mind ("Exercent animum") is a point Prosper makes even more strongly in the accompanying *Sententia*: "Bonae sunt in Scripturis sanctis mysteriorum profunditates, quae ob hoc teguntur, ne uilescant, ob hoc quaeruntur, ut exerceant, ob hoc aperiuntur, ut pascant" (Good are the depths of mysteries in the Holy Scriptures, which are concealed lest they become worthless; which are sought so as to train; which are opened so as to nurture).⁸⁸ This *Sententia* is derived from Augustine's commentary on Psalm 140:1, but as Katherine O'Brien O'Keeffe has shown, in the context of Prosper's *Epigramma* it lends itself to novitiates by softening Augustine's otherwise severe point "that the difficult meanings of scriptures are veiled for a purpose—that they may challenge the reader to meditate—and they are laid open that they may nourish the persistent."⁸⁹ Augustine's justification of the obscurity of scripture focuses on the necessity of a balanced form of concealment that does not entirely hide, yet does not allow just anyone to trample over the sacred meaning.

This principle is extremely common in Christian exegesis. We have already seen, for example, how in Rufinus's translation of Origen's *In Numeros homiliae*, the sacred meanings of scripture are protected by the obscurity of words from the trampling feet of inexperienced readers.⁹⁰ Bede makes a similar point, echoing the sentiment and language of Prosper's *Sententia* in his *Explanatio Apocalypsis* when he commands: "Mysteria fidei christianae nec passim cunctis ostenta, ne uilescant, nec probis claude, ne in totum lateant" (Do not everywhere display the mysteries of the Christian faith to everyone, lest they become worthless and do not sequester them from upright persons, lest they lie totally hidden).⁹¹ And as Augustine recognized, this balanced form of concealment is the very definition of the trope known as *aenigma*: "Velamen quippe omnimodo intercludit aspectum, aenigma uero tamquam per speculum, sicut idem apostolus ait: *Videmus nunc per speculum in enigmate*, nec euidentissimam detegit speciem nec prorsus obtegit ueritatem" (Indeed, a veil entirely blocks vision; an enigma, as if through a mirror—like the Apostle says: "we see now through a glass in a dark manner"—does not uncover the most evident part, nor does it entirely cover the truth).⁹²

If the obscurities of scripture were understood to protect, first and foremost, sacred meaning from those uninitiated or otherwise profane readers, then the interpretation of those obscurities primarily depends on a reader's belief that those obscurities belong and point back to a Christian God who can resolve the obscurities for faithful readers, or if not resolve them then at least open them up to the rational, interpretive enterprises of a reader who possesses faith. These practical and spiritual approaches to interpretation are neither unrelated nor mutually exclusive; in fact, the former was often understood to rely on and follow the latter. But the relationship between them—between practical and spiritual hermeneutics, between a hermeneutic of force and a hermeneutic of faith—remained ambiguous and unstable throughout the early medieval period. In examining, for instance, the variance that O'Brien O'Keeffe noticed between Prosper's *Epigramma* and the accompanying *Sententia*, it becomes evident that Prosper emphasizes faith more than Augustine. While maintaining Augustine's notion that working through obscurities in scripture nurtures the mind, Prosper's *Epigramma* thus adds an emphasis on hope ("Gratior est fructus quem spes productior edit"), stressing that although the text may be difficult, God will provide understanding to those who seek it: "Qui dedit ut quaeras, addet ut invenias" (may he, who has granted that you seek, also grant that you find).[93] Like the search for the Cross in *Elene*, interpreting the enigmas of scripture was thought, at the most basic and fundamental level, to require a degree of divine assistance.

Faith and Understanding

This interdependent relationship between faith and understanding runs deep in early Christian theology. Augustine, for example, repeatedly posits an opposition between *fides*, on the one hand, and *intellectus* and *ratio*, on the other, treating the former as a necessary prerequisite for obtaining the higher goal of the latter. He addresses this relationship most directly in his *Epistola ad Consentium*, where he responds to Consentius's claim that truth is to be grasped by faith rather than by reason. In the *Epistola*, Augustine argues that while faith must precede reason ("fides antecedat rationem"), the search for rational understanding is still of utmost importance; because God made nothing without reason and specifically gave humans the greatest rational capacity, the use of our minds in the pursuit of understanding must therefore be good.[94] However, Augustine is quick to explain—in a move we have seen before—that "quorundam mirabilium operum eius etiam expedit tantisper occultam esse rationem, ne apud animos fastidio languidos eiusdem rationis cognitione uilescant" (it is presently expedient for the cause of some of his [*scil.* God's] wondrous works to be hidden, lest, in the presence of our minds, weak with fastidiousness, they be cheapened by knowledge of that cause).[95] The process, therefore, of laboring toward an understanding of those mysteries previously accepted only by faith is an honorable endeavor:

porro autem qui uera ratione iam, quod tantum modo credebat, intellegit, profecto praeponendus est ei, qui cupit adhuc intellegere, quod credit; si autem nec cupit et ea, quae intellegenda sunt, credenda tantum modo existimat, cui rei fides prosit, ignorat.[96]

[Moreover, he who now understands by true reason what before he merely used to believe is certainly to be preferred over him who still desires to understand what he believes; but if he does not even desire to do so and thinks that they are to be understood by merely believing, then he is ignorant of that thing that faith serves.]

According to Henri de Lubac's analysis, Augustine tends here and elsewhere to understand this transition from *fides* to *intellectus* as a movement that corresponds to the passage, for instance, from the letter to the spirit or from the Old Testament to the New, as the reader moves into an enlightened state of understanding that comes out of an antecedent faithfulness.[97] In *Elene*, we have seen this transformation take place around Judas's conversion. And in Chapter 5, we learned how a similar kind of faith underlies the ethics of discovery; to seek out the secrets of God or to spy on the hidden actions of a saint demands a movement toward understanding that begins with faith rather than doubt. When the search for understanding is motivated by doubt—as, for instance, in the spy's attempt to test Saint Cuthbert by following him to the seashore—then the hermeneutic act of discovery becomes ethically illicit; if that act is carried out with indifference to God's omniscience, as such acts must necessarily be, then it would constitute an attempted inversion of God's role as the one who sees in secret. And the Augustinian movement from faith to understanding should sound especially familiar because we have already encountered a similar logic in the *Epigrammata* of Prosper of Aquitaine and the *Proslogion* of Anselm of Canterbury, who holds that the process of coming to understand God's mysteries must begin with faith and belief: "neque enim quæro intelligere ut credam, sed credo ut intelligam" (for I do not seek to understand in order that I might believe; rather I believe in order that I might understand).[98] But this logic, as we will see, not only governs attempts at rationalizing and understanding the divine but also reflects a more fundamental process of the human mind as it grapples with complex mysteries or wonders such as those we find in Anglo-Latin *aenigmata*.

We encounter this complex relationship between faith and understanding boiled down in the pseudo-Bedan *Collectanea*, where—alongside riddles and biblical trivia—a pithy extract from Gregory the Great asserts that "Diuinae autem uirtutis mysteria quae comprehendi non possunt, non intellectu discutienda sunt, sed fide ueneranda" (the mysteries of divine power which cannot be comprehended are not to be examined by the intellect, but to be venerated in faith).[99] The logic of this extract loosely resembles the argument proposed by Consentius and refuted by Augustine in the *Epistola* discussed above. That is to be expected, given Gregory's general inversion of Augustine's view: whereas Augustine holds faith as a channel for understanding, Gregory holds understanding as a channel for advancing one's faith.[100] Yet earlier in the *Collectanea*, one also finds the more Augustinian line of thought: "Fides intellectum aperit, infidelitas claudit" (Faith opens understanding, lack of faith closes it).[101] Augustinian in more than just sense, this statement is derived almost verbatim from Augustine's *Epistola* 137.[102] The *Collectanea* is always a good place to turn for diverse and conflicting kernels of wisdom, but these two brief examples demonstrate the particular liquidity of the conceptual relationship between faith and understanding. And in the *Collectanea*, that relationship is explored within a textual context designed to challenge both faith and understanding with its wealth of riddles and trivia. It demonstrates that regardless of whether an Augustinian or Gregorian theory of faith's relation to understanding prevails, and regardless of how accurately these complex views were understood by later readers (the *Old English Soliloquies* suggests that they had become somewhat muddled), the process of interpretation—especially in biblical exegesis, but also in literary methods as well—cannot be separated from an idea that faith is integral to the process of gaining understanding, and vice versa.

Faith and the Interpretation of Riddles

Alcuin of York directly applies these hermeneutic concepts to the playfully didactic task of solving riddles. During his time as an advisor to Charlemagne, he wrote his *Disputatio Pippini*, a short instructional dialogue with Charlemagne's son, Pippin. Like the pseudo-Bedan *Collectanea*, Alcuin's *Disputatio* intertwines wisdom dialogues ("What is a word?—The revealer of the mind") with curiosity dialogues (catechetical riddles based on the Bible such as, "who died and was never born?—Adam"), and concludes with a set of prose riddles or *mira* (wonders) (such as, "Who is it that can only see with his eyes closed? He who snores shows him to you").[103] In the catechetical buildup to Alcuin's culminating series of riddles, Pippin asks:

P. Quid est fides?—A. Ignotae rei et mirandę certitudo.
P. Quid est mirum?—A. Nuper vidi hominem stantem, molientem, ambulantem, qui numquam fuit.

P. Quomodo potest esse? pande mihi.—A. Imago est in aqua.
P. Cur hoc non intellexi per me, dum toties vidi hunc ipsum hominem?—A. Quia bone indolis es iuvenis et naturalis ingenii, proponam tibi quaedam alia mira; tempta si per te ipsum possis conicere illa.
P. Faciemus ita tamen, ut si secus quam est dicam, corriges me.—A. Faciam ut vis.[104]

[P. What is faith?—A. Certainty about something that is both unknown and wondrous.
P. What is a wonder?—A. Not long ago, I saw a man who never was, who stood, moved and walked.
P. How is this possible? Explain it to me.—A. It is an image in water.
P. Why did I not understand this myself, given that I have so often seen this very man?—A. Since you are a young man of good ability and natural intelligence, I shall set out for you some other wonders; see if you can figure them out yourself.
P. Let us do this, so long as you correct me if I make a mistake.—A. I shall do as you wish.]

The very definition of faith in this passage is bound to the *mira*, or wonders, exemplified by the riddles in the ensuing dialogue. Here, Alcuin presents Pippin with an example of such a *mirum*, which Pippin fails to understand and which Alcuin must explain. Once Alcuin has explained it, Pippin wonders why he failed to understand it in the first place, even though he knows that he has had the experience of seeing the very thing described in the riddle (a man whose image is reflected in water). This exchange demonstrates that the task of understanding a *mirum* is epistemologically different from the *certitudo* and *fides* that *mira* initially demand, and the *certitudo* and *fides* that Alcuin provides when he reveals (*pandere*) the solution to his pupil. In doing so, Alcuin mediates between the raw form of the wonder and the faith or certainty produced by his act of revelation. Understanding the wonder requires not just the rational experience of having seen the thing described (an image in water) but also the "aha" moment of arriving at the solution, whether by someone else's explication or by reasoning it out oneself.

Like Judas's prayer in *Elene*, Alcuin's exchange operates on the irreversible temporality of the movement from belief into knowledge, in which the knowledge eventually seems like certain knowledge all along. In other words, once a riddle has been solved or a wonder grasped—once its meaning is known—it cannot be unsolved or ungrasped. As Alcuin demonstrates, then, Pippin's initial inability to solve the riddle is not a matter of his skill or intelligence; rather, it arises from Pippin's need to be certain of the wonder's truth (as opposed to suspecting a false figment or deceitful trick) even though the logic of that truth is as yet unknown. Before one can understand that a wonder is true, one must first believe truth to be possible. In this case, that certainty is initially produced by Alcuin's act of revelation (*pandere*). With that confidence and faith, as it were, Pippin is then able to respond to Alcuin's subsequent riddles without further correction. The riddles, coming full circle, ultimately help Pippin understand the mechanics of faith with which the catechesis began—not only the faith used in the interpretation of playful wonders and riddles but also the much stronger faith necessary for approaching the wonders of God.

Although formally quite different from the *mira* in Alcuin's *Disputatio*, Aldhelm's *Aenigmata* has repeatedly been recognized as a collection of wonders or mysteries. Given "the seriousness of Aldhelm's theme," as Michael Lapidge pronounced, the term *aenigmata* "should probably be rendered 'Mysteries' rather than 'Riddles,' for Aldhelm set out to reveal the hidden links between all Creation—animate and inanimate—and by means of an intricate web of interlocking themes and metaphors to lead the reader to contemplate God's Creation afresh."[105] Martha Bayless has made a similar claim in her discussion of the relationship between early medieval riddle collections, wisdom dialogues, and curiosity dialogues, arguing that these texts served "to evoke [wonder at the glory of God and the everyday marvels of his world, which] included his ability to unite opposites in paradox, and to provide pleasure while doing so."[106] A wonder is a miraculous object of observation, but wonder, of course, is also the response that such objects elicit in their readers and viewers. Patricia Dailey has shown how this responsiveness of wonder drives the Old English *Riddles* of the Exeter Book, such that "what is unknown in the riddle serves to provoke something *knowable* about the responder."[107] As an aesthetic and epistemological category, wonder (or *admiratio* in Latin) is often pitted against knowledge, hence Alcuin's definition of faith as certainty about what is wondrous *and* unknown. Caroline Walker Bynum, in her celebrated essay on the topic, elucidates one type of relationship between wonder and knowledge, noting that "philosophers between the thirteenth and eighteenth centuries developed from the opening of Aristotle's *Metaphysics*, which associated wonder with ignorance and doubt, the idea that the goal of *admiratio* was its own destruction: if wonder arose from the desire to seek causes it did not understand, wonder should lead to its own replacement by *scientia* or *philosophia*."[108] But Bynum is working in reference to a much later period and to thinkers who actually had access to Aristotle.

Such scholarship on the tension between knowledge and wonder, while often focused on the later Middle Ages, tends to overlook the important theological relationship between wonder and faith. For without wonder, there can be no faith. My point runs parallel to what Steven Justice has argued about religious belief and the role of medieval miracles, which serve to produce a sort of thoughtful doubt as opposed to apathetic belief: without the potential for such doubt, faith becomes meaningless.[109] If wonder is associated with "ignorance and doubt," as Bynum suggests, then wonder must not merely serve the production of *scientia* and *philosophia* (to its own detriment) but also the production of *fides* (for the sake of its own perpetuation). Knowing and believing are two very different yet interrelated modalities, and wonder appeals to the tension between them both. As a response to something unknown and wondrous, faith constitutes that indefinite intermediary state in which the thing becomes unconcealed yet remains unknown. Faith is produced and reinforced at that moment, in other words, when the wonder is revealed (*pandere*) to Pippin independent of his prior rational experience of a reflection on water.

Alcuin was a reader of Aldhelm's *Aenigmata*, and for both of them such riddles serve in part to inculcate the reader in the process of marveling before an obscured or encrypted wonder, which entails moving from faith to understanding and back again to a richer form of faith.[110] When Aldhelm explains in the preface to his *Aenigmata* that his collection of riddles serves to "pandere rerum . . . enigmata . . . clandistina"[111] (reveal the secret enigmas of things)—a scheme we shall return to in the next chapter—Aldhelm not only gives Alcuin the language (in the word *pandere*) for using *aenigmata* as a tool for instruction, but he similarly positions his own *Aenigmata* as a mediating force between rational understanding and faith produced through the process of revelation (*pandere*).[112] His choice of the phrase *aenigmata clandistina* captures the relationship between the mystery inherent in all things and his own mystification of those things through language. But that mystification is juxtaposed against and constituted by an act of revelation (*pandere*) that functions as the paradoxical driving force at the heart of each *aenigma*: Aldhelm's *aenigmata* (and those of Tatwine and Eusebius and Alcuin, too) treat the reader to an experience of faith—"certainty about something that is both unknown and wondrous"—by virtue of their given and rubricated titles. The solutions that anticipate or follow each riddle entertain certainty while the *aenigma* itself still simultaneously remains wondrous and unknown. For in the moment that certainty, wonder, and ignorance coalesce, faith obtains.

Chapter 8

Reading Hidden Meaning: Between Interpretive Pride and Eschatological Humility

If poems such as Cynewulf's *Elene* avowedly encouraged and taught readers to approach textual concealment with a certain kind of faith, then it still remains to be seen whether readers actually approached texts in such a way. Indeed, we may never know the full picture, for the only vestiges of readership that survive are those made by the compilers, scribes, glossators, and occasional annotators who left their interpretive marks in any given manuscript, and even this broad definition of readership privileges those parties interested just as much in the transmission and preservation of the text as in its interpretation. Readers of riddles who, by contrast, might have given up before arriving at a solution or who moved on to the next poem out of frustration may not have left behind a trace of their failed interpretive attempts, while the traces that do survive are often inadequate to the processes of interpretation that they represent in their eventual form. There are limits, in other words, to what we can garner about the habits of Anglo-Saxon readers, particularly those readers engaging in the interpretation of riddles. However, when these riddles, especially the highly influential collection of *aenigmata* by Aldhelm of Malmesbury, are examined in their manuscript contexts, we begin to see how Anglo-Saxons viewed reading as an exchange not only between poet and reader but also with God. In this context, riddles can tempt the reader into intellectual pride while simultaneously commending intellectual humility. And in this chapter, we will encounter the very readers who teetered between these two states of mind as they read in the face of larger cosmic forces of concealment and revelation—that is, in the face of God's ultimate act of Judgment.

Reading and Judging *Aenigmata clandestina*

Formally brilliant and complex, the verse preface to Aldhelm's *Aenigmata*—his series of one hundred Latin riddles—is essentially an extravagant prayer. It begins with an address neither to the reader nor to its dedicatee but to God, the eternal Judge and almighty Ruler of heaven and earth. It ends—echoing the rhetoric of serving and solving discussed in Chapter 6—with a request that God loose us from the bonds of sin:

> Arce poli, genitor, seruas qui saecula cunctA
> Soluere iam scelerum noxas dignare nefandaS.
>
> [O Father, who holds the universe together from the citadel of heaven, now deign to resolve the evil injuries of sins.][1]

God holds together ("seruas") and scatters apart ("soluere"), binding and loosing just as Aldhelm's reader will need to do on a much smaller scale when reading the *aenigmata* that follow, holding together each word and each paradox in order to solve a given *aenigma* in its entirety.[2] But Aldhelm goes on to put this otherwise trifling task into cosmic perspective.

The preface is not just a prayer for God's protection against sin. At the core of these opening lines, Aldhelm beseeches God's assistance in the composition of poetry, pleading that his "dull mind" ("stolidae . . . menti") might be inspired and his "dactylic style" ("ritu dactilico") might be free of errors.[3] He rejects the inspiration of the Muses (as the cleansing of sin would fall outside of their jurisdiction) and instead invokes God as the ultimate source of poetic inspiration, having already successfully inspired the words of David and Moses.[4] The *Arbiter* invoked here thus governs not only the universe but also the creation of verse:

> Arbiter, aethereo iugiter qui regmine sceptrA
> Lucifluum que simul caeli regale tribunaL
> Disponis moderans aeternis legibus illuD,
> (Horrida nam multans torsisti membra vehemotH,
> Ex alta quondam rueret dum luridus arcE), 5
> Limpida dictanti metrorum carmina praesuL
> Munera nunc largire, rudis quo pandere reruM
> Versibus enigmata queam clandistina fatV:
> Sic, Deus, indignis tua gratis dona rependiS.
>
> [O Judge, you who with celestial authority govern perpetually both the scepters and the glorious royal throne of heaven, ruling it with eternal laws (for in punishment you tortured the terrible limbs of Behemoth when the ghastly creature once fell from the high citadel): now as my protector, bestow your bright gifts upon me as I compose (bright) poems

in meter, whereby I, unskilled, may seek to lay open the secret mysteries of things by speaking in verses: in return, you, God, thus freely give your gifts to the unworthy.][5]

One brilliantly complex feature of the preface is the double acrostic that runs vertically down both the first and last letters of each line, spelling out "ALDHELMVS CECINIT MILLENIS VERSIBVS ODAS" (Aldhelm has sung songs in a thousand [i.e., many] verses). In the passage above, the word "ALDHELMVS" is visible down the left and right edges of the text. In most manuscripts, the presentation of the acrostic stands out even more clearly, often with capital letters and spaced away from the main text so that the letters run in straight vertical lines (a typical medieval *mise en page* for acrostic verses).[6] The rubricated and sometimes zoomorphic initial *A*, moreover, draws attention to the striking—if patently obvious—fact that the first letter of "Arbiter" aligns with the first letter of Aldhelm's own name (fig. 10).[7]

To all appearances, this poetic gesture is a conceited display of intelligence and self-admiration: the intersection of *Arbiter* and *Aldhelmus* only aggrandizes the sheer difficulty of producing a hexametrical double acrostic. But this gesture, viewed from a different perspective, also subtly allows Aldhelm to demonstrate his own intellectual subjection to God. Not only does *Arbiter* temporally precede *Aldhelmus* (if one reads the text horizontally first), but the poem also suggests that just as God, the divine *Arbiter*, created and rules the universe, Aldhelm shall compose verses about it; the preface, in other words, attributes creative power to God, while the acrostic seems to attribute it to Aldhelm. This inspirational relationship between God and the poet hinges, for example, on the ambiguity of the word "Limpida" (bright, line 6), which modifies either "carmina" (songs, line 6) or "Munera" (gifts, line 7). This ambiguity allows Aldhelm to request that God's bright gifts ("Limpida . . . Munera") aid in his composition of bright poems ("Limpida . . . carmina"). He can thus humbly eschew the presumption that his own poems are bright in themselves by cleverly insinuating instead that the brightness transfers from God to poem as the verses take on the gift of God's illumination. And yet, the grammatical temporality of this ambiguous illumination means that the reader encounters "Limpida . . . carmina" (bright songs) before encountering "Limpida . . . Munera" (bright gifts) on the next line. That is, unless one reads the poem vertically down the acrostic and accordingly finds "Limpida" directly above "Munera" and "Munera" directly above "Versibus."[8] Where the acrostic seems to claim Aldhelm as a poetic genius, and the text of the preface seems to attribute that genius to God, this play around the word *limpida* inverts these claims: simultaneously, the acrostic can thus visually imply that God's bright gifts supersede Aldhelm's *versus*, while the preface temporally lures the

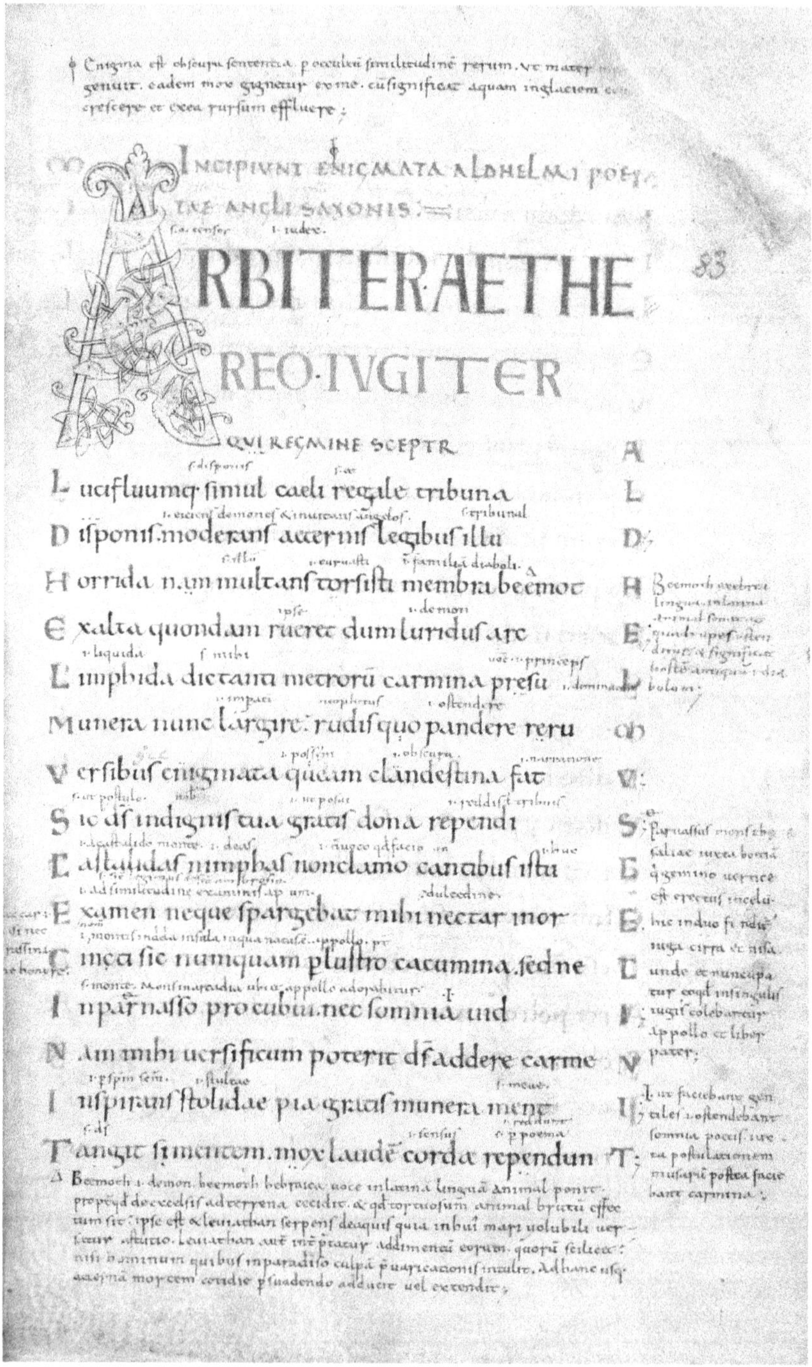

Ænigma est obscura sententia, p[er] occultam similitudinem rerum, ut mater
genuit, eadem mox gignetur ex me, cui significat aquam in glaciem e[t]
crescere et e[ti]a[m] rursum effluere;

INCIPIVNT ENIGMATA ALDHELMI POETÆ
ANGLI SAXONIS

ARBITER AETHE
REO·IVGITER

QVI REGMINE SCEPTR[A]

Lucifluumq[ue] simul caeli regale tribunal   L
Disponis moderans aeternis legibus illa   D
Horrida n[on] nu[m]qua[m] multans torsisti membra behemot   H
Exalta quondam rueret dum luridus arce   E
Limphida dictanti metroru[m] carmina praesul   L
Munera nunc largire rudis quo pandere reru[m]   M
Versibus aenigmata queam clandestina fat[u]   V
Sic deus indignis tua gratis dona rependi[s]   S
Castalidas nimphas non clamo canibus ista   C
Examen neque spargebat mihi nectar in or[e]   E
Cinthi sic numquam plustro cacumina, sed ne   C
In parnasso procubui nec somnia uid[i]   I
Nam mihi uersificum poterit d[eu]s addere carme[n] N
Inspirans stolidae pia gratis munera ment[i]   I
Tangit si mentem mox laude corda rependun[t]   T

A Beemoth i[d est] demon. beemoth hebraica uoce in latina lingua animal ponit[ur]
prop[ter] q[uo]d de cœlis ad terrena cecidit. Et q[uo]d copiosum animal brutu[m] effec-
tum sic ipse est & leuiathan serpens de aquis quia inhuit mari uolubili uer-
titur astutio. Leuiathan cui mę tracui[t] addime[n]te[m] eorum quor[um] scilicet
nisi dominum quib[us] in paradiso culpa p[er]suasione[m] insulit. Ad hanc usq[ue]
aeternam mortem cordis p[er]suadendo adducere uel extendit.

Figure 10. London, British Library, Royal 12. C. xxiii, fol. 83r,
Preface to Aldhelm's *Aenigmata*. © British Library Board.

reader into thinking that Aldhelm's *carmina* are bright in themselves before realizing that the brightness might actually belong to God's *munera* instead.

In other words, Aldhelm seems like a tactician of humility. By acknowledging the aid of divine illumination, he can boldly yet safely claim that his *Aenigmata* will treat a theme even greater than those treated by David and Moses. But while one can certainly be a tactician in the rhetorical deployment of humility, the calculating quality of that deployment risks pushing Aldhelm's efforts back into the realm of pride: not only does he sign his name in a display of formal ingenuity associated with God's ordering of the universe, but he is also doing so with rhetoric that brilliantly deflects the accusation of pride the display conjures. By cleverly attributing this brilliance to divine assistance, Aldhelm's potentially prideful investments reemerge even as he seems to be attempting to safeguard against them. This raises a fundamental question about Aldhelm's project: is he attempting to safeguard himself and his readers from prideful intellectual activity? Or might he be offering this *Aenigmata* as something other than a safe pedagogy, something that draws the reader to the edge of pride to teeter there alongside the poet?

Its overarching purpose, by God's decree and according to Aldhelm's assertion, is to reveal, to lay open, to explain, to announce the secret mysteries of things ("pandere rerum . . . enigmata . . . clandistina fatu").[9] As Aldhelm submits to God and his laws—moral, physical, and perhaps even metrical—he positions himself as a mediator or, better, an *arbiter*, an eyewitness, a judge, an interpreter of the secret mysteries of created things, and from those mysteries he produces new enigmas to be arbitrated in turn by the reader.[10] In the course of this chapter, we will return several times to the implications of this crucial phrase, "pandere rerum . . . enigmata . . . clandistina." But at this point, let us simply note the important and paradoxical role that Aldhelm gives to his own *Aenigmata*. In claiming to lay open the "enigmata . . . clandistina" of created things, Aldhelm grants poetry, as one form of *aenigma*, the capacity to reveal through its own decipherable concealment those divine *aenigmata* that are in themselves beyond the immediate hermeneutic reach of human observers. In doing so, Aldhelm builds on the biblical tradition (established, for instance, in Job 38–40) of using inquisitive language to represent the potency of God's Creation and the infinite reach of divine knowledge and wisdom.[11] For Aldhelm, these *aenigmata* thus become the textual medium, the textual *arbiter*, through which one learns to approach and read these mysteries of God.

For Aldhelm, then, the author of a riddle may serve as a mediator and judge—to facilitate the movement between openness (the unconcealed solution), concealment (the riddle), and a return to openness (the interpreted solution)—but only insofar as that mediation is ultimately subject to God's role as *Arbiter*. He acknowledges that his own *aenigmata* are necessarily restricted in their capacity to conceal, that the process of laying open these mysteries can only be catalyzed by God's decree (in one possible interpretation of the word *fatum*), and that God—as the ultimate *Arbiter*—always gets the final say. By way of comparison, we might think back to Antiochus's riddle in the Old English *Apollonius of Tyre* and consider the king's absolute power to judge the solution to his riddle; he even presumes to judge as false Apollonius's truly correct interpretation and thereby unjustly sentence him to death.[12] The process of producing a riddle and adjudicating its solution—for Antiochus—might exemplify an absolute form of power and judgment, even if that power and judgment ultimately fails. But for Aldhelm the process is much more delicate.

If producing riddles about Creation requires judgment on the part of the poet, then reading them requires judgment on the part of the reader as well. And such judgment fits within the early medieval process of reading as its fundamental goal and culmination. As M. B. Parkes has shown, the Anglo-Saxons tended to approach reading through the methods established in classical *grammatica*, beginning with *lectio* or *rædan*, the most basic form of reading individual letters and words, and working through *ennaratio* or *areccan* (interpretation) to arrive ultimately at *iudicium* or *smeagan* (judgment).[13] Although such forms of interpretation and judgment were most directly applicable to the reading and study of scripture—in which one sought to arrive at the spiritual sense and then internalize it so that it could be applied to one's own life—these modes of reading operated in other literary contexts as well, as Parkes demonstrates with texts such as Boethius's *Consolation of Philosophy* and Old English heroic poetry. But riddles, too, were no exception, not only because of their intellectual proximity to the enigmas of scripture, which we examined in the previous chapter, but also because they invite at the most basic level an act of judgment on the part of the reader. For Aldhelm, that judgment is clearly set in relation to the judgment of the divine *Arbiter*, but not all readers necessarily saw it that way.

Reading and Glossing Aldhelm's *Creatura*

We find just such a reader in one of the scribes responsible for Cambridge, Cambridge University Library Gg. 5. 35, a massive codex of 446 folios compiled at Saint Augustine's, Canterbury, in the mid-eleventh century. It is commonly referred to as the "Cambridge Songs" manuscript after the collection of Latin lyrics it contains, but it also boasts a spectacular range of early Christian, Carolingian, and Anglo-Latin prose and verse, including works by Sedulius, Arator, Prudentius, and Boethius, among others. Most importantly for our purposes, the manuscript preserves complete copies of the Latin *aenigmata* by Symphosius,

Aldhelm, Tatwine, Eusebius, and Boniface, as well as several smaller anonymous groups of riddles.[14] Together, these collections of *aenigmata* are confined to the same section of the manuscript and were written and glossed by the manuscript's two main scribes.[15] The glossing is heavy and demonstrates both the perpetuation of particular intellectual traditions (in the copying of glosses from exemplars) and the formation of new readings (in the production of unique glosses found only here).[16] Naturally, these glosses range from vestiges of basic *lectio* to more advanced engagements with the meaning of the text. When we get to Aldhelm's *Aenigmata*, however, the scribe tests the limits of his own intellectual ingenuity, betraying a tension between the two modes of interpretation outlined in the previous chapter. Here, intellectual force and spiritual faith chafe against one another as the poet and the scribe grapple with the semantics of individual letters and alphabets, the mystery of prayers and judgment, and the potency of God as the almighty Judge.

Aldhelm's *Aenigma* 100 (*De Creatura*) is one of the more heavily glossed texts in Gg. 5. 35.[17] This final poem begins, echoing some of the imagery in Aldhelm's preface, by registering God as the Creator and Ruler of a varied and manifold Creation:

> Conditor, aeternis fulcit qui saecla columnis,
> rector regnorum, frenans et fulmina lege,
> pendula dum patuli uertuntur culmina caeli,
> me uarium fecit, primo dum conderet orbem.[18]

> [The Creator who supports the world on eternal columns, the ruler of all kingdoms, restraining lightning bolts with his law while the suspended summits of the wide skies revolve, made me various when he first created the world.]

The poem proceeds to describe Creation as a series of paradoxes: colder than winter, yet hotter than Vulcan's flaming heat; sweeter than fresh lilies in a field, yet stinking with filthy nastiness; and so forth. Although Aldhelm assembles these incommensurable features of Creation under a single name, the scribe in Gg. 5. 35 takes a different approach. Among the numerous syntactical and lexical glosses, we find a series of glosses that reshape the *aenigma* by compartmentalizing it. For example, above the words "me uarium fecit" (made me various) in the fourth line of the poem (see fig. 11), the scribe notes that "creatura mundi hic multiformis loquitur" (here is mentioned the multiform creation of the world).[19] He then proceeds to mark each time a new creature appears to be introduced, at first with the phrase "Alia creatura" (another creature), twice shortened to the word "alia," and then eventually abbreviated to a series of crosses (+). In figure 12, nineteen crosses run down the left margin, marking almost two-thirds of the lines on the page as lines that each introduce another supposedly new creature. Rather than treating *Aenigma* 100 as a single cohesive riddle with one solution, the glossator treats it as a series of individual riddles and annotates it as though it were a summary compilation of the preceding riddles in the manuscript, including several by authors other than Aldhelm.

We can imagine why the scribe may have been tempted to do so. As a whole, the last of Aldhelm's *aenigmata* is incredibly difficult to solve in the way we typically assume riddles are meant to be solved; that is, it is incredibly difficult to unravel all of the different paradoxes and components, address each paradox and component in turn, and then put them back together so as to arrive at a sensible solution that accounts for each component and paradox. In other words, the *aenigma* resists straightforward logical explication. One cannot turn to Isidore, for example, to explain how these paradoxes relate to one another or fit into the larger scheme of the riddle, even if the material for each isolated side of a given paradox can clearly be found in the *Etymologiae* and other encyclopedic sources. As we have seen, paradoxes are a foundational riddling technique, but here their sheer amalgamation makes the work of solving the riddle impossible. In a sense, that is exactly Aldhelm's point. This final *aenigma* displays the impossibility of comprehending and rationalizing a coherent whole in the mystery of Creation. It requires simply believing in the truth of Creation even though it remains incomprehensible: Creation is thus one form of *aenigmata clandestina*. At the same time, part of Aldhelm's goal, we will recall, is to translate those "enigmata . . . clandistina" into a different kind of *aenigma*, a kind that *can* be interpreted and understood through the human intellect.

The scribe's unique *alia creatura* glosses are one inventive way to solve the *aenigma*, but his other glosses are even more playful. Supplementing many of his *alia creatura* notations, the scribe has provided marginal "solutions" naming the creatures or objects to which individual lines of the *aenigma* seem to refer, as though each verse were an individual riddle. Sometimes, he writes these solutions in Latin, as in the gloss "ut cinamomu*m* & balsamu*m*" (such as cinnamon and balsam), which responds to line 13: "Prorsus odorato ture flagrantior halans" (Truly, I, who emit vapors, am more fragrant than frankincense).[20] But other times, the glossed solutions are encrypted. A simple example is found above line 10, where he writes "ut mfp," replacing each letter in the word *leo* (lion) with the subsequent letter in the alphabet: a simple substitution scheme, sometimes called a Caeser cipher.[21] Elsewhere, he offers more complicated cryptographic glosses, such as those in the margin next to Aldhelm's description of cold more frigid than winter ("frigidior brumis") and the burning heat of Vulcan ("Vulcani flammis torrentibus ardens").[22] Here,

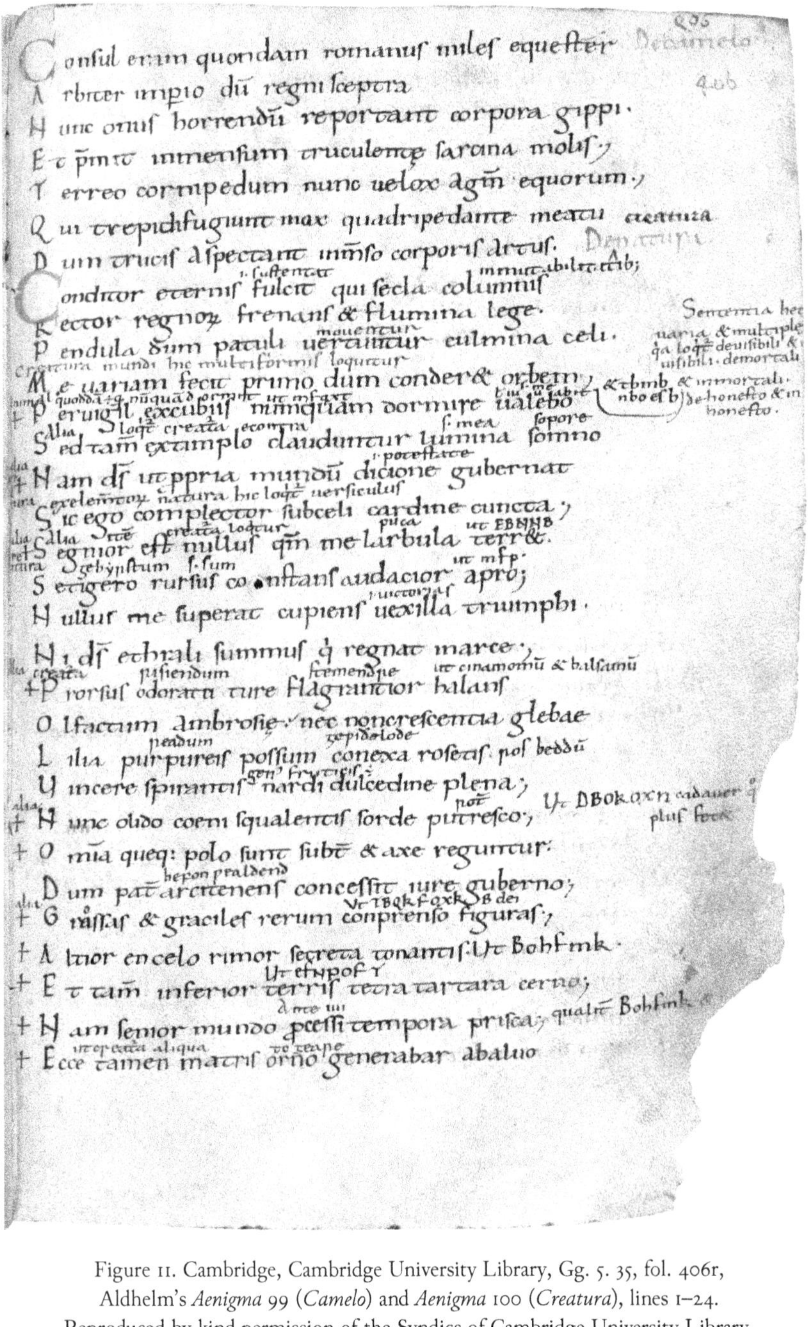

Consul eram quondam romanus miles equester
Arbiter impio dum regni sceptra
Hunc omnis horrendum reportant corpora gippi·
Et primum immensum truculentaque sarcina molis·
Terreo cornipedum nunc uelox agmen equorum·
Qui trepidi fugiunt max quadripedante meatu creatura
Dum trucis aspectant inmenso corporis artus.
  sustentat   inmutabilitatib;
Conditor eterni fulcit qui secla columnis
Rector regnorum frenans & flumina lege·   Sententia hec
                  mouentur   naria & multiple
Pendula dum patuli uerruntur culmina celi·   ga loq̃ de uisibili &
  creatura mundi hic multiformis loquitur·   usibili· demorali
Me uariam fecit primo dum conder & orbem   &tbmb & immortali·
  animal quodā·i·q̃ niquad ornēt ut m̄fare   in ui·tbi· nbo et b·de honesto & in
Peruigil excubiis numquam dormire ualebo   honesto·
  Alia   loq̃ creata ocompta   si mea sopore
Sed tam exemplo clauduntur lumina somno
                    potestate
Nam ds ut ppria mundu dicione gubernat
  ura exelemcov·natura hic loq̃· uersiculus
Sic ego complector subcelí cardine cuncta·
  Alia sue   creata loq̃tur   pūca   ut EBNNB
Segnior est nullus qin me larbula terre&·
  Sebynstum s·sum   ut mfp·
Setigero rursus co·nstans audacior apro;
                                punctorzi·
Nullus me superat cupiens uexilla triumphi·

Nil ds ethrali summus q̃ regnat marce·
  creata   pusiendum   fremendq̃;   ut cinamomu & balsamū
Prorsus odorata ture flagrantior halans
  Olfactum ambrosie· nec noncrescentia glebae
              pendum   tepidolode
Lilia purpureis possum conexa roseas· pos beddū
                        gen´ frytegfis·
Uincere spirantis nardi dulcedine plena·
   alia   not   Y· DBokaxn cadauer q
Hunc olido coeni squalentis sorde putresco·   plus sock
+ Omnia queq; polo sunt subt̄ & axe reguntur·
             hepon pralderd
Dum pat̄ arcitenens concessit iure guberno·
                              Ut TBokfoxkSB dei
+ Grassus & graciles rerum conprenso figuras·
+ Altior en celo rimor secreta tonantis·Ut Bohfmk·
                   Ut ethpof r
+ Et tū inferior terris tecta tartara cerno·
                              à ntē uī   qualē Bohfnk
+ Nam senior mundo pcessi tempora prisca·
   ut epcreata aliqua   to teane
+ Ecce tamen matris orno generabar abaluo

Figure 11. Cambridge, Cambridge University Library, Gg. 5. 35, fol. 406r,
Aldhelm's *Aenigma* 99 (*Camelo*) and *Aenigma* 100 (*Creatura*), lines 1–24.
Reproduced by kind permission of the Syndics of Cambridge University Library.

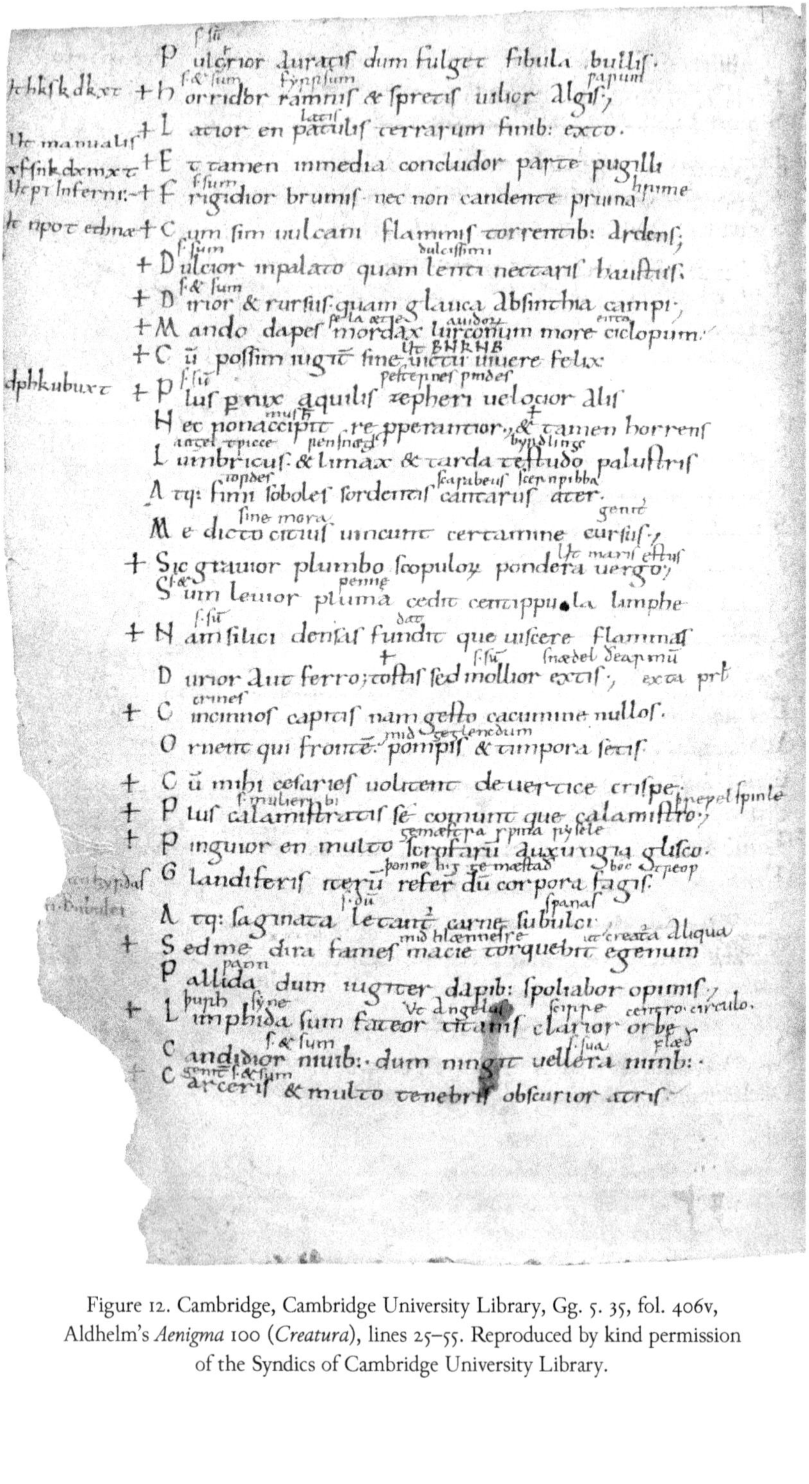

Figure 12. Cambridge, Cambridge University Library, Gg. 5. 35, fol. 406v, Aldhelm's *Aenigma* 100 (*Creatura*), lines 25–55. Reproduced by kind permission of the Syndics of Cambridge University Library.

the glossator writes "Vt pt (= *os*) inferni" (such as the mouth of hell) and "Vt npot (= *mons*) ethnæ" (such as Mount Etna): the first gloss is a clever reference to the common conception of hell as both extremely hot and extremely cold,[23] and the second gloss refers to both the iciness of Mount Etna's summit and its nature as a volcano, for Aldhelm's word *uulcanus* can mean either a volcano or Vulcan, the Roman god of fire. The scribe has searched and found the very paradoxes he believes Aldhelm to be describing, and he records them so they remain still partially obscured from the reader.

Cryptograms such as these would have been relatively familiar to the intellectual world of the early Middle Ages. Isidore, for example, describes an almost identical Roman practice of transposing letters for the purpose of secret ("secreta") communications between Emperor Augustus and his (step-)son.[24] And in his *De temporum ratione*, Bede similarly lays out a system of letter substitution in which each letter of the alphabet is replaced with a number, allowing people to communicate secretly and silently by using their hands to signify letters and form words ("occultius innuendo significans") or dupe the uninitiated as if by magic ("imperitos . . . quasi diuinando deludens").[25] Such encryption can be tremendously powerful, worthy of an emperor's communications or urgent communication between friends.[26] But there are other uses as well. The obscure seventh-century Irish pseudo-grammarian Virgilius Maro Grammaticus thus offers three justifications for what he calls "the scrambling of sounds" (*scinderatio fonorum*):

> Prima est, ut sagacitatem discentium nostrorum in inquirendis atque inueniendis his quae obscura sunt adprobemus; secunda est propter decorem aedificationemque eloquentiae; tertia ne mistica quaeque et quae solis gnaris pandi debent, passim ab infimis ac stultis facile reperiantur.

> [First, so that we may test the cleverness of our students in searching out and identifying obscure points; secondly, for ornamentation and the edification of eloquence; thirdly, lest mystical matters that should only be revealed to the initiated be discovered easily by base and stupid people.][27]

Aside from Virgilius's defense of ornamentation and eloquence, the other two justifications should sound familiar: like riddles, textual encryption serves as a didactic tool and defense against unworthy readers. Both scrambled letters and riddles train and prepare the reader for more difficult texts to come, but they also keep out those readers who should not have access to certain secrets or mysteries in the first place.[28]

The word Virgilius uses by contrast for legitimate access to those secrets and mysteries is *pandere*—the same word used by Pippin in his request that

Alcuin reveal the wonder (*mira*) to him in the *Disputatio Pippini*, and the same word Aldhelm uses in proposing the purpose of his *Aenigmata*.[29] For Virgilius such mysteries should only be laid out (*pandere*) before those who are *already* wise, those who are initiated, who are *gnari*. And yet such initiation and access requires that the student follow a particular didactic path that begins with enigmas and other forms of encryption. Enigmatic texts thus serve a paradoxical role both as the material of elementary study and as the destination opened up by persistent intellectual training. Indeed, Aldhelm seems to echo Virgilius's sentiment and language in *Aenigma* 81, which ends by suggesting that a state of wisdom is the prerequisite for deciphering the *aenigma*, the solution to which "*Gnarus* quos poterit per biblos *pandere* lector" (the *wise* reader will be able to *reveal* through books).[30] But at the end of *Aenigma* 100, as we will discover below, Aldhelm reverses that sentiment, taunting those same *lectores gnari* who think they can *pandere* the meaning of the riddle, which even the wise teacher is scarcely capable of explaining through speech ("*Pandere* quae poterit *gnarus* uix ore magister").[31] We can begin to see how the words "pandere rerum . . . enigmata . . . clandistina" in the preface to Aldhelm's *Aenigmata* now bear even more weight, insinuating Aldhelm himself as just such a *magister gnarus* attempting to reveal some secret mysteries.

The glossator of Aldhelm's *Aenigmata* in Gg. 5. 35 seems to situate himself in a similar position, as a *lector gnarus* who can both understand the intricacies of Aldhelm's *aenigma* and, in response, produce new cryptographic *aenigmata* of his own. To that end, he has inscribed seventeen of these cryptographic glosses in the margins and between the lines of Aldhelm's *Aenigma* 100. I have argued elsewhere that some of these cryptograms depart from the standard and predictable patterns of encryption with ostensible errors.[32] For example, the cryptogram "BNKNB" (on fol. 406v, fig. 12, corresponding to line 34 of *Aenigma* 100) results in the nonsensical word *amima* in place of *anima* (soul). This snag may appear to have been a simple error in which the glossator carelessly forgot to encrypt the letter *n* in *anima*, thus resulting in "BNKNB" instead of the hypothetically correct *BOKNB*. However, I have suggested that the error could also have been a deliberate way to add an additional layer of encryption to the otherwise rather unsophisticated letter-substitution paradigm; by leaving the occasional letter unencrypted, the glossator ends up with a more robust form of encryption and a cryptogram slightly more difficult to solve.

The solubility of these cryptograms depends primarily on the reader's intimate and intuitive knowledge of Latin, knowledge that recognizes not just *amima* for *anima* but also more complicated orthographic deviations as well. Yet at the same time, their solubility also depends on a certain kind of hermeneutic faith, in which the reader must fully trust that the glossator has concealed a real Latin word and that the concealed word contains meaning germane to the adjacent lines of poetry. Akin to the hermeneutics of faith discussed in the previous chapter, this kind of readerly faith is demanded not just by the scribe's interpretive and enigmatic glosses but also by Aldhelm's *aenigmata* themselves. In order for any riddle to work as a scheme that both conceals *and* remains open to interpretive decryption, the reader must trust that the text actually conceals some true and sensible meaning *and* that the medium through which it is concealed has been accurately presented and preserved. This need for trusting in the accuracy of the text is the reason why errors of the sort ostensibly produced by the glossator in his cryptograms (e.g., *amima*) are so problematic for the interpretation of riddles. These apparent corruptions and departures from the accepted rules of encryption introduce doubt into the equation, and they make it harder for the reader to work through the various paradoxes and apparent nonsense that are the very keystones of the riddling genre. As when a student discovers a typo in *Wheelock's Latin*, a reader who has encountered an error in a cryptogram or riddle will naturally begin to question the authority of any text that subsequently seems, on the surface, to be wrong or inconsistent. And on the surface, riddles always *seem* wrong and inconsistent.

These cryptographic glosses in Gg. 5. 35 reveal one reader's attempt to grapple with the mechanics of concealment in Aldhelm's *Aenigmata*. But they do more than simply clarify Aldhelm's diction and references (such clarification is accomplished with the occasional Old English gloss or the copious syntactic glosses). For this glossator, solving a riddle entails encrypting the solution in a new way. The glossator thus tasks himself with an extension of Aldhelm's own original objective; if Aldhelm set out to reveal the "enigmata . . . clandistina" of Creation by means of his own *aenigmata,* then our glossator has set out to reveal Aldhelm's *aenigmata* with his own unique and inspired efforts at encryption. Those efforts serve to exalt Aldhelm's created verses, just as Aldhelm's verses serve to exalt God's creative power.

These multiple forms of glossing, moreover, add to the linguistic variety at play in Aldhelm's poems: one created thing can be described in multiple ways, with different words, in different languages, using different alphabets. The same kind of variety that Aldhelm's *Aenigma* 100 depicts in the paradoxical expansiveness of all of Creation our glossator then conveys in the field of language, playfully scrambled and reinvented. Together, these cryptographic glosses—with their potential insolubility and their concealment from human readers, with their role as encrypted revelations, and with their veneration of the concealed object—position the glossator himself as a kind of Aldhelmian *arbiter*, as one who mediates between the *aenigmata clandestina* of the universe and the literary *aenigmata* in which they are represented, and who then mediates between the literary *aenigmata* and the encrypted solutions in which they are reconcealed.

The Worm and the Philosopher

To place the work of this one medieval scribe within the larger context of Aldhelm's *Aenigmata*, we should turn to the end of *Aenigma* 100. There the scribe seems to have recognized some weighty implications for reading the *Aenigmata* as a whole. In the right margin on fol. 407r of Gg. 5. 35, the glossator has written the cryptogram "Vt ukofb," which can be resolved (following the methods discussed above) as *Vt tinea* (such as a moth [or worm]). This cryptogram corresponds to lines 70–72 of Aldhelm's *Aenigma* 100:

> Sic mea prudentes superat sapientia sophos, 70
> <Nec tamen in biblis docuit me littera diues>
> Aut numquam quiui, quid constet sillaba, nosse.

> [Thus does my wisdom surpass the skilled philosophers;
> <yet, nevertheless, the rich letters in books did not teach me,>
> nor was I ever able to learn what a syllable consists of.]³³

In Gg. 5. 35, the text jumps from "sophos" at the end of line 70 to "Aut" at the beginning of line 72 with no indication that anything is missing. We might speculate (and that is all we might do) that instead of a classic example of scribal eye-skip, the missing line is an ingenious joke on the part of the scribe, making palpable the *tinean* consumption of letters implied in the marginal cryptographic "solution." Speculation aside, without that middle verse and its image of rich letters in books, the reference to a book moth (*tinea*) becomes entirely abstracted, since what remains is a nonsensical paradox consisting merely of something that is wiser than philosophers yet ignorant of syllables. While the gloss could have been inspired by Symphosius's *Aenigma* 16 (which the scribe copied out only a few folios back [on fol. 390r] with the rubricated solution "De tinea"), its significance in the margin of Aldhelm's poem still rests on the crucial reference to books (*bibli*) and letters (*litterae*) in the missing line.

Together, the cryptographic gloss and the omitted line obscure their reference to an otherwise common feature of medieval scribal and literary culture, attested not only by the countless tiny holes bored through pages and pages of parchment but also by the delightfully familiar Exeter Book *Riddle* 47:

> Moððe word fræt.   Me þæt þuhte
> wrætlicu wyrd,   þa ic þæt wundor gefrægn,

þæt se wyrm forswealg   wera gied sumes,
þeof in þystro,   þrymfæstne cwide
ond þæs strangan staþol.   Stælgiest ne wæs   5
wihte þy gleawra,   þe he þam wordum swealg.³⁴

[A worm ate words. That seemed to me a strange thing when I heard of that wonder, that the worm, a thief in the darkness, swallowed a man's song, his glory-fast sayings and the strong tradition. The visiting thief was not the wiser for having swallowed those words.]

This is a profound riddle, for it seems to reflect not merely the material prevalence of wormholes in books but also the monastic intellectual tradition of *ruminatio*, a careful process of reading and internalizing scripture represented through the metaphor of chewing and digestion.³⁵ As such, it invites the reader to consider the implicit connection between the interpretation of the riddle and the related practices of scriptural interpretation. At the same time, scholars such as Mercedes Salvador-Bello and Martin Foys have elucidated the thematic proximity between *Riddle* 47 and numerous Latin *aenigmata*, including Symphosius's *Aenigma* 16 (*De tinea*) and Aldhelm's *Aenigma* 100 (*Creatura*), as well as Aldhelm's *Aenigma* 89 and Eusebius's *Aenigma* 33 (which are solved as *arca libraria* [book chest] and *scetha* [book satchel], respectively). The *ut tinea* gloss in Gg. 5. 35 is only further evidence that the entangled relationships between these riddles were evidently recognized by medieval readers as well.

But each of these riddles uses the figure of a book moth to draw slightly different conclusions. For example, Martin Foys reads *Riddle* 47 as a reversal of Symphosius's *Aenigma* 16, arguing that although both riddles turn "on the thin zone of qualities the larval insect and the unstudious human reader share," Symphosius uses the image of the reader to point toward a moth, whereas the Exeter Book riddle uses the moth to point toward the unstudious reader.³⁶ Foys thus proposes that the solution to *Riddle* 47 is not the moth announced in the first line of the poem but rather those "undesiring learners" represented by "the immature creature who devours a learned man's sayings with no intellectual gain." In this interpretation, *Riddle* 47 both portrays and addresses "a monastic schoolboy who cannot or will not learn the wisdom set before him."³⁷ But as Jordan Zweck has argued more positively, the riddle might also be celebrating the worm for its silent *ruminatio*.³⁸

The pedagogical tension in *Riddle* 47 finds a precedent in Aldhelm's *Aenigmata*, a collection originally included alongside his treatises on meter and envisioned partly as an aid for learning one's spondees and dactyls. Given that Aldhelm's *Aenigmata* in part served to train the reader in Latin metrics, one who makes it as far as the final lines of *Aenigma* 100 would encounter the poem's implicit interrogation: your wisdom may surpass that of the wisest philosophers, but if you cannot recognize a syllable ("quid constet sillaba") that wisdom is meaningless. The interrogation works the other way around, too: you might be able to recognize syllables, and yet you lack wisdom. This proposition moves the poem beyond the technical minutia of syllabification (recall that many of Aldhelm's aenigmata depend on keen linguistic sensibility) and pushes the reader to think about more substantial forms of knowledge, which escape language and the rich letters of books.

At this point in the poem, the paradox of Creation is thus represented by a form of intelligence that is simultaneously more learned than wise philosophers, yet unlearned in meter, orthography, and the other basics of language that typically precede any kind of philosophical thinking. It turns out that Aldhelm's *Aenigmata* functions in the same paradoxical way: the goal of metrical instruction is decidedly different from the goal announced in the verse preface, where Aldhelm beseeches God's assistance in revealing the "enigmata . . . clandistina" of Creation. On the one hand, the *Aenigmata* serves to teach linguistic skills; on the other, it serves to reveal (*pandere*) the secret, spiritual mysteries of God's Creation as a way to teach the importance of faith in the practice of interpretation. These two objectives play in tension on the space of each page. Without the former, the latter becomes inaccessible; without the latter, the former becomes meaningless. Between them, the reader of Aldhelm's *Aenigmata* must navigate.

Arriving at the final lines of *Aenigma* 100, the reader is thrust from a *tinean* focus on enigmatic details into a much larger intellectual frame of reference:

> Auscultate mei credentes famina uerbi,   80
> Pandere quae poterit gnarus uix ore magister
> Et tamen infitians non retur friuola lector!
> Sciscitor inflatos, fungar quo nomine, sophos.³⁹

[Listen, trusting in the utterances of my words, which the wise teacher is scarcely capable of explaining in speech; and yet that reader who doubts them ought not to think them trifles! I ask the puffed-up philosophers to inform me what name I bear.]

Who are these *sophi inflati*? these *lectores infitiantes*? these *magistri gnari*? This culminating challenge addressed to the reader—whether *sophus*, *lector*, or *magister*—seems to call into question the underlying justification for Aldhelm's own *Aenigmata*. If skilled and knowledgeable teachers cannot reveal ("pandere") the subject of the *aenigma*, then perhaps the subject simply cannot be reached through language or reason. Yet that is precisely what Aldhelm, himself a wise intellectual *par excellence*, proposes to do in the preface to the *Aenigmata* when he beseeches God's assistance in creating verse (a technique that requires, *inter alia*, a keen sense of syllabification) so as to reveal ("pandere") those secret mysteries ("enigmata . . . clandistina") that are manifested through God's Creation and mediated through Aldhelm's poetry. And that is precisely what the ninety-nine preceding riddles do, inviting the reader to reason through their paradoxical language and references. Both Aldhelm and the glossator in Gg. 5. 35 seek to render, in their own unique ways, certain *aenigmata clandestina* through another form of *aenigma*: God's secret mysteries are represented through creatures and phenomena on earth, the obscurities of which are represented through Aldhelm's poetic *aenigmata*, which are then reobscured through the glossator's cryptograms.[40]

The tone of these final lines, however, is clearly critical of those *magistri*, *lectores*, and *sophi* who propound the possibility of knowing and revealing these kinds of divine mysteries through such rational means. Vivien Law has speculated that Aldhelm's scorn may have been directed at intellectuals such as Virgilius Maro Grammaticus, who not only praised the practice of cryptographic *scinderatio fonorum* (discussed above) but also propounded a Creation doctrine that assumes we have access to the "knowledge of higher things," which Aldhelm here consigns as unknowable.[41] According to Law, Aldhelm clearly disdains the ranks of such *philosophi* and "insists that the mysteries remain mysteries, divine wonders inaccessible to rational investigation."[42] Emily Thornbury has read these lines in more positive terms, as Aldhelm's challenge to his readers who "struggle with the solutions" and "are possibly not as clever as they think themselves," a challenge that hinges on the brilliantly fine reading of a distinction between the reader (*lector*) and the puffed-up philosophers (*sophi inflati*), a distinction that gives the former a chance to avoid becoming the latter.[43] These lines, as Thornbury rightly understands them, are certainly "a hyperbolically aggressive challenge to Aldhelm's own readers."[44] But the reason they seem like a challenge to his readers is because it is difficult to imagine how Aldhelm could be divorced, even theoretically, from the wise persona he so actively seems to cultivate in himself (whether as *magister*, *lector*, or *sophus*) and at times seems to admire in others.[45] The difficulty of imagining Aldhelm as something other than a wise intellectual—even if wisely critical of his own intellect and the intellect of others—would explain why, for instance, Foys gives those *magistri* and *lectores* the benefit of the doubt by arguing that Aldhelm reproves the lazy student, while maintaining "the necessity of understanding the text, the importance of wisdom, the explicatory role of a knowledgeable teacher." But even Foys draws a conclusion similar to Law's, as he notes that Creation "remains a theological mystery that, while superficially solved in Aldhelm's riddle, can never truly be understood by a human mind."⁴⁶ The solution, in other words, lies in Creation's enigmatic insolubility.

This insolubility, however, is missed by the glossator of Gg. 5. 35, who reads these final four lines instead as an epilogue, noting "EPILOGVS" in the margin and commenting that "hic conuertit se poeta ad lectores" (here the poet turns himself to the readers).⁴⁷ While a poet, of course, always directs the various movements of a poem, here it is not Aldhelm who turns to the reader (as some critics, including our glossator, assume). Rather, it is Creation whose personification throughout the poem persists until the last line when it finally asks for its name to be spoken. It is not the poet, therefore, but Creation who commands that the reader "Auscultate mei credentes famina uerbi" (Listen, trusting in the utterances of my words) and who asks the *sophi inflati* to speak its name.⁴⁸ All along, the glossator treats *Aenigma* 100 as a collection of individual riddles describing a variety of individual objects, creatures, and phenomena (hence his use of the phrase "alia creatura" to mark each apparent reference to a new creature). The glossator explains away the inexplicable paradoxes by finding things in the natural world (such as Mount Etna) that fit both sides of a given paradox (hot and icy). But the solution to *Aenigma* 100 can only be understood from a different perspective, one that attempts to witness all of the variety and paradoxes—and the limitless possibilities they enable—together at once and under a single name: *Creatura*.

Each of these four final lines therefore speaks to a different kind of reader who might encounter and attempt to solve the *aenigma*. The first line addresses all readers, establishing what is necessary for a proper reading of the poem and, moreover, of Creation: it commands the reader to have faith, to believe (*credere*), as he or she encounters and listens to the words of the poem. The next two lines describe failing readers: the *magister* who can scarcely reveal the meaning of the poem in his own words and the *lector* who doubts their significance.⁴⁹ The act of faith suggested in the first line is thus directly opposed to the rational knowledge in the second line, which fails to aid the *magister* in revealing the words, words that must be believed (*credere*) before they can be understood. It moreover serves as a warning to those doubtful, unfaithful, denying readers (*lectores infitiantes*),⁵⁰ urging them not to think these words mere frivolities ("non retur friuola"), a temptation to which readers of other riddles might easily succumb. By contrast, for instance, Symphosius considers his own *Aenigmata* to invite just such frivolity:

Tum uerbosa cohors studio sermonis inepti
Nescio quas passim magno de nomine nugas
Est meditata diu; sed friuola multa locuta est.⁵¹

[Then the verbose crowd, in its enthusiasm for foolish talk, in ignorance contemplated those trifles with grand titles here and there for a long time; yet the crowd uttered many frivolous things].

Indeed, such *lectores infitiantes* and *magistri gnari* even show up in Aldhelm's *Aenigma* 81, where the setting of the Morning Star (*Lucifer*) is characterized as a fall recklessly perpetuated by his pride of mind ("cecidi proterua mente superbus"). The *aenigma* ends by inviting readers wise in books to explain and reveal this proud fall ("*Gnarus* quos poterit per biblos *pandere* lector"), for who better to know "mente superbus" (pride of mind) than such wise readers? It is scarcely a frivolous matter. The final verse of *Aenigma* 81 thus anticipates the impotent *lector* and *magister gnarus* who by contrast cannot *pandere*, who cannot reveal or explain the words of *Aenigma* 100.

The final line of Aldhelm's *Aenigma* 100 then challenges these *sophi inflati* to name a solution, to pick a single word that fully and accurately characterizes all of those paradoxes and varieties of Creation. But here Aldhelm seems to lay a trap for those proud and inflated philosophers who will want to reason toward and arrive at a precise and rational solution, a solution that will only in turn make them more inflated and more proud. Indeed, pride is at the heart of the final line of Aldhelm's *Aenigma* 100: "Sciscitor inflatos, fungar quo nomine, sophos" (Now I ask the puffed-up philosophers what name I bear).[52] Aldhelm is clearly referencing 1 Corinthians 8:1, Paul's oft-cited injunction against prideful knowledge: "Scientia inflat, caritas vero aedificat" (knowledge puffeth up, but charity edifieth). Paul's "scientia inflat" is initially mirrored in Aldhelm's "sciscitor inflatos," but Aldhelm's syntax twists Paul's words so that the *sophus inflatus* is denied any agency of inquiry. Instead, Creation controls the interrogation ("sciscitor") from the very start, while the state of inflated pride remains adjectively bound to the identity of the philosopher. Aldhelm may have tweaked Paul's rhetoric, but the point remains the same: *scientia* risks producing an empty form of growth, inflation, and pride—all of which Paul opposes to the solid edification produced by *caritas*.[53]

Anyone who has solved a difficult riddle will know that unavoidable feeling of pride and accomplishment that accompanies such a moment of triumph. Scholars who have not spent much time puzzling over riddles or who have never tried writing their own (a similarly inflating experience) will nevertheless be familiar with the same feeling upon the discovery of a new idea or the solving of an old conundrum.[54] This drive to intellectual superiority is somewhat inherent to scientific thought (*scientia*). And Paul and Aldhelm are not the only ones who saw it that way. Even Albert Einstein famously suggested that many scientists "take to science out of a joyful sense of superior intellectual power."55 To approach riddles with such a pretense of scientific superiority and thus without humility is to dismiss Paul's injunction ("scientia inflat") and overlook Aldhelm's implied jab at those *sophi inflati* trying to decipher the *aenigma*. Put another way, the moment when the reader assumes interpretive control over the concealed or mysterious meaning of the text is the moment the reader assumes the position of *arbiter*, trying to govern the known and the unknown. Pride both generates and is generated by this assumption of control, and accordingly such inflated acts of interpretation not only negate the virtue of wisdom but also give way to sin.

Pride is commonly conceived as the beginning of all sin (e.g., Ecclus. 10:15), and for Aldhelm, it is also the "ceterarum uirtutum deuoratricem" (devourer of the other virtues).[56] In other words, pride is the sin that carries the power to produce each of the other deadly sins but also has the potential to usurp otherwise well-intentioned and virtuous actions, turning them to evil.[57] Even *humilitas* thus always bears a tinge of *superbia*: from the *Regula Sancti Benedicti* to Bernard of Clairvaux, for instance, the steps of humility involve a mode of ascendancy that is necessarily susceptible to pride until one reaches the complete humility of the final step.[58] Likewise, in the final lines of *Aenigma* 100, reason and wisdom come into similar contact with pride. *Sapientia* is clearly a virtue, and as its inverse, ignorance is often treated as a vice.[59] Pride not only tends to usurp virtue but also specifically interferes with wisdom and rationality, as Proverbs 11:2 makes clear: "Ubi fuerit superbia, ibi erit et contumelia; ubi autem est humilitas, ibi et sapientia" (Where pride is, there also shall be reproach: but where humility is, there also is wisdom).[60] By the end of the *Aenigmata*, then, Aldhelm's final injunction against prideful acts of scientific reading should thus serve to remind the reader that wisdom itself is not as important as the means by which it is obtained, as even innocent or playful acts have the potential to be judged harshly.

Indeed, the scribe in Gg. 5. 35 seems to have noticed Aldhelm's concern for prideful knowledge acquisition, for he glossed "inflatos" with the word "superbos" and "sophos" with the word "sapientes." Together, these glosses make the final lines of Aldhelm's poem reverberate with line 70 above—"mea prudentes superat sapientia sophos"[61] (my wisdom surpasses the skilled philosophers)—by stressing the etymological relationship between the verb *superare* (to surpass) and the sin of *superbia* (pride).

For Aldhelm, the goal of his *Aenigmata* was therefore not merely to initiate the reader into the intricacies of poetic meter, nor was it merely to teach the hermeneutic skills necessary for interpreting the enigmas of scripture, but to encourage the reader toward the humility necessary for a faithful approach to interpretation. Such interpretation was to be both faithful to the meaning of the text *and* trusting that the meaning of that text remains entirely subject to

God's judgment and knowledge, trusting that God remains the ultimate *Arbiter*. For the reader to think otherwise, to think that his or her hermeneutic judgment supersedes the judgment of God is to risk falling into pride.

The forcefulness of this final warning is anticipated as early as Aldhelm's acrostic preface, where God is responsible as *Arbiter* for two things. First, he punished Behemoth when that ghastly creature once fell from the high citadel ("Ex alta quondam rueret dum luridus arcE"), a conflation of the fallen Satan with the enormous Behemoth that conveys Satan's inflated pride.[62] And second, it is Aldhelm's hope that God might act as his protector ("praesul") and aid in his composition of the poems that follow.[63] At first this image of the fallen Behemoth may seem unrelated to Aldhelm's subsequent petition for God's aid in revealing the "enigmata . . . clandistina" through his poetic verses; indeed, it may just seem like a convenient Latin word ending in the letter *H* (a rarity) without which Aldhelm's acrostic would collapse. However, in light of those final lines of *Aenigma* 100, Aldhelm's hermeneutics and Satan's pride become profoundly linked and yet profoundly at odds.

On the other hand, the glosses in Gg. 5. 35 note not only the risk of pride but also the virtue of humility represented by that creature who is ignorant of syllables. The *tinea* (encrypted in the margin of lines 70–72) may represent a degraded form of idle ignorance (as scholars have proposed), but it can also represent the most positively humble form of learning. Psalm 21:7, for example, famously equates such a creature with the virtue of humility: "Ego autem sum vermis, et non homo" (But I am a worm, and no man).[64] And most monks (including Aldhelm and our glossator) would have been familiar with this psalmic expression, especially if they lived in a house that closely followed the *Regula Sancti Benedicti*, which instructs monks to recite it as part of the seventh degree of humility.[65] It is worth noting, though, that the Old English word *wyrm* often translates the humble *uermis* of Psalm 21:7 as well as snakes and serpents, which can symbolize not humility but prideful wisdom or hellish torture.[66] For an Anglo-Saxon scribe cognizant of the ambiguities around the creature (particularly in the vernacular), the encrypted *tinea* gloss becomes another perfect representation of Creation's paradoxes: not merely between humble ignorance and exalted wisdom, but also between angelic humility and satanic pride. As the pride of the wise philosopher is tempted in the final lines of Aldhelm's *Aenigma* 100, that pride is contrasted with the humble ignorance of the worm. And yet both are subsumed under God's Creation.

Indeed, humility itself becomes a token of the very paradoxes that structure Aldhelm's *Aenigma* 100, where Creation is described in one pairing as "Altior, en, caelo rimor secreta Tonantis / Et tamen inferior terris tetra Tartara cerno" (Behold, higher than heaven, I explore the secrets of the Thunderer; yet, lower than earth, I examine the foul underworld).[67] While the Gg. 5. 35

glossator takes these two lines to refer to angels and demons ("Vt Bohfmk" and "Vt efNPOfT," respectively),⁶⁸ other readers seem to have recognized the central paradox of humility. In his *Aenigma* 24 (*De humilitate*), for example, Tatwine borrows Aldhelm's phrasing to conclude his description of humility: "Inferior terris et celis altior exsto" (I am lower than earth and higher than heaven).⁶⁹ And although his borrowing is not verbatim, Boniface makes a similar claim in his *aenigma* on the virtue of Christian humility (*De humilitate cristiana*): "Ima solo quantum, tantum fio proxima caelo" (so much as I am made deepest in the soil, so much am I made nearest to heaven).⁷⁰ Curiously, however, pride can also fit within the same paradoxical structure, as Eusebius puts it in his *Aenigma* 27 (*De humilitate et superbia*):

> Curua licet maneam uel strata soloque depressa,
> Me tamen hinc omnes nunc exaltabo tenentes;
> Effera stans inimica mea sustollitur alta,
> Atque suos sternit uel comprimit illa sequaces.
>
> [Although I remain depressed, stooped or even prostrate on the ground, yet I shall henceforth exalt all who hold to me now; my enemy is cruel, elevated she is raised on high, but scatters and crushes those who follow her.]⁷¹

In Aldhelm and Tatwine, the lowliness of humility is signified by the earth (*terra*), while in Boniface and Eusebius it is signified by the soil (*solum*): the implied etymological connection is deep-rooted, as the word *humilitas* is itself derived from *humus* (soil, earth, ground).⁷² But in these poems we witness a kind of vertiginous subjectivity, whereby what distinguishes the exalted lowliness of humility from the lowly exaltedness of pride is the order in which the lowliness is sought; to be lowly now will lead to exaltation later (e.g., Luke 14:11). The worm is thus a perfect characterization of that humble lowliness with its dwelling place in the *humus*, in the earth and soil with its inferior grasp of learning, which later will become exalted.

Death, Worms, and the Imposition of Silence

While worms often signify humility, in Anglo-Saxon England they were also often thought to play a fundamental role in imposing silence on the dead.⁷³ We have already seen in Chapter 2 how the silence of death was thought to correspond with the most absolute—although still not entirely inviolable—form of secrecy. This corporal silence and secrecy physically manifested in the decomposition of dead bodies in their earthen graves, where (according to the *Soul and*

Body poems) the corpse becomes "wyrmum to wiste" (nourishment for worms) in a grotesque reversal of the kind of consumption that characterized the life of the sinful, proud, and inflated body ("þrymful þunedest").[74] But death is humbling, as the greedy consumption is now carried out by lowly earthworms:

> ond þe sculon her moldwyrmas   manige ceowan,
> slitan sarlice   swearte wihta,
> gifre ond grædige.[75]

> [And here the many earthworms must gnaw on you, must rend you sorrowfully, those dark creatures, ravenous and greedy.]

The image of these earthworms gnawing on the flesh of the body returns us to the image of the larval book moth chewing through the parchment in Exeter Book *Riddle* 47. Darkness surrounds both species as they eat their respective meals. The thief working in the dark ("þeof in þystro") evokes the secrecy inherent to the act of stealing (see Chapters 1 and 3), while the darkness of the earthworms at work evokes an altogether different kind of subterranean concealment.[76] In *Riddle* 47, the worm swallows the songs of men ("se wyrm forswealg wera gied sumes"), but the worms in a grave impose silence another way.

In the Vercelli Book poem *Soul and Body I* (like *Soul and Body II* in the Exeter Book), worms tear out and destroy—among other body parts—the tongues of their victims:

> Rib reafiað   reðe wyrmas,
> beoð hira tungan totogenne   on tyn healfa
> hungregum to frofre;   forþan hie ne magon huxlicum
> wordum wrixlian   wið þone werian gast.   115

> [Ferocious worms ravage the ribs; as nourishment for those hungry ones, their tongues are torn into ten pieces; therefore it (*scil.* the body) cannot disgracefully exchange words with the wretched spirit.][77]

Much like the end of Aldhelm's *Aenigma* 100, the end of *Soul and Body I* then turns to warn the reader who thinks himself too wise ("þæt mæg æghwylcum / men to gemynde, modsnotra gehwam"), urging him to be mindful of the fact that mere worms have the power to undo that wisdom.[78] Worms are thus both humble and humbling, as they destroy the worldly mechanisms for gaining and distributing knowledge and thereby prevent their victims from ever exchanging words again.

Indeed, "wordum wrixlian" is a common epithet for the production of riddles, verse, and those *gydd* (songs) swallowed by the book moth in *Riddle* 47.[79] This connection between the words of wise men and the practice of exchanging words ("wordum wrixlan") is made especially clear in the opening lines of the Exeter Book poem *Maxims I*:

> Frige mec frodum wordum!   Ne læt þinne ferð onhælne,
> degol þæt þu deopost cunne!   Nelle ic þe min dyrne gesecgan,
> gif þu me þinne hygecræft hylest   ond þine heortan geþohtas.
> Gleawe men sceolon gieddum wrixlan.[80]

> [Question me with wise words! Do not let your heart be concealed, that which you most deeply know to be secret! I will not tell you my secret if you conceal your understanding and the thoughts of your heart from me. Wise men must exchange songs.]

The exchange of words is precisely what wise men ("gleawe men") do when they conceal and disclose their enigmatic and secret wisdom, particularly (we might imagine) in the form of riddles. These various worms that consume the songs and tongues of wise men (but are none the *gleawera*, none the wiser, as a result), signify not only the humbling of proud philosophers but also the foreclosure of speech; the tearing of the tongue and the theft of words produce a deadly silence. They sabotage the very means by which wise men would otherwise proudly exchange their secrets.

However, despite the irresistible tendency to view death and the decomposition that inevitably follows as the indelible silencing of a human being, many riddles challenge the permanence of that deadly silence. In the Exeter Book, for example, the book moth *Riddle* (47) is immediately succeeded by *Riddle* 48, and several scholars have noticed the interaction between these two riddles, both in their manuscript context where they appear as one continuous riddle and in their shared language and imagery.[81] By reading the two poems together, the damaging problems introduced in *Riddle* 47 (where, for instance, the creature consumes the words of men) are, in *Riddle* 48, miraculously reversed and resolved:

> Ic gefrægn for hæleþum   hring endean,
> torhtne butan tungan,   tila þeah he hlude
> stefne ne cirmde,   strongum wordum.
> Sinc for secgum   swigende cwæð:
> "Gehæle mec,   helpend gæsta."   5

> Ryne ongietan   readan goldes
> guman galdorcwide,   gleawe beþencan
> hyra hælo to gode,   swa se hring gecwæð.⁸²

> [I learned about a ring that delivered a message for men, clearly yet without a tongue, perfectly though he did not cry out with a loud voice or strong words. The treasure spoke silently before men: "Save me, O helping spirit." Let men understand the mystery of the red gold, the powerful saying; let the wise entrust their salvation to God, as the ring said.]

The object (either a paten or chalice) is able to convey a message clearly, although it has no tongue ("butan tungan"); and it is able to speak, although it does so silently ("swigende cwæð"). This tongueless speech is often interpreted as an inscription on the surface of the object, yet it also represents a kind of mystery ("ryne") for wise men to contemplate and understand. The indirect mode of understanding is predicated on a prior move of entrusting one's salvation to God, and the mysterious prayer becomes both the call and the means to salvation, which depends on faith. Such faithful prayer becomes one way to work toward salvation and to invert the silence inevitably imposed by the gnawing of worms.⁸³ These riddles are not alone in giving the dead the power to speak.⁸⁴ Others, such as Eusebius's *Aenigma* 32 (*De membrano*), allow parchment to speak only because the animal, although once alive, is dead:

> Antea per nos uox resonabat uerba nequaquam,
> Distincta sine nunc uoce edere uerba solemus;
> Candida sed cum arua lustramur milibus atris;
> Viua nihil loquimur, responsum mortua famur.⁸⁵

> [Once we had no voice of any kind to say a word; now we produce words without an audible voice; But we, although white fields, are wandered over by a thousand black figures; alive we do not speak, but dead we give answers.]

And *Riddle* 60 in the Exeter Book, for instance, likewise gives a reed pen the capability to exchange words, despite being mouthless:

>   Lyt ic wende
> þæt ic ær oþþe sið   æfre sceolde
> ofer meodubence   muðleas sprecan,
> wordum wrixlan.⁸⁶   10

[I hardly expected that, sooner or later, I would ever speak mouthless over the benches in the mead hall, exchange words.]

These enigmatic depictions of dead and mouthless objects speaking are all the more profound in light of those riddles and poems that imagine the intricate feeding habits of worms and their capacity to deflate the pride of wise men. But while the spectacle of speech acts by the dead and tongueless is a frequent occurrence in early medieval riddles, it is even more common still in the literature of the Day of Judgment.

Judgment, Humility, and the Eschatology of Interpretation

As the time in which the lowliness of the humble and the exaltedness of the proud will be swiftly inverted, in which sins (almost all of which were thought to stem from pride) will be revealed and punished, the Day of Judgment was also believed to be the day in which the silence of the dead and the secrecy of the living would be reversed. Indeed, Anglo-Saxon Christians believed that at the Last Judgment, the body—although tongueless and worm-infested on earth—would be reunited with the soul and thus perfected. The body and soul would be forced to testify, as all the secrets of the present life come to be revealed, not just before God but before everyone: the silence produced by the worms' consumption of all these corporeal tongues will thus be overridden by the universal revelation.[87] Where riddles imagine the possibility of posthumous speech, they implicitly confront the eschatological dimensions of human secrecy, but they also confront the eschatology of concealment and interpretation in more subtle ways as well.

The preface to Aldhelm's *Aenigmata* begins with an invocation of God as *Arbiter*, as the Judge who oversees his Creation and, eventually, as the Judge who will oversee the judgment at the end of time. In the context of the *Aenigmata*, this juridical image adds initial weight to the eschatological significance of reading these kinds of texts. We have now seen how riddles—despite their often ludic nature—could easily occasion intellectual pride, and we have seen how Aldhelm in particular is keen to remind the reader that such pride produces an empty form of wisdom that further impairs the reader's ability to understand the mysteries in the riddle and their true relation to the mysteries of God's Creation.

For medieval Christians, the Day of Judgment was of considerable interest and speculation; it was naturally a subject taken up in countless homilies and poems, as well as in treatises and illustrations.[88] Given that the production and interpretation of riddles could become occasions of sinful pride, and given that several riddles urge readers to be humbly mindful of the transience of their inflated wisdom, it should come as little surprise that many riddles and many of the manuscripts that preserve them in fact present readers with frequent reminders of this impending Judgment.

The first three riddles of the Exeter Book are sometimes interpreted as a single riddle, and the final lines of *Riddle* 3 present an awe-inspiring image of captivity at the hands of an all-powerful lord:

> Hwilum mec min frea fæste genearwað,
> sendeð þonne under salwonges
> bearm þone bradan, ond on bid wriceð,
> þrafað on þystrum þrymma sumne,
> hæste on enge, þær me heord siteð 5
> hruse on hrycge. Nah ic hwyrftweges
> of þam aglace, ac ic eþelstol
> hæleþa hrere; hornsalu wagiað,
> wera wicstede, weallas beofiað,
> steape ofer stiwitum. Stille þynceð 10
> lyft ofer londe ond lagu swige,
> oþþæt ic of enge up aþringe,
> efne swa mec wisaþ se mec wræde on
> æt frumsceafte furþum legde,
> bende ond clomme, þæt ic onbugan ne mot 15
> of þæs gewealde þe me wegas tæcneð.[89]

[Sometimes my Lord tightly confines me, then sends me under the broad bosom of fertile fields, and holds me in wait, presses me, one of the glorious things, into the darkness, forced into prison, there earth sits hard on my back. I have no escape from that misery, yet I stir the noble city of men, the horned halls shake, the dwelling place of men; the walls tremble, tall above the household. The air seems still over the land and the sea seems quiet, until I break out of confinement, just as He instructs me, He who laid me in bonds at the Creation, in fetter and chain, so that I could not stir from the power of the one who shows me the paths.]

The storm described here carries particular eschatological weight, as it takes the form of an earthquake. On the one hand, this image is consonant with the early medieval understanding that earthquakes were caused by winds trapped and running through subterranean caves, shaking the spongelike earth.[90] On the other hand, earthquakes were considered to be one of the signs that the Day of Judgment was near.⁹¹ With shaking halls and trembling (*beofian*) walls, the stormy earthquake in *Riddle 3* thus recalls a scene much like the one depicted in the Exeter Book poem *Judgment Day I*:

> Lixeð lyftes mægen,   leg onetteð,   55
> blæc byrnende,   blodgyte weorþeð
> mongum gemeldad,   mægencyninges þrea;
> *beofað* eal beorhte gesceaft,   brondas lacað
> on þam deopan dæge,   dyneð upheofon.⁹²

[Tempests of air flash, fire hurtles forth, blazing as it burns; bloodshed is charged to many, the rebuke of the mighty King. The whole bright Creation *trembles*, flames dance, heaven thunders on that awful day.]

Likewise, in the Exeter Book poem *Christ III*: "*Beofað* middangeard, / hruse under hæleþum" (the earth *trembles*, the ground under men).⁹³ The earth also trembles in *Judgment Day II* (a translation of Bede's *De die iudicii*): "Eall eorðe bifað, eac swa þa duna / dreosað and hreosað" (All the earth will *shake*, every hill will then crumble and collapse).⁹⁴ These are mild examples of the terrifying sort of scene into which the reader of the Exeter Book *Riddles* is immediately thrown, a horrifying picture that frames and puts into perspective the entire experience of reading the nearly one hundred riddles that follow.

But the apocalyptic and eschatological implications of *Riddle 3* run deeper still, as the storm's burial and resurrection both transpire at the will of God, whose power holds the storm in wait ("on bid wriceð," line 3b), confining it underground in the darkness ("þrafað on þystrum," line 4a) with the weight of earth on its back ("hruse on hrycge," line 6a). It can only finally break free when the lord decides it is time ("efne swa mec wisaþ," line 13a). This imagery of subterranean confinement and revived ascension is common to a number of other Old English poetic treatments of the Day of Judgment. The Exeter Book poem *Judgment Day I* again, for example, explains,

> Hwæþre þæt gegongeð,   þeah þe hit sy greote beþeaht,
> lic mid lame,   þæt hit sceal life onfon,
> feores æfter foldan.   100

[Although one will be covered by clay, the body by soil, it will happen nevertheless that it (*scil.* the body) will receive life, its vital spirit, after the earthen grave.]⁹⁵

And *Christ III* depicts this familiar image, not once:

> Daga egeslicast
> weorþeð in worulde, þonne wuldorcyning
> þurh þrym þreað þeoda gehwylce,
> hateð arisan reordberende
> of foldgrafum.[96]   1025

[It will prove the most terrifying day in the world when the King of glory with his might punishes everyone, and orders the speech bearers to rise from their earthen graves.]

but twice:

> þætte eorðe ageaf þa hyre on lægun.   1155
> Eft lifgende up astodan
> þa þe heo ær fæste bifen hæfde,
> deade bibyrgde, þe dryhtnes bibod
> heoldon on hreþre.[97]

[. . . that earth gave up those who lay in it. Living once again, those whom it had formerly confined tight rose up, the buried dead who had held the Lord's commandment in their breasts.]

Resuscitating the storm—which was previously confined—God raises it up from beneath the earth, just as he raises up the dead bodies on the Day of Judgment.

    The eschatological rhetoric of *Riddle* 3 thus sets the stage for interpreting the subsequent riddles. And its language, for instance, takes hold in *Riddle* 47, where the book moth is described as a "þeof in þystro" (thief in the darkness, line 4a), a half-line sonically evocative of the storm's confinement in the darkness of the earth ("þrafað on þystrum," line 4a) and conceptually evocative of the biblical motif of death and Judgment as a nocturnal thief.[98] Other images related to Judgment Day crop up elsewhere in the *Riddles* as well. For example, as Brandon Hawk has shown, *Riddle* 30a presents the Cross alongside "eschatological images of penitential fire" that are "associated with the Judgment," suggesting that a reader's meditation on these images would "urge personal penitence" in anticipation of the Last Judgment.[99]

    Utilizing generic techniques akin to those found in the *Riddles*, all four of Cynewulf's runic signatures reflect in some way on the theme of Judgment. It is common, of course, for epilogues and colophons to contain an author's thoughts on death and posterity, but in his epilogues Cynewulf interweaves eschatology with the concealment of his name, which has the particular effect of rendering his efforts at textual concealment relatively trifling. At the end of *Juliana*, for example, he reflects on the unknown journey of his approaching death:

>   Min sceal of lice
> sawul on siðfæt,   nat ic sylfa hwider,   700
> eardes uncyðgu.[100]

[My soul must depart from my body on a journey to where I myself do not know, ignorant of its dwelling place.]

He then immediately juxtaposes this ignorance against his concealed name, which he asks the reader to remember ("noman minum / gemyne") in prayers for God's mercy on the Day of Judgment.[101] In *Fates of the Apostles*, Cynewulf invites the reader to "findan . . . hwa þas fitte fegde" (discover who created this poem) and then concludes his runic signature with confidence:

>   Nu ðu cunnon miht   105
> hwa on þam wordum wæs   werum oncyðig.[102]

[Now you might know who was revealed to men with these words.]

With that knowledge discovered, the reader is asked to pray for Cynewulf's journey from this world, again to a destination undisclosed ("nat ic sylfa hwær") and habitations unknown ("wic sindon uncuð").[103] In *Elene*, Cynewulf embeds his signature in an apocalyptic scene where the wind rushes about until it is suddenly "in nedcleofan nearwe geheaðrod" (narrowly restrained in its prison), reminiscent of the wind "fæste genearwað" (tightly restrained) in Exeter Book *Riddle 3*.[104]

Although implicit in the messages of just judgment and punishment that permeate his epilogues, Cynewulf takes this opportunity to reflect on the clear and distinctly Anglo-Saxon notion that the end of this journey and the accompanying judgment of God would necessarily entail the revelation of *all* secrets to *everyone*:

>   Sceall æghwylc ðær
> reordberendra   riht gehyran
> dæda gehwylcra   þurh þæs deman muð.[105]

[There every speech bearer must hear the truth about every deed through the mouth of the Judge.]

The immediacy and absoluteness of this universal revelation seems to play against the creative textual concealment for which Cynewulf is so well known. Why else would he juxtapose them in such close proximity? And such proximity, moreover, asks us to read the encryption of his signatures (and perhaps other similarly encrypted texts as well) in light of God's absolute power to reveal secrets both great and small.

In their manuscript contexts, even riddles that are not explicitly eschatological often appear in close proximity to texts concerned with the theme of Judgment. Sometimes the connection is loose: for example, in the Vercelli Book, *Soul and Body I* falls immediately after Cynewulf's enigmatic and eschatological signature to *Fates of the Apostles*. Other times it is almost indiscernible: there is reason to believe that Aldhelm, for example, may have modeled the acrostic verse preface to his *Aenigmata* on a poem about the Day of Judgment attributed to the Sibyl (*Versus sibyllae de iudicio Dei*), and the *Versus sibyllae* survives alongside the *Aenigmata* in at least one manuscript.[106] And other times the connection is more distant: in London, British Library, Royal 12 C. xxiii, copies of the *Aenigmata* of Aldhelm, Symphosius, Eusebius, and Tatwine are preceded by a glossed copy of the *Prognosticum futuri saeculi* by Julian of Toledo (d. 690), an enormous collection of material organized as answers to questions concerning death, the status of the soul prior to resurrection, and the Last Judgment.[107]

Although not as narrowly focused as Royal 12 C. xxiii, the Exeter Book also contains numerous eschatological poems in the pages surrounding the *Riddles*. For example, *Christ III* is the third part of the first poem in the manuscript, and its depiction of the coming Judgment parallels *Riddle 3* as the third part of the opening storm riddles later in the manuscript. The first set of fifty-nine riddles, moreover, is closely preceded by *Soul and Body II* and closely followed by *Judgment Day I*. To be sure, the Exeter Book covers a breathtaking variety of both religious and secular topics, which necessarily frustrates any search for unity and any efforts to imagine how an Anglo-Saxon reader may have approached the material.[108] But it would have nevertheless been difficult for a reader to ignore the familiar theme of Judgment, even while turning to the playfully enigmatic riddles elsewhere in the book.

Finally, we might consider the compilation of Gg. 5. 35, more than three times the size of the Exeter Book and containing an even greater variety of material.[109] Codicologically, the manuscript has been shown to comprise four parts.[110] In Part III (fols. 370–431, following the analysis of Rigg and Wieland), we find all of the collections of *Aenigmata* (Eusebius [18], Tatwine [19], Boniface [22], Symphosius [25], and Aldhelm [26]), along with an assortment of other shorter texts, all of which I have detailed and numbered in an Appendix below.[111] Several common threads emerge in this diverse assortment of texts. There are the main collections of *aenigmata* as well as the smaller sets of riddles, such as those attributed to Bede (29b), a medical riddle (39), and the *Bibliotheca magnifica* (42). A number of the other items are concerned with letters, the alphabet, and the Greek language: the *Versus cuiusdam Scoti de alfabeto* (21) (which also appears at the end of Royal 12 C. xxiii) is a series of riddles based on each letter of the alphabet; the Hisperic abecedarian poem *Rubisca* (32) is intermingled with Greek and Hebrew words, as is the immediately subsequent abecedarian poem, *Adelphus Adelpha* (33);[112] and a copy of the Greek alphabet is then followed by transliterated Greek prayers. These items may also more broadly be considered didactic texts, a category to which we could add the *Epistola* and *Disticha Catonis* (27), Alcuin's *Dogmata ad Carolum Imperatorem* (20a), Columbanus's *Versus de bonis moribus observandis* (28), and perhaps Oswald's *Centum concito* (30) and *Terrigene bene* (31).[113] Other items in this part of the manuscript can be categorized as versified prayers (36), hymns (23, 31), and poems about prayers (38, 41). This interest in prayers sometimes overlaps with the interest in language, as exemplified by the prayers written in Greek (35, 37) and Oswald's retrograde hymn (31). The verses on the Creed (38) and the metrical versions of the Pater Noster (36) may have overlapped with an interest in the mysterious power of prayer.[114] Many of these items also betray an interest in versification, as they transform prayers (31, 36) and medical lore (40) into verse, or reflect on the mechanics of metrical production (30).

The collections of *aenigmata* in this section of Gg. 5. 35—with their pedagogical and spiritual interest in language and etymology, in poetic meter, in the praise of God's Creation, and in the decoding of difficult and obscure meaning—easily fall within any of the categories above and, in fact, appear to tie together this otherwise disparate set of items.[115] However, what remains unaccounted for is the inclusion of Bede's *De die iudicii* (29a), an extremely popular 162-line poem devoted to the topic of the Last Judgment.[116] While the poem's inclusion could be explained by its proximity to the riddles attributed to Bede (29b), those Bedan riddles were only (and erroneously) ascribed to him in the twelfth-century contents list, likely as a result of their proximity to the more widely recognized Bedan poem (*De die iudicii* (29a]). That argument fast becomes circular. Alternatively, Bede's *De die iudicii* could have been included to complement the various hymns and prayers, which one might turn to in anticipation of the Day of Judgment. But what immediately follows *De die iudicii* is not a prayer or hymn (those are isolated to nos. 35–38 and

41)¹¹⁷ but rather a series of brief riddles (29b), heavily glossed with solutions, explanations, and references.¹¹⁸ It seems that the only explanation left—even if the glossator seems to have ignored the edifying reminders of *De die iudicii* in favor of the more frivolous toils of riddling on the nature of letters and syllables—is that at some point a compiler thought the topic of Judgment Day to be an appropriate and wise companion to the ostensibly playful and occasionally trifling pedagogy of the surrounding texts.¹¹⁹

The dual emphasis in *De die iudicii* on the importance of confessing one's secret sins in this life and on the inevitable revelation of all those secrets on the Day of Judgment, pairs strongly with the logic of Aldhelm's *Aenigmata*. The poem thus exhorts the reader to the urgency of revealing all concealed sins prior to death and before Judgment:

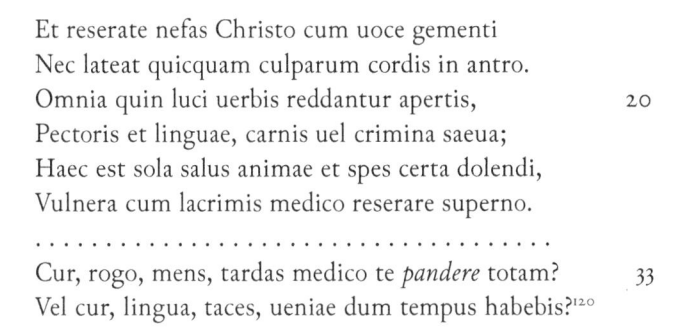

> Et reserate nefas Christo cum uoce gementi
> Nec lateat quicquam culparum cordis in antro.
> Omnia quin luci uerbis reddantur apertis,   20
> Pectoris et linguae, carnis uel crimina saeua;
> Haec est sola salus animae et spes certa dolendi,
> Vulnera cum lacrimis medico reserare superno.
> . . . .
> Cur, rogo, mens, tardas medico te *pandere* totam?   33
> Vel cur, lingua, taces, ueniae dum tempus habebis?¹²⁰

[And reveal your sins with a lamenting voice to Christ, and do not conceal any fault in the cave of your heart. In fact, let everything be brought to light with open words: the severe crimes of the heart, the tongue, and the flesh. This is the only salvation for the soul and certain hope for him who grieves, to open up his wounds with tears to the heavenly doctor. . . . I ask, why, mind, are you so slow to *reveal* yourself completely to the doctor? Or, tongue, why are you silent while you still have time for forgiveness?]

While salvation depends on the resistant mind revealing itself completely to God, that act of resistant revelation echoes Aldhelm's self-proclaimed purpose of his *Aenigmata*: to reveal (*pandere*) the secret mysteries of things through a process of concealment. Bede's *De die iudicii* thus recommends clarity and openness, yet acknowledges the mind's resistance. The riddles and *aenigmata* recommend decipherment and understanding, yet they operate through the resistance of textual concealment. But ultimately, both the concealment of riddles and the mind's refusal to confess, or by contrast, acts of revelation or confession, will pale in comparison to the total revelation to come, when, as Bede puts it:

Cunctaque cunctorum cunctis archana patebunt.
Quod cor, lingua, manus, tenebrosis gessit in antris
Et quod nunc aliquem uerecundans scire uerebat,   70
Omnibus in patulo pariter tunc scire licebit.[121]

[Everyone's every secret will be revealed to everyone. What the heart, tongue, or hand has done in dark caves, and then everyone will be equally permitted to know openly that which the shamefaced one now dreads for anyone to know.]

The absolute completeness of this eventual revelation is evident in Bede's triple use of the word *cunctus*: "Cunctaque cunctorum cunctis."[122] A conviction so ubiquitous means that, just as in those riddles where the dead and tongueless are made to speak, the lifeless bodies will be made to testify, and speech bearers will rise from their graves to speak.[123] Or to borrow from the imaginative words of one Blickling Homily, they will simply become as transparent as glass.[124] The openness envisioned in Bede's poem thus stands in stark contrast to the encrypted texts in its company and profoundly alters the meaning of their textual encryption by reminding the reader to approach the interpretation of such ostensibly trivial forms of concealment with serious anticipation of the inevitable transparency and disclosure to come.

Bede's *De die iudicii* is not alone in this effect: a short poetic Epitaph on Alcuin (24), although naturally concerned with death, also reaches out to the proud intellectual with an Aldhelmian admonition. In a couplet evocative of the worms and their consumption of the proud, the poet thus asks, "Cur Tyrio corpus inhias vestirier ostro, / Quod mox esuriens pulvere vermis edet?" (Why do you desire your body to be clothed in Tyrian purple, because soon hungry worms will eat it and turn you to dust?).[125] The imperial superiority associated with the purple clothing is shredded by the humble yet hungry worm. The poem then ends with the eschatological sound of heavenly trumpets, signaling a riddlelike resuscitation of the dust ("pulvere") created in the lines above: "Qui iaces in tumulo, terrae de pulvere surge, / Magnus adest iudex milibus innumeris" (You who lie in the grave, rise up out of the dust of the earth; the great Judge is near, with innumerable thousands).[126] Alcuin was certainly a reader of Aldhelm, and so we might imagine that his fondness for riddles and wonders, such as those in his *Disputatio ad Pippini*, would have been characterized by a certain Aldhelmian recognition of the limits to linguistic and textual forms of concealment.[127] By recognizing those limits, one can come to appreciate wonders and mysteries that are ultimately unknowable but can nevertheless be approached and laid open with faith and humility.

The genre of Anglo-Saxon riddles covers an astonishing vastness of intellectual and cultural terrain. But even allowing for its variety, that terrain saw frequent confrontations between the human mechanics of secrecy and the divine, from the mystery of Creation to the certainty of the Last Judgment. Whether these confrontations manifested in the tenuous secrecy of master and servant or between the profound secrecy of death and the radical transparency at the end of time, they present the reader with a conflict: the immediate and trivial task of discovering and deciphering their hidden meaning becomes either all the more trivial or all the more serious in the face of the divine. But the conflict rests in the reader. For such interpretation always seems to invite pride, piqued by a reader's natural appetite for discovery when texts, riddles, and mysteries are read with an inflated mind as mere trivia or tests of one's knowledge and intellectual bravado. Such prideful interpretation was thought to be facilitated by a mind that temporarily tunes out divine omniscience and judgment, as Aldhelm seems to have forewarned in his prefatory address to God as *Arbiter*. At the same time, then, riddles—even ones not directly concerned with death or servitude or God or judgment—invite the sensitive reader to approach them with a humble awareness of their place (intellectually and codicologically) and, indeed, the reader's own place in relation to God's knowledge and his power to reveal at will whatever we as humans have attempted to conceal. To approach textual enigmas with such humble faith—trusting in the bright yet enigmatic utterances, trusting a mystery even if it is not fully understood, trusting that even the most absolute forms of encryption will inevitably be laid open—was a powerful ideal that, while sometimes chafing against the trifling work of proud and inflated readers, would render the human experience of secrecy unavoidably penetrable, fragile, fleeting.

Appendix to Chapter 8

Contents of CUL, Gg. 5. 35, Part III, fols. 370–431

These contents are numbered and cited per Rigg and Wieland, "Canterbury Classbook," 124–28, who provide additional details (such as incipits for all items and standard editions when available). I have silently corrected errors.

18. Eusebius
370r   *ENIGMATA EUSEBII DE DEO*

19. Tatwine
374v   *ENIGMATA TAUTUINI*

20. Alcuin
378r   a. *DOGMATA ALBINI AD CAROLUM IMPERATOREM*
379v   b. *DISTICA EIUSDEM AD EUNDEM REGEM*

21. Scotus quidam
381r   *VERSUS CUIUSDAM SCOTI DE ALFABETO*

22. Boniface
382r   a. *BONIFACII AENIGMATA*
385r   b. *DE ACERBISSIMIS MALIS*

23. Hymn
388v   Inc. *Sancte sator legis lator suffragator largus dator*

24. Epitaph on Alcuin
388v   *EPITAPHIUM ALBINI*

25. Symphosius
389r   *ENIGMATA SIMPHOSII*

26. Aldhelm
394r   *ALTHELMI ENIGMATA MILLE VERSIBVS CURRENTIA*

27. Pseudo-Cato
407r   a. *EPISTULA CATONIS*
407v   b. *DISTICHA CATONIS*

28. Columbanus
412v   *VERSUS COLUMBANI ABBATIS DE BONIS MORIBUS OBSERVANDIS*

29. Bede
416r   a. *VERSUS BEDE DE DIE JUDICII*
418v   b. Riddles (Pseudo-Bede)

30. Oswald of Ramsey
419r   *Centum concito* (poem on metrical composition in retrograde verse)
      Inc. Centum concito sic qui novit condere versus

31. Oswald of Ramsey
419v   *Terrigene bene* (hymn in retrograde verse)
      Inc. Terrigene bene nunc laudent, ut condecet almum

32. *Rubisca*
419v   *Inc. Parce domine digna narranti Indigna licet palam peccanti*

33. *Abecedarius*
420r   *Inc. Adelphus adelpha meter alle philus hius tigater*

34. Greek alphabet
420v   Greek alphabet with the names of the letters written above in Roman characters

35. Liturgical prayers in Greek
420v   a. *Inc. O theos istin boythian mu proskis kyrrie* (a series of liturgical incipits)
421r   b. *Inc. Patir imon o en tis uranis* (= *Pater noster*)

36. Metrical versions of the *Pater noster*
421r   a. *Inc. Sancte pater summa celi qui sedis in aula*
421r   b. *Inc. O genitor nostri celi qui in sede moraris*

37. Liturgical prayers in Greek
421v   a. *Inc. Doxa enipsistis theo ke epis gis* (= the *Gloria*)
421v   b. *Inc. Pisteugo is enan theon patiran* (= the Creed)

38. Verses on the Creed
422r   *Inc. Confiteor dominum nunc patrem cunctipotentem*

39. Medical riddle
422v   *Inc. Dic duo que faciunt pronomina nomina cunctis* (followed by the student's responses, which are linked to the riddle with letters of the alphabet)

40. Medical expressions in verse
423r   *Inc. Flegmon apoplexis reuma liturgia spasmus*

41. Verses on the "Te Deum"
423r   *Inc. Te eternum patrem tellus veneratur et omnis*
423v   *Inc. Omnipotentem semper adorant et benedicunt omne per evum*

42. Bibliotheca magnifica
423v   BIBLIOTHECA MAGNIFICA DE SAPIENTIA (a series of riddles on school subjects)

Afterword

Secrets have afterlives. They can be remembered or forgotten, hidden or discovered, exhibited, manipulated, judged: they can vanish with only some trace persisting in the silence that remains behind or the narrative that records their history, in memory, text, or artifact, passing on as a secret long after that vital and original act of concealment ceases to constitute, protect, and constrain it. But the concept of secrecy, too, has its lives and afterlives. We stand now, for instance, in a moment of modernity when the limits of secrecy are as often technological as psychological: a moment when the concept of secrecy tends to imply autonomy and individual responsibility and power; when rights to privacy are assumed; access to privileged information, traded; transparency, venerated; when state and corporate surveillance operates pervasively, yet often unseen (concealed, as it were, by algorithms most of us can neither access nor comprehend). These are generalizations of a contentious moment, an afterlife, a mere blip on secrecy's historical map. From here, we might look back on the discrete secrecies of the past, noticing their continuities and detours, taking the opportunity to reflect on the meaning and function of secrecy as a fundamental, complex, and necessarily changing phenomenon in human social life, unique and distinct at any given historical moment or cultural milieu.

To study the past is to encounter numerous difficulties, one of which—a challenge in the writing of any history, whether literary or cultural or intellectual—is that when we observe and describe historical phenomena that have contemporary iterations and relevance, our studies are limited and shaped by the current range of our language and terminology. Understanding thus requires a supple mode of translation that moves between not only linguistic but also conceptual differences without reifying the past in its imagined alterity. Since the concept of secrecy attracts such contemporary interest and is a matter of such contemporary concern, writing its history in the culture, literature, and intellectual climate of early medieval England, then, becomes an attempt to describe something that we already tend to perceive as familiar in one form or another, or else tend to perceive its otherness in contrast to which modernity defines itself. Perceived familiarity and assumed alterity always risk distorting the process of translation, for as we look back on the past and encounter a given iteration of secrecy, we either misread it as an instantiation of the secrecy familiar to us, attribute it to some grand and universal human phenomenon, or inadvertently pass it over because it diverges from our preconceived definition of the term. The peril is compounded, of course, by the fact that "our" conception of secrecy, although perhaps assumed as familiar, is itself hardly singular.

At the start of this book, I suggested that we approach the phenomenon of secrecy in early medieval England as a *tabula rasa* and begin with the broadest possible definition, one that hinges on separation (*secernere*) rather than, say, intention or calculation or power or possession. Doing so has allowed us to see experiences of secrecy where we might not have otherwise looked: for instance, in one monk's secluded openness to God and in another's futile act of hiding something from his superiors; in the unknown arrival of death and in the silence imposed by the grave; in the concealment of a riddle and the radical unknowability of the divine Judge. Some might object that I have expanded the scope of secrecy too broadly, applying the modern concept and language of secrecy to situations that might not warrant the term. Some of the situations examined in this book may thus seem like mere unknowns (such as death) or accidental concealments (such as a forgotten hoard of treasure): diluted forms of secrecy, if secrecy at all.

But the profound belief in God's omniscience fundamentally alters these mere unknowns and accidental concealments, rendering them in early medieval England somewhat closer to our contemporary sense of secrecy as a tactical and deliberate act of concealing something from someone. If God knows when death will come (as Anglo-Saxons tended to believe), then the vague unknowability of mortality becomes something deliberately concealed from humans by God: thus, a secret. A hoard of treasure might be accidentally lost or forgotten, but to God its location remains entirely known and its rediscovery depends on that knowledge: thus, a secret. In order to understand the secrecy of the past, we must therefore constantly reevaluate and readjust our assumptions about its mechanics, its functions, and its limitations.

Over the course of writing this book, I discovered that one of the challenges in confronting these assumptions is the sheer number and variety of references to secrets, secrecy, and other related acts of hiding, covering, concealing, revealing, and discovering. Often these references are brief and made in passing; they refer to myriad forms, concepts, experiences, and circumstances of concealment, broadly conceived; and they survive across a diversity of genres and media, from law codes to church architecture to the wildly popular genre of riddles. The primary obstacle to the study of secrecy, in other words, is not so much that secrets are innately evasive but rather that they show up so frequently and are so often unmarked by those experiencing and writing about them. This obstacle is felt with particular force in the present study, since the Anglo-Saxons left behind no treatise that theorizes nor any document that explains their thoughts about the nature of secrecy or the mechanics of concealment. What remains are a scattering of offhand statements, material traces, and disparate narratives where secrecy is set in relief or plays in the background.

Given the challenge of writing these statements, traces, and narrative into a coherent history of secrecy, much room still remains for future research. I am aware, for instance, that although I have examined a variety of Old English and Anglo-Latin poems, my study of textual concealment and literary interpretation in these pages has been primarily directed toward riddles and *aenigmata*. I have focused on these texts partly because they constituted a vibrant and important early medieval literary genre and, moreover, because their diversified and playful engagement with textual secrecy allows us to begin to see the particularly unique hermeneutic climate of this period in its most direct and candid form.[1] While I have elsewhere explored the function of secrecy in relation to the hermeneutics of discovery in *Beowulf*,[2] this relationship between secrecy and the literary deserves to be explored further in other genres (such as allegory and exegesis) and across other Anglo-Saxon and even Scandinavian literary sources, as scholars such as Steven Justice and Karma Lochrie have done in their two different approaches to the later Middle Ages, as Katherine Eisaman Maus has done for early modern drama, and as Michael McKeon has done for the literature of seventeenth- and eighteenth-century England, to name only a few of the scholars who have contributed to our understanding of secrecy in the literatures of the past.[3] More work in this area remains ahead—both in the sphere of early medieval studies and in other periods of literary history—with special attention to the ways in which religious belief, especially the belief in divine omniscience, shapes the experience of secrecy.[4]

———•———

The more limited aim of this book has been to begin reorienting the expectations and assumptions we might bring to bear on the idea of secrecy as it took shape in early medieval England, roughly between the years 600 and 1100. My central argument has been that two of the period's major institutions—secular law and monastic life—produced a culture of scrutiny that relied heavily on the belief in God's omniscience and thereby conditioned the experience of secrecy during this period, not only informing Anglo-Saxon notions of mental activity and ideas about the mind but also shaping the ethics of literary interpretation in the process.

This culture of scrutiny depended on and fostered the idea that secrets could be forced open at any time by divine intervention, as we have seen in Chapter 1 with the legal practice of trial by ordeal (in which the healing of an irremediable wound, for example, serves as a divinely authenticated form of testimony in cases where witnesses are lacking or unreliable); or in Chapter 3, with those demons and demoniacs such as Ægelward who are capable of penetrating a person's secret thoughts and broadcasting them to the wider community; or in Chapter 5, with those humble saints who, despite their best attempts to conceal their pious and miraculous actions, find their secret activities revealed to others by the will of God. If a person manages to retain some thought within the secret recesses of his or her mind, as poems such as *The Wanderer* seem to encourage ("ferðlocan fæste binde"), those recesses were nevertheless considered easily penetrable; the secrecy of servants and the textual knots of riddles, even more so; death, the most absolute form of secrecy, was not impervious, either; and any remaining secrets, many Anglo-Saxons seem to have believed, would be revealed before everyone on the Day of Judgment. For secrets belonged, ultimately, to God.

The weakness of human concealment and the impossibility of *keeping* secrets in the face of God's prior and complete knowledge paradoxically made secrets into possessors (rather possessions) that bound and enslaved those who sought to conceal them. This logic is reflected in the rhetoric of bondage and servitude that, as I have shown, pervades Anglo-Saxon law codes, monastic rules, hagiographic narratives, and riddles. But more importantly, it produced a distinct ethics of secrecy in which the moral acceptability of an act of concealment depended on the individual's orientation toward God. Accordingly, to attempt to hide from God was not only to attempt the impossible but to commit a serious sin, whereas to seclude oneself from other human beings while remaining deliberately open to God's constant observation was often upheld as an exemplary form of spiritual virtue. We see this ethical distinction in monastic life, for instance, where monks are strictly forbidden from keeping a secret from the abbot, yet they are encouraged to pray in private (*in secreto*); we see it in law codes that severely punish the harboring of a thief and yet allow for sanctuary in churches; and we see it in the way Bede uses the phrase *locus secretior* to describe both the location of Cain's fratricide (a secluded field) and the places that saints visit in order to pray alone, the remoteness of which nevertheless brings them closer to God.

This ethics of secrecy operates in a variety of contexts—from legal documents to church architecture—but in a rather surprising way it also comes to govern the ethics of discovery and interpretation. If a morally acceptable act of concealment depends on a faithful openness to God's omniscience, then so, too, do acts of interpretation. This ethics of discovery is most clearly legible in the hagiography discussed in Chapter 5, where the hagiographer who sets out to write a saint's *uita* shares some similarities with the illicit spy who sets out to uncover and disseminate the unknown activities of the saint—activities the saint would humbly want to conceal so as to avoid the traps of hypocrisy and pride. The difference, however, is that the spy tends to be motivated by doubt and guided by the false assumption that his actions are unseen by God, whereas the hagiographer is motivated by faith in his deliberate submission to God's aid and supervision.

Just as the Anglo-Saxons left behind no coherent theories of secrecy, so they likewise left behind no coherent theories of literary interpretation or any evaluative surveys concerning the principles of interpretation beyond strictly theological and exegetical contexts. Essays by George H. Brown, Nicholas Howe, and M. B. Parkes have enriched our understanding of how the Anglo-Saxons thought of the practices of reading and interpretation.[5] To go beyond these important studies based on examples of interpretation *qua* interpretation and reading *qua* reading, my goal has been to discern Anglo-Saxon approaches to the interpretation of literary texts by considering how the Anglo-Saxons conceived of the experience and mechanics of secrecy and concealment more generally. As we have seen, secrecy and concealment—what Michel de Certeau considered the "precondition for hermeneutics"—were experiences both pervasive and variegated, paving an inroad for understanding the diverse ways early medieval intellectuals and readers might have approached the process of interpretation.[6] Some of the poems we have examined, such as Cynewulf's *Elene*, thus embrace and proclaim this ethics of discovery, making a strong case for a hermeneutic of faith as opposed to a forceful, proud, interrogative form of doubt. But the hermeneutic tension between force and faith becomes all the more contentious, as we have seen, in the extremely popular genre of riddles, some of which require small-scale faith on the part of the reader as she pieces together their various paradoxes and incongruities, while others tempt the reader into a prideful mode of *scientia*, and a few subtly admonish the reader away from such an approach, encouraging instead humility in the face of the unknown.

Getting from the mechanics of secrecy to the mechanics of interpretation is a big jump, but the jump seems not to have been all that distant for early medieval readers. Indeed, Gregory the Great made use of the tactical and interpersonal experience of secrecy as an analogy for reflecting on the challenge of interpreting scripture:

> Sicut enim ignotorum hominum facies cernimus et corda nescimus, sed si familiari eis locutione coniungimur, usu colloquii eorum etiam cogitationes indagamus. Ita cum in sacro eloquio sola historia aspicitur, nihil aliud quam facies uidetur; sed si huic assiduo usu coniungimur, eius nimirum mentem quasi ex collocutionis familiaritate penetramus.[7]

[In the same way that we see the faces of strangers and know nothing of their hearts, but if we connect ourselves to them with intimate speech, through the practice of conversation we also discover their thoughts, thus when in scripture only the story is observed, nothing other than the face is seen; but if we connect ourselves to it with diligent practice, we can without doubt penetrate its mind as if in intimate conversation.]

For Gregory, this experience of secrecy—when an individual conceals something from someone else—translates to the way a text can conceal its own meaning from the reader, requiring in turn a kind of engagement on the part of the reader that operates much like a conversation. The face that Gregory looks behind and the mind that he penetrates are just different metaphors for the literary surface that in recent years has become a locus for self-reflection in the field of literary criticism.[8] To perform close reading in one model is to dig below the surface of a text and extract its hidden meaning, what the Middle Ages would refer to as the letter and the spirit, respectively. As scholars continually evaluate alternative methods of interpretation that, for instance, seek to read the surface on its own terms rather than as some concealing barrier to something more significant, and as scholars recognize the medieval origins of such methodological questions, these conversations would be enriched by considering how humility in particular was long an integral feature of interpretation: it was thought to enable and animate the process of moving from letter to spirit or, in Gregory's metaphor, from the face to the mind.

In reading Gregory's analogy, we might be thus struck by the easy power that he seems to assign to the "intimate conversation" that enables a reader to "penetrate" the mind of the text. But really, the power of this hermeneutic conversation just needs context: immediately before equating scripture to the face of a stranger, Gregory establishes what is truly necessary for the conversation to be at all productive: "Quae nimirum ueritatis intellegentia cum per cordis humilitatem quaeritur, legendi assiduitate penetratur" (Doubtless, when this understanding of truth is sought with humility of heart, it is penetrated by the diligence of reading).[9] Alone, reading is not enough to access what texts hide; it also takes a kind of faithful humility, "per cordis humilitatem," which opens up the very possibility of a more diligent practice of interpretation.

In the last chapter of this book, we examined a variety of riddles in their manuscript contexts, where two hermeneutic modes subtly chafed against one another: prideful force against humble faith. As the dominant and positive discourses of humility excoriate the pride that readers sometimes felt and texts sometimes induced, the friction between these two interpretive modes not only illuminates Anglo-Saxon tensions around the practice of interpretation but also, I think, speaks to our own literary critical moment as well. A crucial distinction thus emerges between Anglo-Saxon approaches to reading and present-day assumptions about literary criticism, for the former ineluctably operates alongside the belief that if God already knows the secrets hidden beneath the surface of a text, then for a human reader to divine those secrets requires either an act of humble piety or a potentially dangerous act of presumption—not merely, as for some modern varieties of reading, an exertion of hermeneutic force.

——— • ———

Given this realization, what responsibility do we have to the hermeneutic logics of the past? And what are the risks, moreover, of allowing this historicized understanding of early medieval practices of interpretation to influence our readings of their texts?

The first thing to realize in attempting to answer these questions is that literary criticism still very much negotiates similar tensions between faith and suspicion, tolerance and aggression, pride and humility, surfaces, depths, description, explication, nearness, distance, and so forth. The terms and the stakes are slightly different, yet we talk about the latent or symptomatic meanings of a text and answer its need for explication, or we turn to its surface and answer its need for description, just as exegetes of the past attended to their own surfaces and symptoms in the four senses of scripture. While today's interpretive paradigms are myriad, this analogy is often more than mere analogy—a matter of tradition, albeit distant and at times disconnected. The fierce commitments to one framework over another seem to have faded into a broader openness to mixed forms of critical inquiry and the desire to test and reinvent our critical assumptions.[10] Along the way, however, the underlying philosophies of hermeneutics have often drawn inspiration from medieval religiosity, even, for instance, from versions of the hermeneutic faith that I have sought to recover in this book.

Think of Paul Ricoeur's use of Anselm of Canterbury to frame his recuperative hermeneutic in opposition to the school of suspicion: "Believe in order to understand, understand in order to believe."[11] Or go back a little further to Friedrich Schleiermacher (1768–1834), a pioneering philosopher of hermeneutics, who recognized the circularity of the hermeneutic process, noting, for instance, that "the image of the whole becomes more complete via the understanding of the particular, and the particular is more and more completely understood the more one gets an overall view of the whole."[12] Or consider the critique of Schleiermacher offered by Hans-Georg Gadamer (1900–2002), who posited that hermeneutics is always subject to the unavoidable "prejudices and fore-meanings that occupy the interpreter's consciousness."[13] These are all different ways of saying that belief conditions understanding. For the Anglo-Saxons, this conditioning happened in a very particular way—in relation to God's omniscience. I would argue that this period was therefore a critical moment in the evolution of hermeneutics as it worked through the experience of faithful humility both in the face of concealment and in the practice of interpretation.

In trying to think through the stakes of this critical realization and the responsibility that it places on scholars and interpreters of the past, I have found Gadamer to be especially helpful. On the one hand, he argues that temporal distance is central to the process of understanding, for the meaning of a text "is always co-determined also by the historical situation of the interpreter and hence by the totality of the objective course of history."[14] In other words, it is impossible for us to escape our own historical moment, nor can we hope to inhabit fully that moment of the texts we read. The medievalist Paul Zumthor grappled with precisely this dilemma for the field of medieval studies in his elegant 1980 book, *Parler du moyen age*, as did one of Gadamer's pupils, another medievalist, Hans Robert Jauss.[15] At the center of these inquiries—so central themselves to the study of the Middle Ages—is the idea that the conditions of understanding are always subject to those involuntary prejudices that, again, as Gadamer puts it, "occupy the interpreter's consciousness." And because the interpreter "cannot separate in advance the productive prejudices that enable understanding from the prejudices that hinder it and lead to misunderstandings," these prejudices—which Enlightenment thinkers such as Schleiermacher sought to discredit and overcome with the advancement of a historical science—must be subject to another level of hermeneutic consideration and interrogation altogether.

This interrogation, I would then add, also requires us to bear in mind the hermeneutic assumptions of the period we are studying—insofar as we can discern them. If the role Gadamer assigns to "prejudices" and "self-reflection" can be loosely equated to what medieval Christians called "faith" and "humility," then together these principles demand an acknowledgment of our own hermeneutic limitations, an acknowledgment that—just as a secret does not belong to its keeper—interpretation does not entirely *belong* to the interpreter. As Gadamer famously put it, "history does not belong to us; we belong to it."[16] Or said another way, those aforementioned prejudices are never at the interpreter's "free disposal," and the conditions of understanding "do not amount to a 'procedure' or method which the interpreter must of himself bring to bear on the text; rather they must be given."[17] This idea can be most compellingly seen when Gadamer, in a strikingly Gregorian moment, analogizes "understanding a text and reaching an understanding in a conversation," suggesting that we might "say that we 'conduct' a conversation, but the more genuine a conversation is, the less its conduct lies within the will of either partner. Thus a genuine conversation is never the one that we wanted to conduct. Rather, it is generally more correct to say that we fall into conversation, or even that we become involved in it."[18]

The way one falls into interpretation as one falls into conversation—contingent on factors outside of one's control—demands an acknowledgment on our part as scholars that we in fact have little chance today of fully accessing and inhabiting the interpretive mindsets that past readers took up in encounters with poetry or saint's lives or riddles. But one way to begin discerning these mindsets is by treating secrecy and concealment as the basis for most hermeneutic endeavors. However, that gives us only a partial picture, and even if we could fully access the interpretive minds of the past, I am not convinced doing so would do much good. Just because Gregory prescribes humility of the heart or Cynewulf professes the hermeneutic power of faith does not mean that we should necessarily embrace such humility and faith as such. Even so, I have come to realize that an awareness of these hermeneutic paradigms, their contentiousness, and their role in framing the period's engagement with hidden and concealed meaning in all its various forms has the radical potential to shape our own approach to these texts.

I am not suggesting that we should start interpreting like Augustine—D. W. Robertson, Jr., tried that and bore more eventual chastisement than he probably deserved for doing so, given that he also seemed to recognize, like Gadamer, that we can neither leave behind nor contravene our own historically contemporary moment in our thinking. The point, then, is certainly not that readers today should somehow do away with their own sophisticated and novel methods of inquiry, even as some of those methods have exegetical and medieval roots. Indeed, our diversity of opinions and approaches and backgrounds only makes our acts of interpretation more fruitful in the end and points optimistically toward a future of vivacious inquiry. Instead, I am proposing that we can learn much from how a culture thinks about the unknown and unknowable, the secret and the concealed. For Anglo-Saxons, the unknown demanded humility and faith. Although perhaps uncomfortable, an appreciation for this humility and faith—the combination is crucial, for faith without humility risks becoming too self-certain—will ultimately provoke more meaningful interpretive work.

From various perspectives, this need for humility in contemporary criticism is already being recognized. In his history of the long and intertwined relationship between faith and hermeneutics, for instance, James Simpson ultimately makes a case for a friendlier mode of interpretation "based in faith in persons as ethical agents" that "does not do away with suspicion" but instead respects "the alterity of its subjects."[19] Scholars of more modern literatures are taking similar approaches: Heather Love's respectful observation comes to mind, as does D. A. Miller's confessed tendency toward pride in moments of interpretive discovery and in readings that are, perhaps, too close.[20] If the early Middle Ages tells us something in this respect, it is that this humility is crucial but often difficult to achieve.

What connects us, then, is the profoundly human experience of secrecy, reasoned as universal even as the complexity of that experience remains historically and culturally contingent. Whether we follow Bede or Gregory, or the sociologist Georg Simmel or the moral philosopher Sissela Bok, we find a governing tendency to recognize secrecy as a natural and proper part of human life.[21] Even Aldhelm embraced this possibility: "naturali quadam, ut mihi insitum fertur, latentium rerum curiositate" (a certain natural curiosity about hidden things, as, it is said, is innate in me).[22] On the one hand, such innateness—conceptually indebted, as it is, to the sayings of others—necessarily remains variable and impossible as such; but on the other, something akin to Aldhelm's innate curiosity has persisted to motivate me—perhaps you, too—in the ways I have come to read the past, leaving me the more curious and humbled by all that yet remains hidden.

Notes

Introduction

1. The shelf-mark is BL, Cotton Claudius B. iv; Gneuss-Lapidge, no. 315; Ker, no. 142. The manuscript is available in digital facsimile: British Library Digitised Manuscripts, "Cotton MS Claudius B. iv."

2. The phrase is used by Gregory the Great, *Moralia in Iob*, ed. Adriaen, vol. 143a, lib. XXII, cap. 15, §30, p. 1113, line 8: "augmenta nequitiae."

3. Ibid., §32, p. 1115, lines 58, 60–61; §30, p. 1113, line 5; §32, p. 1115, lines 61–62.

4. Bede, *In Genesim*, ed. Jones, lib. I, p. 63, lines 2017–21; *On Genesis*, trans. Kendall, 130.

5. This phrase and its cousin, *internus iudex*, are particularly popular with Bede (who uses them twenty-four and five times, respectively) and Gregory (who uses them eleven and twenty-two times, respectively).

6. Gregory the Great, *Moralia in Iob*, ed. Adriaen, vol. 143a, lib. XXII, cap. 15, §31, p. 1114, lines 39–40.

7. Simmel, "Sociology of Secrecy," 464. See Urban, "Adornment of Silence," who takes up Simmel and Pierre Bourdieu to argue that secrecy functions as a kind of adornment whose scarcity value gives its possessor symbolic capital and thus power.

8. *Maxims I*, ASPR 3, p. 161, line 121a; *The Wanderer*, ASPR 3, p. 134, lines 13–14a.

9. See, for example, Godden, "Anglo-Saxons on the Mind," 288; Harbus, *Life of the Mind*, 74–77.

10. Sedulius Scottus, *Collectaneum miscellaneum*, ed. Simpson, div. IV, no. 12, p. 13, lines 19–20. The precept comes from Pseudo-Seneca, *De moribus*, ed. Friedrich, §16, p. 262, and therefore, like much of Sedulius Scottus's material, is not known to have had a significant and original impact on early medieval English thought. However, the precept is also reproduced in Pseudo-Bede, *Collectanea Pseudo-Bedae*, ed. and trans. Bayless and Lapidge, no. 201.

11. Boas, ed., *Disticha Catonis*, lib. I, dist. 3, p. 36. Readers of Smaragdus's commentary on the *Regula Sancti Benedicti* (cap. 6) would have encountered a similar extrapolation on the idea that one must guard one's tongue so as not to let slip evil speech. Smaragdus thus quotes Sir. 20:7: "homo sapiens tacebit usque ad tempus lascivus autem et inprudens non servabunt tempus" (A wise man will hold his peace till he see opportunity: but a babbler, and a fool, will regard no time). See Smaragdus, *Smaragdi Abbatis Expositio in Regulam S. Benedicti*, ed. Spannagel and Engelbert, cap. 6, §1, p. 157. Smaragdus was an important Frankish transmitter of patristic ideas, particularly influential in early medieval England; see Joyce Hill, "Ælfric and Smaragdus."

12. Lockett, *Anglo-Saxon Psychologies*; *Traditional Subjectivities*; "Manipulations of the Mind-as-Container Motif"; "Representation of the Mind."

13. I have made a similar argument with respect to King Alfred's Old English translation of Gregory the Great's *Regula pastoralis* in Saltzman, "Mind, Perception and the Reflexivity of Forgetting."

14. While rarely considering the human experience of secrecy in relation to the belief in divine omniscience, numerous studies of secrecy in religion, esotericism, and secret societies thoroughly attend to the phenomenon of religious mystery and human participation in divine knowledge; see, for example, Wolfson, "Introduction," in *Rending the Veil*, ed. Wolfson, 2, who views secrecy as central to "the phenomenology of religious experience" and to "the human condition" but makes no

mention of divine omniscience; Bolle, "Secrecy in Religion," likewise asks broadly how secrecy is "present in our human existence" but makes no mention of divine omniscience, merely divine mystery (the same is true for the other contributors to this volume on secrecy in religions); and similarly, Lochrie, *Covert Operations*, 136, does not consider God's omniscience (even in her discussion of confessional practices), although she notes the important correspondence between human forms of secrecy and divine mystery. Khan, *Self and Secrecy in Early Islam*, 31, is a notable exception, addressing on several occasions the themes of "divine omniscience and human accountability" in the Abrahamic religions more generally.

15. *Maxims I*, ASPR 3, p. 156, lines 2a and 2b.

16. Cavell, *Weaving Words and Binding Bodies*; this excellent study of binding and weaving surveys almost every instance of the phenomenon in Anglo-Saxon literature but does not examine its relationship to the concept or experience of secrecy.

17. Bentham, *Panopticon Writings*, 31.

18. Ibid., 34.

19. Ibid., 11–20.

20. Foucault, *Discipline and Punish*, 203–6.

21. Ibid., 225.

22. Carl Schmitt's concept of "political theology" also rests on a similar argument about the origins of modern jurisprudence as a secularized form of divine omnipotence; see Schmitt, *Political Theology*.

23. See, for example, Bok, *Secrets*, whose premise is that, unlike lying—which is always ethically wrong—secrecy is more ambiguous.

24. Simmel, "Sociology of Secrecy," 463.

25. The relationship between secrecy and privacy is complex; see, for example, Bellman, "Paradox of Secrecy."

26. For an important study of this shift, see MacIntyre, *After Virtue*.

27. But cf. Boethius, *Philosophiae consolatio*, ed. Bieler, lib. I, prosa 4, p. 11, §43: "existimatio plurimorum non rerum merita sed fortunae spectat euentum" (the judgment of many men looks not upon the merit of actions, but upon the outcome of chance). The point Boethius is trying to make here—that the results of an action are often judged prior to the merit of the action itself (as in his own particular case)—was lost in the Old English translation of the *Consolatio*. See Godden and Irvine, eds., *Old English Boethius*, vol. 1, B Text, cap. 3, pp. 245–46; vol. 1, C Text, prose 3, pp. 388–89.

28. Gen. 4:8.

29. Bede, *In Genesim*, ed. Jones, lib. II, 4:8, p. 77; translation based on Bede, *On Genesis*, trans. Kendall, 144.

30. Alfred the Great, *King Alfred's Old English Prose Translation of the First Fifty Psalms*, ed. O'Neill, p. 109, Ps. 9:29–31.

31. Goscelin of Saint-Bertin, *Liber Confortatorius*, ed. Talbot, p. 26, line 12.

Chapter 1

1. Giving false testimony is, of course, forbidden in the Ten Commandments (Exod. 20:16), which are reproduced in King Alfred's preface to his law code (§8: "Ne sæge ðu lease gewitnesse" [Thou shalt not bear false witness]). The act is also condemned in secular legislation. For example, II Æthelstan §26 states that anyone who is proven to have sworn a false oath will forfeit his right to swear an oath in the future and to being buried in consecrated burial grounds when he dies.

Unless otherwise noted, all quotations of Anglo-Saxon laws are from vol. 1 of Liebermann, ed., *Die Gesetze der Angelsachsen*, cited by king (or by title, in the case of anonymous codes) and by law number. When Liebermann gives multiple manuscripts, I have quoted from the oldest manuscript available. For example, unless I am discussing variants in other manuscripts, Alfred and Ine's laws are always quoted from MS *E* (CCCC, MS 173; Gneuss-Lapidge, no. 52; Ker, no. 39). Throughout this book, translations of early Anglo-Saxon laws (up to those of King Æthelstan) are based, with occasional and silent modification, on Attenborough, ed. and trans., *Laws of the Earliest English Kings*. Translations of later Anglo-Saxon laws (from Edmund to Henry I) are based, with occasional and silent modification, on Robertson, ed. and trans., *Laws of the Kings of England*.

2. Of course, the nature of these rights varies by legal system, but most modern legal systems have some version of the right to silence (i.e., the right not to incriminate oneself). See Bradley, "Interrogation and Silence"; Ma, "Comparative View."

3. See, for example, Dershowitz, *Is There a Right to Remain Silent?*

4. Derrida, *Poétique et politique du témoignage*, 37–39; "Poetics and the Politics of Witnessing," 78–79.

5. *Poétique et politique du témoignage*, 14; "Poetics and the Politics of Witnessing," 68 (emphasis in original).

6. *Poétique et politique du témoignage*, 49; "Poetics and the Politics of Witnessing," 83. On the integral relationship between faith (*fides*) and the oath, see Agamben, *Sacrament of Language*, 25–34.

7. See also Derrida, *Demeure*, 27, where he makes a similar point, but he does so by looking backward to the "Christian-Roman meaning" of "passion" and its implication of testimony, which "goes hand in hand with at least the *possibility* of fiction, perjury, and lie."

8. Derrida, "Poetics and the Politics of Witnessing," 83.

9. See below for a discussion of the mechanics of the ordeal.

10. Bartlett, *Trial by Fire and Water*, 33.

11. For example, I Edward §3.

12. See discussion in the Introduction.

13. Wormald, *Making of English Law*, 481.

14. For an example of this approach, see Warren Brown, *Unjust Seizure*.

15. This debate is addressed in numerous studies; see, for example, the overview by Williams, "Introduction," in *Kingship, Legislation and Power*, ed. Owen-Crocker and Schneider, 1–14. The debate is refined in Molyneaux, *Formation of the English Kingdom*.

16. II Cnut §29.2.

17. Hyams, *Rancor and Reconciliation*, 97–98.

18. Wormald, *Papers Preparatory*, 126–29.

19. On the former, see, for example, Æthelberht §4; Ine §6 and §45; Alfred §4. On the latter, see, for example, Æthelberht §§2, 3, and 5; Alfred §7. On forfeiture to the king (and in general the argument that Anglo-Saxon law distinguished between crimes that involve a greater degree of royal punishment and wrongs that are resolved outside of royal jurisdiction), see Wormald, "Giving God and King Their Due," 339. Similar punishments, which are not aimed at redressing the wrong but rather at penalizing the criminal, include incarceration and execution. On the former, see Daniel Thomas, "Incarceration as Judicial Punishment," 92–112. On the latter, see Rabin, "Capital Punishment," 181–200; Reynolds, *Anglo-Saxon Deviant Burial Customs*.

20. E.g., Æthelberht §9; Ine §12. See below for further discussion. On the punishment of theft as a crime, see Lambert, "Theft, Homicide and Crime."

21. Hyams, *Rancor and Reconciliation*, 220–24.

22. The oath is contained in III Edmund, also known as the Colyton code, which was likely the last of Edmund's codes and which survives only in the *Quadripartitus* (the twelfth-century Latin translation of the early English law codes). Its unknown date opens the possibility that it may have actually laid the groundwork for the code known as II Edmund (date also unknown), which is often regarded by scholars as instrumental in restructuring Anglo-Saxon law away from the destructive and violent culture of blood feud or at least in developing a system for resolving feuds speedily—tasks that require a strong institutionalization of political epistemology. Alternatively, if III Edmund did not precede II Edmund (a scenario just as likely), then at least it certainly solidified it. On the importance of II Edmund, see Hyams, *Rancor and Reconciliation*, 82–84. On the development of the oath of allegiance, see Wormald, *Papers Preparatory*, 112–26.

23. III Edmund §1.

24. III Edmund §2.

25. III Edmund §5 and §6.

26. III Edmund §6.2.

27. Sawyer, *Anglo-Saxon Charters*, no. 1457; edited in Campbell, ed., *Charters of Rochester*, §36, pp. 53–54.

28. Asser, *Asser's Life of King Alfred*, ed. Stevenson, p. 923, §106; emendations and translation after Asser, *Alfred the Great*, trans. Keynes and Lapidge, 109.

29. Aldhelm, *Aenigm.* 65 (*Muriceps* [Cat]), p. 467, lines 2–4. A translation of the *Aenigmata* is available in Aldhelm, *Poetic Works*, trans. Lapidge and Rosier, 70–94.

30. Isidore, *Etymologiae*, vol. 1, lib. V, cap. 26, §18, lines 16–17.

31. *Maxims II*, ASPR 6, p. 56, line 42a.

32. Aldhelm, *Aenigm.* 97 (*Nox* [Night]), p. 523, line 9.

33. *Beo*, p. 79, lines 2289b–90.

34. *Christ III*, ASPR 3, p. 27, lines 871–72a.

35. Ælfric of Eynsham, *Angelsächsische Homilien und Heiligenleben*, ed. Assmann, hom. 4 (*Sermo in natale unius confessoris*), p. 54, lines 96–98.

36. Morris, ed. and trans., *Blickling Homilies*, hom. 11 (*On Þa Halgan Þunres Dei*), p. 117. Also available in Kelly, ed. and trans., *Blickling Homilies*, hom. 11, p. 82, lines 25–28.

37. For a survey of the Anglo-Saxon laws on theft, see Schwyter, *Old English Legal Language*; however, Schwyter does not comment on the relationship between theft and concealment. For an explanation of the legal implications of the secrecy of theft, see Lambert, *Law and Order*, 89n93.

38. E.g., Hlothhere & Eadric §16.3.

39. Ine §17.

40. Cockayne, ed., *Leechdoms, Wortcunning, and Starcraft*, 1:392; the charm is also edited in Storms, ed., *Anglo-Saxon Magic*, no. 12, p. 206. This charm and the next one come from CCCC, MS 41 (Gneuss-Lapidge, no. 57; Ker, no. 32), p. 206. The text was later copied into three manuscripts containing legal texts: CCCC, MS 190 (Gneuss-Lapidge, no. 59; Ker, no. 45), CCCC, MS 383 (Gneuss-Lapidge, no. 102; Ker, no. 65), and the *Textus Roffensis* (Strood, Medway Archive and Local Studies Centre MS DRc/R1). It also survives in BL, Cotton Tiberius A. iii (Gneuss-Lapidge, no. 363; Ker, no. 186). Although these charms might not seem like traditional legal texts, Andrew Rabin has argued that we should expand our understanding of Anglo-Saxon law to include them within its purview. See Rabin, "Ritual Magic or Legal Performance," 177–95; see also Hollis, "Old English 'Cattle-Theft Charms.'"

41. Cockayne, ed., *Leechdoms, Wortcunning, and Starcraft*, 1:391–92; Storms, ed., *Anglo-Saxon Magic*, no. 13, p. 206.

42. Eckhardt, ed., *Pactus legis Salicae*, MGH LL nat. Germ. 4.1, §85, p. 251; Drew, ed. and trans., *Laws of the Salian Franks*, 139. Similarly, see *Pactus legis Salicae*, §33.1, p. 123. The *Pactus legis Salicae* is the sixth-century Merovingian form (close to the original produced by Clovis, ca. 466–ca. 511) of the later, Frankish *Lex Salica*, as reedited and authorized by Charlemagne (ca. 742–814). For a history of the *Lex Salica* and its relation to Anglo-Saxon law, see Wormald, *Making of English Law*, 40–42.

43. As suggested by Drew, ed. and trans., *Laws of the Salian Franks*, p. 237, n. 79.

44. In his Letter to Wulfgeat, for instance, Ælfric distinguishes between "dyrnan stala" (secret theft) and "opene reaflac" (open robbery); Ælfric of Eynsham, *Angelsächsische Homilien und Heiligenleben*, ed. Assmann, no. 1, pp. 1–12, lines 186–88. On this passage and the semantics of *reaflac*, see Cowen, "*Byrstas and bysmeras*," 400. But cf. II Cnut §26.1, which concerns the crime of "openre ðyfðe"; although the phrase appears to be an oxymoron referring to the act of stealing committed in the open, it is referring rather to an act of stealing that has been discovered and proven, which parallels the terminology of the phrase "ebæra ðeof" (proven thief) in II Cnut §26. It therefore confirms the notion that an act of theft is one committed under concealment, waiting to be made manifest and proven by the law. See also Andersson, "Thief in *Beowulf*," 496–98, who finds a similar distinction in Icelandic law, where a person who seizes something in secret and a person who does so in the open both receive the same punishment, but the one who seizes in secret is prosecuted for theft, not merely seizure, and prohibited from filing a suit *post hoc* against the accuser for libel.

45. The language of the two laws is nearly identical. Wihtred's code dates to 695, and Ine's code is from early in his reign (688–726). Liebermann, ed., *Die Gesetze der Angelsachsen*, 3:30, suggests that Wihtred is borrowing from Ine, but Oliver, *Beginnings of English Law*, 179–80, interprets the laws as two iterations of a common, "quasi-universal" custom (in use even in the American Wild West).

46. Found only in these two laws, the Old English verb *profian* is a borrowing from Latin *probare*; see Holthausen, *Altenglisches etymologisches Wörterbuch*, s.v. *profian*. The Latin *probare*, however, has the primary sense of "to try, test, examine, inspect, judge of anything in respect to its goodness, fitness, etc."; see Lewis and Short, *Latin Dictionary*, s.v. *probare*, sense I. But *probare* also has the juridical sense of "to prove or demonstrate" or to put to the test/prove by a judicial process such as by the ordeal; see *DMLBS*, s.v. *probare*, senses 3, 5, and 8.

47. Ine §12. See O'Brien O'Keeffe, "Body and Law," for the argument that in lieu of the death penalty, later Anglo-Saxon law sought punishment for thieves that would mark their bodies with a sign of their guilt and thereby give them a chance at repentance and salvation.

48. Wihtred §26.1. Execution could still be profitable, since after the owner of the stolen property had been compensated, the thief's property would have been divided between the king and the slain thief's family and associates (e.g., VI Æthelstan §1.1). However, it would be difficult to acquire the property of a foreign traveler other than what was in his possession at the time of death.

49. Ine §21.

50. A similar condition is given in Ine §35 for the killing of a thief who tries to escape; if he conceals the killing ("gif he hit þonne dierne"), then he becomes responsible for paying the thief's wergild.

51. Pollock and Maitland, *History of English Law*, 1:52. As the authors recognized, in Anglo-Saxon laws "we find a rudiment of the modern distinction between murder and manslaughter, but the line is drawn not between willful and other killing, but between killing openly and in secret."

52. Nordal, ed., *Egils saga Skalla-Grímssonar*, cap. 59, p. 181.

53. Finsen, ed., *Grágás*, vol. 1, cap. 88, p. 154; translated in Dennis et al., eds. and trans., *Laws of Early Iceland*, vol. 1, cap. 88, p. 146. These Icelandic laws were not codified until the early twelfth century, but they still offer many useful comparisons with Anglo-Saxon law, especially since they are both part of the same Germanic legal tradition, and since there would have been mutual influence between early English and Scandinavian law.

54. Finsen, ed., *Grágás*, vol. 1, cap. 87, pp. 153–54.

55. Eckhardt, ed., *Pactus legis Salicae*, MGH LL nat. Germ. 4.1, §70, p. 240; Drew, ed. and trans., *Laws of the Salian Franks*, 130.

56. Eckhardt, ed., *Pactus legis Salicae*, MGH LL nat. Germ. 4.1, §41.3, p. 155. The composition for killing in the open ("si non fallaniuit" [sic] [if it is not concealed]) is 200 solidi.

57. Eckhardt, ed., *Pactus legis Salicae*, MGH LL nat. Germ. 4.1, §28, pp. 110–11.

58. BT, s.v. *morþ*.

59. BT, s.v. *morþ*, sense 3.a.

60. Liebermann, ed., *Die Gesetze der Angelsachsen*, 2:149, s.v. *morð*, defines the word as "heimlicher Mord, Tötung nicht in offenem Kampfe (Rache oder Streit)" (secret murder; killing not done in an open fight [in an act of revenge or dispute]). Schmid, ed., *Die Gesetze der Angelsachsen*, 633, s.v. *morð*, associates the term with "Hexereien und Zaubereien" (witchcraft and magic); Thorpe, ed., *Ancient Laws and Institutes*, glossary, s.v. *morð*, defines the term as "homocidium clandestinum, murdrum" as opposed to *slege*, "which signifies open homicide, and therefore not murdrum. Morð answers exactly to the french *assassinat*, or *muerte de guet-apens*, both with regard to its secrecy, and from the circumstance that, to constitute it, the consequent death of the object is not necessary."

61. O'Brien, "From *Morðor* to *Murdrum*," 343–44.

62. Hyams, *Rancor and Reconciliation*, 84–85; see also Wormald, *Papers Preparatory*, 159.

63. II Cnut §56. Although sometimes taken to suggest that the crime of *morð* is one committed in the open, the phrase "open morð weorðe" is similar to others in Cnut's codes where the word *open* describes a concealed crime that has been discovered or confessed or in some other way made manifest (e.g., I Cnut §26; II Cnut §37), suggesting a daunting awareness of the impossibility of

resolving crimes that remain concealed. For further justification for this interpretation, see Jurasinski, "*Reddatur Parentibus*," 171.

64. Ine §52. For further discussion, see below, pp. 35–36.

65. On the importance of loyalty oaths, see Wormald, *Papers Preparatory*, 120–21.

66. Pseudo-Theodore, *Die Canones Theodori Cantuariensis*, ed. Finsterwalder, lib. I, cap. 4, §4, p. 294.

67. *Scriftboc* in Spindler, ed., *Das altenglische Bußbuch*, cap. 19, §20a, p. 186.

68. Jurasinski, "Old English Penitentials," 103–4.

69. On this code, see Wormald, *Making of English Law*, 367–68, 379. He suggests that the law is a product of "local initiative rather than central guidance. . . . It is not easy," Wormald concludes, "to imagine what else could have spawned something so pertinent yet so mundane" (367). But Wormald argues in his discussion on the anonymous code *Hundred* that it along with *Be blaserum* and *Forfang* were laws written by those "entrusted with law enforcement and its rewards," and they were added to Cnut's code by the author's "own initiative," since "Cnut had not said enough about arson, rewards for tracing stolen goods, or even Hundreds" (379).

70. *Be blaserum* in Liebermann, ed., *Die Gesetze der Angelsachsen*, 1:388; translation from Wormald, *Making of English Law*, 367.

71. Ine §43.1. Henry Sweet explains that "fire is a thief, because it does its work silently, while the axe is an informer, because it betrays its wielder by the noise it makes"; see *Sweet's Anglo-Saxon Reader*, 245. I think Sweet's logic is correct, but it is disputed by Beechy, *Poetics of Old English*, 83–84, who reads the law as a riddle and proposes that its "solution" lies in a pun between *fyr* and *feorran/fyrran* (she gives both forms of the word and defines the former as "to remove, withdraw, alienate"). This interpretation is doubtful. First, *feorran/fyrran* is an adverb meaning "from afar" or "far away" (not a verb, as Beechy defines it). Second, the verb *feorrian* (to which Beechy likely intended to refer) is an uncommon word that rarely carries the specific sense required here, making it particularly inhospitable to paronomasia. The *DOE*, s.v. *feorrian*, sense 2, only offers "to remove, take away, withdraw" as a definition to the word when found in a gloss to *elongare* in Ps. 102:12. Now, even if *fyr* is a pun with *ferian* (the much more common transitive verb, meaning "to carry, transport, convey"), the link to theft is diminished by the fact that *ferian* is never used in the sense of moving stolen goods *and* by the fact that the morphological link between *fyr* and *fyrran* (originally posited by Beechy) no longer holds. Although unmentioned by Beechy, the only possible remaining link between *fyr* and *fyrran* (the adverb, meaning "from afar") is really too obscure to be useful; *fyr* could be linked to the foreigner (the "feorcund man") who is proven a thief according to Ine §20 if he fails to make noise while traveling through the forest. Aside from the fact that there is no way to find even a poetic relationship between fire and foreignness (other than the fact that they both travel through the forest), this interpretation would only return us to Sweet's logic that fire is a thief because it is silent.

72. Liebermann, ed., *Die Gesetze der Angelsachsen*, 3:76; Liebermann also points to *Grágás* (Finsen, ed., vol. 2, cap. 199, p. 110), which allows for someone who fells a tree, removes it, and covers the stump to be punished as a thief.

73. BT, s.v. *morþsliht*, "murder, assassination." Attenborough, ed. and trans., *Laws of the Earliest English Kings*, 171, translates it as "to secretly compass death"; Liebermann, ed., *Die Gesetze der Angelsachsen*, 1:388, translates it as "die heimlichen Morde"; Wormald, *Making of English Law*, 367, translates it as "underhand killings" to capture the "furtiveness" of "killings out of reach of immediate reprisal."

74. It is also possible that *Be blaserum* concerns not the destruction of property but rather the act of killing people by burning: we see a cultural distaste for such forms of killing in *Njal's Saga*, for example. However, *Be blaserum* begins with a terminological distinction between arson and murder, the former unqualified, the latter qualified as secretive. This distinction is repeated in the twelfth-century Latin translation known as the *Quadripartitus* ("de blaseriis et murdritoribus" [of arsonists and murderers]; Liebermann, ed., *Die Gesetze der Angelsachsen*, 1:389) and refined in another twelfth-century translation known as the *Consiliatio Cnutii III* ("de balatronibus [*sic*] et de *furtiuis*

mortificatoribus" [of arsonists and *secretive* murderers]; Liebermann, ed., *Die Gesetze der Angelsachsen*, 1:389, emphasis added). If the arson involved murder, it would presumably just be included, categorically, under the term *morþslyht*. Instead, a *blæsere* is treated as one kind of secretive actor, and one who commits *morþslyht*, another; both receive the same punishment.

75. Wormald, *Making of English Law*, 379.

76. II Æthelstan §6 makes a similar arrangement, stating that if someone causes death by witchcraft, sorcery, or murder ("wiccecræftum 7 be liblacum 7 be morðdædum") and wishes to deny it, he must undergo the ordeal and remain in prison; the same is applied in II Æthelstan §6.2 for arsonists ("blysieras") and for those who avenge the death of a thief ("ðeof wrecen"), and in II Æthelstan §7 for those often accused of theft ("oft betihtlede wæron"). Likewise, Edward & Guthrum §11 and II Cnut §4 both group together "wiccan oððe wigleras, mansworan oððe morðwyrhtan oððe fule, afylede, æbere horcwenan" (wizards or sorcerers, perjurers or those who murder, or vile, polluted, notorious prostitutes), and command them to be driven from the land unless they reform themselves. Aside from the fact that each of these vocations is clearly considered morally corrupt, they are also united by the fact that they all entail an evasion of the law whether by magic, by false testimony, or, in the case of prostitutes, by the secrecy associated with fornication and adultery (as illustrated, for example, in the assortment of compound words derived from and related to *dyrneliger* [adultery, fornication, lit. secret fornication]).

77. Hyams, *Rancor and Reconciliation*, suggests that the disappearance of the Roman legal distinction between fact and law (a distinction that would later resurface in the beginning of the thirteenth century) "never posed a problem in the Early Middle Ages because [the linked postulates of fact and law] were unknown to secular law. This was not merely a matter of the disappearance of Roman law from northern Europe but a function also of God's omniscience. Men conceptualized legal proof largely in terms of God's judgment, although they sought this by a variety of means (ordeal, duel, oaths, and so forth)" (219).

78. Green, *Crisis of Truth*, has argued that fourteenth-century England saw a shift in the nature of evidence and proof, "from a truth that resides in people to one located in documents" (xiv). But although the oath and the ordeal were certainly the primary forms of proof used in Anglo-Saxon law, the survival of just over 1,500 charters demonstrates that documents were also often used as evidence and carried legal value long before the reign of Richard II. On the (literary) nature and the important social role of these documents (especially those dealing with the ownership and transfer of land), see Smith, *Land and Book*.

79. E.g., perjurers in I Edward §3.

80. For an overview and history of the varieties of the practice, see Bartlett, *Trial by Fire and Water*, 4–33; Hyams, "Trial by Ordeal."

81. See Green, *Crisis of Truth*, 92.

82. Green provides an extremely helpful flowchart that lays out the various scenarios of Anglo-Saxon litigation. Ibid., 97.

83. Ine §52 set the fine for such extrajudicial resolutions at 120 shillings. On the Continent, these secret compositions were actually treated as a form of theft, since judicial authorities lost profits that they would have otherwise earned for resolving a given case: "Si quis furtum uult celare et occulte sine iudice conpositionem fecerit, et qui acceperit latroni similis est illi" (If anyone tries to conceal a theft and secretly pays composition without the judgment of a judge, both he who made the composition and he who accepts it are alike to the thief); see Eckhardt, ed., *Pactus legis Salicae*, MGH LL nat. Germ. 4.1, §80, p. 250; Drew, ed. and trans., *Laws of the Salian Franks*, 137. This law is derived from the sixth-century (pre-588) Merovingian *Pactus Childeberti regis* and *Decretio Chlotharii regis*; see *Pactus Childeberti regis* in Boretius, ed., *Capitularia Merowingica*, MGH Capit. 1, §3, p. 5; on the date, see Van Dam, "Merovingian Gaul," 201.

84. VI Æthelstan §11.

85. On the Continent, the *Pactus legis Salicae* makes this connection especially transparent, stating that "Si quis occulte de rem sibi furatam a quolibet latrone conpositionem acceperit, utraque latronis culpa subiaceant. Fures tamen iudicibus presententur; nullus latrones aut quemlibet culpabilem

occultare praesumat. Cui si fecerit, similis illi subiaceat culpae" (If anyone secretly accepts from a thief composition for stolen property, let them both be guilty of theft. Thieves must be presented before the judges; no one shall presume to conceal anyone guilty of theft. He who does this shall be guilty of the same offense); Eckhardt, ed., *Pactus legis Salicae*, MGH LL nat. Germ. 4.1, §89, p. 252; Drew, ed. and trans., *Laws of the Salian Franks*, 140. See also the similar law in *Decretio Chlotharii regis* in Boretius, ed., *Capitularia Merowingica*, §13, p. 6.

86. Ine §28.8. See also Ine §73.

87. Ine §36. The translation of this law in the *Quadripartitus* renders the phrase "ðiefðe gedierne" as "furtum celauerit" (Liebermann, ed., *Die Gesetze der Angelsachsen*, 1:105), which recalls the phrasing of *Pactus legis Salicae*, §80 ("Si quis furtum uult celare"), discussed above, n. 83.

88. II Edward §4, IV Æthelstan §6.5, and VI Æthelstan §1.2.

89. Wormald, *Papers Preparatory*, 121.

90. IV Edgar §14.

91. Ine §7.1.

92. Liebermann, ed., *Die Gesetze der Angelsachsen*, 3:69; Attenborough, trans., *The Laws of the Earliest English Kings*, 184.

93. *Maxims I*, ASPR 3, line 86a, p. 159.

94. Alfred & Guthrum §4 suggests that the *getyma* did not necessarily have to be the person from whom the goods were purchased; it could also have been a trustworthy third party.

95. I Edward §1, §1.2, §1.3; Hlothhere & Eadric §16.3; see also II Cnut §§23, 24.

96. *Swerian* §8. For background on this anonymous tract, see Wormald, *Making of English Law*, 383–84.

97. Hlothhere & Eadric §5; I Edgar §8.

98. Ine §43.1. We might also note that Beowulf learns of the reason for the dragon's wrath through the hand of an informer ("þurh ðæs meldan hond"); *Beo*, p. 82, line 2405.

99. III Æthelred §2.

100. III Æthelred §2.1.

101. See, for example, the anonymous tract known as *Swerian* (Liebermann, ed., *Die Gesetze der Angelsachsen*, 1:396–99), where each oath formula begins with the phrase, "On ðone Drihten" (On the Lord), "On ælmihtiges Godes naman" (In the name of Almighty God), or "On lifiendes Godes naman" (In the name of the living God).

102. See Oakley, *English Penitential Discipline*, 158–60.

103. I Edward §3 and II Æthelstan §26. Presumably, perjurers would lose the privilege to stand as oath helpers as well.

104. Ine §37 implies that a thief often accused will become subject to the ordeal.

105. II Æthelstan §14.1.

106. See, for example, O'Brien O'Keeffe, "Body and Law"; Hyams, "Trial by Ordeal"; Keefer, "Anglo-Saxon Lay Ordeal," 353–63.

107. Whitman, *Origins of Reasonable Doubt*, 56–57.

108. Wormald, *Papers Preparatory*, 82.

109. On the role of fear and apprehension in the efficacy of the judicial ordeal, see Keefer, "*Corsnæd* Ordeal," esp. 252.

110. *Iudicia Dei II* in Liebermann, ed., *Die Gesetze der Angelsachsen*, 1:406 (emphasis added).

111. Translation based on Wormald, *Papers Preparatory*, 81 (emphasis added).

112. *Iudicia Dei II* in Liebermann, ed., *Die Gesetze der Angelsachsen*, 1:407.

113. Wormald, *Papers Preparatory*, 82.

114. Bartlett, *Trial by Fire and Water*, 33.

115. Ibid., 30.

116. O'Brien O'Keeffe, "Body and Law," 216–17.

117. Ibid., 218–19.

118. Yet the ordeal still required the practitioner or priest to interpret the outcome, as O'Brien O'Keeffe, "Body and Law," 224, has shown.

Chapter 2

1. Ine §53.

2. Ine §25 (on the process of vouching in this law, see Oliver, *Beginnings of English Law*, 141–42); Hlothhere & Eadric §16.3.

3. II Æthelstan §24 states that after vouching the previous owner, the current owner must return the property to the previous owner, who then implicitly takes on the responsibility of proving that he, too, legally purchased the property in question.

4. Ine §75.

5. II Æthelred §§9.1, 9.4.

6. II Æthelred §9. But cf. III Æthelred §6.1, which stipulates that the vouching must take place "on þæs kyninges byrig" (in the king's manor). Liebermann translates it as "im königlichen (Gericht in reichsunmittelbarer) Stadt" (*Die Gesetze der Angelsachsen*, 1:231).

7. Alfred §14, for example, allows a father to pay composition on behalf of his son if his son cannot confess or deny his wrongdoings because he was born dumb or deaf.

8. Liddell and Scott, *Greek-English Lexicon*, s.vv. κρύπτω, κρύπτη.

9. *The Wanderer*, ASPR 3, p. 134, lines 22–23a.

10. The verb *bewreon* denotes an act of covering, but it is also frequently used to describe the act of burial. See *DOE*, s.v. *bewreon*, sense 1.a.ii; cf. senses 2 and 3, which reflect an even more specific notion of concealment and secrecy. For another instance of *heolstor* used in the sense of earthen grave, see *Judith*, ASPR 4, p. 102, line 121a.

11. Lockett, *Anglo-Saxon Psychologies*, discusses in detail this process of "cardiocentric restraint" (81).

12. *The Wanderer*, ASPR 3, p. 134, lines 17–23a.

13. This translation between the topographical secrecy of a crypt and the psychological secrecy of the self is explored in Derrida, "*Fors*," xiv, where he reflects on the nature of the crypt as that which both conceals and displays. "Within this forum," writes Derrida in one movement of the foreword, "a place where the free circulation and exchange of objects and speeches can occur, the crypt constructs another, more inward, forum." That more inward forum of the crypt is, Derrida continues, "sealed, and thus internal to itself, a secret interior within the public square, but, by the same token, outside it, external to the interior. Whatever one might write upon them, the crypt's parietal surfaces do not simply separate an inner forum from an outer forum. The inner forum is (a) safe, an outcast outside inside the inside. That is the condition, and the stratagem, of the cryptic enclave's ability to isolate, to protect, to shelter from any penetration, from anything which can filter in from outside along with air, light, or sounds, along with the eye or the ear, the gesture of the spoken word." For Derrida, the crypt represents the interior space *within* the self, yet internally *separated* from the self. I have demonstrated elsewhere how a similar (particularly Heideggerian) concept of reflexive self-concealment was explored and adapted in Alfred's Old English translation of Gregory the Great's *Regula pastoralis*. To be sure, the terms and stakes in Abraham, Torok, and Derrida are radically different from those employed and sought by Alfred and Gregory; for one thing, the role of God in the *Regula pastoralis* ensures that the interior "pith of the mind" remain always open to divine scrutiny, itself the model for an ideal form of perpetually internalized self-perception. However, Alfred's negotiation of this slippage into self-concealment (what I term "completely reflexive forgetting") suggests that a similar notion of selfhood—in which the self can and often does conceal a part of itself from itself—was at least conceptually available during the period. See Saltzman, "Mind, Perception, and the Reflexivity of Forgetting."

14. *The Panther*, ASPR 3, p. 171, lines 61b–63a (emphasis added).

15. Squires, ed., *The Old English Physiologus*, suggests that "*di(e)gol* as a noun rather than an adj. seems more common in prose than verse [where] the usual phrase is *on digle / diglum* 'in secret'" (66). Squires seems to have been considering a possible emendation from "of digle" (from the grave) to "on digle" (in secret), but ultimately leaves the line as is in order to maintain the parallel with line 37a, as discussed below. See also *DOE*, s.v. *digol*, noun, sense 2.a. That the state of death was considered to be a state of secrecy is further evidenced in Gregory the Great, *Dialogues*, ed. de Vogüé,

vol. 2, lib. III, cap. 17, p. 340, §6, where the state of death is referred to as "occulto" and later translated into the Old English word "deogolnesse" in Werferth of Worcester, *Bischofs Waerferth von Worcester Übersetzung der Dialoge Gregors des Grossen*, ed. Hecht, lib. III, cap. 17, p. 217, line 4.

16. Matt. 27:66.
17. Bede, *Homiliarum euangelii libri II*, ed. Hurst, lib. II, hom. 10, pp. 247–48, lines 59–60.
18. *The Panther*, ASPR 3, p. 170, line 37.
19. Ibid., p. 171, lines 64b–65a.
20. *Paris Psalter*, ASPR 5, pp. 139–40, Ps. 142, verses 1 and 4.
21. *El*, p. 86, lines 722–24a.
22. *Beo*, lines 445b–47.
23. *Maxims I*, ASPR 3, p. 159, line 78. The phrase "deop deada wæg" poses some philological difficulty, but some scholars resolve "deada" as a substantive genitive plural, thus "the deep way of the dead." See Krapp and Dobbie, eds., ASPR 3, p. 306; Muir, ed., *Exeter Anthology of Old English Poetry*, 2:558. Wyatt, *Anglo-Saxon Reader*, 138, emended to "deadra," the form we would expect to find for the genitive plural.
24. Christie, "Sméagol and Déagol," 97. Christie argues, for instance, that the statement in *Maxims I* that a wife must "rune healdan" (hold secrets, line 86a) indicates a form of secrecy necessary for "a harmonious society." However, the statement is, I think, less imperative than it is gnomically descriptive: wives are expected to hold secrets, a fact that, as we have seen, determines how Anglo-Saxon law codes account for the role of a wife's knowledge of and complicity in a crime (e.g., in Ine §7). On the gnomic nature of this half-line, see Fell et al., *Women in Anglo-Saxon England*, 36–37; Fell suggests that the half-line refers to a woman's ability to "preserve" or keep a "hand on knowledge."
25. Not unreasonably, Christie, "Sméagol and Déagol," 98, conflates these three forms of secrecy by, for example, interpreting *Maxims I*, lines 114–16, as a simple analogue to the representations elsewhere of death as a secret thief (e.g., in Ælfric's *Sermo in natale unius confessoris*, discussed above, Chapter 1, n. 35), when in fact they are devoted specifically to the secrecy of murder ("morþor"). He thus takes the line "ne biþ þæt gedefe deaþ, þonne hit gedyrned weorþeð" to mean "that is not an honest death, when it comes in secret" (line 116). However, the second half-line is perhaps better translated as "when it takes place in secret," since the passage is clearly referring to the perversity of killing secretly ("þe hit forhelan þenceð"), rather than the always secret and unpredictable nature of death's approach (which will come secretly regardless of whether it takes place in a noble or public fashion). See BT, s.v. *weorþan*, sense II.2.
26. Morris, ed. and trans., *Blickling Homilies*, hom. 5 (*Dominica V in Quadragesima*), p. 59; see also Kelly, ed. and trans., *Blickling Homilies*, hom. 5, p. 40, lines 64–67.
27. *Soul and Body I*, ASPR 2, p. 56, line 65a; *Soul and Body II*, ASPR 3, p. 176, line 60a.
28. *Soul and Body II*, ASPR 3, pp. 177–78, lines 108–10a. Cf. *Soul and Body I*, ASPR 2, pp. 57–58, lines 113–15a.
29. *The Soul's Address to the Body* in Jones, ed. and trans., *Old English Shorter Poems*, frag. C, p. 212, lines 16–17a. Elsewhere and in other fragments of the poem, the Soul repeatedly points out the sealed lips and shut mouth of the dead Body (e.g., frag. C, p. 212, line 19a; frag. E, p. 220, lines 38–39; frag. F, p. 222, lines 1–18).
30. II Æthelred §9.2. Liebermann considers II Æthelred §§8 and 9 to have been an appendix, which he dates to between 930 and 1030, or more precisely 950–1000. The rest of II Æthelred is dated to 991. See Liebermann, ed., *Die Gesetze der Angelsachsen*, 3:150, 3:154–55.
31. Ine §53.1 (a subsection of the law quoted above) dictates that if the current owner knows the heir of the dead man's estate, then he must vouch the estate, and the heir shall attest to the transfer of title. But, of course, doing so would subsequently make the heir responsible for proving that the property was rightfully purchased by the dead man.
32. The Fonthill Letter has been most recently edited and translated in Brooks and Kelly, eds., *Charters of Christ Church, Canterbury*, vol. 2, no. 104, pp. 852–62; Sawyer, *Anglo-Saxon Charters*, no.

1445. See also Roberts, "What Did Anglo-Saxon Seals Seal When?" 134. Roberts argues that although the letter and the seal were often separate objects (the latter denoted by the *insigle*), this passage in the Fonthill Letter possibly refers to an early form of a "sealed document."

33. For example, see Keynes, "Fonthill Letter," 88. Alternatively, Smith, "Of Kings and Cattle Thieves," 457–59, reads the Fonthill episode as a sort of legal bildungsroman in which the visit to Alfred's grave "facilitates some recuperation of Helmstan's character" while also invoking the political influence of Edward's father and the authoritative model of justice that he represented. Likewise, Rabin, "Testimony and Authority in Old English Law," argues that the visit to Alfred's body "claims a direct and unmediated connection to a particular source of authority or authenticity, and thereby asserts the essential naturalness and truthfulness of its testimony" (169).

34. Thorpe, ed., *Ancient Laws and Institutes*, 59; the notes were written by Richard Price.

35. Hywel Dda, *Ancient Laws and Institutes of Wales*, ed. and trans. Owen, vol. 1, lib. II, §18, pp. 430–31; cf. vol. 1, lib. II, §20, pp. 430–31 and (in the Latin *Leges Hyweli Boni*) vol. 2, lib. II, §19.2, p. 842. The law code is also available in a newer edition, but without translation: Hywel Dda, *Cyfreithiau Hywel Dda yn ôl Llyfr Blegywryd*, ed. Williams and Powell, p. 41, lines 20–25. I thank Annalee Rejhon for her assistance with this passage.

36. Altars were often used to validate the oath of a witness (e.g., Wihtred §17–22).

37. Eckhardt, ed., *Schwabenspiegel*, MGH Fontes iuris N.S. 4.1/2, §5b, p. 53; cf. §290, p. 371. A similar law is also found in Eckhardt and Hübner, eds., *Deutschenspiegel und Augsburger Sachsenspiegel*, MGH Fontes iuris N.S. 3, §10, p. 87. It should be noted that these codes do not prescribe new legal practices but rather record ones already in use.

38. Schlyter, ed., *Codex Iuris Uplandici*, cap. 7, §1, p. 136 (*Manhælghis balken*). I thank Molly Jacobs Bauer for her assistance with interpreting this law.

39. The instructions are found in BL, Additional MS 14252, a compilation of charters and laws pertaining to the city of London; see Bateson, "A London Municipal Collection of the Reign of John," 493 (cap. IV, §5, fols. 98r–98v).

40. Ballard and Tait, eds., *British Borough Charters*, 185.

41. Ibid., xviii, 185. See also Gross, "Modes of Trial," 700.

42. See, for example, Whitman, *Origins of Reasonable Doubt*, 53. The decline of the practice, however, took centuries. From 1100, the ordeal was "under sustained attack from church reformers," who criticized the practice for illicitly tempting God to perform miracles and "polluting those involved in it with blood."

43. Lea, *Superstition and Force*, 42.

44. It finds a more developed, explicitly Christian form well into the sixteenth century, when on the Isle of Man there was "an old custom concerning debts, which is now abolished. When the debtor died, and was buried, and there remained no writings to prove the debt, the creditor came to the grave of the deceased, and laid himself all along with his back upon the grave, with his face towards heaven, and a bible on his breast, and there he protested before God that is above him, and by the contents of the bible on his breast, that the deceased there buried under him did owe him so much money; and then the executors were bound to pay him. But in 1609 this custom was abolished, and such controversies ordered to be tried according to the form of law, by witnesses or otherwise." This quotation is from an elaborated and amended edition of William Camden's *Britannia* by Harrison, *Old Historians of the Isle of Man*, 24.

45. In II Cnut §§36 and 36.1, for example, "gyf hwa mæne að on haligdome swerige, 7 he oferstæled weorðe, þolige þæra handa oððe healfes weres . . . 7 na beo he þannon forð aðes wyrðe, butan he for Gode þe deoppar gebete 7 him borh finde, þæt he æfre eft swylces gewice" (if anyone swears a false oath on the relics, and is confuted, he is to forfeit his hands or half his wergild . . . and from thenceforth he is not to be entitled to an oath, unless he atones for it very deeply with God, and finds surety for himself that he will desist from such ever afterward). See also III Æthelred §2.1. For further discussion and examples of the practice of swearing on relics, see Rollason, "Relic-Cults," 97.

46. For example, II Cnut §§36, 36.1.

47. It must be noted that although Ine's code belongs to the seventh century, it only survives alongside (as a sort of appendix to) Alfred's late ninth-century code. But there is no reason to believe Ine's code not to have originated in the period of his reign.

48. See Pelteret, *Slavery in Early Mediaeval England*, 73–74, who provides evidence that the theft of slaves was a common practice.

49. On the legal personhood of slaves, see ibid., 244.

50. II Æthelstan §24 states that if anyone buys cattle and later has to vouch the person from whom he purchased the cattle, he must afterward return the cattle to the person whom he vouched (who sold him the cattle), regardless whether that person is a freeman or a slave ("beo he swa freoh swa ðeow").

51. On the right of slaves to own a small amount of movable goods, see Jurasinski, "Old English Penitentials," 109. See also Pelteret, *Slavery in Early Mediaeval England*, 104. This allowance is not exclusively made in late sources (although it certainly becomes more widespread in later Anglo-Saxon England); it is also found in Pseudo-Theodore, *Die Canones Theodori Cantuariensis*, ed. Finsterwalder, lib. II, cap. 3, §3, p. 331: "Non licet homini a servo suo tollere pecuniam quam ipse labore suo adquesierit" (A man may not take away from his slave money which he earned by his labor). I have quoted from the latest recension known as the *discipulus Umbrensium* (Finsterwalder's U), but the rule also occurs in the earlier recensions, the *Canones Gregorii* (G, §164, p. 268) and *Iudicium de penitentia Theodori episcopi* (Co, §179, p. 282). The textual history of the Theodoran Penitentials is severely complicated; see Charles-Edwards, "Penitential of Theodore," 141–74.

52. ". . . ut nouem testes iurent, quod seruum ipsum equaliter per tres mallos super plagiatorem audierint dicentem" (. . . so that there will be nine witnesses in all who can attest that they heard the slave himself speaking about his kidnapper in the same way in three courts); Eckhardt, ed., *Pactus legis Salicae*, MGH LL nat. Germ. 4.1, §39.2, pp. 142–44; Drew, ed. and trans., *The Laws of the Salian Franks*, 101, 204.

53. Hlothhere & Eadric §5. On the uncertain meaning of the hapax legomenon *stermelda*, see Oliver, *Beginnings of English Law*, p. 129, n. b.

54. But note that the thief in *Beowulf* might also be considered a *meldan*; *Beo*, line 2405b ("þurh ðæs meldan hond"). See Biggs, "Beowulf and Some Fictions," 63–64.

55. Ine §47.

56. E.g., Ine §24; VI Æthelstan §6.3.

57. Wihtred §23.

58. Lantfred of Winchester, *Translatio et miracula Sancti Swithuni*, ed. and trans. Lapidge, in *The Cult of St Swithun*, cap. 20, p. 302.

59. For the date, see Wilmart, "Ève et Goscelin (II)," 62.

60. Goscelin of Saint-Bertin, *Liber Confortatorius*, ed. Talbot, lib. III, p. 85. This story comes from Leontios of Neapolis, *Vita S. Ioannis Eleemosinarii* (PL 73.380–82), cap. 51, and a similar story (also mentioned by Goscelin) is found in Amphilochio of Iconium, *Vita S. Basilii Caesareae Cappadociae Archiepiscopi* (PL 73.307–9), cap. 10.

61. Goscelin of Saint-Bertin, *Liber Confortatorius*, ed. Talbot, lib. IV, p. 104.

62. Ibid., lib. IV, p. 104.

63. Lewis and Short, *Latin Dictionary*, s.v. *festuca*, sense I.B, note that the word can refer to "a rod with which slaves were touched in the ceremony of manumission."

64. On the agency of silence invoked by this scene, see O'Brien O'Keeffe, *Stealing Obedience*: "Alexander's redemption by the wordless gesture of the buried girl fantasizes a larger order, where transgression is not merely forgiven, but spiritually undone, by an act of interpreting silence" (237).

65. Revenants are another good example of the kind of belief that at once confirms and troubles not only the boundary between the living and the dead but also more generally the secrecy of death; see Blair, "Dangerous Dead," 539–59.

66. This notion finds a parallel in Derrida's analysis of the notion of the crypt and of Abraham and Torok's notion of cryptonymy (Derrida, "Fors," esp. xix). In his discussion, Derrida suggests that the crypt is a site of not only concealment but also testimony. While for Derrida the notion of

the crypt is one in which testimony is outwardly displayed, although encrypted, in Ine §53 the testimony of the grave and its truth-bearing authority do not exclusively come from within the crypt but come instead from without, from God.

Chapter 3

1. *Conlationes*, lib. II, cap. 11, p. 49, line 7–p. 50, line 10. See Lake, "Knowledge of the Writings of John Cassian," who has shown that although Cassian's direct influence on early Anglo-Saxon monastic thought was not expansive, it is substantially evidenced in the writings of Aldhelm, Bede, and the Leiden Glossary, as well as possible echoes in the anonymous *Vita Sancti Cuthberti* and the ninth *Responsio* from Pope Gregory to Augustine of Canterbury. Two extant Anglo-Saxon manuscripts contain excerpts from the *Conlationes* that include Serapion's anecdote: Oxford, Bodleian Library, Hatton 23, fols. 24r–25r (Gneuss-Lapidge, no. 627), and Salisbury, Cathedral Library, MS 10 (Gneuss-Lapidge, no. 700); I have not been able to consult the Salisbury manuscript. See below for a discussion of Cassian's influence on the *Regula Sancti Benedicti*.

2. *Conlationes*, lib. II, cap. 10, p. 48, lines 12–16.

3. *Conlationes*, lib. II, cap. 10, p. 48, line 24–p. 49, line 2.

4. On the relationship between law and monastic rules, see the discussion in Agamben, *Highest Poverty*, 28–47, who argues that the monastic rule (as exemplified by Basil and Pachomius), which has the Gospel as its model, "cannot therefore have the form of law, and it is probable that the very choice of the term *regula* implied an opposition to the sphere of the legal commandment" (46).

5. *RSB*, cap. 2, commands that "non convertenti ex servitio praeponatur ingenuus, nisi alia rationabilis causa exsistat . . . . quia siue seruus siue liber omnes in Christo unum sumus" (a man born free is not to be given higher rank than a slave who becomes a monk, except for some good reason. . . . Whether slave or freeman, we are all one in Christ). *RM*, cap. 2, makes an identical statement. *RSB*, cap. 63, further explains that monks "ordines suos in monasterio ita conservent ut conversationis tempus ut vitae meritum discernit utque abbas constituerit" (keep their ranks in the monastery according to the date of their entry, the virtue of their lives, and the decision of the abbot).

6. On the problematic question of will and choice in the decision to enter a monastery, see O'Brien O'Keeffe, *Stealing Obedience*, esp. chap. 1, "Dunstan in the Theatre of Choice," who shows that although entrance to monastic life was often considered a fulfillment of God's will, it sometimes played out in a "theatre of choice." On the forcible tonsure of kings on the Continent (where it was more common), see de Jong, "Monastic Prisoners." On the practice in England, see Pratt, "Illnesses of King Alfred," 53; Yorke, "Burial of Kings," in *Kingship, Legislation and Power*, ed. Owen-Crocker and Schneider, 249.

7. Ine §1.

8. Foot, *Monastic Life*, 7.

9. On the *circa*, see *RegC*, cap. 57; Lanfranc, *Decreta Lanfranci*, 78–80.

10. See Saltzman, "Writing Friendship," 258–64.

11. *RSB*, cap. 33. This rule then refers to Acts 4:32, and an aspect of its logic can be traced to Rufinus's translation of Basil of Caesarea, *Asceticon parvum* (PL 103.510), cap. 29: "Si quis vero proprium sibi esse dicit aliquid, sine dubio alienum se facit ab electis Dei et a charitate Domini, qui docuit verbo, et opere complevit, et animam suam posuit pro amicis suis. Si ergo ipse animam suam pro amicis dedit, quomodo nos etiam ea quae extra animam sunt, propria vindicamus?" (Indeed, if anyone claims something to be proper to himself, without doubt he makes himself alien to the elect of God and to the charity of the Lord, who taught in word and accomplished in deed and laid down his life for his friends. If, therefore, he gave his very life for his friends, how shall we defend as our own those things that are extraneous to life?). The notion that monastic life requires the monk to forfeit personal possessions and personal will is also found in Cassian's *De institutis*, lib. II, cap. 3, p. 19, lines 4–9, where the same principle is a prerequisite for becoming an abbot: "non enim quisquam conuenticulo fratrum, sed ne sibi quidem ipsi praeesse conceditur, priusquam non solum uniuersis facultatibus suis reddatur externus, sed ne sui quidem ipsius esse se dominum uel potestatem habere

cognoscat" (For no one is allowed to rule over a community of brothers, or even over himself, unless he not only renders himself estranged from all his possessions, but also recognizes that he is in fact not his own master and has no power over himself).

12. See O'Brien O'Keeffe, *Stealing Obedience*, 44–45, for a discussion of the *Verba seniorum* story of Abba Pambo and his theory that the negation of a monk's self-will as a servant (*seruus*) in total obedience to the will of another is the highest of monastic virtues.

13. Foot, *Monastic Life*, 12–24; Blair, *Church in Anglo-Saxon Society*, esp. 246–90; Pestell, *Landscapes of Monastic Foundation*, 18–64.

14. Foot, *Monastic Life*, 5–6; on the diversity of rules, see also Sims-Williams, *Religion and Literature*, 115–43.

15. Gretsch, *Ælfric and the Cult of Saints*, 129–33, shows that the *Regula Sancti Benedicti* had been the dominant rule in England and on the Continent between the years 800 and 1000.

16. For instance, a monk at Wenlock was permitted to own a slave girl with his biological brother, which would have constituted a serious violation on several counts in any reformed monastery; see Boniface, *Die Briefe des heiligen Bonifatius und Lullus*, ed. Tangl, MGH Epp. sel. 1, ep. 10, p. 13. See Sims-Williams, *Religion and Literature*, 117.

17. *RegC*, prol. 4.

18. The most direct reference to humility through secrecy is found in the preface to the *VCA*, lib. I, cap. 2, p. 62. For further discussion, see Chapter 5.

19. Basil of Caesarea, *Regulae fusius tractatae* (PG 31.985–88), cap. 26. Although scholars now generally see Cassian as the bridge between Basil and Benedict, in his *Life of Saint Basil*, Ælfric of Eynsham viewed Basil as Benedict's direct model. See Ælfric of Eynsham, *Ælfric's "Life of Saint Basil the Great,"* ed. and trans. Corona, 45–46.

20. *RSB*, cap. 7.

21. *RSB*, cap. 42.

22. *RSB*, cap. 4.

23. When this Benedictine command is translated into Old English by Æthelwold, the role of God's all-seeing perception of human secrets receives even greater emphasis; Schröer, ed., *Die angelsächsischen Prosabearbeitungen der Benediktinerregel*, cap. 4, p. 17, line 23–p. 18, line 4: "his weorca he sceal giman on ælce tide, þæt þa gode sien, and he sceal geþencan, þæt he nahwer Gode dygle ne bið, ac he hine æghwær gesihþ; þa yflan geþohtas, þe him on mod becumað, he sceal sona on Criste toslean and his gastlican lareowe andedtan" (he [*scil.* the monk] must observe his deeds at all times, just as they are seen by God, and he must understand that nowhere is he secret from God, but he sees him everywhere; the evil thoughts, which come into his mind, he must quickly smash them against Christ and confess them to his spiritual teacher). Where the Latin simply reminds the monk that God's gaze is always and everywhere fixed on him ("Deum se respicere pro certo"), the Old English adds that nowhere is secret (*dygle*) from God. The ninth-century commentary on the *Regula Sancti Benedicti* by Smaragdus, *Smaragdi Abbatis Expositio in Regulam S. Benedicti*, ed. Spannagel, lib. IV, cap. 49, p. 129, lines 22–25, explains that "Inmensitas divinae magnitudinis tanta est ut omnia videat, omnia impleat et sit super omnia et subtus omnia et infra omnia et extra omnia, et nullus sit locus contentus, ubi deus non sit" (so immense is the divine greatness that it sees everything, fills everything, and is above everything and below everything, and inside everything and outside everything, and therefore is no place so shut in that God is not there). On Æthelwold's use of Smaragdus's commentary in his translation of the *Regula Sancti Benedicti*, see Lapidge, "Æthelwold as Scholar and Teacher," 101 (who cites Gretsch, *Die "Regula Sancti Benedicti" in England*), and Gretsch, "Æthelwold's Translation," 144–46. On the language of God as the internal or inward judge, see Saltzman, "The Mind, Perception and the Reflexivity of Forgetting." The phrases *internus arbiter* and *internus iudex* are frequently used by Bede and Gregory.

24. *RM*, cap. 15, addresses the situation in which a subordinate must reveal evil thoughts to his superiors; the logic for doing so depends on a series of metaphors in which containing something evil within an interior space is not only counterproductive to the very purpose of the interior space but also quite dangerous: "Nec enim dignum est, mundatis foris regiis, cubiculum intus inquinari

de sordibus, sed decenter efficitur, si de intrinsecus foris eiecta sorditie, iam tum demum et foras iuste mundetur. Non enim secura possunt esse fossata, ubi intus est hostis. Simul et porta clusura sua captiua est, ubi muri non repellunt, sed inclusum continent inimicum" (It is inappropriate that a palace should be cleansed on the outside while the room within is soiled with filth. Instead, the correct thing to do is to throw out the filth from inside, and only then ought the outside to be cleansed. Indeed, entrenchments cannot be secure when the enemy is within. So also a bolted door is its own captor when the walls do not keep the enemy out, but hold him enclosed). The image of captivity here is significant.

25. *RSB*, cap. 2; *RM*, cap. 2.

26. *De institutis*, lib. IV, cap. 9, p. 53, lines 9–14.

27. *RSB*, cap. 4.

28. *RSB*, cap. 2; see also *RM*, cap. 2. Cassian also employs a similar use of Ps. 136:9 in *De institutis*, lib. VI, cap. 13, p. 122, line 24–p. 123, line 1: "emergentes etiam peccatores terrae nostrae, id est sensus carnales, in matutinis sui ortus nos oportet extinguere, et dum adhuc paruuli sunt adlidere filios Babylonis ad petram" (It is also necessary for us to destroy the sinners emerging in our land—that is, our fleshly senses—on the morning of their birth and while they are still young, to dash the children of Babylon against the rock).

29. The best-known and patent late-medieval conceptualization of confession as a "handling of sin" occurs in the early fourteenth-century poem by Robert Mannyng of Brunne, *Handlyng Synne*, edited in 1901 by Frederick J. Furnivall. Idele Sullens's 1983 edition introduces numerous errors but accounts for three manuscripts unknown to Furnivall. D. W. Robertson, Jr., in "The Cultural Tradition of *Handlyng Synne*," was the first to argue that *Handlyng Synne* was primarily a text dealing with the work of confession.

30. Alfred the Great, *King Alfred's West-Saxon Version of Gregory's Pastoral Care*, ed. Sweet, cap. 16, p. 105, lines 18, 22; Gregory the Great, *Règle pastorale*, ed. Judic et al., lib. 2, cap. 5, pp. 200–202. See Saltzman, "The Mind, Perception and the Reflexivity of Forgetting," 169. On the linguistic development of this metaphor, see Healey, "Taking *hand* in Hand," 48–49. The Gregorian metaphor of the washbasin references not only the laver at Solomon's temple (3 Kings 7:23) but also the cleansing of iniquity described in 1 John 1:9.

31. Morris, ed. and trans., *Blickling Homilies*, hom. 4 (*Dominica tertia in quadragesima*), p. 43. Also available in Kelly, ed. and trans., *Blickling Homilies*, hom. 4, p. 28, lines 63–65.

32. *VCP*, cap. 9, p. 186; also recounted in *HE*, lib. IV, cap. 27, p. 432. See Meens, "Frequency and Nature," who notes that although Bede's description might be of an idealized past, "the picture of pastoral care as presented here, carried out from a monastic setting with preaching and confession as main instruments, must somehow have been familiar to Bede's audience" (51).

33. *CH* II, hom. 10, pp. 84–85, lines 126–36. The nature of the secret atonement will be discussed below. Malcolm Godden in *CH* III, 421, points out the odd placement of this passage in Ælfric's narrative and that it is "perhaps based" on cap. 9 of Bede's *VCP*.

34. Boniface, *Die Briefe*, ed. Tangl, ep. 59, p. 111; translation based on Boniface, *Letters of Saint Boniface*, trans. Emerton, 79.

35. Columbanus, *Regula monachorum*, ed. and trans. Walker, cap. 9, pp. 138–40. The quotation is from Sir. 32:24. Although Columbanus's *Regula monachorum* does contain a separate chapter on *discretio*, and although the final conference of Cassian's *Conlationes* is on the topic of *mortificatio*, Columbanus's notion of *mortificatio* seems to be subsumed by Cassian's notion of *discretio*. The two concepts as discussed by both thinkers necessarily overlap. Cassian was an important source for Irish monastic practices, and he was one of the main avenues by which the Irish absorbed monastic traditions from Egypt. See Frantzen, *Literature of Penance,* 25–26; Mayr-Harting, *Coming of Christianity*, 79–86; Riché, *Education and Culture*, 324–36.

36. Columbanus, *Regula monachorum*, ed. and trans. Walker, cap. 9, p. 138, line 10.

37. Columbanus, *Regula coenobialis*, ed. and trans. Walker, cap. 15, p. 164, lines 1–11.

38. Gildas, *De poenitentia*, ed. and trans. Winterbottom, 146–47; also available in Bieler, ed. and trans., *Irish Penitentials*, 60–65.

39. *RSB*, cap. 23.

40. *RSB*, cap. 69. Although it is difficult to show that this rule would have been observed in the monasticism practiced by Columbanus and/or Gildas, it can be traced to Basil of Caesarea, *Asceticon parvum* (PL 103.509–10), cap. 26; and to Pachomius, *Regula coenobiorum* (PL 23.88–89), cap. 176.

41. Or at least, as Benedict does, toward a senior monk who might witness the sin of a fellow monk and who ought to reprimand him privately rather than before the entire community. Even in *RSB*, cap. 27, where the abbot sends in "senpectas" to console a wavering monk "quasi secrete," the abbot is centrally aware of the secret consolation carried out by the senior monks. Also, in *RSB*, cap. 58.6, the senior monk who "aptus sit ad *lucrandas* animas" (is skilled in winning souls) is assigned to a novice, echoing Matt. 18:15, "si te audierit *lucratus* es fratrem tuum" (If he shall hear thee, thou shalt gain thy brother) (emphasis added).

42. *RegC*, cap. 57.

43. Lanfranc, *Decreta Lanfranci*, ed. and trans. Knowles, 78–79.

44. See Kornexl, "Ein benediktinischer Funktionsträger."

45. Hildemar of Civate, *Expositio regulae ab Hildemaro tradita*, ed. Mittermüller, cap. 48, p. 484.

46. The practice seems to have originated in Carolingian monastic legislation, where the *circa* was established as an official post and expected to report to the community. See, for example, Leccisotti, ed., *Ordo Casinensis I dictus Ordo regularis*, caps. 7–12, pp. 102–4; Frank and Laach, eds., *Capitula notitiarum*, cap. 13, p. 344. Michael Lapidge and Michael Winterbottom suggest that, when producing the *Regularis concordia*, Æthelwold must have received these customs from his Fleury informants; see their editorial introduction to Wulfstan of Winchester (Wulfstan Cantor), *The Life of St Æthelwold*, ed. and trans. Lapidge and Winterbottom, p. lx. For a historical survey of the office of the *circa*, see Feiss, "Circatores."

47. Feiss, "Circatores," 356–57.

48. *Circatores* are, however, mentioned twice by Ekkehard of Saint Gall, *Casus S. Galli*, ed. Pertz, MGH SS 2, 97–98, 111–12. The practice is also mentioned in Strecker, ed., *Ecbasis cuiusdam captivi per tropologiam*, MGH SS rer. Germ. 24, p. 17, line 468. I have found no direct references to a *circa* in Anglo-Saxon England other than in the *Regularis concordia*.

49. Gregory the Great, *Dialogues*, ed. de Vogüé, vol. 2, lib. II, cap. 3, §7, p. 144, lines 61–62 (emphasis added).

50. Early medieval practices of penance were diverse, and the traditions that fashioned them were complex. For a survey, see Meens, "Remedies for Sins." In particular, the rise of private penance has now been reconsidered by scholars such as Meens, *Penance in Medieval Europe*, and de Jong, "Transformations of Penance," who have challenged the long-held narrative that private penance originated in the monasticism of early Ireland and was disseminated to England and the Continent by Columbanus. This older narrative is one of decline, in which the rigorous public penance of late antiquity was slowly replaced by weaker private forms of penance, which eventually came to be required by the Fourth Lateran Council in 1215 (giving the decline of public penance its telos). This narrative was influentially advanced in the late 1920's by Poschmann, *Die abendländische Kirchenbusse im Ausgang des christlichen Altertums* and *Die abendländische Kirchenbusse im frühen Mittelalter*. For a historiographical survey, see Hamilton, *Practice of Penance*, 4; Frantzen, *Literature of Penance*, 19–60. On Columbanus's *Penitential*, see Charles-Edwards, "Penitential of Columbanus." On the division between public and private penance in Anglo-Saxon England, see Frantzen, *Literature of Penance*, 100, 141; Bedingfield, "Public Penance," 226; Meens, "Early Medieval Penance," 47–52; de Jong, "What Was Public," 863–902; Hamilton, "Remedies for 'Great Transgressions,'" 83–89. On the division in Carolingian practice, see Vogel, *Le pécheur et la pénitence au moyen âge*, 24–27.

51. *CH* I, hom. 33 (Seventeenth Sunday after Pentecost), p. 462, lines 113–16.

52. This logic can also be found in *RSB*, cap. 46: "Si animae vero peccati causa fuerit latens, tantum abbati aut spiritalibus senioribus patefaciat, qui sciat curare et sua et aliena vulnera, non detegere et publicare" (If the cause of the sin lies hidden in his soul, he must disclose it only to the

abbot or to the spiritual seniors, who know how to heal both their own wounds and those of others without exposing them and making them public).

53. Ælfric's source is Bede, *In Lucae euangelium expositio*, ed. Hurst, cap. 3.8, pp. 193–94, lines 1086–87: "publica noxa, publico eget remedio, levia autem peccata leviori et secreta queunt poenitentia deleri" (a public crime requires a public remedy, while trivial sins require lighter remedies and are able to be erased through private penance). A similar construction also occurs in Ælfric's "Homily on a Servant's Failure to Forgive," in Irvine, ed., *Old English Homilies*, hom. 2, p. 45, lines 208–15: "Gif ðe gylt beo digle, bet þu hine digollice, and ne mælde þu nateshwon hine oðrum monnum; and gif openlice agulte, bed þu hine openlice" (If a sin is committed in secret, you should atone for it privately, and you should not speak of it at all to anyone else; and if you sin openly, you should atone for it openly). Ælfric's source here is Augustine, *Sermones* (PL 38.519), Sermo 83: "si peccatum in secreto est, in secreto corripe. si peccatum publicum est et apertum, publice corripe: ut ille emendetur, et caeteri timeant" (If a sin is committed in secret, atone for it in secret. If a sin is committed in public and in the open, atone for it publicly: so the sinner may be corrected and the others might grow fearful). In both Bede and Augustine, the adjectives are *secretus* and *publicus*, which evoke the modern distinction between public and private. However, Ælfric notably employs the adjectives *diglan* and *openan*, respectively, which suggest less of a distinction between public and private and more of a distinction between concealment and openness. In other words, the difference between the two modes of penance has less to do with the potential audience (as implied by the word *publicus* or the Old English *folclic*, for example) and more to do with the state of the thing concealed. Furthermore, in several Carolingian sources, *occultus* is the adjective of choice for those secret sins (especially sexual ones) and their corresponding requirement of penance. See, for example, the Council of Mainz in 852 in Hartmann, ed., *Concilium Mainz, a. 852, Oct. 3*, MGH Conc. 3, cap. 10 ("De adulterio"), p. 247; Theodulf of Orléans, *Capitula 2*, ed. Brommer, MGH Capit. episc. 1, cap. 8, p. 169.

54. On the Carolingian use of this monastic logic, see de Jong, "Transformations of Penance," 220.

55. *CH* II, hom. 10, pp. 84–85, lines 126–36.

56. Isidore of Seville, *Sententiae*, ed. Cazier, lib. II, cap. 20.1–3, pp. 135–36.

57. Pseudo-Bede, *Collectanea Pseudo-Bedae*, ed. and trans. Bayless and Lapidge, no. 192.

58. Gregory the Great, *Moralia in Iob*, ed. Adriaen, vol. 143a, lib. XXII, cap. 15, §30, p. 1113. See Introduction.

59. Dunn, "Paradigms of Penance."

60. *RM*, cap. 80.

61. Odo of Cluny, *Vita sancti Geraldi Auriliacensis comitis* (PL 133.662–63), cap. 34. On Gerald's piety and Odo's depiction of it, see Airlie, "Anxiety of Sanctity."

62. BL, Cotton Faustina A. x. (fols. 102–51); Ker, no. 154b, s. xii^1. The addendum is inserted as cap. 62 and printed as appendix II in Schröer, ed., *Die angelsächsischen Prosabearbeitungen der Benediktinerregel*, pp. 140–41, lines 15–18 (emphasis added).

63. See Osbern of Canterbury, *Miracula Sancti Dunstani*, ed. Stubbs, cap. 19, pp. 144–51. Eadmer's version is also edited by Stubbs (cap. 16, pp. 234–38); however, a superior edition is now available in Eadmer of Canterbury, *Lives and Miracles*, ed. and trans. Turner and Muir, cap. 19 (cap. 16 in Stubbs), pp. 182–88.

64. We can roughly date the event since it had to have happened after the appointment of Prior Henry in 1076 but before the consecration of Gundulf as bishop of Rochester on 19 March 1077. See Rodney Thompson, ed., *Life of Gundulf*, cap. 11.

65. Osbern of Canterbury, *Miracula Sancti Dunstani*, ed. Stubbs, 145; Eadmer of Canterbury, *Miracula Sancti Dunstani* in *Lives and Miracles*, ed. Turner and Muir, 182.

66. Osbern of Canterbury, *Miracula Sancti Dunstani*, ed. Stubbs, 146.

67. Ibid., 147.

68. The event is possibly (and enigmatically) mentioned in an undated letter to Bishop John of Rouen from Lanfranc, *Letters of Lanfranc*, ed. and trans. Clover and Gibson, ep. 15, p. 90, where

Lanfranc merely indicates that the messenger will tell all about it: "De iuuene cuius euentum usque ad aures uestras fama uulgauit lator presentium, qui uidit et interfuit, qualiter gestum sit uobis ueraciter enarrabit" (As for the young monk, rumors of whose experience have reached you, the man who brings this letter witnessed the affair himself; he will tell you what actually happened).

69. Perhaps the questionable value of the episode as a miracle pertaining to Saint Dunstan is the reason it was left out of (or removed from) three manuscripts; see Stubbs, *Memorials of St. Dunstan*, xliii.

70. O'Brien O'Keeffe, "Writing Community," 202–18, reads this episode as demonstrating both the "painful limits" of Lanfranc's "temporal power as abbot" and the "between-ness" of Christ Church just after the Norman Conquest.

71. *Conlationes*, lib. VII, cap. 16, p. 195, lines 11–22.

72. Eadmer of Canterbury, *Miracula Sancti Dunstani* in *Lives and Miracles*, ed. and trans. Turner and Muir, 184–85.

73. Rubenstein, "Life and Writings of Osbern of Canterbury," 30.

74. Eadmer of Canterbury, *Miracula Sancti Dunstani* in *Lives and Miracles*, ed. and trans. Turner and Muir, 184.

75. Osbern of Canterbury, *Miracula Sancti Dunstani*, ed. Stubbs, 146.

76. All quotations here are from ibid.; similar rhetoric of tangibility is used in Eadmer of Canterbury, *Miracula Sancti Dunstani* in *Lives and Miracles*, ed. and trans. Turner and Muir, 184.

77. Wulfstan of Winchester, *Life of St Æthelwold*, ed. and trans. Lapidge and Winterbottom, cap. 33, pp. 48–52. The monk is unnamed in Wulfstan's version, but Ælfric records his name as Eadwine in his *Vita Sancti Æthelwoldi*, printed as an appendix in *Life of St Æthelwold*, ed. and trans. Lapidge and Winterbottom, 77. The *Vita* was probably composed in the year 996 or shortly thereafter, coinciding with the translation of Saint Æthelwold on 10 September 996 (see p. xvi).

78. Wulfstan of Winchester, *Life of St Æthelwold*, ed. and trans. Lapidge and Winterbottom, cap. 33, p. 50.

79. Ibid. A similar episode occurs in Abbo of Fleury, *Passio Sancti Edmundi*, ed. Winterbottom, cap. 15, p. 83: eight thieves attempt, under the cover of nocturnal silence ("sub nocturno silentio"), to break into the tomb of Saint Edmund, only to be miraculously bound ("ligat") in place by the power of the saint and thereby caught red-handed the next morning.

80. *Conlationes*, lib. II, cap. 11, p. 49, line 11.

81. This scene gives O'Brien O'Keeffe, *Stealing Obedience*, 3–5, the title of her monograph, and it is central to her argument about agency and obedience in the monasticism of the Benedictine Reform.

82. Wulfstan of Winchester, *Life of St Æthelwold*, ed. and trans. Lapidge and Winterbottom, cap. 14, pp. 26–28.

83. O'Brien O'Keeffe, *Stealing Obedience*, pp. 5–6, n. 10, cites Foucault, "About the Beginning of the Hermeneutics of the Self," who observes: "Obedience in the monastic institutions must bear on all the aspects of life; there is an adage, very well known in the monastic literature, which says, 'everything that one does not do on order of one's director, or everything that one does without his permission, constitutes a theft'" (174). O'Brien O'Keeffe has documented several possible sources for this adage, some of which I have reproduced in my discussion here.

84. Wulfstan of Winchester, *Life of St Æthelwold*, ed. and trans. Lapidge and Winterbottom, cap. 14, pp. 26. O'Brien O'Keeffe, *Stealing Obedience*, 48n139, directs us to Lewis and Short, *Latin Dictionary*, s.v. *praevideo*, sense II.B, with the late Latin meaning "to provide."

85. O'Brien O'Keeffe, *Stealing Obedience*, 48–49.

86. Ibid., 51.

87. *RSB*, cap. 46.

88. Basil of Caesarea, *Sermo asceticus de renuntiatione saeculi* (PG 31.633 = CPG 2889), cap. 4; translation based on Basil of Caesarea, *Ascetic Works*, trans. Clarke, 64.

89. Only Rufinus's translation of Basil's *Homiliae in Psalmos* survives in a manuscript from Anglo-Saxon England: Winchester, Winchester College MS 40A (Gneuss-Lapidge, no. 759.5; s. viii^2,

possibly from France). However, Basil was known from other sources, primarily in early Anglo-Saxon England through the school of Theodore and Hadrian in Canterbury and through a few references to him in works by Aldhelm, Bede, and Alcuin. A Latin translation by Rufinus of the *Regula Sancti Basilii* survives in an eighth- or ninth-century manuscript from "a German center under Anglo-Saxon influence" (Basle, Universitätsbibliothek F. III. 15c, fols. 28–64; see *CLA* 7.846). Ælfric's *Life of Saint Basil the Great*, ed. Corona, also exposes an interest in Basil's contribution to monastic life in later Anglo-Saxon England. For a discussion of the knowledge of Basil in Anglo-Saxon England, see Corona's introduction to ibid., pp. 29–50. For a discussion of Basil in the school of Theodore and Hadrian, see Bischoff and Lapidge, ed., *Biblical Commentaries*, 206–8. Lapidge, *Anglo-Saxon Library*, notes that "of the works of Basil which were available and widely circulated in Latin translation, the *Hom. in Hexaemeron*, trans. Eustathius, [was] a work frequently used by Bede, or perhaps the *Asceticon paruum* or *Regula S. Basilii*, trans. Rufinus or *Sermo* xii (*De scetica disciplina*), both of which circulated in Latin translation" (230). Locherbie-Cameron, "From Caesarea to Eynsham," also offers a brief discussion of the knowledge of Basil in Anglo-Saxon England.

90. Basil of Caesarea, *Regulae fusius tractatae* (PG 31.949–52), cap. 14: "Ὁ γὰρ ἀναθεὶς ἑαυτὸν τῷ Θεῷ, εἶτα πρὸς ἄλλον βίον ἀποπηδήσας, ἱερόσυλος γέγονεν, αὐτὸς ἑαυτὸν διακλέψας, καὶ ἀφελόμενος τοῦ Θεοῦ τὸ ἀνάθημα" (For a man who dedicates himself to God and then springs away to another form of life has committed sacrilege, for he has stolen himself away and robbed God of His votive offering). Also see the eighth-century commentary on the *Regula Sancti Benedicti* by Hildemar of Civate, *Expositio regulae ab Hildemaro tradita*, ed. Mittermüller, 142, where the category of theft is expanded to include not only the secret taking of another person's property (*alienam rem absconse tollit*) but also the withdrawal of oneself from God's service or the leading of a bad example for others.

91. E.g., *RSB*, cap. 4: "In primis Dominum Deum diligere ex toto corde, tota anima, tota uirtute; deinde proximum tamquam seipsum. Deinde non occidere, non adulterare, non facere furtum, non concupiscere, non falsum testimonium dicere, honorare omnes homines, et quod sibi quis fieri non vult, alio ne faciat" (First of all, love the Lord God with your whole heart, your whole soul, and all your strength, and love your neighbor as yourself. Then the following: you are not to kill, not to commit adultery; you are not to steal nor covet; you are not to bear false witness. You must honor everyone, and never do to another what you do not want done to yourself). Smaragdus, *Expositio in Regulam S. Benedicti*, ed. Spannagel and Engelbert, lib. IV, cap. 5, p. 90, line 10–p. 91, line 3, interprets *RSB*, cap. 4, "non facere furtum" (not to steal) to mean that one who withdraws himself from the service of the Lord and subjects himself to the devil is automatically a thief and will be punished as a slave of sin. See also Kleist, "Division of the Ten Commandments."

92. *RM*, cap. 21.

93. Columbanus, *Regula coenobialis*, ed. and trans. Walker, cap. 1, pp. 144–45. The saying is attributed to Antony; Athanasius (trans. Evagrius), *Vita Beati Antonii Abbatis* (PL 73.151), cap. 28. Note that the verb *proferre* is the same as the verb used by Cassian to describe the young Serapion's act of placing the stolen biscuit before the abbot and the brothers, "in medium proferens" (*Conlationes*, lib. II, cap. 11, p. 50, line 7; see above, pp. 65–66), and by Bede in describing the way the townsfolk would confess their sins to Cuthbert, "confitendo proferrent" (*VCP*, cap. 9, pp. 186–87; see above, pp. 74–75). The other word used by Benedict and Cassian in similar situations is *patefacere*, which suggests more an act of opening up than that of carrying forward.

94. A more extreme form of this idea is advanced in the Evagrian translation of Athanasius's *Vita Sancti Antonii* (PL 73.151), cap. 28: "sæpe nostra non posse nos intelligere peccata, sæpe falli in ratione gestorum; aliud esse Dei cuncta cernentis judicium qui non ex superficie corporum, sed ex mentium judicat arcanis" (often we cannot perceive our own sins, often we manage to be deceived in our reasoning concerning our deeds; the judgment of the all-seeing God is different, as he judges not from the surface of the body but from the secrets of the mind).

Chapter 4

1. Alcuin of York, *Epistolae*, ed. Dümmler, MGH Epp. 4.18–481, ep. 138, pp. 216–18; "De penitentia" in Alcuin, *De virtutibus et vitiis* (PL 101.622–23), cap. 13. Frantzen, *Literature of Penance*, 158,

notes that "Ælfric endorsed the three forms of reconciliation accepted by the Franks: confession to God alone was permitted for minor sins; confession to the priest was preferred for both major and minor sins; sins of public consequence required public penance." See, for instance, *CH* I, hom. 8 (*Dominica III post Epiphania Domini*), p. 243, lines 65–71: "Swa sceal eac se þe mid heafodleahtrum wiðinnan reoflig bið. cuman to godes sacerde & geopenian his digelnysse þam gastlican læce: & be his ræde. & fulteme his sawle wunda dædbetende gelacnian. Sume men wenað þæt him genihtsumie to fulfremedum læcedome: gif hi heora synna mid onbryrdre heortan gode anum andettað. & ne þurfon nanum sacerde geandettan gif hi yfeles geswicað" (So should he who is leprous within with mortal sins also go to God's priest and open his secret to that spiritual doctor, and by his counsel and aid heal the wounds of his soul with penance. Some men believe that it will suffice for a complete cure if he confesses his sins with compunction of heart to God alone and that they do not need to confess to a priest if they extinguish their evil). See also Ælfric of Eynsham, *Homilies of Ælfric*, ed. Pope, vol. 1, hom. 11 (*Sermo ad populum in octavis Pentecosten dicendus*), pp. 436–37, lines 391–99.

2. Osbern of Canterbury, *Miracula Sancti Dunstani*, ed. Stubbs, cap. 19, p. 146.

3. The liturgical Secret (*Secretum*)—which, in the order of the Mass, follows after the Offertory and comes before the *Sursum corda* and Preface—according to Harper, *Forms and Orders of Western Liturgy*, is an offertory prayer that "belongs to the Proper, but only the conclusion of the doxology at the end of the prayer was sung aloud by the celebrant (the remainder was silent as the name suggests). All sang *Amen*" (119).

4. Osbern of Canterbury, *Miracula Sancti Dunstani*, ed. Stubbs, cap. 19, p. 182; on Ægelward, see Chapter 3 above. Bede, *In Genesim*, ed. Jones, lib. II, 4:8, p. 77; for discussion of Cain's secret field, see the Introduction above.

5. Lochrie, *Covert Operations*, 31.

6. The point of the field's remoteness, according to Bede, is exactly that it can hide Cain's murder from society but not from God.

7. See Foot, *Monastic Life*, 210.

8. See Alison Goddard Elliott, *Roads to Paradise*, 85–91.

9. Licence, *Hermits and Recluses*, 22–27, on early Anglo-Saxon examples of reclusion. It is important to note also the passing references to hermits: e.g., Hereberht of Huntingdon, a Mercian hermit mentioned in Bede's *VCP*, cap. 28, p. 248; and St. Ecgberht, a hermit mentioned in the *Old English Martyrology* entry for Chad (available in Rauer, ed. and trans., *Old English Martyrology*, §37, p. 60).

10. *HE*, lib. IV, cap. 3, p. 338. John of Beverly, bishop of Hexham, similarly built himself a private oratory (*clymiterium*), where he and a few others would devote themselves to prayer and reading (*HE*, lib. V, cap. 2, p. 456). On the ways in which bishops and other clerics found time for private contemplation in spite of their ecclesiastical duties, see Foot, *Monastic Life*, 208–9. On the practice of bishops building *mansiones remotiores* and *secretiores*, see Blair, *Church in Anglo-Saxon Society*, 217–18.

11. But see Chapter 5 for a discussion of Saint Cuthbert, who manages to move between a life of solitude and a life of administration.

12. *HE*, lib. III, cap. 16, p. 262.

13. Alcuin of York, *Bishops, Kings, and Saints of York*, ed. and trans. Godman, p. 120, line 1524.

14. *HE*, lib. V, cap. 12, pp. 496, 488.

15. *HE*, lib. V, cap. 12, p. 496.

16. Blair, *Church in Anglo-Saxon Society*, 144–45, 217–20. But cf. Beckery Chapel, an early satellite hermitage associated with the church at Glastonbury and about a mile from the abbey; its name comes from Old Irish *Becc-Ériu*, meaning "little Ireland" (reinforcing the view that such hermitages were more common in the north and were often the product of Irish influence); see Abrams, *Anglo-Saxon Glastonbury*, 56. This mode of isolation was also emulated later in the Anglo-Saxon period: Dunstan, for example, built and dwelt in a small cell (*cellam*; *domunculam*) near Saint Mary's Chapel at Glastonbury; the cell, according to Eadmer, measured four by two and a half feet with a ceiling just high enough for a person to stand up, while according to Osbern it was like a tomb

("formam gerat sepulcri") and so confined it seemed uninhabitable. Eadmer of Canterbury, *Vita Sancti Dunstani* in *Lives and Miracles*, ed. and trans. Turner and Muir, cap. 11, p. 66; Osbern of Canterbury, *Vita Sancti Dunstani*, ed. Stubbs, cap. 13, p. 83.

17. *VCA*, lib. III, cap. 1, p. 94.

18. *VCP*, cap. 17, p. 214.

19. *VCP*, cap. 17, p. 214.

20. *VCP*, cap. 17, p. 216.

21. *VCP*, cap. 18, p. 220.

22. Even after he became bishop of Lindisfarne, Cuthbert would still visit Farne Island and "secretus Domino solita deuotione militaret" (fight in secret with his customary devotion to the Lord); *VCP*, cap. 25, p. 238; also recounted in *HE*, lib. IV, cap. 30, p. 444.

23. On Ælfric's anxiety about hermits, for example, see Clayton, "Hermits and the Contemplative Life," 163–67.

24. For example, Felix (Guthlac's earliest biographer) writes of his surroundings that "nullus hanc ante famulum Christi Guthlacum solus habitare colonus valebat, propter videlicet illic demorantium fantasias demonum" (on account of the phantoms of the demons who dwelt there, no one had been able to dwell alone upon this island before Guthlac the servant of Christ), but draws this description almost verbatim from Bede's prose *Vita Sancti Cuthberti*, essentially only replacing the name "Domini Cuthbertum" with "Christi Guthlacum." Felix, *Vita Sancti Guthlaci*, ed. and trans. Colgrave, cap. 25, p. 88; *VCP*, cap. 17, p. 214.

25. *Guthlac A*, ASPR 3, p. 54, lines 157b–59a and p. 55, line 215. In the *Vita Sancti Guthlaci* by Felix (*Life of Saint Guthlac*, ed. and trans. Colgrave, cap. 25, p. 88), Tatwine tells Guthlac of "aliam insulam in abditis, remotioris heremi partibus" (a certain island in the hidden regions, namely in the more remote parts of the desert), and once Guthlac began to inhabit it "adamato illius loci abdito situ velut a Deo sibi donato" (he fell in love with the secrecy of the place, neglected just as it had been given to him by God).

26. Accordingly, *digla stowa* are not always places of worship; they also, outside of a monastic context, often signal a space that is dangerous, forbidden, or evil. When Beowulf's troop seeks out Grendel's mother, for instance, the land is ominously described as "dygel lond" (*Beo*, line 1357). References to the secret nature of monsters and their habitats abound. The very first lines of the *Liber monstrorum*, for example, read: "de occulto orbis terrarum situ interrogasti et si tanta monstrorum essent genera credenda quanta in abditis mundi partibus . . . monstrantur" (you have asked about the secret region of the lands of the earth and if as many kinds of monsters are to be accepted as true as are demonstrated in the hidden parts of the world). An edition and translation of the *Liber monstrorum* is provided in appendix III of Orchard, *Pride and Prodigies*, 254–317. As Orchard points out, *situ* could also mean "filthiness." Lewis and Short, *Latin Dictionary*, s.v. *situs*, also gives "idleness" as a possible definition, but since the passage is pertaining to parts of the world, "region" is probably the best translation.

27. Clark, "More Permanent Homeland," 76.

28. *Guthlac A*, ASPR 3, p. 62, lines 465–66.

29. *Conlationes*, lib. VII, cap. 16, p. 195, lines 11–22.

30. *Guthlac B*, ASPR 3, p. 80, lines 1082b–86a (emphasis added).

31. *DOE*, s.v. *gastgeryne*; see also Fell, "Runes and Semantics."

32. BT, s.v. *gæstgeryne*.

33. *Gæstgeryne* is a compound of *gast* (which carries a meaning similar to Latin, *anima*; *DOE*, s.v. *gast*: breath, air, wind, spirit, ghost, soul) and *geryne* (which is related to Old English *run*, meaning "whisper," "mystery," "secret"). BT, s.v. *gæstgeryne*, defines the word as "a ghostly or spiritual mystery; a mystery of the mind." The second BT definition comes closer to the meaning implied in these passages of *Guthlac B*. *DOE*, s.v. *gastgeryne*, gives "spiritual mystery" as its only definition, and records eight occurrences in the *DOE Corpus*, always in poetry. More specifically, save for its use in line 246 of *Guthlac A* and *Andreas* (ASPR 2, p. 26, line 857), the word is only elsewhere found in poems by Cynewulf (*Christ II*, ASPR 3, p. 15, line 440 and p. 23, line 713; *El*, p. 71, line 189 and p. 98, line

1147) or tentatively attributed to him (*Guthlac B*, ASPR 3, p. 80, line 1084 and p. 81, line 1113). I have translated the term here and elsewhere as "spiritual secrecy," the ambiguity and slight awkwardness of which draws attention to that human experience of secrecy in a way that other translations do not. Despite my use of the singular phrase "spiritual secrecy," the Old English term is always used in the dative plural; its plural sense must be inferred by the reader.

34. *Guthlac B*, ASPR 3, p. 81, lines 1112–13a.
35. Ibid., lines 1121–23a.
36. Ibid., lines 1112–13a.
37. *Guthlac A*, ASPR 3, p. 56, lines 246–51a (emphasis added).
38. See Dendle, *Satan Unbound*, 112–13.
39. Byrhtferth of Ramsey, *Byrhtferth's Enchiridion*, ed. and trans. Baker and Lapidge, 247, explains that once we have been baptized, God entrusts us to his angels, who continually supply information to God about our sins and deeds while on earth.
40. Rauer, ed. and trans., *Old English Martyrology*, §63, p. 80.
41. *RegC*, cap. 7, forbids monks from entering the "secreta santimonialium" (i.e., the nunneries), which the Old English gloss renders as "diglu mynecyna" in Kornexl, ed., *Die "Regularis Concordia,"* 8.
42. *RM*, cap. 24.
43. Magennis, ed. and trans., *The Old English Life*, p. 66, lines 130–32.
44. Ælfric of Eynsham, *Ælfric's Lives of Saints*, ed. Skeat, vol. 2, no. 31 (Saint Martin, Bishop and Confessor), p. 238, lines 312–14.
45. Werferth of Worcester, *Bischofs Waerferth von Worcester Übersetzung der Dialoge Gregors des Grossen*, ed. Hecht, preface, p. 3, lines 10–16.
46. Foot, *Monastic Life*, 96–108.
47. An exception may have been Saint Augustine's monastery at Canterbury, where Augustine seems to have intended the intermural cathedral for the clerics with pastoral duties and reserved the extramural monastery for monks; see Blair, *Church in Anglo-Saxon Society*, 68. See also Brooks, *Early History*, 87–91.
48. See Chapter 3.
49. Foot, *Monastic Life*, 210, suggests that early Anglo-Saxon monasteries must have been unfavorable to contemplation on account of numerous distractions.
50. This pattern is more frequently seen in early Anglo-Saxon monasticism than in the monasticism of the Reform period. See ibid.
51. See Gittos, *Liturgy, Architecture, and Sacred Places*, 147.
52. *RSB*, cap. 52.
53. de Vogüé, *Rule of Saint Benedict*, 253.
54. *RegC*, cap. 6. A similar phrase occurs in *RegC*, cap. 67, which concerns the Office of the Dead: "His tamen triginta diebus cotidie sacerdotum unusquisque secretis oratorii locis specialiter pro eo Missas celebret" (During these thirty days each priest shall say a special Mass daily for the dead brother, in the secret places of the oratory). In the Old English gloss of the *Regularis concordia* the phrase is "on diglum gebedhuses stowum" (Kornexl, ed., *Die "Regularis Concordia,"* 8, 140).
55. Kate Heulwen Thomas, "Meaning, Practice and Context," argues that many forms of private prayer were reflective of and based on the communal parts of the liturgy.
56. Matt. 6:6.
57. Ibid.
58. Günzel, ed., *Ælfwine's Prayerbook*, no. 52.10, p. 139.
59. The prayer to Saint Augustine, from which this reference is taken, is included in Holthausen, ed., "Altenglische Interlinearversionen," no. 17, p. 242, but he does not print the prayer itself on account of it being "unglossiert." However, the text of the prayer (which clearly is glossed) is located in Logeman, "Anglo-Saxonica Minora," p. 119, line 65.
60. Alcuin of York, *Alcuins Gebetbuch*, ed. Waldhoff, no. 3a (*Confessio: Deus inestimabilis misericordiae*), p. 344, verse 29. For Alcuin's disapproval of nonsacerdotal confession, see *Epistolae*, ed.

Dümmler, ep. 138, pp. 216–18; "De penitentia" in Alcuin of York, *De virtutibus et vitiis* (PL 101.622–23). On this confessional prayer and its relation to Alcuin's theories of confession as well as its use in later prayer books, see Bullough, "Alcuin and the Kingdom of Heaven," 15.

61. One even finds such examples in specifically communal prayers such as the Collect to be said in the second prayer of the *Trina oratio*, as outlined in *RegC*, cap. 27: "Deus, cui omne cor patet et omnis uoluntas loquitur, et nullum latet secretum" (O God to whom every heart is open, every desire speaks, and from whom no secret is hidden). The Collect is from the "Missa de gratia Sancti Spiritus postulanda" in Alcuin of York, *Liber Sacramentorum* (PL 101.446), which is also recorded in the Leofric Missal (A) as the "Missa de cordis emundatione per Spiritum Sanctum postulanda," in Nicholas Orchard, ed., *Leofric Missal*, vol. 2, no. 1935, pp. 325–26. The *Praefatio* of this mass (unmentioned in *RegC*, cap. 27) further reemphasizes God's constant inspection of the secrets of the mind: "Qui inspicis cogitationum secreta, et omnis nostrae mentis intentio, prouidentiae tuae patescit intuitu. Respice propitius archana cordis nostri cubilia" (You who examine the secrets of our thinking—the intent of all our minds also lies open for your providence to gaze upon—look favorably upon the secret recesses of our hearts). The mass is also printed in Deshusses, ed., *Le Sacramentaire Grégorien*, no. 109, pp. 125–26.

62. The text is edited by Fowler, "Late Old English Handbook," 30.

63. Napier, ed., "Old English Vision of Leofric," p. 182, lines 23–25; more recently reedited by Stokes, ed., "Vision of Leofric," 48. See Gatch, "Miracles in Architectural Settings," 229–43, who discusses the architectural details implied by the *Visio Leofrici* but does not consider what might be meant by "dihlum stowum."

64. B., *Vita Sancti Dunstani*, ed. and trans. Winterbottom and Lapidge, cap. 36, p. 100.

65. Ibid.

66. Kate Heulwen Thomas, "Meaning, Practice and Context of Private Prayer."

67. Lapidge goes on to discuss the one private prayer that could have possibly been composed by Æthelwold. But such prayers, as Lapidge himself points out, "were usually passed anonymously into prayer-books" (Introduction to Wulfstan of Winchester, *Life of St Æthelwold*, ed. and trans. Lapidge and Winterbottom, lxxxiv–lxxxv). On this basis alone, it is hard to say that the Benedictine Reform under Æthelwold suppressed the practice of private prayer, even if it did regulate the diurnal procedures with greater formality and stricture.

68. The earlier evidence of Anglo-Saxon private devotion (from the mid-eighth century to the early ninth century) tends to be Irish in origin, whereas the later evidence tends to have more Continental and early Anglo-Saxon parallels. See Kathleen Hughes, "Some Aspects of Irish Influence"; Bestul, "Continental Sources."

69. The Galba Prayerbook is BL, Cotton Galba A. xiv + Nero A. ii (fols. 3–13), which dates to the first half of the eleventh century; Ker, no. 157; Gneuss-Lapidge, nos. 333 and 342. The text is edited by Muir, ed., *Pre-Conquest English Prayer-Book*.

70. The *Portiforium of St. Wulfstan* is CCCC, MS 391 (Ker, no. 67; Gneuss-Lapidge, no. 104). It was owned by Wulfstan, bishop of Worcester (1062–95) and is dated to the late 1060s. The text is edited by Anselm Hughes, ed., *Portiforium of Saint Wulstan*.

71. Ælfwine, the dean of the New Minster at Winchester in the early eleventh century, owned a small-format prayer book (ca. 130 mm x 95 mm, suitable for traveling with its owner) datable to between the years 1023 and 1032. The manuscript was separated into two volumes by Sir Robert Cotton and now carries the shelf-marks BL, Cotton Titus D. xxvi and Titus D. xxvii; Ker, no. 202; Gneuss-Lapidge, no. 380). The manuscript has been edited by Günzel, ed., *Ælfwine's Prayerbook*; see p. 4 for a description of the format of the manuscripts and pp. 1–2 for the dating of the manuscripts. The private prayers are contained under item no. 52 and no. 76.

72. Günzel, ed., *Ælfwine's Prayerbook*, no. 53.6, p. 143.

73. For a list of manuscripts containing private prayers, see Günzel, ed., *Ælfwine's Prayerbook*, 205–6.

74. Ibid., no. 53.8, p. 143. The language here is similar to Ælfric's in *CH* I, hom. 1 (*De initio creaturae*), p. 178, lines 13–14: "ne mæg nan gesceaft fulfremedlice smeagan ne understandan ymbe

god" (no creature can fully inquire nor understand about God); the logic is similar to that found in the preface to Alcuin of York, *De psalmorum usu* (PL 101.465–68).

75. See Carruthers, *Book of Memory*, 112. See also Riché, *Education and Culture*, 464.

76. Alcuin of York, *Epistolae*, ed. Dümmler, ep. 31, p. 72, lines 24–25. The letter dates to before October 797, but according to Bullough, "What Has Ingeld to Do with Lindisfarne?" pp. 98–99, esp. n. 21, "It must remain uncertain whether in Alcuin's eyes the Hexham community was or was not at that date a monastic one," since he does not use the phrase *regularis uita* or "any other specifically monastic language."

77. Bede, *Homiliarum euangelii libri II*, ed. Hurst, lib. I, hom. 18, p. 130, lines 79–80.

78. *RegC*, cap. 67.

79. Günzel, *Ælfwine's Prayerbook*, no. 53.6, p. 143.

80. Isidore, *Etymologiae*, vol. 2, lib. XV, cap. 4, §2, line 15, describes the most holy part of sacred buildings as a *locus secretior*: "sancta autem sanctorum locus templi secretior" (but the sacred place of the sacred temple is a *locus secretior*).

81. On the Anglo-Latin ecclesiastical significance of the word *locus*, which tends to be used in order to describe a particular monastic or religious space, see Blair, *Church in Anglo-Saxon Society*, 110; on OE *stow* as a common term for religious establishments, see 217n145. In Old English, the adjective *digol* is the only word used to designate a space (*stow*) as secret; it is also the primary word used to describe divine secrecy. See *DOE*, s.v. *digol*, senses 2 and 1.b.i, respectively. Sometimes, *locus remotus* is used in place of *locus secretus*, but the sense is the same.

82. This detail is according to the *Vita Ceolfridi*, likely authored by Bede available in Bede, *Historia abbatum*, ed. Plummer, vol. 2, cap. 15, p. 379.

83. Alcuin of York, *Bishops, Kings, and Saints of York*, ed. and trans. Godman, p. 120, lines 1512–14.

84. Blair, *Church and Anglo-Saxon Society*, 220.

85. One might turn to the famous ninth-century Saint Gall Plan for understanding where the *loci secreti* might have been located within an idealized monastic layout, but by my assessment the only spaces reserved in the plan for private prayer are the chapels located along the nave in typical fashion. However, as Foot, *Monastic Life*, has noted, "it is hard to draw close parallels between the injunctions of monastic legislators about the best way in which to order a religious enclosure and the evidence for formal planning of monastic enclosures" (110). Blair, "Anglo-Saxon Minsters," 260, has similarly suggested we should instead study these plans as part of a tradition "in which formal main buildings co-existed with a high density of informal lesser ones." For an edition of the Saint Gall Plan, see UCLA Digital Library, "St. Gall Monastery Plan."

86. Gittos, *Liturgy, Architecture, and Sacred Places*, esp. 4–6.

87. Ó Carragáin, "Term *Porticus*," 13–34, gives a thorough picture of the full range of meaning implied by the term *porticus*, which could refer to a spectrum of architectural features ranging from open passageways or private chapels along the sides of a basilica; Ó Carragáin concludes that "instead of being an insular peculiarity, the early Anglo-Saxon use of the word *porticus* is an example of the community of culture that in the seventh and eighth centuries linked the Anglo-Saxon Church to Rome" (34).

88. Adomnán, *Life of Columba*, ed. and trans. Anderson and Anderson, lib. III, cap. 19, p. 210. The *Vita Sancti Columbae* was written in Ireland likely between 697 and 704. For a discussion of the term *exedra*, the exact meaning of which in the context of Iona is unclear, see pp. xlvi–xlvii. Although the editors suggest that it might refer to a sacristy, the logistics of the episode in which the word appears seem to imply a space very much like a *porticus* (for further discussion of the episode, see Chapter 5). For a discussion of the similarity and differences between the *porticus* and the *secretarium* (sacristy), see Ó Carragáin, "Term *Porticus*," 20–21.

89. Adomnán, *De locis sanctis*, ed. Meehan, cap. 1, p. 7.

90. See Parsons, *Books and Buildings*, 24–27 (752–54 in reprint). Meyvaert, "Book of Kells and Iona," 11n22, reiterated Parson's argument with additional evidence from Adomnán's *Vita Sancti Columbae* and *De locis sanctis*.

91. Walahfrid Strabo, *Libellus de exordiis*, ed. and trans. Harting-Correa, p. 66, lines 19–20, 25–26. Harting-Correa notes that "insular sources have used both *exedra* and *porticus* to mean a sort of side chapel" (221).
92. Ælfric of Eynsham, *Ælfric's Letter to the Monks of Eynsham*, ed. and trans. Jones, §33, p. 126.
93. Klukas, "Liturgy and Architecture," 86–87.
94. See Clapham, *English Romanesque Architecture*, 18–19; Taylor and Taylor, *Anglo-Saxon Architecture*, 1:134–39.
95. *HE*, lib. I, cap. 26, p. 76. On the early use of the Church of Saint Martin, see Brooks, *Early History*, 6–8, 17–23.
96. According to Bede (*HE*, lib. I, cap. 26, p. 76), it was built "dum adhuc Romani Brittaniam incolerent" (while the Romans were still in Britain). For a survey of the different arguments about the dating of the church, see Fisher, *Greater Anglo-Saxon Churches*, 360–62.
97. Fisher, *Greater Anglo-Saxon Churches*, 362.
98. Gittos, *Liturgy, Architecture, and Sacred Places*, 157.
99. Taking these photographs, I was reminded of some of the stories told by Howe, *Writing the Map*, e.g., 23–24. The afternoon that I spent at Saint Augustine's also happened unpleasantly to be the day for spraying herbicide on the ruins. The weeds in the photographs, which were certainly not there when the building was in its prime, would be gone the next day.
100. More people could certainly fit in the room, but if we allow for any furnishings along the interior walls, then the space seems ideally suited for use by a single supplicant or perhaps for sacerdotal confession.
101. *HE*, lib. II, cap. 3, p. 144. Such private masses are rare but nonetheless attested in other sources as well. Similarly, Stephen of Ripon writes of a priest who would say Mass privately every day for Bishop Wilfrid; *Life of Bishop Wilfrid*, ed. and trans. Colgrave, cap. 65, p. 410. See also Foot, *Monastic Life*, 206.
102. While Northumbrian churches tended not to have *porticus* like their Kentish counterparts, there is evidence of many pre-Conquest English abbeys that boasted multiple churches, such as Saint Augustine's, Canterbury, Glastonbury, Jarrow, and Hexham. Monkwearmouth also had at least two churches and an oratory. Nevertheless, based on literary sources, a number of other buildings might have also been two stories with small chapels on the second story, although such features are difficult to prove from the archeological record. See Taylor and Taylor, *Anglo-Saxon Architecture*, 1:13–14.
103. Anglo-Saxon church architecture can be divided into two periods that correspond roughly to the periods of heightened monastic activity discussed above. During the later period, the architectural style is more nationalized; during the earlier period, there was a clear difference between Northumbrian-type and Kentish-type styles. The Kentish-type churches tended to have *porticus*, while the Northumbrian ones did not. See Fisher, *Greater Anglo-Saxon Churches*, 31, 46n3.
104. Archaeological evidence in all cases, however, makes it hard to rule out the possibility that these could have been aisles rather than discrete chapels. See Taylor and Taylor, *Anglo-Saxon Architecture*, 1:110 (Brixworth) and 1:340 (Jarrow).
105. Ædiluulf (Æthelwulf), *De abbatibus*, ed. and trans. Campbell, cap. 14, p. 35, lines 436–37. For a discussion of the architectural implications of this poetic description, see Taylor, "Architectural Interest," 169.
106. Ædiluulf (Æthelwulf), *De abbatibus*, ed. and trans. Campbell, cap. 22, p. 57, lines 714–15.
107. Ibid., cap. 22, p. 61, lines 759–66.
108. Ibid., cap. 22, p. 61, line 772.
109. Ibid., cap. 18, p. 45, lines 562–66.
110. In his *Vita Sancti Dunstani*, William of Malmesbury describes these additions as "alas uel porticus quas uocant adiecit" (wings or what they call *porticus*); see William of Malmesbury, *Saints' Lives*, ed. and trans. Winterbottom and Thomson, lib. I, cap. 16.1, p. 204.
111. *RegC*, cap. 6 and 67.
112. Wulfstan of Winchester, *Epistola specialis*, ed. and trans. Lapidge, pp. 374–77, lines 45–58.
113. On the *Regula magistri* and efforts to conceal the Rule from outsiders, see p. 103.

114. Quirk, "Winchester Cathedral," 44–56, draws comparisons between this passage and Continental and English examples of similar west work.

115. Wulfstan of Winchester, *Epistola specialis*, ed. and trans. Lapidge, pp. 380–83, lines 127–44.

116. Klukas, "Liturgy and Architecture," 87, suggests that the "secretis oratorii locis" in the *Regularis concordia* refers to upper chapels, such as those at Deerhurst. This seems a very reasonable possibility, although it should not discount the possibility that other chapels at the ground level could have been just as suitable.

117. Wulfstan of Winchester, *Epistola specialis*, ed. and trans. Lapidge, pp. 386–89, lines 177–80, 189–92.

118. Other churches had similar towers and upper chapels. For example, New Minster had a tower with six so-called *segmentorum caelaturae* (celatures of the segments); see Birch, ed., *Liber vitae*, 9–10. The sense of this term is obscure, but it seems to refer to six stories, the first of which was a *porticus* dedicated to Mary (the dedication mass was celebrated by Dunstan); the second *segmentum* was dedicated to the Holy Trinity, the third to the Holy Cross, the fourth to All Saints, the fifth to Michael the archangel, and the final one to the four evangelists. The design of such a tower would have allowed the supplicant to enter a space of prayer that becomes more secret the higher one climbs, approaching closer to the angels (e.g., Michael) and God at every level.

119. *Vita Sancti Wulfstani* in William of Malmesbury, *Saints' Lives*, ed. and trans. Winterbottom and Thomson, lib. I, cap. 3, p. 24. It is not known which of the two pre-Conquest churches at Worcester contained the *porticus* referred to here, although Winterbottom and Lapidge suggest it was Saint Mary's Church (p. 26, n. 3). Wulfstan's beating at the door to heaven is a reference to Matt. 7:7 and Luke 11:9 ("pulsate et aperietur vobis" [knock, and it shall be opened to you]).

120. *Vita Sancti Wulfstani* in William of Malmesbury, *Saints' Lives*, ed. and trans. Winterbottom and Thomson, lib. I, cap. 4, p. 26.

121. *Conlationes*, lib. IX, cap. 35, p. 282, line 25–p. 283, line 5. Columbanus, *Regula monachorum*, ed. and trans. Walker, cap. 7, p. 130, line 17, also directs its monks to pray alone in their cells ("unusquisque in cubiculo suo orare debet").

122. The Continental reformer Peter Damian (c. 1007–1072) made use of a similar metaphor, encouraging his reader both to "mentis sue latibulum petat, ubi ad videndam creatoris sui faciem totis nisibus inardescat" (seek the secret place of his mind, where he may burn with all his efforts to see the face of his Creator) and, later in the letter, to "Scrutentur anguli, remotionum recessuum abdita penetrentur" (search for nooks and enter into the secret places of remote retreats), for "Furtivae quippe orationes vim inferunt caelo et indulgentiam rapiunt, dum frequenter in tenebris caelesti lumine perfunduntur" (secret prayers, of course, bring power down from heaven and carry off forgiveness, provided that in darkness they are often imbued with the light of heaven); Peter Damian, *Die Briefe des Petrus Damiani*, ed. Reindel, MGH Briefe d. dt. Kaiserzeit 4.1–4, vol. 4, ep. 153, p. 37, lines 15–16; p. 57, lines 12–13, 13–15.

123. A counterargument, however, is found in Job 13:10, where Job reminds his friends that "ipse vos arguet quoniam in abscondito faciem eius accipitis" (He shall reprove you, because in secret you accept his person). Gregory interprets this verse to mean that one should not attempt to flatter God with tears when in his presence and slight him behind his back, as it were, assuming that God sees with bodily sight. Gregory the Great, *Moralia in Iob*, ed. Adriaen, vol. 143a, lib. XI, cap. 29, p. 608, lines 1–21.

Chapter 5

1. *VCA*, lib. II, cap. 3, pp. 78–82; *VCM*, cap. 8, pp. 74–76, lines 220–51; *VCP*, cap. 10, pp. 188–90. For easy comparison between the three Anglo-Latin versions of the episode, they are printed with translations in Bolton, *History of Anglo-Latin Literature*, 1:136–38.

2. *CH* II, hom. 10, p. 83, lines 74–94.

3. *VCA*, lib. II, cap. 3, pp. 80–82.

4. Phil. 2:12.

5. Kierkegaard, *Fear and Trembling*, 39–42, in reflecting on God's command that Abraham sacrifice his son, argues that the movement of faith is carried out by virtue of the absurd. In other words, the absurdity of God's command renders Abraham's actions evidence of his faith.

6. See the Introduction, for a discussion of the interpretation of this passage in Bede, *In Genesim*, ed. Jones, lib. 2, §4.8, pp. 76–78, lines 137–96.

7. *VCA*, lib. II, cap. 3, p. 80.

8. *VCP*, cap. 10, p. 188.

9. *VCM*, cap. 8, p. 74, lines 221–22.

10. *CH* II hom. 10, p. 83, lines 77–78. Note that *stalcung* has as its root OE *stelan* (to steal); OED, s.v. stalk, v. 1. See Chapter 1, for a discussion of the relationship between theft and secrecy.

11. *VCM*, cap. 8, p. 75, line 236. The image of the "curved cave" occurs in a few fairly obscure texts: the Roman poet Valerius Flaccus (d. ca. AD 90) writes in his *Argonautica*: "cum sese Martia tigris / abstulit aut curvo tacitus leo condidit antro" (when the warlike tiger withdrew or the silent lion hid in the curved cave); Valerius Flaccus, *Argonautica*, ed. Ehlers, lib. III, p. 444, lines 635–36. Silius Italicus, another Roman poet contemporary to Valerius Flaccus, uses the phrase to describe the cave of a giant serpent on the bank of the river Bagrada: "intus dira domus curuoque immanis in antro / sub terras specus et tristes sine luce tenebrae" (within it was the terrible dwelling place and the vast subterranean hollow in the curved cave where gloomy darkness lets in no light); see Silius Italicus, *Punica*, ed. Delz, lib. VI, p. 143, lines 149–50. It is unlikely that either text was known in early medieval England; see Lapidge, *Anglo-Saxon Library*, 84. However, the image could have come to Bede through Aldhelm's *Aenigmata*, where he describes the *mustela* (weasel) as follows: "Discolor in curuis conuersor quadripes antris / Pugnas exercens dira cum gente draconum" (A variegated quadruped, I dwell in curved caves / making war with the snakes, a hateful species); see Aldhelm, *Aenigm*. 82, p. 501, lines 1–2.

12. But Gretsch, *Ælfric and the Cult of Saints*, 117–22, argues that Ælfric's Old English version of this episode follows more closely on Bede's *VCM* than on his *VCP*. Also see Blokhuis, "Bede and Ælfric."

13. *VCP*, cap. 10, p. 190; *VCM*, cap. 8, p. 74, line 222.

14. *VCA*, lib. II, cap. 3, p. 80.

15. *VCP*, cap. 10, p. 190.

16. On the date of *VCA*, see the introduction in Anonymous, *Two Lives of Saint Cuthbert*, ed. and trans. Colgrave, 13. On the date of Adomnán's *Vita Sancti Columbae*, see the introduction in Adomnán, *Life of Columba*, ed. and trans. Anderson and Anderson, xlii.

17. Scholars have generally concluded that many of the similarities between the two texts arise from mutually held ideals of sanctity, cultural interchange between Iona and Lindisfarne, and a shared body of source material rather than a direct relationship between the two *uitae*. However, none of their sources—or any other earlier source to my knowledge—contains a story such as the one we find in the *Vita Sancti Cuthberti* and the *Vita Sancti Columbae* in which a saint is secretly spied upon. On the relationship between the two *uitae*, see Stancliffe, "Cuthbert and the Polarity," 23n12. On the sources for the anonymous *Vita Sancti Cuthberti* and Adomnán's *Vita Sancti Columbae*, see, respectively, the introduction to Anonymous, *Two Lives of St Cuthbert*, ed. and trans. Colgrave, 11, and the introduction to Adomnán, *Life of Columba*, ed. and trans. Anderson and Anderson, lxvii–lxviii. Whether Bede knew of the *Vita Sancti Columbae* is a question shaped by a greater body of evidence. Scholars have long assumed that Bede did not have access to Adomnán's *Vita*; see, for example, Picard, "Bede, Adomnán, and the Writing of History," and Picard, "Purpose of Adomnán's *Vita Columbae*," 164n3. However, McCready, *Miracles and the Venerable Bede*, 169–75, has argued that Bede probably did have access to Adomnán's *Vita Sancti Columbae* and shows that at several points Bede draws more closely on Adomnán's *Vita* than even the Anonymous might have done. Nevertheless, the conclusion most often returned in these debates is, as Thacker, "Lindisfarne," puts it, "the ambiguous relationship between the *Vita Columbae* and the *Vita Cuthberti* reflects the complexity of Iona's relations with Northumbria in the late seventh century" (113).

18. Thacker, "Lindisfarne," 112.

19. Adomnán, *Life of Columba*, ed. and trans. Anderson and Anderson, lib. III, cap. 16, p. 204.

20. Ibid., lib. III, cap. 16, pp. 204–6.

21. Ibid., lib. III, pref., p. 182.

22. For a discussion of this term, see Chapter 4, p. 111.

23. Adomnán, *Life of Columba*, ed. and trans. Anderson and Anderson, lib. III, cap. 19, p. 210.

24. Ibid.

25. Ibid., lib. III, cap. 20, p. 212.

26. Ibid., lib. III, cap. 21, p. 212 (emphasis added).

27. Ibid., lib. III, cap. 21, pp. 212–14 (emphasis added).

28. In *VCP*, cap. 10, p. 188, Bede refers to the cleric as an *explorator*, perhaps following Adomnán's language in the *Vita Sancti Columbae*. For commentary on this connection, see McCready, *Miracles and the Venerable Bede*, 172–75.

29. This suggestion is made by Anderson and Anderson in their edition of Adomnán, *Life of Columba*, 215n234.

30. This feature of the narrative (that the unfaithful, spying brother is not asked to keep silent) is also found in the Irish *Vita* of Saint Fintan of Clonenagh (ca. 524–ca. 594), part of the so-called O'Donohue group (datable to before or around the year 800). Rather than experiencing self-induced fear, the brothers in both *uitae* encounter fear externally as the saints approach them with "magna seueritate" (great severity) (in the case of Columba) and a "minaci vultu" (threatening countenance) (in the case of Fintan). Together, these two secret witnesses assume that their actions would remain unknown—hidden from the saint and from God—and thereby prove themselves to possess neither faith nor the fear that activates it. The passage from the *Vita Sancti Fintani* is found in Plummer, ed., *Vitae Sanctorum Hiberniae*, vol. 2, cap. 16, p. 102. With slight alterations, the same story is also found in the *Vita Sancti Fintani abbatis de Cluain Edhnech* in Heist, ed., *Vitae Sanctorum Hiberniae*, cap. 18, p. 150. On the composition and dating of the O'Donohue group, see Sharpe, *Medieval Irish Saints' Lives*, 297–339, esp. 338–39.

31. *Vita Sancti Oswaldi* in Eadmer of Canterbury, *Lives and Miracles*, ed. and trans. Turner and Muir, cap. 7, pp. 232–34. The *Vita* was written between 1095 and 1116. See Gretsch, *Ælfric and the Cult of Saints*, 99, on Oswald's embrace of Cuthbert's cult.

32. On the type of monastic space evoked in this scene, see Chapter 4.

33. The editors seem to be confused about the liturgy referred to here, since they do not note the fact that the *Secretum* is what is implied by this incipit and by the phrase "in secretis orationibus," which they translate as "the secret prayers." The phrase "intenta mente ad Deum praemitteret," they translate as "recited to God . . . with total concentration," which misses the distinct silence of the verb and the emphasis on the mental connection with God. A few sentences later, at the end of the *Secretum*, Oswald says aloud the conventional formula, "Per omnia saecula saeculorum," which is typically sung aloud by the celebrant. See Andrew Hughes, *Medieval Manuscripts*, 88. Nevertheless, the reference to the part of the Mass following the *Secretum* (in which the priest returns to a normal voice directed at the congregation) is translated by the editors as "the other things usually said within the hearing of the congregation during the order of the mass." The phrase "et alia quae in audientia populi dici solent . . . in ordine missae" is perhaps better translated as "and the other parts in the order of the Mass, which are typically spoken to the listening congregation."

34. Ædiluulf, *De abbatibus*, ed. and trans. Campbell, cap. 15, p. 39, lines 478–89.

35. Tyrannius Rufinus, *Historia monachorum sive de Vita Sanctorum Patrum*, ed. Schulz-Flügel, cap. 31 (*De Paulo*), §4, p. 379.

36. Jerome, *Vita S. Pauli primi eremitae* (PL 23.25).

37. *VCP*, cap. 10, p. 188.

38. Bede, *Expositio Actuum apostolorum*, ed. Laistner, cap. 5.8, p. 29, lines 9–10. Bede takes this phrase verbatim from Jerome's translation of Didymus Alexandrinus's *Liber de Spiritu Sancto*, which suggests even wider readership and range of influence; see Jerome, *Liber Didymi Alexandrini de Spiritu Sancto* (PL 23.159). On the passage from Bede's commentary, see Dendle, *Satan Unbound*, 25–26.

39. Aldhelm, *Aenigm.* 88, p. 507, line 1.

40. Peter Chrysologus, *Collectio sermonum*, ed. Olivar, vol. 24, cap. 11, §5, p. 74, line 73. On the knowledge of Peter Chrysologus in Anglo-Saxon England (which is limited to the citation of three sermons in the *Old English Martyrology* and the citation of one sermon by Ælfric), see Lapidge, *Anglo-Saxon Library*, 325.

41. Peter Damian, *Die Briefe des Petrus Damiani*, MGH Briefe d. dt. Kaiserzeit 4.1–4, vol. 3, ep. 137, p. 468, line 30; vol. 4, ep. 165, p. 229, lines 11–12.

42. Ibid., vol. 2, ep. 86, p. 501, lines 19–20; vol. 2, ep. 69, p. 300, line 13; vol. 3, ep. 119, p. 376.

43. Bieler, ed. and trans., *Four Latin Lives of Saint Patrick*, cap. 5, p. 56, lines 17–19; on the date, see pp. 7–12; on the author, see pp. 6–7. This is a version of the *Vita Sancti Patricii* by a possibly French redactor written sometime after the middle of the eighth century and surviving in one manuscript dated to the end of the eleventh century.

44. Adomnán, *Life of Columba*, ed. and trans. Anderson and Anderson, lib. III, cap. 16, p. 204; *VCM*, cap. 8, p. 74, lines 221–22.

45. *Vita Sancti Oswaldi* in Eadmer of Canterbury, *Lives and Miracles*, ed. and trans. Turner and Muir, cap. 12, p. 240.

46. *CH* I, hom. 36, p. 486, lines 16–17.

47. *CH* I, hom. 36, p. 486, lines 19–21.

48. *CH* I, hom. 24, p. 375, lines 134–35.

49. *CH* I, hom. 36, p. 487, lines 41–44. This homily is a close translation of an anonymous Latin homily, printed in Cross, "Legimus in ecclesiasticis historicis," 105–21; see *CH* III, p. 301.

50. The connection to speech is also evident in Isidore's etymology: prophets are so-called "quasi praefatores, quia porro fantur et de futuris vera praedicunt" (as if they were "pre-speakers" [*praefator*] because indeed they speak [*fari*, ppl. *fatus*] and make true predictions about the future); Isidore, *Etymologiae*, vol. 1, lib. VII, cap. 8, §1, lines 1–3.

51. Lapidge, "Study of Latin Texts," 466.

52. Prosper of Aquitaine, *Liber sententiarum*, ed. Gastaldo, cap. 171, p. 297, lines 1–3. For *Epigramma* 90 (91), see Prosper of Aquitaine, *Liber epigrammatum*, ed. Horsting, 143–44; also available in PL 51.526 (*Epi*. 91).

53. Prosper of Aquitaine, *Liber epigrammatum*, ed. Horsting, pp. 143–44, *Epi*. 90, lines 1–2 and 9; also available in PL 51.526 (*Epi*. 91).

54. This vernacular adaptation of Augustine's *Soliloquia* is available in Carnicelli, ed., *King Alfred's Version*, lib. I, p. 67, lines 3–5. However, I am very grateful to Leslie Lockett for allowing me to consult the text of her forthcoming edition and translation of *The Old English Soliloquies*, in which the quoted passage will be found in lib. I, tentatively §47.

55. Carnicelli, ed., *King Alfred's Version,* lib. I, p. 59, line 4; Lockett, ed. and trans., *Old English Soliloquies*, lib. I, tentatively §31.

56. Carnicelli, ed., *King Alfred's Version*, lib. II, p. 86, lines 22–23; Lockett, ed. and trans., *Old English Soliloquies*, lib. II, tentatively §9.

57. Carnicelli, ed., *King Alfred's Version*, lib. II, p. 91, lines 12–15; Lockett, ed. and trans., *Old English Soliloquies*, lib. II, tentatively §20.

58. Writing in a quite different intellectual world, Anselm of Canterbury similarly works through the ineffability of the supreme being using logic and reason, arguing that the process of reaching God ultimately depends on faith and belief: "neque enim quæro intelligere ut credam, sed credo ut intelligam" (for I do not seek to understand in order that I might believe; rather I believe in order that I might understand); *Proslogion* by Anselm of Canterbury, *Anselmi Opera Omnia*, ed. Schmitt, vol. 1, cap. 1, p. 100, line 18. For a discussion of this idea, see Simpson, "Faith and Hermeneutics."

59. Adomnán, *Life of Columba*, ed. and trans. Anderson and Anderson, lib. III, cap. 16, p. 204.

60. Morris, ed. and trans., *Blickling Homilies,* hom. 14 (*Seo Gebyrd S. Johannes þæs Fulwihteres*), p. 161. Also available in Kelly, ed. and trans., *Blickling Homilies*, hom. 14, p. 114, lines 9–13.

61. Gregory the Great, *Dialogues*, ed. de Vogüé, vol. 2, lib. II, cap. 16, §3, p. 186, lines 23–24.

62. Ibid., vol. 2, lib. II, cap. 16, §§3–5, pp. 186–88, lines 26–38.

63. Ibid., vol. 2, lib. II, cap. 16, §§7–8, p. 190, lines 61–79.

64. Augustine employs similar logic in his *De cura pro mortuis gerenda*, ed. Zycha, §15.18, p. 651, lines 9–15, when explaining that the dead are like the prophets in their capacity to know only as much as God judges best for them to know: "Possunt etiam spiritus mortuorum aliqua, quae hic aguntur, quae necessarium est eos nosse et quos necessarium est ea nosse, non solum praesentia uel praeterita, uerum etiam futura spiritu dei reuelante cognoscere, sicut non omnes homines, sed prophetae, dum hic uiuerent, cognoscebant, nec ipsi omnia, sed quae illis esse reuelanda dei prouidentia iudicabat" (Indeed, the souls of the dead are able to know, when the Spirit of God reveals the truth, some of the things that happen here, not only present or past things, but even future things which need to be known by them and which they need to know. Likewise, not just any other men, but the prophets, while they were living here, did not even know all things, but only what the providence of God decided to reveal to them). The passage is also reproduced verbatim in Julian of Toledo, *Prognosticorum futuri saeculi*, ed. Hillgarth, lib. II, cap. 29, p. 67, lines 13–19. On the knowledge of these two texts in Anglo-Saxon England, see Lapidge, *Anglo-Saxon Library*, 284, for Augustine's *De cura pro mortuis gerenda*, and 317–18 for Julian of Toledo's *Prognosticum futuri saeculi*, which is listed in several Anglo-Saxon book inventories and extant in several manuscripts from the period. The *Prognosticum* is cited twice by Bede and numerous times by Ælfric, although neither author cites the chapter discussed here. More importantly, the *Old English Soliloquies* is a text that actually incorporates portions of Gregory the Great's and Julian of Toledo's views on the *visio Dei* that directly contradict what Augustine himself says in *Soliloquia* and elsewhere (including in *De cura pro mortuis gerenda*). See Godden, "Text and Eschatology," esp. 192–96; Whitelock, "Prose of Alfred's Reign," 86–89.

65. This is an especially Gregorian construction, found in his *Moralia in Iob*, *Regula pastoralis*, *Dialogi*, and *Epistolae*. Alfred the Great, *King Alfred's West-Saxon Version of Gregory's Pastoral Care*, ed. Sweet, translates the term at pref., p. 25, line 5; cap. 1, p. 27, line 20; cap. 4, p. 39, line 19; cap. 14, p. 87, line 7; cap. 15, p. 93, line 10; cap. 28, p. 191, lines 2–3; cap. 43, p. 315, line 10; and cap. 54, p. 421, line 25. See Saltzman, "Mind, Perception and the Reflexivity of Forgetting," 158.

66. Straw, *Gregory the Great*, 98.

67. For this sense of proper interpretation, see Augustine, *De doctrina Christiana*, ed. and trans. Green, lib. I, cap. 86–96, pp. 48–54.

68. Adomnán, *Life of Columba*, ed. and trans. Anderson and Anderson, lib. I, cap. 1, pp. 16–18.

69. Ibid., lib. I, cap. 1, p. 18.

70. Gregory the Great, *Dialogues*, ed. de Vogüé, vol. 2, lib. II, cap. 35, §3, p. 238, lines 24–26.

71. Ibid., vol. 3, lib. IV, cap. 8, p. 42.

72. Ibid., vol. 2, lib. II, cap. 18–20, pp. 194–98. The story of Exhilaratus is replicated in the episode of Isaac of Spoleto and a servant who brings him a gift basket, then hides the second along the roadside for himself only to find a snake in it as Isaac had predicted (ibid., vol. 2, lib. III, cap. 14, §9, p. 310, lines 99–114).

73. Ibid., vol. 2, lib. II, cap. 18, p. 194, lines 6–7.

74. Adomnán, *Life of Columba*, ed. and trans. Anderson and Anderson, lib. I, cap. 1, pp. 16–18.

75. Felix, *Life of Saint Guthlac*, ed. and trans. Colgrave, cap. 50, p. 156.

76. Gregory the Great, *Dialogues*, ed. de Vogüé, vol. 2, lib. II, cap. 19, §2, p. 196, line 13.

77. Ibid., vol. 2, lib. II, cap. 20, §2, p. 198, lines 17–18.

78. Straw, *Gregory the Great*, 99, refers to the monk as a "murmurer."

79. Gregory the Great, *Dialogues*, ed. de Vogüé, vol. 2, lib. II, cap. 20, §2, p. 198, lines 18–20.

80. Gregory the Great, *Règle pastorale*, ed. Judic et al., vol. 1, lib. I, cap. 11, pp. 170–72; Alfred the Great, *King Alfred's West-Saxon Version of Gregory's Pastoral Care*, ed. Sweet, cap. 11, p. 71. See Saltzman, "Mind, Perception and the Reflexivity of Forgetting," 172–73.

81. *VCP*, cap. 9, p. 186. For a discussion of this episode in another context, see Chapter 3.

82. *CH* II hom. 10, p. 83, lines 90–93.

83. Gregory the Great, *Dialogues*, ed. de Vogüé, vol. 2, lib. II, cap. 37, §1, p. 242, lines 4–5.

84. Athanasius (trans. Evagrius), *Vita Beati Antonii Abbatis* (PL 73.153–54).

85. *VCP*, cap. 24, p. 236.

86. Adomnán, *Life of Columba*, ed. and trans. Anderson and Anderson, lib. I, cap. 43, p. 78; lib. III, cap. 6, p. 190; lib. III, cap. 22, pp. 214–16; lib. III, cap. 23, p. 220.

87. Felix, *Life of St. Guthlac*, cap. 50, p. 156.

88. *HE*, lib. IV, cap. 3, p. 342.

89. *HE*, lib. V, cap. 19, p. 526.

90. Wulfstan of Winchester, *Life of St Æthelwold*, ed. and trans. Lapidge and Winterbottom, cap. 14, p. 28.

91. See Watson, *Honor Among Christians*, who argues that Jesus's concealment of his deeds and identity, especially in Mark, arises out of conceptions of honor and shame in ancient Mediterranean culture.

92. The Anonymous of Lindisfarne does compare Cuthbert to Daniel—or more precisely, the sea animals that minister to Cuthbert are compared to the lions that minister to Daniel (Dan. 6). And he compares Cuthbert's ability to see the hidden monk with Peter's detection of Ananias and Sapphira when they tempted the Holy Spirit (Acts 5).

93. *VCM*, cap. 8, pp. 75–76, lines 244–46.

94. Translation by Lapidge, "Bede's Metrical *Vita S. Cuthberti*," 91n46.

95. *VCP*, cap. 10, p. 190.

96. Stancliffe, "Cuthbert and the Polarity," 40–41.

97. Bede, *Homiliarum euangelii*, ed. Hurst, lib. II, hom. 6, pp. 223–24, lines 133–41 (on Mark 7:31–37), emphasis added.

98. *VCP*, cap. 10, p. 188.

99. *VCA*, lib. I, cap. 2, p. 62; Sulpicius Severus, *Vie de Saint Martin*, ed. Fontaine, cap. 1.7, p. 252. Fontaine comments (at 2:424) that "C'est l'idéal évangélique de la 'vie cachée' que Sulpice développe pour se justifier lui-même d'une relative brièveté: isolement du μόναχος, seul avec Dieu et sa conscience; fuite de la glorie humaine; désir de cacher totalement ses dons spirituels," suggesting that this path of the private life is juxtaposed against the public life of Martin as a bishop.

100. Adomnán, *Life of Columba*, ed. and trans. Anderson and Anderson, lib. I, cap. 50, p. 92. See also lib. III, cap. 7, p. 192, where using similar language Adomnán explains that not all of the "celata sacramenta" (secret mysteries), "arcana ab aliis" (hidden from others) but revealed to him by God, were allowed to reach the knowledge of men, and that Columba gave two reasons for this: to avoid boasting and to avoid intolerable crowds. A similar metaphor of new wine (versus old wine) is used in Luke 5:36–39 to describe the Old and New Testaments.

101. This agreement further supports McCready's argument in *Miracles and the Venerable Bede*, 169–75, that Bede had access to Adomnán's *Vita Sancti Columbae*.

102. Bede, *Homilarum euangelii*, ed. Hurst, lib. II, hom. 6, p. 224, lines 141–44 (on Mark 7:31–37).

103. *VCA*, lib. II, cap. 3, p. 82.

104. *VCA*, lib. II, cap. 3, p. 82.

105. *VCP*, cap. 10, p. 190.

106. *VCM*, cap. 8, p. 76, lines 248–51.

107. Translation based with modifications on that of Lapidge, "Bede's Metrical *Vita S. Cuthberti*," 91n46.

108. Lantfred of Winchester, *Translatio et miracula Sancti Swithuni*, ed. and trans. Lapidge, 254.

109. *VCA*, lib. I, cap. 2, p. 62.

110. For example, *VCA*, lib. IV, cap. 7, p. 121 ("nec silentio praetereundum existimo") and lib. IV, cap. 17, p. 136 ("silentio non praetereo"), but cf. *VCA*, lib. I, cap. 7, p. 72, where the Anonymous explains that he must "silentio pretereo" (pass over in silence) much of Cuthbert's youth. Cicero seems to have been particularly fond of the phrase (especially in paralipsis). Jerome, Augustine, Gregory the Great, Bede, and others used the phrase as well.

111. For example, *VCP*, cap. 10, p. 188. The verb *tegere* (to cover, conceal) is, of course, different from *praeterire* (to pass over), but we do find the former used on occasion, as in the phrase "non est

tegendum silentio" (we must not cover over in silence) found in the Anonymous of Whitby, *Earliest Life of Gregory the Great*, cap. 9, p. 90.

112. As discussed earlier (pp. 135–36), Eadmer would have almost certainly been aware of the episode of Cuthbert on the shore, which he echoes in his depiction of the pauper spying on Saint Oswald in the *confessio* of the church.

113. Eadmer of Canterbury, *Life of St Anselm*, ed. and trans. Southern, cap. 72, p. 150.

114. Ibid., pp. 150–51.

115. The incident between Anselm and Eadmer took place around the year 1100, but on the treatment of disobedience in the reformed monasteries of England prior to the year 1100 and the idea that obedience requires an act of interpretation on the part of the subject, see O'Brien O'Keeffe, *Stealing Obedience*, e.g., 8.

116. Matt. 9:31, emphasis added.

Chapter 6

1. Several book-length studies of the Anglo-Saxon riddle traditions provide excellent introductions to the genre and its literary importance during the period. See, for example, Murphy, *Unriddling the Exeter Riddles*; Bitterli, *Say What I Am Called*; Borysławski, *Old English Riddles*; and Niles, *Old English Enigmatic Poems*, who notes, at pp. 3–4, that the enigmatic elements common to the riddles can be found across the Old English poetic corpus more broadly.

2. Goolden, ed., *Old English "Apollonius of Tyre,"* cap. 1, p. 2, lines 15–19. In the Old English translation, it is unclear whether it is the king or the "ongeanwinnendan fæmnan" (resisting woman [*scil.* his daughter]) who wishes to conceal the crime. Goolden (p. 45) notes that the earliest Latin recension (RA) of the *Historia Apollonii regis Tyri* specifies that it is the daughter who wishes to conceal the crime, graphically conveying the brutal loss of her virginity and the impossibility of concealing it: "fluentem sanguinem coepit celare; sed guttae sanguinis in pavimento ceciderunt" (she began to hide the flow of blood, but drops of blood fell to the floor); Kortekaas, ed., *Story of Apollonius*, cap. 1, p. 104, lines 17–18. Recension RB tones down the scene by replacing "guttae sanguinis" with "certa" (certain things); ibid., cap. 1, p. 105, line 16. By the time the text arrives in English manuscripts, the scene has been trimmed further, leaving behind only an ambiguous reference to the fact that one of them wishes the crime to be concealed: "perfectoque scelere cupit celare secrete" (and he/she wished to conceal the crime in complete secrecy); Raith, ed., *Die alt- und mittelenglischen Apollonius-Bruchstücke*, cap. 1, p. 92. The Old English translation retains the ambiguity.

3. For other instances of servants who are privy to the secrets of their masters, see Chapter 2.

4. Goolden, ed., *Old English "Apollonius of Tyre,"* cap. 3, p. 4, line 25.

5. Ibid., cap. 4, p. 6, lines 11–12.

6. Ibid., cap. 4, p. 6, lines 17–18.

7. Ibid., cap. 6, p. 8, lines 5–6.

8. The Latin source is similar: "Thaliarche, secretorum meorum fidelissime minister" (Thaliarcus, servant most trustworthy of my secrets); Raith, ed., *Die alt- und mittelenglischen Apollonius-Bruchstücke*, cap. 6, p. 93.

9. Goolden, ed., *Old English "Apollonius of Tyre,"* cap. 50, p. 40, lines 6–7 (emphasis added).

10. Ibid., cap. 4, p. 6, line 18; cap. 50, p. 40, line 12.

11. Ibid., cap. 50, p. 40, lines 16–17.

12. I will use the term "servant" as the most general category to describe those individuals who are bound in some way to a master or superior. The category is slippery and can be expanded to include radically different degrees of freedom and unfreedom; advisors have vastly more freedom than servants, and servants have more freedom than enslaved people. What these figures share is that they are bound by greater or lesser degrees of obligation and force to serve their masters, and I am interested in how the nature of such obligation and force enacts a form of secrecy on the part of the servant. On the full range of Old English terminology of servitude and slavery, see Pelteret, *Slavery in Early Mediaeval England*, appendix 1, pp. 261–330.

13. For an example of a slave being subject to the ordeal, see, for example, Wulfstan of Winchester, *Narratio metrica de S. Swithuno*, ed. and trans. Lapidge, 510–12.

14. Ælfric of Eynsham, *Ælfric's Lives of Saints*, ed. Skeat, vol. 1, no. 2 (Saint Eugenia), p. 30, line 103.

15. The word *asecretis* is relatively rare. Latham, *Medieval Latin Word-List*, s.v. *a secretis*, p. 1, dates the usage of the word to c. 1125. But see Niermeyer and van de Kieft, *Mediae Latinitatis lexicon minus*, vol. 1, s.v. *a secretis*, pp. 83–84, who supply several late ninth- and early tenth-century sources from the Continent. OED, s.v. secretary, n.1 and adj., sense A.1.a.

16. BT, s.v. *rædels*.

17. Porter, ed., *Antwerp-London Glossaries*, p. 129, line 2924; Priscian, *Excerptiones de Prisciano*, ed. Porter, lib. II, cap. 336, p. 150; for the gloss, see the Scholia to the *Excerptiones* (appendix I), p. 371. The phrase "Asecretis est consiliarius regum intimus" occurs in an eleventh-century manuscript of Ælfric's *Grammar*, BL, Harley 3271, fol. 92v (Ker, no. 239, art. 12; Gneuss-Lapidge, no. 435). See the introduction to Priscian, *Excerptiones de Prisciano*, ed. Porter, 36.

18. *Beo*, line 1325.

19. Goolden, ed., *Old English "Apollonius of Tyre,"* cap. 6, p. 8, line 5.

20. E.g., ibid., cap. 9, p. 14, lines 2–4; cap. 8, p. 12, lines 8–9.

21. The etymological relationship between the noun *seruus* and the verb *seruare* is not especially transparent. Walde and Hofmann, *Lateinisches Etymologisches Wörterbuch*, s.v. *servo*, for instance, suggest that their relation to one another does not fit the usual system because *seruare* can be either denominative or causative. But according to de Vaan, *Etymological Dictionary*, s.v. *servus*, the verbs *seruare* ("to watch over, look after, observe"), *conseruare* ("to keep from danger, keep unchanged"), and *obseruare* ("to observe, watch, abide by") are all in fact derivatives of *seruus*. However, de Vaan also cites the argument of Rix, *Die Termini der Unfreiheit*, 81–87, "that the original meaning of **serwo-* probably was 'guard, shepherd', which underwent a pejorative development to 'slave' in Italy between 700 and 450 BC. *Servīre* would be the direct derivative of *servus,* hence 'be a slave'; *servāre* would in his view be derived from an older noun **serwā-* or **serwom* 'observation, heedance'" (559).

22. Augustine, *De ciuitate Dei*, ed. Dombart and Kalb, vol. 2, lib. XIX, cap. 15, p. 862, lines 12–15; Isidore, *Etymologiae*, vol. 1, lib. V, cap. 28, §32.

23. Origen, *Homilien zum Hexateuch*, ed. Baehrens, hom. 18, §4.6, p. 175 (emphasis added). Two Anglo-Saxon manuscripts of this text survive (one from the eighth-century missionary activity in Germany and the other a tenth-century manuscript possibly from Winchester); see Lapidge, *Anglo-Saxon Library*, 162, 322.

24. On the translation method, see the introduction to Goolden, ed., *Old English "Apollonius of Tyre,"* xx–xxvii. But see Townsend, "Naked Truth," 174–76, who makes an ingenious case for the hermeneutic and cultural value of the translation by examining its handling of the gymnasium/bathhouse scene in which Apollonius plays ball with the king in the nude. On the role of the translation in relation to the Latin, see also Lees, "Engendering Religious Desire," 37.

25. See Copeland, *Rhetoric, Hermeneutics, and Translation*, who has shown how translation was understood in the Middle Ages to be a richly creative endeavor.

26. See Raith, ed., *Die alt- und mittelenglischen Apollonius-Bruchstücke*, 87–88; see also the introduction to Goolden, ed., *Old English "Apollonius of Tyre,"* xxxiv.

27. Archibald, *Apollonius of Tyre*, 26. In his commentary, Goolden, ed., *Old English "Apollonius of Tyre,"* 45, notes that "the posing of a riddle would have had a special appeal to an Anglo-Saxon audience." But cf. Stanley, "Rev. of *The Old English* Apollonius of Tyre," 428, who questions this notion, supposing that the "taste of the audience of MS. CCCC. 201 need not have been the same as that of those who sniggered at the obscenities of the Exeter Book." Of course, as we will see below, not all riddles of the period are obscene, and many examples of the genre (including the obscene ones) were in fact of a monastic and spiritual orientation. On the centrality of riddles to the narrative of the Latin source, see Laird, "Metaphor and the Riddle of Representation," 225–44.

28. Goolden, ed., *Old English "Apollonius of Tyre,"* cap. 8, p. 12, lines 8–9.

29. Ibid., cap. 2, p. 2, line 24. See above, p. 286, n. 2, on the ambiguity in the Old English concerning whether it is the king or the daughter who initially wishes the crime to be concealed ("to bediglianne"); given the riddles that the daughter puts to her nurse, the Old English may in fact be playing with this ambiguity and their mutual desire for concealment.

30. Goolden, ed., *Old English "Apollonius of Tyre,"* cap. 2, p. 4, lines 4–5, 5–6.

31. Raith, ed., *Die alt- und mittelenglischen Apollonius-Bruchstücke*, cap. 43, pp. 112–14.

32. CCCC MS 318, which dates to twelfth-century Rochester, is the manuscript on which Raith bases his Latin edition of the *Historia Apollonii*. On the Latin source for the Old English *Apollonius*, see Hollis et al., *Old English Prose*, 90–93. As for the manuscript context, Raith (p. 49) insinuates that the *Apollonius* had its counterpart in contemporary works of hagiography, both in Old English (such as the *vita* of Saint Andreas in the Blickling Homilies) and in Latin (such as the *Vita Sancti Thecle*, which survives alongside the Latin *Historia Apollonii* in CCCC MS 318). For additional details about the manuscript, see the description in Parker on the Web, "CCCC MS 318: Manuscript Description."

33. Archibald, *Apollonius of Tyre*, 26.

34. The *aenigmata* in the *Historia Apollonii* correspond to Symphosius, *Aenigm.* 12 (*Flumen et piscis* [River and fish]), *Aenigm.* 2 (*Harundo* [Reed]), *Aenigm.* 13 (*Nauis* [Ship]), *Aenigm.* 90 (*Balneum* [Bathhouse]), *Aenigm.* 61 (*Ancora* [Anchor]), *Aenigm.* 63 (*Spongia* [Sponge]), *Aenigm.* 59 (*Pila* [Ball]), *Aenigm.* 69 (*Speculum* [Mirror]), *Aenigm.* 79 (*Rotae* [Wheels]), and *Aenigm.* 78 (*Scalae* [Stairs]).

35. Aldhelm, *Aenigm.*, 358–540. The best translation of the *Aenigmata* is that in *Poetic Works*, trans. Lapidge and Rosier, 70–94. The reference to Symphosius in the prose prologue is to be found on p. 371, lines 1–4, of Glorie's edition of Aldhelm's *Aenigmata*.

36. Tatwine, *Aenigm.*, 165–208.

37. Eusebius, *Aenigm.*, 209–71. Eusebius is believed to be a pseudonym for Hwætberht, the abbot of Monkwearmouth-Jarrow from 716 until his death; see Lapidge, "Hwætberht," 250–51.

38. Symphosius, *Aenigm.*, pref., p. 621, line 1. This phrase is taken from the first two lines of Symphosius's preface, lines that do not survive in two of the manuscripts (Glorie's *sigla P¹* and *S³*) but do appear in all of the other manuscripts, including the two to be discussed below: CUL, Gg. 5. 35, and BL, Royal 12 C. xxiii (Glorie's *sigla G* and *L*).

39. Nearly one hundred Old English riddles survive in the Exeter Book: Exeter, Cathedral Library, 3501 (Ker, no. 116; Gneuss-Lapidge, no. 257). The Exeter Book is a manuscript of 131 folios likely produced in the south of England in the second half of the tenth century. For an overview of the Exeter Book, see Scragg, "Exeter Book," 183–84. The riddles are separated into three sections (1–59, 30b and 60, 61–95), but scribal inconsistency with respect to the divisions between poems, uncertainty as to which poems count as riddles, and damage to the manuscript make it impossible to determine the exact number of riddles originally contained therein. In their edition of the Exeter Book, Krapp and Dobbie count ninety-five riddles, close enough to one hundred for scholars to postulate an overall design modeled on the earlier Latin collections. While other editions offer different numbering systems, Krapp and Dobbie's numbering is the most widely accepted and is therefore used here. Williamson, ed., *Old English Riddles*, counts ninety-one; Muir, ed., *Exeter Anthology*, counts ninety-four.

40. Bitterli, *Say What I Am Called*, 4–5. In fact, several of the Exeter Book riddles echo ones by Symphosius, and two of them are translations of Aldhelm, *Aenigm.* 33 and 100; Exeter Book *Rid.* 35 and *Rid.* 40 are translations of Aldhelm, *Aenigm.* 33 (*Lorica* [Coat of mail]) and *Aenigm.* 100 (*Creatura* [Creation]), respectively. Exeter Book *Rid.* 16, *Rid.* 47, *Rid.* 60, *Rid.* 85, and *Rid.* 86 share similarities with Symphosius, *Aenigm.* 61 (*Ancora* [Anchor]), *Aenigm.* 16 (*Tinea* [Book-moth]), *Aenigm.* 2 (*Harundo* [Reed]), *Aenigm.* 12 (*Flumen et piscis* [River and fish]), and *Aenigm.* 95 (*Luscus alium uendens* [One-eyed seller of garlic]). Note that Symphosius's *Aenigm.* 61, *Aenigm.* 2, and *Aenigm.* 12 also occur in the *Historia Apollonii*.

41. Ker, no. 49; Gneuss-Lapidge, no. 65.5.

42. For example, Heyworth, "*Apollonius of Tyre*," argues that there is a unifying concern with marriage and incest in the manuscript; Wormald, *Making of English Law*, 208–9, argues that the story

may have been judged exemplary by both laymen and monks alike, since it appears in library catalogs of Frankish abbeys; Robins, "Ancient Romance," 91–128, argues that the *Apollonius* may have been included in reaction to the "tensions and anxieties of eleventh-century England" (particularly those produced by the Danish invasions) elsewhere depicted through the genre of biographical narrative; and Anlezark, "Reading the 'Story of Joseph,'" 72–73, reads the *Apollonius* alongside the *Joseph* fragment as examples of the compiler's interest in laying out a model for good Christian government.

43. Whitbread, "MS. C.C.C.C. 201," 109n9, for example, judged that the *Apollonius* must have been considered suitable monastic reading on the basis of a lost English version listed in a twelfth-century catalog of the library of the Benedictine abbey at Burton-on-Trent.

44. Pelteret, *Slavery in Early Mediaeval England*, 51–53; David Wyatt, *Slaves and Warriors*, 240–41; Irving, "Heroic Experience," 207–8. See also Denno, "Oppression and Voice," who draws our attention to what he calls a "discourse of servitude" and argues that the riddles permit the exiled and captive objects to have a momentary "voice" (35).

45. Cavell, *Weaving Words and Binding Bodies*, 172.

46. Aldhelm, *Aenigm.* 28, 42; Howe, "Aldhelm's *Enigmata*," 41–42.

47. Pelteret, *Slavery in Early Medieval England*, 53–54.

48. With the exception of Cavell, *Weaving Words and Binding Bodies*, 157–91, who discusses many of these riddles, divides them into two categories ("agricultural slaves" and "servants in the hall"), and suggests that the primary reason for this concern with servitude and slavery in the riddles (and less so elsewhere in the poetic corpus) is due to the genre's interest in everyday objects and phenomena.

49. The Exeter Book riddles that contain references to servitude (including metaphorical references to binding and fettering) are *Rid.* 1 (wind), *Rid.* 3 (storm controlled by God), *Rid.* 4 (bell), *Rid.* 6 (sun), *Rid.* 11 (cup of wine), *Rid.* 12 (ox and its hide), *Rid.* 20 (sword), *Rid.* 21 (plow), *Rid.* 22 (Ursa Major, or the month of December), *Rid.* 23 (bow), *Rid.* 25 (onion), *Rid.* 27 (mead), *Rid.* 33 (iceberg), *Rid.* 38 (bull calf), *Rid.* 43 (soul and body), *Rid.* 44 (key), *Rid.* 45 (dough, with a possible reading of *wincel* [line 1] as a variant spelling of *wencel* [slave or servant] proposed by Rudolf, "Riddling and Reading," 514), *Rid.* 49 (bread and oven), *Rid.* 50 (fire), *Rid.* 52 (flail), *Rid.* 53 (gallows or cross), *Rid.* 54 (churn and butter, or sex), *Rid.* 58 (well-sweep), *Rid.* 63 (?drinking vessel), *Rid.* 64 (ship, with a possible reference to "þeow" in the runic puzzle; see Krapp and Dobbie, eds., *Exeter Book*, ASPR 3, 367–68), *Rid.* 72 (ox), *Rid.* 73 (spear), *Rid.* 83 (gold, ore), and *Rid.* 87 (bellows). See Pelteret, *Slavery in Early Mediaeval England*, 51n6, for a survey of the references to slavery in the Exeter Book Riddles, although several of the riddles mentioned above are not included in his list because they refer abstractly to servitude or binding rather than specifically to slavery.

50. For a discussion of this formula and its relation to the Latin *aenigmata*, see Andy Orchard, "Enigma Variations," 286–87. The formula (in various forms) is found in Riddles 1, 3, 8, 10, 11, 12, 14, 16, 19, 23, 26, 27, 62, 66, 73, 80, 83, and 86.

51. On stylistic grounds, the riddles of the Exeter Book seem not to have been the work of a single author, and most scholars "doubt the unity of the riddle collection as a whole," which changes markedly from one riddle to the next (Krapp and Dobbie, eds., *Exeter Book*, ASPR 3, lxv–lxvi). However, Salvador-Bello, "Patterns of Compilation," has shown how the structure of the first forty riddles in the Exeter Book is modeled on the structures of the Anglo-Latin collections, which suggests at least a cohesive plan in the assembly of the riddles; in *Isidorean Perceptions of Order*, Salvador-Bello makes a more comprehensive argument for the structural link between the Old English riddles and the Anglo-Latin tradition.

52. Lapidge, "Stoic Cosmology," for example, makes a compelling case for reading the text as a single riddle to be solved with the stoic concept of *pneuma* or *spiritus*. See also Salvador-Bello, "Patterns of Compilation," 353–56, who argues that "the solution of Riddle 1-2-3 therefore involves a three-phase process in which the solver must first determine the type of '"storm"'—be it on land, at sea, or in the air; secondly, identify the wind as the cause of those atmospheric disturbances, an intellectual task which would certainly require knowledge of encyclopedic meteorological lore; and thirdly, be able to answer that God is the omnipotent force behind those awesome events" (353).

53. *Rid.* 1, p. 180, lines 2b–3a.
54. *Rid.* 1, p. 180, lines 12–15.
55. *Rid.* 3, p. 183, lines 67a and 65a.
56. *Rid.* 3, p. 181, lines 1–6a. This passage is also profoundly apocalyptic, a point that will be discussed in Chapter 8.
57. See, for example, Bede, *De natura rerum*, ed. Jones, cap. 48, p. 232 (Bede has Pliny and Isidore as sources).
58. Aldhelm, *Aenigm.* 2, p. 385, line 1. Cf. Eusebius, *Aenigm.* 8 (*De uento et igne* [On wind and fire]), p. 218, line 2, in which wind can be touched but not seen.
59. Acts 16:30.
60. *Rid.* 4, p. 183, lines 2a and 1b. Niles, *Old English Enigmatic Poems*, 144n2, solves the riddle as water bucket (*wæter-stoppa*), following Stewart, "Solution to the Old English Riddle 4," and Doane, "Three Old English Implement Riddles." The riddle has also been solved as "bell," "millstone," "lock," "flail," and "quill pen," deemed "probably the most perplexing riddle in the Exeter Book collection" by Williamson, *Feast of Creatures*, 162. On the translation of *þegn*, recall that Antiochus refers to his unfree servant, Thaliarcus, as "myn se getrywesta þegn" (see above, pp. 162–63).
61. Stewart, "Solution to the Old English Riddle 4," 53, translates *þegn* as "servant/master." See BT, s.v. *þegen*, which gives "servant, one who does service for another" as the primary definition. See also Pelteret, *Slavery in Early Medieval England*, appendix 1, p. 304, s.v. *þegn*, who gives only three possible senses to the word (none of which refers to a position of dominance): "one who serves another," "a freeman who serves a noble or a king," and "a slave."
62. Doane, "Three Old English Implement Riddles," 246.
63. *Rid.* 12, p. 186, lines 1–15.
64. BT, s.v. *wealh*, sense 2.
65. Bitterli, *Say What I Am Called*, 27–34, helpfully charts the relationships between each of the ox riddles in the Old English and the Latin collections, including parallels in the *Aenigmata* of Aldhelm and of Eusebius, in the *Lorsch Riddles*, and in the pseudo-Bedan *Collectanea*.
66. *Rid.* 72, p. 232, lines 11a and 13a.
67. On the connotations of *swearte*, see Pelteret, *Slavery in Early Medieval England*, 52–53. See also Banham, "Anglo-Saxon Attitudes," 151–52.
68. Brady, "'Dark Welsh.'"
69. *Rid.* 38, p. 199, lines 5–7.
70. Clemoes, *Interactions of Thought and Language*, 105.
71. For a brief discussion of this "unusual narrative structure" and the critical responses to it, see Bitterli, *Say What I Am Called*, 30.
72. Eusebius, *Aenigm.* 37 (*De uitulo* [Calf]), p. 247, line 4. A close parallel also occurs in Pseudo-Bede, *Collectanea Pseudo-Bedae*, ed. and trans. Bayless and Lapidge, no. 194, p. 144.
73. Aldhelm, *Aenigm.* 83 (*Iuuencus* [Bull calf]), p. 503, lines 5–6.
74. Eusebius, *Aenigm.* 32 (*De membrano* [Parchment sheets]), p. 242, line 4.
75. *Rid.* 52, p. 207, lines 1–7. Note that Runlon-Miller, "Sexual Humor and Fettered Desire," argues that the solution to *Riddle* 52 refers to a "yoke of oxen led by a female slave" (117).
76. *Rid.* 21, p. 191, line 7b. *Cræft* either refers to the skill with which the plow is manufactured or the power with which it is made to till the fields.
77. *Rid.* 21, p. 191, lines 14b–15.
78. Symphosius, *Aenigm.* 5 (*Catena* [Chain]), p. 626, lines 1–3 (emphasis added).
79. Symphosius, *Aenigm.* pref., p. 621, line 10 (emphasis added).
80. Raith, ed., *Die alt- und mittelenglischen Apollonius-Bruchstücke*, cap. 43, p. 112.
81. Orchard, "Enigma Variations," 284–86.
82. Ibid., 286–87.
83. Howe, "Aldhelm's *Enigmata* and Isidorian Etymology," 37.
84. Dailey, "Riddles, Wonder and Responsiveness," 455.
85. *Rid.* 42, pp. 203–4, lines 1–17.

86. Translation based on Dailey, "Riddles, Wonder and Responsiveness," 455.
87. The word *hæmedlac* is a hapax legomenon, which most likely refers to sexual intercourse. See Coleman, "Sexual Euphemism."
88. See *DOE*, s.vv. *dyrn-hæmende*, *dyrne-forlegennes*, and *dyrne-liger*.
89. This solution was first proposed by Dietrich, "Die Räthsel des Exeterbuches," 473.
90. Dailey, "Riddles, Wonder, and Responsiveness," 456.
91. Lerer, *Literacy and Power*, 120–23. This interpretation has been maintained by subsequent scholars as well. See, for example, Bitterli, *Say What I Am Called*, 131. But for a different reading, see Lees and Overing, *Double Agents*, 54–62.
92. *Rid.* 26, p. 193, lines 11b–14.
93. Lerer, *Literacy and Power*, 119.
94. Salvador-Bello, "Key to the Body," 60–96.
95. *DOE*, s.v. *clam*.
96. Ælfric of Eynsham, *Ælfrics Grammatik und Glossar*, ed. Zupitza, pref., p. 2, lines 16–17.
97. Anlezark, ed. and trans., *Old English Dialogues*, p. 78, lines 6–7.
98. *Exodus*, ASPR 1, p. 106, line 525b.
99. Note that only one riddle comes between *Riddle* 44 and the cock and hen riddle (42). Salvador-Bello, "Key to the Body," argues that *Riddles* 42 through 46 together form a "cohesive series" of seemingly obscene texts that are in actuality moralizing and instructional about the "spiritual and bodily nature of human beings" (95).
100. *Rid.* 44, pp. 204–5, lines 1–7.
101. See Pelteret, *Slavery in Early Medieval England*, 271–74; *DOE*, s.v. *esne*, sense 1a.
102. Symphosius, *Aenigm.* 4 (*Clauis* [Key]), p. 625, lines 2–3 (emphasis added).
103. See also Matt. 18:18. On binding and loosing in a monastic context, see Chapter 3.
104. *DOE*, s.v. *cræft*. The headnote captures the word's complexity: "The most frequent Latin equivalent of *cræft* is *ars*, yet neither 'craft' nor 'art' adequately conveys the wide range of meanings of *cræft*. 'Skill' may be the single most useful translation for *cræft*, but the senses of the word reach out to 'strength,' 'resources,' 'virtue' and other meanings in such a way that it is often not possible to assign an occurrence to one sense in ModE without arbitrariness and the attendant loss of semantic richness." For a more detailed discussion of the word, see Discenza, "Power, Skill and Virtue," 82–89.
105. *Rid.* 33, p. 197, lines 7b–13.
106. This notion falls in line with the second principle for the valid interpretation of riddles, as set out by Niles, *Old English Enigmatic Poems*, 30. The principle holds that "a valid solution is *comprehensive*"; in other words, "no potentially important aspect or detail of the text is left out."

Chapter 7

1. The exact Latin source for Cynewulf's *Elene* is not known, but it seems to be related to the version published by Mombritius, ed., *Sanctuarium seu Vitae Sanctorum*, 1:376–79. Although he follows the narrative of the Latin source closely, Cynewulf does elaborate and embellish particular details, especially emphasizing the concealment of the Cross. For a more detailed discussion of Cynewulf's source, see Gradon's edition of *Cynewulf's Elene*, 15–20; Whatley, "Figure of Constantine the Great." For comparison of the Latin with Cynewulf's poem, see Bodden, ed. and trans., *Old English Finding of the True Cross*, 37–45.
2. *El*, p. 88, line 792a; p. 82, line 602b. Elsewhere the Cross is described as "hyded" (line 218b), "behyded" (line 987a; line 1081a), and "gehyded" (line 1091b); it is very frequently described with variations on the word *dyrnan*, many of which will be discussed below.
3. *El*, p. 72, line 218; p. 83, line 625a; p. 89, 842a.
4. The nails that pinned Christ to the Cross likewise are "in foldan gen / deope bedolfen dierne sindon, / heolstre behyded" (still in the earth, deeply buried and concealed, hidden in darkness); *El*, p. 96, lines 1079b–1081a.
5. *El*, p. 89, line 844a; p. 93, line 973a.
6. See Chapter 2.

7. *El*, p. 73, lines 280, 283b–84a.

8. *El*, p. 80, line 522b; the word "leoðorune" could also refer to the counsel his father gives him, thus a kind of dialogue with advice. However, given that Cynewulf uses the word *geryne* in reference to precisely that secret that Judas received from his father (lines 566a and 589a), "leoðorune" seems at least to connote the secrecy of their dialogue.

9. *El*, p. 77, lines 426b–30a.

10. See Chapter 1.

11. *El*, pp. 80–81, lines 538–41a.

12. *El*, p. 81, lines 565–66.

13. *El*, p. 82, line 589.

14. *El*, p. 73, line 254a.

15. Klein, *Ruling Women*, 67–68.

16. *El*, pp. 71–72, lines 215–18.

17. *El*, p. 74, lines 317–19.

18. *El*, pp. 74–75, lines 322b–25.

19. *El*, p. 77, lines 406b–410.

20. *El*, p. 77, lines 413b and 414a.

21. *El*, p. 77, lines 419b–420a.

22. *El*, p. 81, line 568b.

23. *El*, p. 82, line 583b–84a.

24. *El*, p. 82, lines 588b–89a.

25. *El*, p. 83, lines 640b–41.

26. *El*, p. 84, lines 673b–74a.

27. *El*, p. 85, lines 690b and 683b.

28. *El*, p. 85, line 696a.

29. *El*, p. 86, lines 721b–22.

30. *El*, p. 85, lines 703a and 706a.

31. *El*, p. 74, line 289a.

32. Heckman, "Things in Doubt," 469, suggests that Elene "reaches the limits of reason."

33. Ricoeur, *Freud and Philosophy*, 525.

34. Ibid., 28.

35. E.g., the notion of prejudice (as the inevitable judgments or foremeanings arrived at prior to understanding) is integral to the philosophical hermeneutics outlined by Gadamer, *Truth and Method*, 306. On the medieval precedent, see Simpson, "Faith and Hermeneutics," who briefly points to Ricoeur as a parallel to his larger argument that "all interpretation demands faith of a kind," which he traces through medieval sources in order to question the ethics of starting an act of interpretation from a position of faith.

36. *El*, p. 88, lines 790–92a.

37. On the well-recognized importance of conversion to the narrative, see Stepsis and Rand, "Contrast and Conversion;" Calder, "Strife, Revelation, and Conversion."

38. *El*, p. 88, lines 795b–801.

39. E.g., Cynewulf, *Old English Poems of Cynewulf*, ed. and trans. Bjork, 199.

40. For Heckman, "Things in Doubt," 462–63, the Cross provides a rational argument that converts doubt into belief, following Anselm and Boethius's notion that an argument "is a reason that produces belief regarding a thing in doubt."

41. Ælfric places a similar emphasis on the importance of faith in the discovery of the Cross, although he assigns it to Elene "mid fullum geleafan"; see *CH* II, hom. 18 (*Inventio sanctae crucis*), p. 175, lines 39–40.

42. *El*, p. 88, line 807.

43. *El*, p. 88, lines 814b–15.

44. *El*, p. 92, lines 959–60.

45. *El*, p. 94, lines 1035b–36a.
46. *El*, p. 96, lines 1080–81a, 1090–91.
47. *El*, pp. 95–96, lines 1072b, 1087a, and 1100a.
48. E.g., "georne secan" at *El*, p. 71, line 216b; p. 96, lines 1096b–98.
49. *El*, p. 98, lines 1147–49a.
50. *El*, p. 98, lines 1156b, 1159b, and 1162b.
51. *El*, p. 98, lines 1167–68a and 1170a.
52. *Georne* and *secan* are both exceedingly common words, but the frequency with which they are collocated in *Elene* is higher than normal. The metrical translation of Ps. 50–150 in the *Paris Psalter* also sees the two words collocated with some frequency (nine times), but overall it is a text roughly four times the length of *Elene*.
53. Heckman, "Things in Doubt," 479–80; Klein, *Ruling Women*, 85; R. W. V. Elliott, "Coming Back to Cynewulf"; Martin Irvine, "Anglo-Saxon Literary Theory."
54. Martin Irvine, "Anglo-Saxon Literary Theory," 47–48.
55. *El*, p. 100, lines 1239b–42a.
56. *El*, p. 100, lines 1242b–50a.
57. The word *lar* in this passage (line 1245a) parallels *wisdom* in the passage above (line 1242a). On the rhetoric of binding in this passage, see Cavell, *Weaving Words and Binding Bodies*, 234–35.
58. For a facsimile of *Elene* and Cynewulf's signatures, see Sisam, *Vercelli Book*, fol. 133r.
59. *El*, p. 101, lines 1257b and 1259b.
60. Niles, *Old English Enigmatic Poems*, 297–302.
61. Ibid., 299–300.
62. Thomas D. Hill, "Failing Torch"; R. W. V. Elliott, "Coming Back to Cynewulf," 242.
63. Symons, *Runes and Roman Letters*, 85.
64. For a discussion of the meditative reading invited by Cynewulf's epilogue, see Ó Carragáin, "Cynewulf's Epilogue," 187–201.
65. See generally Niles, *Old English Enigmatic Poems*, on the ludic nature of the genre. The idea is more broadly argued by Huizinga, *Homo Ludens*, 104–35. See also Borysławski, *Old English Riddles*, who makes a similar argument with respect to the Old English *Riddles*.
66. Symphosius, *Aenigm.*, pref., p. 621, line 7.
67. Aldhelm, *Aenigm.*, prologue, p. 371, lines 1–4. Also available in Aldhelm, *Opera Omnia*, ed. Ehwald, MGH Auct. ant. 15, p. 75. Generally, translations here of Aldhelm's *Aenigmata* follow *Poetic Works*, trans. Lapidge and Rosier, 70–94, but the prose prologue (this section of Aldhelm's *Epistola ad Acircium*) is not available in translation.
68. See the translators' introduction to the *Aenigmata* in *Poetic Works*, trans. Lapidge and Rosier, 62.
69. Andy Orchard, *Poetic Art of Aldhelm*, 158.
70. For example, CUL, Gg. 5. 35 (which dates to the mid-eleventh century) contains the *Epistola* and *Disticha Catonis* (immediately following Aldhelm's *Aenigmata*) on fols. 407r–412v and preserves Prosper of Aquitaine's *Epigrammata* earlier in the manuscript, beginning on fol. 126v. Rigg and Wieland, "Canterbury Classbook," proposed that the manuscript was used for schoolroom instruction; however, Lapidge, "Study of Latin Texts," argues that it was more likely used as a library book for private monastic study. For a response to Lapidge, see Wieland, "Glossed Manuscript." For more on the contents and use of CUL, Gg. 5. 35, see Chapter 8.
71. Lockett, *Anglo-Saxon Psychologies*, 261–62n102.
72. Aldhelm's *Aenigmata* was a part of his lengthy *Epistola ad Acircium*, sandwiched between two treatises on Latin hexameter and metrical feet known as *De metris* and *De pedum regulis*, respectively. See the translators' introduction in Aldhelm, *Poetic Works*, trans. Lapidge and Rosier, 61.
73. See, for example, the translators' introduction in Aldhelm, *Poetic Works*, trans. Lapidge and Rosier, 63; Stork, *Through a Gloss Darkly*, 59–65.
74. For a complete list and discussion, see Stork, *Through a Gloss Darkly*, 60–61.

75. Augustine, *De doctrina Christiana*, ed. and trans. Green, lib. II, cap. 58, p. 82 and lib. II, cap. 110, p. 108. On the importance of knowing such information, see the classic study by Leclercq, *Love of Learning*, 77–78.

76. Cassiodorus, *Expositio psalmorum*, ed. Adriaen, vol. 2, Ps. 96:6, p. 873, lines 132–36.

77. Donatus, *Ars Maior*, ed. Holtz, lib. III, cap. 6, p. 672, line 10.

78. Ibid.

79. Aldhelm, *Opera Omnia*, ed. Ehwald, p. 77, line 12; Gneuss-Lapidge, no. 478. On the gloss, see Stork, *Through a Gloss Darkly*, 96. For an image of the gloss, see fig. 10 in Chapter 8.

80. Bede, *De arte metrica et de schematibus et tropis*, ed. Kendall, p. 162, lines 191–92; Bede, *Libri II De Arte Metrica et De Schematibus et Tropis*, ed. and trans. Kendall, 194.

81. Aldhelm, *Aenigm.*, prologue, p. 372. Also available in Aldhelm, *Opera Omnia*, ed. Ehwald, 76–77.

82. Pseudo-Bede, *Collectanea Pseudo-Bedae*, ed. and trans. Bayless and Lapidge, no. 6, pp. 122–23.

83. Tatwine, *Aenigm.* 3, p. 170.

84. Aldhelm's *Aenigmata* is frequently referred to by scholars as a collection of "mysteries." See the translators' introduction to Aldhelm, *Poetic Works*, trans. Lapidge and Rosier, 11.

85. The *Epigrammata* and Aldhelm's *Aenigmata* both survive in CUL, Gg. 5. 35 (Gneuss-Lapidge, no. 12). On the *Epigrammata* in Anglo-Saxon England, see Chapter 5; see also Lapidge, "Study of Latin Texts," 466.

86. Prosper of Aquitaine, *Liber epigrammatum*, ed. Horsting, Epi. 69, p. 129; also available in PL 51.519–20, *Epi.* 70.

87. Translation based on O'Brien O'Keeffe, *Stealing Obedience*, 135; "dona morata" in line 4 could also mean "gifts to which attention has been devoted" if one takes "morata" as the past participle of *moror*.

88. Prosper of Aquitaine, *Liber sententiarum*, ed. Gastaldo, Sent. 67, p. 273. This *Sententia* is derived from Augustine, *Enarrationes in Psalmos*, ed. Dekkers and Fraipont, vol. 3, p. 2026, lines 6–9 (Ps. 140:1).

89. O'Brien O'Keeffe, *Stealing Obedience*, 135.

90. See Chapter 6, p. 166. Origen, *Homilien zum Hexateuch*, ed. Baehrens, hom. 18, §4.6, p. 175.

91. Bede, *Explanatio Apocalypsis*, ed. Gryson, lib. II, cap. 15, p. 363, lines 32–33 (Apoc. 10:4).

92. Augustine, *De diuersis quaestionibus ad Simplicianum*, ed. Mutzenbecher, lib. II, praef., p. 57, lines 8–11.

93. Prosper of Aquitaine, *Liber epigrammatum*, ed. Horsting, Epi. 69, p. 129; also available in PL 51.519–20, *Epi.* 70.

94. Augustine, *Epistulae*, ed. Goldbacher, vol. 34.2, ep. 120, §1, p. 707, line 4. There is no evidence, however, that *Epistola* 120 was known in Anglo-Saxon England.

95. Ibid., §1, p. 708, lines 15–17.

96. Ibid., §2, p. 711, lines 19–23.

97. de Lubac, *Medieval Exegesis*, 2:115–17.

98. *Proslogion* by Anselm of Canterbury, *Anselmi Opera Omnia*, ed. Schmitt, vol. 1, cap. 1, p. 100, line 18.

99. Pseudo-Bede, *Collectanea Pseudo-Bedae*, ed. and trans. Bayless and Lapidge, no. 290, pp. 160–61. The sentence is taken verbatim from Gregory the Great, *Homiliae in Hiezechihelem prophetam*, ed. Adriaen, lib. II, hom. 8, p. 344, lines 300–302.

100. See de Lubac, *Medieval Exegesis*, 2:114.

101. Pseudo-Bede, *Collectanea Pseudo-Bedae*, ed. and trans. Bayless and Lapidge, no. 69, pp. 130–31.

102. The phrase is only slightly different in Augustine, *Epistulae*, ed. Goldbacher, vol. 44, ep. 137, §4, p. 117, lines 7–8 ("sed intellectui fides aditum aperit, infidelitas claudit" [faith opens the pathway of understanding; faithlessness closes it]). It is also reproduced in Prosper of Aquitaine's

Liber sententiarum, a more likely source for the *Collectanea*: Prosper of Aquitaine, *Liber sententiarum*, ed. Gastaldo, cap. 128, p. 286, line 1 ("Intellectui fides uiam aperit, infidelitas claudit").

103. Alcuin of York, *Disputatio*, ed. Suchier, 137–43. The portion of the text containing the riddles (nos. 86–104) is also reprinted, translated, and discussed in relation to early medieval riddles in Bayless, "Alcuin's *Disputatio Pippini*," 157–78. On these three subgenres as found in the *Disputatio*, see ibid., 160. The examples here are taken from Alcuin of York, *Disputatio*, ed. Suchier, nos. 2, 102, and 99, pp. 138 and 142.

104. Alcuin of York, *Disputatio*, ed. Suchier, nos. 85–89, p. 141.

105. Lapidge, "Anglo-Latin Background," 12. This view was first (briefly) advanced in the translators' introduction in Aldhelm, *Poetic Works*, trans. Lapidge and Rosier, 11. It has since been adopted by numerous other scholars; for example, Andy Orchard, *Poetic Art of Aldhelm*, 158.

106. Bayless, "Alcuin's *Disputatio Pippini*," 160.

107. Dailey, "Riddles, Wonder and Responsiveness," 453.

108. Bynum, "Wonder," 40.

109. Justice, "Eucharistic Miracle and Eucharistic Doubt."

110. That Alcuin read Aldhelm's *Aenigmata* is evidenced by the fact that he borrows line 3 of Aldhelm's *Aenigm.* 22 (p. 405), "Spurca colore tamen sed non sum spreta canendo" (For all that I am dusky in color, yet I am not to be scorned for my singing), almost verbatim in his poem "De luscinia." Alcuin of York, *Carmina*, ed. Dümmler, MGH Poetae 1, Carm. 61, p. 274, line 7. Further evidence is found in Alcuin's *Versus de Patribus Regibus et Sanctis Euboricensis Ecclesiae*, where at line 111 he scans the word *statim* as a spondee (where it would traditionally be scanned as a trochee); in doing so, Alcuin seems to be following Aldhelm's usage in line 4 of his *Aenigm.* 62 (p. 461), according to Andy Orchard, *Poetic Art of Aldhelm*, 79n26. See also Godman's introduction to Alcuin of York, *Bishops, Kings, and Saints of York*, cix. Godman states that Alcuin knew "every one of [Aldhelm's] metrical works" (lxviii).

111. Aldhelm, *Aenigm.*, pref., p. 381, lines 35–36.

112. Law, *Wisdom, Authority and Grammar*, 102, suggests that Aldhelm's explanatory phrase means "not the allegorical or scientific explanation of long-pondered mysteries, demystification of the mysteries, but the revelation of the presence of mysteries even in familiar things." I think Law is correct that Aldhelm's goal is one of mystification rather than demystification; after all, he has not written a treatise on the natural world (such as Bede's *De natura rerum*) but a collection of *aenigmata* whose obscurity is the defining feature.

Chapter 8

1. Aldhelm, *Aenigm.*, pref., p. 381, lines 35–36.

2. The word *soluere*, as we have seen in Chapter 6, is semantically rich. I translate it above as "resolve" in order to convey the range of this richness, from the more passive loosing of literal or figurative fetters, to the more active scattering apart, and finally to the explaining or solving of riddles; see Lewis and Short, *Latin Dictionary*, s.v. solvo, senses I.A.1, I.A.2, I.B.2, and II.2.h. In their translation, Lapidge and Rosier take the word to mean "forgive," but while that is certainly a perspicuous rendering, it does restrict the greater variety of meaning suggested by Aldhelm's choice of the word. Aldhelm, *Poetic Works*, trans. Lapidge and Rosier, 71.

3. Aldhelm, *Aenigm.*, pref., p. 378, line 15 and p. 380, line 27.

4. On the literary effect of this rejection, see Thornbury, "Aldhelm's Rejection."

5. Aldhelm, *Aenigm.*, pref., p. 377, lines 1–9.

6. For example, see CUL, Gg. 5. 35, fol. 398v (Gneuss-Lapidge, no. 12); Oxford, Bodleian Library, Rawlinson C. 697, fol. 1r (Gneuss-Lapidge, no. 661); BL, Royal 12. C. xxiii, fol. 83r, fig. 10 (Gneuss-Lapidge, no. 478; Ker, no. 263).

7. BL, Royal 12. C. xxiii has a zoomorphic initial "A."

8. "Versibus" is a significant word here, as it is repeated in the acrostic itself.

9. The phrase could also be read as "the mysteries of things spoken in secret," ambiguously conflating the secret mysteries of things (God's creations) with the secrecy of Aldhelm's own verses.

10. On the semantic correspondence between *arbiter* and the word *interpres* (interpreter), see George H. Brown, "Meanings of *Interpres*," 44–45.

11. On the use of this technique in Anglo-Saxon England, see Wehlau, "Power of Knowledge," 292.

12. See Chapter 6.

13. Parkes, "*Rædan, areccan, smeagan.*"

14. Other riddles in the manuscript include nineteen *aenigmata* (or "*Joca-seria*") attributed to Bede in the manuscript's twelfth-century table of contents; see Tupper, "Riddles of the Bede Tradition," 565–71. There is also a series of riddles on school subjects such as music, ethics, and grammar titled *Bibliotheca magnifica*; see Giles, ed., *Anecdota Bedæ*, 50–53.

15. Part III of the manuscript and Scribes A and B, according to the codicological and paleographical analysis by Rigg and Wieland, "Canterbury Classbook," 113–14.

16. For example, the text of Aldhelm's *Aenigmata* and some (although not all, as many are unique) of its glosses in CUL, Gg. 5. 35 share a common exemplar with the version in BL, Royal 12 C. xxiii. On the glossing tradition of Aldhelm's *Aenigmata*, see Stork, *Through a Gloss Darkly*, esp. 19–24.

17. The glosses in Bremen, Staats- und Universitätsbibliothek, MS 651 and BL, Royal 15 A. XVI (Gneuss-Lapidge, no. 489) also showed a heightened interest in Aldhelm's *Aenigma* 100.

18. Aldhelm, *Aenigm.* 100 (*Creatura* [Creation]), p. 529, lines 1–4.

19. CUL, Gg. 5. 35, fol. 406r.

20. Ibid.

21. Ibid.

22. Aldhelm, *Aenigm.* 100 (*Creatura* [Creation]), p. 533, lines 27–30.

23. See, for example, Bede's description in *HE*, lib. V, cap. 12, pp. 488–90.

24. Isidore, *Etymologiae*, vol. 1, lib. I, cap. 25, §2, lines 12–16.

25. Bede, *De temporum ratione*, ed. Jones, cap. 1, p. 272, lines 85–89; Bede, *Reckoning of Time*, trans. Wallis, 11.

26. On the powerful nature of alphabets and encrypted writing of this sort, see Christie, "By Means of a Secret Alphabet."

27. Virgilius Maro Grammaticus, *Opera Omnia*, ed. Löfstedt, *Epitoma* X, p. 213, lines 5–10; translation based, with modifications, on Law, *Wisdom, Authority and Grammar*, 83.

28. Doležalová, "On Mistake and Meaning," argues that the purpose of *scinderatio fonorum* is principally didactic.

29. On Alcuin's *Disputatio Pippini*, see Chapter 7, pp. 203–4.

30. Aldhelm, *Aenigm.* 81 (*Lucifer* [Morning star]), p. 499, line 10 (emphasis added). Evidence that Aldhelm read Virgilius is found at the end of Aldhelm's *Epistola ad Heahfrith*, in *Opera Omnia*, ed. Ehwald, 494. See Michael Herren's comments in the notes to Aldhelm, *Prose Works*, trans. Lapidge and Herren, 202n37; and in Herren, "Some New Light," 43–46.

31. Aldhelm, *Aenigm.* 100 (*Creatura* [Creation]), p. 539, line 81 (emphasis added).

32. Saltzman, "*Vt hkskdkxt*"; see the article's appendix for a detailed list of the cryptograms in CUL, Gg. 5. 35.

33. Aldhelm, *Aenigm.* 100 (*Creatura* [Creation]), p. 539, lines 70–72. Glorie gives "umquam" for "numquam" in line 72; but CUL, Gg. 5. 35 has "numquam."

34. *Rid.* 47, p. 205, lines 1–6.

35. See Salvador-Bello, *Isidorean Perceptions of Order*, 356; Scattergood, "Eating the Book"; Niles, *Old English Enigmatic Poems*, 142, who interprets the solution to *Riddle* 47 as "maða ond sealm-boc" (maggot and psalter). On *ruminatio* as formative of early Anglo-Saxon monastic identity, see DeGregorio, "*Interpretatio Monastica*," and generally, Carruthers, *Book of Memory*, 164–67.

36. Foys, "Undoing of Exeter Book Riddle 47," 108.

37. Ibid., 122.

38. Zweck, "Silence in the Exeter Book Riddles," 326–31.

39. Aldhelm, *Aenigm.* 100 (*Creatura* [Creation]), p. 539, lines 80–84.

40. Anselm of Canterbury uses a similar logic in his *Monologion* to explain why riddles can be used to signify things that are not fully understood; see *Anselmi Opera Omnia*, ed. Schmitt, vol. 1, cap. 65, p. 76, lines 12–18.

41. Law, *Wisdom, Authority and Grammar*, 103–4.

42. Ibid., 103.

43. Thornbury, *Becoming a Poet*, 107.

44. Ibid.

45. We see this admiration in the opening passages of Aldhelm's *Prosa de uirginitate*, where he praises the intellectual skills of the nuns at Barking. Comparing them to talented athletes, Aldhelm notes that their skills are "non exterioris hominis motibus aguntur, sed interioris gestibus geruntur" (not performed with the motions of the outer man, but with the actions of the inner man). Later, he compares the nuns to bees (a typical metaphor) skilled in biblical exegesis as well as the "grammaticorum regulas et ortograforum disciplinas" (the rules of the grammarians and the teachings on orthography) and various aspects of poetic meter. See Aldhelm, *Aldhelmi Malmesbiriensis Prosa de uirginitate*, ed. Gwara, cap. 3, p. 43, lines 4–5; cap. 4, p. 61, lines 44–45.

46. Foys, "Undoing of Exeter Book Riddle 47," 112.

47. CUL, Gg. 5. 35, fol. 407v.

48. Aldhelm, *Aenigm.* 100 (*Creatura* [Creation]), p. 539, line 80.

49. Lerer, *Literacy and Power*, 107, argues that this line does not refer to the teacher's inability to explain the words, but rather that "engagement with these words is to be done in writing instead of speech" corresponding to Aldhelm's own commitment to the mechanics of literacy. However, the very words to be explained are themselves characterized not as writing but as speech: "famina uerbi" (utterances of words) in line 80. Blaise, *Dictionnaire*, s.v. *famen*, defines the word as "parole, langage, expression, discours, éloquence."

50. The relationship between the verb *infitiari* and unfaithfulness is in sense only; etymologically, *infitiari* is derived from *in-* + **fātos* (said) (Greek φατός) + *-ia*. See Glare, *Oxford Latin Dictionary*, vol. 1, s.v. *infitias*.

51. Symphosius, *Aenigm.*, pref., p. 621, line 8.

52. Aldhelm, *Aenigm.* 100 (*Creatura* [Creation]), p. 539, line 84.

53. Augustine had a similar experience of becoming puffed up with knowledge ("inflabar scientia"); see Augustine, *Confessions*, ed. O'Donnell, lib. VII, cap. 20, p. 86.

54. Miller, "Hitchcock's Hidden Pictures," for example, considers a similar kind of academic pride, albeit in a very different context.

55. The quotation is from a speech that Einstein delivered in 1918 in honor of Max Planck's sixtieth birthday; "Principles of Research," 1. He goes on to praise Planck as a scientist of the third order: "The state of mind which enables a man to do work of this kind is akin to that of the religious worshiper or the lover; the daily effort comes from no deliberate intention or program, but straight from the heart" (5). Extracts of this speech are famously quoted in Pirsig, *Zen and the Art of Motorcycle Maintenance*, 109–10.

56. Aldhelm, *Prosa de uirginitate*, ed. Gwara, cap. 10, p. 121, line 37.

57. See McDaniel, "Pride Goes Before a Fall," who argues that Aldhelm follows Gregory the Great and John Cassian in imagining Pride as the "conqueror and destroyer of the citadel of the virtuous soul" (103).

58. *RSB*, cap. 7; Bernard of Clairvaux, *De gradibus humilitatis et superbiae*, ed. Leclercq and Rochais, 13–59.

59. Boniface, *Aenigm.*, *De uitiis* 9 (*De ignorantia* [Ignorance]), p. 339.

60. Prov. 11:2; see Wallis, *Bede and Wisdom*, esp. 22–31, for a discussion of Bede's views on humility as a prerequisite for wisdom: "Humbly acknowledging God as the source of wisdom, while diligently pursuing wisdom, purges learning of vanity and self-indulgence, and the quest for knowledge of any stain of pride" (22). This humble acknowledgment is precisely, I think, what Aldhelm is trying to do in his *Aenigmata* all while tempting the reader toward pride in that quest for knowledge—although

it should be noted that Wallis views Aldhelm's *Aenigmata* as trying to accomplish something different than Bede's "refusal to play the philosophers' wisdom-game by their rules" (31).

61. Aldhelm, *Aenigm.* 100 (*Creatura* [Creation]), p. 539, line 70.

62. Aldhelm, *Aenigm.* pref., p. 377, lines 4–5.

63. Ibid., pref., p. 377, lines 6–9.

64. Victoria Thompson, *Dying and Death*, 137, suggests that the notion that worms represent humility was "ignored by Anglo-Saxon writers" (despite the fact that the psalm was translated into English). However, it seems clear that Aldhelm is playing with the idea here.

65. *RSB*, cap. 7. See also *RM*, cap. 10.

66. BT, s.v. *wyrm*, sense 1. For an example of a serpent as a symbol for pride, see Boniface, *Aenigm., De uitiis* 4 (*De superbia* [On Pride]), pp. 325–27. The psalm is translated in the prose section of the *Paris Psalter*; see Alfred the Great, *King Alfred's Old English Prose Translation*, ed. O'Neill, 122. For the Old English translation of the *Regula Sancti Benedicti*, see Schröer, ed., *Die angelsächsischen Prosabearbeitungen*, cap. 7, p. 29, lines 10–14.

67. Aldhelm, *Aenigm.* 100 (*Creatura* [Creation]), p. 531, lines 21–22.

68. The glossator seems to have derived this reference to angels and demons from Eusebius, *Aenigm.* 2 (*De angelo* [On an Angel]), p. 212; and *Aenigm.* 3 (*De demone* [On a Demon]), p. 213. However, note the glossator's ingenious use of capitalization in the second cryptogram, where the capitalized letters (NPOT) are deciphered as *mons* (mountain), so that the solution to Aldhelm's paradoxical lines is captured even within a single cryptogram: a demon and a mountain.

69. Tatwine, *Aenigm.* 24 (*De humilitate* [On Humility]), p. 191, line 5.

70. Boniface, *Aenigm., De uirtutibus* 9 (*De humilitate cristiana* [On Christian humility]), p. 301, line 6.

71. Eusebius, *Aenigm.* 27 (*De humilitate et superbia* [On Humility and Pride]), p. 237. See also Eusebius, *Aenigm.* 1 (*De Deo* [On God]), p. 211, which describes God as both beneath (*infra*) and above (*sublimior*) all things.

72. de Vaan, *Etymological Dictionary of Latin*, s.v. *humus*, p. 292. See also Isidore, *Etymologiae*, vol. 1, lib. X, §115, line 1.

73. A specimen of great semantic diversity, the Old English word *wyrm* can describe creatures large and small, from the deadly dragon in *Beowulf* (e.g., *Beo*, line 2287) to intestinal parasites (*smeawyrmas*) in Cockayne, ed., *Leechdoms, Wortcunning, and Starcraft*, vol. 2, lib. III, cap. 39, p. 332. But as Victoria Thompson has shown, images of worms often arise in conjunction with scenes of death, where they symbolize "the many different kinds of transformation connected with literal and spiritual death, burial and rebirth." See *Dying and Death*, chap. 5, 132–69, esp. 169.

74. *Soul and Body I*, ASPR 2, p. 55, lines 25a, 40a.

75. Ibid., p. 56, lines 72–74a. See also *Soul and Body II*, ASPR 3, p. 176, lines 67–69.

76. *Rid.* 47, p. 205, line 4a. In *Soul and Body I*, ASPR 2, p. 56, line 73, it is equally possible that "swearte" is an adverb modifying "slitan" instead of an adjective modifying "wihta," but either reading allows for darkness as a key feature of the worm and its behavior.

77. Quoted from *Soul and Body I*, ASPR 2, pp. 57–58, lines 112–15; translation based on Jones, ed. and trans., *Old English Shorter Poems*, 199. See also *Soul and Body II*, ASPR 3, p. 177, lines 106–10.

78. *Soul and Body I*, ASPR 2, p. 58, lines 125b–26.

79. Ibid., p. 58, lines 120a. The half-line is also used in *Vainglory*, ASPR 3, p. 147, line 16a; *Rid.* 60, p. 225, line 10a; *Beo*, lines 366a and 874a.

80. *Maxims I*, ASPR 3, p. 156–57, lines 1–4a.

81. Anderson, "Two Spliced Riddles," has proposed an integrated reading of *Riddles* 47 and 48, which (although traditionally read as two separate riddles) are presented in the manuscript with none of the markers typically used to signify the division of texts. Salvador-Bello, *Isidorean Perceptions of Order*, 359–61. See also Foys, "Undoing of Exeter Book Riddle 47," who argues that "both halves of Riddle 47/48 work together to address concerns about physical and intellectual ruin, and they modify mechanisms of human communication, mutating the appropriate sensory organs for the production and reception of language to do so. Mouths make works but should not consume them; this is the

domain of the eyes and the ears. But this is precisely and uncharacteristically what happens in the first half of this conjoined text. Real speech cannot transpire in silence, or without a tongue, and yet this is precisely and miraculously what occurs in its second half" (129).

82. *Rid.* 48, pp. 205–6.
83. A similar point is made by Anderson, "Two Spliced Riddles," 62.
84. On this literary phenomenon, see Hayes, *Divine Ventriloquism*, 25–52.
85. Eusebius, *Aenigm.* 32, p. 242.
86. *Rid.* 60, p. 225, lines 7b–10a.
87. For example, see Ælfric of Eynsham, *Homilies of Ælfric*, ed. Pope, vol. 1, hom. 11 (*Sermo ad populum in octavis Pentecosten dicendus*), pp. 436–37, lines 391–99: "Ne mæg þonne nan man nahwar beon behydd, ac ealle beoð þær þe æfre cuce wæron, and þær beoð æteowde ure eallra geðohtas, and ealle ure dæda eallum þam werodum" (Nor then will any man be hidden anywhere, but all who were ever alive will be there, and there all our thoughts and all our deeds will be revealed to all men).
88. Anglo-Saxon illustrations of the Day of Judgment are rare, but see, for example, the depiction in the New Minster *Liber Vitae*, BL, Stowe 944, fol. 6r (Ker, no. 274; Gneuss-Lapidge, no. 500); available in facsimile in Keynes, ed., *Liber Vitae*. Also available online at British Library Digitised Manuscripts, "Stowe MS 944." For a discussion of the Judgment illustration, see Karkov, "Judgment and Salvation," 151–64.
89. *Rid.* 3, p. 181, lines 1–16. Taking *Riddles* 1–3 as a single riddle, Lapidge, "Stoic Cosmology," has proposed the brilliant solution and source in the Stoic notion of *pneuma* or *spiritus* as described in Seneca's *Naturales quaestiones*.
90. See, for example, Bede, *De natura rerum*, ed. Jones, cap. 48, p. 232 (Bede has Pliny and Isidore as sources); however, as Lapidge, "Stoic Cosmology," 23, has argued, it is possible that the poet is not working from an assortment of Bede, Lucretius, Pliny, and Isidore, but rather from their Stoic source (Seneca) even though no manuscript of it survives from Anglo-Saxon England. Foley, "How Genres Leak in Traditional Verse," suggests that the solution to *Riddle* 1 is "both Storm (in the person of the pagan Germanic storm-giant) and Apocalypse (in the person of Christ on Judgment Day)" (92).
91. Apoc. 6:12, 8:5, 11:13, 11:19, 16:18. See Darby, *Bede and the End of Time*, 102–3, for commentary on how Bede figures trembling earth as a sign of the events to come.
92. *Judgment Day I*, ASPR 3, p. 213, lines 55–59 (emphasis added).
93. *Christ III*, ASPR 3, p. 27, lines 881b–82a (emphasis added).
94. *Judgment Day II*, ASPR 6, p. 60, lines 99–100 (emphasis added).
95. *Judgment Day I*, ASPR 3, p. 214, lines 98–100a. Translation based on Jones, ed. and trans., *Old English Shorter Poems*, 239. Similar imagery is used in *The Soul's Address to the Body*, available in Jones, ed. and trans., *Old English Shorter Poems*, pp. 204–29, at frag. E, pp. 218–19, lines 7–13.
96. *Christ III*, ASPR 3, p. 31, lines 1021b–1025a.
97. Ibid., p. 35, lines 1155–59.
98. Perhaps coincidentally, the parallel phrases both fall on the fourth on-verse of their respective poems (if we take *Riddle* 3 to be a discrete poem). For a discussion of the nocturnal thief motif, see Chapter 1.
99. Hawk, "'Id est, crux Christi,'" 66.
100. *Juliana*, ASPR 3, p. 133, lines 699b–701a.
101. Ibid., p. 133, lines 720b–721a.
102. *Fates of the Apostles*, ASPR 2, p. 54, lines 105b–106.
103. Ibid., p. 54, lines 111b and 112b.
104. *El*, p. 101, line 1275; *Rid.* 3, p. 181, line 1b. On the eschatological elements of this epilogue, see Hawk, "'Id est, crux Christi,'" 71–72.
105. *El*, p. 101, lines 181b–183.
106. Leipzig, Stadtbibliothek, Rep. I.74, fols. 24r–25r and 1r–13r, respectively. The *Versus sibyllae* is edited in Bulst, "Eine anglo-lateinische Übersetzung." This Sibylline poem was probably available to Aldhelm while at the Canterbury school of Theodore and Hadrian, and Aldhelm quotes it three

times in the *Epistola ad Acircium* (the six-part series of didactic texts that surround and include the *Aenigmata*, which Aldhelm addressed to Aldfrith, king of Northumbria [r. 685–705]). Lapidge and Rosier, in the introduction to Aldhelm, *Poetic Works*, trans. Lapidge and Rosier, 16, speculate that the poem may not have even been composed by Aldhelm himself. Orchard, *Poetic Art of Aldhelm*, 195–200, argues that the *Versus sibyllae* was not written by Aldhelm, even though it likely did originate in the aforementioned Canterbury school, where it made an impression on Aldhelm and his early poetics. Orchard also suggests (165–66) that Aldhelm's acrostic preface to the *Aenigmata* may have instead been influenced by two poems that circulate in manuscripts alongside work by Sedulius.

107. On the relationship between Aldhelm's *Aenigmata* and Julian of Toledo's *Prognosticum* in BL, Royal 12 C. xxiii (fols. 1v–79v), see Stork, "Spanish Bishop Remembers the Future."

108. Leofric's inventory describes what scholars take to be the Exeter Book as follows: ".i. mycel Englisc boc be gehwilcum þingum on leoðwisan geworht" (one large book in English about various things composed in verse). The inventory is edited in Conner, *Anglo-Saxon Exeter*, appendix V, 226–35, esp. 232.

109. Lerer, *Literacy and Power*, considers the Exeter Book an "illuminating homology with the Cambridge manuscript" (105).

110. The parts are as follows: I(*a*), fols. 1–209; I(*b*), fols. 210–76; II, fols. 280–369; III, fols. 370–431; and IV, fols. 432–46. The contents of each part are catalogued and described in Rigg and Wieland, "Canterbury Classbook."

111. Ibid., 113–15.

112. Both *Rubisca* and *Adelphus Adelpha* are edited in Herren, ed., *Hisperica Famina*.

113. Oswald's poem and hymn are not strictly curriculum texts like the *Disticha Catonis* or Prosper's *Epigrammata* and could be considered didactic only in the sense that they teach the reader how to compose in an unfamiliar verse form. Since they are both written in retrograde verse (meaning they are "metrically and syntactically viable when read both forwards and backwards, word by word" [Lockett, "Oswald's *uersus retrogradi*," 158]), they can function as a kind of riddle, since their meter masquerades as normal hexameters and pentameters, requiring the reader to figure out their true form from some cue, much like those cues and solutions that serve as paratexts to the Old English riddles. In the opening lines of *Centum concito*, Oswald offers such a cue for the reader to appreciate the difficulty and magnitude of his poetic accomplishment: "laudis munera dat dictanti scansio lucens: / Virgilianus hic dicetur maxime uates" (the resplendent scansion confers the bounty of praise on the poet: let this poet by all means be called 'Vergilian'"); edited and translated in Lapidge, "Hermeneutic Style," 106–7. Yet despite the pride that comes with such a poetic accomplishment, Oswald then goes on to make multiple claims of humility, ultimately inviting the corrector of his errors to accrue the true glory of the poet himself. For a discussion of Oswald's desire that "his audience appreciate his poetic virtuosity," see Lockett, "Oswald's *uersus retrogradi*," 161–62. Oswald's texts seem therefore to play multiple roles in this section of CUL, Gg. 5. 35: didactic, enigmatic, and also a reflection on the pull of pride and the need for humility that emerge in these genres.

114. *Rid*. 48, pp. 205–6, lines 6a–7a. See also, for example, the treatment of the Pater Noster in *Solomon and Saturn I*, where the letters P-A-T-E-R N-O-S-T-E-R are scrambled, signified by runes, personified, and given mystical power to fight against the devil. Christie, "By Means of a Secret Alphabet," has argued that they represent a sort of secret, cryptographic form of communication. The poem is edited in Anlezark, ed. and trans., *Old English Dialogues*, 60–71.

115. In isolation, Symphosius's *Aenigmata* may not fall into these categories as easily as Aldhelm's *Aenigmata* does. However, Aldhelm's collection is at the center of the genre, as it pulls together Symphosius's collection as archetype and the Tatwine-Eusebius collection as corollary, shaping their collective reception and intellectual value in the process.

116. In CUL, Gg. 5. 35, the poem ends at line 155: "Ac dominum benedicere secla per omnia Christum" (And give praise to Christ the Lord through all ages).

117. That is, with two exceptions: the hymn *Terrigene bene nunc laudent* (31) (which immediately follows Oswald of Ramsey's *Centum concito* [30]) and the prayer *Sancte sator* (23) (which immediately

follows Boniface's *Aenigmata* [22]). However, the placement of *Terrigene bene nunc laudent* can be explained by the fact it was likely authored by Oswald; Dronke et al., "Die unveröffentlichten Gedichte," 66–68, edit the hymn and argue that the two poems are both authored by Oswald (even though Oswald's name only appears in the body of *Centum concito*). The reasoning behind the placement of the prayer *Sancte sator* is less evident. However, the prayer "enjoyed wide circulation in monastic centres associated with the Anglo-Saxon mission in Germany" according to Bischoff and Lapidge, *Biblical Commentaries*, 188, which might explain its placement following Boniface's *Aenigmata*. The prayer also circulated in several manuscripts alongside Alcuin's *Enchiridion* (which Alcuin originally sent to Arno of Salzburg in 802); this might explain the prayer's placement preceding the Epitaph on Alcuin (24). See Gretsch and Gneuss, "Anglo-Saxon Glosses," 9–16.

118. *De die iudicii*, by contrast, has only one gloss (on fol. 418r, line 11; line 124 in the poem): "s. erit" (indicating futurity by supplying the future tense of the verb "to be") above "semperque in saecula" (and always forever).

119. It is important to note that an incomplete version of Bede's *De die iudicii* also survives next to, inter alia, the *Disticha Catonis* and Prosper's *Epigrammata* (much like the organization of CUL, Gg. 5. 35) in Cambridge, Trinity College O. 2. 31 (1135) (Gneuss-Lapidge, no. 190).

120. Bede, *De die iudicii*, ed. Caie, pp. 29–30, lines 18–23 and 33–34.

121. Ibid., pp. 30–31, lines 68–71.

122. This idea of total and absolute revelation before everyone seems to have been especially influential in Anglo-Saxon England. In the *Old English Soliloquies*, for example, we find an eschatology distinct from that advanced by Gregory and Augustine himself. Godden, "Text and Eschatology," 189–90, has argued that in book III the translator utilized Julian of Toledo's *Prognosticon* in stressing "the knowledge that all will have in the afterlife, both the good and the wicked, both of this life and the next, both of the past and the future."

123. *Christ III*, ASPR 3, p. 31, lines 1021b–1025a: "hateð arisan reordberende / of foldgrafum."

124. Morris, ed. and trans., *Blickling Homilies*, hom. 10, p. 109: "se flæscoma ascyred swa glæs." Also available in Kelly, ed. and trans., *Blickling Homilies*, hom. 10, p. 78, line 48. For a similar picture, see also Scragg, ed., *Vercelli Homilies*, hom. IV, pp. 90–104.

125. *Epitaphium Alchuuini* in Alcuin of York, *Carmina*, ed. Dümmler, MGH Poetae 1, pp. 350–51, lines 13–14. The inclusion of the epitaph is clearly in connection with the two Alcuinian items presented ten folios back (the *Dogmata* [20a] and the *Distica* [20b]).

126. *Epitaphium Alchuuini* in Alcuin of York, *Carmina*, ed. Dümmler, MGH Poetae 1, p. 351, lines 21–22.

127. See Chapter 7, n. 110.

Afterword

1. Literary riddles are, of course, not unique to Anglo-Saxon England, having existed long before (e.g., in the Greek tradition) and continued long after—my colleagues remind me of Jane Austen's fondness for riddles in *Emma*, for instance—nor are they only to be found in the European West. But by the start of the twelfth century in England, the popularity of riddles quickly dissipates, and few poets show an interest in creating new collections with the same kind of vigorously inventive energy exemplified and sparked by Aldhelm. During this later period riddles were occasionally copied out in manuscripts of rhetorical treatises and found their place in some university settings. It is not until the late fourteenth and fifteenth centuries that the literary invention of riddles comes somewhat back into fashion, chiefly with William Langland, who takes up these rhetorical riddles and employs them in a more literary and theological context. See Galloway, "Rhetoric of Riddling"; Gruenler, "How to Read Like a Fool"; and especially Gruenler, *"Piers Plowman."*

2. Saltzman, "Secrecy and the Hermeneutic Potential in *Beowulf*."

3. Justice, *Adam Usk's Secret*; Lochrie, *Covert Operations*; Maus, *Inwardness and Theater*; McKeon, *Secret History of Domesticity*.

4. Along these lines, see Nuttall, *Overheard by God*, who reads Herbert, Milton, and Dante, asking: what would God think as a reader of poetry?

5. George H. Brown, "Meanings of *Interpres*"; Howe, "Cultural Construction of Reading"; Parkes, "*Rædan, areccan, smeagan.*"

6. de Certeau, *Mystic Fable*, 99. See also Kermode, *Genesis of Secrecy*, esp. 23–47, for whom the obscurity of narrative invites interpretation in a process very closely tied up with the history of biblical exegesis.

7. Gregory the Great, *Moralia in Iob*, ed. Adriaen, vol. 143, lib. IV, praef., p. 158, lines 19–24.

8. For a helpful and concise survey of the status of reading in the twenty-first century, especially in light of the move from the late twentieth-century modes of symptomatic reading to the twenty-first-century modes of reading that "attend to the surfaces of texts rather than plumb their depths," see Best and Marcus, "Surface Reading," 1–2.

9. Gregory the Great, *Moralia in Iob*, ed. Adriaen, vol. 143, lib. IV, praef., p. 158, lines 17–18.

10. For example, Felski, *Limits of Critique*, has argued that critique, as a hermeneutic of suspicion, is "not always the best tool for the job" and advocates for a pragmatic use of critique that, among other things, allows art its own agency as a coactor in the work of interpretation (8).

11. Ricoeur, *Freud and Philosophy*, 28; *Prosologion* by Anselm of Canterbury, *Anselmi Opera Omnia*, ed. Schmitt, vol. 1, cap. 1, p. 100, line 18. Ricoeur could also be referring to Is. 7:9, which Anselm makes reference to here. For a discussion of Ricoeur's hermeneutics of faith, see Chapter 7.

12. Schleiermacher, *Hermeneutics and Criticism*, 232.

13. Gadamer, *Truth and Method*, 306.

14. Ibid., 307.

15. Zumthor, *Speaking of the Middle Ages*, 43. See also, for example, Jauss, *Alterität und Modernität* and *Ästhetische Erfahrung und literarische Hermeneutik* (along with the English versions provided in the bibliography). On the intellectual relationship between these three thinkers—Zumthor, Jauss, and Gadamer—in the context of the study of medieval texts, see Saltzman, "Hermeneutics and the Medieval Horizon."

16. Gadamer, *Truth and Method*, 288–89.

17. Ibid., 306.

18. Ibid., 386, 401. It is fascinating how in a medieval way, Gadamer's construction here complicates the active-passive dichotomy that continues to be articulated in the differences between, for example, the aggressiveness of symptomatic reading and the receptiveness of surface reading (at least in some formulations); see Best and Marcus, "Surface Reading."

19. Simpson, "Faith and Hermeneutics," 236; see also Felski, *Limits of Critique*, who argues for a more pragmatic and limited use of suspicion.

20. Love, "Close but Not Deep"; Love, "Close Reading and Thin Description"; Miller, "Hitchcock's Hidden Pictures," 113, 124.

21. Simmel, "Sociology of Secrecy"; Bok, *Secrets*.

22. Aldhelm, *Aldhelmi Malmesbiriensis Prosa de uirginitate*, ed. Gwara, cap. 2, p. 31, lines 1–4; translation based on Aldhelm, *Prose Works*, trans. Lapidge and Herren, 59.

Bibliography

Facsimiles

British Library Digitised Manuscripts. "Cotton MS Claudius B. iv."
———. "Stowe MS 944."
Keynes, Simon, ed. *The "Liber Vitae" of the New Minster and Hyde Abbey, Winchester: British Library Stowe 944, Together with Leaves from British Library Cotton Vespasian A. viii and Cotton Titus D. xxvii*. Early English Manuscripts in Facsimile 26. Copenhagen: Rosenklide & Bagger, 1996.
Sisam, Celia, ed. *The Vercelli Book: A Late Tenth-Century Manuscript Containing Prose and Verse (Vercelli Biblioteca Capitolare CXVII)*. Early English Manuscripts in Facsimile 19. Copenhagen: Rosenkilde & Bagger, 1976.

Reference Works

Blaise, Albert. *Dictionnaire Latin-Français des auteurs Chrétiens*. Turnhout: Brepols, 1954–1967. Revised and corrected by Paul Tombeur, 2005.
Bosworth, Joseph, and T. Northcote Toller. *An Anglo-Saxon Dictionary* (London, 1898), with *Supplement* by T. Northcote Toller (1921), with revised and enlarged addenda by Alistair Campbell. Oxford: Oxford University Press, 1972.
de Vaan, Michiel. *Etymological Dictionary of Latin and the Other Italic Languages*. Leiden Indo-European Etymological Dictionary Series 7. Leiden: Brill, 2008.
Dictionary of Old English: A to I. Edited by Angus Cameron, Ashley Crandell Amos, Antonette diPaolo Healey, and Haruko Momma. Toronto: Dictionary of Old English Project, 2018.
Dictionary of Old English Web Corpus. Compiled by Antonette diPaolo Healey with John Price Wilkin and Xin Xiang. Toronto: Dictionary of Old English Project, 2009.
Glare, P. G. W., ed. *Oxford Latin Dictionary*. 2nd ed. 2 vols. Oxford: Oxford University Press, 2012.
Gneuss, Helmut, and Michael Lapidge. *Anglo-Saxon Manuscripts: A Bibliographical Handlist of Manuscripts and Manuscript Fragments Written or Owned in England up to 1100*. Toronto: University of Toronto Press, 2014.
Holthausen, Ferdinand. *Altenglisches etymologisches Wörterbuch*. Heidelberg: C. Winter, 1963.
Ker, N. R. *Catalogue of Manuscripts Containing Anglo-Saxon*. New York: Oxford University Press, 1957, reprint 1990.
Latham, R. E. *Medieval Latin Word-List from British and Irish Sources*. London: Oxford University Press, 1983.
Latham, R. E., and D. R. Howlett. *Dictionary of Medieval Latin from British Sources*. London: Oxford University Press, 1975–2013.
Lewis, Charlton Thomas, and Charles Short. *A Latin Dictionary*. Oxford: Clarendon Press, 1966.
Liddell, H. G., and R. Scott. *Greek-English Lexicon*. Oxford: Clarendon Press, 1996.
Niermeyer, J. F., and C. van de Kieft. *Mediae Latinitatis lexicon minus*. 2 vols. Revised by J. W. J. Burgers. Leiden: Brill, 2002.
Oxford English Dictionary Online. Oxford: Oxford University Press.
Parker on the Web: Manuscripts in the Historic Parker Library at Corpus Christi College, Cambridge. Stanford, CA: Stanford University Libraries.

Sawyer, P. H. *Anglo-Saxon Charters: An Annotated List and Bibliography.* Royal Historical Society Guides and Handbooks 8. London: Royal Historical Society, 1968.
Taylor, H. M., and Joan Taylor. *Anglo-Saxon Architecture.* 3 vols. Cambridge: Cambridge University Press, 1965, 1978.
Walde, A., and J. B. Hofmann. *Lateinisches Etymologisches Wörterbuch.* 3rd ed. 3 vols. Heidelberg: Carl Winter, 1938–56.

Primary Sources

Abbo of Fleury. *Passio Sancti Edmundi.* In *Three Lives of English Saints,* edited by Michael Winterbottom. 65–88. Toronto: Pontifical Institute of Medieval Studies, 1972.
Adomnán. *Life of Columba.* Edited and translated by Alan Orr Anderson and Marjorie Ogilvie Anderson. OMT. Oxford: Clarendon Press, 1991.
Ædiluulf (Æthelwulf). *De abbatibus.* Edited and translated by Alistair Campbell. Oxford: Clarendon Press, 1967.
Ælfric of Eynsham. *Ælfric's Catholic Homilies: The First Series, Text.* Edited by Peter Clemoes. EETS s.s. 17. Oxford: Oxford University Press, 1997.
———. *Ælfric's Catholic Homilies: The Second Series, Text.* Edited by Malcolm Godden. EETS s.s. 5. Oxford: Oxford University Press, 1979.
———. *Ælfrics Grammatik und Glossar: Text und Varianten.* Edited by Julius Zupitza. 4th ed. Hildesheim: Weidmann, 2003.
———. *Ælfric's Letter to the Monks of Eynsham.* Edited and translated by Christopher A. Jones. CSASE. Cambridge: Cambridge University Press, 1999.
———. *Ælfric's "Life of Saint Basil the Great": Background and Context.* Edited and translated by Gabriella Corona. Anglo-Saxon Texts. Cambridge: D. S. Brewer, 2006.
———. *Ælfric's Lives of Saints.* Edited by Walter W. Skeat. EETS o.s. 76, 82, 94, 114. Oxford, 1881–1900. Reprint, 2 vols., Oxford: Oxford University Press, 1966.
———. *Angelsächsische Homilien und Heiligenleben.* Edited by Bruno Assmann. Kassel, 1889. Reprint, with supplementary introduction by Peter Clemoes, Darmstadt: Wissenschaftliche Buchgesellschaft, 1964.
———. *Homilies of Ælfric: A Supplementary Collection.* Edited by John C. Pope. 2 vols. EETS 259 and 260. London: Oxford University Press, 1967, 1968.
Alcuin of York. *Alcuins Gebetbuch für Karl den Großen: Seine Rekonstruktion und seine Stellung in der frühmittelalterlichen Geschichte der "libelli precum."* Edited by Stephan Waldhoff. Liturgiewissenschaftliche Quellen und Forschungen 89. Münster: Aschendorff, 2003.
———. *The Bishops, Kings, and Saints of York.* Edited and translated by Peter Godman. OMT. Oxford: Clarendon Press, 1982.
———. *Carmina.* Edited by Ernst Dümmler. MGH Poetae 1. Berlin, 1881.
———. *De psalmorum usu.* PL 101.465–508.
———. *De virtutibus et vitiis.* PL 101.613–38.
———. *Disputatio.* Edited by Walther Suchier. In Lloyd William Daly and Walther Suchier, eds., *Altercatio Hadriani Augusti et Epicteti Philosophi.* Urbana: University of Illinois Press, 1939.
———. *Epistolae.* Edited by Ernst Dümmler. MGH Epp. 4.18–481. Berlin, 1895.
———. *Liber Sacramentorum.* PL 101.445–66.
Aldhelm. *Aenigmata.* In *Variae collectiones aenigmatum merouingicae aetatis,* edited by Fr. Glorie. CCSL 133. Turnhout: Brepols, 1968.
———. *Aldhelmi Malmesbiriensis Prosa de uirginitate.* Edited by Scott Gwara. CCSL 124 and 124A. Turnhout: Brepols, 2001.
———. *Opera Omnia.* Edited by Rudolf Ehwald. MGH Auct. ant. 15. Berlin: Weidmann, 1919.
———. *The Poetic Works.* Translated by Michael Lapidge and James L. Rosier. Cambridge: D. S. Brewer, 1985. Reprint, with addenda, 2009.

———. *The Prose Works*. Translated by Michael Lapidge and Michael W. Herren. Cambridge: D. S. Brewer, 1979, reprint 2009.

Alfred the Great. *King Alfred's Old English Prose Translation of the First Fifty Psalms*. Edited by Patrick P. O'Neill. Cambridge, MA: Medieval Academy of America, 2001.

———. *King Alfred's West-Saxon Version of Gregory's Pastoral Care*. Edited by Henry Sweet. EETS o.s. 45, 50. London, 1871–72. Reprint, with corrections by N. R. Ker, London: Oxford University Press, 1958.

Amphilochio of Iconium. *Vita S. Basilii Caesareae Cappadociae Archiepiscopi*. PL 73.293–320.

Anlezark, Daniel, ed. and trans. *The Old English Dialogues of Solomon and Saturn*. Anglo-Saxon Texts. Cambridge: D. S. Brewer, 2009.

Anonymous of Lindisfarne. *Vita Sancti Cuthberti*. In *Two Lives of Saint Cuthbert*, edited and translated by Bertram Colgrave. Cambridge: Cambridge University Press, 1940.

Anonymous of Whitby. *The Earliest Life of Gregory the Great*. Edited and translated by Bertram Colgrave. Cambridge: Cambridge University Press, 1968.

Anselm of Canterbury. *Anselmi Opera Omnia*. Edited by F. S. Schmitt. 6 vols. Edinburgh: Thomas Nelson & Sons, 1946–61.

Asser. *Alfred the Great: Asser's "Life of King Alfred" and Other Contemporary Sources*. Translated by Simon Keynes and Michael Lapidge. Harmondsworth: Penguin, 1983.

———. *Asser's Life of King Alfred, Together with the Annals of Saint Neots*. Edited by William Henry Stevenson, with an introduction by Dorothy Whitelock. Oxford: Clarendon Press, 1959.

Athanasius (trans. Evagrius). *Vita Beati Antonii Abbatis*. PL 73.125–94.

Attenborough, F. L., ed. and trans. *The Laws of the Earliest English Kings*. Cambridge: Cambridge University Press, 1922.

Augustine. *Confessions*. Edited by J. J. O'Donnell. 3 vols. Oxford: Clarendon Press, 1992.

———. *De ciuitate Dei*. Edited by Bernardus Dombart and Alphonsus Kalb. CCSL 47 and 48. Turnhout: Brepols, 1955.

———. *De cura pro mortuis gerenda*. Edited by Joseph Zycha. CSEL 41, 621–59. Turnhout: Brepols, 1900.

———. *De diuersis quaestionibus ad Simplicianum*. Edited by Almut Mutzenbecher. CCSL 44. Turnhout: Brepols, 1970.

———. *De doctrina Christiana*. Edited and translated by R. P. H. Green. Oxford: Clarendon Press, 1995.

———. *Enarrationes in Psalmos*. Edited by Eligius Dekkers and I. Fraipont. 3 vols. CCSL 38–40. Turnhout: Brepols, 1956.

———. *Epistulae*. Edited by Al. Goldbacher. CSEL 34 (2 parts), 44, 57, and 58. Vienna, 1895–1898.

———. *Sermones*. PL 38.

B. *Vita Sancti Dunstani*. In *The Early Lives of St Dunstan*, edited and translated by Michael Winterbottom and Michael Lapidge. OMT. Oxford: Clarendon Press, 2012.

Ballard, Adolphus, and James Tait, eds. *British Borough Charters, 1216–1307*. Cambridge: Cambridge University Press, 1923.

Basil of Caesaria. *The Ascetic Works*. Translated by W. K. L. Clarke. Translations of Christian Literature. London: Society for Promoting Christian Knowledge, 1925.

———. *Asceticon parvum*. PL 103.483–554.

———. *Regulae fusius tractatae*. PG 31.890–1052.

———. *Sermo asceticus de renuntiatione saeculi*. PG 31.619–92.

Bede. *Bedas metrische Vita Sancti Cuthberti*. Edited by Werner Jaager. Palaestra 198. Leipzig: Mayer & Müller, 1935.

———. *De arte metrica et de schematibus et tropis*. Edited by Calvin B. Kendall. In *Bedae Venerabilis opera didascalica*, CCSL 123A. Turnhout: Brepols, 1975.

———. *De die iudicii*. In *The Old English Poem "Judgment Day II": A Critical Edition with Editions of "De die iudicii" and the Hatton 113 Homily "Be domes dæge,"* edited by Graham D. Caie. Anglo-Saxon Texts 2. Cambridge: D. S. Brewer, 2000.

———. *De natura rerum*. Edited by Ch. W. Jones. *Bedae Venerabilis opera didascalica*. CCSL 123A. Turnhout: Brepols, 1975.

———. *De temporum ratione*. Edited by Ch. W. Jones. *Bedae Venerabilis opera didascalica*. CCSL 123B. Turnhout: Brepols, 1977.

———. *Ecclesiastical History of the English People*. Edited and translated by Bertram Colgrave and R. A. B. Mynors. OMT. Oxford: Clarendon Press, 1969.

———. *Explanatio Apocalypsis*. Edited by R. Gryson. In *Bedae Venerabilis opera exegetica*. CCSL 121A. Turnhout: Brepols, 2001.

———. *Expositio Actuum apostolorum*. Edited by M. L. W. Laistner. In *Bedae Venerabilis opera exegetica*. CCSL 121. Turnhout: Brepols, 1983.

———. *Historia abbatum*. In *Venerabilis Bedae opera historica*, edited by Charles Plummer. 2 vols. Oxford, 1896.

———. *Homiliarum euangelii libri II*. Edited by D. Hurst. In *Bedae Venerabilis opera homiletica*. CCSL 122. Turnhout: Brepols, 1955.

———. *In Genesim*. Edited by Ch. W. Jones. In *Bedae Venerabilis opera exegetica*. CCSL 118A. Turnhout: Brepols, 1967.

———. *In Lucae euangelium expositio*. Edited by D. Hurst. In *Bedae Venerabilis opera exegetica*. CCSL 120. Turnhout: Brepols, 1960.

———. *Libri II De Arte Metrica et De Schematibus et Tropis: The Art of Poetry and Rhetoric*. Edited and translated by Calvin B. Kendall. Bibliotheca Germanica, Series Nova. Saarbrücken: AQ-Verlag, 1991.

———. *On Genesis*. Translated by Calvin B. Kendall. Translated Texts for Historians 48. Liverpool: Liverpool University Press, 2008.

———. *The Reckoning of Time*. Translated by Faith Wallis. Translated Texts for Historians 29. Liverpool: Liverpool University Press, 1999.

———. *Vita Sancti Cuthberti*. In *Two Lives of Saint Cuthbert*, edited and translated by Bertram Colgrave. Cambridge: Cambridge University Press, 1940.

Benedict of Nursia. *Benedicti Regula*. Edited by Rudolph Hanslik. 2nd ed. CCEL 75. Vienna: Hoelder-Pichler-Tempsky, 1960.

———. *The Rule of St. Benedict in Latin and English with Notes*. Edited and translated by Timothy Fry. Collegeville, MN: Liturgical Press, 1981.

Bernard of Clairvaux. *De gradibus humilitatis et superbiae*. Edited by J. Leclercq and H. Rochais. *Sancti Bernardi Opera*, vol. 4, 13–59. Rome: Editiones Cistercienses, 1963.

Bieler, Ludwig, ed. and trans. *Four Latin Lives of Saint Patrick*. Scriptores Latini Hiberniae. Dublin: Dublin Institute for Advanced Studies, 1971.

———, ed. and trans. *The Irish Penitentials*. Scriptores Latini Hiberniae. Dublin: Dublin Institute for Advanced Studies, 1963.

Birch, Walter de Gray, ed. *Liber vitae: Register and Martyrology of New Minster and Hyde Abbey, Winchester*. London, 1892.

Boas, Marcus, ed. *Disticha Catonis*. Revised by H. J. Botschuyver. Amsterdam: North-Holland, 1952.

Bodden, Mary-Catherine, ed. and trans. *The Old English Finding of the True Cross*. Cambridge: D. S. Brewer, 1987.

Boethius. *Philosophiae consolatio*. Edited by Ludwig Bieler. CCSL 94. Turnhout: Brepols, 1957, reprint 1984.

Boniface. *Aenigmata*. Edited by Fr. Glorie. *Variae collectiones aenigmatum merouingicae aetatis*. CCSL 133. Turnhout: Brepols, 1968.

———. *Die Briefe des heiligen Bonifatius und Lullus*. Edited by Michael Tangl. MGH Epp. sel. 1. Berlin: Weidmann, 1916.

———. *The Letters of Saint Boniface.* Translated by Ephraim Emerton. New York: Columbia University Press, 1940, reprint 1976.
Boretius, Alfred, ed. *Capitularia Merowingica.* MGH Capit. 1. Hannover, 1883.
Brooks, N. P., and S. E. Kelly, eds. *Charters of Christ Church, Canterbury.* 2 vols. Anglo-Saxon Charters 17–18. Oxford: Oxford University Press, 2013.
Bulst, Walther. "Eine anglo-lateinische Übersetzung aus dem Griechischen um 700." *Zeitschrift für deutsches Altertum* 75 (1938): 105–14.
Byrhtferth of Ramsey. *Byrhtferth's Enchiridion.* Edited and translated by Peter S. Baker and Michael Lapidge. EETS s.s. 15. Oxford: Oxford University Press, 1995.
Campbell, A., ed. *Charters of Rochester.* Anglo-Saxon Charters 1. London: Oxford University Press, 1973.
Carnicelli, Thomas A., ed. *King Alfred's Version of St. Augustine's "Soliloquies."* Cambridge, MA: Harvard University Press, 1969.
Cassian, John. *The Conferences.* Translated by Boniface Ramsey. New York: Paulist Press, 1997.
———. *Conlationes XXIIII.* Edited by Michael Petschenig. CSEL 13. Vienna, 1886.
———. *De Institutis Coenobiorum et de Octo Principalium Vitiorum Remediis Libri XII.* Edited by Michael Petschenig. CSEL 17. Vienna, 1888.
———. *The Institutes.* Translated by Boniface Ramsey. New York: Newman Press, 2000.
Cassiodorus. *Expositio psalmorum.* Edited by M. Adriaen. CCSL 97 and 98. Turnhout: Brepols, 1958.
Cockayne, Oswald, ed. *Leechdoms, Wortcunning, and Starcraft of Early England.* 3 vols. London, 1864.
Columbanus. *Regula coenobialis.* In *Sancti Columbani Opera,* edited and translated by G. S. M. Walker. Scriptores Latini Hiberniae. Dublin: Dublin Institute for Advanced Studies, 1957.
———. *Regula monachorum.* In *Sancti Columbani Opera,* edited and translated by G. S. M. Walker. Scriptores Latini Hiberniae. Dublin: Dublin Institute for Advanced Studies, 1957.
Cynewulf. *The Old English Poems of Cynewulf.* Edited and translated by Robert E. Bjork. DOML. Cambridge, MA: Harvard University Press, 2013.
———. *Cynewulf's Elene.* Edited by P. O. E. Gradon. Exeter: University of Exeter Press, 1977.
Dennis, Andrew, Peter Foote, and Richard Perkins, eds. and trans. *Laws of Early Iceland, Grágás: The Codex regius of Grágás with Material from Other Manuscripts.* Winnipeg: University of Manitoba Press, 1980, 2000.
Deshusses, Jean, ed. *Le Sacramentaire Grégorien: Ses principales formes d'après les plus anciens manuscrits.* 2nd ed. Spicilegium Friburgense 24. Saint Paul, Fribourg: Éditions Universitaires Fribourg Suisse, 1988.
de Vogüé, Adalbert, ed. *La Règle du Maître.* 3 vols. SC 105–7. Paris: Éditions du Cerf, 1964–65.
Dobbie, Elliott Van Kirk, ed. *The Anglo-Saxon Minor Poems.* Anglo-Saxon Poetic Records 6. New York: Columbia University Press, 1985.
———, ed. *Beowulf and Judith.* Anglo-Saxon Poetic Records 4. New York: Columbia University Press, 1953, reprint 2003.
Donatus, Aelius. *Ars Maior.* In *Donat et la tradition de l'enseignement grammatical: Étude sur l'*Ars Donati *et sa diffusion (ive–ixe siècle) et édition critique,* edited by Louis Holtz. Paris: Centre national de la recherche scientifique, 1981.
Drew, Katherine Fisher, ed. and trans. *The Laws of the Salian Franks.* Philadelphia: University of Pennsylvania Press, 1991.
Eadmer of Canterbury. *The Life of St Anselm, Archbishop of Canterbury.* Edited and translated by R. W. Southern. OMT. Oxford: Clarendon Press, 1962.
———. *Lives and Miracles of Saints Oda, Dunstan, and Oswald.* Edited and translated by Andrew J. Turner and Bernard J. Muir. OMT. Oxford: Clarendon Press, 2006.
Eberle, Luke, trans. *The Rule of the Master.* Kalamazoo, MI: Cistercian Publications, 1977.
Eckhardt, Karl August, ed. *Pactus legis Salicae.* MGH LL nat. Germ. 4.1. Hannover: Hahnsche Buchhandlung, 1962.

———, ed. *Schwabenspiegel: Kurzform*. MGH Fontes iuris N.S. 4.1/2. Hannover: Hahnsche Buchhandlung, 1974.
Eckhardt, Karl August, and Alfred Hübner, eds. *Deutschenspiegel und Augsburger Sachsenspiegel*. MGH Fontes iuris N.S. 3. Hannover: Hahnsche Buchhandlung, 1933.
Ekkehard of Saint Gall. *Casus S. Galli*. Edited by Georg Heinrich Pertz. MGH SS 2. Hannover, 1829.
Eusebius. *Aenigmata*. Edited by Fr. Glorie. Translated by Erika von Erhardt-Siebold. *Variae collectiones aenigmatum merouingicae aetatis*. CCSL 133. Turnhout: Brepols, 1968.
Felix. *Life of Saint Guthlac*. Edited and translated by Bertram Colgrave. Cambridge: Cambridge University Press, 1956.
Finsen, Vilhjálmur, ed. *Grágás: Islændernes Lovbog i Fristatens Tid*. 3 vols. Copenhagen, 1852.
Fowler, Roger. "A Late Old English Handbook for the Use of a Confessor." *Anglia* 83 (1965): 1–34.
Frank, D. H., and M. Laach, eds. *Capitula notitiarum*. In *Initia consuetudinis benedictinae*, ed. K. Hallinger. CCM 1. Siegburg: F. Schmitt, 1963.
Gildas. *De poenitentia*. In *The Ruin of Britain and Other Works*, edited and translated by Michael Winterbottom. Arthurian Sources. Chichester: Phillimore, 2002.
Giles, John A., ed. *Anecdota Bedæ, Lanfranci, et aliorum*. Publications of the Caxton Society 7. London, 1851.
Godden, Malcolm, and Susan Irvine, eds. and trans. *The Old English Boethius: An Edition of the Old English Version of Boethius's "De Consolatione Philosophiae."* 2 vols. Oxford: Oxford University Press, 2009.
Goolden, Peter, ed. *The Old English "Apollonius of Tyre."* London: Oxford University Press, 1958.
Goscelin of Saint-Bertin. *The Liber Confortatorius of Goscelin of Saint Bertin*. Edited by C. H. Talbot. Studia Anselmiana 37, Analecta Monastica, 3rd ser. Rome: Herder, 1955.
Gregory of Tours. *Libri historiarum X*. Edited by Bruno Krusch and Wilhelm Levison. MGH SS rer. Merov. 1.1. Hannover: Hahnsche Buchhandlung, 1951.
Gregory the Great. *Dialogues*. Edited by Adalbert de Vogüé. Translated by Paul Antin. 3 vols. SC 251, 260, and 265. Paris: Éditions du Cerf, 1979–1980.
———. *Homiliae in Hiezechihelem prophetam*. Edited by M. Adriaen. CCSL 142. Turnhout: Brepols, 1971.
———. *Moralia in Iob*. Edited by Marc Adriaen. 3 vols. CCSL 143, 143a, 143b. Turnhout: Brepols, 1979.
———. *Règle pastorale*. Edited by Bruno Judic, Floribert Rommel, and Charles Morel. 2 vols. SC 381 and 382. Paris: Éditions du Cerf, 1992.
Günzel, Beate, ed. *Ælfwine's Prayerbook (London, British Library, Cotton Titus D. xxvi + xxvii)*. Henry Bradshaw Society 108. Woodbridge, Suffolk: Boydell Press, 1993.
Hartmann, Wilfried, ed. *Concilium Mainz, a. 852, Oct. 3*. MGH Conc. 3. Hannover: Hahnsche Buchhandlung, 1984.
Heist, W. W., ed. *Vitae Sanctorum Hiberniae*. Subsidia Hagiographica 28. Brussels: Société des Bollandistes, 1965.
Herren, Michael W., ed. *The Hisperica Famina: II. Related Poems: A Critical Edition with English Translation and Philological Commentary*. Studies and Texts 85. Toronto: Pontifical Institute of Medieval Studies, 1987.
Hildemar of Civate. *Expositio regulae ab Hildemaro tradita*. Edited by Rupert Mittermüller. *Vita et Regula SS. P. Benedicti una cum expositione regulae*, vol. 3. Regensburg, 1880.
Holthausen, Ferdinand, ed. "Altenglische Interlinearversionen lateinischer Gebete und Beichten." *Anglia* 65 (1941): 230–54.
The Holy Bible: Douay-Rheims Version. Charlotte, NC: Saint Benedict Press, 2009.
Hughes, Anselm, ed. *The Portiforium of Saint Wulstan (Corpus Christi College, Cambridge, MS. 391)*. 2 vols. Henry Bradshaw Society 89–90. London: Henry Bradshaw Society, 1958, 1960.
Hywel Dda. *Ancient Laws and Institutes of Wales*. Edited and translated by Aneurin Owen. 2 vols. London, 1841.

———. *Cyfreithiau Hywel Dda yn ôl Llyfr Blegywryd*. Edited by Stephen J. Williams and J. Enoch Powell. Cardiff: University of Wales Press, 1942, reprint 1961.

Irvine, Susan, ed. *Old English Homilies from MS Bodley 343*. EETS o.s. 302. Oxford: Oxford University Press, 1993.

Isidore of Seville. *Etymologiarum sive Originum libri XX*. Edited by W. M. Lindsay. 2 vols. Oxford: Clarendon Press, 1911.

———. *The "Etymologies" of Isidore of Seville*. Translated by Stephen A. Barney, W. J. Lewis, J. A. Beach, and Oliver Berghof. Cambridge: Cambridge University Press, 2006.

———. *Sententiae*. Edited by P. Cazier. CCSL 111. Turnhout: Brepols, 1998.

Jerome. *Liber Didymi Alexandrini de Spiritu Sancto*. PL 23.109–62.

———. *Vita S. Pauli primi eremitae*. PL 23.17–28.

Jones, Christopher A., ed. and trans. *Old English Shorter Poems: Religious and Didactic*. DOML. Cambridge, MA: Harvard University Press, 2012.

Julian of Toledo. *Prognosticorum futuri saeculi libri tres*. Edited by J. N. Hillgarth. CCSL 115. Turnhout: Brepols, 1976.

Kelly, Richard J., ed. and trans. *The Blickling Homilies*. New York: Continuum, 2003.

Klaeber, Friedrich. *Klaeber's "Beowulf" and the Fight at Finnsburg*. Edited by R. D. Fulk, Robert E. Bjork, and John D. Niles. 4th ed. Toronto: University of Toronto Press, 2008.

Kornexl, Lucia, ed. *Die "Regularis Concordia" und ihre altenglische Interlinearversion*. Texte und Untersuchungen zur Englischen Philologie 17. Munich: Wilhelm Fink, 1993.

Kortekaas, G. A. A., ed. *The Story of Apollonius, King of Tyre: A Study of Its Greek Origin and an Edition of the Two Oldest Latin Recensions*. Leiden: Brill, 2004.

Krapp, George Philip, ed. *The Junius Manuscript*. Anglo-Saxon Poetic Records 1. New York: Columbia University Press, 1931.

———, ed. *The Paris Psalter and the Meters of Boethius*. Anglo-Saxon Poetic Records 5. New York: Columbia University Press, 1932, reprint 1970.

———, ed. *The Vercelli Book*. Anglo-Saxon Poetic Records 2. New York: Columbia University Press, 1932, reprint 2004.

Krapp, George Philip, and Elliott Van Kirk Dobbie, eds. *The Exeter Book*. Anglo-Saxon Poetic Records 3. New York: Columbia University Press, 1936, reprint 2004.

Lanfranc. *Decreta Lanfranci: The Monastic Constitutions of Lanfranc*. Edited and translated by David Knowles. London: Thomas Nelson & Sons, 1951.

———. *The Letters of Lanfranc, Archbishop of Canterbury*. Edited and translated by Helen Clover and Margaret Gibson. Oxford: Clarendon Press, 1979.

Lantfred of Winchester. *Translatio et miracula Sancti Swithuni*. In *The Cult of St Swithun*, edited and translated by Michael Lapidge. Winchester Studies 4.ii. Oxford: Clarendon Press, 2003.

Leccisotti, T., ed. *Ordo Casinensis I dictus Ordo regularis*. In *Initia consuetudinis benedictinae*, ed. K. Hallinger. CCM 1. Siegburg: F. Schmitt, 1963.

Leontios of Neapolis. *Vita S. Ioannis Eleemosinarii*. PL 73.337–92.

Liebermann, F., ed. *Die Gesetze der Angelsachsen*. 3 vols. Halle: Max Niemeyer, 1903–1916.

Lockett, Leslie, ed. and trans. *The Old English Soliloquies*. DOML. Cambridge, MA: Harvard University Press, forthcoming.

Logeman, H. "Anglo-Saxonica Minora." *Anglia* 11 (1889): 97–120.

Magennis, Hugh, ed. and trans. *The Old English Life of St. Mary of Egypt: An Edition of the Old English Text with Modern English Parallel-Text Translation*. Exeter: University of Exeter Press, 2002.

Mombritius, Boninus, ed. *Sanctuarium seu Vitae Sanctorum*. 2 vols. Paris: Fontemoing, 1910.

Morris, R., ed. and trans. *The Blickling Homilies of the Tenth Century*. EETS 58, 63, and 73. London, 1874–1880. Reprint, as single volume, London: Oxford University Press, 1967.

Muir, Bernard J., ed. *The Exeter Anthology of Old English Poetry: An Edition of Exeter Dean and Chapter MS 3501*. 2nd ed. 2 vols. Exeter Medieval English Texts and Studies. Exeter: University of Exeter Press, 2000.

———, ed. *A Pre-Conquest English Prayer-Book (BL MSS Cotton Galba A.xiv and Nero A.ii [ff. 3–13])*. Henry Bradshaw Society 103. Woodbridge, Suffolk: Boydell Press, 1988.
Napier, A. S., ed. "An Old English Vision of Leofric, Earl of Mercia." *Transactions of the Philological Society* 26, no. 2 (1908): 180–88.
Nordal, Sigurður, ed. *Egils saga Skalla-Grímssonar*. Íslenzk fornrit 2. Reykjavík: Hið íslenzka fornritafélag, 1933.
Odo of Cluny. *Vita sancti Geraldi Auriliacensis comitis*. PL 133.639–704.
Oliver, Lisi. *The Beginnings of English Law*. Toronto: University of Toronto Press, 2002.
Orchard, Andy, ed. *Liber monstrorum*. In *Pride and Prodigies: Studies in the Monsters of the "Beowulf"-Manuscript*, by Andy Orchard. 254–317. Cambridge: D. S. Brewer, 1995.
Orchard, Nicholas, ed. *The Leofric Missal*. 2 vols. Henry Bradshaw Society 113. Woodbridge, Suffolk: Boydell Press, 2002.
Origen. *Homilien zum Hexateuch: In Numeros homiliae*. Edited by W. A. Baehrens. Vol. 7, Die griechischen christlichen Schriftsteller der ersten Jahrhunderte 30. Leipzig: J. C. Hinrichs, 1921.
Osbern of Canterbury. *Miracula Sancti Dunstani*. Edited by William Stubbs. *Memorials of St. Dunstan, Archbishop of Canterbury*. Rolls Series 63. London, 1874.
Pachomius. *Regula coenobiorum*. PL 23.65–90.
Peter Chrysologus. *Collectio sermonum*. Edited by Alexander Olivar. CCSL 24, 24A-B. Turnhout: Brepols, 1975.
Peter Damian. *Die Briefe des Petrus Damiani*. Edited by Kurt Reindel. MGH Briefe d. dt. Kaiserzeit 4.1–4. Munich: Monumenta Germaniae Historica, 1983–1993.
Plummer, Charles, ed. *Vitae Sanctorum Hiberniae*. 2 vols. Oxford: Clarendon Press, 1910.
Porter, David W., ed. *The Antwerp-London Glossaries: The Latin and Latin–Old English Vocabularies from Antwerp, Museum Plantin-Moretus 16.2—London, British Library Add. 32246*. Publications of the Dictionary of Old English 8. Toronto: Pontifical Institute of Medieval Studies, 2011.
Priscian. *Excerptiones de Prisciano: The Sources for Ælfric's Latin–Old English Grammar*. Edited by David W. Porter. Anglo-Saxon Texts 4. Cambridge: D. S. Brewer, 2002.
Prosper of Aquitaine. *Epigrammata*. PL 51.497–532.
———. *Liber epigrammatum*. Edited by Albertus G. A. Horsting. CSEL 100. Berlin: Walter de Gruyter, 2016.
———. *Liber sententiarum*. Edited by M. Gastaldo. CCSL 68A. Turnhout: Brepols, 1972.
Pseudo-Bede. *Collectanea Pseudo-Bedae*. Edited and translated by Martha Bayless and Michael Lapidge. Scriptores Latini Hiberniae. Dublin: Dublin Institute for Advanced Studies, 1998.
Pseudo-Seneca. *De moribus*. Edited by O. Friedrich. *Publilii Syri Mimi Sententiae*, 261–73. Berlin, 1880.
Pseudo-Theodore. *Die Canones Theodori Cantuariensis und ihre Überlieferungsformen*. Edited by Paul Willem Finsterwalder. Untersuchungen zu den Bussbüchern des 7. 8. und 9. Jahrhunderts I. Band. Weimar: Böhlaus, 1929.
Raith, Josef, ed. *Die alt- und mittelenglischen Apollonius-Bruchstücke: mit dem Text der "Historia Apollonii" nach der englischen Handschriftengruppe*. Studien und Texte zur englischen Philologie 3. Munich: Max Hueber, 1956.
Rauer, Christine, ed. and trans. *The Old English Martyrology*. Cambridge: D. S. Brewer, 2013.
Robert Mannyng of Brunne. *Handlyng Synne*. Edited by Idelle Sullens. Binghamton, NY: Medieval and Renaissance Texts and Studies, 1983.
———. *Handlyng Synne*. Edited by Frederick J. Furnivall. EETS o.s. 119. London: Kegan Paul, Trench, Trübner and Co., 1901.
Robertson, A. J., ed. and trans. *The Laws of the Kings of England from Edmund to Henry I*. Cambridge: Cambridge University Press, 1925.
Rufinus, Tyrannius. *Historia monachorum sive de Vita Sanctorum Patrum*. Edited by Eva Schulz-Flügel. Patristische Texte und Studien 34. Berlin: Walter de Gruyter, 1990.

Schlyter, D. C. J., ed. *Codex Iuris Uplandici.* Codex Iuris Sueo-Gotorum Antiqui 3. Stockholm, 1834.
Schmid, Reinhold, ed. *Die Gesetze der Angelsachsen.* Leipzig, 1858.
Schröer, Arnold, ed. *Die angelsächsischen Prosabearbeitungen der Benediktinerregel.* Bibliothek der angelsächsischen Prosa 2, 2nd ed. with a supplement by Helmut Gneuss. Darmstadt: Wissenschaftliche Buchgesellschaft, 1964.
Scragg, D. G., ed. *The Vercelli Homilies.* EETS o.s. 300. Oxford: Oxford University Press, 1992.
Sedulius Scottus. *Collectaneum miscellaneum.* Edited by D. Simpson. Corpus Christianorum Continuatio Mediaevalis 67. Turnhout: Brepols, 1988, with a Supplementum by François Dolbeau, 1990.
Silius Italicus. *Punica.* Edited by Joseph Delz. Bibliotheca scriptorum Graecorum et Romanorum Teubneriana. Stuttgart: Teubner, 1987.
Smaragdus. *Smaragdi Abbatis Expositio in Regulam S. Benedicti.* Edited by Alfred Spannagel and Pius Engelbert. CCM 8. Siegburg: F. Schmitt, 1974.
Spindler, Robert, ed. *Das altenglische Bußbuch (sog. Confessionale Pseudo-Egberti).* Leipzig: B. Tauchnitz, 1934.
Squires, Ann, ed. *The Old English Physiologus.* Durham Medieval Texts 5. Durham: Durham Medieval Texts, 1988.
Stephen of Ripon. *The Life of Bishop Wilfrid by Eddius Stephanus.* Edited and translated by Bertram Colgrave. Cambridge: Cambridge University Press, 1927.
Stokes, Peter A. "The Vision of Leofric: Manuscript, Text and Context." *Review of English Studies* 62, no. 256 (2011): 529–50.
Storms, G., ed. *Anglo-Saxon Magic.* The Hague: Nijhoff, 1948.
Strecker, Karl, ed. *Ecbasis cuiusdam captivi per tropologiam.* MGH SS rer. Germ. 24. Hannover: Hahnsche Buchhandlung, 1935.
Stubbs, William, ed. *Memorials of St. Dunstan, Archbishop of Canterbury.* Rolls Series 63. London, 1874.
Sulpicius Severus. *Vie de Saint Martin.* Edited by Jacques Fontaine. SC 133–35. Paris: Éditions du Cerf, 1967–1969.
Symons, Dom Thomas, ed. and trans. *Regularis Concordia.* London: Thomas Nelson & Sons, 1953.
Symphosius. *Aenigmata.* Edited by Fr. Glorie. Translated by R. Th. Ohl. *Variae collectiones aenigmatum merouingicae aetatis.* CCSL 133A. Turnhout: Brepols, 1968.
Tatwine. *Aenigmata.* Edited by Fr. Glorie. Translated by Erika von Erhardt-Siebold. *Variae collectiones aenigmatum merouingicae aetatis.* CCSL 133. Turnhout: Brepols, 1968.
Theodulf of Orléans. *Capitula 2.* Edited by Peter Brommer. MGH Capit. episc. 1, 103–84. Hannover: Hahnsche Buchhandlung, 1984.
Thompson, Rodney, ed. *The Life of Gundulf, Bishop of Rochester.* Toronto Medieval Latin Texts 7. Toronto: University of Toronto Press, 1977.
Thorpe, Benjamin, ed. and trans. *Ancient Laws and Institutes of England.* London, 1840.
UCLA Digital Library. "St. Gall Monastery Plan: Codex Sangallensis 1092, Content and Context." University of California, http://www.stgallplan.org.
Valerius Flaccus. *Argonautica.* Edited by W. W. Ehlers. Bibliotheca scriptorum Graecorum et Romanorum Teubneriana. Stuttgart: Teubner, 1980.
Virgilius Maro Grammaticus. *Opera Omnia.* Edited by B. Löfstedt. Bibliotheca scriptorum Graecorum et Romanorum Teubneriana. Munich: K. G. Saur, 2003.
Walahfrid Strabo. *Libellus de exordiis & incrementis quarundam in observationibus ecclesiasticis rerum.* Edited and translated by Alice L. Harting-Correa. Leiden: Brill, 1996.
Weber, Robert, and Roger Gryson, eds. *Biblia Sacra iuxta vulgatam versionem.* 5th ed. Stuttgart: Deutsche Bibelgesellschaft, 2007.
Werferth of Worcester. *Bischofs Waerferth von Worcester Übersetzung der Dialoge Gregors des Grossen.* Edited by Hans Hecht. 2 vols. Bibliothek der angelsächsischen Prosa 5. Leipzig: G. H. Wigland, 1900–1907. Reprint, Darmstadt, 1965.

William of Malmesbury. *Saints' Lives: Lives of SS. Wulfstan, Dunstan, Patrick, Benignus and Indract*. Edited and translated by Michael Winterbottom and R. M. Thomson. OMT. Oxford: Clarendon Press, 2002.

Williamson, Craig, ed. *The Old English Riddles of the Exeter Book*. Chapel Hill: University of North Carolina Press, 1977.

Wulfstan of Winchester (Wulfstan Cantor). *Epistola specialis ad Ælfegum Episcopum*. In *The Cult of St Swithun*, edited and translated by Michael Lapidge. Winchester Studies 4.ii. Oxford: Clarendon Press, 2003.

———. *The Life of St Æthelwold*. Edited and translated by Michael Lapidge and Michael Winterbottom. OMT. Oxford: Clarendon Press, 1991.

———. *Narratio metrica de S. Swithuno*. In *The Cult of St Swithun*, edited and translated by Michael Lapidge. Winchester Studies 4.ii. Oxford: Clarendon Press, 2003.

Secondary Sources

Agamben, Giorgio. *The Highest Poverty: Monastic Rules and Form-of-Life*. Translated by Adam Kotsko. Stanford, CA: Stanford University Press, 2013.

———. *The Sacrament of Language: An Archaeology of the Oath*. Translated by Adam Kotsko. Stanford, CA: Stanford University Press, 2011.

Airlie, Stuart. "The Anxiety of Sanctity: St Gerald of Aurillac and His Maker." *Journal of Ecclesiastical History* 43, no. 3 (1992): 372–95.

Anderson, James E. "Two Spliced Riddles in the Exeter Book." *In Geardagum* 5 (1983): 57–75.

Andersson, Theodore. "The Thief in *Beowulf*." *Speculum* 59, no. 3 (1984): 493–508.

Anlezark, Daniel. "Reading the 'Story of Joseph' in MS Cambridge, Corpus Christi College 201." In *The Power of Words: Anglo-Saxon Studies Presented to Donald G. Scragg on His Seventieth Birthday*, edited by Hugh Magennis and Jonathan Wilcox. 61–94. Morgantown: West Virginia University Press, 2006.

Archibald, Elizabeth. *Apollonius of Tyre: Medieval and Renaissance Themes and Variations*. Cambridge: D. S. Brewer, 1991.

Banham, Debby. "Anglo-Saxon Attitudes: In Search of the Origins of English Racism." *European Review of History* 1, no. 2 (1994): 143–56.

Bartlett, Robert. *Trial by Fire and Water: The Medieval Judicial Ordeal*. Oxford: Clarendon Press, 1986.

Bateson, Mary. "A London Municipal Collection of the Reign of John." *English Historical Review* 17, no. 67 (1902): 480–511.

Bayless, Martha. "Alcuin's *Disputatio Pippini* and the Early Medieval Riddle Tradition." In *Humour, History and Politics in Late Antiquity and the Early Middle Ages*, edited by Guy Halsall. 157–78. Cambridge: Cambridge University Press, 2001.

Bedingfield, Brad. "Public Penance in Anglo-Saxon England." *ASE* 31 (2002): 223–55.

Beechy, Tiffany. *The Poetics of Old English*. Farnham, UK: Ashgate, 2010.

Bellman, Beryl L. "The Paradox of Secrecy." *Human Studies* 4 (1981): 1–24.

Bentham, Jeremy. *The Panopticon Writings*. Edited by Miran Božovič. London: Verso, 1995.

Best, Stephen, and Sharon Marcus. "Surface Reading: An Introduction." In "The Way We Read Now," special issue edited by Stephen Best and Sharon Marcus. *Representations* 108 (2009): 1–21.

Bestul, Thomas H. "Continental Sources of Anglo-Saxon Devotional Writing." In *Sources of Anglo-Saxon Culture*, edited by Paul E. Szarmach, with the assistance of Virginia Darrow Oggins. 103–26. Kalamazoo, MI: Medieval Institute Publications, 1986.

Biggs, Frederick M. "Beowulf and Some Fictions of the Geatish Succession." *ASE* 32 (2003): 55–77.

Bischoff, Bernhard, and Michael Lapidge. *Biblical Commentaries from the Canterbury School of Theodore and Hadrian*. CSASE 10. Cambridge: Cambridge University Press, 1994.

Bitterli, Dieter. *Say What I Am Called: The Old English Riddles of the Exeter Book and the Anglo-Latin Riddle Tradition*. Toronto: University of Toronto Press, 2009.

Blair, John. "Anglo-Saxon Minsters: A Topographical Review." In *Pastoral Care Before the Parish*, edited by John Blair and Richard Sharpe. 226–66. Leicester: Leicester University Press, 1992.
———. *The Church in Anglo-Saxon Society*. Oxford: Oxford University Press, 2005.
———. "The Dangerous Dead in Early Medieval England." In *Early Medieval Studies in Memory of Patrick Wormald*, edited by Stephen Baxter, Janet Nelson, and David Pelteret. 539–59. Farnham, UK: Ashgate, 2009.
Blokhuis, B. A. "Bede and Ælfric: The Sources of the Homily on St Cuthbert." In *Beda Venerabilis: Historian, Monk, and Northumbrian*, edited by L. A. J. R. Houwen and A. A. MacDonald. 107–38. Groningen: Egbert Forsten, 1996.
Bok, Sissela. *Secrets: On the Ethics of Concealment and Revelation*. New York: Vintage Books, 1984.
Bolle, Kees W. "Secrecy in Religion." In *Secrecy in Religions*, edited by Kees W. Bolle. 1–24. Leiden: Brill, 1987.
Bolton, Whitney F. *A History of Anglo-Latin Literature, 597–1066*. Vol. 1. Princeton, NJ: Princeton University Press, 1967.
Borysławski, Rafał. *The Old English Riddles and the Riddlic Elements of Old English Poetry*. Studies in English Medieval Language and Literature 9. Frankfurt: Peter Lang, 2004.
Bradley, Craig M. "Interrogation and Silence: A Comparative Study." *Wisconsin International Law Journal* 27, no. 2 (2009): 271–97.
Brady, Lindy. "The 'Dark Welsh' as Slaves and Slave Traders in Exeter Book Riddles 52 and 72." *English Studies* 95, no. 3 (2014): 235–55.
Brooks, Nicholas. *The Early History of the Church of Canterbury: Christ Church from 597 to 1066*. Leicester: Leicester University Press, 1984.
Brown, George H. "The Meanings of *Interpres* in Aldhelm and Bede." In *Interpretation: Medieval and Modern*, edited by Piero Boitani and Anna Torti. 43–65. Cambridge: D. S. Brewer, 1993.
Brown, Warren. *Unjust Seizure: Conflict, Interest, and Authority in an Early Medieval Society*. Ithaca, NY: Cornell University Press, 2001.
Bullough, Donald A. "Alcuin and the Kingdom of Heaven: Liturgy, Theology, and the Carolingian Age." In *Carolingian Essays: Andrew W. Mellon Lectures in Early Christian Studies*, edited by Uta-Renate Blumenthal. 1–69. Washington, DC: Catholic University of America Press, 1983.
———. "What Has Ingeld to Do with Lindisfarne?" *ASE* 22 (1993): 93–125.
Bynum, Caroline Walker. "Wonder." In *Metamorphosis and Identity*, by Caroline Walker Bynum. 37–75. New York: Zone Books, 2001.
Calder, Daniel G. "Strife, Revelation, and Conversion: The Thematic Structure of *Elene*." *English Studies* 53, no. 3 (1972): 201–10.
Carruthers, Mary. *The Book of Memory: A Study of Memory in Medieval Culture*. 2nd ed. CSML 70. Cambridge: Cambridge University Press, 2008.
Cavell, Megan. *Weaving Words and Binding Bodies: The Poetics of Human Experience in Old English Literature*. Toronto: University of Toronto Press, 2016.
Charles-Edwards, T. M. "The Penitential of Columbanus." In *Columbanus: Studies of the Latin Writings*, edited by Michael Lapidge. 217–39. Woodbridge, Suffolk: Boydell Press, 1997.
———. "The Penitential of Theodore and the *Iudicia Theodori*." In *Archbishop Theodore: Commemorative Studies on His Life and Influence*, edited by Michael Lapidge. 141–74. Cambridge: Cambridge University Press, 1995.
Christie, E. J. "By Means of a Secret Alphabet: Dangerous Letters and the Semantics of *Gebregdstafas* (*Solomon and Saturn I*, Line 2b)." *Modern Philology* 109, no. 2 (2011): 145–70.
———. "Sméagol and Déagol: Secrecy, History, and Ethical Subjectivity in Tolkien's World." *Mythlore* 121/122 (2013): 83–101.
Clapham, A. W. *English Romanesque Architecture Before the Norman Conquest*. Oxford: Clarendon Press, 1930.
Clark, Stephanie. "A More Permanent Homeland: Land Tenure in *Guthlac A*." *ASE* 40 (2012): 75–102.

Clayton, Mary. "Hermits and the Contemplative Life in Anglo-Saxon England." In *Holy Men and Holy Women: Old English Prose Saints' Lives and Their Contexts*, edited by Paul E. Szarmach. 147–75. Albany: State University of New York Press, 1996.

Clemoes, Peter. *Interactions of Thought and Language in Old English Poetry*. New York: Cambridge University Press, 1995.

Coleman, Julie. "Sexual Euphemism in Old English." *Neuphilologische Mitteilungen* 93 (1992): 93–98.

Conner, Patrick W. *Anglo-Saxon Exeter: A Tenth-Century Cultural History*. Studies in Anglo-Saxon History 4. Woodbridge, Suffolk: Boydell Press, 1993.

Copeland, Rita. *Rhetoric, Hermeneutics, and Translation in the Middle Ages: Academic Traditions and Vernacular Texts*. CSML 23. Cambridge: Cambridge University Press, 1991.

Cowen, Alice. "*Byrstas* and *bysmeras*: The Wounds of Sin in the *Sermo Lupi ad Anglos*." In *Wulfstan, Archbishop of York: The Proceedings of the Second Alcuin Conference*, edited by Matthew Townend. 397–411. Turnhout: Brepols, 2004.

Cross, J. E. "*Legimus in ecclesiasticis historicis*: A Sermon for All Saints and Its Use in Old English Prose." *Traditio* 33 (1977): 101–35.

Dailey, Patricia. "Riddles, Wonder and Responsiveness in Anglo-Saxon Literature." In *The Cambridge History of Early Medieval English Literature*, edited by Clare A. Lees. 451–72. Cambridge: Cambridge University Press, 2013.

Darby, Peter. *Bede and the End of Time*. Farnham, UK: Ashgate, 2012.

de Certeau, Michel. *The Mystic Fable*. Vol. 1, *The Sixteenth and Seventeenth Centuries*. Translated by Michael B. Smith. Chicago: University of Chicago Press, 1992.

DeGregorio, Scott. "*Interpretatio Monastica*: Biblical Commentary and Monastic Identity." In *Latinity and Identity in Anglo-Saxon Literature*, edited by Rebecca Stephenson and Emily V. Thornbury. 38–53. Toronto: University of Toronto Press, 2016.

de Jong, Mayke. "Monastic Prisoners or Opting Out? Political Coercion and Honour in the Frankish Kingdoms." In *Topographies of Power in the Early Middle Ages*, edited by Mayke de Jong and Frans Theuws with Carine van Rhijn. 291–328. Leiden: Brill, 2001.

———. "Transformations of Penance." In *Rituals of Power: From Late Antiquity to the Early Middle Ages*, edited by Frans Theuws and Janet L. Nelson. 185–224. Leiden: Brill, 2000.

———. "What Was Public about Public Penance? *Paenitentia publica* and Justice in the Carolingian World." In *La Giustizia nell'Alto medioevo II (secoli IX–XI)*. 863–902. Spoleto: Presso la sede del Centro, 1997.

de Lubac, Henri. *Medieval Exegesis: The Four Senses of Scripture*. Translated by E. M. Macierowski. Vol. 2. Grand Rapids, MI: Wm. B. Eerdmans, 2000.

Dendle, Peter. *Satan Unbound: The Devil in Old English Narrative Literature*. Toronto: University of Toronto Press, 2001.

Denno, Jerry. "Oppression and Voice in Anglo-Saxon Riddle Poems." *CEA Critic* 70, no. 1 (2007): 35–47.

Derrida, Jacques. *Demeure: Fiction and Testimony*. Translated by Elizabeth Rottenberg. Stanford, CA: Stanford University Press, 2000.

———. "*Fors*: The Anglish Words of Nicholas Abraham and Maria Torok." In *The Wolf Man's Magic Word: A Cryptonymy*, by Nicholas Abraham and Maria Torok, foreword, xi–xlviii. Minneapolis: University of Minnesota Press, 1986.

———. "Poetics and the Politics of Witnessing." In *Sovereignties in Question: The Poetics of Paul Celan*, edited by Thomas Dutoit and Outi Pasanen. 65–96. New York: Fordham University Press, 2005.

———. *Poétique et politique du témoignage*. Paris: Éditions de L'Herne, 2005.

Dershowitz, Alan M. *Is There a Right to Remain Silent? Coercive Interrogation and the Fifth Amendment After 9/11*. Oxford: Oxford University Press, 2008.

de Vogüé, Adalbert. *The Rule of Saint Benedict: A Doctrinal and Spiritual Commentary*. Translated by John Baptist Hasbrouck, Cistercian Studies Series 54. Kalamazoo, MI: Cistercian Publications, 1983.

Dietrich, Franz. "Die Räthsel des Exeterbuches: Würdigung, Lösung und Herstellung." *Zeitschrift für deutsches Altertum* 11 (1859): 448–90.
Discenza, Nicole Guenther. "Power, Skill and Virtue in the Old English *Boethius*." *ASE* 26 (1997): 81–108.
Doane, A. N. "Three Old English Implement Riddles: Reconsiderations of Numbers 4, 49, and 73." *Modern Philology* 84 (1987): 243–57.
Doležalová, Lucie. "On Mistake and Meaning: *Scinderationes fonorum* in Medieval *artes memoriae*, Mnemonic Verses, and Manuscripts." *Language and History* 52, no. 1 (2009): 26–40.
Dronke, Peter, Michael Lapidge, and Peter Stotz. "Die unveröffentlichten Gedichte der Cambridger Liederhandschrift (CUL Gg.5.35)." *Mittellateinisches Jahrbuch* 17 (1982): 54–95.
Dunn, Marilyn. "Paradigms of Penance." *Journal of Medieval Monastic Studies* 1 (2012): 17–39.
Einstein, Albert. "Principles of Research." In *Essays in Science,* translated by Alan Harris. 1–5. New York: Philosophical Library, 1934. Reprint, Mineola, NY: Dover, 2009.
Elliott, Alison Goddard. *Roads to Paradise: Reading the Lives of the Early Saints.* Hanover, NH: Brown University Press, 1987.
Elliott, R. W. V. "Coming Back to Cynewulf." In *Old English Runes and Their Continental Background,* edited by Alfred Bammesberger. 231–47. Heidelberg: Carl Winter, 1991.
Feiss, Hugh. "*Circatores*: From Benedict of Nursia to Humbert of Romans." *American Benedictine Review* 40, no. 4 (1989): 346–79.
Fell, Christine E. "Runes and Semantics." In *Old English Runes and Their Continental Background,* edited by Alfred Bammesberger. 195–229. Heidelberg: Carl Winter, 1991.
Fell, Christine E., Cecily Clark, and Elizabeth Williams. *Women in Anglo-Saxon England and the Impact of 1066.* London: British Museum, 1984.
Felski, Rita. *The Limits of Critique.* Chicago: University of Chicago Press, 2015.
Fisher, E. A. *The Greater Anglo-Saxon Churches: An Architectural-Historical Study.* London: Faber & Faber, 1962.
Foley, John Miles. "How Genres Leak in Traditional Verse." In *Unlocking the Wordhoard: Anglo-Saxon Studies in Memory of Edward B. Irving, Jr.,* edited by Mark C. Amodio and Katherine O'Brien O'Keeffe. 76–108. Toronto: University of Toronto Press, 2003.
Foot, Sarah. *Monastic Life in Anglo-Saxon England, c. 600–900.* Cambridge: Cambridge University Press, 2006.
Foucault, Michel. "About the Beginning of the Hermeneutics of the Self." In *Religion and Culture by Michel Foucault,* edited by Jeremy R. Carrette. 158–81. Manchester: Manchester University Press, 1999.
———. *Discipline and Punish: The Birth of the Prison.* Translated by Alan Sheridan. New York: Vintage Books, 1995.
Foys, Martin. "The Undoing of Exeter Book Riddle 47: 'Bookmoth.'" In *Transitional States: Change, Tradition, and Memory in Medieval Literature and Culture,* edited by Graham Caie and Michael D. C. Drout. 101–30. Tempe: Arizona Center for Medieval and Renaissance Studies, 2018.
Frantzen, Allen J. *The Literature of Penance in Anglo-Saxon England.* New Brunswick, NJ: Rutgers University Press, 1983.
Gadamer, Hans-Georg. *Truth and Method.* 2nd rev. ed. Translated by Joel Weinsheimer and Donald G. Marshall. New York: Bloomsbury, 2013.
Galloway, Andrew. "The Rhetoric of Riddling in Late-Medieval England: The 'Oxford' Riddles, the *Secretum philosophorum*, and the Riddles in *Piers Plowman*." *Speculum* 70, no. 1 (1995): 68–105.
Gatch, Milton McC. "Miracles in Architectural Settings: Christ Church, Canterbury and St Clement's, Sandwich in the Old English *Vision of Leofric*." *ASE* 22 (1993): 227–53.
Gittos, Helen. *Liturgy, Architecture, and Sacred Places in Anglo-Saxon England.* Oxford: Oxford University Press, 2013.
Godden, Malcolm. *Ælfric's Catholic Homilies: Introduction, Commentary and Gloss.* EETS s.s. 18. Oxford: Oxford University Press, 2000.

———. "Anglo-Saxons on the Mind." In *Learning and Literature in Anglo-Saxon England: Studies Presented to Peter Clemoes on the Occasion of His Sixty-fifth Birthday*, edited by Michael Lapidge and Helmut Gneuss. 271–98. Cambridge: Cambridge University Press, 1985.

———. "Text and Eschatology in Book III of the Old English *Soliloquies*." *Anglia* 121, no. 2 (2003): 177–209.

Green, Richard Firth. *A Crisis of Truth: Literature and Law in Ricardian England*. Philadelphia: University of Pennsylvania Press, 1999, reprint 2002.

Gretsch, Mechthild. Ælfric and the Cult of Saints in Late Anglo-Saxon England. CSASE 34. Cambridge: Cambridge University Press, 2005.

———. "Æthelwold's Translation of the *Regula Sancti Benedicti* and Its Latin Exemplar." *ASE* 3 (1974): 125–51.

———. *Die "Regula Sancti Benedicti" in England und ihre altenglische Übersetzung*. Texte und Untersuchungen zur englischen Philologie 2. Munich: Wilhelm Fink, 1973.

Gretsch, Mechthild, and Helmut Gneuss. "Anglo-Saxon Glosses to a Theodorean Poem." In *Latin Learning and English Lore: Studies in Anglo-Saxon Literature for Michael Lapidge*, edited by Katherine O'Brien O'Keeffe and Andy Orchard. 9–46. Toronto: University of Toronto Press, 2005.

Gross, Charles. "Modes of Trial in the Mediæval Boroughs of England." *Harvard Law Review* 15, no. 9 (1902): 691–706.

Gruenler, Curtis. "How to Read Like a Fool: Riddle Contests and the Banquet of Conscience in *Piers Plowman*." *Speculum* 85, no. 3 (2010): 592–630.

———. *"Piers Plowman" and the Poetics of Enigma*. Notre Dame, IN: University of Notre Dame Press, 2017.

Hamilton, Sarah. *The Practice of Penance, 900–1050*. Woodbridge, Suffolk: Boydell Press, 2001.

———. "Remedies for 'Great Transgressions': Penance and Excommunication in Late Anglo-Saxon England." In *Pastoral Care in Late Anglo-Saxon England*, edited by Francesca Tinti. 83–105. Woodbridge, Suffolk: Boydell Press, 2005.

Harbus, Antonina. *The Life of the Mind in Old English Poetry*. Amsterdam: Rodopi, 2002.

Harper, John. *The Forms and Orders of Western Liturgy: From the Tenth to the Eighteenth Century*. Oxford: Clarendon Press, 1991, reprint 1995.

Harrison, William. *The Old Historians of the Isle of Man*. The Manx Society 18. Isle of Man, 1871.

Hawk, Brandon W. "'Id est, crux Christi': Tracing the Old English Motif of the Celestial Rood." *ASE* 40 (2011): 43–73.

Hayes, Mary. *Divine Ventriloquism in Medieval English Literature: Power, Anxiety, Subversion*. New York: Palgrave Macmillan, 2011.

Healey, Antonette diPaolo. "Taking *hand* in Hand: Mapping Its Meaning in Old English and Later." In *More than Words: English Lexicography and Lexicology Past and Present: Essays Presented to Hans Sauer on the Occasion of His 65th Birthday, Part I*, edited by Renate Bauer and Ulrike Krischke. Münchener Universitäts-Schriften, Texte und Untersuchungen zur Englischen Philologie 39–58. Frankfurt am Main: Peter Lang, 2011.

Heckman, Christina M. "Things in Doubt: *Inventio*, Dialectic, and Jewish Secrets in Cynewulf's *Elene*." *JEGP* 108, no. 4 (2009): 449–80.

Herren, Michael. "Some New Light on the Life of Virgilius Maro Grammaticus." *Proceedings of the Royal Irish Academy* 79 (1979): 27–71.

Heyworth, Melanie. "*Apollonius of Tyre* in Its Manuscript Context: An Issue of Marriage." *Philological Quarterly* 86, no. 1/2 (2007): 1–26.

Hill, Joyce. "Ælfric and Smaragdus." *ASE* 21 (1992): 203–37.

Hill, Thomas D. "The Failing Torch: The Old English *Elene*, 1256–1259." *Notes and Queries*, n.s., 52 (2005): 155–60.

Hollis, Stephanie. "Old English 'Cattle-Theft Charms': Manuscript Contexts and Social Uses." *Anglia* 115, no. 2 (2009): 139–64.

Hollis, Stephanie, and Michael Wright. *Old English Prose of Secular Learning*. Annotated Bibliographies of Old and Middle English Literature 4. Cambridge: D. S. Brewer, 1992.

Howe, Nicholas. "Aldhelm's *Enigmata* and Isidorian Etymology." *ASE* 14 (1985): 37–59.

———. "The Cultural Construction of Reading in Anglo-Saxon England." In *The Ethnography of Reading*, edited by Jonathan Boyarin. 58–79. Berkeley: University of California Press, 1993.

———. *Writing the Map of Anglo-Saxon England: Essays in Cultural Geography*. New Haven, CT: Yale University Press, 2008.

Hughes, Andrew. *Medieval Manuscripts for Mass and Office: A Guide to Their Organization and Terminology*. Toronto: University of Toronto Press, 1982.

Hughes, Kathleen. "Some Aspects of Irish Influence on Early English Private Prayer." *Studia Celtica* 5 (1970): 48–61.

Huizinga, J. *Homo Ludens: A Study of the Play-Element in Culture*. London: Routledge & Kegan Paul, 1949, reprint 1980.

Hyams, Paul R. *Rancor and Reconciliation in Medieval England*. Ithaca, NY: Cornell University Press, 2003.

———. "Trial by Ordeal." In *On the Laws and Customs of England: Essays in Honor of Samuel E. Thorne*, edited by Morris S. Arnold, Thomas A. Green, Sally A. Scully, and Stephen D. White. Chapel Hill: University of North Carolina Press, 1981.

Irvine, Martin. "Anglo-Saxon Literary Theory Exemplified in Old English Poems: Interpreting the Cross in *The Dream of the Rood* and *Elene*." *Style* 20 (1986): 157–81. Reprinted in Katherine O'Brien O'Keeffe, ed., *Old English Shorter Poems: Basic Readings*. 31–63. New York: Garland Press, 1994.

Irving, Edward B., Jr. "Heroic Experience in the Old English Riddles." In *Old English Shorter Poems: Basic Readings*, edited by Katherine O'Brien O'Keeffe. 199–212. New York: Garland, 1994.

Jauss, Hans Robert. *Aesthetic Experience and Literary Hermeneutics*. Translated by Michael Shaw. Minneapolis: University of Minnesota Press, 1982.

———. *Alterität und Modernität der mittelalterlichen Literatur: Gesammelte Aufsätze 1956–1976*. Munich: W. Fink, 1977.

———. "The Alterity and Modernity of Medieval Literature." Translated by Timothy Bahti. *New Literary History* 10, no. 2 (1979): 181–229.

———. *Ästhetische Erfahrung und literarische Hermeneutik*. 2nd ed. Frankfurt: Suhrkamp, 1982.

Jurasinski, Stefan. "The Old English Penitentials and the Law of Slavery." In *English Law Before Magna Carta: Felix Liebermann and "Die Gesetze der Angelsachsen,"* edited by Stefan Jurasinski, Lisi Oliver, and Andrew Rabin. 97–118. Leiden: Brill, 2010.

———. "*Reddatur Parentibus*: The Vengeance of the Family in Cnut's Homicide Legislation." *Law and History Review* 20 (2002): 157–80.

Justice, Steven. *Adam Usk's Secret*. Philadelphia: University of Pennsylvania Press, 2015.

———. "Eucharistic Miracle and Eucharistic Doubt." *JMEMS* 42, no. 2 (2012): 307–22.

Karkov, Catherine E. "Judgment and Salvation in the New Minster Liber Vitae." In *Apocryphal Texts and Traditions in Anglo-Saxon England*, edited by Kathryn Powell and Donald Scragg. 151–64. Cambridge: D. S. Brewer, 2003.

Keefer, Sarah Larratt. "Ðonne se cirlisca man ordales weddigeð: The Anglo-Saxon Lay Ordeal." In *Early Medieval Studies in Memory of Patrick Wormald*, edited by Stephen Baxter, Janet Nelson, and David Pelteret. 353–63. Farnham, UK: Ashgate, 2009.

———. "*Ut in omnibus honorificetur Deus*: The Corsnæd Ordeal in Anglo-Saxon England." In *The Community, the Family, and the Saint: Patterns of Power in Early Medieval Europe*, edited by Joyce Hill and Mary Swan. 237–64. Turnhout: Brepols, 1998.

Kermode, Frank. *The Genesis of Secrecy: On the Interpretation of Narrative*. Cambridge, MA: Harvard University Press, 1980.

Keynes, Simon. "The Fonthill Letter." In *Words, Texts, and Manuscripts: Studies in Anglo-Saxon Culture: Presented to Helmut Gneuss on the Occasion of His Sixty-Fifth Birthday*, edited by Michael Korhammer, Karl Reichl, and Hans Sauer. 53–97. Cambridge: D. S. Brewer, 1992.

Khan, Ruqayya Yasmine. *Self and Secrecy in Early Islam*. Columbia: University of South Carolina Press, 2008.

Kierkegaard, Søren. *Fear and Trembling*. Edited by C. Stephen Evans and Sylvia Walsh. Cambridge Texts in the History of Philosophy. Cambridge: Cambridge University Press, 2006, reprint 2010.

Klein, Stacy. *Ruling Women: Queenship and Gender in Anglo-Saxon Literature*. South Bend, IN: University of Notre Dame Press, 2006.

Kleist, Aaron J. "The Division of the Ten Commandments in Anglo-Saxon England." *Neuphilologische Mitteilungen* 103 (2002): 227–40.

Klukas, Arnold W. "Liturgy and Architecture: Deerhurst Priory as an Expression of the *Regularis concordia*." *Viator* 15 (1984): 81–106.

Kornexl, Lucia. "Ein benediktinischer Funktionsträger und sein Name: Linguistische Überlegungen rund um den *circa*." *Mittellateinisches Jahrbuch: Internationale Zeitschrift für Mediävistik* 31, no. 1 (1996): 39–60.

Laird, Andrew. "Metaphor and the Riddle of Representation in the *Historia Apollonii regis Tyri*." In *Metaphor and the Ancient Novel*, edited by Stephen Harrison, Michael Paschalis, and Stavros Frangoulidis. 225–44. Groningen: Barkhuis Publishing and Groningen University Library, 2005.

Lake, Stephen. "Knowledge of the Writings of John Cassian in Early Anglo-Saxon England." *ASE* 32 (2003): 27–41.

Lambert, Tom. *Law and Order in Anglo-Saxon England*. Oxford: Oxford University Press, 2017.

———. "Theft, Homicide and Crime in Late Anglo-Saxon Law." *Past and Present* 214 (2012): 3–43.

Lapidge, Michael. "Æthelwold as Scholar and Teacher." In *Bishop Æthelwold: His Career and Influence*, edited by Barbara Yorke. 89–118. Woodbridge, Suffolk: Boydell Press, 1988. Reprint, *ALL* 2:183–211.

———. "The Anglo-Latin Background." In *A New Critical History of Old English Literature*, edited by Stanley B. Greenfield and Daniel G. Calder. 5–37. New York: New York University Press, 1986. Reprint, *ALL* 1:1–36.

———. *Anglo-Latin Literature, 600–899*. London: Hambledon Press, 1996.

———. *Anglo-Latin Literature, 900–1066*. London: Hambledon Press, 1993.

———. *The Anglo-Saxon Library*. Oxford: Oxford University Press, 2006.

———. "Bede's Metrical *Vita S. Cuthberti*." In *St Cuthbert, His Cult and His Community to A.D. 1200*, edited by Gerald Bonner, Clare Stancliffe, and David Rollason. 77–93. Woodbridge, Suffolk: Boydell Press, 1989.

———. "The Hermeneutic Style in Tenth-Century Anglo-Latin Literature." *ASE* 4 (1975): 67–111. Reprint, *ALL* 2:105–49.

———. "Hwætberht." In *The Wiley Blackwell Encyclopedia of Anglo-Saxon England*, 2nd ed., edited by Michael Lapidge, John Blair, Simon Keynes, and Donald Scragg. 250–51. Malden, MA: John Wiley & Sons, 2014.

———. "Stoic Cosmology and the Source of the First Old English Riddle." *Anglia* 112, no. 1 (1994): 1–25.

———. "The Study of Latin Texts in Late Anglo-Saxon England: The Evidence of Latin Glosses." In *Latin and the Vernacular Languages in Early Medieval Britain*, edited by Nicholas Brooks. Leicester: Leicester University Press, 1984. Reprint, *ALL* 1:455–98.

Law, Vivien. *Wisdom, Authority and Grammar in the Seventh Century: Decoding Virgilius Maro Grammaticus*. Cambridge: Cambridge University Press, 1995.

Lea, Henry C. *Superstition and Force: Essays on The Wager of Law, The Wager of Battle, The Ordeal, Torture*. Philadelphia, 1866.

Leclercq, Jean. *The Love of Learning and the Desire for God: A Study of Monastic Culture.* Translated by Catharine Misrahi. New York: Fordham University Press, 1982.
Lees, Clare A. "Engendering Religious Desire: Sex, Knowledge, and Christian Identity in Anglo-Saxon England." *JMEMS* 27, no. 1 (1997): 17–46.
Lees, Clare A., and Gillian R. Overing. *Double Agents: Women and Clerical Culture in Anglo-Saxon England.* Philadelphia: University of Pennsylvania Press, 2001.
Lerer, Seth. *Literacy and Power in Anglo-Saxon Literature.* Lincoln: University of Nebraska Press, 1991.
Licence, Tom. *Hermits and Recluses in English Society, 950–1200.* Oxford: Oxford University Press, 2011.
Locherbie-Cameron, M. A. "From Caesarea to Eynsham: A Consideration of the Proposed Route(s) of the *Admonition to a Spiritual Son* to Anglo-Saxon England." *Heroic Age* 3 (2000).
Lochrie, Karma. *Covert Operations: The Medieval Uses of Secrecy.* Philadelphia: University of Pennsylvania Press, 1999.
Lockett, Leslie. *Anglo-Saxon Psychologies in the Vernacular and Latin Traditions.* Toronto: University of Toronto Press, 2011.
———. "Oswald's *uersus retrogradi*: A Forerunner of Post-Conquest Trends in Hexameter Composition." In *Latinity and Identity in Anglo-Saxon England*, edited by Emily V. Thornbury and Rebecca Stephenson. 158–67. Toronto: University of Toronto Press, 2016.
Love, Heather. "Close but Not Deep: Literary Ethics and the Descriptive Turn." *New Literary History* 41 (2010): 371–91.
———. "Close Reading and Thin Description." *Public Culture* 25, no. 3 (2013): 401–34.
Ma, Yue. "A Comparative View of the Law of Interrogation." *International Criminal Justice Review* 17, no. 1 (2007): 5–26.
MacIntyre, Alasdair. *After Virtue.* 3rd ed. Notre Dame, IN: University of Notre Dame Press, 2007.
Maus, Katharine Eisaman. *Inwardness and Theater in the English Renaissance.* Chicago: University of Chicago Press, 1995.
Mayr-Harting, Henry. *The Coming of Christianity to Anglo-Saxon England.* 3rd ed. University Park: Pennsylvania State University Press, 1991.
McCready, William D. *Miracles and the Venerable Bede.* Toronto: Pontifical Institute of Mediaeval Studies, 1994.
McDaniel, Rhonda L. "Pride Goes Before a Fall: Aldhelm's Practical Application of Gregorian and Cassianic Conceptions of *Superbia* and the Eight Principal Vices." In *The Seven Deadly Sins: From Communities to Individuals*, edited by Richard Newhauser. 95–109. Leiden: Brill, 2007.
McKeon, Michael. *The Secret History of Domesticity: Public, Private, and the Division of Knowledge.* Baltimore: Johns Hopkins University Press, 2007.
Meens, Rob. "The Frequency and Nature of Early Medieval Penance." In *Handling Sin: Confession in the Middle Ages*, edited by Peter Biller and A. J. Minnis. 35–63. York: York Medieval Press, 1998.
———. *Penance in Medieval Europe, 600–1200.* Cambridge: Cambridge University Press, 2014.
———. "Remedies for Sins." In *Cambridge History of Christianity, III: Early Mediēval Christianities, c. 600–c. 1100*, edited by Thomas F. X. Noble and Julia M. H. Smith. 399–415, 736–47. Cambridge: Cambridge University Press, 2008.
Meyvaert, Paul. "The Book of Kells and Iona." *Art Bulletin* 71, no. 1 (1989): 6–19.
Miller, D. A. "Hitchcock's Hidden Pictures." *Critical Inquiry* 37, no. 1 (2010): 106–30.
Mize, Britt. "Manipulations of the Mind-as-Container Motif in *Beowulf*, *Homiletic Fragment II*, and Alfred's Metrical Epilogue to the *Pastoral Care*." *JEGP* 107 (2008): 25–56.
———. "The Representation of the Mind as an Enclosure in Old English Poetry." *ASE* 35 (2006): 57–90.
———. *Traditional Subjectivities: The Old English Poetics of Mentality.* Toronto: University of Toronto Press, 2013.

Molyneaux, George. *The Formation of the English Kingdom in the Tenth Century*. Oxford: Oxford University Press, 2015.
Murphy, Patrick J. *Unriddling the Exeter Riddles*. University Park: Pennsylvania State University Press, 2011.
Niles, John D. *Old English Enigmatic Poems and the Play of the Texts*. Studies in the Early Middle Ages 13. Turnhout: Brepols, 2006.
Nuttall, A. D. *Overheard by God: Fiction and Prayer in Herbert, Milton, Dante and St John*. New York: Methuen, 1980.
Oakley, Thomas Pollock. *English Penitential Discipline and Anglo-Saxon Law in Their Joint Influence*. Studies in History, Economics and Public Law 107. New York: Columbia University Press, 1923.
O'Brien, Bruce R. "From *Morðor* to *Murdrum*: The Preconquest Origin and Norman Revival of the Murder Fine." *Speculum* 71, no. 2 (1996): 321–57.
O'Brien O'Keeffe, Katherine. "Body and Law in Late Anglo-Saxon England." *ASE* 27 (1998): 209–32.
———. *Stealing Obedience: Narratives of Agency and Identity in Later Anglo-Saxon England*. Toronto: University of Toronto Press, 2012.
———. "Writing Community: Osbern and the Negotiations of Identity in the *Miracula S. Dunstani*." In *Latinity and Identity in Anglo-Saxon Literature*, edited by Rebecca Stephenson and Emily V. Thornbury. 202–18. Toronto: University of Toronto Press, 2016.
Ó Carragáin, Éamonn. "Cynewulf's Epilogue to *Elene* and the Tastes of the Vercelli Compiler: A Paradigm of Meditative Reading." In *Lexis and Texts in Early English: Studies Presented to Jane Roberts*, edited by Christian J. Kay and Louise M. Sylvester. 187–201. Amsterdam: Rodopi, 2001.
———. "The Term *Porticus* and *Imitatio Romae* in Early Anglo-Saxon England." In *Text and Gloss: Studies in Insular Learning and Literature Presented to Joseph Donovan Pheifer*, edited by Helen Conrad-O'Briain, Anne-Marie D'Arcy, and John Scattergood. 13–34. Dublin: Four Courts Press, 1999.
Orchard, Andy. "Enigma Variations: The Anglo-Saxon Riddle-Tradition." In *Latin Learning and English Lore: Studies in Anglo-Saxon Literature for Michael Lapidge*, edited by Katherine O'Brien O'Keeffe and Andy Orchard. 284–304. Toronto: University of Toronto Press, 2005.
———. *The Poetic Art of Aldhelm*. Cambridge: Cambridge University Press, 1994.
———. *Pride and Prodigies: Studies in the Monsters of the "Beowulf"-Manuscript*. Cambridge: D. S. Brewer, 1995.
Parkes, M. B. "*Rædan, areccan, smeagan*: How the Anglo-Saxons Read." *ASE* 26 (1997): 1–22.
Parsons, David. *Books and Buildings: Architectural Description Before and After Bede*. Jarrow Lecture. Jarrow: Jarrow Parish Council, 1987. Reprinted in Michael Lapidge, ed., *Bede and His World*, 2 vols. (Aldershot, UK: Variorum, 1994), 2:729–74.
Pelteret, David A. E. *Slavery in Early Mediaeval England: From the Reign of Alfred until the Twelfth Century*. Woodbridge, Suffolk: Boydell Press, 1995, reprint 2001.
Pestell, Tim. *Landscapes of Monastic Foundation: The Establishment of Religious Houses in East Anglia c. 650–1200*. Anglo-Saxon Studies 5. Woodbridge, Suffolk: Boydell Press, 2004.
Picard, Jean-Michel. "Bede, Adomnán, and the Writing of History." *Peritia* 3 (1984): 50–70.
———. "The Purpose of Adomnán's *Vita Columbae*." *Peritia* 1 (1982): 160–77.
Pirsig, Robert M. *Zen and the Art of Motorcycle Maintenance: An Inquiry into Values*. New York: Perennial, 2000.
Pollock, Frederick, and Frederic William Maitland. *The History of English Law Before the Time of Edward I*. 2nd ed. 2 vols. London: Cambridge University Press, 1923.
Poschmann, Bernhard. *Die abendländische Kirchenbusse im Ausgang des christlichen Altertums*. Munich: Kösel & Pustet, 1928.

———. *Die abendländische Kirchenbusse im frühen Mittelalter.* Breslauer Studien zur historischen Theologie 16. Breslau: Müller und Geiffert, 1930.
Pratt, David. "The Illnesses of King Alfred the Great." *ASE* 30 (2001): 39–90.
Quirk, R. N. "Winchester Cathedral in the Tenth Century." *Archaeological Journal* 114 (1957): 28–68.
Rabin, Andrew. "Capital Punishment and the Anglo-Saxon Judicial Apparatus: A Maximum View?" In *Capital and Corporeal Punishment in Anglo-Saxon England*, edited by Jay Paul Gates and Nicole Marafioti. 181–200. Woodbridge, Suffolk: Boydell Press, 2014.
———. "Ritual Magic or Legal Performance? Reconsidering an Old English Charm Against Theft." In *English Law Before Magna Carta: Felix Liebermann and "Die Gesetze der Angelsachsen,"* edited by Stefan Jurasinski, Lisi Oliver, and Andrew Rabin. 177–95. Leiden: Brill, 2010.
———. "Testimony and Authority in Old English Law: Writing the Subject in the 'Fonthill Letter.'" In *Law and Sovereignty in the Middle Ages and the Renaissance*, edited by Robert S. Sturges. 153–71. Turnhout: Brepols, 2011.
Rauer, Christine. *Beowulf and the Dragon: Parallels and Analogues.* Cambridge: D. S. Brewer, 2000.
Reynolds, Andrew. *Anglo-Saxon Deviant Burial Customs.* Oxford: Oxford University Press, 2009.
Riché, Pierre. *Education and Culture in the Barbarian West: From the Sixth through Eighth Century.* Translated by John J. Contreni. Columbia: University of South Carolina Press, 1976.
Ricoeur, Paul. *Freud and Philosophy: An Essay on Interpretation.* Translated by Denis Savage. New Haven, CT: Yale University Press, 1970.
Rigg, A. G., and G. R. Wieland. "A Canterbury Classbook of the Mid-Eleventh Century (the "Cambridge Songs" Manuscript)." *ASE* 4 (1975): 113–30.
Rix, Helmut. *Die Termini der Unfreiheit in den Sprachen Altitaliens.* Stuttgart: Steiner, 1994.
Roberts, Jane. "What Did Anglo-Saxon Seals Seal When?" In *The Power of Words: Essays in Lexicography, Lexicology and Semantics in Honour of Christian J. Kay*, edited by Graham D. Caie, Carole Hough, and Irené Wotherspoon. 131–57. Amsterdam: Rodopi, 2006.
Robertson, D. W., Jr. "The Cultural Tradition of *Handlyng Synne*." *Speculum* 22, no. 2 (1947): 162–85.
Robins, William Randolph. "Ancient Romance and Medieval Literary Genres: *Apollonius of Tyre*." PhD diss., Princeton University, 1995.
Rollason, D. W. "Relic-Cults as an Instrument of Royal Policy c. 900–c. 1050." *ASE* 15 (1986): 91–104.
Rubenstein, Jay. "The Life and Writings of Osbern of Canterbury." In *Canterbury and the Norman Conquest: Churches, Saints and Scholars, 1066–1109*, edited by Richard Eales and Richard Sharpe. 27–40. London: Hambledon Press, 1995.
Rudolf, Winfried. "Riddling and Reading: Iconicity and Logographs in Exeter Book *Riddles* 23 and 45." *Anglia* 130, no. 4 (2012): 499–525.
Runlon-Miller, Nina. "Sexual Humor and Fettered Desire in Exeter Book Riddle 12." In *Humor in Anglo-Saxon Literature*, edited by Jonathan Wilcox. 99–126. Cambridge: D. S. Brewer, 2000.
Saltzman, Benjamin A. "Hermeneutics and the Medieval Horizon: Zumthor, Jauss, Barthes, and Gadamer." In *Thinking of the Middle Ages: Postwar Scholarship and the Medieval*, edited by R. D. Perry and Benjamin A. Saltzman. (Cambridge: Cambridge University Press, forthcoming).
———. "The Mind, Perception and the Reflexivity of Forgetting in Alfred's *Pastoral Care*." *ASE* 42 (2013): 147–82.
———. "Secrecy and the Hermeneutic Potential in *Beowulf*." *PMLA* 133, no. 1 (2018): 36–55.
———. "*Vt hkskdkxt*: Early Medieval Cryptography, Textual Errors, and Scribal Agency." *Speculum* 94, no. 4 (2019): 975–1009.

———. "Writing Friendship, Mourning the Friend in Late Anglo-Saxon *Rules of Confraternity.*" *JMEMS* 41, no. 2 (2011): 251–91.
Salvador-Bello, Mercedes. *Isidorean Perceptions of Order: The Exeter Book Riddles and Medieval Latin Enigmata.* Morgantown: West Virginia University Press, 2015.
———. "The Key to the Body: Unlocking Riddles 42–46." In *Naked Before God: Uncovering the Body in Anglo-Saxon England,* edited by Benjamin C. Withers and Jonathan Wilcox. 60–96. Morgantown: West Virginia University Press, 2003.
———. "Patterns of Compilation in Anglo-Latin *Enigmata* and the Evidence of a Source-Collection in Riddles 1–40 of the *Exeter Book.*" *Viator* 43, no. 1 (2012): 339–74.
Scattergood, John. "Eating the Book: *Riddle 47* and Memory." In *Text and Gloss: Studies in Insular Learning and Literature Presented to Joseph Donovan Pheifer,* edited by Helen Conrad-O'Briain, Anne-Marie D'Arcy, and John Scattergood. 119–27. Dublin: Four Courts Press, 1999.
Schleiermacher, Friedrich. *Hermeneutics and Criticism: And Other Writings.* Edited and translated by Andrew Bowie. Cambridge Texts in the History of Philosophy. Cambridge: Cambridge University Press, 1998.
Schmitt, Carl. *Political Theology: Four Chapters on the Concept of Sovereignty.* Translated by George Schwab. Chicago: University of Chicago Press, 2005.
Schwyter, J. R. *Old English Legal Language: The Lexical Field of Theft.* Odense: Odense University Press, 1996.
Scragg, Donald. "Exeter Book." In *The Wiley Blackwell Encyclopedia of Anglo-Saxon England,* 2nd ed., edited by Michael Lapidge, John Blair, Simon Keynes, and Donald Scragg. 183–84. Malden, MA: John Wiley & Sons, 2014.
Sharpe, Richard. *Medieval Irish Saints' Lives: An Introduction to "Vitae Sanctorum Hiberniae."* Oxford: Clarendon Press, 1991.
Simmel, Georg. "The Sociology of Secrecy and of Secret Societies." *American Journal of Sociology* 11, no. 4 (1906): 441–98.
Simpson, James. "Faith and Hermeneutics: Pragmatism Versus Pragmatism." *JMEMS* 33, no. 2 (2003): 215–39.
Sims-Williams, Patrick. *Religion and Literature in Western England, 600–800.* CSASE 3. Cambridge: Cambridge University Press, 1990.
Smith, Scott Thompson. *Land and Book: Literature and Land Tenure in Anglo-Saxon England.* Toronto: University of Toronto Press, 2012.
———. "Of Kings and Cattle Thieves: Rhetorical Work of the Fonthill Letter." *JEGP* 106, no. 4 (2007): 447–67.
Stancliffe, Clare. "Cuthbert and the Polarity Between Pastor and Solitary." In *St Cuthbert, His Cult and His Community to A.D. 1200,* edited by Gerald Bonner, Clare Stancliffe, and David Rollason. 21–44. Woodbridge, Suffolk: Boydell Press, 1989.
Stanley, E. G. "Rev. of *The Old English* Apollonius of Tyre, by Peter Goolden." *Modern Language Review* 55, no. 3 (1960): 428.
Stepsis, Robert, and Richard Rand. "Contrast and Conversion in Cynewulf's *Elene.*" *Neuphilologische Mitteilungen* 70, no. 2 (1969): 273–82.
Stewart, Ann Harleman. "The Solution to the Old English Riddle 4." *Studies in Philology* 78 (1981): 52–61.
Stork, Nancy Porter. "A Spanish Bishop Remembers the Future: Oral Traditions and Purgatory in Julian of Toledo." *Oral Tradition* 23, no. 1 (2008): 43–70.
———. *Through a Gloss Darkly: Aldhelm's Riddles in the British Library MS Royal 12.C.xxiii.* PIMS Studies and Texts 98. Toronto: Pontifical Institute of Mediaeval Studies, 1990.
Straw, Carole. *Gregory the Great: Perfection in Imperfection.* Berkeley: University of California Press, 1988.
Sweet, Henry. *Sweet's Anglo-Saxon Reader in Prose and Verse.* Revised by Dorothy Whitelock. Oxford: Clarendon Press, 1967.
Symons, Victoria. *Runes and Roman Letters in Anglo-Saxon Manuscripts.* Berlin: Walter de Gruyter, 2016.

Taylor, H. M. "The Architectural Interest of Æthelwulf's *De abbatibus*." *ASE* 3 (1974): 163–73.
Thacker, Alan. "Lindisfarne and the Origins of the Cult of St Cuthbert." In *St Cuthbert, His Cult and His Community to A.D. 1200*, edited by Gerald Bonner, Clare Stancliffe, and David Rollason. 103–22. Woodbridge, Suffolk: Boydell Press, 1989.
Thomas, Daniel. "Incarceration as Judicial Punishment in Anglo-Saxon England." In *Capital and Corporal Punishment in Anglo-Saxon England*, edited by Jay Paul Gates and Nicole Marafioti. 92–112. Woodbridge, Suffolk: Boydell Press, 2014.
Thomas, Kate Heulwen. "The Meaning, Practice and Context of Private Prayer in Late Anglo-Saxon England." PhD diss., University of York, 2011.
Thompson, Victoria. *Dying and Death in Later Anglo-Saxon England*. Anglo-Saxon Studies 4. Woodbridge, Suffolk: Boydell Press, 2004.
Thornbury, Emily V. "Aldhelm's Rejection of the Muses and the Mechanics of Poetic Inspiration in Early Anglo-Saxon England." *ASE* 36 (2007): 71–92.
———. *Becoming a Poet in Anglo-Saxon England*. CSML. Cambridge: Cambridge University Press, 2014.
Townsend, David. "The Naked Truth of the King's Affection in the Old English *Apollonius of Tyre*." *JMEMS* 34, no. 1 (2004): 173–95.
Tupper, Frederick, Jr. "Riddles of the Bede Tradition." *Modern Philology* 2 (1904–5): 561–72.
Urban, Hugh B. "The Adornment of Silence: Secrecy and Symbolic Power in American Freemasonry." *Journal of Religion and Society* 3 (2001): 1–29.
Van Dam, Raymond. "Merovingian Gaul and the Frankish Conquests." In *The New Cambridge Medieval History*, vol. 1, *c. 500–c. 700*, edited by Paul Fouracre. 193–231. Cambridge: Cambridge University Press, 2005.
Vogel, Cyrille. *Le pécheur et la pénitence au moyen âge*. Paris: Éditions du Cerf, 1969.
Wallis, Faith. *Bede and Wisdom*. Jarrow Lecture. Jarrow: Jarrow Parish Council, 2016.
Watson, David F. *Honor Among Christians: The Cultural Key to the Messianic Secret*. Minneapolis, MN: Fortress Press, 2010.
Wehlau, Ruth. "The Power of Knowledge and the Location of the Reader in *Christ and Satan*." In *The Poems of MS Junius 11: Basic Readings*, edited by R. M. Liuzza. 287–301. New York: Routledge, 2002.
Whatley, Gordon E. "The Figure of Constantine the Great in Cynewulf's *Elene*." *Traditio* 37 (1981): 161–202.
Whitbread, L. "MS. C.C.C.C. 201: A Note on Its Character and Provenance." *Philological Quarterly* 38 (1959): 106–12.
Whitelock, Dorothy. "The Prose of Alfred's Reign." In *Continuations and Beginnings: Studies in Old English Literature*, edited by Eric G. Stanley. London: Nelson, 1966.
Whitman, James Q. *The Origins of Reasonable Doubt: Theological Roots of the Criminal Trial*. New Haven, CT: Yale University Press, 2008.
Wieland, Gernot R. "The Glossed Manuscript: Classbook or Library Book?" *ASE* 14 (1985): 153–73.
Williams, Ann. "Introduction." In *Kingship, Legislation and Power in Anglo-Saxon England*, edited by Gale R. Owen-Crocker and Brian W. Schneider. 1–14. Woodbridge, Suffolk: Boydell Press, 2013.
Williamson, Craig. *A Feast of Creatures: Anglo-Saxon Riddle-Songs*. Philadelphia: University of Pennsylvania Press, 1982.
Wilmart, André. "Ève et Goscelin (II)." *Revue Bénédictine* 50 (1938): 42–83.
Wolfson, Elliot R. "Introduction." In *Rending the Veil: Concealment and Secrecy in the History of Religions*, edited by Elliot R. Wolfson. 1–10. New York: Seven Bridges Press, 1999.
Wormald, Patrick. "Giving God and King Their Due: Conflict and Its Regulation in the Early English State." In *Legal Culture in the Early Medieval West*, by Patrick Wormald. London: Hambledon Press, 1999.
———. *The Making of English Law: King Alfred to the Twelfth Century*. Vol. 1. Oxford: Blackwell, 1999.

———. *Papers Preparatory to The Making of English Law: King Alfred to the Twelfth Century.* Vol. 2, *From God's Law to Common Law*. Edited by Stephen Baxter and John Hudson. London: University of London, 2014.

Wyatt, A. J. *An Anglo-Saxon Reader.* Cambridge: Cambridge University Press, 1919.

Wyatt, David. *Slaves and Warriors in Medieval Britain and Ireland, 800–1200.* Leiden: Brill, 2009.

Yorke, Barbara. "The Burial of Kings in Anglo-Saxon England." In *Kingship, Legislation and Power in Anglo-Saxon England*, edited by Gale R. Owen-Crocker and Brian W. Schneider. 237–57. Woodbridge, Suffolk: Boydell Press, 2013.

Zumthor, Paul. *Parler du moyen age.* Paris: Les Éditions de Minuit, 1980.

———. *Speaking of the Middle Ages.* Translated by Sarah White. Lincoln: University of Nebraska Press, 1986.

Zweck, Jordan. "Silence in the Exeter Book Riddles." *Exemplaria* 28, no. 4 (2016): 319–36.

Index

Abbo of Fleury: *Passio Sancti Edmundi*, 272 n.79
abbot, role of, 8, 9, 70, 72–73, 77, 80, 137
Abel (OT), 11–12, 199
Abraham (OT), 41–42, 281 n.5
Acca, bishop of Hexham, 149
Adam (OT), 1–3, 6, 11–12, 145, 203
Adelbert of Egmond, 75
Adelphus Adelpha, 238, 243
Adomnán of Iona: *De locis sanctis*, 111; *Vita Sancti Columbae*, 111, 128–35, 138–39, 142, 145–46, 149, 152–53; *Vita Sancti Columbae* (relation to *Vita Sancti Cuthberti*), 281 n.17
adultery, 41–43, 138, 178, 261, 271 n.53, 273 n.91
Æbbe, abbess of Coldingham, 125
Ædiluulf: *De abbatibus*, 111, 115–16, 136–37, 139
Ægelward (monk at Canterbury), 82–85, 87–89, 93–96, 104, 247
Ælberht, archbishop of York, 98
Ælfflæd of Whitby, 149
Ælfheah, archbishop of Canterbury, bishop of Winchester, 116, 118–20
Ælfric (son of Æscwyn), 25
Ælfric of Eynsham, 71, 275 n.23, 283 n.40, 284 n.64; Assmann hom. **4**, 27, 264 n.25; *CH* I.**1**, 277 n.74; *CH* I.**8**, 96; *CH* I.**24**, 140; *CH* I.**33**, 80; *CH* I.**36**, 139–40; *CH* II.**10**, 75, 80–81, 125, 127–28, 149–50; *CH* II.**18**, 292 n.41; *Grammar*, 180, 287 n.17; Irvine hom. **2** (on a servant's failure to forgive), 80, 271 n.53; Letter to the Monks of Eynsham, 111; Letter to Wulfgeat, 29, 258 n.44; *Life of Saint Basil*, 268 n.19, 272 n.89; *LS* I.**2**, 164; *LS* II.**31**, 103; *Suppl.* hom. **11**, 96, 299 n.87; *Vita Sancti Æthelwoldi*, 272 n.77
Ælfstan, abbot of Old Minster, Winchester, 25, 89–91, 105, 149–50
Ælfwine, abbot of New Minster, Winchester, 277 n.71
Ælfwine's Prayerbook, 107–9
aenigmata. *See* riddles, Latin; *Riddles* (Exeter Book)

Æschere (in *Beowulf*), 164–65
Æscwyn (widow of Ælfhere), 25
Æthelberht, king of Kent, 24, 111–12. *See also under* legislation, Anglo-Saxon
Æthelred, king of Mercia, 31. *See also under* legislation, Anglo-Saxon
Æthelstan, king of Wessex, 8, 36, 256 n.1. *See also under* legislation, Anglo-Saxon
Æthelwold, bishop of Winchester, 25, 88–92, 95, 108, 116–20, 149–50, 268 n.23, 270 n.46, 277 n.67
Agamben, Giorgio, 257 n.6, 267 n.4
Aidan, bishop of Lindisfarne, 98–99
Alcuin of York: as reader of Aldhelm, 206, 240, 295 n.110; *Carmina*, 295 n.110; *De psalmorum usu*, 277 n.74; *De virtutibus et vitiis*, 96, 276 n.60; *Disputatio Pippini*, 203–6, 217–18, 240; *Dogmata ad Carolum Imperatorem*, 238, 242, 301 n.125; *Enchiridion*, 300 n.117; *Epistolae*, 96, 109, 276 n.60; *Epitaphium Alchuuini*, 240, 242; *Liber Sacramentorum*, 277 n.61; prayer book (Waldhoff), 107; *Versus de patribus regibus et sanctis Euboricensis ecclesiae* (York Poem), 110–11, 295 n.110
Aldfrith, king of Northumbria, 299 n.106
Aldhelm of Malmesbury, bishop of Sherborne, 267 n.1, 272 n.89; *Aenigmata*, 14, 26, 168–69, 176, 184–85, 197–99, 205–8, 211–14, 218–26, 232, 237–39, 242, 290 n.65; *Aenigm*. pref., 198, 207–8, 218; *Aenigm*. prose prologue, 197–99; *Aenigm*. **2**, 171; *Aenigm*. **22**, 295 n.110; *Aenigm*. **28**, 169; *Aenigm*. **33**, 221, 288 n.40; *Aenigm*. **42**, 169; *Aenigm*. **62**, 295 n.110; *Aenigm*. **65**, 26–27; *Aenigm*. **81**, 218, 225; *Aenigm*. **82**, 281 n.11; *Aenigm*. **83**, 173; *Aenigm*. **88**, 138; *Aenigm*. **89**, 221; *Aenigm*. **97**, 27; *Aenigm*. **100**, 213–29, 288 n.40; *De metris*, 198, 293 n.72; *De pedum regulis*, 198, 293 n.72; *Epistola ad Acircium*, 293 n.72, 299 n.106; *Epistola ad Heahfrith*, 296 n.30; *Prosa de uirginitate*, 226, 253, 297 n.45

Alexander the hermit, 59–60
Alfred the Great, king of Wessex, 8, 24, 25–26, 36, 52; *Pastoral Care*, 74, 147, 255 n.13, 263 n.13, 284 n.65; *Prose Translation of the First Fifty Psalms*, 11. See also *Boethius* (OE); *Soliloquies* (OE); *under* legislation, Anglo-Saxon
allegory, 49, 109, 199, 246, 295 n.112
Ammon (in the *Vita Sancti Antonii*), 149
Ananias (NT), 153
anchoretism. *See* monasticism, eremitic
Andreas, 275 n.33
Andrew, St., *porticus* of (Glastonbury), 116–17
anger. *See under* emotion
Anonymous of Lindisfarne: knowledge of *Vita Sancti Columbae*, 281 n.17; *Vita Sancti Cuthberti*, 98, 125–28, 139, 150–53, 155, 267 n.1, 268 n.18
Anonymous of Whitby, *Vita Sancti Gregorii*, 285 n.111
Anselm of Canterbury, 108, 155–58, 190–91, 250; *Monologion*, 297 n.40; *Proslogion*, 202, 250, 283 n.58
Antiochus (in *Apollonius of Tyre*), 161–67, 171, 178, 181, 212, 290 n.60
Antony, St., 138–39, 273 nn.93–94
Antwerp-London glossaries, 164
Apollonius of Tyre (OE), 13, 161–71, 176, 178, 181–82, 212
Arator, 212
Arbiter. *See under* judgment
architecture, 6, 12; of Anglo-Saxon churches, 9, 110–22; of the heart, 122–23
Aristotle: *Metaphysics*, 205
Arno of Salzburg, 300 n.117
arson, 33–34
Asser: *Life of King Alfred*, 25–26
Athanasius: *Vita Beati Antonii*, 149, 273 nn.93–94
Augsburg (Germany), 52
Augustine of Canterbury, 111–13, 267 n.1, 276 n.47, 276 n.59
Augustine of Hippo, 140, 252, 276 n.59, 285 n.110, 301 n.122; *Confessiones*, 225, 297 n.53; *De ciuitate Dei*, 166; *De cura pro mortuis gerenda*, 284 n.64; *De diuersis quaestionibus ad Simplicianum*, 200; *De doctrina Christiana*, 198, 284 n.67; *Enarrationes in Psalmos*, 200, 294 n.88; *Epistola* **137**, 203; *Epistola ad Consentium*, 201–3; *Sermones*, 271 n.53; *Soliloquia*, 283 n.54
Austen, Jane: *Emma*, 301 n.1

B.: *Vita Sancti Dunstani*, 107–8
Bald: *Leechbook*, 298 n.73
Barking Abbey, nuns of, 297 n.45
Basil of Caesarea, 76, 78, 81, 267 n.4, 272 n.89; *Asceticon parvum*, 78, 267 n.11, 270 n.40, 272 n.89: *Homiliae in Hexaemeron*, 272 n.89; *Homiliae in Psalmos*, 272 n.89; *Regulae fusius tractatae*, 72, 92, 272 n.89; *Sermo asceticus*, 91–92, 272 n.89
Beccel (disciple of St. Guthlac), 102, 149
Bede, monk of Monkwearmouth and Jarrow, 7, 70–71, 111, 267 n.1, 272 n.89, 284 n.64, 285 n.110; knowledge of *Vita Sancti Columbae*, 281 n.17; on wisdom, 297 n.60; *De die iudicii*, 234, 238–40, 243; *De natura rerum*, 171, 290 n.57, 295 n.112, 299 n.90; *De schematibus et tropiis*, 198; *De temporum ratione*, 217; *Explanatio Apocalypsis*, 200; *Expositio Actuum apostolorum*, 138; *Historia ecclesiastica*, 98, 113, 125, 149, 268 n.32, 274 n.10, 296 n.23; *Homiliarum euangelii*, 48–49, 109, 151–53; *In Genesim*, 2–4, 11–12; *In Lucae euangelium expositio*, 271 n.53; *Vita Ceolfridi*, 110; *Vita Sancti Cuthberti* (metrical), 125–28, 138–39, 150–51, 153–54; *Vita Sancti Cuthberti* (prose), 74–75, 81, 98–99, 125–28, 138–39, 148–51, 153–54, 269 n.33, 273 n.93, 274 n.9, 275 n.24
Bede, Pseudo-: *aenigmata* (*Joca-seria*), 212–13, 238, 243, 296 n.14; *Collectanea*, 81, 199, 202–3, 255 n.10, 290 n.65
Behemoth (OT), 208, 227
belief. *See* faith
Bellman, Beryl L., 256 n.25
Benedict of Aniane, 108
Benedict of Nursia, 76, 79, 142–45, 149, 154, 273 n. 93. See also *Regula Sancti Benedicti*
Benedictine Reform, 70–71, 75, 78, 82, 91–92, 104–5, 108–9, 116, 122, 135, 272 n.81, 276 n.50, 277 n.67, 286 n.115
Bentham, Jeremy, 6–7, 22
Beowulf, 27, 49, 164–65, 246, 262 n.98, 266 n.54, 275 n.26, 298 n.73, 298 n.79
Berchán (in Adomnán's *Vita Sancti Columbae*), 133–34, 137–38, 149
Bernard of Clairvaux: *De gradibus humilitatis et superbiae*, 226
Bertha, wife of King Æthelberht of Kent, 111
Bible, 186, 198, 202–3; Gen. **3:1**, 138; Gen. **3:8**, 1; Gen. **4:8**, 11–12, 96–97, 127, 247; Exod. **20:16**, 256 n.1; Judges **9:8**, 199; 3 Kings **7:23**, 268 n.30; Job **13:10**, 280 n.123; Job

13:17, 198; Job 38–40, 211; Ps. 9:29–31, 12; Ps. 21:7, 227; Ps. 67:14, 198; Ps. 68:6, 107; Ps. 96, 198; Ps. 118:13, 143; Ps. 136:9, 73, 268 n.28; Ps. 142:1, 49; Ps. 142:4, 49; Ps. 140:1, 200; Prov. 1:6, 198; Prov. 11:2, 226; Ecclus. 10:15, 226; Sir. 20:7, 255 n.11; Ez. 17:2, 198; Matt. 5:14, 153; Matt. 6:20, 150; Matt. 6:6, 95, 100, 106, 123–24; Matt. 7:7, 280 n.119; Matt. 8:4, 150; Matt. 9:27–30, 150–51, 155; Matt. 9:31, 151, 157; Matt. 16:19, 181; Matt. 17:1–9, 150–51; Matt. 18:15–16, 76–77, 79, 85, 93; Matt. 27:66, 48; Mark 1:41–45, 150; Mark 7:31–37, 150–51, 155; Mark 8:30, 150; Mark 9:2–8, 150; Luke 2:24, 109; Luke 3:22, 198; Luke 5:14, 150; Luke 5:36–39, 285 n.100; Luke 8:56, 150; Luke 9:21, 150; Luke 9:28–36, 150; Luke 11:9, 280 n.119; Luke 14:11, 228; John 14:6, 21; Acts 4:32, 69; Acts 5:3, 138; Acts 16:26–30, 171; Rom. 11:33, 143; 1 Cor. 2:11, 143; 1 Cor. 6:17, 143, 145; 1 Cor. 8:1, 225–26; 1 Cor. 13:12, 200; 2 Cor. 12:4, 146; Galatians 2:19, 70; Phil. 2:12, 126; 1 Thess. 5:2, 28; 1 John 1:9, 268 n.30; Apoc. 6:12, 8:5, 11:13, 11:19, 16:18, 233–34; Apoc. 16:15, 28

Biblical Commentaries, Canterbury, 272 n.89
Bibliotheca magnifica, 212–13, 238, 243, 296 n.14
Blickling Homilies: hom. **4**, 74, 86; hom. **5**, 50; hom. **10**, 240; hom. **11**, 28; hom. **14**, 142; hom. **19**, 288 n.32
body, 4–5, 12, 40–43, 89, 130, 144–45, 147, 180, 232, 234–36, 265 n.33, 273 n.94; as corpse, 30, 47, 50–52, 59–60, 229; decomposition of, 228–30
Boethius: *Philosophiae consolatio*, 212, 256 n.27
Boethius (OE), 256 n.27
Bok, Sissela, 11, 253, 256 n.23
bonds: of the devil, 87–89; loosing of (*soluere*), 13, 208; of foliage, 1–2; of knowledge, 195; metaphors of, 5, 13, 161, 169, 171, 175; of the mind, 4–5, 13, 48, 247; of riddles, 167, 175–83; of secrecy, 6, 59, 87–89; of servitude, 13, 161–75; of sin, 9, 67, 92, 181, 195, 208, 273 n.91
Boniface: *Aenigmata*, 212–13, 226, 228, 238, 242, 298 n.66; *Epistolae*, 75, 268 n.16
Bourdieu, Pierre, 255 n.7
Brixworth (Mercia), Church of All Saints, 115–16
Bromley, estate of, 25
Burton-on-Trent, monastery of, 289 n.43
Byrhtferth of Ramsey: *Enchiridion*, 102
Byrhtwaru (Ælfric's widow), 25

Cain (OT), 11–12, 96–97, 127, 247
callidus explorator, 128–29, 132, 134, 138, 282 n.28
Camden, William: *Britannia*, 265 n.44
Canterbury: Christ Church, 272 n.70; Church of Saint Martin, 111–12; Church of Saint Pancras, 112–16, 122; Church of Saint Peter and Saint Paul, 113–15; monastic center of, 1, 70, 108, 111–15, 299 n.106; Saint Augustine's Abbey, 1, 107, 112–15, 276 n.47
Capitula notitiarum, 270 n.46
cardiocentrism. *See* mind, cardiocentric model of
caritas, 79, 145, 225
Cassian, John, 72, 76, 81, 91, 273 n.93; *Conlationes*, 9, 65–68, 72, 85–86, 89, 100–101, 123, 273 n.93; *De institutis*, 73, 267 n.11, 269 n.28
Cassiodorus: *Expositio psalmorum*, 198
Cato, Pseudo-. See *Disticha Catonis*; *Epistola Catonis*
Ceolfrith, abbot of Monkwearmouth-Jarrow, 110
Chad, bishop of Lichfield, 97–99, 149, 274 n.9
Charlemagne, 107, 203, 258 n.42
charms (OE), 28–29
charters, 23; Sawyer no. **1457**, 25
Christ, 72–73, 106, 122, 155, 157, 239, 291 n.4; abbot in role of, 67, 80; crucifixion of, 28, 191–92; healing the sick, 150–51, 155, 157; as mediator of secrets, 12–13, 80; as model for saintly behavior, 149; resurrection of, 48–50, 59
Christ III, 27, 234–35, 237, 240, 301 n.123
Cicero, 285 n.110
circa (monastic occupation), 9, 69, 78–80, 135
Clovis, king of the Salian Franks, 258 n.42
Cnut, king of England, 8, 23–24, 31, 36. *See also under* legislation, Anglo-Saxon
Codex Iuris Uplandici, 52–53
Codex Theodosianus, 55
Colcu (in Adomnán's *Vita Sancti Columbae*), 132–34
Coldingham, monastery of, 125, 136
Columba, St., 13, 128–39, 142, 145–46, 149, 152–53
Columbanus, 77–78, 80, 91; *Regula coenobialis*, 76, 93; *Regula monachorum*, 76; *Versus de bonis moribus observandis*, 238, 242
Colyton code. *See* legislation, Anglo-Saxon, III Edmund

confession: legal, 41, 255 n.14, 259 n.63, 263 n.7; spiritual, 8–9, 58–59, 65–69, 72–89, 93–96, 107, 127, 130, 134–36, 148, 156, 239, 268 n.23, 269 n.29, 269 n.32, 273 n.1, 273 n.93, 276 n.60, 279 n.100
Consentius, 201, 203
Consiliatio Cnutii III, 260 n.74
Constantine, Emperor, 14, 185, 187
corpse. *See* body; death
Council of Mainz (852), 271 n.53
counterfeiting, 39–40, 44
Creation, 184, 205, 211–14, 219, 222–27, 232–33, 238, 241
crime, 29–43; *botleas*, 31; of concealment, 8–9, 12, 19–20, 23, 26–34, 39, 42–43, 60, 91; complicity in, 38, 76, 58; concealment of, 22–23, 40, 59, 81, 162, 165; crucifixion as, 188; of the heart, 239; open, 20, 30–31; as opposed to wrong, 24
Cross, True, 14, 185–97
cryptography, 214, 217–20, 223
cryptonymy, 266 n.66
crypts. *See* graves
curiosity, 126, 253
Cuthbert, St., 13, 71, 74–75, 80–81, 95, 98–100, 104, 125–28, 130–32, 135–36, 138–39, 142, 148–55, 202, 273 n.93
Cynewulf: *Christ II*, 275 n.33; *Elene*, 14, 49, 185–97, 201–4, 207, 236, 248, 275 n.33; *Elene* (Latin source), 291 n.1; *Fates of the Apostles*, 236–37; *Juliana*, 235–36; signatures, 14, 185, 194–97, 235–37

Dante Alighieri, 301 n.4
David (OT), 143, 208, 211
Day of Judgment. *See* judgment, Last Judgment
de Certeau, Michel, 248
death: as absolute form of secrecy, 9, 47–51, 163–65, 186, 228–32, 247; civil, 57, 70; of a saint, 126, 148–58; as secret, 27–28, 47–51; as thief, 27–28
death penalty, 29, 31, 37, 259 n. 48
Decretio Chlotharii regis, 261 n.83, 261 n.85
Deerhurst, Church of St. Mary, 111, 280 n.116
demoniacs, 5, 84, 89, 96, 247
demons, 5, 83–89, 96, 97, 99–101, 228, 247
deontology, 11
Derrida, Jacques, 20–21, 257 n.7, 263 n.13, 266 n.66
devil, 59, 74, 87–89, 92–93, 100–102, 138, 142, 227, 273 n.91, 300 n.114

didacticism, 4, 140, 161, 168, 184, 197–201, 217–18, 238 (*see also under* riddles)
Didymus Alexandrinus: *Liber de Spiritu Sancto*, 282 n.38
Dimetian Code (*Llyfr Blegywryd*), 52, 55
Dionysias (in *Apollonius of Tyre*), 163, 167, 171
discretio (monastic), 66–68, 72–73, 76, 79, 93, 269 n.35
disobedience, 57, 77, 90–92, 130, 134, 137, 139, 156–57
Disticha Catonis, 4, 197, 238, 242, 293 n.70
Donatus, Aelius: *Ars Maior*, 198
doubt, 44, 126, 128, 136–37, 139, 142, 156–58, 161, 191, 202, 205–6, 219, 222–24, 248
Dream of the Rood, The, 185
Dryhthelm (monk at Melrose), 98–99
Dunstan, St., 25, 84, 107–8, 116–17, 139, 274 n.16, 280 n.118

Eadfrith (teacher to Sigbald), 115–16
Eadmer of Canterbury: *Miracula Sancti Dunstani*, 82–83, 86–89; *Vita Sancti Anselmi*, 155–57; *Vita Sancti Dunstani*, 274 n.16; *Vita Sancti Oswaldi*, 135, 139, 155
Ecgberht, St. (hermit), 274 n.9
Ecgfrith, king of Northumbria, 149
Eden, 1–3
Edgar, king of England, 25–26. *See also under* legislation, Anglo-Saxon
Edmund, king of East Anglia, 24–25, 256 n.1, 272 n.79. *See also under* legislation, Anglo-Saxon
Edward the Confessor, king of England, 53
Edward the Elder, king of Wessex, 38. *See also under* legislation, Anglo-Saxon
Egils Saga, 30
Einstein, Albert, 225–26
Eirik, King, 30
Ekkehard of Saint Gall: *Casus Sancti Galli*, 270 n.48
Elene. *See under* Cynewulf
emotion: anger, 4; fear, 41–42, 130–33, 135–36, 271 n.53, 282 n.30
enigmata. *See* Riddles (Exeter Book); riddles, Latin
Enlightenment, the, 4, 6–7, 11, 251
epistemology: divine, 22, 74–75, 107, 125, 139–43, 146 (*see also* omniscience, divine); of faith, 185, 197; of interpretation, 190; legal, 34, 44, 45; political, 19–22, 23–26, 257 n. 22; of servitude, 162; testimonial, 20–21
Epistola Catonis, 238, 242, 293 n.70

Epitaphium Alchuuini, 240, 242
esoteric knowledge, 5, 255 n.14
ethics of secrecy. *See under* secrecy
Eusebius (Hwætberht): *Aenigmata*, 168, 176, 206, 212–13, 237–38, 242, 290 n.65; *Aenigm.* 1, 298 n.71; *Aenigm.* 2, 298 n.68; *Aenigm.* 3, 298 n.68; *Aenigm.* 8, 290 n.58; *Aenigm.* 27, 228; *Aenigm.* 32, 174, 231; *Aenigm.* 37, 173
Eva of Wilton, 12–13, 58
Evagrius: trans. of *Vita Beati Antonii*, 149, 273nn.93–94
Eve (OT), 1–2, 6, 11–12
Exeter Book, 4, 13, 27, 168–77, 180, 182, 205, 229–34, 237. *See also* Riddles (Exeter Book)
Exhilaratus of Montecassino, 146–47
Exodus, 180
Ezekiel (OT), 198

faith: Christian (as opposed to Jewish), 186, 191; in God, 6, 20–21, 41; in God's omniscience, 3, 22, 40–41, 67, 127, 161, 247; hermeneutics of (*see* interpretation, hermeneutics of faith); lack of, 11–12, 41–42, 128, 130, 134–35, 139, 149, 203 (*see also* doubt); in observing a saint, 126–28, 130, 134, 136–42, 156–57; psychology of, 3, 6, 126–39; in testimony, 20–21; and understanding, 141–42, 190–92, 201–4, 206, 250–51, 283 n.58, 294 n.102
family, as privy to secrets, 37
Farne Island, Northumbria, 98–99
Fawkham, estate of, 25
fear and trembling, 126, 130–31. *See also under* emotion
Felix: *Vita Sancti Guthlaci*, 9, 100, 146, 149
feud, 257 n.22
Fintan of Clonenagh: *Vita* of, 149, 282 n.30
Fleury, monastery of, 270 n.46
Fonthill Letter, 26, 52, 55
foreigners, secrecy associated with, 29, 259 n.48, 260 n.71
forgetting, completely reflexive form of, 263 n.13
Foucault, Michel, 7, 272 n.83
Fourth Lateran Council, 53, 270 n.50
Freud, Sigmund, 190–91

Gadamer, Hans-Georg, 190–91, 250–52, 292 n.35
Galba Prayerbook, 108
gaze. *See* vision
Gerald of Aurillac, 82

Germanus, bishop of Capua, 145–46, 154
Gildas: *De poenitentia*, 77, 80
Glastonbury: Beckery Chapel, 274 n.16; Ine's Church, 116; monastery of, 116–17, 274 n.16, 279 n.102
glosses, 14, 198, 207, 213–28, 237, 239. *See also* Antwerp-London glossaries; Leiden Glossary
Goscelin of Saint-Bertin: *Liber confortatorius*, 12–13, 58–60
Grágás, 30
grammatica, classical, 212
graves, 45–61, 84, 117, 163, 186, 189, 228–29, 234–35, 240, 245, 263 n.10, 263 n.13, 265 n.33, 266 n.66, 272 n.79, 274 n.16
Greek language, 47, 238, 243
Gregory the Great, 202–3, 285 n.110, 301 n.122; *Dialogi*, 79, 103–4, 106, 142–45, 149, 154, 263 n.15, 284 n.65; *Epistolae*, 284 n.65; *Homiliae in Hiezechihelem prophetam*, 202–3; *Moralia in Iob*, 2–4, 11, 81, 93, 248–49, 252–53, 280 n.123, 284 n.65; *porticus* of (Canterbury), 113; *Regula pastoralis*, 74, 147, 255 n.13, 263 n.13, 284 n.65; *Responsio* (to Augustine of Canterbury), 267 n.1
Gundoforus, King (in Goscelin of Saint-Bertin's *Liber confortatorius*), 59–60
Gundulf, bishop of Rochester, 271 n.64
Guthlac A, 9, 100, 275 n.33
Guthlac B, 9, 100–102, 275 n.33
Guthlac of Crowland, 9, 100–104, 146, 149

Hadrian, abbot of St. Augustine's Canterbury, 70, 89, 272 n.89, 299 n.106
hagiography, 9, 12–13, 26, 52, 69, 71, 82, 87, 98, 100–102, 124–25, 139, 149–60, 185, 247–48; and the obligation to announce the deeds of a saint, 154–58; writing process, 155–56
Handbook for the Confessor (OE), 107
harboring of criminals, 25, 36, 60, 247
heart, 4–5, 10, 12, 69–70, 97, 140, 189, 230, 239–40; secrets of, 12, 66–67, 70, 72–73, 75, 86–87, 107, 122–23, 148, 164, 193
Hebrew language, 191, 198, 238
Heidegger, Martin, 263 n.13
Helena, mother of Constantine, 14, 185
Helmstan. *See* Fonthill Letter
Henry (prior of Christ Church, Canterbury), 271 n.64
Henry I, king of England, 256 n.1
Henry III, king of England, 53–54
Herbert, George, 301 n.4

Hereberht of Huntingdon (hermit), 274 n.9
hermeneutics. *See* interpretation
hermeneutics of suspicion. *See under* interpretation
hermits. *See* monasticism, eremitic; *see also names of individual hermits*
heroic poetry (OE), 212
Hexateuch, 1–2, 6, 12
Hexham, monastery of, 109, 278 n.76, 279 n.102
hiding: from God, 1–3, 6, 11–12, 41, 44, 81, 125, 127, 132, 134, 137, 156, 247; from saints, 127–28, 147, 156, 282 n.30
Hildemar of Civate: *Expositio regulae*, 79, 273 n.90
Historia Apollonii regis Tyri, 166–68, 176, 286 n.2, 288 n.32, 288 n.34, 288 n.40
history, study of, 244
homilies, anonymous Latin, homily on All Saints, 283 n.49
Hrothgar (in *Beowulf*), 164–65
hue and cry, 23
humility: and confession, 72; in the desire to conceal good deeds, 154–58; and interpretation, 14, 193, 207, 226, 240–41, 249–51; monastic, 66, 69, 72, 227; and private prayer, 106, 124–25, 193; relationship to pride, 226–28; and sanctity, 71, 130, 138–39, 152–57, 247; steps of, 226–28; tactical poetics of, 211, 300 n.113; and the unknown, 14, 252–53; and wisdom, 226–27; and worms, 227–28, 240
Hwætberht. *See* Eusebius (Hwætberht)
Hywel Dda, king of Deheubarth (Wales), 52, 55

ignorance, 65, 89–90, 130, 139, 143, 154–55, 192, 202, 205–6, 220, 225–27, 236, 297
incest, 162, 165, 178, 288 n.42
Ine, king of Wessex, 8–9, 45, 51, 56, 68, 116, 117. *See also under* legislation, Anglo-Saxon
informants (*meldan*), 33, 36, 38, 56, 186–87, 234, 262 n.98, 266n nn.53–54
institutions, 4, 6, 21–22. *See also* monasticism; law
intention, 11, 32, 99, 101, 131–33, 157, 226, 245, 297 n.55
interiority, 5, 12, 21–22, 81
internus arbiter. *See under* judgment
interpretation: of the commands of a superior, 90–91, 157; as conversation, 248–52; of divine secrets, 21, 40, 101–2, 139–48, 184, 208, 214; early medieval notions of, 212, 248; and eschatology, 232–41; ethics of, 14–15, 161, 185, 202, 246–47; exegesis, 12, 101, 150–51, 185, 198–200, 203, 246, 248, 250, 252; as expression of monastic agency, 90–91, 157; God's assistance in, 184, 191–92, 195–97, 204; hermeneutics of faith, 14–15, 145, 190–97, 200–201, 203–6, 207, 218–19, 224–26, 248; hermeneutics of force, 14–15, 185–97, 248; hermeneutics of suspicion, 14, 190–91, 250, 252; of human behavior, 21–22, 91, 132, 147; legal, 9, 21–22, 26, 40, 60; literary, 8, 13, 203, 247–53; of monastic rules, 71, 79; pride in, 207, 222–27, 248–53; of riddles, 162–65, 175–83, 184–85, 198–99, 203–7, 219, 221, 232–41; *ruminatio*, 221; of runes, 178, 195–96; of scripture, 73, 101, 166, 186, 193–94, 198–201, 221, 226, 248–52; of secrets, 14, 162; textual, 161, 184–85; as unbinding/unfettering, 175–83
Ioca monachorum, 199
Iona, monastic community of, 281 n.17
Isidore of Seville, 214, 299 n.90; *Etymologiae*, 27, 110, 166, 169, 214, 217, 283 n.50; *Sententiae*, 81
Islam, 255 n.14
Isle of Man, 265 n.44
Israelites, 67, 191, 198

Jarrow, monastery of, 70, 110, 115, 279 n.102
Jauss, Hans Robert, 251
Jerome, St., 285 n.110; *Liber Didymi Alexandrini de Spiritu Sancto*, 282 n.38; *Vita Sancti Pauli primi eremitae*, 138
Jews, as concealers of the Cross, 28, 186–90, 193–94, 196
Job (OT), 198
John, king of England, 53
John of Beverly, bishop of Hexham, 274 n.10
John of Rouen, 84
John the Almoner, 58–59
John the Baptist, *porticus* of (Glastonbury), 116–17
Judas Cyriacus, 186–97, 202, 204
judgment: *Arbiter*, 208–9, 211–12, 219, 226–27, 232, 241; divine, 7, 21, 35, 39–40, 143–44, 207–9, 213, 245; as highest level of reading, 212; interpretation as, 212; of inward Judge (*internus arbiter*), 2–5, 7, 255 n.5, 268 n.23; of the king, 25–26; Last Judgment, 5, 14, 27–28, 35, 72, 96, 207, 232–39, 241, 299

n.88; legal, 19, 21, 26, 39–40; of the unseen (or secret) judge, 144
Judgment Day I, 234–35, 237
Judgment Day II, 234
Judith, 263 n.10
Julian of Toledo: *Prognosticorum futuri saeculi*, 237, 284 n.64, 301 n.122

keeping secrets. *See* secrets, posession of
Kermode, Frank, 302 n.6
Kierkegaard, Søren, 126
knowledge: divine (*see under* epistemology; omniscience); and faith (*see* faith, and understanding); *scientia*, 205–6, 225–26, 248. *See also* epistemology; esoteric knowledge; ignorance; witness(es)

Lanfranc, archbishop of Canterbury, 82–89, 93, 96, 104; *Decreta*, 78, 267 n.9; *Epistolae*, 84
Langland, William, 301 n.1
Lantfred of Winchester: *Miracula Sancti Swithuni*, 57; *Translatio et miracula Sancti Swithuni*, 154
Last Judgment. *See under* judgment
law, 6, 68, 70, 164, 145; canon, 23; Carolingian, 55; divine, 208, 211, 213; English common, 53; Germanic 52, 54; Icelandic, 30, 258 n.44, 259 n.53; late medieval, 7; *lex euangelium*, 76, 80, 85; of Moses, 186; Roman, 55; Scandinavian, 52, 54; Welsh, 52, 54. *See also* charters; lawsuits; legislation, Anglo-Saxon
lawsuits, 23
learning. *See* didacticism
legislation, Anglo-Saxon, 19, 23, 26; Æthelberht §§2–5, 24, 257 n.19; Æthelberht §9, 24, 257 n.20; II Æthelred §9, 46–47, 51–52, 55; III Æthelred §2, 39, 54, 265 n.45; III Æthelred §6, 263 n.6; II Æthelstan §§6–7, 261 n.76; II Æthelstan §14, 40–41; II Æthelstan §24, 46, 56, 263 n.3; II Æthelstan §26, 39, 256 n.1; VI Æthelstan §1, 37, 259 n.48; VI Æthelstan §6, 57; VI Æthelstan §11, 36; Alfred pref. §8, 256 n.1; Alfred §4, 24, 257 n.19; Alfred §7, 24, 257 n.19; Alfred §14, 47, 263 n.7; Alfred §43, 56; Alfred & Guthrum §4, 37, 262 n.94; *Be blaserum* (anonymous), 33–34, 260 n.69; I Cnut §26, 259 n.63; II Cnut §4, 261 n.76; II Cnut §§23–24, 262 n.95; II Cnut §26, 258 n.44; II Cnut §29, 23, 25; II Cnut §36, 54,
265nn.45–46; II Cnut §37, 259 n.63; II Cnut §56, 31; I Edgar §8, 38, 56; IV Edgar §14, 36; II Edmund, 257 n.22; III Edmund §§1–2, 24–25, 257 n.22; III Edmund §§5–6, 25, 257 n.22; Edward & Guthrum §11, 261 n.76; I Edward §1, 38; I Edward §3, 39, 257 n.11, 261 n.79; *Forfang* (anonymous), 260 n.69; Hlothhere & Eadric §5, 38, 56; Hlothhere & Eadric §16, 28, 38, 46; *Hundred* (anonymous), 260 n.69; Ine §1, 68; Ine §6, 24, 257 n.19; Ine §7, 36–37, 58; Ine §12, 24, 29, 37, 257 n.20; Ine §17, 28; Ine §20, 29; Ine §21, 29; Ine §24, 57; Ine §25, 46; Ine §28, 36; Ine §35, 259 n.50; Ine §36, 36; Ine §37, 39; Ine §43, 33, 38, 56; Ine §45, 24, 257 n.19; Ine §47, 57; Ine §52, 32, 35–36, 261 n.83; Ine §53, 9, 45–47, 51–58, 60, 266 n.66; Ine §73, 36; Ine §75, 46; *Iudicia Dei II* (anonymous), 41–42; *Swerian* (anonymous) §8, 38, 262 n.101; Wihtred §§17–22, 265 n.36; Wihtred §23, 57; Wihtred §26, 29; Wihtred §28, 29
Leiden Glossary, 267 n.1
Leofric, bishop of Exeter, 300 n.108
Leofric Missal, 277 n.61
Leofric of Mercia, 107
lex euangelium, 76, 80, 85
Lex Salica, 55; §28, 30–31; §33, 258 n.42; §39, 56; §41, 30; §70, 30; §80, 261 n.83; §85, 28–29; §89, 261 n.85
libel, 258 n.44
Liber monstrorum, 275 n.26
Liber Vitae, New Minster, 299 n.88
Lichfield, monastery of, 98
Lindisfarne, monastic community of, 97–99, 115, 281 n.17
liturgy, 96, 106, 108–11, 135–36, 243, 277 n.61
loci secretiores, 9, 11–12, 83, 95–99, 103–6, 110, 113, 122, 124, 247, 278 n.80
London, 25, 53, 265 n.39
Lorsch Riddles, 290 n.65
Lot (OT), 41–42
Love, Heather, 253
Lucretius, 299 n.90

manuscripts, by shelfmark: Basle, Universitätsbibliothek, F. III. 15c, 272 n.89; Bremen, Staats- und Universitätsbibliothek, MS 651, 296 n.17; Cambridge, Corpus Christi College, MS 173, 256 n.1; MS 190, 258 n.40; MS 201, 168–69, 287 n.27; MS 318, 288 n.32; MS 383, 258 n.40; MS 391, manuscripts, by shelfmark *(continued)* 277 n.70; **MS 41,** 258 n.40; University Library, **Gg. 5. 35,** 209, 212–28, 288 n.38, 293 n.70, 294 n.85, 295 n.6, 296 n.16; *Exeter*, Cathedral Library, **MS 3501** (*see* Exeter Book); *Leipzig*, Stadtbibliothek, **Rep. I.74,** 237; *London*, British Library, **Additional MS 14252,** 53, 265 n.39; **Cotton Claudius B. iv,** 1–3, 255 n.1; **Cotton Faustina A. x,** 271 n.62; **Cotton Galba A. xiv + Nero A. ii,** 277 n.69; **Cotton Tiberius A. iii,** 258 n.40; **Cotton Titus D. xxvi and Titus D. xxvii,** 277 n.71; **Harley 3271,** 287 n.17; **Royal 12 C. xxiii,** 198, 209–10, 237–38, 288 n.38, 295 n.6, 296 n.16; **Royal 15 A. XVI,** 296 n.17; **Stowe 944,** 299 n.88; *Oxford*, Bodleian Library, **Hatton 23,** 267 n.1; **Rawlinson C. 697,** 209, 295 n.6; *Salisbury*, Cathedral Library, **MS 10,** 267 n.1; *Strood*, Medway Archive and Local Studies Centre, **MS DRc/R1,** 258 n.40; *Vercelli*, Biblioteca Capitolare di Vercelli, **MS CXVII** (*see* Vercelli Book); *Winchester*, Winchester College, **MS 40A,** 272 n.89

Martin of Tours, 103–4, 152, 285 n.99; *porticus* of (Canterbury), 113

Marx, Karl, 190–91

Mary, the Blessed Virgin: chapel of (Canterbury), 107; *porticus* of (New Minster, Winchester), 280 n.118

Mary of Egypt: OE *Vita* of, 103

Maxims I, 4–5, 37, 49–50, 230

Maxims II, 27

Meaux, city of, 149

Melrose, monastery of, 98

Michael the archangel, chapel of (New Minster, Winchester), 280 n.118

Miller, D. A., 253, 297 n.54

Milton, John, 301 n.4

mind: as container, 4–5, 47–48; cardiocentric model of, 4–5; concealment of, 47–48, 75, 100, 147, 239; and concealment, 11; in confession, 74–75; control over, 6–7; directed toward God, 99, 123, 141, 144–45; early medieval notions of, 4–5, 246; of God, 100–101, 154; God's access to, 5, 101, 123, 147, 263 n.11; intention of, 11, 32, 99; in interpretation, 182, 200–202, 241, 249, 252; limits of, 141, 184; of a monk, 73; in prayer, 101, 123; pride of, 225, 241; restraint of, 4–5, 47–48, 177–78, 247; of saints, 154; Satan's entrance into, 138; as metaphor for text, 248–49; and wisdom, 194–95, 199–200; words of (*uerba cogitationis*), 145–48, 203. *See also* didacticism; psychology

miracles, 41–42, 84, 86, 104, 151–55, 206, 265 n.42; visions, 115–16, 128–34, 139

missionaries, in Germany, Anglo-Saxon, 197, 287 n.23, 300 n.117

monasticism, 6, 9, 65, 95, 118; coenobitic, 9, 68–73, 77–80, 97; eremitic, 9–11, 13, 95–101, 104, 109, 122, 124, 155; historical periods of, 68–70; monastic rules, 3, 8, 68–71, 77, 79–80, 85, 93, 95, 103, 105, 118; secrecy of, 103–4, 118; traditions of, 9, 68–72; vows, 68. *See also individual monastic rules*

Monkwearmouth, monastery of, 70, 110, 279 n.102

mortificatio (monastic), 76–78

Moses (OT), 41–42, 186, 208, 211

Mount Etna, 217, 224

murder: of Abel, 11–12, 96–97, 127; and arson, 33–34; of Christ, 186; crime of, 8, 12, 23; in narrative, 163–64, 167; secrecy of, 8, 30–32, 43, 50–51, 60, 127, 165

Muses, 208

mutilation, 43

mysteries: of Christianity, 148, 166; divine, 5, 14, 102–3, 143, 146, 152–53, 184, 186, 193, 202–3, 211–12, 214, 222–23, 232, 255 n.14; of the mind, 101; spiritual, 101, 166, 186, 193, 222; textual, 82, 166, 177, 182, 199–202, 205–6, 211–12, 217–18, 223, 226, 231–32, 240–41

Nietzsche, Friedrich, 190–91

nighttime, 30, 65, 85, 107–8, 120–22, 125–28, 131–34, 137–38, 148; association with theft, 26–28, 43, 50, 100–101

Njal's Saga, 260 n.74

nocturnal emission, 81–82

Norman Conquest, 70, 272 n.70

Northumbria, 70, 97–98, 111, 115, 135, 279 n.102, 281 n.17

oath (judicial), 7–9, 19–21, 30, 33–40, 43, 45–46, 52–60, 256 n.1, 257 n.6, 265 n.36

oath of allegiance, 24–25, 36

Odo of Cluny: *Vita Sancti Geraldi*, 82

Old English Illustrated Hexateuch, 1–3, 6, 12

Old English Martyrology, 102–3, 274 n.9, 283 n.40

Old Norse language, 31

omniscience, divine: disbelief in, 3–4, 11, 40, 127, 134–35, 202, 241; and epistolary

secrecy, 12–13; faith in, 40, 67, 91–93, 105, 161, 185, 247; God as witness, 34–35; hiding from, 1–3, 134; impossibility of escaping the infinite loop of, 3–4; influence on human behavior, 7–8, 22, 245–47; influence on literary interpretation, 8, 14, 22, 161, 185, 241, 247, 251; influence on psychological mechanics of secrecy, 6, 161, 246; internalization of, 22; and judicial oaths, 38, 60; and the judicial ordeal, 40–42, 60; versus the knowledge of demons, 85–86, 100–101; in *loci secretiores*, 97, 101, 106; in monastic life, 67, 72, 79–81, 91; mystery of, 1, 5; and penance, 81; and private prayer, 106–7, 124; reliability of, 21; role in early medieval law, 9, 21–22, 34–35, 40, 43–44; saints as extensions of, 140, 145–47; secret witnesses in relation to, 139, 202; and seeing in secret (*videt in abscondito*), 124–25, 127, 156; as shaping the nature of concealment and secrecy, 245–46; similarity to the panopticon, 6–8; and the study of secrecy, 255 n.14
openness, to God, 9, 11, 13, 81, 93, 97, 99, 101, 121–22, 245, 247. *See also* secrecy, spiritual
oratory, 81–82, 97, 104–6, 109–10, 116, 118, 122–23, 131, 274 n.10, 276 n.54, 279 n.102
ordeal, judicial, 5, 7, 9, 21, 33–35, 39–44, 53–54, 60, 90–91, 246–47, 259 n.46, 261 nn.76–78, 265 n.42, 287 n.13. *See also* judgment; law
Ordo Casinensis, 270 n.46
Origen: *In Numeros homiliae*, 166, 200
Original Sin. *See under* sin
Osbern of Canterbury: *Miracula Sancti Dunstani*, 82–85, 87–89, 96; *Vita Sancti Dunstani*, 274 n.16
Oswald, bishop of Worcester, archbishop of York, 13, 135–36, 139
Oswald of Ramsey: *Centum concito*, 238, 243, 300 n.113, 300 n.117; *Terrigene bene*, 238, 243, 300 n.113, 300 n.117
Owine, monk, 149

Pachomius, 78, 267 n.4; *Regula coenobiorum*, 78
Pactus Childeberti regis, 261 n.83
Palestine, 103
Pambo, Abbo, 268 n.12
panopticon, 6–7, 22
Panther, The, 48–49, 59
Paradise. *See* Eden
Paris Psalter, 49, 293 n.52, 298 n.66
Pater Noster, 238, 243, 300 n.114

Patrick, St.: *Vita* of, 138
Paul of Thebes, 138–39
Paul the Apostle (NT), 28, 70, 74, 126, 143, 171, 225–26
Paul the Simple, 138
pedagogy. *See* didacticism
penance, 59, 76, 80, 86, 93, 105, 270 n.50. *See also* confession
Penitential of Finnian, 81
Penitential of Theodore, 32
perception. *See* vision
perjury, 19–21, 23, 34–35, 39–40, 44, 60, 247, 256 n.1, 257 n.7, 273 n.91
Peter Chrysologus: *Collectio sermonum*, 138
Peter Damian: *Epistolae*, 138, 280 n.122
Peter the Apostle (NT), 153, 181
pharaoh, 65, 67
Pippin, son of Charlemagne, 203–6
Pirsig, Robert M., 297 n.54
Plan of St. Gall, 278 n.85
Planck, Max, 297 n.54
Pliny the Elder, 299 n.90
pneuma, Stoical concept of, 289 n.52, 299 n.89
Pontius Pilate (NT), 48
porticus, 110–17, 119, 122–23
Portiforium of Saint Wulfstan, 108
possession: personal, 4, 9; of personal property, 69, 92; of secrets (*see under* secrets); of soul, 9, 87–89, 180
prayer, private, 9–11, 95–96, 104–11, 120–23, 247
prejudice, 191, 250–51, 292 n.35
pride, 14, 79, 147, 152, 211, 225–28, 232, 241, 248–50, 253
Priscian: *Excerptiones*, 164
privacy, 256 n.25; right to, 11, 19–20, 244
proof (judicial), 7–8, 19–21, 28–29, 34–35, 43, 54, 259 n.46, 261 n.77
prophecy, 126, 139–40, 142–46, 149, 154, 190, 283 n.50, 284 n.64
Prosper of Aquitaine: *Epigrammata*, 140–41, 197, 199–202, 293 n.70; *Liber sententiarum*, 140–41, 200, 294 n.102
proverbs, 4, 5. See also *Maxims I*; *Maxims II*
Prudentius, 212
Psalms, 107–9. *See also under* Bible
Pseudo-Bede. *See* Bede, Pseudo-
Pseudo-Seneca. *See* Seneca, Pseudo-
Pseudo-Theodore. *See* Theodore, Pseudo-
psychology: of concealment, 4–6, 161, 244; early medieval notions of, 4–5; materialist, 4–5; of the ordeal, 40. *See also* mind

Quadripartitus, 257 n.22, 260 n.74, 262 n.87

reading: forms of, 14–15, 194, 212, 248–49; manuscripts, 220, 232–34; proper monastic methods of, 169, 196, 224–26. *See also* interpretation
reasonable doubt, legal concept of, 40
Regula magistri, 68, 104, 109, 11; **2**, 68, 72–73; **10**, 227, 298 n.65; **15**, 72; **21**, 92–93; **24**, 103, 106; **80**, 81–82
Regula Sancti Benedicti, 9, 68, 70, 104, 226, 268 n.15; **2**, 68, 72–73, 267 n.5; **4**, 72–73, 92, 273 n.91; **7**, 72, 226–27; **42**, 72; **23**, 77; **33**, 69–70; **46**, 80, 91, 270 n.52; **48**, 79; **52**, 104–5; **63**, 68, 267 n.5; **69**, 78; OE translation of, 82, 268 n.23, 298 n.66
Regularis concordia, 9, 68, 111, 116–17, 280 n.116; prol. **4**, 71; **6**, 105–6, 108, 116; **7**, 103; **27**, 277 n.61; **57**, 78, 267 n.9; **67**, 109, 116, 276 n.54; OE gloss to, 276 n.41, 276 n.54
relics, 39, 47, 52–55, 58, 60, 84, 120, 265 n.45
remote spaces. *See loci secretiores*
restraint: failure of, 186; virtue of, 4–6
resurrection, 165, 171, 234, 237. *See also under* Christ
reticence, virtue of, 4–6
revelation (*pandere*), 204–6, 208, 211, 217–18, 222–25, 239
Richard II, king of England, 261 n.78
Ricoeur, Paul, 190–91, 250
riddles, 13–15, 161–83, 197–207, 211–41, 246; as didactic, 161, 184, 197–201, 203; and metaphors of servitude, 161, 169–75; obscene, 179–80, 287 n.27, 291 n.99; as play, 168, 184, 195–97, 203, 205, 214, 219, 226, 232, 237, 239, 246; solving, 13, 161, 165, 175–83, 184, 196, 201, 203–4, 208, 214, 218–19, 224–25
Riddles (Exeter Book), 13, 161, 168–69, 175–76, 205, 234, 288 n.39; *Rid.* **1**, 169–70, 289 nn.49–50, 289 n.52, 299 n.90; *Rid.* **2**, 170, 289 n.52; *Rid.* **3**, 169–71, 174, 179, 233–37, 289 nn.49–50, 289 n.52; *Rid.* **4**, 169, 171–72, 289 n.49; *Rid.* **6**, 169, 289 n.49; *Rid.* **8**, 169, 289 n.50; *Rid.* **10**, 169, 289 n.50; *Rid.* **11**, 169, 289 nn.49–50; *Rid.* **12**, 169, 172–74, 289 nn.49–50; *Rid.* **14**, 169, 289 n.50; *Rid.* **16**, 288 n.40, 289 n.50; *Rid.* **19**, 169, 289 n.50; *Rid.* **20**, 169, 289 n.49; *Rid.* **21**, 169, 174–75, 181, 289 n.49; *Rid.* **22**, 169, 289 n.49; *Rid.* **23**, 169, 289 nn.49–50; *Rid.* **25**, 169, 289 nn.49–50; *Rid.* **26**, 169, 178–79, 289 n.50; *Rid.* **27**, 169, 289 n.49; *Rid.* **30a**, 235; *Rid.* **33**, 169, 181–82, 289 n.49; *Rid.* **35**, 288 n.40; *Rid.* **38**, 169, 173, 289 n.49; *Rid.* **40**, 288 n.40; *Rid.* **42**, 177–82; *Rid.* **43**, 169, 180, 289 n.49; *Rid.* **44**, 169, 180–81, 289 n.49; *Rid.* **45**, 169, 289 n.49; *Rid.* **47**, 220–21, 229–30, 235, 288 n.40; *Rid.* **48**, 230–31, 300 n.114; *Rid.* **49**, 169, 289 n.49; *Rid.* **50**, 169, 289 n.49; *Rid.* **52**, 169, 173–74, 289 n.49; *Rid.* **53**, 169, 289 n.49; *Rid.* **54**, 169, 289 n.49; *Rid.* **58**, 169, 289 n.49; *Rid.* **60**, 231–32, 288 n.40, 298 n.79; *Rid.* **62**, 169, 289 n.50; *Rid.* **63**, 169, 289 n.49; *Rid.* **64**, 169, 289 n.49; *Rid.* **66**, 169, 289 n.50; *Rid.* **72**, 169, 173, 289 n.49; *Rid.* **73**, 169, 289 nn.49–50; *Rid.* **80**, 169, 289 n.50; *Rid.* **83**, 169, 289 nn.49–50; *Rid.* **85**, 288 n.40; *Rid.* **86**, 288 n.40, 289 n.50; *Rid.* **87**, 169, 289 n.49
riddles, Latin, 14, 161, 168–69, 184–85, 197. *See also under* Aldhelm of Malmesbury; Boniface; Eusebius (Hwætberht); Tatwine, archbishop of Canterbury; Symphosius
Robert Mannyng of Brunne: *Handlyng Synne*, 269 n.29
Robertson, D. W., Jr., 252
Rochester, Kent, 25, 288 n.32
Rubisca, 238, 243
Rufinus, 166, 200, 267 n.11, 272 n.89
run, 37, 101–3, 182, 186–90, 193, 231, 275 n.33, 292 n.8
runic letters, 178, 182, 195–96, 300 n.114
Ruthwell Cross, 138

Sachsenspiegel, 265 n.37
saints, 8, 13, 124–25, 139; desire to conceal the deeds of, 154–58; hierarchy of, 139; impossibility of hiding from, 127–28, 147–48; *vitae* of, 9. *See also names of individual saints*
Sancte sator (hymn), 242, 300 n.117
Sapphira (NT), 153, 285 n.92
Schleiermacher, Friedrich, 250–51
Schmitt, Carl, 256 n.22
Schwabenspiegel, 52, 55
Scriftboc (OE), 32
scripture. *See* Bible; interpretation
scrutiny: communal, 69, 93; culture of, 6–8, 246; divine, 1, 3, 158, 263 n.13; human, 12; judicial, 9, 19, 60; monastic, 9, 67. *See also* omniscience; vision
seal (*insigle*), 52
secrecy: as basis for interpretation, 248; as captivity, 59–60, 65–67, 88–89, 93; definition of, 10, 245; divine, 98, 103, 124–25, 130, 137, 139–44, 148, 161, 202, 278 n.81; epistolary, 12–13; ethics of, 3–4, 10–14, 20, 161,

184–85, 247–48; etymology of, 10; historical contingency of, 10, 244–45; humble forms of, 154–58; legal regulation of, 20, 22; legal toleration of, 19; monastic regulation of, 8–9, 11, 20, 22, 65–94; as separation, 10; of slaves/servants, 57–58, 162, 164–67; spatiality of, 12; spiritual, 9–11, 13, 95–100, 102, 106, 109, 121–23, 124, 157, 247, 275 n.34; tactical, 4, 69, 166, 248; textual, 13, 248–50; as theft, 89–94; as universal, 10, 244–45. *See also under* bonds; death; foreigners; monasticism; murder; secrets; theft

secret compositions (extrajudicial conflict resolution), 32, 35–36

secret flight (hagiographic motif), 96–97

secret societies, 255 n.14

secret witness (hagiographic motif), 125–39, 142, 149–54, 156, 158, 202, 247–48

secretarius, 164, 287 n.15

secrets: as belonging to God, 5–6, 67, 93; as belonging to the devil, 86–87, 93; forbidden, 8–9, 11, 76, 95, 247; posession of, 4–6, 9, 14, 74, 163, 165, 247; public revelation of, 5, 7, 8, 14, 58, 67–68, 232–41; of the state, 11. *See also* secrecy

Secretum (liturgical), 96, 106, 108, 135, 282 n.33

Sedulius Scottus, 108, 212, 299 n.106; *Collectaneum miscellaneum*, 4

Seneca: *Naturales quaestiones*, 299 n.89

Seneca, Pseudo-: *De moribus*, 4

Serapion, Abba, 65–67, 72, 86–91, 94–95, 273 n.93

servitude, to God (monastic), 9, 68, 88, 92, 164, 268 n.12; and mastery, 22, 56–58, 162, 164, 170–74; metaphors of, 5, 13, 169; representations of in Exeter Book *Riddles*, 169–75; terminology of, 286 n.12, 287 n.21; and the Welsh, 172–74

shame, 1, 65–67, 73, 76–77, 81, 83–84, 86, 93, 155, 240, 285 n.91

Sigbald (in Ædiluulf's *De abbatibus*), 115

Sigwine (in Ædiluulf's *De abbatibus*), 136–37, 139

Silas the Apostle (NT), 171

silence, 4–5, 57–61, 76, 244, 298 n.81; agency in, 266 n.64; in death, 47–51, 58–61, 228–32, 245; legal right to, 20, 257 n.2; of the night, 133, 272 n.79; of objects, 199, 231–32; in prayer, 96, 98, 104–6, 109, 122–23 (*see also* prayer, private); *silentio tegere*, 151–52, 154–56, 285 n.110, 286 n.111; of slaves/servants, 45, 55–58; vow of, 126, 135–37, 148–49; of witnesses, 45, 57–58, 76

Silius Italicus: *Punica*, 281 n.11

Simmel, Georg, 4, 10–11, 253

sin, 58–59, 74, 76–83, 86–88, 179; as bondage, 9, 67, 92, 181, 195, 208, 273 n.91; and concealment, 2–4, 11–14, 80–81, 93, 96, 105, 130, 247, 271 n.53; of disobedience, 91–92, 157; Original, 2; of pride, 226

slaves and slavery: legal status of slaves, 56; punitive slavery, 37; stolen slave, 9, 45–47. *See also* servitude

Smaragdus of St. Mihiel: *Expositio in Regulam Sancti Benedicti*, 255 n.11, 268 n.23, 273 n.91

Snodland, Kent, 25

Sodom and Gomorrah (OT), 41–42

Soliloquies (OE), 141–42, 203, 284 n.64, 301 n.122

solitude. See *loci secretiores*; monasticism, eremitic

Solomon and Saturn I, 300 n.114

Solomon and Saturn II, 180

soul, 50–51, 69, 72–73, 142, 154, 170, 180, 232, 236–37

Soul and Body I, 50, 228–29, 237

Soul and Body II, 50, 228–29, 237

Soul's Address to the Body, The, 50–51, 299 n.95

sovereignty, 7, 9, 19, 22–23, 34

spiritual secrecy. *See under* secrecy

spying. *See* secret witness (hagiographic motif)

Stephen of Ripon: *Vita Sancti Wilfrithi*, 279 n.101

Stranguillo (in *Apollonius of Tyre*), 163, 167

Sulpicius Severus: *Vita Sancti Martini*, 152

surveillance, 6–7, 11, 35, 48, 93, 244. *See also* scrutiny

Swithun, St., 154–55; tomb of (Old Minster, Winchester), 117, 119

Symphosius, 168, 176, 197; *Aenigmata*, 176, 197, 212–13, 237–38, 242; *Aenigm.* pref. 175–76, 224–25, 288 n.38; *Aenigm.* **2**, 168, 288 n.34, 288 n.40; *Aenigm.* **4**, 180–81; *Aenigm.* **5**, 175–76; *Aenigm.* **12**, 168, 288 n.34, 288 n.40; *Aenigm.* **13**, 168, 288 n.34; *Aenigm.* **16**, 220–21, 288 n.40; *Aenigm.* **59**, 168, 288 n.34; *Aenigm.* **61**, 168, 288 n.34, 288 n.40; *Aenigm.* **63**, 168, 288 n.34; *Aenigm.* **69**, 168, 288 n.34; *Aenigm.* **78**, 168, 288 n.34; *Aenigm.* **79**, 168, 288 n.34; *Aenigm.* **90**, 168, 288 n.34; *Aenigm.* **95**, 288 n.40

Tatwine, archbishop of Canterbury, *Aenigmata*, 168, 176, 206, 212–13, 237–38, 242; *Aenigm.* **3**, 199; *Aenigm.* **24**, 228

terrorism, 20
testimony (judicial), 8–9, 19–21, 34–44, 47, 53–60, 247; chain of, 46–47; false (*see* perjury); of slaves/servants, 45–46, 164–65, 187
Thaliarcus (in *Apollonius of Tyre*), 162–65, 290 n.60
Thasia (in *Apollonius of Tyre*), 163, 165, 167, 176
theft, 19, 21–25, 27, 29, 36–40, 44, 50, 55–57, 65–66, 88–89, 95, 230; and arson, 33–34; concealment of, 24, 67, 261 n.85; by demons, 86; distinguished from robbery, 29; legal treatment of, 28–30, 45–47; of obedience, 90–92; of persons, 45–47, 163; and secrecy, 8–9, 24–30, 31, 42–43, 60, 89–93, 229; of self, 56, 90–93; as treason, 23–24
Theodore, archbishop of Canterbury, 32, 70, 272 n.89, 299 n.106
Theodore, Pseudo-: Penitentials of, 266 n.51
Theodore (in the *Vita Sancti Antonii*), 149
Theodulf of Orléans: *Capitula*, 271 n.53
Theonas, Abba, 65, 89, 91
tombs. *See* graves
torture, 43, 196–97, 208, 227
translation, 167, 244, 287 n.25
treason, 23–24, 31, 36
trial by jury, 53
Tyrannius Rufinus: *Historia monachorum sive de Vita Sanctorum Patrum*, 138

Uppland (Sweden), 52–53
utilitarianism, 11

Vainglory, 298 n.79
Valerius Flaccus: *Argonautica*, 281 n.11
Verba seniorum, 268 n.12
Vercelli Book, 185, 229, 237
Vercelli Homilies: hom. **4**, 301 n.124
Versus cuiusdam Scoti de alfabeto, 238, 242
Versus sibyllae de iudicio Dei, 237
Virgilius Maro Grammaticus, 217–18, 223
Virgno, abbot of Iona, 131–34, 136
virtue ethics, 11
Visio Leofrici, 107
vision: of cats, 27; Christ's healing of the blind, 150–51, 155; divine (*visio Dei*), 1–3, 12, 79–80, 121, 124–25, 268 n.23 (*see also* omniscience, divine); human, 1, 13, 121; loss of, 132–34, 136, 139, 142; of saints, 139–48, 153–54 (*see also* miracles, visions; prophecy); seeing in secret, 95, 106, 124–25, 127, 202; spiritual vs. bodily, 146. *See also* panopticon

Vita Sancti Thecle, 288 n.32
Vitae patrum, 58, 149
vouching to warranty (judicial process), 37–38, 45–47, 51–60, 266 n.50
Vulcan (Roman deity), 213–14, 217

Walahfrid Strabo: *Libellus de exordiis*, 111
walls, 99, 104, 110–13, 115–16, 118, 121–22, 131, 233–34, 268 n.24. *See also* architecture
Wanderer, The, 4–5, 47–48, 247
Wearmouth-Jarrow, monastic community of, 70
Wenlock Abbey, 268 n.16
Werferth of Worcester: trans. Gregory's *Dialogi*, 103–4, 263 n.15
wergild, 29, 31, 36, 259 n.50, 265 n.45
Wilfrid, bishop of Northumbria, 149, 279 n.101
William of Malmesbury, 111; *Vita Sancti Dunstani*, 116, 279 n.110; *Vita Sancti Wulfstani*, 122
Winchester, monastery of, 57, 108, 116, 287 n.23; New Minster, 280 n.118 (see also *Liber Vitae*, New Minster); Old Minster, 116–22, 154
witness(es): distinguished from accessories, 37; dead, 9, 45–47, 51; divine (*see* omniscience); false (*see* perjury); judicial, 19–22, 34–44; slaves as, 55–58; to property transactions, 25, 28, 36–38, 46–47; warrantors (class of witness), 37–38, 45–47, 51–53, 56–58, 60. *See also* informants (*meldan*); secret witness (hagiographic motif)
wonders, 202–6, 218, 223, 240
Worchester, Church of Saint Mary, 122
wrongs (judicial), 8, 19
Wulfsig (in Ædiluulf's *De abbatibus*), 116
Wulfstan, bishop of Worcester, 122–23; *Portiforium* of, 108
Wulfstan of Winchester (Wulfstan Cantor): *Epistola specialis*, 117–18, 120–22; *Narratio metrica de Sancti Swithuno*, 287 n.13; *Vita Sancti Æthelwoldi*, 88–93, 149–50, 270 n.46
Wulfstan the Homilist, archbishop of York, 31, 168–69

York, Basilica of Alma Sophia, 110–11

Zosimus of Palestine, 103–4
Zumthor, Paul, 251

Acknowledgments

It is truly a privilege to record my gratitude to the many individuals and institutions who helped bring this book into the world. The research and writing here have been supported by fellowships and grants from a number of organizations: the National Endowment for the Humanities; the Division of the Humanities and the Visiting Committee to the Division of the Humanities at the University of Chicago; the Division of Humanities and Social Sciences at the California Institute of Technology; the UC Berkeley Department of English, Center for British Studies, and Institute of East Asian Studies; the Lynne Grundy Memorial Trust; and the Mellon Foundation and American Council of Learned Societies. I also wish to thank the Cambridge University Library, the British Library, and the Bodleian Library for opening their collections to me; images of their manuscripts are reproduced here by the kind permission of the Syndics of Cambridge University Library and the British Library Board.

I owe my greatest and gladdest debt to Katherine O'Brien O'Keeffe, who championed this project from the start and has always been a dedicated and scrupulous reader of my work—all with her natural generosity, care, kindness, and grace. Emily Thornbury showed me what it means to be a scholar, a colleague, and a devoted teacher. From ambling conversations to precision adjustments to absolutely crucial skepticism, her input on this book has been challenging and thoughtful and, indeed, character-building. I admire you both beyond measure. And for all you have given to me, I am beyond grateful.

In direct and indirect ways, and over the course of more than a decade, this book has been shaped by and in the company of so many great minds: Oliver Arnold, Stephanie Bahr, Chris Baswell, Stephen Best, Frank Bezner, Dan Blanton, George Brown, Sean Curran, Kathleen Davis, Martha Driver, Marcos Garcia, Jacob Hobson, Mary Kate Hurley, Molly Jacobs-Bauer, Eleanor Johnson, Steven Justice, Stacy Klein, Geoff Koziol, Leslie Lockett, Jennifer Lorden, Jennifer Miller, Maureen Miller, Hal Momma, Rebecca Munson, Maura Nolan, Spencer Strub, Elaine Treharne, James Grantham Turner, Norman Underwood, Claude Willan, and Evan Wilson. Thank you.

Patricia Dailey: thank you for your friendship, for introducing me to gewürztraminer and Lyotard, and for inspiring the second chapter of this book and from there, the rest. Mo Pareles, Ryan Perry, Matthew Sergi, and Micha Lazarus: you are dear friends, truly, and I so profoundly value our conversations, your words on my work, and the varieties of wisdom—justice, theory, performance, Aristotle—you bring to bear on my life. Jonathan Montgomery and Andy Holmes, thank you for your friendship and your legal advice. Del Kolve and Larry Luchtel: thank you for your warm kindness, for sharing your office, and for all the delightful meals together.

This book saw its completion at two institutions. Caltech has a kind of electric tranquility and is a place that—to the surprise of many—genuinely supports humanities research in a rare and serious way: certainly a model for other academic institutions to emulate. There, Warren Brown, Jennifer Jahner, Keith Pluymers, Cindy Weinstein, and Leah Klement were the best colleagues and readers one could wish for. Keith, thank you for our many conversations, both in the office and during all those early mornings at El Porto. I also wish to thank Jean Laurent-Rosenthal, Cathy Jurca, and Tom Rosenbaum for making Caltech so intellectually hospitable during my time there.

The University of Chicago—it is true—has a way of pushing one's thinking further than ever seemed possible. My colleagues here, particularly Michael Allen, Sophia Azeb, Alexis Chema, Daisy Delogu, Maud Ellmann, Frances Ferguson, Timothy Harrison, Patrick Jagoda, Sarah Johnson, Aden Kumler, Jonathan Lyon, Ellen MacKay, Jo McDonagh, Mark Miller, Benjamin Morgan, David Nirenberg, Julie Orlemanski, Kaneesha Parsard, Lucy Pick, Tina Post, Zach Samalin, Josh Scodel, Joe Stadolnik, and Chris Taylor, have in short time become generous interlocutors. I thank William Donovan for his last-minute research assistance, expertly conducted. And since I joined the faculty here, Debbie Nelson and Anne Walters Robertson have been exceedingly supportive of my work; I am truly proud and grateful to be a part of the rich and happy intellectual community they have fostered.

Each of the chapters of this book has benefited from exchanges with audiences and colleagues at various conferences and lectures. My great thanks to the hosts and many participants: the UC Berkeley Medieval Studies Colloquium; the Haas Junior Scholars at the UC Berkeley Institute for East Asian Studies, especially Scott McGinnis, Alexandre Roberts, and Shao-Yun Yang; the Anglo-Saxon Studies Colloquium and Columbia University; the California Medieval History Seminar at the Huntington Library; the Center for Religion and Civic Culture at the University of Southern California, especially Lisa Bitel and also Amy Hollywood and Richard Kieckhefer; the Division of Humanities and Social Sciences at Caltech; the Department of English at Harvard University, especially James Simpson, Daniel Donoghue, and Nicholas Watson; the Department of English at the University of Chicago; the Franke Institute for the Humanities at the University of Chicago; and the Program in

Medieval Studies at the University of Wisconsin–Madison, especially Martin Foys, Jordan Zweck, and Thomas E. A. Dale. I would also like to thank Jerry Singerman for seeing the potential in this book and for so expertly navigating it into print, in spite of all my idiosyncratic requests. I am very grateful to the two anonymous readers for their extremely generous and careful feedback.

Above all, I thank my family: to Betty and Peter Langs for your continual support and encouragement (and for the gift of a 1941 Royal KLM on which some of this book was written); to my parents, Steven Saltzman and Katherine Brown-Saltzman, for your love and unfaltering faith from the beginning, somehow managing to prepare me for this work even when such a path may have seemed so improbable in my youth (and indeed inadvertently enabling me to write a book on ethics that pales in comparison to the *real* ethical work you do every day); to my sister, Julia, for inspiring me nearly every day with her creativity and endless talent; to Oliver and Sidney, for making me smile, giving me purpose, and taking my sleep (all errors that remain in this book are surely theirs alone); and above all, to Ashleigh: everything positive I have ever done has been motivated by you, and it is no secret that for all these years you have been my supreme inspiration and joy.